SOURCES FOR LATIN AMERICA
IN THE MODERN WORLD

SOURCES FOR LATIN AMERICA IN THE MODERN WORLD

EDITED BY

Nicola Foote

FLORIDA GULF COAST UNIVERSITY

NEW YORK   OXFORD
OXFORD UNIVERSITY PRESS

Oxford University Press is a department of the University of Oxford.
It furthers the University's objective of excellence in research, scholarship,
and education by publishing worldwide. Oxford is a registered trade mark of
Oxford University Press in the UK and certain other countries.

Published in the United States of America by Oxford University Press
198 Madison Avenue, New York, NY 10016, United States of America.

For titles covered by Section 112 of the US Higher Education
Opportunity Act, please visit www.oup.com/us/he for the latest
information about pricing and alternate formats.

Library of Congress Cataloging-in-Publication Data

Sources for Latin America in the Modern World
Library of Congress Cataloging in Publication Control Number: 2018013898
CIP data is on file at the Library of Congress
ISBN 978-0-19-934024-8

9 8 7 6 5 4 3 2 1

Printed by Sheridan Books, Inc., United States of America

CONTENTS

ACKNOWLEDGMENTS

This book was a highly collaborative process and thanks are due to many people for helping it come to fruition. I am deeply grateful to Charles Cavaliere, Peter Henderson, Ginny Garrard and Bryan McCann for inviting me to create this volume as a companion to their important new book *Latin America in the Modern World*. Thanks especially to Peter—my longtime mentor and sometime research assistant!—for providing so many generous suggestions on potential sources. Ginny and Bryan were also very helpful in expanding the source selections related to Central America and Brazil. The Florida Gulf Coast University Library provided essential help with securing materials via Interlibrary Loan and UBorrow. Rachel Tait-Ripperdan and Sheila Allen were especially important to this process, and I am especially grateful for the implementation of Library Express Delivery, which made the later stages of work on this book much easier. Bob Gregerson fostered a supportive environment in which I could continue to advance my scholarly interests as a Department Chair. Dawn Kirby supported me in continuing in this project when I moved into a new role as her associate dean, and provided me with some much-needed leave time at a key point in the semester. It was such a pleasure to finally work with Charles Cavaliere as my editor, and I am grateful for his guidance, enthusiasm, and support through an unexpectedly long process. Thanks also to Rowan Wixted, who has been invaluable in doing amazing work to secure permissions. I am thankful to my amazing mentors Chris Abel and Nicola Miller for providing me with such a thorough grounding in Latin American history as a student, as well as to my own students in LAH 3200 who have helped advance my own knowledge and insight. I am grateful for my many supportive friends and colleagues at FGCU, including Paul Bartrop, Elizabeth Bouldin, Diane Bova, Erik Carlson, Jackie Chastain, Mike Cole, Frances Davey, Mari De Wees, Kris De Welde, Mike Epple, Melodie Eichbauer, billY Gunnels, Jan Meij, Joanna Salapska-Gelleri and Ted Thornhill. Special thanks to Eric Strahorn for his mentoring. Thanks to Erin O'Connor for introducing me to the value of pedagogical work, and for supporting me in all my endeavors. Finally, thank you to my family, Carlos King and Margaret, Jeff, and Chris Foote, for your love and support.

HOW TO READ A PRIMARY SOURCE

This sourcebook is composed of sixty-seven primary sources. A primary source is any text, image, or other source of information that gives us a firsthand account of the past by someone who witnessed or participated in the historical events in question. While such sources can provide significant and fascinating insight into the past, they must also be read carefully to limit modern assumptions about historical modes of thought. Here are a few elements to keep in mind when approaching a primary source.

AUTHORSHIP

Who produced this source of information? A male or a female? A member of the elite or of the lower class? An outsider looking in at an event or an insider looking out? What profession or lifestyle does the author pursue, which might influence how he is recording his information?

GENRE

What type of source are you examining? Different genres—categories of material—have different goals and stylistic elements. For example, a personal letter meant exclusively for the eyes of a distant cousin might include unveiled opinions and relatively trivial pieces of information, like the writer's vacation plans. On the other hand, a political speech intended to convince a nation of a leader's point of view might subdue personal opinions beneath artful rhetoric and focus on large issues like national welfare or war. Identifying genre can be useful for deducing how the source may have been received by an audience.

AUDIENCE

Who is reading, listening to, or observing the source? Is it a public or private audience? National or international? Religious or nonreligious? The source may be geared toward the expectations of a particular group; it may be recorded in a language that is specific to a particular group. Identifying audience can help us understand why the author chose a certain tone or included certain types of information.

HISTORICAL CONTEXT

When and why was this source produced? On what date? For what purposes? What historical moment does the source address? It is paramount that we approach primary sources in context to avoid anachronism (attributing an idea or habit to a past era where it does not belong) and faulty judgment. For example, when considering a medieval history, we must take account of the fact that in the Middle Ages, the widespread understanding was that God created the world and could still interfere in the activity of mankind—such as sending a terrible storm when a community had sinned. Knowing the context (Christian, medieval, views of the world) helps us to avoid importing modern assumptions—like the fact that storms are caused by atmospheric pressure—into historical texts. In this way we can read the source more faithfully, carefully, and generously.

BIAS AND FRAMING

Is there an overt argument being made by the source? Did the author have a particular agenda? Did any political or social motives underlie the reasons for writing the document? Does the document exhibit any qualities that offer clues about the author's intentions?

STYLISTIC ELEMENTS

Stylistic features such as tone, vocabulary, word choice, and the manner in which the material is organized and presented should also be considered when examining a source. They can provide insight into the writer's perspective and offer additional context for considering a source in its entirety.

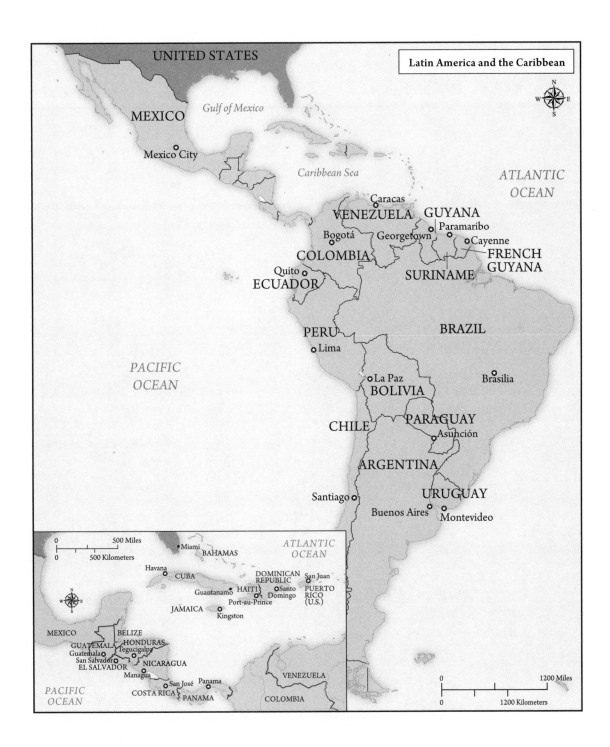

Latin America and the Caribbean

UNITED STATES

MEXICO

Gulf of Mexico

Mexico City

Caribbean Sea

ATLANTIC OCEAN

Caracas

VENEZUELA GUYANA

Paramaribo

Bogotá Georgetown

Cayenne

COLOMBIA FRENCH GUYANA

Quito SURINAME

ECUADOR

PERU BRAZIL

Lima

PACIFIC OCEAN

La Paz Brasilia

BOLIVIA

PARAGUAY

CHILE Asunción

ARGENTINA

URUGUAY

Santiago

Buenos Aires Montevideo

0   500 Miles
0   500 Kilometers

Miami

BAHAMAS

ATLANTIC OCEAN

Havana

CUBA

DOMINICAN REPUBLIC San Juan

Guantanamo HAITI Santo Domingo PUERTO RICO (U.S.)

JAMAICA Port-au-Prince

Kingston

MEXICO BELIZE

GUATEMALA HONDURAS

Guatemala Tegucigalpa

San Salvador NICARAGUA

EL SALVADOR

Managua

PACIFIC OCEAN

San José Panama

COSTA RICA PANAMA VENEZUELA

COLOMBIA

0   1200 Miles
0   1200 Kilometers

xv

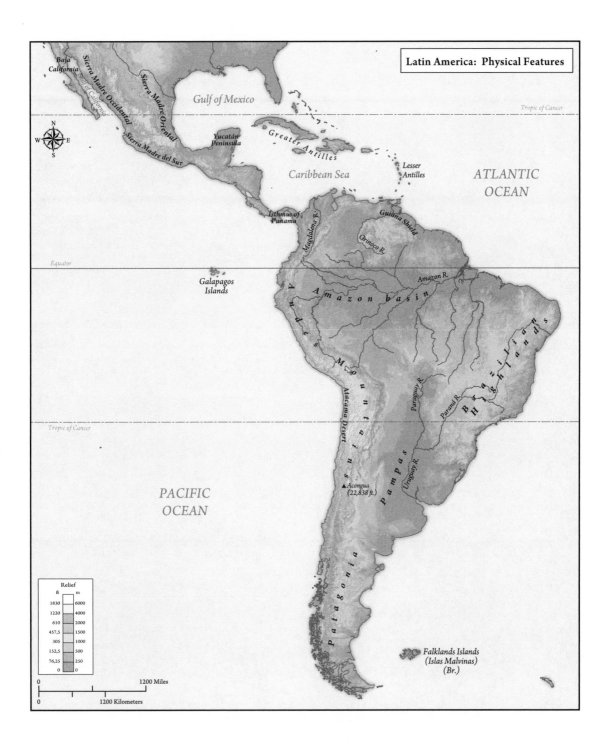

Latin America: Physical Features

Baja California
Sierra Madre Occidental
Gulf of California
Sierra Madre Oriental
Sierra Madre del Sur
Gulf of Mexico
Yucatán Peninsula
Greater Antilles
Caribbean Sea
Lesser Antilles
ATLANTIC OCEAN
Tropic of Cancer

N
W   E
S

Isthmus of Panama
Magdalena R.
Guiana Shield
Orinoco R.
Equator
Galapagos Islands
A m a z o n   b a s i n
Amazon R.
A n d e s
M o u n t a i n s
Atacama Desert
Paraguay R.
Paraná R.
B r a z i l i a n   H i g h l a n d s
Tropic of Cancer
Uruguay R.
P a m p a s
▲ Acongua (22,838 ft.)

PACIFIC OCEAN

P a t a g o n i a

Falklands Islands
(Islas Malvinas)
(Br.)

Relief
ft   m
1830   6000
1220   4000
610   2000
457,5   1500
305   1000
152,5   500
76,25   250
0   0

0   1200 Miles
0   1200 Kilometers

SOURCES FOR LATIN AMERICA
IN THE MODERN WORLD

CHAPTER 1

LATIN AMERICA IN THE AGE OF REVOLUTION, 1789–1820s

TOUSSAINT L'OUVERTURE

1.1 LETTER TO THE FRENCH DIRECTORY, 1797

The Haitian Revolution is the defining moment of the Age of Revolution: through the only successful slave rebellion in history, Europe's most economically prolific sugar colony became the world's first black republic. The Haitian revolution would serve simultaneously as a beacon of freedom and hope and a symbol of elite fear of the consequences of mass rebellion. The Haitian revolution serves as an essential backdrop to understanding the differing trajectories of independence in continental Latin America and the Hispanic Caribbean.

This document is one of the key texts of the Haitian Revolution. Toussaint L'Ouverture was a former slave whose life prior to the Haitian Revolution underlines the complexity of Caribbean slave societies. The son of an African prince who was shipped to the French colony of Saint-Domingue as a slave, Toussaint was born into slavery, but due to his intellectual and physical abilities was given a series of prestigious skilled roles on the plantation, ultimately becoming steward of all livestock, before receiving manumission and becoming a small landowner and slave-owner himself. Yet when the slave rebellion broke out in 1791, Toussaint joined with the slave rebels and became the key military and intellectual leader of the revolution, until his death in a French prison in 1802. Significantly, Toussaint was not always pro-independence; instead antislavery was his main philosophy and motivation, and he formed shifting strategic alliances with European powers based on this goal.

Toussaint L'Ouverture was a prolific correspondent, frequently composing as many as three hundred letters per day. Yet this letter from November 5, 1797, stands out as the most significant and enduring articulation of his political philosophy. Written at a moment when the French Directory was becoming increasingly conservative following the French parliament's abolition of slavery in 1794, with proslavery voices resurging (notably that of Representative Vaublanc, named in the letter), the letter underlines L'Ouverture's commitment to universal human rights and republicanism, and provides emphatic insistence that the formerly enslaved would never be slaves again. L'Ouverture's warnings would ultimately come to fruition in the scorched earth campaign that followed Napoleon's reintroduction of slavery in 1800 and led to the Haitian Declaration of Independence in January 1804.

Source: Nick Nesbitt (ed.) *Toussaint L'Ouverture, The Haitian Revolution* (London: Verso Books, 2008), pp. 32–35.

TOUSSAINT L'OUVERTURE
TO THE FRENCH DIRECTORY

When the people of St-Domingue first tasted the fruit of liberty that they hold from the equity of France; when to the violent upheavals of the revolution that announced it succeeded the pleasures of tranquility; when finally the rule of law took the place of anarchy under which the unfortunate colony had too long suffered, what fatality can have led the greatest enemy of its prosperity and our happiness still to dare to threaten us with the return of slavery? The impolitic and incendiary speech of Vaublanc has threatened the blacks less than the certainty of the plans meditated upon by the property owners of St-Domingue. Such insidious declamations should have no effect upon the wise legislators who have decreed liberty to humanity. The attacks the colonists propose against this liberty must be feared all the more insofar as they hide their detestable projects under the veil of patriotism. We know that illusory and specious descriptions have been made to you of the renewal of terrible violence. Already, perfidious emissaries have crept among us to foment destruction at the hands of the liberticides. They will not succeed, this I swear by all that is most sacred in liberty. My attachment to France, the gratitude that all the blacks conserve for her, make it my duty to hide from you neither the plans being fomented nor the oath that we renew to bury ourselves beneath the ruins of a country revived by liberty rather than suffer the return of slavery.

It is for you, Citizen Directors, to remove from over our heads the storm that the eternal enemies of our liberty are preparing in the shades of silence. It is for you to enlighten the Legislature, it is for you to prevent the enemies of the present system from spreading themselves on our unfortunate shores to sully them with new crimes. Do not allow our brothers, our friends, to be sacrificed to men who wish to reign over the ruins of the human species. But no, your wisdom will enable you to avoid the dangerous snares which our common enemies hold out for you. . . .

I send you with this letter a declaration which will acquaint you with the unity that exists between the proprietors of St-Domingue who are in France, those in the United States, and those who serve under the English banner. You will see there a resolution, unequivocal and carefully constructed, for the restoration of slavery; you will see there that their determination to succeed has led them to envelop themselves in the mantle of liberty in order to strike it more deadly blows. You will see that they are counting heavily on my willingness to espouse perfidious views out of fear for my children. It is not astonishing that these men who sacrifice their country to their interests are unable to conceive how many sacrifices a true love of country can support in a better father than they, since I unhesitatingly base the happiness of my children on that of my country, which they and they alone wish to destroy.

I shall never hesitate in choosing between the safety of St-Domingue and my personal happiness, but I have nothing to fear. It is to the solicitude of the French government that I have confided my children. . . . I would tremble with horror if it was into the hands of the colonists that I had sent them as hostages; but even if it were so, let them know that in punishing them for the fidelity of their father, they would only add one degree more to their barbarism, without any hope of making me fail in my duty. . . .

Blind as they are, they cannot see how this odious conduct on their part can become the signal of new disasters and irreparable misfortunes, and that far from it helping them regain what in their eyes liberty for all that has made them lose, they expose themselves to total ruin and the colony to its inevitable destruction. Could men who have once enjoyed the benefits of liberty look on calmly while it is taken from them! They bore their chains when they knew no condition of life better than that of slavery. But no, the hand that has broken our chains will not subject us to them again. France will not renounce her principles. She shall not permit the perversion of her sublime morality and the destruction of the principles that honour her the most, and the degradation of her most beautiful accomplishment, by rescinding the degree of 16 Pluviôse [February 4, 1794, abolishing slavery in the French colonies] that honours so well all of humanity. But if, in order to re-establish servitude to St-Domingue this were to be done, I declare to you that this would be to attempt the impossible. We have known how to confront danger to obtain our liberty, and we will know how to confront death to preserve it. This, Citizens and Directors, is the morality of the people of St-Domingue, these are the principles I transmit to you on their behalf.

Let me renew to you the oath that I have made: to cease to exist before gratitude is stricken from my heart and to remain faithful to France, to my duty, and before the land of liberty be profaned and blackened by the liberticides, before they can wrest from my hands this glaive, these arms that France has confided in me for the defence of her rights, for those of humanity, and for the triumph of liberty and equality.

Greetings and respect

Toussaint L'Ouverture

STUDY QUESTIONS

1. What insight does the letter provide into the relationship between political ideas and movements in Europe and revolutionary currents in Latin America and the Caribbean?
2. How does L'Ouverture define freedom?
3. How does L'Ouverture represent his relationship to the Haitian people? What insight does this give us about the types of political hierarchies and structures being forged in the crucibles of revolutionary wars?

LUCAS ALAMÁN

1.2 THE SIEGE OF GUANAJUATO, 1849

This document recounts one of the most significant events in the struggle for Mexican Independence—the aftermath of Miguel Hidalgo's famous "Grito de Dolores," issued on September 16, 1810, in which the parish priest proclaimed revolution in the name of Ferdinand VII and the Catholic Church (now celebrated as Mexico's Independence Day). Tens of thousands of Indians and peasants listened to Hidalgo's call for rebellion and joined his movement. This excerpt documents the armed siege of Guanajuato—a prosperous mining town, home to many Spanish elites—by Hidalgo's peasant army. The skirmish in Guanajuato lasted only hours but was marked by intense brutality and extreme violence against both civilians and soldiers defending the city, and was followed by extensive looting. Although Hidalgo's army successfully took the city, the looting and violence led many creole elites to withdraw their support from the rebel cause out of fear of the popular masses. Hidalgo himself was later captured and executed in 1811. This piece is written by Lucas Alamán, the son of a wealthy and aristocratic Guanajuato family, who was seventeen at the time of the siege, and who subsequently became a distinguished historian and one of the most important Conservative thinkers in early republican Mexico. Alamán was a direct eyewitness to the siege, although this account was written as part of a history of Mexico more than three decades after the event.

Source: Gilbert M. Joseph and Timothy J. Henderson (eds.) *The Mexico Reader: History, Culture and Politics* (Durham, NC: Duke University Press, 2002), pp. 169–188.

A little before twelve o'clock, in the avenue of Our Lady of Guanajuato, which is the entrance to the city from the plains of Marfil, there appeared a huge crowd of Indians with few rifles; most were carrying lances, sticks, slings, and arrows. The first of this group passed the bridge . . . and arrived in front of the adjoining trench, at the foot of Mendizábal Hill. Gilberto de Riaño—to whom his father had entrusted the command of that point, which he deemed the most hazardous—ordered them to stop in the name of the king, and since the crowd continued to advance, he gave the order to open fire, whereupon some Indians fell dead and the rest retreated hurriedly. In the avenue, a man from Guanajuato said they should go to El Cuarto Hill, and he showed them the way. The remaining groups of Hidalgo's footsoldiers, perhaps 20,000 Indians, joined by the people from the mines and lower classes of Guanajuato, were occupying the heights and all of the houses around [the Alhóndiga de] Granaditas (the public granary in which the corn harvest was stored), in which they placed soldiers from Celaya armed with rifles; meanwhile a corps of around two thousand cavalrymen, composed of country people with lances, mixed in among the ranks of the dragoons of the Queen's regiment led by Hidalgo, climbed along the road called Yerbabuena and arrived at [the top of San Miguel Hill], and from there went down to the city. Hidalgo went to the headquarters of the Prince's cavalry regiment, where he remained throughout the action. The column continued crossing through the town in order to station itself at Belén Street, and as they passed by they sacked a store that sold sweets, and they freed all the prisoners of both sexes who were locked up in the jail—no fewer than three or four hundred persons, among them serious criminals. They made the male prisoners march on the Alhóndiga.

The intendant, noting that the largest number of the enemy rushed to the side of the trench at the mouth of Los Pozitos Street . . . thought it necessary to reinforce the point. He took twenty infantrymen from the company of the peasants to join the battalion, and with more boldness than prudence he went with them to station them where he wanted them to be, accompanied by his assistant, José María Bustamante. Upon returning, as he was climbing the stairs to the door of the Alhóndiga, he was wounded about the left eye by

a rifle bullet and he immediately fell dead. The shot came from the window of one of the houses of the little plaza to the east of the Alhóndiga, and is said to have been fired by the corporal of the infantry regiment from Celaya. Thus, a glorious death ended the spotless life of the retired frigate captain Don Juan Antonio de Riaño, knight of the Order of Caltrava, intendant, *correjidor*, and the commandant of the armies of Guanjuato. . . .

The intendant's death introduced division and discord among the defenders of the Alhóndiga at the moment when it was most necessary that they act in unison and with firm resolution. The counselor of the intendancy, Manuel Pérez Valdés, citing the fact that in ordinance of the intendancy leadership falls to the counselor when the [intendant] is accidentally removed, claimed that since he was now the superior authority of the provinces, nothing should be done except by his command. He was inclined to surrender. Major Berzabal argued that, since this was a purely military situation, according to the ordinance he should take charge, since he was the veteran officer of the highest rank. He was resolved to keep up the defense. While this dispute could not be resolved, the confusion of the attack meant that everyone was giving commands and no one was obeying them, except for the soldiers who always recognized their old leaders. The crowd on El Cuarto Hill began a barrage of stones, hurling them by hand and shooting them with slings, a barrage that was so continuous it exceeded the thickest hail storm. In order to keep the combatants supplied with stones, swarms of Indians and the people of Guanajuato unceasingly picked up the round stones that covered the bottom of the Cata River. So great was the number of stones launched in the short time that the attack lasted, that the floor of the Alhóndiga's balcony was raised about a quarter above its ordinary level. It was impossible to defend the trenches, and the troops that garrisoned them were ordered to withdraw; Captain Escalera of the guard ordered that the door of the Alhóndiga be closed. With that, the Europeans who occupied the Hacienda of Dolores were left isolated and with no recourse but to sell their lives dearly, and the cavalry on the slope of the Cata River was in the same situation or worse. Nor could the people on the roof defend themselves for long, since it was dominated by the hills El Cuarto and San Miguel, although since the latter was farther away, less damage was done from there. And despite the havoc caused by the continuous fire of the troops from the garrison, the number of assailants was so great that those who fell were very promptly replaced by others, and they were not missed.

Once the trenches were abandoned and the troops who defended the roof withdrawn, that wild mob rushed to the base of the building: those in front were pushed by those who followed, unable to turn around, as in an ocean storm when some waves are impelled by others till they dash against the rocks. The brave man could not show his mettle, nor could the coward find a way to flee. The cavalry was completely routed, unable to use its weapons and horses. Captain Castilla died, some soldiers perished; the rest joined the conquerors. The valiant José Francisco Valenzuela, turning his horse about, rode up on the hill three times, opening a path with his sword; he was dragged from his saddle and suspended on the points of the lances of those who surrounded him in large numbers; even so, he killed some of those closest to him before receiving his death blow, shouting "Long live Spain!" until he gave up his final breath. He was a native of Irapuato and a lieutenant of the company of that village.

There was a store at the corner of Los Pozitos Street and Mount Los Mandamientos where they sold *ocote* [pine] chips, which the men who worked the mines by night used to illuminate the road. The crowd broke down the doors [of the store] and, loading up that fuel, they brought it to the door of the Alhóndiga and set it ablaze. Others, who were experienced at subterranean labors, approached the back of the building, which was surrounded by earthen walls . . . and they began to drill holes to undermine the foundation. Those inside the building hurled iron flasks, of which we have spoken, through the windows down into the crowd. These would explode and bring down many people, but immediately the mob would close in tight and snuff out the flasks that had fallen under their feet, which is why there were so few wounded among the assailants, even though a large number were killed. The discord among those under siege was such that, at the very moment when Gilberto Riaño (who was thirsty for vengeance on his father's death), Miguel Bustamante, and others were hurling flasks at the assailants, the counselor held up a white handkerchief

as a sign of peace. The people, attributing to perfidy what was nothing more than the effect of the confusion that prevailed inside the Alhóndiga, redoubled their furor and began to fight with greater cruelty. The counselor then ordered a soldier to climb down from the window to parley; the unfortunate man fell to the ground, broken to bits. Then Martín Septiem tried to leave, confident in his priestly vocation and in the Holy Christ he carried in his hands; the image of the Savior flew into splinters as stones struck it, and the priest, using the crucifix in his hand as an offensive weapon, managed to escape through the crowd, though badly wounded. The Spaniards, meanwhile, hearing only the voice of terror, tossed money from the windows in hopes of sparking the people's greed and thus placating the mob; others shouted their capitulation, and many, persuaded that their final hour had arrived, threw themselves at the feet of the priests to receive absolution.

Berzabal, seeing the door ablaze, gathered what soldiers he could of the battalion and stationed them at the entrance: as the door was consumed by flames, he ordered his soldiers to fire at close range, and many of the assailants perished. Still, those in the back of the crowd pushed forward, and the ones in front trampled over the dead, sweeping everything from before them with an irresistible force. The patio, stairs, and corridors of the Alhóndiga were very soon filled with Indians and common people. Berzabal, retreating with a handful of men who remained with him to a corner of the patio, defended his battalion's banners along with the standard-bearers Marmolejo and González. When these men fell dead at his side, he gathered up the banners and held them tightly with his left arm, and he held out with a sword—even though it had been destroyed by a pistol shot—against the multitude that surrounded him, until he fell pierced by many lances, still without abandoning the banners he had sworn to defend.

[With Berzabal's death] all resistance ceased, and no more than a few isolated shots were heard from some who still held out, such as the Spaniard Raymayor, who did not let the Indians come near till all of his cartridges were spent. The Europeans at the Hacienda of Dolores tried to save themselves through a back door that opened upon the log bridge over the Cata River, but they found that the assailants had already taken that bridge. They then retired to the well, where—since it was a high, strong spot—they defended themselves until the last of their ammunition ran out, causing much carnage among the insurgents . . . The few Europeans who remained alive at the end fell or were thrown into the well, and they drowned.

The taking of the Alhóndiga de Granaditas was entirely the work of the common people of Guanajuato, together with the numerous bands of Indians led by Hidalgo. As for Hidalgo and his fellow leaders, there was not, nor could there have been any disposition other than to lead the people to the hills and begin the attack. But once it had begun, it was impossible to maintain any order at all: there was no one to receive or follow orders, for there was no organization at all in that riotous crowd, nor were there lesser chiefs to lead the people. They rushed with extraordinary valor to take part in the first action of the war, and, once committed to combat, the Indians and people of the villages could not turn back, for the crowd surged forward upon those who went first, obliging them to win land and to instantaneously occupy any space left by those who died. The resistance of the besieged defenders, though intrepid, was without order or plan, since the intendant died before anyone else, and it is to this we may attribute the quick termination of the action, for by five in the afternoon it was all over.

The insurgents, after taking over the Alhóndiga, gave free reign to their vengefulness. Those who had surrendered begged their conquerors in vain for clemency; on their knees, they prayed that their lives be spared. Many of the soldiers of the battalion were dead; others escaped by taking off their uniforms and mixing with the crowd. Of the officers, many young men of the city's most distinguished families perished, and others were gravely wounded, among them Gilberto Riaño who died a few days later, and José María and Benigno Bustamante. Of the Spaniards, many of the richest and most important citizens died . . . Some managed to hide in granary number 21, where the corpses of the intendant and several others lay, but they were discovered and killed without mercy. All were despoiled of their clothes. When the rebels stripped the corpse of José Miguel Carrica, they found he was covered with haircloth, which gave rise to the rumor that a *gachupín* saint had been found. Those

who remained alive—naked, covered with wounds, tied up with rope—were taken to the public jail, which had been empty since the prisoners were freed. To get there, they had to cross the long expanse from the Alhóndiga while the unruly crowd threatened them with death at each step.

There are various calculations of the number of dead on both sides. The insurgents took pains to hide their dead, burying them that night in ditches they dug in the Cata River bottom. The city council, in its statement, estimated the dead at three thousand; Abásolo, at his trial, said that there were very few. The latter claim does not strike me as plausible, and the former I think is rather exaggerated. Some two hundred soldiers died, as well as one hundred and fifty Spaniards. Their naked corpses were seized by the feet and hands and carried or dragged to the nearby cemetery of Belén, where they were buried. The intendant's body spent two days exposed to the mockery of the mob: the people wished to investigate for themselves an absurd fable that had been circulating, which said that the intendant had a tail because he was a Jew. (This same ridiculous fable ran through the mob with respect to all of the Spaniards, even among those who had seen their naked corpses. Such is the ignorance of the common people!) . . . The [intendant's] body was then buried in a mean shroud that had been placed there by the monks of that convent, receiving none of the honor that should have been due the mortal remains of a noble conqueror. No sign of compassion was permitted: one woman in the crowd, who expressed sympathy for when the corpse of a European was carried by, was wounded in the face by the men who carried it.

The people devoted themselves to pillaging everything that had been gathered at the Alhóndiga, and it all disappeared within a few moments. Hidalgo wanted to reserve the ingots of silver and money for himself, but he could not prevent the people from taking them. Later some of the ingots were found and taken back, for they belonged to the army's treasury and so could not be included in the general looting. The Alhóndiga presented the most dreadful spectacle; the food that had been stored there was scattered all around; naked corpses were found half-buried in corn and money, all of it stained with blood. The looters killed one another fighting among themselves for booty. A rumor spread that the granaries holding the stores of gunpowder had been burned, and that the castle—which is what the people called the Alhóndiga—was about to blow up; the Indians fled, and the people on horseback sped through the streets to escape. With that, the common people of Guanajuato, who may have been the ones who spread this rumor, remained sole owner of the prize—at least until the rest, their fear having evaporated, came back to take their share.

The people who had stayed on the hilltops awaiting the results now came down to take part in the despoliation, even though they had not been involved in the combat. Together with the rest of the townspeople and the Indians who had come with Hidalgo, they began the general looting of the stores and homes of the Europeans of the city, which began that same afternoon and continued all through the night and all the next day. They ransacked more pitilessly than any foreign army could have done. The sad scene on that mournful night was lit by many torches of candlewood and *ocote*, and nothing was heard but the blows of doors being battered down, and the ferocious howls of the rabble who applauded upon seeing them fall and then charged as if in triumph to steal the merchandise, furniture, clothing, and all kinds of things. Women fled in terror to their neighbor's homes, crawling across the roads, and, still not knowing if they had lost a father or a husband in the Alhóndiga that afternoon; they watched as the treasures their men had collected during many years of work, industry, and economy were snatched away in an instant. Whole families who had awakened that day under the protection of a father or husband, some enjoying opulence, others taking pleasure in an honorable yet moderate lifestyle, lay down that night in a deplorable orphanhood and misery. It was not as if many people ceased being rich while just as many emerged from poverty; no, all those treasures that in active and industrious hands fomented commerce and mining, now went up in smoke without leaving any trace but a memory of ancient prosperity. It has taken many years to recover that prosperity, plus the great boost that Guanajuato later received from foreign mining companies and the fortuitous bonanzas some of these have enjoyed.

The looters grabbed the most valuable things from one another. The astute and clever people of Guanajuato took advantage of the ignorance of the Indians to take their loot away from them, or to buy it at a low price. They persuaded the Indians that ounces of gold were not coins, but copper medallions, and they bought them for two or three reales; they did the same with the jewelry, the value of which they themselves did not know. On the 29th, Hidalgo's birthday, Guanajuato presented the most lamentable aspect of disorder, ruin, and desolation. The plaza and the streets were full of fragments of furniture, the remains of the goods looted from the stores, and liquor that had been spilled once the people had drunk their fill. The people abandoned themselves to all manner of excess. Hidalgo's Indians made the strangest figures of all, for on top of their own clothing they wore the clothes they had taken from the homes of the Europeans, including the uniforms of magistrates, so that the Indians adorned themselves with embroidered dress-coats and gilded hats while barefoot and in the most complete state of inebriation.

The pillage was not limited to the homes and stores of the Europeans of the city; the same thing was done in the mines, and the looting became extensive at the metal-refining haciendas. The commoners of Guanajuato, having already killed in the Alhóndiga the industrious men of these establishments—the men who had enabled them to earn their keep by paying them considerable wages—now ruined the establishments themselves, dealing the death blow to that branch of mining that had been the source of the wealth not just of the city of Guanajuato, but of the whole province.

Hidalgo wanted to put a stop to this disorder, so he published a proclamation on Sunday, September 30. Not only was this proclamation not obeyed, but inasmuch as there was nothing left to loot in the houses and stores, the commoners began to drag the iron trellises down from the balconies, and they broke into the homes of Mexicans whom they suspected of hiding goods belonging to Spaniards. Among the homes so threatened was that of my own family, which was located atop a store that had belonged to a Spaniard who had died in the well at Dolores, a man named José Posadas. Although the home had already been sacked, one of Posadas's trusted porters let it be known that in an interior patio there was a storeroom that he himself had stocked with money and goods. It was very difficult to hold the people back; they entered through the mezzanine and made their way to the foot of the stairway. I was in no little danger myself, having been raised European. Amid this conflict, my mother resolved to go and see the priest Hidalgo, with whom she had longtime friendly relations, and I went with her. It was quite risky for a decently dressed person to walk the streets among that mob, drunk with rage and liquor. We nonetheless arrived without incident at the headquarters of the Prince's regiment, where Hidalgo was staying. We found Hidalgo in a room filled with people of all classes. In one corner there was a considerable stack of silver ingots that had been recovered from the Alhóndiga, and which were still stained with blood; in another corner was a stack of lances, and haphazardly suspended from one of the walls was the painting of the image of Guadalupe, which served as a symbol of this enterprise. The priest was seated on his field cot with a small table in front of him, wearing his ordinary costume, but with a purple shoulder-belt on top of the jacket, assuring my mother of their longtime friendship. Once made aware of our fears for the house, he gave us an escort commanded by a muleteer from the Cacalote Ranch near Salvatierra, Ignacio Centeno, whom Hidalgo had made a captain and whom he ordered to defend my house and to guard the belongings of Posadas. Hidalgo told the escort to bring those things to his lodgings as soon as possible, for he needed them to meet the expenses of the army. Centeno thought it would be impossible to hold back the growing tumult, for at each instant more and more people gathered, determined to join in the looting. He sent one of his soldiers to Hidalgo, thinking the priest's presence would contain the disorder which the public proclamation had not been sufficient to do.

Hidalgo came on horseback to the plaza where my house was located, accompanied by his generals. At the head of the group was the painting of the image of Guadalupe, and an Indian on foot banging a drum. Some country people followed on horseback, along with some of the Queen's dragoons in two ranks. The priest and his generals presided over this procession-of-sorts, dressed in jackets like those worn by small town militia officers; in place of insignia of the Queen's regiment, they had hung silver cords and tassels from their epaulets, which no doubt they had seen in some picture of the French generals' aides-de-camp; they all wore the image of the Virgin of Guadalupe on their hats. When Hidalgo's retinue arrived in front of the Posadas store where the largest mob was gathered, they ordered the mob to withdraw. When the people did not obey, [one of the officers] tried to keep them away from the doors of the store by forcing his way into the midst of the crowd. Nearby, the flagstones formed a sharp slope, and at the moment they were covered with all sorts of filth and were very slippery. [The officer] fell off his horse, and while trying to get up, he angrily drew his sword and began to wield it at the crowd; people fled in terror, leaving one man gravely wounded. Hidalgo continued circling the plaza, ordering that the men who were dragging the balconies off the houses be fired upon. With that the crowd began to disperse, though for some time large groups remained selling the objects they had ransacked for outrageous prices.

Hidalgo did his best to keep some things hidden from the people. Captain Centeno and the guards stayed for several days in my house at my family's expense, and they spent those days removing the money and other belongings from Posadas's interior storeroom and bringing them to the cavalry headquarters. It was determined that they were worth around 40,000 pesos. As Centeno became a familiar presence in my house, he was once asked for his views of the revolution in which he had taken part. He replied, with the sincerity of a humble man of the country, that his wishes could easily be summed up as follows: to go to Mexico City and place the priest on the throne, and then, with the rewards the Hidalgo would pay him for his services, he would return to working in the fields. What happened in my house with the belongings of Posadas was repeated in many other houses, since although there were faithful servants who helped to salvage what remained of their masters' treasures, others betrayed their masters and denounced the places where they had hidden their money and jewelry. . . .

When the tumult of the siege and sacking of the city had calmed somewhat, Hidalgo lodged his cavalrymen in the ransacked haciendas. The Indians remained scattered throughout the streets, and many of them, content with the loot they had taken, returned to their villages and *rancherías*. Desertion did not bother the priest at all, however, because he was sure he would find plenty of new recruits in all the villages he passed through. . . .

STUDY QUESTIONS

1. In what ways does Alamán's social standing impact his view of the siege? Does Alamán's elite background affect the reliability of the source?
2. Does the source provide insight into what motivated Hidalgo's troops into battle? Is it possible to distinguish between class-based and political interests?

SIMÓN BOLÍVAR

1.3 THE JAMAICA LETTER, 1815

Simón Bolívar is an iconic figure of South American independence. Born in Venezuela into a family of enormous privilege and wealth, he became the most important military strategist and intellectual visionary of the independence movement. The Jamaica letter is the most famous and significant of Simón Bolívar's voluminous writings, and is considered one of the foundational documents of Latin American history. Written at a moment of defeat, during his exile to Jamaica that followed the retaking of Venezuela by independence forces in 1814, the letter lays out his vision for the future of an independent Spanish America and was written in the hope of attracting British support for his movement. The document articulates a vision of "Spanish Americans" as a unified and distinct people, and envisages a political union stretching the full span of the South American continent. The letter is the foundation for the political vision Bolívar later sought to implement (unsuccessfully) as president of Gran Colombia.

Kingston, 6 September 1815

I hasten to reply to the letter of 29 August, which you [Henry Cullen] honored me by writing and which I received with the greatest satisfaction. . . .

As I feel obliged to address the concerns of your kind and well-meaning letter, I am inspired to send these lines to you, in which you will find not the brilliant ideas you hope for but merely the candid expression of my thoughts.

"Three centuries ago," you write, "marked the beginning of the atrocities committed by the Spaniards in the vast hemisphere of Columbus." Atrocities discounted as fables by contemporary historians, simply because they seem to transcend the limits of human perversity. Modern critics would never have accepted such horrors as true had they not been verified by an endless stream of texts documenting the events. The philanthropic bishop of Chiapas, the apostle of American, [Bartolomé de] Las Casas, has bequeathed to posterity a brief account of them, extracted from the summaries of the indictments brought against the conquistadores in Seville, with testimony by every respectable person living in the New World at the time, and with the detailed records of the accusations the tyrants leveled at each other, all of this documented by the most sublime historians of the period. All impartial accounts support the integrity and passion for truth of that friend of humanity, who so fervently and forcefully denounced before his own government and contemporaries the most depraved acts of that bloodfest.

Source: David Bushnell (ed.) *El Libertador: Writings of Simón Bolívar* (Oxford: Oxford University Press, 2003), pp. 12–30.

How deeply grateful I am to read the passage from your letter where you write, "May the good fortune experienced at that time by the Spanish armies now favor the armies of their enemies, the terribly oppressed South Americans!" I take this wish as a prediction, if justice has any part in the conflicts between men. Success will crown our efforts because the destiny of America is irrevocably fixed; the tie that bound her to Spain is severed, for it was nothing but an illusion binding together the two sides of that vast monarchy. What formerly united them now separates them. The hatred we feel for the Peninsula is greater than the sea separating us from it; it would be easier to bring the two continents together than to reconcile the spirits and minds of the two countries. The habit of obedience, a commerce of shared interests, knowledge, and religion; mutual goodwill; a tender concern for the birthland and glory of our ancestors; in brief, everything that constituted our hopes came to us from Spain. This was the source of a principle of adhesion that seemed eternal, even though the behavior of our rulers undermined that sympathy, or to put it more accurately, that closeness imposed on us by rule of force. Today, the opposite is true: death, dishonor, everything harmful threatens us and makes us fearful. That wicked stepmother is the source of all our suffering. The veil has been rent, and now we can see the light now she wants to return us to darkness. The chains have been broken, we've been liberated, and now our enemies want to make us slaves. This is why America fights with such defiance, and it would be rare should such desperate intensity not bring victory in its wake.

Just because our successes have been partial and intermittent is no reason to doubt our fortune. In some places the independents win victories, while in others the tyrants seem to be gaining ground. But what is the final outcome? Is not the entire New World stirred into action and armed for defense? If we look around, we observe a simultaneous struggle throughout this hemisphere.

Ah, the madness of our enemy, to want to conquer America once again, without a navy, with no money in the treasury, almost without any soldiers! The few she has are scarcely enough to keep her own people in a state of forced obedience and to defend herself against her neighbors. Besides, is there any way that this nation could control the commerce of half the world without a manufacturing base, with no productivity from the land, with no art, no sciences, no clear policy? Even if such a mad project were realized, and even supposing that they managed to pacify their empire, would not the children of today's Americans, allied with the children of their European conquerors, within a single generation, feel a resurgence of the same patriotic aspirations for which they now struggle and die?

Europe could do Spain a favor by dissuading her from this reckless course; she would at the very least avoid the waste of funds and the shedding of blood, so that by focusing on her own immediate interests she could begin to rebuild her prosperity and power on foundations far more solid than these uncertain conquests, precarious commercial enterprises, and violent pillaging in lands that are remote, hostile, and powerful. Europe herself, with an eye to rational foreign relations, should have prepared and carried out the project of American independence, not only because world equilibrium demands it but because this is the legitimate and sure way to acquire overseas markets. Europe, unafflicted by the violent passions of vengeance, ambition, and greed motivating Spain, would have been fully justified by reasons of fairness and enlightenment to proceed on this course dictated by her own best interests.

There is unanimous agreement in this regard among all the writers who have treated the topic. Consequently, we were justified in expecting all civilized nations to rush to our aid, helping achieve a goal whose advantages are mutual to both hemispheres. Never were reasonable hopes so frustrated! Not only the Europeans but even our brothers to the north stood apart as idle spectators of this struggle, which is in essence the most just and in outcome the most beautiful and important of any ever undertaken in ancient or modern times. Truly, is there any way to calculate the transcendent effects of freedom for Columbus's hemisphere?. . .

It is even more difficult to predict the future lot of the New World, or to make definitive statements about its politics, or to make prophecies about the form of government it will adopt. Any idea relative to the future of this land seems to me to be purely speculative. Could anyone have foreseen, when the human race was in its infancy, besieged by so much uncertainty, ignorance, and error, what particular regime it would embrace for its own survival? Who would have dared predict that one nation would be a republic or another a monarchy, that this one would be unimportant, that one great? In my opinion, this is the image of our situation. We are a small segment of the human race; we possess a world apart, surrounded by vast seas, new in almost every art and science, though to some extent old in the practices of civil society. I consider the current state of America similar to the circumstances surrounding the fall of the Roman Empire, when each breakaway province formed a political system suitable to its interests and situation or allied itself to the particular ambition of a few leaders, families, or corporations. There is, though, this notable difference, that those dispersed members reestablished their former nations with the changes demanded by the circumstances or events, while we, who preserve only the barest vestige of what we were formerly, and who are moreover neither Indians nor Europeans, but a race halfway between the legitimate owners of the land and the Spanish usurpers—in short, being American by birth and endowed with rights from Europe—find ourselves forced to defend these rights against the natives while maintaining our position in the land against the intrusion of the invaders. Thus, we find ourselves in the most extraordinary and complicated situation. Even though it smacks of divination to predict the outcome of the political path America is following, I venture to offer some conjectures, which of course I characterize as arbitrary guesses dictated by rational desire, not by any process of probable reasoning.

The posture of those who dwell in the American hemisphere has been over the centuries purely passive. We were at a level even lower than servitude, and by that very reason hindered from elevating ourselves to the enjoyment of freedom. Allow me to offer these considerations to place the question in context. Slave states are identified as such by virtue of their constitution or the abuse of it. People are slaves when the government, by its essence or through its vices, tramples and usurps the rights of the citizen or subject. Applying these principles, we will find that America was not only deprived of its freedom but deprived as well of the opportunity to practice its own active tyranny. Let me explain what I mean. In absolute regimes, no limits are acknowledged in the exercise of governmental powers: The will of the great sultan, khan, bey, and other despots is the supreme law, and this is executed almost arbitrarily by the lesser pashas, khans, and satraps of Turkey and Persia, who have organized a system of oppression in which subordinates participate according to the authority entrusted to them. They are in charge of the civil, military, and political administration as well as the treasury and the religion. But there is this difference: The rulers of Isfahan are, after all, Persians; the viziers of the Grand Vizier are Turks; the sultans of Tartary are Tartars. China does not seek her military commanders and judges from the country of Ghengis Khan, who conquered her, even though the present-day Chinese are direct descendants of those subjugated by the ancestors of the present-day Tartars.

How different it was in our case. From the beginning we were plagued by a practice that in addition to depriving us of the rights to which we were entitled left us in a kind of permanent infancy with respect to public affairs. If we had even been allowed to manage the domestic aspects of our internal administration, we would understand the processes and mechanisms of public affairs; then we would enjoy the personal esteem in the eyes of the public that derives from a certain automatic respect so necessary to maintain during revolutions. This is why I said that we were deprived of an active tyranny, since we were not allowed to practice those functions.

The Americans, within the Spanish system still in force, and perhaps now more than ever, occupy no other place in society than that of servants suited for work, or that of simple consumers, and even this role is limited by appalling restrictions: for instance, the prohibition against the cultivation of European crops or the sale of products monopolized by the king, the restriction against the construction of factories that don't even exist on the peninsula, exclusive privileges for engaging in commerce even of items that are basic necessities, the barriers between American provinces, preventing them from establishing contact, or communication, or doing business with one another. In short, would you like to know the extent of our destiny? Fields for the cultivation of indigo, grain, coffee, sugar cane, cacao, and cotton, empty prairies for raising cattle, wilderness for hunting ferocious beasts, the bowels of the earth for excavating gold that will never satisfy the lust of that greedy nation.

So negative was our situation that I can find no other like it in any other civilized society, no matter how much I peruse the succession of epochs and political systems of all nations. To expect that a land so abundantly endowed, so extensive, rich, and populous should remain merely passive, is this not an outrage and a violation of the rights of humanity?

We were, as I just explained, lost, or worse, absent from the universe in all things relative to the science of government and the administration of the stat. We were never viceroys, never governors, except in extraordinary circumstances; hardly ever bishops or archbishops; never diplomats; soldiers, only in lower ranks; nobles, but without royal privileges. In short, we were never leaders, never fanciers, hardly even merchants— all in direct contravention of our institutions. . . .

The events on the [South American] mainland have demonstrated that perfectly representative institutions are not appropriate to our character, our customs, and our current level of knowledge and experience. In Caracas, party spirit had its origins in the social groups, assemblies, and popular elections, and these parties returned us to slavery. And just as Venezuela has been the American republic most advanced in her political institutions, she has also been the clearest example of the impracticality of the democratic and federalist model for our emerging states. In New Granada, the excessive power of the provincial governments and the lack of centralization in general have led that previous country to the situation it finds itself in today [1815]. For this reason, its weak enemies have managed to survive, against all probability. Until our compatriots acquire the political skills and virtues that distinguish our brothers to the north, entirely popular systems, far from being favorable to us, will, I greatly fear, lead to our ruin. Unfortunately, the acquisition of these qualities to the necessary level would seem to be very remote from us; on the contrary, we are dominated by the vices contracted under the rule of a nation like Spain, which has shown itself to excel only in pride, ambition, vengeance, and greed.

"It is harder," says Montesquieu, "to rescue a country from slavery than to enslave a free one." This truth is verified by the annals of every period in history, which show most free nations being subjected to the yoke and very few subject nations recovering from their freedom. Despite this convincing evidence, the people of South America have manifested the inclination to establish liberal and even perfect institutions, an effect,

no doubt, of the instinct all men share of aspiring to the highest possible degree of happiness, which is invariably achieved in civil societies founded on the principles of justice, freedom, and equality. But are we capable of maintaining in proper balance the difficult undertaking of a republic? Is it conceivable that a newly liberated people can be launched into the sphere of freedom without their wings disintegrating and hurling them into the abyss, like Icarus? Such a wonder has never been seen, is inconceivable. In consequence, there is no rational basis for such a hope.

More than anyone, I would like to see America become the greatest nation on earth, regarded not so much for its size and wealth as for its freedom and glory. Although I aspire to a perfect government for my country, I can't persuade myself that the New World is ready at this time to be governed by a grand republic. Since this is impossible, I dare not wish it, and even less do I desire a universal American monarchy, because such a project, without even being practical, is also impossible. The abuses that currently exist would not be reformed, and our regeneration would be fruitless. The American states need the stewardship of paternalistic governments to cure the wounds and ravages of despotism and war. The metropolis, for example, would be Mexico, which is the only country capable of assuming that role, because of her intrinsic power, without which there can be no metropolis. Let us imagine that the Isthmus of Panama were the metropolis, being the central point for all the extremes of this vast land. Would these not persist in their current state of lethargy and disorder? For a single government to bring to life, to animate, to marshal all the resources of a public prosperity, and to correct, enlighten, and perfect the New World, it would have to have the powers of a God, or at least the enlightenment and virtues of all human beings.

The partisan spirit vexing our states would then flare up more fiercely, since the only source of power capable of quenching it would be far away. Besides, the notables of the [regional] capitals would balk at the domination of the metropolitans, whom they would regard as just so many tyrants. Their jealousy would be so intense that they would compare them to the hateful Spaniards. In short, such a monarchy would be a monstrous colossus, whose own weight would bring it down at the least convulsion.

M. de Pradt has wisely divided America into fifteen or seventeen independent states, each governed by its own monarch. I concur with such a division, because America is large enough to support the creation of seventeen nations. As for his second point, although it would be quite simple to achieve, it is less practical, so I am opposed to the idea of American monarchies. Here are my reasons: Rightly understood, the interest of a republic is limited to concerns about its preservation, prosperity, and glory. Since freedom exercises no power, because it is directly opposed to it, there is nothing to motivate republicans to extend the borders of their nation, in detriment of their own resources, for the mere purpose of forcing their neighbors to participate in a liberal constitution. They acquire no new rights; they derive no advantage by defeating them, unless they follow Rome's example in reducing them to colonies, either conquered or allied. Such notions and examples are in direct opposition to the principles of justice of republican systems. I will go even further: They are in clear opposition to the interests of their citizens, because a state that is too large in itself or in conjunction with its dependent territories ultimately falls into decadence and converts its freedom into tyranny. It relaxes the principles that were meant to preserve it and lapses ultimately into despotism. The unique quality of small republics is their permanence while large ones suffer a variety of changes, always tending toward empire. Almost all small republics have been long-lasting; the only large one that lasted for several centuries was Rome, but that was because the capital was a republic while the rest of its possessions were governed by different laws and institutions.

The politics of a king is quite different, his inclination being directed constantly to the increase of his possessions, wealth, and powers—with good reason, because his authority grows with these acquisitions both in the eyes of his neighbors and in those of his own subjects, who come to fear him as a power as formidable as his empire, which is maintained through war and conquest. For these reasons I believe that Americans, desirous of peace, sciences, art, commerce, and agriculture, would prefer republics to kingdoms, and it seems to me that these desires are also in keeping with the aspirations of Europe.

Of all popular and representative systems I find the federalist system too perfect, in that it requires political virtues and skills far superior to ours. For the same reason I reject the monarchical blend of aristocracy and democracy, which has brought such fortune and splendor to England. Since the most perfected form of republic and monarchy is beyond our capacity, let us avoid falling into demagogic anarchy or monocratic tyranny. Let us seek a middle way between these opposite extremes, either of which will lead us to a founder on the identical reefs of misery and dishonor. In an effort to resolve my doubts about the future lot of America, I will venture the following suggestion: Let us strive not for the best but for the most likely of attainment.

For reasons of geography, wealth, population, and character, I imagine that the Mexicans will initially attempt to establish a representative republic, granting great power to the executive, concentrating it in a single individual who, if he performs his duties properly and fairly, will almost certainly hold his authority for life. Should he, through incompetence or violent exercise of power, stir up a successful popular revolt, this same executive power may end up being conferred on an assembly. If the ruling party is military or aristocratic, it will likely demand a monarchy, which will at first be limited and constitutional but inevitably deteriorate into absolutism, for we have to concede that nothing is more difficult to maintain in the political order than a mixed monarchy and that only people as patriotic as the English could contain the authority of a king and sustain the spirit freedom under a scepter and a crown.

The states of the Isthmus of Panama as far north as Guatemala will perhaps form a confederation. Its magnificent strategic position between two great oceans may in time result in a universal emporium, its canals shortening the distances between worlds and reinforcing commercial ties between Europe, America, and Asia, bringing tribute to this happy region from the four quarters of the globe. Here alone, perhaps, it will be possible to establish a world capital, as Constantine aspired for Byzantium to become for the ancient world.

New Granada will unite with Venezuela if they can agree to form a central republic, whose capital might be Maracaibo. Or perhaps a new city named for the philanthropic hero, Las Casas, will be built on the border of the two countries near the magnificent port of Bahía-Honda. This site, although little known, is advantageous in all respects. It is easily accessible, yet in such a dominant position that it can be made impregnable. It has a pure, healthy climate, terrain as suitable for agriculture as for raising cattle, and an abundance of wood for construction. The natives who inhabit it would become civilized, and our possessions would grow with the acquisition of the Goajira [Peninsula]. This nation would be named Colombia in fair and grateful tribute to the creator of our hemisphere. Its government might be modeled on the English, though in place of a king there would be an executive power elected for life, never hereditary, assuming that a republic is the goal. The senate or upper legislative body would be hereditary, and during times of political turmoil it would mediate between the frustrations of the people and unpopular governmental decrees. Finally, there would be a legislative body, freely elected, as unencumbered by restrictions as the English House of Commons. This constitution would borrow elements from all political forms, though I would hope it would not partake of their vices. As this Colombia is my country, I have an inalienable right to wish for it what I believe is best. It is quite possible that New Granada, being intensely addicted to the federalist system, would not wish to subject itself to a centralized government. It might, then, form its own state that, if it survived, would attack great prosperity because of the abundance and variety of its resources.

We know little about the opinions prevailing in Buenos Aires, Chile, and Peru; judging by what can be surmised from appearances, in Buenos Aires there will be a centralized government dominated by the military as a consequence of internal divisions and wars abroad. This system will inevitably degenerate into an oligarchy, or a monarchy with greater or lesser restrictions, these being impossible to characterize or predict. Such an outcome would be painful to behold, because the people living there deserve a more glorious destiny.

The kingdom of Chile is destined, by the nature of its geography, by the innocent and virtuous customs of its inhabitants, by the example of its neighbors, the indomitable republicans of Arauco, to enjoy the blessings conferred by the just and gentle laws of a republic. If any American republic is to endure, I am inclined to believe it will be Chile. There, the spirit of freedom has never waned; the vices of Europe and Asia will come late or never to corrupt the customs of that far corner of the world. Its territory is limited; it will always be free of contagion from other peoples; it will not alter its laws, its customs, or its habits; it will preserve its uniformity in political and religious ideas; in a word, Chile can be free.

Peru, to the contrary, is marked by two elements that are inimical to any just and liberal regime: gold and slaves. The first corrupts everything; the second is inherently corrupt. The soul of a slave rarely manages to appreciate the wholesome condition of freedom. It turns to rage during uprisings or to servility in its chains.

Although these truths could be applied to all of America, I believe they are most justified with regard to Lima, because of the concepts I have presented and because of her collusion with her Spanish masters against her own brothers, the illustrious sons of Quito, Chile, and Buenos Aires. Obviously, to win freedom, some degree of effort is required. I assume that in Lima, the rich will not tolerate democracy, nor will the slaves and free pardos tolerate aristocracy. The rich would prefer the tyranny of a single individual, so as not to suffer the violence of the mob, and also to establish a somewhat peaceful order. It will be a wonder if Peru manages to recover her independence.

From the foregoing, we can deduce certain consequences: The American provinces are involved in a struggle for emancipation, which will eventually succeed; a few will constitute themselves as conventional federal and centralized republics; almost inevitably the larger territories will establish monarchies, some so wretched that they will devour their natural and human resources in present and future revolutions, for it will be difficult to consolidate a great monarchy, impossible to maintain a great republic.

The idea of merging the entire New World into a single nation with a single unifying principle to provide coherence to the parts and to the whole is both grandiose and impractical. Because it has a common origin, a common language, similar customs, and one religion, we might conclude that it should be possible for a single government to oversee a federation of the different states eventually to emerge. However, this is not possible, because America is divided by remote climates, diverse geographies, conflicting interests, and dissimilar characteristics. How beautiful it would be if the Isthmus of Panama could be for us what Corinth was for the Greeks! I hope that someday we will have the good fortune to install there an august congress of the representatives of these republics, kingdoms, and empires for the purpose of considering and discussing the important issues of peace and war with the nations of the rest of the world. Such a corporation might conceivably emerge at some felicitous moment in our regeneration; any other thought is as impractical as the praiseworthy delirium of the Abbé de Saint-Pierre, who proposed assembling a European congress to decide the fate and interests of those nations.

Undoubtedly, unity is what we need to complete our project of regeneration. However, our division is not surprising, for such is the nature of civil wars, usually fought between two factions: conservations and reformers. Generally, the former are more numerous, because the rule of custom inclines us to obedience to established powers; the latter are always less numerous but more passionate and enlightened. In this way physical mass is balanced by moral force, so that the conflict is prolonged and the results are uncertain. Fortunately, in our case, mass has followed intelligence.

I will tell you exactly what we need to ready ourselves to expel the Spaniards and form a free government:

unity, of course; however, such unity will not come to us through divine miracle but through sensible action and well-organized effort. America has come together here because it feels itself abandoned by all other nations, isolated in the world, without diplomatic relations or military support, and besieged by a Spain that wields more machinery for war than anything we can amass in secret.

When success is uncertain, when the state is weak, and when the undertaking is still remote in time and space, all men vacillate; opinions are divided, inflamed by passion and by the enemy, which seeks to win easy victory in this way. When we are at last strong, under the auspices of a liberal nation that lends us its protection, then we will cultivate in harmony the virtues and talents that lead to glory; then we will follow the majestic path toward abundant prosperity marked out by destiny for South America; then the arts and sciences that were born in the Orient and that brought the enlightenment to Europe will fly to a free Colombia, which will nourish and shelter them.

Such, sir, are the observations and thoughts that I am honored to submit for your consideration and which you may correct or reject according to their merit. I implore you to understand that I have expressed myself forthrightly, not to be discourteous but because I believe I am in a position to inform you on these matters.

Yours,

Simón Bolívar

STUDY QUESTIONS

1. How does Bolívar represent Spanish colonialism? How did Spanish rule impact South American political and economic development, in his opinion?
2. What characteristics does Bolívar see as distinguishing Spanish Americans from Spaniards? How does he grapple with racial and ethnic difference?
3. What type of government does Bolívar see as most suitable for implementation in South America? What rationale does he use to support his arguments?

SIMÓN BOLÍVAR

1.4 DECREE FOR THE EMANCIPATION OF THE SLAVES, JUNE 2, 1816

One of the decisive moments in Bolívar's leadership was his decision to abolish slavery in 1816. Bolívar was born into a slave-owning family, but liberty and freedom were the central planks of his political philosophy. He had also directly benefited from antislavery when the newly independent state of Haiti provided him with refuge and supplies following his army's defeat in Cartagena in 1815. Yet Bolívar's abolitionism was motivated by pragmatism and strategy as well as idealism and moral values. Bolívar recognized the need to gain the support of the black and mixed-race masses that formed the majority of Venezuela's population, and notably opened his officer ranks to non-whites, creating a critical avenue for black social mobility. In his abolition decree, Bolívar linked emancipation to military service, ensuring that all freed slaves would form part of his army.

Carúpano, 2 June 1816
Simón Bolívar
Commander in Chief and Captain General of the Armies of Venezuela and New Granada, etc.
To the Inhabitants of the Río Caribe, Carúpano, and Cariaco
Greetings:
Considering that justice, policy, and the country imperiously demand the inalienable rights of nature, I have decided to formally decree absolute freedom for the slaves who have groaned under the Spanish yoke during the three previous centuries. Considering that the Republic needs the services of all her children, we must impose on these new citizens the following conditions:

Article 1—Every healthy man between the ages of fourteen and sixty shall appear in the parish church of his district to enlist under the flag of Venezuela, within twenty-four hours of the publication of this decree.

Article 2—Old men, women, and children, and all invalids shall be exempt from this day forth from military service exempt as well from any domestic or field service in which they were previously employed for the benefit of their masters.

Article 3—The new citizen who refuses to bear arms in fulfillment of the sacred duty to defend his freedom shall be subject to servitude, not only for himself but also for his children under the age of fourteen, his wife, and his aged parents.

Article 4—The relatives of the military occupied in the army of liberation shall enjoy the rights of citizens and the absolute freedom granted to them by this decree in the name of the Republic of Venezuela.

The present regulation shall have the force of law and be faithfully executed by the Republican Authorities of Río Caribe, Carúpano, and Cariaco.

Signed into law in the General Headquarters of Carúpano on 2 June 1816.

Bolívar

Source: David Bushnell (ed.) *El Libertador: Writings of Simón Bolívar* (Oxford University Press, 2003), pp.177–178.

STUDY QUESTIONS

1. What conditions were placed on the emancipation of the slaves? How would this impact former slaves' experiences of freedom?
2. How does Bolívar account for the existence of slavery as an institution in South America? How does this correlate to his position as a former slave-owner?

AUGUSTIN DE ITURBIDE

1.5 THE PLAN OF IGUALA, FEBRUARY 24, 1821

The Plan of Iguala was a revolutionary decree passed in the final stages of the war for Mexican Independence. It laid out the constitutional framework for an independent Mexican government. Promulgated in February of 1821 by Augustin de Iturbide, a creole landowner who had assumed leadership of the revolutionary army, the Plan of Iguala was ratified into law by the Treaty of Córdoba in August 1821, thus establishing an independent Mexico with Iturbide as monarch. The document is notable for the three central principles it laid out (often referred to as the "Three Guarantees"): the primacy of Roman Catholicism, the political independence of Mexico as a constitutional monarchy, and equal rights under the law for all citizens of Mexico. As a framework for governance it was short-lived: the ratification of 1821 established Iturbide as emperor of Mexico, but this was not recognized by Spain, and Iturbide's monarchy was opposed by many other Mexican generals, governors, and high-ranking officials. In 1823, facing far-reaching rebellion, Iturbide abdicated the throne and went into exile, reinstating the Congress. The first Mexican republic was established the following year. Yet the document remains critically important for understanding the political ideals and philosophies that shaped Mexican independence, as well as the ascendancy of a more conservative approach to political governance as contrasted with independence movements in South America.

PLAN OF THE COLONEL
D.DON AGUSTIN ITURBIDE

Plan or indications to the government that must be provisionally installed with the objective of ensuring our sacred religion and establishing the independence of the Mexican Empire: and it will have the title of the North American Government Junta, proposed by Colonel. D.Don Agustin de Iturbide to his Excellency, the Viceroy of N.S. New Spain, Count de Venadito.

1. The religion of New Spain is and shall be Catholic, apostolic and Roman, without toleration of any other.
2. New Spain is independent of the old and of any other power, including those within our Continent.
3. Its Government shall be a Monarchy moderated by the Kingdom's particular and flexible Constitution.
4. Its Emperor will be D.Don Fernando VII, and if he does not personally present himself to take the oath in Mexico within the term prescribed by the

Source: Center for Digital Scholarship, Rice University. Translated by Cecilia Bonnor

Courts, his Most Serene Highness, the Prince Carlos D.Don Francisco de Paulo, Archduke Carlos, or another individual of the Royal Household that the Congress considers suitable will be called upon to take his place.

5. While the courts convene, a Junta will meet to assure compliance with the plan in all extents.

6. Said Junta. Which will be designated as Governing, must be composed of representatives, as dictated by his Excellency, the Viceroy's official letter.

7. While D.Don Fernando VII presents himself in Mexico to be sworn in, the Junta will govern in the name of His Majesty by virtue of its oath to remain loyal to the nation; however the orders that he may have imparted will be suspended during the time in which he is not sworn in.

8. If D.Don Fernando VII does not consider it worthwhile to come to Mexico, the Junta or the Regency shall rule in the name of the nation while the issue of the Emperor to be crowned is resolved.

9. This government shall be supported by the army of the three guaranties that will be discussed later.

10. The courts shall resolve the continuation of the Junta, or its substitution with a Regency if deemed necessary, while awaiting the person who should be crowned.

11. The courts shall immediately establish the constitution of the Mexican Empire.

12. All the inhabitants of New Spain, without any distinction between Europeans, Africans, or Indians, are citizens of this Monarchy, and have access to all employment according to their merits and virtues.

13. Every citizen's person and his properties shall be respected and protected by the government.

14. The secular and regular cleric will be preserved in all its rights and pre-eminences.

15. The Junta shall assure that all the branches of the state remain without any alteration and that all the political, ecclesiastic, civil, and military personnel [remain] in the same state as they exist today. Only those that manifest dissent with the plan shall be removed, replaced by those more distinguished by virtue and merit.

16. A protective army will be formed that shall be called [the army] of the three guarantees, and it will take under its protection: first, the conservation of the Roman Catholic apostolic religion, cooperating

by all means that are within its reach so that there will be no mixing with any other sect and opportunely attacking the enemies that could damage it; second, the independence under the manifested system; third, the intimate union of Americans and Europeans, thereby guaranteeing the bases so fundamental to the happiness of New Spain, sacrificing their lives for all individuals, from the first to the last, before consenting to their infringement.

17. The troops of the army will strictly observe the ordinances to the letter, and the chiefs and officers will continue to operate under the same laws as they do today: that is, in their respective classes that access to open employment as well as any posts that will be vacated by those who do not wish to toe the line, or for any other cause, and with access for those that are considered regular troops.

18. The troops of said army shall be considered regular troops.

19. The same will take place with those that follow this plan. Those that do not differ, those of the system prior to the independence that join said army immediately, and the countrymen who intend to enlist, shall be considered national militia troops, and the Courts shall dictate all forms for the kingdom's domestic and foreign security.

20. Employment will be granted according to the true merit by virtue of reports from the respective chiefs and provisionally in the name of the Nation.

21. While the Courts are being established, delinquencies will be processed in total agreement with the Spanish Constitution.

22. Conspiring against independence shall result in imprisonment without progressing to any other action until the Courts decide the penalty for the gravest of the delinquencies after that of Divine Majesty.

23. Those who encourage disunion shall be watched and shall be considered conspirators against independence.

24. Since the Courts to be installed shall be constituent, it is necessary that the deputies receive sufficient powers to that effect; and furthermore as it is of great importance that the voters know that their representatives will be for the Mexican Congress, and not for Madrid, the Junta shall prescribe the just rules for the elections and shall indicate the time necessary for them and for the

opening of Congress. Since the elections may not be verified in March, the terms will be stretched as long as possible.

Iguala, February 24, 1921—This is a copy—Iturbide. Printed in Puebla and reprinted in Mexico in the office of D. J. M, Benavente and Associates. Year 1821.

STUDY QUESTIONS

1. To what extent does the plan reveal its origins as a compromise between Liberal and Conservative governing philosophies? Which clauses best highlight the conservative and Liberal perspectives, respectively?
2. The Plan of Iguala is often credited as ushering in the concept of equality of all Mexicans before the law. How are issues of race and ethnicity engaged in the Plan?

WILLIAM MILLER

1.6 DESCRIPTION OF BATTLE OF AYACUCHO, 1828

William Miller was an English-born solider who was one of many British and Irish mercenaries who joined revolutionary armies and came to play a key role in the independence struggle in South America. Here Miller describes the Battle of Ayacucho, which took place on December 9, 1824, and was the decisive battle that assured the victory of the independence movement in Peru. The document reminds us of the centrality of battlefield strategy and military contingencies to the political outcomes of independence, and highlights the military skill and valor of the generals who would overcome extreme logistical challenges to become the first leaders of the independent states. The document also highlights the complex role of indigenous peoples in the struggle for independence, with Indians fighting with both rebels and royalists.

On the 6th, the patriots reached the village of Quinua. The royalists continued their parallel movement to the heights of the Pacaycasa. In consequence of the road between this place and Guamanga being intersected by two deep *quebradas* and many ravines, and the paths being, in most places, extremely narrow, their line of march extended over a distance of from two to three leagues. The patriots, already in Quinua, upon perceiving this, formed for the purpose of attacking their opponents, the foremost of whom were only three miles distant from them; the intervening space being an open country with a gradual descent, seemed to afford them a favourable opportunity of avenging the losses they had sustained at Corpaguayeo. Previous to ordering the intended advance, Sucre and La Mar rode forward to reconnoitre. But this operation occupied so much of their time, that they considered it was too late to attack the royalists that evening. On the next

Source: William Miller, "Description of Battle of Ayacucho," *William Miller's Memoirs of General Miller in the Service of Peru* (London: Rees, Orne, Brown & Green, 1828), II, pp. 190–203.

morning, the latter entered Guamanguilla, and thus once more cut off the farther retreat of the independents, whose situation then became extremely critical.

Sucre conducted the retreat with skill, but his numbers were so alarmingly reduced, that nothing but some desperate effort was likely to save his army from destruction. The viceroy sent detachments to Marca, Mayoc, and other defiles, to render them impassable, and to destroy the bridges.

The Indians of Guanta, Huanacavelica, Chincheros, Huando, and the adjacent villages, had been induced to rise against the liberating army. They had assassinated upwards of one hundred sick with their escorts, together with the escorts of some of the baggage. An aide-de-camp of Miller, Captain Smith, was taken by those of Guanta, but after receiving a severe beating, and three days' imprisonment, he escaped to the coast. His life was spared only on the intercession of an inhabitant at whose house Miller had been billeted. The hills which overlook the village of Quinua were occupied by hostile Indians, who had the boldness to approach within half a mile of the patriot encampment, and succeeded in capturing several head of oxen from a party of dragoons. During the preceding fortnight, the casualties of the liberating army had not been less than twelve hundred, so that at Quinua it amounted to less than six thousand effective men. The cavalry, having lost their mules at Corpaguayco, were obliged to walk and lead their horses, many of which became disabled in consequence of having cast their shoes.

A patriot battalion, and some detachments of convalescents, on their way home from Xauxa to join the liberating army, were attacked in the dark by the Indians of Huando, and obliged to retreat with loss. Every circumstance concurred to increase the gloom which overhung the prospects of the patriots. They could not retreat; they could not attack the royalists, on account of the abrupt ravine, two hundred yards deep, between the two armies; and want of provisions would have rendered their remaining in that position, five days longer, impossible. All was now ominous and fearful, but the spirits and courage of the republicans appeared to rise in proportion as their affairs became more desperate; and it will soon be seen what brave men, ably led on, can effect in the cause of liberty.

In the afternoon of the 8th, the viceroy moved from Guamanguilla, and occupied, with his whole forces, the heights of Condorkanki,[1] just without gun-shot of the encampment of the independents. Two hours before sunset, a royalist battalion of light-infantry descended the hill, and extended itself at the foot. It was opposed by a light-infantry battalion of the patriots; and some sharp skirmishing, in extended files, took place. The evolutions were performed at the sound of the bugle, and nothing could exceed the coolness and good conduct of the men engaged on both sides.

The general effect of the skirmishing was extremely fine. The interest of the scene was much varied and enhanced by the occasional cessations of firing by tacit consent. During which intervals, several officers of the opposite parties approached each other and conversed. In one of these parleys, Brigadier-General Tur, of the Spanish service, sent a message to his brother, who, having married a beautiful woman of Lima, had become virtually an American, and was now a lieutenant-colonel in the independent army. The two brothers met. The elder began the conversation by expressing his regret that a Spaniard should be seen in the ranks of the insurgents, but added that, notwithstanding his sorrow on that account, he felt impelled by the recollections and feelings of other times to assure his brother, that he might reckon upon his protection when the coming battle should place him in the power of the royalists, who otherwise might not deal lightly with a Spaniard taken in such company. The lieutenant-colonel observed, in reply, that if he had sent for him for the purpose of offering an insult, it were better they had never met, and then turned round to walk away. Upon this, the royalist general rushed forward, made an apology, and, in view of the two armies, the brothers embraced in the most affectionate manner. In a few hours afterwards General Tur was a prisoner of war, and the welcome guest of his brother, the lieutenant-colonel.

Quinua, an Indian village, is on the western extremity of the plain of Ayacucho, the shape of which is nearly square, about a league in circumference, and flanked right and left by deep, rugged, ravines. In the rear of the plain, or towards the west, is a gradual descent of two leagues to the main road from Guamanga to Guanta, which runs along the base of a mountain

---

1   Condorkanki, or Condorcanqui, is a Quichus term, which means "worthy of the condor."

range, that rises like a wall with no apparent outlet. The eastern boundary of the plain is formed by the abrupt and rugged ridge of Condorkanki; which gigantic bulwark, running north and south, overlooks the field of Ayacucho. A little below the summit of this ridge was perched the royalist army.

The liberating army was drawn up on the plain, in front of the Spaniards, at an interval of about a mile, having Quinua in the rear, each corps being formed in close column, to await the attack of the royalists. It was disposed in the following order:

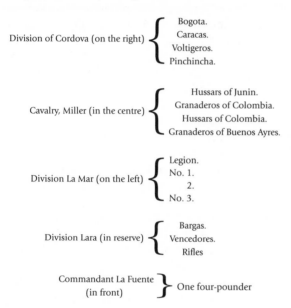

Division of Cordova (on the right) { Bogota. Caracas. Voltigeros. Pinchincha.

Cavalry, Miller (in the centre) { Hussars of Junin. Granaderos of Colombia. Hussars of Colombia. Granaderos of Buenos Ayres.

Division La Mar (on the left) { Legion. No. 1. 2. No. 3.

Division Lara (in reserve) { Bargas. Vencedores. Rifles

Commandant La Fuente (in front) } One four-pounder

General Gamarra, Chief of Staff.
Colonel O'Connor, Second to Gamarra on the staff.

During the night of the 8th, a brisk fire was maintained between the royalist and the patriot outposts. It was the object of Sucre to prevent the royalists descending in the night. For this purpose the bands of two battalions were sent with a company near to the foot of the ridge, and continued playing for some time whilst a sharp fire was kept up. This feint had the desired effect, for the royalists did not stir from their lines.

The viceroy's position in the night of the 8th was very much exposed: his infantry, occupying the front of the ridge of Condorkanki, was within musket-range of the foot of the hill. The fire from two or three battalions, deployed into line, might have obliged the royalists to abandon their position. As it was, a lieutenant-colonel

and two or three men, within the Spanish encampment, were killed, as they sat round their fires, by chance balls from the patriot company at the foot of the hill.

The night of the 8th was one of deep and anxious interest. A battle was to decide the destinies of South America. The patriots were aware that they had to contend with twice their own numbers; and that nothing but a decisive victory could save them and their country from ignominious servitude. The patriot *soldier* might indeed expect to escape with *life*, reduced to the condition of a slave; but with the patriot generals and officers, it was only a choice between death and victory. They knew full well what would be the cruel policy of the Spaniards if they proved victorious. The viceroy was, it is true, a man of human disposition, but the individual who counselled Monet to shoot two patriot officers in the pass of San Mateo, and the other man (if such he may be called) who ran his sword through the wounded and defenceless Major Gumer, on the field at Ica, were, with others, of a character equally sanguinary, amongst the advisers of La Serna; and it is extremely probable that unsparing executions would have been resorted to in the hope of destroying the very germ of future insurrection. Every one felt that the approaching battle was to have no common result.

The morning of the 9th dawned particularly fine. At first there was a chillness in the air which seemed to influence the minds of the men, but when the sun rose above the mountain, the effects of its genial warmth became manifest in the renovated spirits of the soldiers. The men on both sides were observed rubbing their hands, and exhibiting every token of content and satisfaction. At nine A.M. the division Villalobos began to descend. The viceroy, on foot, placed himself at its head; and the files wound down the craggy side of the Condorkanki, obliquing a little to their left. The division Monet, forming the royalist right, commenced at the same time to defile directly into the plain. The cavalry, leading their horses, made the same movement, though with greater difficulty, between the infantry of each division. As the files arrive on the plain, they formed into columns. This was a moment of extraordinary interest. It appeared as though respiration were suspended by feelings of anxiety, mingled with doubts and hope.

It was during this operation, which had an imposing effect, that Sucre rode along his own line, and, addressing a few emphatic words to each corps, recalled to memory its former achievements. He then placed himself in a central point, and, in an inspiring tone of voice, said, "that upon the efforts of that day depended on the fate of South America"; then pointing to the descending columns, he assured his men, "that another day of glory was about to crown their admirable constancy." This animating address of the general produced an electric effect, and was answered by enthusiastic *"vivas."*

By the time that rather more than half the royalist divisions, Monet and Villalobos, had reached and formed upon the arena, Sucre ordered the division of Cordova and two regiments of cavalry to advance the charge. The gallant Cordova placed himself about fifteen yards in front of his division, formed into four parallel columns with the cavalry in the intervals. Having dismounted, he plunged his sword into the heart of his charger, and turning to the troops, exclaimed, "There lies my last horse; I have now no means of escape, and we must fight it out together!" Then waving his hat about his head, he continued, *"Adelante, con paso de Vencedores"* (onwards with the step of conquerors). These words were heard distinctly throughout the columns, which, inspired by the gallant bearing of their leader, moved to the attack in the finest possible order. The Spaniards stood firmly and full of apparent confidence. They viceroy was seen, as were also Monet and Villalobos, at the head of their columns as they reached the plain. The hostile bayonets crossed, and for three or four minutes the two parties struggled together, so as to leave it doubtful which would give way. At this moment the Colombian cavalry, headed by Colonel Silva, charged. This brave officer fell covered with wounds, but the intrepidity of the onset was irresistible. The royalists lost ground, and were driven back with great slaughter. The viceking was wounded and taken prisoner. As the fugitives climbed the sides of Condorkanki, the patriots, who had deployed, kept up a well-directed fire, and numbers of the enemy were seen to drop and roll down, till their progress was arrested by the brush-wood, or some jutting crag.

Miller, who had followed up on Cordova's division, perceiving its complete success, returned to the regiment of Usares de Junin, which fortunately had been left in reserve.

At dawn of day, the royalist division Valdez commenced a detour of nearly a league. Descending the sides of Condorkanki on the north, Valdez had placed himself on the left of the patriots at musket-shot distance, separated by a ravine. At the important moment of the battle, just described, he opened a heavy fire from four field-pieces and a battalion in extended files. By this, he obliged two battalions of the Peruvian division La Mar to fall back. The Colombian battalion Bargas, sent to support the Peruvian division, also began to give way. Two royalist battalions crossed the deep ravine, already spoken of, on the left, and advanced in double quick time in pursuit of the retiring patriots. At this critical juncture, Miller took it upon himself to lead the hussars of Junin against the victorious Spaniards, and by a timely charge drove them back, and followed them across the ravine, by which time he was supported by the granaderos à caballo and by the division of La Mar, which had rallied. The brave Colonel Plaza crossed the ravine at the head of the legion on the left. Lieutenant-Colonel Moran, at the head of the battalion Bargas, made a similar movement on the right of the cavalry. These two battalions and the cavalry, mutually supporting and rivalling each other in valour, repeated their charges with such resolution, that the division Valdez was broken; its artillery taken; its cavalry obliged to fly in disorder; and its infantry dispersed.

The royalists had now lost the battle, and fled to the ridge from which they had descended, in the morning, with so much confidence.

The action lasted an hour. Fourteen hundred royalists were killed, and seven hundred wounded, and they lost fifteen pieces of artillery.

The loss on the part of the patriots was three hundred and seventy killed, and six hundred and nine wounded.[2]

---

2 Names of officers killed. Colonel Carreño, Lieutenant-Colonel Medina†, Captain Urquiola; Lieutenants, Oliva, Colmenares, Ramirez, Bonilla, Sevilla, Prieto, Ramonet.

Wounded. Colonels. Silva, Luque, Leal; Lieutenant-Colonels, Leon, Blanco, Castillo, Gerardino; Majors, Torres, Sornoza; Captains, Ximenes, Coquis, Dorronzoro, Brown, Gil, Cordova, Urena, Dorronsoro, Landacia, Troyano, Alcala, Grenados, Miro; Lieutenants, Infantes, Silva, Suares, Vallaríno, Otarola, French, Pedrahita, Pazaga,

The single piece of artillery belonging to the patriots did considerable execution on the royalist columns, and was of service also in attracting a heavy fire from their artillery, which if it had been directed upon the patriot columns, would have occasioned the loss to be more considerable.

The plan of the royalists was to wait until Valdez had outflanked the left of Sucre's position, from which having driven him, the whole army was to advance and complete the victory. The mistake of the viceroy in attacking at all, originated in suffering himself to be impelled to it by the eagerness of his troops. Their patience had been worn out, by the terrible marches, which appeared to them to be endless. At Guamanguilla, a system of pasquinading had been adopted. The tents of La Serna, Canterac, and others, had various lampoons posted on them, and it may be fairly said that they were goaded by their own soldiers into a general action contrary to their own judgement.

The royalists, upon regaining the heights of Condorkanki, rallied as many of their defeated troops as they possibly could. The patriot divisions La Mar and Lara gained the summit of the heights at about 1 P.M. Before sunset Canterac sued for terms, and an hour afterward rode down to the tent of Sucre, where a capitulation was agreed upon. The viceroy La Serna, Generals

Canterac, Valdez, Carratalà, Monet, Villalobos, Ferras, Bedoya, Somocursio,[3] Cacho, Atero, Landazuri, Garcia-Camba, Pardo, Vigil, and Tur; 16 colonels, 68 lieutenant-colonels, 484 officers, 3200 rank and file, became prisoners of war. The rest had dispersed.

The battle of Ayacucho was the most brilliant ever fought in South America. The troops on both sides were in a state of discipline which would have been creditable to the best European armies. The ablest generals and chiefs of either party were present, and it is difficult to say which army most panted for an appeal to the sword, as every man fought with undaunted bravery. What the patriots wanted in numbers was made up by enthusiasm, and by a perfect knowledge that, if beaten, retreat was utterly impracticable. It was not a victory of mere chance, but the result of the most determined valour, and of an irresistible onset, conceived and executed at the proper moment.

Sucre exposed himself during the action whenever his presence was required with the utmost *sang froid*, and his example produced its full effect. La Mar displayed the same qualities, and with energetic eloquence he rallied some corps that had given way, and reconducted them to the attack.

The heroism of General Cordova was the admiration of every one, and they beheld with satisfaction his promotion upon the field of battle to the rank of general division, at the age of twenty-five years. General Lara was conspicuous for activity and exertion. General Gamarra displayed his usual tact. Colonel O'Connor, adjutant-general, Colonel Plaza, the commanding officers of corps, and indeed the officers and men, with hardly an exception, behaved with a valour and zeal as if each imagined that the issue of the battle depended upon his own individual exertion. Colonels Caravajal and Silva, Lieutenant-Colonels Suares, Blanco, Braun, Medina, and Olavarria, who displayed so much valour at Junin, again distinguished themselves at Ayacucho. Captain Don Juan Alarcon, aide-de-camp to General Miller, behaved extremely well upon this occasion, as he had done on many others. He was of aboriginal descent, but very well educated. He was unassuming, meritorious, and hard-working.

Ariscum, Otarola, J. Suares, Ornas, Posadas, Miranda, Montoya, Morena; Ensigns, Galindo, Chabur, Rodriguez, Malabe, Jeran, Perez, Calles, Marquina, Paredes, Sabino, Isa, Alvarado.

ABSTRACT

	killed	wounded
Colonels	1	3
Lieutenant-Colonels	1	4
Majors	0	2
Captains	1	13
Lieutenants	7	16
Ensigns	0	12
Rank and file	360	559
Total	370	609

† Killed by the Indians of Huando on his way to Lima with General Sucre's despatch of the battle. Lieutenant-Colonel Medina was one of the bravest officers in the Colombian army. He had greatly distinguished himself at the affair of Junin.

3 Struck dead by lightning on his way from Guamanga to Arequipa.

STUDY QUESTIONS

1. What were the key military strategies that facilitated the independence victory, according to Miller? Was the victory of the independence side assured, or even likely, in his telling?
2. What can we learn from the source about the position of Peruvian indigenous peoples vis-à-vis independence?
3. Does the source help us understand why military leaders from the independence wars came to play such a key role in postindependence politics?

VICENTE GREZ

1.7 *LAS MUJERES DE LA INDEPENDENCIA, 1878*

Women played a critically important role in the struggle for independence in Latin America, providing support for proindependence politics. While some women did fight (often disguised as men), more common was for women to provide other types of support for military efforts. The excerpt presented here comes from a book first published in 1878 by the renowned Chilean writer and politician Vicente Grez, in which Grez sought to commemorate the lives of prominent women among the "Generation of 1810" that had led the independence movement, and to underline their contribution to the creation of the Chilean nation.

Here, Grez relays the contributions of two women: Mercedes Fuentecilla, the wife of General José Miguel Carrera, the most important leader of the Chilean War for Independence during the period of the "Old Republic" (1810–1814); and Paula Jara Quemeda, an upper-class Chilean woman who famously gave refuge to San Martin's army following their defeat at the Battle of Cancha Rayada in 1818—an act that is credited with allowing San Martin to regroup and continue to victory. Historians and literary scholars have argued that some elements of Grez's account are exaggerated—for example, his claim that Mercedes Fuentecilla gave birth to her son in the desert does not seem to accord with the documentary record. Yet his book remains important for providing insight into how women's roles were remembered and commemorated in the decades following independence.

MERCEDES FUENTECILLA

Among the beautiful women of 1810, Mercedes Fuentecilla towers above all. Her features were delicate and gracious; her skin the purest white; her hair and eyes black; her eyes, especially, were an expression of her soul, burning with dazzling passion; it was impossible to look into them without bending to their will. The enchantment of her face was united with the majesty of her figure. . . .

The most notable man of that era, José Miguel Carrera, fell in love with this woman and made her his wife. She, in love also, and seduced at the same time by the

Source: Vicente Grez, *Las Mujeres de la Independencia* (Santiago: Imp. De la "Gratitud Nacional", 1910 [1878]), pp. 64–68, 75–77. Translated by Nicola Foote

brilliant position that he offered her, united her beautiful destiny with this good gentleman, which was to launch her into all the abysses and misfortunes of life. From the steps of the altar itself, before she could even remove her white wedding dress, José Miguel Carrera led his spouse to the banishment of the battlefields, their honeymoon delights the terrors and dangers of nocturnal assaults, and the groans and cries of the dying.

His wife followed him through the whole length of the immense Argentine pampa, taking part of the experience of his army, sharing all the tremendous danger of that situation, giving birth to her son in the middle of the desert, suffering from hunger and thirst—she, who had been born surrounded by all life's comforts and pleasures of good fortune!—she happily and contentedly put up with all these terrible tests.

Never did the annoyances of errant life, the loss of material pleasures, of fortune, of family, of family, of her changed social position, upset the dream of this heroic woman: never did a complaint or a reproach escape from her lips. At times sick, caring for two children, sleeping between two cradles, her soul suffering for the uncertain future for those children and the shadow over her husband's destiny. She loved this disgraced man, that fiery spirit, this forbidden genius, with all the force of her soul. . . .

The demands of the battle in which Carrera was engaged one day separated the two spouses; she returned to live on a ranch alone, while he continued his series of victories and defeats. Only occasionally did destiny unite the two spouses for even an hour. Then a ray of sunshine would descend over the humble house of Mercedes. . . .

Carrera never sacrificed . . . the least of his projects, the smallest of his ambitions. [Fuentecilla] understood this all too well and maintained a heroic silence . . . generous souls are always thus, preferring to sacrifice their own lives completely; in sublime tranquility and silence, rather than . . . being an obstacle to the glory of a beloved man.

PAULA JARA QUEM

In the afternoon of 19 March, 1818, San Martin, surrounded by some officials and soldiers, was deep in the Maipo Valley, heading towards Santiago. The appearance of the general and his troops was marked by gloom; a cloud of sadness and doubt shrouded those manly features. This was the sadness of the defeat that the patriotic army had suffered at Cancha Rayada.

Suddenly the general is arrested in his march. A strange group of riders intercepted his path, and a woman mounted on an elegant horse, a true Amazon, gave the word offering this group of brave men that they could replenish the casualties suffered by their ranks at their recent defeat.

This unexpected feminine apparition was Señora Paula Jara Quemada, who was an opulent woman and an enthusiastic patriot, who knew about the surprising disgrace suffered by the Chilean army. She gathered together all the tenant farmers and overseers on her hacienda and placed herself at the head of them with her sons and daughters to go out and meet the defeated men, leading them with the example of her valor and selflessness.

And it was not just this small contingent of men that the Señora Jara Quemeda offered to the defeated men, but also all of her estate, the magnificent horses and spacious houses, which were transformed into general quarters for the new and reorganized army.

STUDY QUESTIONS

1. How did gender expectations and family relationships mediate the contributions of elite women to Chilean independence?
2. What do we learn from these biographies about how gender ideologies were taking shape in the decades following independence?

MANUELA SÁENZ

1.8 LETTER TO THE COLOMBIAN AMBASSADOR, 1827

One of the most iconic women of the Independence era is Manuela Sáenz, the lover of Simón Bolívar, is often referred to as "The Liberatrix of the Liberator" because of her role in saving Bolivar's life on multiple occasions. Yet Sáenz is of interest far beyond her romantic relationship with Bolivar; she was also an important actor in her own right in the liberation of South America. She served as a military strategist, soldier, politician, and archivist and became an important figure in the early Republic. In this document, Sáenz protests her imprisonment by the Peruvian army following the collapse of Bolívar's rule in Peru. The context for her imprisonment was a military uprising in Lima in opposition to Bolívar's efforts to integrate Peru into the Gran Colombia federation and against the constitution he had sought to introduce. The uprising began on January 26, 1827, and quickly led to Bolívar's ousting and the installation of a new anti-Bolivarian Peruvian government and constitution. Troops were sent to Magdalena to expel Sáenz to Colombia after a minister accused her of being present in Peru to provoke a counterrevolution among veterans of Bolívar's army who were unhappy with the uprising against him. She was later accused of writing letters hostile to the Peruvian government, and taking visitors who included officials with "Bolivarian sentiments" while under surveillance at the Nazarenas Convent. While historians debate the exact nature of Sáenz's role in these political and military maneuverings, her arrest underlines the extent to which she was perceived by her contemporaries as a central actor in independence politics.

Dear Honorable Ambassador of Colombia,

Before you, as the agent of the Republic to which I have the honor to belong . . . I write to you to expose that at midnight on the seventh of the current month, my house was raided by police, I was in the town of Magdalena, where I have always resided, and I was ordered to immediately abandon it and march in any capacity to this capital, an order I could not comply with because of the poor state of my health, as a result of which an official was assigned to observe me during the night, in my room, and . . . my house and the roads that immediately led to it, were full of troops, until the following day, when they drove me to the Nazarenas Convent, like a prisoner of war, or a criminal; in truth, I am not the latter, and I do not know what reason could have motivated me becoming the former.

Even now I don't know the reason for my imprisonment, nor who is my accuser, and the behavior towards me is entirely inquisitorial. I have made clear that I am Colombian, and that there is a lack of consideration and gratitude owed to this nation, and further, that I demand the treatment that the law of nations dispenses towards people pressed with justice, or without it.

I place my cause in the well accredited hands of Your Excellency. . . . The government has forgotten article 117 of the constitution of this country,[1] surely

1   Article 117 held that within 24 hours of an arrest any individual would be informed of the reason for their arrest and any evidence against them. Failure to comply with this would be grounds for the immediate release of an individual.

Source: Vicente Lecuna (ed.) *Papeles de Manuela Sáenz, Boletín de la Academia Nacional de Historia* (Caracas), Vol. 28, Oct–Dec 1945: 507–508. Translated by Nicola Foote

this has been an oversight, and I have no doubt that the Interim President, given his diligence and pride in enforcing laws, will today itself take all necessary steps towards its end. . . . My vindication is of absolute necessity, and permit me to remind Your Excellency, that as an agent of the Republic of Colombia, you have the right to demand, with the energy vested in you as a representative, my release, and that the result of my case will gain favor with all men of thought, and any competent judge will see that I have committed no more crime than that of belonging to a republic that has done so much good to that of Peru.

STUDY QUESTIONS

1. How does Manuela Sáenz present her situation to the ambassador? Do you believe her insistence that she knew nothing about why she was imprisoned?
2. To what extent does her letter typify or challenge gendered expectations for women in the independence era?

PEDRO I

1.9 DECLARATION OF BRAZILIAN INDEPENDENCE, 1822

Independence in Brazil followed a different, less militarized, path than in Spanish America. When Napoleon invaded Portugal in 1807, the Portuguese royal family took refuge in Brazil, establishing Rio de Janeiro as the de facto capital of Portugal. After Napoleon was defeated in 1815, to assuage the fears of local elites about a return to colonial rule, King John IV of Portugal changed the legal status of Brazil, creating the United Kingdom of Portugal, Brazil, and the Algarves, in which all three territories held equal status. However, when the kingdom's first formal constitution was created in 1821 it subordinated the government of the Brazilian provinces directly to Portugal and recalled the prince regent Pedro, who had been acting as the king's deputy in Brazil, back to Lisbon. Brazilian elites rejected the changes and pushed Pedro to remain in Brazil and insist on equal political status. After months of negotiations and escalating tensions between Portuguese officials and creole elites, Pedro declared independence for Brazil with himself as king. This declaration was verbal, not written, and so we have no official government record to document the event. Instead, historians rely on the writings of royal courtiers and officials who were present at the declaration and recorded their own recollections in diaries and letters. The most thorough and best known is this account by Belchior Pinheiro de Oliveira, the priest of Minas Gerais and a close confidant of Prince Pedro.

The prince ordered me to read aloud the letters brought by Paulo Bregaro and Antônio Cordeiro. They consisted of the following: an instruction from the Côrtes, a letter from D. João, another from the Princess, another from José Bonifácio and still another from Chamberlain, the secret agent of the Prince. The Côrtes demanded the

Source: Bradford E. Burns, *A Documentary History of Brazil* (NY: Alfred A. Knopf, 1966).

immediate return of the Prince and the imprisonment and trial of José Bonifácio; the Princess recommended prudence and asked the Prince to listen to the advice of his minister; José Bonifácio told the Prince that he must choose one of two roads to follow: leave immediately for Portugal and make himself the prisoner of the Côrtes, as was the situation of D. João VI, or remain and proclaim the independence of Brazil becoming either its Emperor or King; Chamberlain gave information that the part of D. Miguel, in Portugal, was victorious and that they spoke openly of the disinheritance of D. Pedro in favor of D. Miguel; D. João advised his son to obey the Portuguese law. D. Pedro, trembling with rage, grabbed the letters from my hands and crumpled them up and threw them on the ground and stomped on them. He left them lying there, but I picked them up and kept them. Then, after buttoning up and arranging his uniform (he had just been to the edge of the stream of Ypiranga agonized by a painful attack of dysentery), he turned toward me and asked: "What now, Father Belchior?"

I quickly responded, "If your Highness does not declare himself King of Brazil, you will be made a prisoner of the Côrtes and perhaps disinherited by them. The only course is independence and separation."

Accompanied by me, Cordeiro, Bregaro, Carlota, and others, D. Pedro silently walked toward our horses at the side of the road. Suddenly he halted in the middle of the road and said to me, "Father Belchior, they asked for it and they will get it. The Côrtes is persecuting me and calling me an adolescent and a Brazilian. Well, now let them see their adolescent in action. From today on our relations with them are finished. I want nothing more from the Portuguese government, and I proclaim Brazil forevermore separated from Portugal."

With enthusiasm, we immediately answered, "Long live liberty! Long live an independent Brazil! Long live D. Pedro!"

The Prince turned to his adjutant and said, "Tell my guard that I have just declared the complete independence of Brazil. We are free from Portugal."

Lieutenant Canto e Melo rode toward a market where most of the soldiers of the guard remained. He returned to the Prince with them shouting enthusiastically in favor of an independent and separate Brazil, D. Pedro, and the Catholic Religion.

D. Pedro before the guard said, "The Portuguese Côrtes wants to enslave and to persecute us. Henceforth our relations are broken. Not one tie unites us!" And tearing from his hat the blue and white emblem decreed by the Côrtes as a symbol of the Portuguese nation, he threw it on the ground, saying, "Throw away that symbol, soldiers! Long live independence, liberty, and the separation of Brazil!"

We responded with a shout in favor of an independent and separate Brazil and another for D. Pedro.

The Prince unsheathed his sword, and the civilians removed their hats. D. Pedro said, "By my blood, by my honor, and with God's help, I swear to liberate Brazil."

"We all swear to it," shouted the rest.

D. Pedro sheathed his sword, an act repeated by the guard, went to the head of the crowd. Turned, and rose up on the stirrups to cry, "Brazilians, our motto from this day forward will be 'Independence or Death.'"

Seated firmly in his saddle, he spurred his handsome horse and galloped, followed by his retinue, toward São Paulo, where he was lodged by Brigadier Jordão, Captain Antônio Silva Prado, and others, who worked miracles in order to cheer up the prince.

After dismounting D. Pedro ordered his adjutant to go at once to the goldsmith Lessa and have made a small disk in gold bearing the words "Independence or Death" to be fastened on the arm with ribbons of green and gold.

Wearing the emblem he appeared at the theatre where my dear friends Alfêres Aquins and Father Ildefonso acclaimed him the King of Brazil.

Throughout the theatre were yellow and green ribbons. They hung from the walls, from the boxes, from the arms of the men and from the hair and dresses of the women.

STUDY QUESTIONS

1. What factors fed into Pedro's decision to declare independence, according to Pinheiro de Oliveira? Were political or personal considerations more important?
2. What public steps were taken to implement Pedro's private decision? Which do you think were most important to ensuring public understanding of the declaration of independence?

CHAPTER 2

LATIN AMERICA:
Regionalism and Localism

SIMÓN BOLÍVAR

2.1 LETTER TO GENERAL JUAN JOSE FLORES, NOVEMBER 9 1830; AND FINAL PROCLAMATION OF THE LIBERATOR, DECEMBER 10, 1830

As with so many of the themes of independence-era Latin America, Simón Bolívar's writings provide the best insight into the tensions and conflicts over governance in the immediate aftermath of independence. Bolivar believed that Latin America would be strongest if the different regions were united into a single nation, and he pushed for a centralized system of government that spanned the entire Northern Andes. He founded the republic of Gran Colombia, comprising what is today Colombia, Ecuador, and Venezuela, and strove to also integrate Bolivia and Peru (to which he assumed the presidency as separate nations). Many other political and military leaders opposed Bolivar's vision, accusing him of seeking to establish a personal dictatorship, and he suffered a series of setbacks in the years immediately following independence. By the time of his death from tuberculosis in 1830 he had faced a series of rebellions and assassination attempts, been forced to resign his presidencies and sent into exile, and watched the Gran Colombia union he had built dissolve.

The two documents excerpted here are among the most famous and revealing of Bolívar's later writings. The first is a letter in which he expresses his frustration to Juan Jose Flores, who had served as a General in Bolívar's army and who became the first president of Ecuador following the dissolution of Gran Colombia. The second is his final presidential address, in which he resigned his presidency. Together they highlight the challenges facing the leaders of independence in their struggle to establish postcolonial governments.

Source: David Bushnell (ed.) *El Libertador: Writings of Simón Bolívar* (Oxford: Oxford University Press, 2003), pp. 145–149.

LETTER TO GENERAL JUAN JOSE FLORES, NOVEMBER 9, 1830 ("PLOUGHING THE SEA")

Barranquilla, 9 November 1830

My dear General:

I have received your fine letter from Guayaquil, of 10 September placed in my hands by your emissary, [José María] Urbina. You cannot imagine my surprise to see that you took the trouble to send a special envoy to deliver your reply and to inform me of what is happening in the South and with your situation. I never expected that a personal letter could be the object of so much concern and benevolence. By so doing, you have surpassed the usual standard of extraordinary kindness in your dealings with me. Your friendship leaves nothing to be desired. With regard to the country, you conduct yourself like a statesman, always behaving in accordance with the ideas and desires of the people who have entrusted their destiny to you. In this case you fulfill your obligation as a leader and citizen.

I will not respond to the letter in question, because the important letter was the message delivered in person by Mr. Urbina: this procedure is diplomatic, prudent, and consistent with the nature of the revolution, for we never know in what moment and with whom we live our lives; and a voice is most flexible and lends itself to all the alterations one chooses to give it; this is politics. Urbina assures me that the desire of the South, according to the information he has brought, is final with respect to the independence of that country. Let the will of the South be carried out; keep your promises. Those people are in possession of their own sovereignty and will make of it a sack or a smock, depending on their whim. In this, nothing is determined so far, because nations are like children, who soon throw away what they have wept to attain. Neither you nor I nor anyone else knows the will of the people. Tomorrow they may kill each other, split into factions, and let themselves fall into the most powerful or the most ferocious hands. Be sure, my dear General, that you and those generals from the North are going to be ejected from that country, unless you transform yourselves into France, and even that will not suffice, because you know that all the revolutionaries of France died slaughtering their enemies, and that there are very few monsters of that ilk who have escaped the knife or the gallows. I will speak to you in passing and with clear intent. This young man has told me, because I asked him, that the grand destiny of the South is in the hands of the northern generals. This struck me as despicable even before the last revolution. With how much more justification will they not now call this tyranny? Even at this distance I have been hearing that they are still colonists, creatures of foreigners; foreigners from Venezuela, others from New Granada, others English, others Peruvians, and who knows from how many other countries they originate. And then, what manner of men! Some arrogant, some despotic, no doubt others simply thieves; all of them ignorant, with absolutely no talent for administration. Yes, my dear sir, I say this to you because I love you and do not want you to be a victim of this prejudice. I must warn you that [Vicente] Rocafuerte must already be en route to that country and that he is a man who harbors the most sinister intentions against you and against all my friends. He is capable of anything and has the means to carry out his designs. He is full of the most conflicting ideas; he was one of my best friends in our tender youth, one of my admirers until I entered Guayaquil, but then he became my fiercest enemy for the same offenses you have committed, i.e., for attacking La Mar and for not being from Guayaquil, and for other petty matters and opinions. He is the most rapid federalist the world has ever known, the antimilitarist incarnate, and something of a bully. If that gentleman lays his hands on Guayaquil, you will have much to suffer, and beyond this, God only knows. La Mar will join him. [José Joaquín] Olmedo idolizes him, loves only him. Use the past to predict the future. You know that I have ruled for twenty years, and I have derived from these only a few sure conclusions: (1) America is ungovernable, for us; (2) Those who serve revolution plough the sea; (3) The only thing we can do in America is emigrate; (4) This country will fall inevitably into the hands of the unrestrained multitudes and then into the hands of tyrants so insignificant they will be almost imperceptible, of all colors and races; (5) Once we've been eaten alive by every crime and extinguished by ferocity, the Europeans won't even bother to conquer us; (6) If it were possible for any part of the world to revert to primitive chaos, it would be America in her last hour.

My advice to you as a friend is that as soon as you sense your fortune waning, step down yourself and leave your post with honor and on your own: *No one dies of hunger on land.*

Unfortunately, among us, the masses are incapable of independent action, so a few powerful individuals do everything, and the multitude follows their audacity without examining the righteousness or criminality of the leaders, but then they abandon them as soon as others even more treacherous stage a surprise attack. This is the essence of public opinion and national power in our America.

And you can ask yourself whether a man who has drawn the previous conclusions as his only profit from his experience with revolutions is going to want to drown himself again after having emerged from the belly of a whale. The answer would be obvious.

My letter is quite long in comparison with yours, so it is time to close, and I do so by imploring you to tear up this letter as soon as you have read it, because I only wrote it out of consideration for your health, always fearing that it might fall into the hands of our enemies and that they might publish it with atrocious commentaries.

Meanwhile, accept my assurances of friendship and even more my gratitude for your former acts of kindness and loyalty toward me, and lastly, receive my heart.

Bolívar

FINAL PROCLAMATION OF THE LIBERATOR, DECEMBER 10, 1830

Santa Marta, 10 December 1830
Simón Bolívar
Liberator of Colombia, etc.

Colombians! You have been witness to my efforts to establish freedom where tyranny previously reigned. I have worked without thought of personal gain, sacrificing my fortune and even my peace of mind. I relinquished my power when I became convinced that you mistrusted my detachment. My enemies took advantage of your credulity and undermined what is most sacred to me: my reputation and my love of freedom. I have been the victim of my persecutors, who have driven me to the very threshold of my grave. I forgive them.

As I disappear from among you, my affection tells me that I must make clear my final wishes. I aspire to no other glory than the consolidation of Colombia. You must all work for the inestimable good of the Union: the people offering their obedience in the current government in order to save themselves from anarchy; the ministers of the sanctuary directing their prayers to heaven; and the military officers using their swords to defend social guarantees.

Colombians! My final wishes are for the happiness of the country. If my death contributes to the cessation of factions and the consolidation of the Union, I will step peacefully into the grave.

Hacienda of San Pedro [Alejandrino], in Santa Marta, 10 December 1830, in the twentieth year of independence.

Simón Bolívar

STUDY QUESTIONS

1. How does Bolívar characterize his role in the struggle for independence? What reasons does he give for losing popular support?
2. Why is Bolívar so pessimistic about the prospects for South American independence? What does he see as the most important threats to the region's development?

DOMINGO FAUSTINO SARMIENTO

2.2 FACUNDO: CIVILIZATION AND BARBARISM, OR, LIFE IN THE ARGENTINE REPUBLIC IN THE DAYS OF THE TYRANTS, 1845

Facundo is one of the most famous works to emerge from nineteenth-century Latin America. First published in 1845, it was written by Domingo Faustino Sarmiento, an Argentine writer, intellectual, and politician, who was a prominent Liberal and a member of the Unitarian Party, which pushed for strong centralized government. Sarmiento would ultimately become the seventh president of Argentina in 1868, but at the time of writing *Facundo* he was in exile in Chile. The book critiqued the rise of caudillos and military strongmen. Although the subject of the book was Juan Facundo Quiroga, a caudillo from the plains who had dominated the Argentine provinces in the 1820s and 1830s, its publication was intended also as a criticism of the dictatorship of Juan Manuel de Rosas, which had been in power for over a decade at the time of publication. In *Facundo*, Sarmiento drew a strong contrast between cities such as Buenos Aires, which he saw as heirs to the European enlightenment, with the culture of the Argentine countryside, which he characterized as defined by "barbarism." He argued it was the culture and geography of the countryside that led to the devaluation of democracy and intelligent thought, and that paved the way for the rise of military strongmen like Rosas. In this excerpt, Sarmiento lays out this contrast between city and countryside, detailing extensively the culture of the gauchos (cowboys) of the Argentine plains.

Argentine cities have the regular physiognomy of almost all American cities: their streets are cut at right angles and their population disseminated across a broad area, with the exception of Córdoba, which, built within a limited, narrow district, has all the appearances of a European city, made even more striking by the multitude of spires and cupolas of its numerous, magnificent churches. The city is the center of Argentine, Spanish, European civilization; the artisans' workshops are there, the commercial stores, the schools and academics, the courthouses: in short, everything that characterizes cultured peoples.

There, elegant manners, the conveniences of luxury, European clothing, the tailcoat, and the frock coat have their theater and their appropriate place. Not without purpose do I make this trivial enumeration.

The capital city of the pastoral provinces sometimes exists by itself, without any smaller cities, and in more than one of them the uncivilized region reaches right up to its streets. The desert surrounds the cities at a greater or lesser distance, hems them in, oppresses them; savage nature reduces them to limited oases of civilization, buried deep into an uncivilized plain of hundreds of square miles, scarcely interrupted by some little town or other of any consequence. Buenos Aires and Córdoba are the cities that have been able to sprout the greatest number of small towns in the countryside, to be additional focuses of civilization and municipal interests; this in itself is noteworthy.

The man of the city wears European dress, lives a civilized life as we know it everywhere: in the city, there are laws, ideas of progress, means of instruction, some

Sources: University of California Press, 2003. Translated by Kathleen Ross

municipal organization, a regular government, etc. Leaving the city district, everything changes in aspect. The man of the country wears other dress, which I will call American, since it is common to all peoples; his way of life is different, his needs, specific and limited. They are like two distinct societies, two peoples strange to one another. And more still: the man of the country, far from aspiring to resemble the man of the city, rejects with scorn his luxuries and his polite manners; and the clothing of the city dweller, his tailcoat, his cape, his saddle—no such sign of Europe can appear in the countryside with impunity. All that is civilized in the city is blockaded, banished outside of it, and anyone who would dare show up in a frock coat, for example, and mounted on an English saddle, would draw upon himself the peasants' jeers and their brutal aggression.

Now let us study the external physiognomy of the extensive countryside surrounding the cities, and let us penetrate the internal life of its inhabitants. I have already said that, in many provinces, the compulsory border is an interposed, waterless desert. In general, this is not the case for the countryside of a province when the greatest part of its population resides there. In Córdoba, for example, where 160,000 souls live, scarcely 20,000 of them are within the isolated city district; all the rest of the population is in the country, which, since it is commonly a flat plain, is grassy in almost all areas, whether covered with forests or denuded of significant vegetation, and in some areas with such abundance and such exquisite quality that an artificial meadow would not surpass it. Mendoza and San Juan above all are exceptions to this particular characteristic of uncultivated areas, since their inhabitants principally live off the products of agriculture. Everywhere else, with grass in abundance, the raising of livestock is not the occupation of the inhabitants, but rather their means of subsistence. Once again, pastoral life unexpectedly brings to mind the recollection of Asia, whose plains we always imagine to be covered, here and there, with the tents of Kalmyks, Cossacks, and Arabs. The primitive life of the settlers, the eminently barbaric and unchanging life, the life of Abraham which is that of today's Bedouin, looms in the Argentine countryside, although modified by civilization in an odd way.

The Arab tribe, roaming through Asian solitudes, lives united under the command of an elder of the tribe or a warrior chief. A society exists, although it may not be permanently set in a certain place on earth; religious beliefs, traditions immemorial, the invariability of customs, respect for elders, together form a code of law, of customary ways and practices of government, that maintains order, morality as they understand it, and association within the tribe. But progress is suffocated, because there can be no progress without permanent ownership of land, without the city, which develops the capacity of man for industry and permits him to extend his acquisitions.

On the Argentine plains, the nomad tribe does not exist. The herdsman owns the land as a proprietor, he stays in one place which belongs to him; but it has been necessary to dissolve association within the group, and to spread families out over an immense surface, in order for him to occupy it. Imagine an expanse of two thousand square leagues, totally populated but with homesteads set apart from each other by four leagues, sometimes eight, two at the closest. The development of property and furnishings is not impossible; articles of luxury are not totally incompatible with this isolation, and riches could construct a fine edifice in the desert. But the stimulus is lacking, the example has disappeared, the need to maintain a dignified appearance which is felt in the cities, is not felt there, amid isolation and solitude. Unavoidable privations justify natural laziness, and a frugality of pleasures quickly brings with it all the exterior aspects of barbarity. Society has completely disappeared; all that is left is the feudal family, isolated, enclosed within itself, and with no collective society; all forms of government are made impossible, the municipality does not exist, the police cannot do their work, and civil justice has no means of catching delinquents.

I am not aware of the modern world offering a type of association as monstrous as this one. It is the exact opposite of the Roman municipality, which concentrated within one district the whole population, which from there went out to work the surrounding fields. So a strong social organization did exist, and its beneficial effects are felt even today, having prepared the way for modern civilization. The Argentine type is similar to the old Slavonic *sloboda*, the difference being that the latter was agricultural and therefore more easily governed; the spreading out of the population was not as extensive as it is in the former. It is different from the nomad tribe, in that the latter hardly even passes as a society since it does not own land. And finally, it is somewhat similar to the feudal system of the Middle Ages, where barons resided in the country and from there made war on the cities and devastated the countryside; but here, the baron and his feudal castle are missing. If some power rises up in the country, it is momentary, it is democratic; it cannot be inherited or preserved, owing to a lack of mountains and natural strongholds. That is why even the savage tribes of the Pampas are better organized for moral development than is our countryside.

But what is noteworthy in this society, in terms of its social aspects, is its affinity with ancient life, with Spartan or Roman life, were it not for a radical difference. The free citizen of Sparta or Rome lay the burden of material life, the worry of providing for subsistence, upon his slaves, while he himself lived free of worry in the forum and in the public square, occupying himself only with interests of the state, of peace, war, and partisan struggles. Pasturage provides the same advantages, with the inhuman function of the ancient Helot assumed by livestock. Spontaneous procreation makes fortune accumulate indefinitely; the hand of man is unnecessary, his work his intelligence, his time are not needed for the preservation of growth of his means of living. But although he needs none of this for the material side of life, he cannot put to use the effort he saves as the Romans did: he lacks a city, a municipality, intimate association, and therefore lacks the basis for all social development; since the ranchers do not meet together, they have no public needs to satisfy; in a word, there is no *res publica*.

Moral progress, the culture of intelligence neglected in the Arab or Tartar tribe, is thus here not only neglected, but impossible. Where could a school be placed so that children disseminated over ten leagues in every direction could attend classes? Civilization, then can never be attained, barbarism is the norm, and we can be thankful if domestic customs preserve a small measure of morality.[1] Religion suffers the

consequences of society's dissolution; there is only a nominal parish, the pulpit has no audience, the priest flees from his isolated chapel or becomes demoralized by inactivity and solitude; vices, simony, and accepted barbarism penetrate his cell and turn his moral superiority into a source of fortune and ambition, for, in the end, he winds up becoming a partisan caudillo.

I have witnessed a rural scene worthy of primitive times in the world, before the establishment of the priesthood. In 1838, I was in the sierra of San Luis, in the home of a rancher whose two favorite occupations were praying and gambling. He had built a chapel in which, on Sunday afternoons, he himself recited the rosary, to substitute for the priest and the holy service that had been lacking for years. That was a Homeric picture: the sun setting in the west; the sheep returning to the fold, splitting the air with their bleats; the master of the house—a man of sixty with a noble appearance, in which his pure European race was displayed by the whiteness of his skin, his blue eyes, his wide, smooth brow—reciting the service, to which responded a dozen women and a few young boys whose horses, still not entirely broken, were tied up near the chapel door. The rosary concluded, he made a fervent offering. I have never heard a voice more full of devotion, a fervor more pure, a faith more firm, or a prayer more beautiful, more appropriate to the circumstances, than the one he recited. In it, he asked God for rain for the fields, fertility for the livestock, peace for the Republic, safety for travelers. . . . I am very prone to weeping, and that day I wept until I sobbed, because religious sentiment had awakened in my soul with exaltation and like an unknown sensation, for I have never observed a more religious scene. I thought I was back in the times of Abraham, in his presence, in that of God and of the nature which reveals Him. The voice of that honest and innocent man made every fiber in me shake, and penetrated into my very bone.

This, then, is what religion is reduced to in the pastoral countryside: to natural religion. Christianity exists, like the Spanish language, as a sort of tradition that is carried on, but corrupted, embodied in coarse superstitions, with no instruction, rites, or conviction. Almost everywhere in the countryside far from the cities, it happens that, when merchants from San Juan or Mendoza arrive, they are presented with three

---

1   In 1826, during a yearlong stay in the sierra of San Luis, I taught six young men from prominent families to read, the youngest of whom was twenty-two years old.

or four babies a few months or a year old to baptize, people being convinced that because of their education, they can do this validly; and it is not unusual that when a priest arrives, they bring him young boys already breaking colts, so that he may anoint them and administer baptism *sub conditione.*

Lacking all means of progress and civilization, which cannot develop unless men are grouped together in populous societies, consider the education of men in the country. The women keep the home, prepare the meals, shear the sheep, milk the cows, make cheese, and weave the coarse material from which they make clothing. All the domestic chores, all the production of the home is the woman's job; almost all of the burden of work is on her, and she can be thankful if some of the men decide to grow a little corn to feed the family, since bread is unusual as an ordinary staple. The boys exercise their physical strength, and for pleasure become skilled in the handling of the lasso and the bolas, with which they endlessly harass and chase the calves and goats. When they become riders—and this happens almost as soon as they learn to walk—they do a few tasks on horseback; later on, when they have grown in strength, they race through the fields, falling off horses and getting up again, tumbling on purpose over viscacha holes, jumping off cliffs, and becoming skilled horsemen. When puberty arrives, they devote themselves to breaking wild colts, and death is only the least of the punishments that await them, if at any moment they lack the strength or courage. With young manhood comes complete independence—and idleness.

Here is where what I will call the public life of the gaucho begins, for his education is now finished. We must see these men as Spanish only in language, and in the confused religious notions they maintain, to be able to appreciate their indomitable, haughty character, born of the struggle of isolated man with savage nature, of rational man with the brute. We must see these heavily bearded faces, these grave, serious countenances like those of Asian Arabs, to judge the pitying disdain inspired in them by the sight of a sedentary city dweller, who may have read many books but does not know how to provide himself with a horse in the open country, on foot and without help from anyone; who has never stopped a tiger, facing it with a dagger in one hand and a poncho wrapped around the other

to stick in its mouth, while he runs it through the heart and leaves it lying at his feet. This habit of triumphing over all resistance, of always proving himself superior in nature, challenging and conquering it, develops a prodigious feeling of individual importance and superiority. The Argentines, civilized or ignorant, of whatever class they may be, have a high awareness of their worth as a nation; all the other peoples of America accuse them of this vanity and are offended by their presumption and arrogance. I think the charge is not totally unfounded, and it causes me no regret. Woe to the nation without faith in itself! It was not meant for great things! How much did the arrogance of these Argentine gauchos, who have never seen anything under the sun better than themselves, not even learned or powerful men, surely contribute to the independence of a whole region of America? The European, for them, is the least of all, for he cannot even stand a couple of plunges on a horse. If the origin of this national vanity in the lower classes is a mean one, its results are no less noble for that reason, just as the water of a river is no less pure because it may be born at a marshy, infected source. The hatred that cultured men inspire in them is implacable, and their repugnance for the dress, ways, and manners of those men unyielding. From this clay are molded Argentine soldiers, and it is easy to imagine what these sorts of customs can produce in valor and tolerance of war. Add to this that from earliest childhood they are accustomed to slaughtering cattle, and that this act of necessary cruelty familiarizes them with the spilling of blood and hardens their hearts against the victims' moans.

Country life, then, has developed the gaucho's physical faculties, but none of his intelligence. His moral character is affected by his custom of triumphing over obstacles and the power of nature: he is strong, haughty, vigorous. Without instruction, without need of it either, without a means of subsistence and without needs, he is happy in the midst of his poverty and privations, which are not many for one who has never known greater pleasures or set his desires any higher. So, although this dissolution of society deeply implants barbarism because of the impossibility and uselessness of moral and intellectual education, in another way it is not without its attractions. The gaucho does not work; he finds food and clothing at hand in his home. Both of these are provided by his livestock, if he is a proprietor, or the house of his employer or relatives, if he owns nothing. The attention the livestock require boils down to excursions and pleasurable games. The branding, which is like the grape harvest for farmers, is a celebration whose arrival is greeted with transports of joy: this is the place where all the men within a twenty-league radius meet, where they show off incredible skill with the lasso. The gaucho arrives at the branding on his best racing horse with a slow, measured step, halting some distance away, and to better enjoy the spectacle, crosses his leg over the horse's neck. If enthusiasm so moves him, he descends slowly from his horse, unrolls his lasso, and throws it over a bull going by at the speed of lightning, forty paces away: he catches it by a hoof, as he intended, and calmly rolls his rope up again.

STUDY QUESTIONS

1. What are the main differences Sarmiento sees as characterizing city and country life?
2. What are the key characteristics of the people of the countryside in Sarmiento's telling? Is his characterization a reliable one?
3. Does he see the gaucho as a positive or negative force in the development of Argentina? What types of global and historical comparisons does Sarmiento use to develop his arguments in this regard?

2.3 *DÉCIMAS* DEDICATED TO SANTA ANNA'S LEG

One of the most iconic of the Latin American caudillos, and a towering figure of postindependence Mexico, was General Antonio Lopez de Santa Anna, a veteran of the Mexican Wars for Independence who dominated Mexican politics in the subsequent decades, serving eleven nonconsecutive presidential terms over a twenty-two-year period between 1833 and 1855. Santa Anna oversaw some disastrous military defeats, notably the loss of Texas in 1836, but he also led some famous victories, including defeating a French invasion force at Veracruz in 1838. Santa Anna lost half his left leg in the Battle of Veracruz when his horse was shot out from under him, and this personal sacrifice became a key element of the cult of personality he created around himself. In 1842 he ordered his leg dug up and reburied in the national cemetery. An extravagant state funeral ceremony was held, including a full military dress parade, cannon salvos and elaborate speeches. When Santa Anna lost the presidency in 1844, crowds stormed the cemetery, dug up the leg, and dragged it through the streets of Mexico City shouting "Death to the Cripple!" The following documents present the lyrics to two décimas written about Santa Anna's leg in the aftermath of these events. Décimas were popular songs, the predecessor of the topical ballads known as corridos that are still popular in Mexico and Central America today, and they were an important way in which ordinary people heard about national news. Often humorous and satirical in tone, they provide insight into how ordinary people made sense of national events.

Source: Gilbert M. Joseph and Timothy J. Henderson (eds.) *The Mexico Reader: History, Culture and Politics* (Durham, NC: Duke University Press, 2002), pp. 213–217.

I.

Why should anyone criticize
If a funeral is performed
for the foot, arm, or hair
of an illustrious General?
Passions always tarnish
merit with malevolence
and really do not wish
true merit celebrated;
So answer quickly
and with confidence:
Why should we not honor
merit in the lifeless limb
of a great and heroic caudillo?
Why should anyone criticize?
To make this fitting obsequy
to a sacrificed limb—
not to the man, but to what he has given
fearlessly for the Fatherland—
it would be unjust,
ungrateful, foolish and disloyal
to claim it is not lawful and right
that a lone foot have
a tomb or mausoleum,
that a funeral is performed.
Did Artemisia not hide
the ashes of Mausolus[1]
in her breast and believe this
the only remedy?
She did her duty.
So today Mexico erects
a tomb reaching the night sky,
covering with ardent hope
a jewel of History,
and giving glory
to the foot, arm or hair.
There is a maxim which states
a cherished principle:
If one kisses the hem of a robe
it is because of the Saint who wears it;

---

1   Masuolus: Persian satrap who ruled over Caria from c.
376–353 B.C. Known for his personal aggrandizement,
he designed a splendid tomb for himself which his wife,
Artemisia, built after his death. He thus gave his name to
the mausoleum. *Ed.*

thus, it is not for the foot itself, on the
contrary,
through traitors may complain,
that we say, for good, or ill,
"Viva!" and be assured
that the people are grateful
to an illustrious General.

II.

Nothing in life is permanent,
God alone remains,
so the things of this world
are here today and gone tomorrow.
If we search through all of history
we will not find a single soul
whose triumphs and glory
last for all eternity.
Even so, our memory
of great heroes is eternal;
though no one can be constant
in their conduct or their lives
for until death arrives,
nothing in life is permanent.
Such may be said of Santa Anna's foot
which was placed in Santa Paula
with such solemn
pomp and majesty;
and today the Mexican populace,
after rising in rebellion,
full of enthusiasm and zeal,
took the foot from the sepulchre;
so it is clear that on the earth
God alone remains.
At that hour and moment
the foot's owner was far away;
but around here his FOOT was
walking around with the rebels.
It is certain that no one
felt any pain from this;
but I believe
that such an unthinkable act
could only have been done by
the things of this world.
At other times this foot was earnestly respected;
but that was when its owner
still held us in subjugation;
today the people have treated it

like a dirty old bone,
because the nation
no longer wishes to stand for it;

because, in the end, good and evil
are here today and gone tomorrow.

STUDY QUESTIONS

1. How do the two *décimas* differ in their attitude toward Santa Anna and his leg?
2. What insight do the *décimas* provide into the nature of Santa Anna's rule and his personal appeal?

JAMES K. POLK

2.4 TEXAS, MEXICO AND MANIFEST DESTINY, 1845

This document is an excerpt from President James K. Polk's annual Address to Congress on December 2, 1845. It took place just weeks before the official integration of Texas into the United States on December 29, 1845, and several months after an independent Texas voted for annexation in July 1845. In the speech, Polk outlines what he sees as the process through which Texas moved from being part of Mexico to voting to become part of the United States, vociferously denouncing both the Mexican government and European powers for their opposition to Texan annexation. The speech is noted by historians as laying out a clear vision of "Manifest Destiny" and is seen as an important precursor to Polk's declaration of war against Mexico in 1846.

Fellow-Citizens of the Senate and House of Representatives:

. . . In performing for the first time, the duty imposed on me by the constitution, of giving you the information of the state of the Union, and recommending to your consideration such measures as in my judgement are necessary and expedient, I am happy that I can congratulate you on the continued prosperity of our country. Under the blessings of Divine Providence and the benign influence of our free institutions, it stands before the world a spectacle of national happiness. . . .

A constitution for the government of the State of Texas, formed by a convention of deputies, is herewith laid before Congress. It is well known, also, that the people of Texas at the polls have accepted the terms of annexation, and ratified the constitution . . .

This accession to our territory has been a bloodless achievement. No arm of force has been raised to produce the result. The sword has had no part in the victory. We have not sought to extend our territorial possessions by conquest, or our republican institutions over a reluctant people. It was the deliberate homage of each people to the great principle of our federative union.

If we consider the extent of territory involved in the annexation—its prospective influence on America—the means by which it has been accomplished, springing purely from the choice of the people themselves to share the blessings of our union, the history of the

Source: "President's Message." *The Congressional Globe*, 29th Congress, 1st Sess. (Dec. 4, 1845).

world may be challenged to furnish a parallel. . . . We may rejoice that the tranquil and pervading influence of the American principle of self-government was sufficient to defeat the purposes of British and French interference, and that the almost unanimous voice of the people of Texas has given to that interference a peaceful and effective rebuke. From this example European governments may learn how vain diplomatic arts and intrigues must ever prove upon this continent against that system of self-government which seems natural to our soil, and which will ever resist foreign interference. . . . I regret to inform you that our relations with Mexico, since your last session, have not been of amiable character which it is our desire to cultivate with all foreign nations. On the sixth day of March last, the Mexican Envoy Extraordinary and Minister Plenipotentiary to the United States made a formal protest. . . against the joint resolution passed by Congress "for the annexation of Texas to the United States," which he chose to regard as a violation of the rights of Mexico, and, in consequence of it, he demanded his passports. . . . Thus, by the acts of Mexico, all diplomatic intercourse between the two countries was suspended.

Since that time Mexico has, until recently, occupied an attitude of hostility towards the United States—has been marshalling and organizing armies, issuing proclamations, and avowing the intention to make war on the United States, either by an open declaration, or by invading Texas. . . . The independence of Texas is a fact conceded by Mexico herself, and she had no right or authority to prescribe restrictions as to the form of government which Texas might afterwards choose to assume. But though Mexico cannot complain of the United States on account of the annexation of Texas, it is to be regretted that serious causes of misunderstanding between the two countries continue to exist, growing out of unredressed injuries inflicted by the Mexican authorities and people on the persons and property of citizens of the United States, through a long series of years. Mexico has admitted these injuries, but has neglected and refused to repair them. . . . Such a continued and unprovoked series of wrongs could never have been tolerated by the United States, had they been committed by one of the principle nations of Europe. Mexico was, however, a neighboring sister republic, which, following our example, had achieved her independence, and for whose success and prosperity all our sympathies were early enlisted. . . . We have, therefore, borne the repeated wrongs she has committed, with great patience, in the hope that a returning sense of justice would ultimately guide her councils, and that we might, if possible, honorably avoid any hostile collision with her. . . .

The rapid extension of our settlements over our territories heretofore unoccupied; the addition of new States to our confederacy; the expansion of free principles, and our rising greatness as a nation, are attracting the attention of the Powers of Europe; and lately the doctrine has been broached in some of them, a "balance of power" on this continent, to check our advancement. The United States, sincerely desirous of preserving relations of good understanding with all nations, cannot in silence permit any European interference in the North American continent; and should any such interference be attempted, it will be ready to resist it at any and all hazards. . . . The American system of government is entirely different from that of Europe. Jealousy among the different sovereigns of Europe, lest any one of them might become too powerful for the rest, has caused them anxiously to desire the establishment of what they term the "balance of power." It cannot be permitted to have any application on the North American continent, and especially to the United States. We must never maintain the principle, that the people of this continent alone have the right to decide their own destiny. Should any portion of them, constituting an independent State, propose to unite themselves with our confederacy, this will be a question for them and us to determine, without any foreign interposition. . . .

STUDY QUESTIONS

1. How does President Polk represent the actions of the United States in acquiring Texas? Do you agree with Polk's claim that the acquisition of Texas was a "bloodless achievement"?
2. How does President Polk characterize the Mexican governments' response to the annexation of Texas?
3. To what extent do concerns about European intervention in the Americas underpin Polk's speech?

DOMINGOS JOSÉ GONÇALVES DE MAGALHÃES

2.5 UPRISING IN MARANHÃO, 1839–1840

Like Spanish America, Brazil was racked by political and social unrest in the decades following independence. Regionalism was a particular factor: the central government's ability to impose its power was limited by immense distances and varied terrain, and several regions pressed for autonomy from Rio de Janeiro, with local leaders proclaiming that Portuguese rule had been replaced by an equally foreign and distinct power that did not represent their interests. Between 1822 and 1848 there were five major rebellions that threatened secession. This document describes one of the most important of these movements: the Balaiada uprising—a major social rebellion that took place between 1838 and 1841 in the province of Maranhão in the northeast of Brazil. The rebellion began as a conflict between political elites, and its immediate spark was the removal from power of local Liberal officials by Conservative leaders empowered by the ascendance of conservatism within the national government. However, the armed rebellion quickly turned into a popular movement, and subalterns came to take control of the major cities of the state through military actions led by popular leaders, including the black cattle herder Raymundo Gomes; Cosme Bento, an ex-slave with a force of three thousand escaped Africans; and Manuel Francisco dos Anjos Ferreira, a basketweaver nicknamed "el balaiao"—the basket—from whose name the uprising takes its name. The movement underlines how quickly class and race interests could subsume elite politics. The subsequent fear elites developed of empowering the nonwhite masses has been identified by historians as one of the factors explaining the stabilization of Brazilian politics after 1850. This account of the rebellion was written by the acclaimed poet and playwright José Gonçalves de Magalhães in 1848, close to a decade after the movement's end, and was initially published in an elite history journal.

Before telling this history, it is necessary to know the men, classes, practices, and customs of the country that draws our attention, because such things are of great importance for the weighing of facts and understanding of many things, which without this previous knowledge would seem, at first, view, inexplicable. The population of this province is computed at 217,000 souls, amount them whites, mixed peoples, and Negroes, scattered over an area of more than 800 square leagues. Its land, although fertile, as that of the entire Empire, is little cultivated: copious rains wet it from December until June, and in this pluvial time, which only for that reason they call it winter, the weeks are linked without intermission of one dry day; the fields are deluged, the rivers grow, of which there are many; and the flooded highways become difficult transit. Such a pestilence of fevers develop at the beginning and end of the rains that only those accustomed to the humid and hot climate can resist them.

The principle types of cultivation are cotton and rice, and for these they employ numerous arms of African slaves, those who are treated with such barbarous rigor, that even the necessary sustenance they [the landlords] deny to them; one ear of corn is their lunch, rice and manioc meal the dinner, scavenging and hunting furnish the rest for them; they walk naked or embraced with a small loincloth, except for few exceptions; and for that reason, the slaves seek to withdraw from the yoke of the landlord.

Source: Domingos José Gonçalves de Magalhães, "Uprising in Maranhão, 1839–1840."

The plantation owners appropriate everything that is harvested without fretting over the land with means of industry, hardly careful to improve the cultivation; and for that reason, the province is dotted by plantations raising bovine cattle, in whose care and in the salting of meat and hides are occupied throngs of lazy men, without steady homes, for the most part a race crossed by Indians, whites, and Negroes, whom are called *cafusos*: those who are very fond of this semivagrant life, little interested in other trades, and much in scavenging and hunting, distinguishing themselves only from the savages by the use of our language. They are men of cruel temperament by the habit of herding and killing cattle, consuming the rest of life in laziness or brawls. From this brute people, there are great emigrations from this province, and thus the people of Piauí and Ceará are similar to them in practices and customs. Many of the plantation owners, in imitation of the old barons, live without any respect for the authorities, avenging by their own hands particular insults and harboring on their lands the criminals who seek their shelter, and who together lend themselves to their [the landowners'] reprisals. By such people, they [the landowners] are escorted and become feared, and it is as easy for them to arrange a murder as to deny a debt, or at least not to pay creditors, who at their opportunity, if they can, do not hesitate to employ the same means for their own good. This is the people who incited war against us; it is they who compose the army of the rebellion. . . .

This province was found in peace when Senhor Vicente Thomaz Pires de Figueredo Camargo took possession of the presidency [of the province] on March 3, 1838. . . . Strong opposition was manifested against the administration of Senhor Camargo, opposition in part malicious, because those who then composed the part of the government, before rising to the public offices, as oppositionists, had been strongly attacking the government of Senator Antonio Pedro da Costa Ferreira, a person dear to the party that now, in getting even, waged war against them [the people now in office]. A small newspaper with the title of *Bemteví*, written in popular language, attracted a broad party; it attacked the president and the law of the prefects, a new creation that, with the president's indication, had passed in the provincial assembly. . . .

. . . The population was divided into two rancorous parties, the *bemtevís* [hummingbirds] and *cabanos*. (*Cabanos* was the name applied, in Maranahão,

to the people of the interior, or those living in cabins and huts. It denoted a rustic and fierce people.) Into the arms of the second [party], the government offered itself, although it ought to have remained neutral and balanced them [the parties]. Partisan government is always unjust. The repercussions from the complaint in the province had reach the Côrte [the capital], and was repeated by the journalists. All this anger by the parties was excited more by the ambition for power and positions, and by the desire to triumph in the elections; those who were on top because of the party's influence did not want to descend; the others wanted to rise, and insults were traded, until at last the cry of the rebellion and civil war succeeded the infamous war of words.

On December 13, 1838, in the village of Manga, situated on the left bank of the Iguará River, in the *comarca* [judicial district] of Itapucurú, there appeared a certain Raymundo Gomes, a man of sufficiently dark color, accompanied by the nine of his race; they broke into the village jail and freed the criminal inmates. There existed in the village twenty some troops under orders of the subprefect and those who were tempted by the same spirit joined Raymundo Gomes. This rebel soon started to apprehend commissioners, and to proclaim against the prefects and the president, whom he planned to topple and in his place elevate the vice president, known as the oppositionist. That a hidden hand directed this drama cannot be doubted. Raymundo Gomes was incapable of making by himself such a resolution, although by his habits he was very appropriate for executing it. Born in Piauí and son of that race crossed by Indians and Negroes that we described, raised in the country among cattle that he herded, offering his knife to his own and others' vengeances, inexperienced in the human letters, only known for some murders from which he lived unpunished, stained by the perversity of the customs that we related and the ineffectiveness of the laws, he would not commit himself to disturbing the public tranquility for political motives without an outside impulse; and when he might dare to, he would abandon his boldness at not finding the decent support, which was incontestably given to him. Stupid instrument of a blind party that imagined to be able, when it might please them, to close the dike of a popular rage, Raymundo Gomes, the cowboy assassin, was converted into chief of the *bemteví* party, and those who lifted him from the earth's dust shamed themselves by their deed. . . .

Caxias, formerly Aldêas-Atlas, was the flourishing emporium of the interior of Maranahão and Piauí, the richest and most commercial city of the province after the capital, notable for the luxury of its inhabitants and the lack of good manners of many, and still more notable for being the theater of continuous vengeances and murders. Resting on the right and eastern back of the Itapucurú, sixty leagues to the southeast of the capital, it faces on the opposite bank the parish of Trezidella, which dominates it. In all the long extension of this principle river are discovered properties, plantations, towns, and villages; and as the land that it penetrates is the most fertile and much cut by its branches, which they call *igarapés*, it is also the most populated and richest area of all Maranahão. The slaves alone are computed at around 20,000 Africans, which often threatens the public tranquility as some of them, withdrawing from the landlord's yoke and hiding out in the forests, go in sorties to rob the surrounding plantations, and armed force is necessary to capture them. This was not one of the smallest ills of the present rebellion, since the fleeing plantation owners left to the mercy of the rebels their houses and slaves, and the latter made use of the opportunity to escape the labor of the plundered fields, and went to find shelter in that area of the coast between the sandbar at Tutoya and Priá, where in a number exceeding 3,000 and commanded by the Negro Cosme, considered a witch doctor, they made a great havoc. In a more appropriate place, we will address these people, who for the time being were accumulating in that area without attracting the attention of the government, which was totally occupied in the matters of greater cost.

Caxias, the city of crime, refuge of criminals, the domain of minor pashas who at their will determined others' lives, was accustomed to seeing murders every day. Pious souls portended for it a great disgrace as punishment for its crimes, and God wanted it to be the bloody theater for all the horrors of the rebellion, perhaps as a correction for its depraved customs and its future improvement.

Everything in Caxias attracted the rebels; its very central position, its riches, munitions, sympathies, and immortality invited them to besiege it. . . .

The journalists in the national capital started to occupy themselves seriously with the business of Maranahão, which was poorly weighed at the beginning, as always happens, and they gave it no value. Particular reports, cities and villages captured, plantations devastated, continuous horrors, and the ineffectiveness of the provincial government frightened the people and exposed to the ministry the impossibility of pacification of this part of the Empire, if it would continue in the hands in which it was found. Also, the general government recognized the necessity of entrusting to a single man the presidency [of Maranahão] and command of the armed forces, to avoid by this maneuver delays and intrigues observed currently and in other identical circumstances. . . .

Colonel Luiz Alves de Lima was thus named president and commander of the armed forces for Maranahão. . . .

Those who already were familiar with his name and reputation cheered him happily, and the newspapers of the province, to which the eminent qualities of the new chief were not secret, disposed themselves in his favor; and from now on we will note that they never made the least opposition or censure against his government, instead always exalting him, and in this each party always wanted to outdo the other. There is so much certainty that the great man, who in the execution of his sacred duties, did not aim at any other end, that it imposes silence even on jealousy and intrigue. On great occasions, great men stand out while small ones disappear.

We have said that our expeditions did not cease, and it would be verbosity to cite more than thirty gunfights monthly from which there resulted rebel deaths and prisoners, and great losses of their mounts. . . .

With these continuous reversals, the insurgents started to become discouraged and only cared about fleeing, seeing certain harm and death everywhere; and as they deserted and turned themselves in to our forces, they were immediately armed and employed against their own comrades, sorely reducing the insurgents' ranks and invigorating ours.

Raymundo Gomes, appearing so badly spiritless and distrusting his forces, sent a delegation designated by some caudillos asking for a pardon, but nevertheless demanding certain conditions unworthy of attention. The president returned it to him with a proclamation that served as a response, ordering them, without any condition, to lay down all arms in order to be pardoned, and otherwise he would continue to pursue them until exterminating them. Sending this response, at the same time, he made a force from the third column march to uphold it. . . .

Raymundo Gomes, however, who because of his crimes doubted the pardon, escaped without weapons, without baggage, without followers, and almost naked, and went to offer himself to the Negro Cosme, who put him in an iron collar [to chain him to a post], and discovering in him [Gomes] the ability to make gunpowder, employed him in that exercise, always under guard. The Negro Cosme, the criminal fugitive from the jails of the capital, then started to be the important figure who most frightened the plantation owners, since he was found in the leadership of 3,000 slaves stirred up to rebellion by him. He signed his name "Dom Cosme, guardian and emperor of the *bemtevi's* liberties." He proclaimed against slavery, he gave titles and posts, he established a school for reading and writing, and hidden in the headwaters of the Rio Preto, *comarca* of Brejo, on the plantation of Lagôa Amarella, he had forward patrols, and he sent parties to rob from and incite insurrection at the surrounding plantations. . . .

Through the emissary, the president knew that Francisco Ferreira Pedrosa, boss of 1,700 criminals harbored on Bella-Agua, desired to turn himself in because he now could not maintain his position and feared not being pardoned, and he [the president] sent assurance to him that he would accept him with the condition of first doing some service in return for having taken up arms against the government; that he would beat the Negroes and later turn himself in. Thus, he acted; the Negroes, in disarray and fleeing after the attack on Lagôa Amarella, ran toward Bella-Agua supposing there to find support, and they found death and subjugation. It was always the policy of the president to impede the joining of rebels with the slaves, rendering the first averse to the second, which certainly was a joy for the province. Raymundo Gomes, who found himself imprisoned at Lagôa Amarella under the power of Cosme and who, by him, would be in the end sentenced to death, found an opportunity to escape on the same day that, as he later narrated, he ought to have received the punishment for his crimes at the hands of that other criminal; his fate, however, wanted that on that day the Negroes would be attacked; they, as he, only sought in headlong flight to cheat death, and from there he went to hide out in Miritiba. . . .

Then the president continued to Miritiba, where Raymundo Gomes hid, and through an escort, ordered him to seek his presence. Insignificant was his figure—almost Negro, which we call *fula*, short, stocky, bow-legged, long and flat forehead, timid and shifting eyes, hardly polished with reason, low and meek voice, no boldness of the conspirator—and although he might have been chief of the insurgents, he obeyed more than he ordered and never marched in front of his forces at the moment of battle, and he kept himself in the rearguard, always ready to flee and avoid dangers. Out of all of them, he was not even the most criminal and cruel; instead, compared to the others, he seemed humane. Before him, the old Matroá turned himself in, all bent over with the weight of 120 years of age and crime, dragging a long sword, however, bold and boasting of having entered every great and minor revolt of the North during his life; this old man died one month after turning himself in. In Muritiba, more than 700 rebels laid down arms, all of them naked and without munitions for war, except weapons. The number of surrenders in all our points reached 3,000, and when the period given [for a pardon] expired, there was still captured in the *comarca* of Brejo a band of 300 bandits, who had remained in a hostile attitude.

To complement the pacification of the province, there was imprisoned in the place named Calabouço, a district of Miarim, the infamous Negro Cosme and the rest who accompanied him. Some fifty died because of the tenacious resistance that they offered. Cosme was delivered to justice, and Raymundo Gomes, after amnestied, pledged an eight-year term of exile from the province, São Paulo being designated for him as his residence.

On January 19 [1841], the president ordered the pacification of the province.

STUDY QUESTIONS

1. How did popular discontent shape the rebellion according to Gonçalves de Magalhães? What role did slavery play in the uprising?
2. Was Gonçalves de Magalhães sympathetic to the rebellion? What did he think local elites might have done differently to prevent it?

ANONYMOUS

2.6 A REPORT ON PARAGUAY, *THE MORNING CHRONICLE* (LONDON), AUGUST 23, 1824

More than most Latin American countries, Paraguay experienced intense domination by a single leader in the decades after independence, yet this political domination also served as a protectant against intervention by foreign powers. Following independence, the country spent decades under the control of Dr. José Gaspar Rodríguez de Francia, who pursued a policy of near-total isolationism, as a result of fear of potential annexation by Argentina or Brazil. Francia's government limited trade with outside powers and monitored the handful of foreigners who remained in the country. This document is the single news article known to have appeared in the British press about Paraguay in the decades between independence in 1811 and Francia's death in 1840. It provides an overview of the economy and politics of the country that is extremely favorable to Dr. Francia. Although the article is anonymous, historians have suggested that it was written by Francia himself as he weighed the possibility of opening trading relations with Britain—perhaps in the hope of British protection against rival powers.

The independent State of Paraguay, situated on the river Parana, between Peru, Chile and Brazil, and comprehending all those immense and luxuriant tracts of land which stretch East and West from Brazil, nearly as far as the Andes mountains, is divided into six departments, viz. Santiago, Conception, Villareal, Curuguatia, Candelaria, and Assumption. This valuable portion of country, constituting the heart of South America, has always been represented as a perfect garden and its inhabitants as the happiest race in the whole Southern hemisphere. They are extremely fond of their own country, laborious, steady in their pursuits, mild and upright in their disposition, and particularly attached to each other.

Their productions are rich and various, and their forests abound with valuable wood, gums and rosins, entirely unknown in the markets of Europe. The country abounds in cattle, and is intersected by several of the finest rivers in America, and studded with lakes. Amidst the general waste and destruction occasioned by the wars in the herds, which formerly were so abundant

in the contiguous provinces, those of the Paraguayans alone have been preserved and increased. Most of the grains known in Europe are successfully raised in Paraguay, besides a variety of native ones. Fruits of various kinds are abundant, so that the inhabitants live at ease, with few wants, surrounded by plenty, and in the possession of a country that has always been represented as the Arcadia of the New World. Peace, union and concord, reign among them, and Patriots, in the true sense of the word, have no wishes—no ambition— beyond the welfare of their beloved native land.

[In 1811], influenced by the just principle of self-preservation, and unattended by the smallest political commotion, a meeting of the principal inhabitants was convened and assembled, when their situation was fairly laid before them, and discussed, and upwards of one thousand Deputies unanimously declared a favour of total independence, and, as it were, political seclusion, in which state they have remained ever since. They further resolved that the Government should be confided to that person among them, who, from his

Source: Peter Lambert and Andrew Nickson (eds.) *The Paraguay Reader: History, Culture, Politics* (Durham, NC: Duke University Press, 2013), pp. 55–59.

virtues and knowledge, should be found most deserving of the public confidence; but, in order to avoid the conflict of two parties, headed by two individuals, equally entitled to this distinction, they determined to elect Dr. Francia and M. Yegros Joint Governors. These two persons, for some time, administered the affairs of Paraguay, jointly, each having a separate district, and commanding an equal force; till, in the course of time, the inconvenience of this plan was felt, and the ascendancy of Dr. Francia having, in the mean while, increased, at a second meeting of the inhabitants, he was elected sole governor—a command he has held ever since, revered and beloved by the people.

From the peculiar traits of character Dr. Francia has since evinced, it is evident he sought the exercise this supreme command from no interested or ambitious views. His country was early attacked by an enemy from Buenos Ayres; every effort was made to induce the inhabitants to enter into the La Plata coalition, on the one hand, and that of Artigas, on the other, and had Dr. Francia been obstructed by the interference of a colleague, possibly he never would have been able to repel the aggressions of his neighbours, or so successfully shield this territory from civil commotions, and afterwards, by his foresight and perseverance, raise it to a state of prosperity and happiness it now enjoys, beyond any other portion of the same continent.

Dr. Francia is a native of Paraguay, and was bred a lawyer. Not fond of society, and rich enough to live with ease and independence, previous to the revolution, he remained retired on his own estate in the country, principally devoted to study; his pursuits gave him a reputation for learning beyond any of his countrymen, and his virtuous and moral conduct, added to his stern probity and known disinterestedness, subsequently secured their confidence. Gradually Dr. Francia has consolidated his power, and without any of the appendages or expenses of state; he exercises the duties of first magistrate, and his orders are obeyed throughout the whole territory the instant they are received. Justice is his guide, and he derives no emolument from his administration. He sees to everything himself; purchases the clothing and arms for the militia, settles disputes, grants passports, and, in short, superintends each department of government, everything being conducted on the most simple and economical scale. He has no favourites—no enemies—and, by a fair and impartial demeanour, he stands unimpeached in the opinions of his fellow-countrymen, after governing them for a number of years.

Strictly containing themselves to their own territorial limits, and intent only on keeping their rights and property unimpaired, for the last fourteen years the Paraguayans have had no external enemies, nor has their tranquility been once interrupted. Thus concentrated within themselves, their country has served as an asylum for those fleeing from desolation and civil war in the surrounding provinces, by which means their numbers have been considerably increased. Emigrants have flocked thither from Corrientes, Tucuman, and Buenos Ayres; but more particularly from the eastern bank of the River Plata at the time it was desolated by Artigas, who eventually fell into the hands of the Paraguayans, by whom he is still kept a prisoner. These fugitives carried with them the property they were so able to collect in their own provinces, and having thus found a secure asylum, they adopted the habits of their benefactors, and devoted themselves to the pursuits of industry. By this means, and the advantages of peace, and a regular mode of life, the population of Paraguay has increased in a manner unexampled. Numerous tribes of Indians, who formerly refused to submit to the restraints of civilised life, and wandered about without any fixed residence, have also been blended into the general mass, and become useful members of society. According to the last census, taken in the year 1822, the population of Paraguay amounted to upwards of 500,000 souls. They have 30,000 armed militia, occasionally exercised, and only called into the field in case of an external attack. Their regular armed forces consists of three small vessels of war, intended for the defence of the rivers, and four legions of volunteers of 2,000 men each, paid only whilst on duty. This armed force is commanded by Dr. Francia, and the military regulations enacted by the Marshal Beresford in Portugal have been adopted in Paraguay.

Old-established custom and well-authenticated precedents, such as are on record from the time of the Jesuits, together with the laws of the Indies, regulate the administration of justice, and the concerns of Government, in every thing not opposed to the Provisional Code drawn up and ordered to be observed by Dr. Francia, in which he has consulted the habits, wants, and situation of the people he governs, having their peace and prosperity at heart, and being anxious to promote their social improvement by a moral and substantial education. This Provisional Code has been drawn up so as not to clash with the customs and even the prejudices of a people, peculiar in every thing. In order to be lasting, he has been desirous that all changes and reforms should be gradual, and not adopted by the people until they could duly appreciate their value. So great is the simplicity of manners among the Paraguayans, and so prompt the administration of justice, that few or none of those crimes are to be met with which embitter corrupt and overgrown societies, where the means of existence often depend on painful toil or the abuse of ingenuity. Their Governor seems to have followed the substantial part of the old policy of the Jesuits, who, by the most wonderful address, retained, till the time of their expulsion, an absolute dominion, both in spiritual and temporal concerns, over the inhabitants of Paraguay. He foresees and provides for their wants, and by rendering them individually happy and contented at home, he binds them to the support of a Government, the practical advantages of which they have daily before their eyes. He has thus made them united, and consequently strong in case of attack. All are subject to the same laws, and no distinctions are known beyond those which superior merit bestows. Hence the public revenue is regular and secure, and having been imposed by general consent, it is easily collected, without any expense to the Government.

It has been obvious policy of this extraordinary man to preserve his country from anarchy and civil war, and, in order to effect his purpose, he induced the principal proprietors to make a temporary sacrifice, he allowed no other intercourse with foreigners and neighbours, than what was indispensably necessary to procure arms, and such articles as the Government stood in need of, fearful that the influx of strangers might lead to confusion, and counteract his paternal plans. The Paraguayans consented to the privation of external trade,

and the consequent loss of a large portion of their produce, and zealously devoted themselves to the internal improvement of their growing republic. All the surplus revenue was laid out to advantage. The idle hands were employed in opening roads, making bridges, and other useful works, and the few slaves the country possessed were gradually freed, without any loss to their owners. Public liberty is well regulated; yet the printing of the political works has been discouraged until the people shall be better grounded in substantial knowledge, and more removed from the backward state in which they were when they entered on their political career. So readily did the inhabitants submit to these privations, or so efficient rather was the voluntary police, in which each co-operated for the general good, that during the first nine years not a single letter left the country without having been first inspected by the Chief magistrate—a fact perfectly well authenticated.

With the exception of Brazil, the Paraguayans have never attempted to establish relations of amity and commerce with any independent State, not even with those situated in their own neighbourhood, their whole attention having been turned to the means by which their own liberties and tranquility could be preserved. The frequent overtures of Buenos Ayres to enter into a general confederation of all the provinces formerly constituting the Vice-royalty of the River Plate, have uniformly been rejected, from the principle that all engagements of such a nature could not fail to embroil Paraguay in those unhappy dissensions which have so long afflicted the contiguous districts. The Emperor of Brazil lately invited the Paraguayans to form part of his dominions, but the offer was declined in a firm, although respectful manner. The Paraguayans, in short, have formed a peculiar policy of their own, and they seem resolved to continue united among themselves, prepared at the same time to make every sacrifice in order to secure their own tranquility and independence.

STUDY QUESTIONS

1. How does the article characterize Dr. Francia's rule?
2. What explanations are offered for the international isolation of Paraguay? Is isolation viewed as a positive or a negative for Paraguay's economy?
3. Assuming the article is written by Francia, what can we learn from it about the operation of *caudillo* rule in Latin America?

CHAPTER 3

FIRST ATTEMPTS AT STATE FORMATION
The Liberal-Conservative Debate, 1830–1875

TOMÁS CIPRIANO DE MOSQUERA

3.1 LETTER TO PIUS IX, 1862

The role of the Catholic Church was at the center of the divisions between Liberals and Conservatives. The separation between Church and State was a fundamental Liberal principle, while many Liberal thinkers and intellectuals believed that the wealth the Church had accrued during the colonial period needed to be nationalized in the interests of economic development. In this document, the Colombian Liberal Tomás Cipriano de Mosquera writes to Pope Pius IX at the beginning of his third term as president, in a moment of Liberal ascendancy following a major civil war between Liberals and Conservatives. In the letter, Mosquera lays out the rationale for his plans to redefine the traditional rights of the Church in accordance with the newly passed Colombian Constitution, including overturning previous exemptions of the clergy from state legal and police authority. He also addresses the expropriation of certain Church lands, notably the mortmain properties—lands that had been inherited by religious orders but that had been determined not to be used productively. The letter played an important role in Pius IX's later declaration that Spanish American liberalism was "at war" with the Catholic Church.

T.C. Mosquera, president of the United States of Colombia To His Holiness Pius IX, Supreme Pontiff. *Most Holy Fathers,*

It is not the first time that I must address Your Holiness in my role as first Magistrate of a Nation; and thus, I have no doubt that my official letter will be received by Your Holiness with the same trust and benevolence as my previous ones; and that in it you will find the same loyalty with which I have always spoken to the Holy See and the candor and sincerity required by the Supreme Magistrate of a Nation. . . .

Your Holiness knows well the events that took place in this Nation when complications arose in the relationship between the civil interim Government and the Episcopate of Granada in 1852. To bring this complication to an end, the Government of New Granada decided to satisfy the wishes of the Catholics by leaving the Church independent from the Interim Authority. . . .

Source: Ann Farnsworth-Alvear, et al. (eds.) *The Colombian Reader: History, Culture, Politics* (Durham, NC: Duke University Press, 2017), pp. 119–122.

This withholding of public Authority from strictly spiritual matters was not adequately appreciated by a sector of the Episcopate of Granada nor by the Papal Delegate, both of whom became involved in political questions and hoping to identify religious matters with public questions that unfortunately have divided our Nation. . . .

The Bishops of Pasto and Pamplona, along with members of the clergy, have become involved in supporting one party so that religion may serve as an electoral instrument for political Magistrates. A Canon from Bogotá, Father Sucre, joined an electoral club and, disregarding his Prelate the Bishop, addressed a handbill to all the priests of the Archbishopric, so that the candidacy of General Herrán be substituted for that of Julio Arboleda, who was the candidate of the party that destroyed the federal Constitution. Many clergymen have engaged themselves in the revolution, abusing of their pastoral ministry, in order to agitate the masses to rebel against the constitutional State Governments; some of them have even taken up arms, and there is the scandal of a priest who died in combat while heading a guerrilla [band]. I will not describe to your Holiness other such events, as what is stated is enough to make my point.

For some time we Catholics have had to regret, after the intervention of the civil Government to present to Your Holiness ideal priests for the Episcopates, that vacancies have instead in some cases been filled with people who are not fit to honorably represent the Episcopate, lacking in character and rightness, such as the Bishop of Cartagena, Father Medina, whose reference is no other than having fought in the civil war in 1851, spear in hand, at Garrapata; Father Arbeláez, who before being ordained as a Bishop required three months of previous study in order to make him suitable for consecration; and the Bishop of Pamplona, a priest of little schooling concerned solely with a party's victory; all this despite that there is no shortage of priests of science and virtue in Granada's Clergy.

We must generally regret the lack of Seminaries in our Nation where youth can be educated from the priesthood; and the ecclesiastical career has become a lucrative profession, practiced by men without science, and in which many individuals have been ordained without even knowing Latin; so that the priestly ministry is exercised without an understanding of the sacred Scripture nor the prayers said in mass.

It with great feeling that I must tell Your Holiness that a growing number of priests live scandalously with concubines, and they are thus unable to preach morality. It is apparent that their preaching recommends the payment of ecclesiastical contributions, in order to use these goods for their families and not for Worship. . . .

There is more, Most Holy Father: the Catholic devotion in this nation had provided great riches to Worship, and since public authority has not intervened in their conservation, many of these properties have disappeared, unlawfully disposed; and, with few exceptions, Bishops have contributed with condemnable condescension to the destruction of these assets. Thus, it was necessary to order the disentitlement of these assets as mortmain property, and thus be introduced into national commerce, consolidating their value in the national Treasury, so that their interests may be faithfully invested in the purpose for which they were donated. This has been verified, and Churches receive what is needed to cover the expenses of Worship, as the Government recognizes the maxim that in a free and independent Nation the Church must also be equally free and independent. The degree of Tuition [allegiance to the constitution] has been wrongfully understood, and it has been stated that the government is attempting to intervene in strictly ecclesiastical business, and provide authority to priests and Bishops to exercise their ministry. No doubt Your Holiness has been misinformed by the Papal Delegate, whom I had to exile from the country, for having supported the political party that is no longer in power . . .

Several Bishops, among them the Metropolitan, an old personal friend of mine, have opposed the Government by disobeying the Decrees of Tuition and Disentitlement of Mortmain Property; and I have found myself obliged to confine them to other residences or exile them for rebelling against the interim authority, as they should, in accordance to Papal precepts, submit to those in power, and not forget the precepts of the Holy Bishop of Pospona, Doctor of the Church, Saint Augustine, who counseled obedience even to tyrants . . .

After abandoning the metropolitan Church, several virtuous priests have held Catholic Worship in their churches, and the faithful take pride in attending these religious functions; they address God, in Colombia's capital, giving thanks for the aid they receive, while those of the likes of Bishop Arbeláez order disobedience of public authority, thus establishing a division among

Catholics that only Your Holiness can resolve, by calling upon Colombian Prelates to avoid this division among the faithful, as they have been ordained Bishops to guide the happiness of the Christian people, and in compliance with the interim authority, to remain in their Dioceses so they may be of use to Christian peoples, as their main duty is to ensure harmony among the faithful. . . .

I know well, Most Holy Father, that in exercising the Supreme Power of this Nation as I do, it is my duty to respect the independence of the Catholic Church, as it is required by law of me; but I also know that civil Power cannot waver in the face of functions that are not ecclesiastic as is practiced by Bishops and priests.

In order for clergy to exercise their ministry with absolute independence, we have provided them with personal exemptions from military service, local offices, and personal contributions from all revenues obtained as alms from the faithful, as well as compensation for all the services they provide in their ministry.

In conclusion, I must express to Your Holiness that the Government of Colombia is willing to allow the return of Bishops to their particular dioceses, as soon as they recognize the Decrees known as Tuition and Disentitlement of Mortmain Property. . . .

With sentiments of filial respect, I reassert myself as a devoted son of Your Holiness,

T. C. DE MOSQUERA
Facatativá, January 15, 1862

STUDY QUESTIONS

1. How does Mosquera characterize the role of Catholic priests and bishops within Colombian politics? How have these political interventions shaped the policies Mosquera plans to develop toward the Church?
2. Why does Mosquera argue that Church *mortmain* property must be nationalized by the State? What benefits does he argue that this change in ownership will bring to both the government and the Church, respectively?
3. How does the source help us understand tensions between Liberals and Conservatives over the role of the Church?

JAMES ORTON

3.2 CATHOLICISM IN CONSERVATIVE ECUADOR, 1870

James Orton was an American naturalist who undertook two major expeditions to South America between 1867 and 1876. These trips became landmarks in the study of the physical geography and geology of the western coast of South America and the Amazon Valley, notably documenting Amazonian fossils for the first time. In addition to hundreds of scientific papers, Orton also published an influential and widely read travelogue about his 1867 trip which reflected on the political and social customs he observed. In this excerpt, he describes the influence of the Catholic Church and the dominance of the Catholic religion in the city of Quito, which he visited at the high point of conservative rule. Orton was especially struck by the overt hostility he argued was displayed toward the Protestant faith.

Source: James Orton, *The Andes and the Amazon: Or, Across the Continent of South America* (New York: Harper and Brothers, 1870), pp. 87–91.

One would suppose that the people who breathe this high atmosphere, and enjoy this delightful climate, and are surrounded by all that is truly grand and beautiful, would have some corresponding virtues. But we find that Nature, here as every where, has mingled base and noble elements. The lofty mountains, bearing in their steadfastness the seal of their appointed symbol—"God's righteousness is like the great mountains"—look down upon one of the lowest and most corrupt forms of republican government on earth; their snowy summits preach sermons on purity to Quitonian society, but in vain; and the great thoughts of God written all over the Andes are unable to lift this proud capital out of the mud and mire of mediæval ignorance and superstition. The established religion is the narrowest and most intolerant form of Romanism. Mountains usually have a more elevating, religious influence than monotonous plains. The Olympian mythology of the Greek was far superior to the beastly worship on the banks of the Nile. And yet at the very feet of glorious Chimborazo and Pichincha we see a nation bowing down to little images of the rudest sculpture with a devotion that reminds us of the Middle Ages.

The belief is called *La Fe*, or the only true one. The oath of a Protestant is not regarded in courts of law. One fourth of Quito is covered by convents and churches. The convents alone number fifty-seven, and are very extensive, sometimes spreading over eight or nine acres. The Church revenue amounts to $800,000. There are more than four hundred priests, monks, and nuns in the capital. The native ecclesiastics are notorious for their ignorance and immorality. "It is a very common thing (says Dr. Terry) for a curate to have a whole flock of orphan nephews and nieces, the children of an imaginary brother." There is one ex-president who has the reputation of tying a spur on the leg of a game-cock better even than a curate. The imported Jesuits are the most intelligent and influential clergy. They control the universities and colleges, and education generally. Active and intellectual, though not learned, they have infused new life into the fat indolence of the Spanish system. Men of this world rather than the next, they have adopted a purely mundane policy, abjured the gloomy cowl, raised gorgeous temples, and say, "He that cometh unto us shall in no wise lose heaven." Their chief merit, however, is the discovery of the turkey and quinine.

The Protestant in Quito is annoyed by an everlasting jingling of bells and blowing of bugles night and day. The latter are blown away every third hour. The bells are struck by boys, not rung. A bishop, returning from a visit to London, was asked if there were any good bells in England. "Very fine," he replied, "but there is not a man there who knows how to ring them." Foreign machinery is sprinkled with holy water to neutralize the inherent heresy; but a miller, for example, will charge more for his flour after the baptism.

Lotteries are countenanced by both Church and State, and in turn help support them; we saw one "grand scheme" carried out on the cathedral terrace and defended by bayonets.

At half past nine in the morning all Quito is on its knees, as the great bell of the cathedral announces the elevation of the Host. The effect is astonishing. Riders stop their horses; foot-passengers drop down on the pavement; the cook lets go her dishes and the writer his pen; the merchant lays aside his measure and the artisan his tool; the half-uttered oath (*carájo!*) dies on the lips of the Cholo; the arm of the cruel Zambo, unmercifully beating his donkey, is paralyzed; and the smart repartee of the lively donna is cut short. The solemn stillness lasts for a minute, when the bell tells again, and all rise to work or play. Holidays are frequent. Processions led by a crucifix or wooden image are attractive sights in this dull city, simply because little else is going on. Occasionally a girl richly dressed to represent the humble mother of God is drawn about in a carriage, and once a year the figures of the Virgin belonging to different churches are borne with much pomp to the Plaza, where they bow to each other like automatons.

"This is a bad country to live in, and a worse one to die in," said Dr. Jameson. But times have changed, even in fossil Quito. Through the efforts of our later minister, Hon. W. T. Coggeshall, the bigoted government has at last consented to inclose a quarter of an acre outside the city for the subterranean burial of heretics. The cemetery is on the edge of the beautiful plain of Iñaquito, and on the same right of the road leading to Guápolo. "What a shame," said a Quitonian lady of position, "that there should be a place to throw Protestant dogs!"

On St. Nathaniel's day died Colonel Phineas Staunton, Vice-Chancellor of Ingham University, New York. An artist by profession, and one of very high order, Colonel Staunton joined our expedition to sketch the glories of the Andes, but he fell a victim to the scourge of the lowlands one week after his arrival in Quito. We buried him at noonday[1] in the new cemetery, "wherein was never man laid," and by the act consecrated the ground. Peace

---

[1] This was a new thing under the sun. Quitonian "bury at dead of night with lanterns dimly burning." The dirges sung as the procession winds through the streets are extremely plaintive, and are the most touching specimens of Ecuadorian music. The corpse, especially of a child, is often carried in a chair in a sitting posture. The wealthy class wall up their dead in niches on the side of Pichincha, hypothetically till the resurrection, but really for two years, when, unless an additional payment is made, the bones are thrown into a common pit and the coffin burnt. To prevent this, a few who can afford it embalm the deceased. One of the most distinguished citizens of

to his ashes; honor to his memory. That 8th of September, 1867, was a new day in the annals of Quito. On that day the imperial city beheld, for the first time in three centuries, the decent burial of a Protestant in a Protestant cemetery. Somewhere, mingled with the ashes of Pichincha, is the dust of Atahuallpa, who was buried in his beloved Quito at his own request after his murder in Caxamarca. But dearer to us is that solitary grave; the earth is yet fresh that covers the remains of one nature's noblemen.

Quito keeps his mummified father at his hacienda, and annually dresses him up in a new suit of clothes!

STUDY QUESTIONS

1. What role does religion play in the exercise of political and social rights in Ecuador in 1867, according to Orton?
2. To what extent does the source help us understand how everyday people in Quito experienced the Catholic religion?

FRIEDRICH HASSAUREK

3.3 *FOUR YEARS AMONG THE ECUADORIANS*, 1867

Friedrich Hassaurek was the American minister to Ecuador between 1861 and 1866, during the early years of the Conservative president Gabriel Garcia Moreno's rule. Hassaurek's book about his time in Ecuador became one of the most widely read Latin American travelogues of the nineteenth century, passing through three editions and receiving critical acclaim in the United States and in Europe. While his book mostly dealt with social customs, he also reflected on political developments. In 1860s Ecuador, the tension between Liberals and Conservatives was becoming ever more acute, as the Conservative Garcia Moreno entwined the Catholic Church ever more deeply into the day-to-day workings of the state, and clamped down on freedom of the press and political assembly to combat his Liberal opponents. In this excerpt, Hassaurek emphasizes the violence of these conflicts between political philosophies, and reflects on the consequences of a cycle of revolution and counterrevolution as rival elites jostled for power.

Source: Friederich Hassaurek, *Four Years among the Ecuadorians* (Carbondale: Southern Illinois University Press, 1967 [1867]), pp. 123–141.

A Spanish-American revolution, to be successful, must originate with, or be supported by, the soldiery. The conspirators begin with bribing a portion of the garrison of an important post. Military barracks will never be attacked without a previous secret understanding with some of the officers and men who are in charge of the post. In the negotiations for such purposes the ladies take a most active part. They are passionate politicians and very energetic secret agents. They carry letters and dispatches, excite discontent, conceal political refugees and facilitate their escape, and keep their banished friends posted as to the state of affairs at home. During my residence in Ecuador, several of these female agitators were banished from the country by President García Moreno. They went, hurling defiance into his teeth. He could imprison or shoot the men, who trembled before him, but he could not break the spirit of the women.

The moment a revolutionary party has secured a foothold somewhere, they resort to the customary mode of Spanish-American warfare. Its principal features are forcible impressments and forced loans and contributions, in addition to which they seize all the horses, mules, cattle, provisions, Indians, and other property they can lay hands on. The government does the same. There is no legal or equitable system of conscription or draft. By common consent, gentlemen (that is to say, white men of good families) are exempt from it; but the poor, the half-breeds, or crossbreeds, the journeymen, mechanics, and farm laborers, are seized and impressed wherever found, and without reference to age, condition, disability, or the time they may have served already. The appearance of the recruiting officers on the street always creates a panic among those liable to be recruited. It is a pitiful spectacle to see those poor fellows run away in all directions, wildly chased by the officers and their men. Compulsory service in the army is a calamity greatly dreaded by the populace, and from which they try to escape in a thousand different ways. They will flee to the mountains, and hide themselves in forests or deserts; they will take refuge in churches or convents, or in the houses of foreign representatives or residents, and they will not show themselves on the streets or public highways until the danger is over. When they are near enough to the frontier, they will leave the country in order to avoid impressment. Ecuadorian soldiers are but poorly clad and poorly paid. Many of them have to go barefoot. When their services are no longer required, they are discharged without the means to return to their homes. Under these circumstances, it cannot appear strange that such soldiers should revenge themselves on society whenever the opportunity offers. When marching from one place to another, they will take from the poor people living along the public highways whatever they can find. Hence, when it becomes known that a regiment or company of soldiers will march through a certain district, the people living along the road, even in times of profound peace, will hide their valuables, drive away their horses, mules, cattle, or sheep, take their provisions, chickens, etc. to some out-of-the-way place in the mountains or forests, making preparations as if they expected the arrival of a savage enemy. The houses along the road will be deserted; the men will carefully keep out of the way of the marching columns; and only now and then an old woman will be found to tell the soldiers how poor she is. Many a time when, during my travels in the cordillera, I stopped at a hut to buy eggs or other provisions, the people told me with a sigh, "We have nothing to sell, sir; the soldiers were here and took all we had."

The first measures of a party which succeeds in a revolution or civil war are generally acts of retaliation or revenge on the vanquished, who may congratulate themselves if only forced contributions are resorted to. The wealthy members of the losing party are notified by the new "government," that within a certain number of days or hours they must pay a certain sum of money. If they refuse, the amount is sometimes raised, and even doubled, and the victims are imprisoned, either in their own houses, or in the military barracks, until they pay up. If they are storekeepers, their goods are seized as security. If they are hacienda owners, their cattle or horses are taken in lieu of money. If they are women, they are placed under a military guard, and not allowed to leave their rooms, or to consult with their friends, until they comply with arbitrary edict of the despot of the day. I shall relate but one instance of the many that came to my knowledge. In 1860 a contribution of several hundred dollars (I do not recollect the exact amount) was imposed upon a gentleman who had held office under the government that had just been overthrown. He being absent from Quito on his hacienda in Esmeraldas, on the coast, a detachment of soldiers was send to his house with a command to his wife to pay the money. The lady protested that her husband had left her no money, and that she was unable to pay the required amount. Her answer was deemed unsatisfactory, and her house was surrounded by soldiers, who did not allow anybody to enter or to leave it. She was not permitted to send for victuals or for water, nor was she allowed to employ counsel or to see her friends. For three days and nights she was kept a prisoner, until, coerced by starvation, she yielded at last, and paid the amount which had been assessed without warrant of law by the caprice of the victorious party.

A political adversary is considered an outlaw, who may with impunity be treated in the most arbitrary and cruel manner by those in power. His haciendas are laid waste by soldiers quartered on them; his cattle and horses are at the mercy of a reckless government. The greatest sufferers, however, are the owners of beasts of burden, whether they take part in political affairs or not. Their horses and mules are taken whenever they are needed for the transportation of military stores. They are used generally without compensation to the owner, who may congratulate himself if they are at last restored to him. Their galled backs and emaciated bodies are the pay he gets, all constitutional and legal provisions to the contrary notwithstanding. Those who own mules or donkeys which they hire out of travelers, or on which they bring their vegetables to market, keep away from cities in times of war or civil commotion, for fear of being robbed of their means of subsistence. Their beasts they send to the fastnesses of the mountains until the danger is over. Thus the city markets will be but scantily supplied, merchants cannot ship their goods, travelers find no means of transportation, and the whole country suffers and decays because governments will not respect individual rights and private property.

When the country is threatened with war, foreign invasion, or revolution, or when a violent change of government has taken place, the houses of foreign ministers, consuls, and other foreigners, are eagerly resorted to by all classes of the population. Not only will ladies and gentlemen take refuge there, but such houses will be depositories for all sorts of valuables— goods, trunks, and boxes belonging to merchants, mechanics, private citizens, and even the government. During the war with New Granada in 1862, when it was feared that General Arboleda, after his victory at Tulcán, would march to Quito and occupy the town, the government made arrangements to deposit the silver bars belonging to the mint in the house of one of the foreign ministers. The houses of foreigners are respected, not only because the governments to which they belong are expected to shield them with a strong arm, but also because even the victorious or ruling party is interested in maintaining the sacredness of asylums to which, perhaps tomorrow, it may be their turn to resort as the vanquished. In Ecuador, foreigners alone enjoy the rights and privileges which the constitution, on paper, guarantees the citizen. The persons of foreigners are secure; their servants are not taken away from them; their beasts are never interfered with; their property is respected; and if they have a diplomatic representative in the country, they are favored in a thousand different ways. They are the only class of persons who can carry on business in safety. Of course, they will suffer from bad times, when the country is desolated by revolutions or civil war, but they have little to fear from the government and party leaders; and while forced contributions of money or goods will be exacted from the native capitalists; while their servants and laborers, horses and cattle will be taken away from them; the person, property, laborers, and servants of a foreigner will be secure. No wonder, therefore, the very extensive landowner, every wealthy merchant in the country wants to make himself a foreigner. I was almost continually troubled by persons who wanted to know how to make themselves North American citizens. Everybody, almost, who has anything to lose, is anxious to abjure his nationality, and place himself under the protection of a foreign flag. Many went to the United States for the sole purpose of taking our first papers, which, as they believed, would protect them against forced contributions and other losses. Others go abroad to make themselves foreign subjects and then return to carry on their business as before. I have heard hundreds who protested their anxiety to clothe themselves in a foreign personality, in which case alone they considered their property secure. Mr. Buckalew, the American minister under Buchanan, once saved a man from a loss which, according to the Ecuadorian himself, would have amounted to at least $10,000, simply by allowing him to hoist the American flag over his farm buildings.

Whenever, even in times of profound peace, the government desires to erect a structure, or to repair a building, a road, or a bridge, orders are given to the police to seize all the masons and carpenter that can be found. From the number thus arrested, the directors will select the ablest, and compel them to work for such wages as it may be convenient to pay them. Political adversaries, who are suspected of revolutionary intentions, are arrested and detained in prison for months, without a charge against them, and without the benefit of a trial before the proper tribunals. Political prisoners are generally treated in a cruel and barbarous manner. I know of many who were kept in heavy irons for weeks and months, during which time their relatives had to feed them, as the government was not in the habit of furnishing meals to prisoners of state. They were generally banished to the unredeemed wilderness on the eastern side of the cordillera, commonly called the Napo Country from the Napo River—one of the affluents of the Amazon—or to Brazil by way of the Napo. To understand fully the inhuman nature of this punishment, it must be borne in mind that the road to the Napo, beginning at the village of Papallacta—about two day's journey from Quito—is a mere footpath, inaccessible to horses or mules. The prisoners, with their limbs sore from the irons in which they had been kept, had to walk over rocks, and scramble through bogs and woods; now descending the cold and snowy summits of the cordillera, then wading through deep and rapid streams; now exposed to the almost incessant and drenching rains of those regions, then again to the burning sun of the equator; with no provisions but those they carried with them, with no bed but the wet earth, and no cover but the sky, until they reached their inhospitable destination, where only the painted Indian's humble hut afforded them shelter, without protection from wild beasts, poisonous snakes, and tropical fevers.

Another shocking practice was the flogging of men by order of the president, and without process or warrant of law, the number of lashes varying from twenty-five to six hundred. In 1860, an old general, a mulatto, who is said to have creditably served in the wars of independence, was seized by order of García Moreno—then chief of the so-called provisional government—and received five hundred lashes, in presence of the garrison, and probably at the hands of the very soldiers who had been under his command. He died a short time after this punishment. He had not been convicted by a court of competent jurisdiction, civil or military. No charges had been preferred against him. He was not allowed to make a defense, but the punishment was inflicted at the command of one man, who had no constitutional or legal right to judge or punish him.

In 1864, General Maldonado had made himself conspicuous as the leader of a conspiracy, the object of which was to rid the country of the tyranny of García Moreno. The plot was discovered, and many of the conspirators were sent to the Napo wilderness. General Maldonado succeeded in making his escape to the mountains, where, after an exciting pursuit of several weeks, he was captured on his way to Peru, and taken to Guayaquil. President García, who was then at Quito, immediately gave orders to the general commanding at Guayaquil to send the prisoner to the capital. The poor fellow knew that this would be his last journey, and begged hard to be allowed to leave the country. The general commanding declared his willingness to let him go in case $30,000 should be deposited in the bank of Guayaquil as security for his future good behavior. This sum the friends of the prisoner were either unwilling or unable to make up. They knew very well that the amount, if deposited by them, would immediately be seized and expended by the government. Thus Maldonado was sent to Quito. On his arrival there, he was at once taken before the president, who upbraided him for his conduct, and ordered him to be led out to the plaza in front of the government palace, for immediate execution. The whole town was amazed, and many a hasty effort was made to save the victim, but the president was inexorable. The sympathies of the people were with Maldonado; even the soldiers who were commanded to shoot him could hardly repress their tears. If Maldonado had snatched the sword from the hands of the officer who commanded the troops on the plaza, he might have made a successful revolution and turned the tables on his enemy. The soldiers would have cheered and obeyed him, and the people would have welcomed him as their deliverer. But his spirit was broken. His wife arrived, and a scene took place on the plaza which those who witnessed it will remember to their dying day. The last farewell of the consorts was heartrending. Mrs. Maldonado had to be torn from her husband's embrace, and was led away most insensible. She could hardly have walked one square, when she heard the discharge of the muskets which took her husband's life. She fell on the pavement with a frantic shriek. President García was at his office in the palace, and may have witnessed, and probably did witness the execution, which took place under his very windows. This horrible event cast a gloom over the whole country. It was but the forerunner of more appalling deeds.

Dr. Viola, a lawyer at Guayaquil, a scholar and a gentleman, was known to sympathize with the opposition. It was known that he disapproved of the high-handed, illegal, and unconstitutional measures of President García Moreno. This was his only crime. Nothing else could have been proved against him. On the day of the president's successful return to Guayaquil, after his naval victory at Jambeli, García Moreno issued a decree of banishment against Dr. Viola, and ordered him to leave the country by the next steamer. That very same night, the president, while perusing the papers found on board the vessels captured by him, discovered a letter addressed by Dr. Viola to a Mr. Yerobi, an Ecuadorian exile in Peru, who, although brother-in-law of General Urbina, the chief of the revolutionary party, had not taken part in his expedition, but, as was subsequently ascertained, had quietly remained at Lima. His family had remained in Ecuador, and as Yerobi was very poor, his relatives occasionally sent him some money to Peru, to enable him to live in his expensive exile. For the transmission of these amounts to Peru, they availed themselves of the services of Dr. Viola, their attorney at Guayaquil. Dr. Viola also transmitted their private correspondence. But as it was generally believed in the country that letters directed to any of the Ecuadorian refugees in Peru would be detained or opened by the Ecuadorian postoffice authorities, it was the general practice to direct such letters to fictitious names, previously agreed upon. Dr. Viola, following this precaution, notified Yerobi in a short note, of the pseudonym to which he would send his letters. This note never reached Yerobi. His brother-in-law, General Urbina, received it for him at Paita, and took it with him unopened when he started on his expedition. Thus it fell into García Moreno's hands, after the engagement at Jambeli. It hardly filled one page of notepaper. I saw and read it with my own eyes, and I recollect its contents distinctly. It proved nothing; it raised no presumption. The jealousy of a despot might have looked upon it as a suspicious circumstance, but it admitted of a satisfactory explanation. At all events, it was not sufficient to overcome, unsupported by other evidence, the legal presumption of the man's innocence. No civilized tribunal would have convicted him on such a document. Not even a court-martial of García Moreno's own selection would have found him guilty. The president's principle officers, with only one exception, were opposed to the execution; but such considerations had no weight on García. Early in the morning of the day following his return from Jambeli, he sent for Viola. He showed him the letter, and asked him whether he had written it. "Is this your signature?" "Yes, sir; it is." "Then you are a traitor, and as such, you will be shot this evening at five o'clock!"

The horrible news spread like wildfire over Guayaquil, and created universal consternation and horror. Everybody felt that the sword of Damocles was suspended over his own head. Capital punishment was prohibited by the constitution in political cases. According to another provision of that same instrument, the president, when beyond a certain distance from the capital, became a mere private citizen, while the executive power remained temporarily vested in the vice-president. And yet García Moreno undertook to take the life of an innocent man, without warrant or authority of law, and without any cause or excuse. Everybody interceded for his life. The able old lady, who had to be carried to the government building in a sedan chair—the principal merchants and bankers, the president's personal and political friends, the foreign consuls and residents, pleased for Viola's life, but García Moreno was inexorable. When somebody suggested that it would be much better to send Viola out of the country, he sneeringly answered, "he goes to the other world!" Viola was, personally, very popular. Everybody knew him, and everybody liked him. The president was besought during the whole day to spare his life, but in vain. No other declaration could be wrung from his lips but the stern sentence: "He will be shot this evening at five o'clock!" When the bishop suggested that such an execution would be a violation of law and an infraction of the constitution, the president replied that, it being impossible to save the country from anarchy by attempting to govern it according to the constitution, he had taken the responsibility to govern it according to his own views of right and public necessity. He said that an example had to be set, and he was determined to set it.

While the whole town were thus besieging the president for commutation of the dreadful sentence, Viola was kept in irons until the fatal hour arrived. He was not allowed to see or take leave of any of his friends. Only one of them was admitted to his prison, and to him he dictated his last will and a few private letters. No one else was permitted to see him, and he refused to see the priest who was sent to him by the government. He was kept in chains until he was led out to execution. When he asked that his manacles be taken off but for a few minutes, so that he may write a letter to a lady friend, his keepers said that they had no authority to comply with his request. At five o'clock he was let to the savanna or pampa, in the rear of the city. Here his chains were taken from him, and he was shot in the back as a traitor. Inadvertently his executioners had made him kneel down near a nest of black ants, which covered his body as soon as he fell, and before life was extinct. A second volley had to be fired, as the first had failed to kill him. Nobody was allowed to attend his funeral. He was even denied a Christian burial. Such is republicanism in Spanish America!

The majority of both houses of Congress was opposed to García Moreno and his policy, and might have become troublesome. But García was not the man to allow himself to be thwarted or molested by the representatives of the people. He at once banished a number of the opposition members to Peru and New Granada, and thus intimidated the few whom he allowed to remain. Hence, when the widow of General Maldonado charged the president with the murder of her husband, and demanded an investigation, Congress refused to consider the accusation, and voted the thanks of the nation to García for the energy and promptness with which he had repelled Urbina's invasion, and defeated the revolutionary party at Jambeli.

In this connection, I must state that García Moreno himself owed his elevation to power to a revolution against a legitimate government. General Robles was the constitutional president of Ecuador in 1860, when the complications arose with Peru which led to a declaration of hostilities. General Urbina, who was commander-in-chief of the army, had marched against the Peruvians, and left the capital almost without a garrison. This auspicious moment was seized by García Moreno and his followers, who rose against the administration, organized a provisional government, and with an extemporized army marched south in pursuit of Urbina. The latter, on hearing of their movements, at once suspended his march to the Peruvian frontier, and marched back in the direction of the capital. He defeated García Moreno at the village of Tumbaco, near Guaranda, reestablished his authority at Quito, and drove the scattered remnants of the provisionals into New Granada, after which he again set out to fight the Peruvians. But, aided by the conservatives of New Granada, the provisionals again invaded the country and took possession of the capital. In the meantime, General Franco, at Guayaquil, had pronounced against Robles and Urbina, and proclaimed himself dictator. Thus Robles and Urbina were compelled to give up the struggle, and fled to Peru. Franco, after a protracted civil war, was in his turn driven out of the country by García Moreno, who thus secured his own elevation to power. In justice to Mr. García Moreno, I must add here that he was not without redeeming qualities. He was entirely disinterested in money matters, and expended all his salary for public purposes. When not blinded by passion and prejudice, he was fair minded, and even distinguished by a high sense of justice; which, however, he marred by his endeavors to meddle with everything, and to regulate everything. He was undoubtedly the bravest man in Ecuador, and probably in Spanish America, and ever ready to sacrifice his life, of which he was as reckless as of the lives of others. He was endowed with wonderful energy and restless activity; neutralized, however, by his heedless and sincere in his fanaticism, and, I have no doubt, really had the good of his country at heart.

That under such circumstances there can be no liberty of the press can easily be imagined. Indeed, it can hardly be said that there is a press in Ecuador. No political papers were regularly published at Quito during my residence there, with the exception of one or two semi-official organs, established for temporary purposes—such as to harangue the people when war was apprehended, and to be discontinued as soon as the danger was over. Peruvian papers were not allowed to circulate in the country. Other foreign papers were virtually excluded by the exorbitant postal charges established by the president. The regular official paper— *El Nacional*— came out once a week, with occasional interruptions and irregularities, and contained nothing but official notices and correspondence, new laws and decrees, the decisions of the auditor's office, and now and then an abusive editorial. Violent and abusive language, and a pompous and almost oriental style, full of exaggerations and hifalutin, characterize the great bulk of Spanish-American journalism. Even governments will not require their organs to employ calm and dignified language; and the editorial productions of cabinet members themselves are as abusive and unmeasured as the secret publications of their persecuted, outlawed, and embittered antagonists.

In the beginning, of García Moreno's administration, a poor devil, a Mr. Riofrio, relying on the professions which the successful party had made before their accession to power, attempted to publish an opposition paper in Quito, but was immediately set upon by the authorities, and saved himself only by a rapid flight over the most unfrequented paths and byways of the cordillera. I saw him when he arrived at Tumaco, New Granada, sore footed and worn out by hardships and fatigue, a melancholy illustration of South American liberty.

There is, however, no special desire to read newspapers among the people in the interior of Ecuador, where we find convents instead of printing presses, and military barracks instead of schoolhouses. Street talk is the means of circulating home news, and about events in foreign countries the people care but little.

For the political affairs of their own country, it is true, a press is hardly needed. They scarcely ever rise above the level of mere personalities. I often listened to political discussions between men belonging to different political parties, and heard a great deal of personal criticism, but it was very seldom that I heard an abstract principle discussed, or a question of statecraft or political economy argued. One party vilified the other; one party charged the other with the very same crimes and acts of tyranny with which it was itself charged in return. When I objected to this mode of political discussion I was told that persons were the representatives of principles, and that by promoting the political claims of certain persons, the principles which they advocated would be furthered. Hence we see these partisans faithfully follow the standard of a favorite leader, no matter how often he changes his principles or belies his professions.

Yet it would be unjust to speak of the tyrannical and arbitrary spirit and practices of South American governments, without considering the great disadvantages at which they are placed. Nothing, of course, could extenuate crimes and outrages like those I have related, yet from what I know of Spanish-American character, I cannot believe that a government which should endeavor to keep itself strictly and conscientiously within the bounds of legal and constitutional obligations would be able to maintain itself for a single week against the anarchical and revolutionary tendencies of the opponents with whom it has to deal. We must likewise consider the peculiar disadvantages under which the political existence of our Latin neighbors began. We must consider the colonial system and policy of Spain, which had unfitted them for constitutional self-government, instead of preparing them for it.

The Spanish American did not know, and has not learned, to abide by majority decisions, or to redress wrongs by legal and constitutional remedies. From the ballot box he invariably appeals to the sword. The restlessness and jealousy of his political leaders are unbounded, the ignorance of the masses is extreme. Those in power will not voluntarily surrender it. Those out of power will strain every nerve to oust their lucky rivals. Bloody executions, forced loans and contributions, tyrannical confiscations and arbitrary banishments, reckless issues of worthless paper money, unjust impressments, and willful destruction of property, mark the path of the victorious party; in all of which outrages, as a general rule, it only follows the previous examples of its vanquished predecessors.

The latter, defeated on the field of battle, will resort to plotting and conspiracy, in which arts they are masters. They will conspire as long as their enemies remain in power. Baffled in one plot, they will immediately concoct another, and, in their own opinion, they are always sure to succeed. Having hardly anything else to do, and hardly ever wishing or intending to do anything else, they can devote the best part of their time to intriguing and fomenting discontent and rebellion. No great commercial schemes or industrial enterprises engage their attention. The business of a Spanish-American republic is periodically paralyzed by a war or revolution. Its agriculture is continually interfered with by the recruiting officers, who carry away farm laborers and beasts of burden. The middle classes always become poorer, the poor remain poor, and the number of wealthy families is continually diminishing. Men whose ancestors belonged to the richest of the land will be found struggling with misery and privation. They can leave nothing to their children but prejudices and aristocratic pride. They may be graduates of colleges or universities, but almost every white man of good family is, and hence liberal professions do not pay. How, then, are these gentlemen to live? It does not become their dignity to stoop to the level of an Indian or half-breed by performing common labor, and they have no capital or energy to engage in commercial enterprises, nor could the anarchical condition of the country encourage them to do so. They are bound, therefore, to live on political employments; and the overthrow of a government that does not provide for them will be their chief object and occupation. They are revolutionists from necessity, and are ready to do the biding of those who are revolutionists from ambition or idleness.

It will now be understood why a government, instead of endeavoring to promote the general welfare and develop the resources of the country, must strain every nerve to maintain its bare existence against the restless and unremitting efforts of its enemies. To detect conspiracies, to prevent insurrection, to watch suspected characters, and to rid itself, by whatever means, of its declared enemies, must be the principal and almost exclusive care of an administration so placed. To this object every other consideration will be sacrificed. Individual rights will be trampled upon, depredations without end will be committed, and the soldiery will have to be kept in good humor, at whatever cost. Hence it is that in a country which bountiful nature has intended for a paradise, crumbling ruins and tottering walls, impassable roads and miserable hovels, neglected fields and uninhabited wastes, lazy vagabonds and filthy beggars cry out against the depravity and culpable incapacity of man.

STUDY QUESTIONS

1. How does Hassaurek account for the prevalence of instability and political violence in Latin America? How convincing is his explanation?
2. What role do ordinary people play in political uprisings according to Hassaurek? Does he believe they are motivated by political ideology in joining armed revolutions?
3. What are some of the ways in which García Moreno seeks to undermine his opponents? Are these methods successful?
4. How does political upheaval impact the lives of women?

JUANA MANUELA GORRITTI

3.4 THE DEAD MAN'S FIANCÉE, 1865

Juana Manuela Gorritti was one of the most important women intellectuals of nineteenth-century Latin America. A truly transnational figure, she was born into a distinguished Argentine family, and her father, José Ignacio de Gorritti, was one of the signers of the Argentine Declaration of Independence and a prominent Liberal. Gorritti's family were forced into exile in Bolivia when she was a teenager, and she married Manuel Isidrio Belzu, a Bolivian general who was forced into exile in Peru before becoming president of Bolivia in 1848. Gorritti and Belzu had a tempestuous relationship marked by separations and infidelities, and Gorritti remained in Peru after Belzu ascended to the Bolivian presidency; moving to Lima, she wrote novels, short stories, and poems and hosted influential literary salons in her home. Gorritti's work paid close attention to the experiences of women. In this excerpt from one of her most well-known short stories, set in Argentina at the time of the civil war between Unitarians and Federalists, Gorritti reflects on the impact of civil war on the women who lost their loved ones.

"Vital! Vital!" the good lady shouted as she came in. "Come with me, my daughter; your father has given permission for you to carry out an act of charity. Do you know what that is? It is to bury the unfortunate Unitarians who were executed by firing squad yesterday afternoon in the plaza. Quiroga has said that they may be buried, but under the condition that it be their mothers and their wives who escort them to their graves. Mother of God! Poor children! All of my hatred has turned to pity. Let us go, my daughter, let us go help carry out this painful duty."

Vital sighed, thinking of the poor souls she was going to see; she followed her aunt, thanking God for having spared her husband.

The city was the site of a desolate scene impossible to describe. The streets were filled with blood, the houses were open and had been pillaged. Long lines of women in mourning-black were heading toward the plaza, moaning as they went to find the bloodied cadavers of their loved ones.

Vital and her companion followed the doleful procession.

When they arrived at the fateful plaza that had been turned into a horrible hecatomb, each one of those unfortunate women searched among the bloody remains for he whom death had taken from her.

All of a sudden, Vital screamed and collapsed unconscious to the ground.

Among the bodies of the two hundred officers executed the day before, she had recognized that of her husband . . .

From that day on, Vital turned into an unreal being who slid among the living like a ghost. She never stayed still; sleep never came over her; her lips were silent; and only when the sun set and she saw her own shadow drawn in long silhouettes on the dry grass of the fields, would she interrupt her perpetual silence and exclaim with an infinite sweetness: "Horacio!"

Source: Sergio G. Waisman, and Francine Masiello, *Dreams and Realities: Selected Fiction of Juana Manuela Gorritti* (New York: Oxford University Press, 2003), pp. 83–84.

STUDY QUESTIONS

1. Why does Quiroga stipulate that the mothers and wives of the executed soldiers must be the ones to bury their bodies?
2. Although this is a fictional account, can we learn from it about the gendered experiences of women in the civil wars of the nineteenth century? How does this account compare with Friedrich Hausserek's depiction of women and political unrest?
3. What can we learn from the excerpt about Gorriti's personal attitude toward military conflict?

WILLIAM WALKER

3.5 *THE WAR IN NICARAGUA*, 1860

William Walker was an American filibuster who organized multiple private military expeditions to Latin America with the goal of establishing English-speaking colonies under his personal control, which could be annexed to the United States as new slave states. After efforts in 1853 to capture the Mexican territories of Baja California and Sonora State failed, Walker turned his attention to Central America. In Nicaragua he was able to take advantage of a civil war between Conservatives and Liberals, and offered his private army of American mercenaries in support of the Liberals against the Conservatives. By conquering the Conservative forces, he was able to take effective control of the country and establish a government under his own authority. Following a rigged election in July 1856, Walker's regime was recognized by US President Franklin Pierce as the official government of Nicaragua. As president, Walker pursued an Americanization campaign in Nicaragua that included reinstating slavery, declaring English an official language, and promoting immigration from the United States. Walker was overthrown by a Central American alliance made up of troops from Costa Rica, Honduras, El Salvador, and Nicaragua and repatriated to the United States in 1857. Walker launched two subsequent invasions of Nicaragua in 1857 and 1860 that were defeated by the British Navy, who had their own strategic interests in Central America. In 1860 Walker was executed by firing squad in Honduras. *The War in Nicaragua* is Walker's personal account of his Central American campaign, written during his imprisonment in 1860. In this excerpt he lays out his argument that the Southern slave states must expand into the tropical areas of Latin America if they are to maintain and expand the institution of slavery.

Is it not time for the South to cease the contest for abstractions and to fight for realities? Of what avail is it to discuss the right to carry slaves into the territories of the Union, if there are none to go thither? These are questions for schoolmen—fit to sharpen the logical faculty and to make the mind quick and keen in the perception of analogies and distinctions; but surely they are not such questions as touch practical life and come home to men's interests and actions. The feelings and conscience of a people are not to be called forth by the subtleties of lawyers or the differences of metaphysicians; nor can their energies be roused into action for

Source: William Walker, *The War in Nicaragua* (New York: S. H. Goetzel and Co, 1860).

the defense of rights none of them care to exercise. The minds of full-grown men cannot be fed on mere discussions of territorial rights; they require some substantial policy which all can understand and appreciate.

Nor is it wise for the weaker party to waste its strength in fighting for shadows. It is only the stronger party which can afford to throw away its force on indecisive skirmishes. At present the South must husband her political power else she will soon lose all she possesses. The same influence she brought to bear in favor of the position she took in Kansas would have secured the establishment of the Americans in Nicaragua. And unless she assumes now an entirely defensive attitude, what else is left for the South except to carry out the policy proposed to her three years ago in Central America? How else can she strengthen slavery than by seeking its extension beyond the limits of the Union? The Republican party aims at destroying slavery by sap and not by assault. It declares now that the task of confining slavery is complete and the work of the miner has already commenced. Whither can the slaveholder fly when the enemy has completed his chambers and filled in the powder and prepared the train, and stands with lighted match ready to apply the fire?

Time presses. If the South wishes to get her institutions into tropical America she must do so before treaties are made to embarrass her action and hamper her energies. Already there is a treaty between Mexico and Great Britain by which the former agrees to do all in her power for the suppression of the slave-trade, and in 1856 a clause was inserted in the Dallas-Clarendon Convention, stipulating for the perpetual exclusion of slavery from the Bay Islands of Honduras. This clause was suggested (as the writer was informed by the person himself who proposed it) by an American, for the purpose of securing the support of England to a projected railway across Honduras; and thus the rights of American civilization were to be bartered away from the paltry profits of a railroad company. And while Nicaragua was to be hemmed in by an anti-slavery treaty between England and Honduras on the north, Costa Rica made an agreement with New Granada that slavery should never be introduced within her limits. The enemies of American civilization—for such are the enemies of slavery—seem to be more on the alert than its friends.

The faith which Walker had in the intelligence of the Southern States to perceive their true policy and in their resolution to carry it out, was one of the causes which led to the publication of the decree of the 22d of September at the time it was given forth. Nor is his faith in the South shaken; though who can fail to be amazed at the facility with which the South is carried off after chimeras? Sooner or later, however, the slaveholding States are bound to come as one man to the support of the Nicaraguan policy. The decree of the 22d September, not the result of hasty passion or immature thought, fixed the fate Nicaragua and bound the Republic to the care of American civilization. For more than two years the enemies of slavery have been contriving and plotting to exclude the naturalized Nicaraguans from their adopted country. But as yet not a single additional barrier has been interposed; and the South has but to resolve upon the task of carrying slavery into Nicaragua in order that the work may be accomplished.

If other appeals than those of interest are required for stimulating the Southern States in the effort to reestablish slavery in Central America they are not lacking. The hearts of Southern youth answer to the call of honor, and strong arms and steady eyes are waiting to carry forward the policy which is now the dictate of duty as well as of interest. The issue between slavery and anti-slavery has been made in Nicaragua, and it is impossible for slavery to retire from the contest without losing some of its courage and character. Nor is the issue one of mere words. It is not a tilt of sport, a joust of reeds; but the knights have touched the shields of their adversaries with the points of their lances, and the tourney is one of mortal strife. And may fortune most favor them who best do their duty in the fray.

Something is due from the South to the memory of the brave dead who repose in the soil of Nicaragua. [In defence of slavery these men left their homes, met with calmness and constancy the perils of a tropical climate, and finally yielded up their lives for the interests of the South.] I have seen these men die in many ways. I have seen them gasping life away under the effects of typhus; I have seen them convulsed in the death agony from the fearful blows of cholera; I have seen them sink to glorious rest from mortal wounds received on honorable fields; but I never saw the first man who repented engaging in the cause for which he yielded his life. These martyrs and confessors in the cause of Southern civilization surely deserve recognition at its hands. And what can be done for their memories while the cause for which they suffered and died remains in peril and jeopardy?

If there, then, be yet vigor in the South—and who can doubt that there is—for further contest with the soldiers of anti-slavery, let her cast off the lethargy which enthralls her, and prepare anew for the conflict. But at the same time she throws aside her languor and indifference, let her, taught by the past, discard the delusions and abstractions with which politicians have agitated her passions without advancing her interests. It is time for slavery to spend its efforts on realities and not beat the air with wanton and ill-advised blows. The true field for the exertion of slavery is in tropical America; there it finds the natural seat of its empire and thither it can spread if it will but make the effort, regardless of conflicts with adverse interests. The way is open and it only requires courage and will to enter the path and reach the goal. Will the South be true to herself in this emergency?

STUDY QUESTIONS

1. How does Walker represent his efforts to reinstitute slavery in Nicaragua? How does he position these efforts within US and international legislative debates over slavery?
2. Why does Walker see Central America as so central to the power of the Southern United States?

3.6 CARTOONS DEPICTING RACIAL TENSIONS IN WAR OF TRIPLE ALLIANCE

The War of the Triple Alliance pitted Paraguay against Brazil, Argentina, and Uruguay over control of the River Plate Basin. It lasted over six years, and was by far the deadliest of the inter-regional border conflicts of the nineteenth century; causing an estimated 400,000 deaths and reducing the population of Paraguay by over 70 percent. The war played a key role in shaping national identities in all of the countries involved. The cartoons presented here provide insight into the connection between war and nationalism in Brazil. Brazil mobilized four times as many men to fight in the Triple Alliance as they had in any previous campaign. While the government sought to persuade male citizens to volunteer out of patriotic duty, to meet deployment needs, the army and navy relied heavily on impressment, using press gangs to hunt down recruits in urban and rural areas, and liberating convicts in exchange for military service. Additionally, men who were called up for service could free themselves from recruitment by presenting substitutes. This meant that in practice the upper and middle classes, as well as the "respectable poor" with powerful patrons, could exempt themselves from going to war. Beginning in 1866, slave recruitment was added to the conscription processes, and slave-owners could provide slave "donations" as an alternative to their own service, with the result that thousands of enslaved Africans were given provisional manumission in exchange for fighting. The cartoons highlight the shifting national attitudes toward conscription and military service and provide important insight into how the war shaped national identity in Brazil. The first depicts slave-owners donating their slaves to the war effort. The second shows guardsmen bidding on a "substitute" recruit. The third is a satirical depiction of the composition of the Brazilian army.

Source: a) Courtesy of the Biblioteca Nacional, Rare Works Division; b) Cabriao, Sao Paulo, Dec. 2, 1866; c) Courtesy of the Biblioteca Nacional, Rare Works Division

STUDY QUESTIONS

1. How does the first image represent the slave-owners who donated their enslaved workers to the war effort?
2. What parallels does the second image seek to draw between slavery and the system of recruitment substitutes?
3. How are the Brazilian armed forces represented in the third image? What role do racial stereotypes play in these depictions?

CHAPTER 4

EXCLUSION AND INCLUSION:
Everyday People, 1825–1880s

SIMÓN BOLÍVAR

4.1 DECREES ON INDIAN RIGHTS, LAND AND TRIBUTE, 1825

The legal status of indigenous peoples was a source of intense political debate in the postindependence era. Nationalist leaders sought to create a definitive break from the colonial era, while equality before the law was a key fundamental principle underlying Liberal philosophy. Furthermore, Liberals believed that the eradication of taxes such as tribute and the granting of individual title to communal lands was key to the advancement of Indians and their integration into the market economy. Simón Bolívar passed the first legislation decreeing changes in indigenous legal status. In 1820 he abolished Indian tribute in Gran Colombia, and in 1825 as president of Peru he passed a series of laws aiming at the legal equality of Indians, which included the abolition of communal land. Notably, these legislative changes were not always popular with indigenous people, who especially resisted changes in communal landholding. In the Andes in particular, opposition to these types of legislative changes led indigenous people to become major supporters of Conservative leaders who pledged to uphold colonial norms.

DECREE ABOLISHING PERSONAL SERVICE IMPOSED ON THE NATIVE AMERICAN PEOPLES: NEW STATUTE GOVERNING THEIR WORK

Rosario de Cúcuta, 20 May 1820
Simón Bolívar
Liberator President, etc.

Wishing to correct the abuses practiced in Cundinamarca in most of the native villages, against their persons as well as their communal lands and their freedom, and considering that this segment of the population of the republic deserves the most paternal attention from the government because they were the most aggrieved, oppressed, and humiliated during the period of the Spanish despotism, in view of the provisions of canonical and civil laws, I have decided to decree and do hereby decree:

Article 1. All the lands whose titles identify them as part of the communal reserves [*resguardos*] shall be returned to the Indians as the legitimate owners, despite any legal claims alleged by the current landholders.

Source: David Bushnell (ed.) *El Libertador: Writings of Simón Bolívar* (Oxford: Oxford University Press, 2003), pp. 184–190.

Article 2. The liens against these reserves, having no approval from the authority empowered to grant it, now or in the past, shall be declared null and void even if they have subsisted since time immemorial.

Article 3. Once the usurped land has been restored to the reserves, the *Jueces políticos* shall allot to each family as much land as it can reasonably farm, taking into consideration the number of people that make up the family and total extent of the reserves.

Article 4. Should there be surplus acreage after the reserve lands have been parceled to the families as specified above, it shall be leased at auction by these same *jueces políticos* to the highest bidder with the best collateral, giving preference in case of equal bids to those currently in possession.

Article 5. The families, or family members, shall not be permitted to lease the allotment they own without first informing the *juez políticos*, so as to avoid any damage and fraud that might ensue.

Article 6. The income from the lands leased according to the provisions of Article 4 above shall be applied in part to the payment of tribute and in part to the payment of the salaries of teachers in the schools to be established in each town. Each teacher shall earn an annual salary of 120 pesos if the rental income equals or exceeds this amount; if it amounts to less, the entire sum shall be for the teacher.

Article 7. The *juez políticos*, in consultation with the priest of each town, shall appoint these teachers and notify the provincial governors of these appointments so that they can notify the governor of the department.

Article 8. The political governors of the provinces shall establish the regulations to be observed in the schools of their respective provinces, detailing the methods to be used in teaching and education.

Article 9. All children between the ages of four and fourteen shall attend schools, where they shall be taught reading, writing, arithmetic, the principles of religion, and the rights and obligations of men and citizens in Colombia according to the laws.

Article 10. When the money for teachers' salaries has been deducted, the remaining income from the land rental shall be applied to the payment of tribute, deducting this sum from the general total owed by the town so benefited on a pro rata basis.

Article 11. In order that these operations shall be carried out with all the method, order, and precision required for the general benefit of the towns, the *jueces políticos* shall be obliged to keep a running account of the rent monies and shall present this along with the account of the tributes to the respective administrators of the public treasury.

Article 12. Neither the priests, nor the *jueces políticos*, nor any other person, employed by the government or not, shall be allowed to exploit native peoples in any manner at any time without paying them a wage previously stipulated in a formal contract witnessed and approved by the *juez político*. Anyone violating this article shall pay double the value of the service performed, and the *jueces políticos* shall exact this fine without exception in favor of the aggrieved person for any complaint, however slight; when the *jueces políticos* themselves are the violators, the political governors shall be responsible for exacting said fines.

Article 13. The same provisions of Article 12 apply to religious confraternities whose cattle shall not be pastured on reserve lands unless they pay rent, nor shall they be herded by Indians except under the terms laid down in Article 12.

Article 14. As of this moment, certain scandalous practices that are contrary to the spirit of religion, to the discipline of the church, and to all law shall be terminated without exception, including the practice of denying the sacraments to parishioners who have not paid dues for guild membership or for maintenance of the priest, as well as the practices of obliging them to pay for festivals in honor of the saints and demanding parish fees from which Indians are exempted in consideration of the stipend given to the priests by the state. Any priest found to be violating the provisions of this article by continuing these abuses shall suffer the full rigor of the law, and the *jueces políticos* shall monitor the conduct of the priests, notifying the government of the slightest infraction observed in this regard so that appropriate action can be taken.

Article 15. The Indians, like all other free men in the Republic, can come and go with their passports, sell their fruit and other products, take them to the market or fair of their choice, and practice their craft and talents freely as they choose to do so and without impediment.

Article 16. Not only shall the present decree be publicized in the usual manner, but the *jueces políticos* shall instruct the Indians as to its contents, urging them to demand their rights even though it be against the judges themselves and to initiate action against any infraction committed.

Article 17. The vice president of Cundinamarca is charged with the observation and execution of this decree.

Issued in the General Headquarters of Rosario de Cúcuta, on 20 May 1820, tenth year of the Republic. Simón Bolívar

PROCLAMATION OF THE CIVIL RIGHTS OF INDIANS AND PROHIBITION OF THEIR EXPLOITATION BY OFFICIALS, PRIESTS, LOCAL AUTHORITIES, AND LANDOWNERS

Cuzco, 4 July 1825
Simón Bolívar
Liberator President of the Republic of Colombia, Liberator and Supreme Commander of Peru, etc.
Considering:

I. That equality among all citizens is the basis of the constitution of the Republic;

II. That this equality is incompatible with the personal service that has been imposed on native peoples, and equally incompatible with the hardships they have endured due to the miserable conditions in which they live and the ill treatment they have suffered at the hands of officials, priests, local authorities, and even landowners;

III. That in the assignment of certain public works and services the Indians have been unfairly burdened;

IV. That they have been denied wages on fraudulent grounds for the work in which they have been traditionally involved, either willingly or by force, whether it be the working of mines or farm labor or crafts;

V. That one of the burdens most harmful to their existence is the payment of excessive and arbitrary fees that are commonly assessed them for the administration of the sacraments, I have decided to decree and do hereby decree:

1. That no person in the state shall demand personal service of the Peruvian Indians, either directly or indirectly, without first negotiating a free contract stipulating the wage for the work.

2. That the department prefects, priests, intendants, governors, and judges, ecclesiastical prelates, priests and their subordinates, landowners, and owners of mines and workshops are prohibited from working the Indians against their will in *faenas, séptimas, mitas, pongueajes,* and other types of domestic and common labor.

3. That when public works are ordered by the government for the general benefit of the community, this burden should not fall on Indians alone but all citizens should be drafted proportionally according to their numbers and abilities.

4. That the political authorities, through the mayors or municipalities, shall arrange for distribution of supplies, provisions, and other materials for the troops or any other purpose without burdening the Indians more than other citizens.

5. That the labor of workers in the mines, workshops, and haciendas should be paid in cash according to the wage specified in the contract, without forcing them to accept other forms of pay against their will and at levels below that commonly paid for such work.

6. That the scrupulous observance of the preceding article shall depend on the vigilance and zeal of the intendants, governors, and the territorial deputies for mining.

7. That the Indians shall not be forced to pay higher parochial fees than those stipulated in existing regulations of those legislated in the future.

8. That the parish priests and their assistances cannot negotiate these fees with the Indians without the mediation of the intendant or governor of the town.

9. Any neglect or omission in the observance of the preceding articles shall be cause for popular complaint and shall result in specific charges being brought before the courts.

10. The provisional secretary general is responsible for the execution and observance of this decree.

To be printed, published, and circulated.

Issued in Cuzco on 4 July 1825, the sixth and fourth years of the republic.

Simón Bolívar

By order of His Excellency, *Felipe Santiago Estenós*

RESOLUTION ON THE REDISTRIBUTION OF COMMUNAL LANDS

Cuzco, 4 July 1825

Liberator President of the Republic of Colombia, vested with Supreme Authority, etc., considering:

I. That despite the stipulations of previous laws the distribution of lands has not been carried out adequately;

II. That the majority of Indians have had no opportunity to enjoy land ownership;

III. That large tracts of these lands, which ought to be owned by the Indians, have been usurped under various pretexts by the caciques and collectors of tribute;

IV. That the provisional use granted them under the Spanish government has been extremely prejudicial to the development of agriculture and the prosperity of the state;

V. That the constitution of the republic does not acknowledge the authority of the caciques but rather that of the intendants of provinces and governors of their respective districts, I have decided to decree, and do hereby decree:

1. That the provisions of articles 3, 4, and 5 of the decree issued on Trujillo on 8 April 1824, concerning the redistribution of communal lands be carried out forthwith.

2. Included in the land to be redistributed shall be those sections appropriated by the caciques and tribute collectors by virtue of their office, those lands being clearly identified by those commissioned to sell and distribute them.

3. The extent, redistribution, and sale of lands in each province shall be carried out by persons of integrity and intelligence whose names shall be presented as candidates to the prefect by the departmental junta holding jurisdiction, the junta to determine the fees and authority granted to those carrying out this commission.

4. Article 2 above does not refer to caciques who have inherited or who have legitimate claims and who have been granted absolute ownership of lands assigned to them during redistribution.

5. The caciques who do not own any land of their own shall receive through their wives and each of their children five topos of land or an equal area in places where the term *topo* is unfamiliar.

6. Each native citizen, regardless of sex or age, shall receive one topo of land in fertile places with adequate water.

7. In barren regions without adequate water, they shall receive two topos.

8. The Indians whose lands were taken from them under the Spanish government in order to pay the so-called pacifiers of the revolution of the year 14, shall be compensated in the redistribution to be made of communal lands by one-third more land than that to be assigned to others who have not suffered such a loss.

9. That the absolute ownership granted to the Indians designated in article 2 of the aforementioned decree be understood to be inalienable until year 50, and never taken by mortmain, under penalty of nullity.

10. The provisional secretary general is charged with the responsibility to carry out and fulfill this decree.

To be printed, published, and circulated.

Executed in Cuzco on 4 July 1825.—the sixth and fourth years of the republic.

Simón Bolívar

By order of His Excellency, *Felipe Santiago Estenós*

Note: Article 5 of this decree was amended as follows:

His Excellency the Liberator has ordered that give topos of land, which Article 5 of the decree executed in Cuzco on 4 July of last year allots to the wife and each of the children of the caciques, also be allotted to the cacique himself, as if the article referred to reads as follows: *The caciques will receive, for themselves, for their wife, and for each of their children, and so on.*

By order of His Excellency, I have the honor of communicating this to you so that it shall be brought to the attention of the Council of Government for its proper fulfillment.

I am, Minister, your most attentive and obedient servant.

Felipe Santiago Estenós

To the Minister of State of the Department of Government

STUDY QUESTIONS

1. How does Bolívar present the condition of indigenous people in the 1820s? Which groups does he see as especially responsible for the challenges facing indigenous people?
2. How do Bolívar's decrees change the legal rights and responsibilities of indigenous people?
3. How are indigenous lands to be redistributed, and why?

THOMAS EWBANK

4.2 SLAVERY IN BRAZIL, 1856

Thomas Ewbank was an Englishman who emigrated to the United States and made his fortune in lead, copper and tin manufacturing before devoting himself to the study of mechanics. He traveled to Brazil in 1845–1846 and wrote an account of his experiences that became widely read in England the United States. *Life in Brazil* reflected extensively on the topic of slavery. Ewbank's writings attracted the interest of international abolitionists and became a factor in campaigns to end Brazilian slavery. In this except he describes some of the technologies used to punish slaves, and reflects on the prevalence of slave suicides.

Among lithographic scenes of life in Rio, designed and published by native artists, those relating to the slaves are not the least conspicuous. There is no more fastidiousness, that I observed, about portraying them in shackles than in their labors and their pastimes.

Common punishments [observed include] a negra in a mask, and a negro wearing the usual pronged collar, with a shackle round one ankle, and secured to a chain suspended from his waist.

Source: Thomas Ewbank, *Life in Brazil, Or, A Journal of a Visit to the Land of Cocoa and the Palm* (New York: Harper and Brothers, 1856), pp. 436–441

It is said slaves in masks are not so often encountered in the streets as formerly, because of a growing public feeling against them. I met but three or four, and in each case the sufferer was a female. The mask is the reputed ordinary punishment and preventative of drunkenness. As the baril is often chained to the slave that bears it, to prevent him from selling it for rum, so the mask is to hinder him or her from conveying the liquor to the mouth, below which the metal is continued, and opposite to which there is no opening.

Observing one day masks hanging out for sale at a tin and sheet iron store, I stopped to examine them, and subsequently borrowed one. Except for a projecting piece for the nose, the metal is simply bent cylinder-wise. Minute holes are punched to admit air to the nostrils, and similar ones in front of the eyes. A jointed strap (of metal) on each side goes round below the ears (sometimes two), and meets one that passes over the crown of the head. A staple unites and a padlock secures them.

At most of the smith's shops collars are exposed, as horseshoes are with our blacksmiths, with gyves, chains, etc. Most of the collars were of five-eights-inch round iron, some with one prong, others with two, and some with none except a short upright tubular lock.

Here, too, were the heaviest and cruelest instruments of torture—shackles for binding the ankles and wrists close together, and consequently doubling the bodies of the victims into the most painful and unnatural positions. Had I not seen them, I could hardly have thought such things were. While making a memorandum of their form and dimensions, the proprietor or his adjutant, a black man, in his shirt sleeves, came from the rear, and handling them, spoke by way of recommending them, supposing I was a customer. They were made of bar iron, *three inches wide and three eights of an inch thick!* Each consisted of three pieces, bent, jointed, and fastened as shown in the margin. The large openings were for the legs, the smaller for the wrists. A screw-bolt drew the straight parts close together. The distance from joint to joint was two feet.

Such are the tortures which slaves privately endure in the cellars, garrets, and out-houses of their masters. T——, a native merchant, says another common punishment is to inclose the legs in wooden shackles

or stocks. Some owners fasten their hands in similar devices, and some, again, retain relics of the old thumb-screws to lock these members together. In the northern provinces, he says, the slaves are much worse used than in Rio; that it is no uncommon thing to tie their hands and feet together, hoist them off the ground, and then "beat them as near to death as possible." A heavy log fastened by a chain to the neck or leg of a slave who has absconded, or who is supposed to be inclined to run away, is a usual punishment and precaution. He is compelled to labor with it, laying it on the ground when at work, and bearing it under his arm or on his shoulder when he moves.

I observed one day a slave wearing a collar, the largest and roughest of hundreds I have seen. Of inch round iron, with a hinge in the middle, made by bending the metal of its full size into loops, the open ends flattened and connected by a half-inch rivet. The upright bar terminated in a *death's head,* which reached above that of the wearer, and to it another piece, in the form of the letter S, was welded. The joint galled him, for he kept gathering portions of his canvas shirt under it. Rest or sleep would seem impossible.

A Bahian planter, the brother of an ex-councilor, dined with us one day, and spoke with much freedom on slavery. With most men, he thinks the land can never be cultivated in the northern provinces by whites. The city slaves of Bahia, he said, are principally Minas. Shrewd and intelligent, they preserve their own language, and by that means organize clubs and mature schemes of revolution which their brethren of Pernambuco have repeatedly attempted to carry out. Some write Arabic fluently, and are vastly superior to most of their masters. In the interior, he remarked, the slaves are badly fed, worse clothed, and worked so hard that the average duration of their lives does not exceed six years. In some districts it reaches to eight, while the number that see ten years after leaving Africa is small indeed. Deceptions are played off on foreign agents of the Slavery Commissions. These visit the Engenhos once or twice a year. The planters, informed when they set out, have their slaves decently garbed and *well oiled,* to make them look supple and in good condition. On a late visit, the examiners were so highly gratified that one left, and wrote home a flattering account of the treatment of the helots. The other continued his inquiries, came to a fazenda where he was not looked for, and there beheld what he did not expect—a negro about to be *boiled to death* for some act of insubordination. His owner had invited, according to custom in such cases, neighboring proprietors to witness the tragedy.

From the little I have seen, I should suppose the country slaves are the worst off. Every morning, while nature was enshrouded in blackness of darkness, did I hear them driving wagons through the thick mist, and as late as ten at night were they shouting at the oxen as the jolting and groaning wheels rolled by. (This was, however, the busiest season.) I often wondered how they found their way over the horrid roads, how their naked feet and limbs escaped unharmed, and how they then worked in the fields, unless their pupils had the expansile and contractile powers of night animals.

On large estates, a few days' rest are given them every three or four weeks during the sugar season, but on smaller ones, where owners commonly have difficulty to keep out of debt, they fare badly, and are worked to death. Staggering into their huts, or dropping where their labors close, hardly do their aching bones allow the Angel of Sleep to drive away the memory of their sorrows, than two demons, lurking in the bell and lash, awaken them to fresh tortures. To say these poor creatures are better off than when ranging their native lands is an assertion that language lacks the power justly to describe. It may be true, if the life of an omnibus hack is better than that of a wild horse of Texas. I would rather, a thousand times, be a sheep, pig, or ox, have freedom, food, and rest for a season, then be knocked on the head, than be a serf on some plantations. I say *some*, because there are in Brazil, as in other lands, humane planters.

Suicides continually occur, and owners wonder. The high-souled Minas, both men and women, are given to self-destruction. Rather than endure life on the terms it is offered, many of them end it. Then they that bought them grind their teeth and curse them, hurl imprecations after their flying spirits, and execrate the saints that let them go. If individuals are ever justified in using the power Heaven has placed in their hands to terminate at once their earthly

existence, it must be these. Those who blame them for putting the only barrier between them and oppression could not endure half their woes. And how characteristic of human frailties! Here are slave-dealers who weep over the legendary sufferings of a saint, and laugh at worse tortures they themselves inflict; who shudder at the names of old persecutors, and dream not of the armies of martyrs they make yearly; who cry over Protestants as sinners doomed to perdition, and smile in anticipation of their own reception in the realms above by Anthony and Loyala, Benedict and Becket.

Rich people who lose a slave by suicide or flight scarcely feel the loss, but to many families the loss is ruinous. There are not a few that live on the earnings of one or two helots. The papers are constantly noticing the flight of slaves who have manumitted themselves by escaping across a river their oppressors dare not attempt, since they there become denizens of a country in which Brazilian process can not be served. They unsheathe their spirits, and leave the scabbards for their masters. It is only suicides reported by the police that become publicly known. Were all recorded, every issue of the daily press would, I am told, contain more or less. Instances that have occurred within the last few weeks are here taken from the *Diario*.

June 22–24. "In the parish of Sta. Anna, an inquest was held on the body of the black, Justo, who killed himself by hanging. He was the slave of Major José de Paiva e Silva. Also on the body of slave, Rita, who destroyed herself by drowning. The body of a black, in a state of putrefaction, was found, thrown ashore by the tide, on the beach near the Public Garden."

July 1. The body of one was found near the Carioco Fountain; another, a female, in another parish, had released her spirit with a rope—"suicidou-se com baraço." *July* 5. Another, in a fit of despair, precipitated himself from an upper window upon a mass of granite. 23d. The slave Luiz Pharoux killed himself with a rope. 24th. The slaves Pedro and Camillo by strangulation. *August* 1. Another drowned himself on the Praya Manoel. On the 4th, my last day in Brazil, one was lying on the rocks at the city end of the Gloria Beach, washed up by the tide. He was apparently under thirty years of age. As I stood looking down on him, a Mozambique girl came along, put her basket on the low wall near me, dropped a tear on the corpse, and passed on.

When the means of suspension are not at hand, it is no unusual thing for the high-minded Africans, of both sexes, to expire under circumstances surpassing aught that history records. Some draw ligatures tight around their throats, lie down, and deliberately die. Others, I am told, have the art of folding back their tongues so as to prevent respiration, and thus resolutely perish.

STUDY QUESTIONS

1. Why are the masks, shackles, and chains Ewbank describes such a prominent feature of Brazilian slavery? What do these technologies tell us about the nature of relationships between enslaved workers and slave-owners?
2. What types of working conditions does Ewbank describe on the plantations he visited? Are there significant differences in the experience of the enslaved on different types of estate?
3. How does Ewbank interpret slave suicides? How might his observations be used by abolitionists seeking to end slavery?

4.3 NEWSPAPER ADVERTISEMENTS FOR BLACK WET NURSES, BRAZIL, 1821–1854

In nineteenth-century Brazil, the use of enslaved wet nurses (amas de leite) was a common practice. Elite and middle-class white women would frequently rent or purchase enslaved African women to breast-feed their babies. Sometimes this was a result of illness or insufficient milk production, but it also reflected racial ideas that held that white women were too "weak" to breast-feed effectively, in contrast to black women, whose perceived "robustness" and adaptation to tropical climates meant that they could produce large quantities of nutritious milk. In the first half of the nineteenth century in particular, the employment of an enslaved wet nurse became a mark of social prestige. Wet nurses were usually young women, teenagers or in their early twenties, and most were without their own babies. This reflected in part the high infant mortality rates among babies born into slavery, but it was also common practice for slave-owners to remove enslaved babies from their mothers or to force them to stop breast-feeding their own child early in order to maximize profits from the rental of the mother as a wet nurse. The following excerpts present selections of advertisements for wet nurses that appeared in nineteenth-century Brazilian newspapers.

Source: Robert Edgar Conrad, *Children of God's Fire: A Documentary History of Black Slavery in Brazil* (University Park: Pennsylvania State University Press, 1994), pp. 133–134.

For rent, a wet nurse with very good milk, from her first pregnancy, gave birth six days ago, in the Rua dos Pescadores, No. 64. Be it advised that she does not have a child [*cria*].

Jornal do Comércio, Rio de Janeiro, December 10, 1827

Will trade a good black boy [*moleque*] 15 to 16 years of age, accustomed to the country, a good cook, does all the work of the house, makes purchases, does washing; for a wet nurse who has good milk, who also knows how to take care of a house, and who is without vices. Our reason [for trading] is that we have more need of the latter than of the former. Apply at house No. 39, Rua de Proposito. Also we will sell the said boy for no less than 350$000 *réis*.

For sale as a wet nurse or simply as a personal servant girl [*mucama*] an African who is twenty years of age, without a child, whose talents aside from the usual ones, are an ability to sew reasonably well, to iron, cook, and wash. She would be especially valuable for the service of any bachelor, or farmer, because she understands everything more or less perfectly, and alone can do all the work which normally employs many slave women. She has a good complexion, a good figure, and is for sale only because we have too many in the house. Her final price, free of tax, is 400$000, and she can be seen in the Rua dos Ferradores next to No. 385.

Jornal de Comércio, Rio de Janeiro, December 12, 1827

In the street behind Rua do Hospicio No. 27 we have for sale or for rent a black woman of the Mina nation with a six-day-old child, with very good milk and healthy. She is without vices or bad habits, since she is new in the country and does not even know how to get about in the streets.

Jornal de Comércio, Rio de Janeiro, December 13, 1827

Whoever wants to buy a creole slave, still a young girl, with good milk and in great quantity, who gave birth twenty days ago, should go to Rua das Marrecas, facing toward the public plaza.

Diario de Rio de Janeiro, June 18, 1821.

For sale a black woman, wet nurse, without a child [*cria*], gave birth ten days ago from first pregnancy, 18 to 19 years of age, without any faults, knows how to wash, iron, cook, has learned the rudiments of sewing, and is capable of the full management of a house, in Rua do Sabão da Quitanda, upper section.

Diario de Rio de Janeiro, July 30, 1821.

For rent two wet nurses, one Brazilian-born, the other African, both first pregnancies. One gave birth forty days ago, and the other twenty-six days ago. Both very healthy and very young with an abundance of milk. Whoever has use for them should go to Rua Estreita de São Joaquim No. 32.

O Mercantil, Rio de Janeiro, March 5, 1845

For rent an eighteen-year-old girl, wet nurse, healthy, and with much good milk for the last two months. She is for rent because her child has died. In the Rua da Candelaria No. 18A.

O Mercantil, Rio de Janeiro, April 30, 1845

In this printing office there is for rent a wet nurse, without a child, very healthy and affectionate.

O Observador, São Luis do Maranhão, March 22, 1854

STUDY QUESTIONS

1. What type of language is used to advertise wet nurses for sale or rent? What types of characteristics are especially emphasized?
2. What can we learn from the advertisements about the realities of enslaved motherhood in nineteenth-century Brazil?

ESTEBAN MONTEJO

4.4 LIVES OF ENSLAVED AFRICANS IN CUBA, 1966

Slavery in Cuba lasted until 1886. As a result of its late abolition, slavery remained in the living memory well into the second half of the twentieth century. One of the most remarkable sources we have on Cuban slavery is the life testimony of Esteban Montejo. Born into slavery, Montejo lived a remarkable life, encompassing stretches as a slave, a maroon, and as a soldier in the Cuban War for Independence. When he was 103 years old, he shared his life testimony with the anthropologist Miguel Barnet, and an edited transcript of these interviews was published in book-length form in 1966. While there are challenges inherent in using the youthful memories of someone so elderly as a source, Montejo's testimony provides an unparalleled window into the internal dynamics of slave life and culture. In this excerpt, Barnet reflects on social life and leisure activities on the sugar estate where he was born, providing important insight into the resilience and vivacity of enslaved Africans and Afro-Cubans.

Strange as it may seem, blacks had fun in the barracoons. They had their pastimes and their games. There were also games in the taverns, but those were different. One of the ones they played the most in the barracoons was *tejo*. You put a corncob, split in half, on the ground. You placed a coin on top of it. You drew a line on the ground a short distance away, and you threw a stone from the line toward the corncob. If the stone hit the corncob, and the coin fell on the stone, the man took the coin as his. If it fell close to the corncob, no coin. *Tejo* caused great disputes. In such cases, you had to measure with a straw to see if the coin was closer to the player than the corncob.

That game was played in the patio like the game of bowling. But bowling wasn't played much. I seen it no more than two or three times. There were some black coopers who made the sticks in the shape of bottles and the wooden balls for playing. It was an open game, and everybody could join in. Except for the Chinese, who were pretty standoffish. You rolled the balls along the flat ground to try to knock down the four or five sticks at the other end. It was the same game as

the one that's played today in the city, but the difference is that with the older one, there were fights over the bets. That surely didn't please the masters. That's why they prohibited some games, and you had to play them when the overseer wasn't looking. The overseer was the one who told the news, news and gossip.

The game of *mayombe* was linked to religion. Even the overseers got involved, hoping to benefit. They believed in ghosts so that's why no one today should be surprised that whites also believe in those things. You played *mayombe* with drums. You put a *nganga* or big pot in the middle of the patio.

All the powers, the saints, were in that *cazuela*. And *mayombe* was a useful game, but the saints had to be present. The players began to play the drums and to sing. They brought things for the *ngangas*. The blacks asked about their health, and their brothers' and sisters' health, and asked for harmony among them. They did *enkangues* which were hexes made with dirt from the cemetery. With that dirt you made four corners in little mounds to resemble the points of the universe. They put star-shake, which was an herb, in the pot with

Source: Miguel Barnet (ed.), *Biography of a Runaway Slave* (Willimantic, CT: Curbstone Press, [1966] 1994), pp. 27–37. Translated by Nick W. Hill

corn straw to hold human beings. When the master punished a slave, all the others picked up a little dirt and put it in the pot. With that dirt they vowed to bring about what they wanted to do. And the master fell ill or some harm came to his family because while the dirt was in the pot, the master was a prisoner in there, and not even the devil could get him out. That was the Congo people's revenge on the master.

There were taverns close to the mill. There were more taverns than ticks in the woods. They were a kind of a small general store where you could buy everything. The slaves themselves traded in the taverns. They sold beef jerky that they stored up in the barracoons. During the day and sometimes even in the evening, the slaves could go to the taverns. But that didn't happen at all the plantations. There was always some master who wouldn't give permission for his slaves to go. The blacks went to the taverns for rum. They drank a lot to keep their strength. A shot of good rum cost a half peso. The owners drank a lot of rum, too, and I can't begin to tell you about the to-do there was. Some of the tavern keepers were old men retired from the Spanish army who got a little pension, some five or six pesos.

The taverns were made of wood and yagua palm fronds. None of that cement you see in stores nowadays. You had to sit on piles of jute sacks, or else stand up. In the taverns they sold rice, beef jerky, lard, and all kinds of beans. I seen hard-case tavern owners who cheated the slaves by charging them fat prices. I seen brawls where a black was beaten up and couldn't return to the tavern. In booklets they noted down all the purchases, and when a slave spent half a peso, they put down one mark, and when he spent two, two marks. That's how the system worked for buying everything else, the flour cookies, round and sweet, salt biscuits, different colored sweets the size of chickpeas made of flour, water, bread, and lard. The water bread cost a half peso a loaf. It was different from the water bread today. I preferred that older kind. I also remember that they sold some candy called *capricho*, made of white flour, sesame seeds, and peanuts. Sesame seeds, you know, were a Chinese thing because their salesmen went around the plantations selling them. Those Chinese peddlers were old indentured workers who couldn't lift up their arms to cut cane any longer, so they started selling things.

The taverns were smelly. They got that strong smell from the goods hanging from the beams, sausages, hams, curing, and red mortadella. Even so, it was where you could fool around to relax. Men spent all their time in that silliness. Black men really wanted to be good in games. I recall a game they called "the cracker." The way that game worked was that four or five hard salt crackers were placed on the wooden counter or any board, and the men had to hit the crackers hard with their dicks to see who could break the crackers. The one who broke the crackers won. That game attracted betting and drinking. Blacks as well as whites played it.

Another pastime was the jug game. They would take a big jug with a whole in the top and stick their do-hickey through it. The one who reached the bottom was the winner. The bottom was covered with a little layer or ash so that when the man took his dick out it was easy to see if he touched the bottom or not.

They played other games too, like cards. It's best to play cards with oil-coated cards, which are the right ones to use. There were many kinds of card games. Some liked to play face cards, others *mico* where you could win a lot, but I preferred monte, which started first in private homes and then spread to the countryside. During slavery, monte was played in the taverns and in the masters' houses. But I picked it up after abolition. Monte is very complicated. You have to put two cards on the table and guess which of those two is higher than the three you keep in your hand. It was always played for money, and that was its attraction. The banker was the one who dealt the cards, and the players bet. You could win a lot. I won money every day. The truth is that monte was my vice. Monte and women. And not for nothing because you would have to look around a lot for a better player than me. Each card had its own name. Like nowadays, but it so happens that cards nowadays are not as colorful. In my day, there were queens, jacks, kings, aces, and then came the numbers from two to seven. The cards had pictures of men on them with crowns or on horseback. You could easily see they were Spaniards because those types with the lace collars and long hair never existed in Cuba. What was here before were Indians.

Sundays were the noisiest days on the plantation. I don't know where the slaves found the energy. The biggest fiestas during slavery took place on that day of the week. There were plantations where the drum began at noon or at one. At Flor de Sagua it started very early. At sunrise the noise began, and the games, and the children began to spin around. The barracoon came to life in a flash. It seemed like the world would come to an end. And, even with all the work, everyone got up happy. The overseer and his assistant came into the barracoon and started fooling around with the women. I noticed that the ones who were least involved were the Chinese. Those bastards didn't have an ear for the drums. They were standoffish. It was that they thought a lot. In my opinion they thought more than the blacks. Nobody paid them any mind. And folks just went on with their dances.

The one I remember best is the *yuka*. In the *yuka* three drums were played: *la caja*, *la mula* and the *cachimbo*, which was the littlest. Behind the drums someone played two hollowed-out cedar trunks with two sticks. The slaves themselves made them, and I think they called them *catá*. *Yuka* was danced in pairs, and the movements were dramatic. Sometimes they swooped like birds, and it even seemed like they were going to fly they moved so fast. They did little jumps with their hands on their hips. Everybody sang to encourage the dancers.

There was another more complicated dance. I don't know if it was a dance or a game because the punches given out were serious. That dance was called the *maní*. The *maní* dancers made a circle of forty or fifty men. And they began to slap at each other. The one who got hit went out to dance. They wore ordinary work clothes and put red kerchiefs with drawings on them around their heads and waists. Those kerchiefs were used to tie up the slaves' clothes to take them to be washed. They were known as *vayajá* or red-checkered kerchiefs. So that the licks of the *maní* would be the most painful kind, their wrists were charged up with any old kind of witchcraft. The women didn't dance but made a handclapping chorus. They would shout from the scare they got, because sometimes a black would fall down and never get up again. The *maní* was a cruel game. The dancers didn't bet on the challenges. At some plantations, the masters themselves bet, but at Flor de Sagua I don't remember them doing it. What the masters did do was to prohibit the blacks from hitting each other too much because sometimes they got so beaten up they couldn't work. Boys couldn't

play, but they took it all in. Take me, for example, I will never forget it.

Every time the announcing drum started up, the blacks would go down to the creek to bathe. Near every mill was a little creek. There were cases where a woman waited behind and met a man as he went into the water. Then they fooled around and began to do their business. Or, if not that, they went to the reservoirs, which were pools at the mill made to store water. They played hide and seek there, and the men chased the women to have sex with them.

The women who didn't play that little game stayed in the barracoon and took a bath in a washtub. Those tubs were big, and there were only one or two for the entire work force.

Men's shaving and haircutting was done by the slaves themselves. They took a big knife, and like you trim a horse, that's how they cut the kinks out of a black's hair. There was always someone who liked to cut hair, and he was the most experienced. He trimmed the way they do it today. And it never hurt because hair is the strangest thing—even though you see it grow and all, it's dead. Women combed their hair in curls in little rows. Their heads would look like Castilian melons. They liked that busy work of combing their hair one way one day and another way the next. One day with rows, another with curls, another, conked. To clean your teeth you used soaptree bristles that left them very white. All that fuss was for Sundays.

On that day, each and every person had his special outfit. The blacks used to buy rawhide boots I haven't seen since. They would buy them in nearby stores, the ones they could go to with the master's permission. They wore kerchiefs of *vayajá* red and green around their necks. They wore them on their heads and around their waists like in the *maní* dance. They also put on earrings, and gold rings on every finger. Pure gold. Some didn't wear gold but had silver bracelets all the way up their elbows. And patent leather shoes.

Slaves of French descent danced in pairs, at arm's length. They did slow turns. If there was an outstanding dancer, silk kerchiefs were tied around his leg. Of all colors. That was the prize. They sang in patois and played two big drums with their hands. It was called "The French Dance."

I knew about an instrument that was called the *marímbula*, and it was tiny. They made it with wicker, and it had a deep sound like a drum. It had a hole where the sound came out. With that *marímbula* they accompanied the Congo drums, and maybe the French drums, but I can't remember. The *marímbulas* sound very strange, and many people, mostly the *guajiros*, didn't like them because they said they were voices from beyond the grave.

As I understand it, at that time the *guajiros* made music using only a guitar. Later, around the year 1890, they played *danzones* on those *pianolas* with accordions and gourds. But the white man has always had music different from the black. White man's music has no drum at all. Tasteless.

The same thing more or less happens with religions. The African gods are different although they seem to resemble the other ones, the gods of the priests, which are stronger and less decorated. Right now, if you up and go to a Catholic church, you see no apples, no rocks, no rooster feathers. But in an African household those are the first things you see. The African is more down to earth.

I knew about two African religions in the barracoons, the Lucumí and the Congo. The Conga was the more important. At Flor de Sagua it was well known because the witches put spells on people. They gained the trust of all the slaves with their fortune-telling. I came to know the older blacks more after Abolition.

But at Flor de Sagua I remember the *chicherekú*. The *chicherekú* was a little Congo man. He didn't speak Spanish. He was a small man with a big head who went running through the barracoons. He would jump up and land on your back. I seen it many times. I heard him squeal like a guinea pig. That's a fact, and even in the Porfuerza sugarmill, up to a few years ago, there was one who ran around that way. People used to run away from him because they said he was the devil himself and was allied with *mayombe* and with death. You couldn't play with *chicherekú* because it was dangerous. As for me, in truth, I don't like to talk much about him because I haven't seen him again, and if by happenstance . . . well, devil take it!

For the work of the Congo religion they used the dead and animals. They called the dead *nkise* and snakes *majases*, or *emboba*. They prepared *cazuelas* and everything, and that's where the scent to make

hexes was. They were called *ngangas*. All the Congos had their *ngangas* for *mayombe*. The *ngangas* had to work with the sun. Because he has always been the intelligence and the strength of men. As the moon is for women. But the sun is more important because he gives life to the moon. The Congos worked with the sun almost every day. When they had a problem with some person, they followed that person along any path and gathered up the dirt they walked on. They saved it and put it in the *nganga* or in a secret little corner. As the sun went down, the life of the person would leave him. And at sunset the person was quite dead. I say this because it happens that I seen it a lot during slave times.

If you think about it, the Congos were murderers. But if they killed someone, it was because some harm was being done to them, too. No one ever tried to work a hex on me because I have always been a loner, and I've never cared to know too much about other people's business.

Witchcraft is more common with the Congos than with the Lucumís. The Lucumís are more allied to the Saints and to God. They liked to get up early with the strength of the morning and look at the sky and pray and sprinkle water on the ground. When you least expect it, the Lucumí is doing his work. I have seen old blacks kneeling on the ground for more than three hours speaking in their tongue and telling the future. The difference between the Congo and the Lucumí is that the Congo does things, and the Lucumí tells the future. He knows everything through the diloggunes, which are snails from Africa. With mystery inside. They're white and a little lumpy. Eleggua's eyes are made from that snail.

The old Lucumís would lock themselves in the rooms of the barracoon, and they would clean the evil a person had done out of him. If there was some black man who had desire for a woman, the Lucumí would calm him down. I think they did that with coconuts, *obi*, which were sacred. They are the same as the coconuts today, which are still sacred and can't be touched. If someone dirtied the coconut, he would get a severe punishment. I always knew when things were going good because the coconut said so. He ordered Alafia to be pronounced so everyone would know there was no tragedy. All the saints spoke through the coconuts. Now the master of all of them was Obatalá. Obatalá was an ancient, so I heard, who was always dressed in white. They said that Obatalá was the one who created you, and who knows what else. People come from Nature, and so does Obatalá.

The old Lucumís liked to have their figurines, their gods, made of wood. They kept them in the barracoon. All those figurines had a big head. They were called *oché*. The Eleggua was made of cement, but Changó and Yemayá were made of wood, and the carpenters made them themselves.

On the walls of the rooms they made marks of the saints with charcoal and whitewash. They were long lines and circles. Even though each was a saint, they said the marks were secret. Those blacks kept everything a secret. Today they've changed a lot, but back then, the hardest thing in the world was to get them to trust you.

The other religion was Catholicism. It was introduced by the priests who wouldn't go into the barracoons during slavery for love or money. The priests were very neat and tidy. They had a serious look that didn't sit well in the barracoons. They were so serious that there were even blacks who hung on their every word and obeyed them to the letter. They learned the catechism, and then they would read it to the others. With all the words and the prayers. Those were the house slaves, and they met with the other slaves, the field slaves, in the *bateyes*. They came to be the priests' messengers. Truth is, I never learned that doctrine because I did not understand it at all. I don't think the house slaves did either but because they were so refined and so well-treated, they became Christians. The household slaves got consideration from the masters. I never seen a severe punishment

for a one of them. When they were sent to the fields to cut cane or take care of the pigs, they pretended to be sick and didn't work. That's why field slaves didn't want to see them at all, not even in a painting. Sometimes they went to the barracoon to visit with a family member. And they took back fruits and 'taters for the master's house. I don't know if the slaves made gifts from their *conucos* or if the house slaves just took them. A lot of problems with fighting in the barracoons were caused by them. The men arrived and wanted to flirt and fool around with the women. That's when the worst pushing and shoving began. I was probably twelve years old, and I figured out the whole mess.

There were other tensions, too. For example, between the Congo witch doctor and the Christian there was no getting along. One was good and the other bad. That still goes on in Cuba. The Lucumí and the Congo don't get along either. They bickered over saints and witchcraft. The only ones who didn't have troubles were the old-timers from Africa. They were special, and you had to treat them different because they knew all about religion.

Many scuffles were avoided because the masters moved the slaves around. They looked for ways to separate people so there wouldn't be a rash of runaways. That's why the work force never had meetings.

The Lucumís didn't like to work with cane, and many ran away. They were the most rebellious and the bravest. Not the Congos. They were mostly cowards, big on work, so they worked real hard without complaining. There is a well-known guinea pig called Conga. She is very cowardly too.

STUDY QUESTIONS

1. What types of leisure activities does Montejo describe? Are these activities open to all enslaved workers equally? To what extent do these activities challenge or uphold the institution of slavery?
2. What insight does Montejo's testimony provide into religious beliefs and practices among the enslaved?

JOHN L. STEPHENS

4.5 GOOD FRIDAY MASS IN GUATEMALA, 1840

John Lloyd Stephens was an American travel writer and explorer. His expedition to the sites of Mayan ruins in Central America and Mexico between 1839 and 1841 played a key role in the "rediscovery" of ancient Mayan civilization among American and European intellectuals. His best-selling book about his travels also provides detailed observations of the cultural practices and traditions he witnessed. Here he provides a description of the Good Friday Mass in the Guatemalan city of Quetzaltenango in 1840. Quetzaltenango had one of the largest concentrations of indigenous *cofradias* (religious groups) in Guatemala, and these groups played a major role in religious celebrations. The Good Friday Mass of 1840 took place just days after a major battle in the city in which the Conservative caudillo Rafael Carrera had defeated a Liberal uprising, with indigenous Guatemalans serving as the bulk of his army. This account by Stephens provides important insight into popular Catholicism as practiced by indigenous people, as well as the conflict between whites and Indians.

To return to the cura: he was about forty-five, tall, stout, and remarkably fine-looking; he had several curacies under his charge, and next to a canonigo's, his position was the highest in the country; but it had its labours. He was at that time engrossed with the ceremonies of the Holy Week, and in the evening we accompanied him to the church. At the door the *coup d'oeil* of the interior was most striking. The church was two hundred and fifty feet in length, spacious and lofty, richly decorated with pictures and sculptured ornaments, blazing with lights, and crowded with Indians. On each side of the door was a grating, behind which stood an Indian to receive offerings. The floor was strewed with pine-leaves. On the left was the figure of a dead Christ on a bier, upon which every woman who entered threw a handful of roses, and near it stood an Indian to receive money. Opposite, behind an iron grating, was the figure of

Christ bearing the cross, the eyes bandaged, and large silver chains attached to the arms and other parts of the body, and fastened to iron bars. Here, too, stood an Indian to receive contributions. The altar was beautiful in design and decorations, consisting of two rows of Iconic columns, one above the other, gilded, surmounted by a golden glory, and lighted by candles ten feet high. Under the pulpit was a piano. After a stroll around the church, the cura led us to seats under the pulpit. He asked us to give them some of the airs of country, and then himself sat down at the piano. On Mr. C.'s suggesting that the tune was from one of Rossini's operas, he said that this was hardly proper for the occasion, and changed it.

At about ten o'clock the crowd in the church formed into a procession, and Mr. C. and I went out and took a position at the corner of a street to

Source: John L. Stephens, *Incidents of Travel in Central America, Chiapas and Yucatan, Vol. II.* (New York: Harper and Brothers, 1841), pp. 209–217.

see it pass. It was headed by Indians, two abreast, each carrying in his hand a long lighted wax candle; and then, borne aloft on the shoulders of four men, came the figure of Judith, with a bloody sword in one hand, and in the other the gory head of Holofernes. Next, also on the shoulders of four men, the archangel Gabriel, dressed in red silk, with large wings puffed out. The next were men in grotesque armour, made of black and silver paper, to resemble Moors, with shield and spear like ancient cavaliers; and then four little girls, dressed in white silk and gauze, and looking like little spiritualities, with men on each side bearing lighted candles. Then came a large figure of Christ bearing the cross, supported by four Indians; on each side were young Indian lads, carrying long poles horizontally, to keep the crowd from pressing upon it, and followed by a procession of townsmen. In turning the corner of the street at which we stood, a dark Mestitzo, with a scowl of fanaticism on his face, said to Mr. Catherwood, "Take off your spectacles and follow the cross." Next followed a procession of women with children in their arms, half of them asleep, fancifully dressed with silver caps and headdresses, and finally a large statue of the Virgin, in a sitting posture, magnificently attired, with Indian lads on each side, as before, supporting poles with candles. The whole was accompanied with the music of drums and violins; and as the long train of light passed down the street, we returned to the convent.

The night was very cold, and the next morning was like one in December at home. It was the morning of Good Friday; and throughout Guatemala, in every village, preparations were making to celebrate, with the most solemn ceremonies of the Church, the resurrection of the Saviour. In Quezaltenango, at that early hour, the plaza was thronged with Indians from the country around; but the whites, terrified and grieving at the murder of their best men, avoided, to a great extent, taking part in the celebration.

At nine o'clock the Corregidor called for us, and we accompanied him to the opening ceremony. On one side of the nave of the church, near the grand altar, and opposite the pulpit, were high cushioned chairs for the Corregidor and members of the municipality, and we had seats with them. The church was thronged

with Indians, estimated at more than three thousand. Formerly, at this ceremony no women or children were admitted; but now the floor of the church was filled with Indian women on their knees, with red cords plaited in their hair, and perhaps one third of them had children on their backs, their heads and arms only visible. Except ourselves and the padre, there were no white people in the church; and, with all eyes turned upon us, and a lively recollection of the fate of those who but a few days before had occupied our seats, we felt that the post of honour was a private station.

At the steps of the grand altar stood a large cross, apparently of solid silver, richly carved and ornamented, and over it a high arbour of pine and cypress branches. At the foot of the cross stood a figure of Mary Magdalen weeping, with her hair in a profusion of ringlets, her frock low in the neck, and altogether rather immodest. On the right was the figure of the Virgin gorgeously dressed, and in the nave of the church stood John the Baptist, placed there, as it seemed, only because they had the figure on hand. Very soon strains of wild Indian music rose from the other end of the church, and a procession advanced, headed by Indians with broad-brimmed felt hats, dark cloaks, and lighted wax candles, preceding the body of the Saviour on a bier borne by the cura and attendant padres, and followed by Indians with long wax candles. The bier advanced to the foot of the cross; ladders were placed behind against it; the gobernador, with his long black cloak and broad-brimmed felt hat, mounted on the right, and leaned over, holding in his hands a silver hammer and a long silver spike; another Indian dignitary mounted on the other side, while the priests raised the figure up in front; the face was ghastly, blood trickled down the cheeks, the arms and legs were moveable, and in the side was a gaping wound, with a stream of blood oozing from it. The back was affixed to the cross, the arms extended, spikes driven through the hands and feet, the ladders taken away, and thus the figure of Christ was nailed to the cross.

This over, we left the church, and passed two or three hours in visiting. The white population was small, but equal in character to any in the republic; and there was hardly a respectable family that was not afflicted by the outrage of Carrera. We knew nothing of the effect of the enormity until we entered domestic circles. The distress of women whose nearest connexions had been murdered or obliged to fly for their lives, and then wandering they knew not where, those can only realize who can appreciate woman's affections.

I was urged to visit the widow of Molina. Her husband was but thirty-five, and his death under any circumstances would have been lamented, even by political enemies. I felt a painful interest in one who had lived through such a scene, but at the door of house I stopped. I felt that a visit from a stranger must be an intrusion upon her sorrows.

In the afternoon we were again seated with the municipality in the church, to behold the descent from the cross. The spacious building was thronged to suffocation, and the floor was covered by a dense mass of kneeling women, with turbaned head-dresses, and crying children on their backs, their imaginations excited by gazing at the bleeding figure on the cross; but among them all I did not see a single interesting face. A priest ascended the pulpit, thin and ghastly pale, who, in a voice that rang through every part of the building, preached emphatically a passion sermon. Few of the Indians understood even the language, and at times the cries of children made his words inaudible; but the thrilling tones of his voice played upon every chord in their hearts; and mothers, regardless of their infants' cries, sat motionless, their countenances fixed in high and stern enthusiasm. It was the same church, and we could imagine them to be the same women who, in a phrensy and fury of fanaticism, had dragged the unhappy vice-president by the hair, and murdered him with their hands. Every moment the excitement grew stronger. The priest tore off his black cap, and leaning over the pulpit, stretched forward both his arms, and poured out a frantic apostrophe to the bleeding figure on the cross. A dreadful groan, almost curdling the blood, ran through the church. At this moment, a signal from the cura, the Indians sprang upon the arbour of pine branches, tore it asunder, and with a noise like the crackling of a great conflagration, struggling and scuffling around the altar, broke into bits the consecrated branches to save as holy relics. Two Indians in broad-brimmed

hats mounted the ladders on each side of the cross, and with embroidered cloth over their hands, and large silver pincers, drew out the spikes from the hands. The feelings of the women burst forth in tears, sobs, groans, and shrieks of lamentation, so loud and deep, that, coming upon us unexpectedly, our feelings were disturbed, and even with sane men the empire of reason tottered. Such screams of anguish I never heard called out by mortal suffering; and as the body, smeared with blood, was held aloft under the pulpit, while the priest leaned down and apostrophized it with frantic fervor, and the mass of women, wild with excitement, heaved to and fro like the surges of troubled sea, the whole scene was so thrilling, so dreadfully mournful, that, without knowing why, tears started from my eyes. Four years before, at Jerusalem, on Mount Cavalry itself, and in presence of the scoffing Mussulman, I had beheld the same representation of the descent from the cross; but the enthusiasm of Greek pilgrims in the Church of the Holy Sepulchre was nothing compared with this whirlwind of fanaticism and phrensy. By degrees the excitement died away; the cracking of the pine branches ceased, the whole arbour was broken up and distributed, and very soon commenced preparations for the grand procession.

We went out with the corregidor and officers of the municipality, and took our place in the balcony of the cabildo. The procession opened upon us in a manner so extraordinary, that, screening myself from observation below, I endeavoured to make a note of it on the spot. The leader was a man on horseback, called the centurion, wearing a helmet and cuirass of pasteboard covered with silver leaf, a black crape mask, black velvet shorts and white stockings, a red sash, and blue and red ribands on his arms, a silver-hilted sword, and a lance, with which, from time to time turning around, he beckoned and waved the procession on. Then came a led horse, having on its back an old Mexican saddle richly planted with silver. Then two men wearing long blue gowns, with round hoods covering their heads, and having only holes for the eyes, leading two mules abreast, covered with black cloth dresses enveloping their whole bodies to their feet, the long trains of which were supported by men attired like the other two. Then followed the large silver cross of the crucifixion, with a richly-ornamented silver pedestal, and ornaments dangling from each arm of the cross that looked like lanterns, supported by four men in long black dresses. Next came a procession of Indians, two abreast, wearing long black cloaks, with black felt hats, the brims six or eight inches wide, all with lighted candles in their hands, and then four Indians in the same costume, but with crowns of thorns on their heads, dragging a long low carriage or bier filled with pine-leaves, and having a naked scull laid on the top at one end.

Next, and in striking contrast with the emblem of mortality, advanced an angel in the attitude of an opera-dancer, borne on the shoulders of six men, dressed in flounced purple satin, with lace at the bottom, gauze wings, and a cloud of gauze over her head, holding in her right hand a pair of silver pincers, and in her left a small wooden cross, and having a train of white muslin ten yards long, supported by a pretty little girl fancifully dressed. Then another procession of Indians with lighted candles; then a group of devils in horrible masquerade. Then another angel, still more like an opera-dancer, dressed in azure blue satin, with rich lace wings, and clouds, and fluttering ribands, holding in her right hand a ladder, and in her left a silver hammer; her train supported as before; and we could not help seeing that she wore black velvet smallclothes. Then another angel, dressed in yellow, holding in her right hand a small wooden cross, and in the other I could not tell what.

The next in order was a beautiful little girl about ten years old, armed cap-a-pie, with breastplate and helmet of silver, also called the centurion, who moved along in a slow and graceful dance, keeping time to the music, turning round, stopping, resting on her sword, and waving on a party worthy of such a chief, being twelve beautiful children fancifully dressed, intended to represent the twelve apostles; one of them carrying in his arms a silver cock, to signify that he was the representative of St. Peter. The next was the great object of veneration, the figure of the Christ crucified, on a bier, in a full length case of plate glass, strewed with roses inside and out, and protected by a mourning canopy of black cloth, supported by men in long black gowns, with hoods covering all but the eyes. This was followed by the cura and priests in their richest robes and bareheaded, the muffled drum, and soldiers with arms reversed; the Virgin Mary, in a long black mourning dress, closed the procession. It passed on to make the tour of the city; twice we intercepted it, and then went to the Church of El Calvario. It stands on an elevation at the extreme end of a long street, and the steps were already crowded with women dressed in white from the head to the feet, with barely an oval opening for the face. It was dark when the procession made its appearance at the foot of the street, but by the blaze of the innumerable lighted candles every object was exhibited with more striking wildness, and fanaticism seemed written in letters of fire on the faces of the Indians. The centurion cleared a way up the steps; the procession, with a loud chant, entered the church, and we went away.

STUDY QUESTIONS

1. How does Stephens describe the role of indigenous people in the Good Friday procession? What insight does his account provide about the meaning of religious ritual within indigenous society? What can we learn from it about indigenous *cofradias*, particularly with regard to the blending of Catholic and Maya traditions?
2. What can we learn from Stephens's account about the racial tensions between whites and Indians in Guatemala? To what extent does religious belief and practice serve as a touchstone for these tensions?

FLORA TRISTAN

4.6 POST-INDEPENDENCE LIMA, 1838

Flora Tristan was a French socialist and influential early feminist. She was the illegitimate daughter of an aristocratic Spanish naval officer, whose family had deep roots in colonial Arequipa. After her father's death, Tristan traveled to Peru in 1833 in an unsuccessful attempt to claim an inheritance from her Peruvian family. She published a travel diary of her time in Peru that became widely read in Europe and helped shape international ideas about postindependence Andean societies. In this excerpt she describes the lives of upper-class women in Lima.

. . . and the dead animal was put on to a cart and removed by four galloping horses. All this time the crowd clapped, stamped and shouted; joy and exultation seemed to have turned everyone's head: eight armed men had just killed a bull, what a fine thing to be enthusiastic about! I found the sight revolting, and as soon as the first bull had been killed I wanted to leave; but the ladies said: "You must wait, the best sport is always at the end; the last bulls are always the most vicious; they might kill the horses or wound some men." And they stressed the word "men" as if to say: "That would be most interesting." We were "very fortunate": the third bull eviscerated a horse and nearly killed its rider; the hamstrings, in their fright, cut all four of its legs, and the creature, panting with fury, fell bathed in its own blood. The horse's entrails were exposed. When I saw this, I left in a hurry, feeling about to be sick. Mr Smith had gone pale, and could only say: "This spectacle is inhumane and disgusting."

I took his arm and we walked for some time on the promenade along the river bank. The fresh air revived me, but the thought of the place I had left still depressed me. The attraction felt by a whole nation to the sight of suffering seemed to me an indication of extreme corruption. I was rapt in these reflections when we saw my beautiful aunt's barouche: she called out to me, "You sensitive girl, Florita, why did you run away at the best moment? Oh, if you'd only seen the last one! What a splendid beast! It was really frightening, everyone got so excited. Oh it was marvelous!" Poor people, I thought, have you then no pity, to delight in such sights?

The Rimac was very like the river at Arequipa: it ran over a stony bed amongst rocks. The bridge was quite fine: it was the haunt of idlers who went there to watch the ladies go by on their way to the Paseo del Agua. I shall now pause to describe the costume peculiar to the women of Lima, how they take advantage of it and the effect it has on their customs, habits and character.

There is no place on earth where women are *freer*, where they are more influential than in Lima. They reign supreme, and all initiative comes from them. One might say that the ladies of Lima absorb all the small quantity of energy available to its fortunate inhabitants in that hot, enervating climate. The women are usually taller and sturdier than the men. By the time they are eleven or twelve they are fully developed. They nearly all marry at that age and are very prolific, most of them having six or seven children. They have healthy pregnancies, and easy childbirths, from which they recover quickly. They nearly all nurse their babies, but always with the help of a wet-nurse

Source: *Pérégrinations d'une Paria*, by Flora Tristan, was first published in France in 1838; This translation and Introduction: The Folio Society Limited 1986, pp. 251–262.

who supplements the feed. This is a custom of Spanish origin, for there well-to-do families always have two nurses. The women are not generally beautiful, but their attractive faces give them an irresistible influence over men, for no man can see a woman of Lima without a beating heart. They are not swarthy, as is thought in Europe; most of them are very fair skinned; the rest, according to their various origins, are dark, but their complexions are smooth and velvety, of a warm colour, full of life. All their colouring is beautiful, with bright red lips and fine, naturally curly black hair and black eyes, brilliant and beautifully shaped, which express a baffling combination of intelligence, pride and languishment. Their whole charm lies in this expression of theirs. They are fluent speakers, and their gestures are as expressive as their words. Their costume is *unique*.

Lima is the only city of the world where it has ever been seen. Its origin has been sought in vain, even in the most ancient chronicles. It is totally unlike any of the various Spanish costumes, and it was certainly not brought from Spain. It was found locally, when Peru was discovered, but it is also certain that it has not existed in any other city of Latin America. It consists of a skirt, called a *saya*, and a kind of bag which covers the shoulders, arms and head, called a *manto*. I can hear Parisian ladies protesting at the simplicity of this costume; they have no idea how coquettishly it can be used. The skirt is made of a variety of materials according to rank and fortune; its design is so extraordinary that it is worthy of being put on display as curiosity. It can only be made in Lima, and they claim that one has to be born Lima to be a *saya*-maker. No one from Chile, Arequipa or Cuzco, they say, could ever learn to *pleat* the *saya*. This claim, which I never bothered to check, shows how unique this costume is. I shall now try to give a rough idea of what it is like.

To make an ordinary *saya* requires twelve to fourteen ells (fourteen to eighteen metres) of satin.[1] It is lined with light taffeta or very fine cotton. The dressmaker, in return for your fourteen ells of satin, comes back with a little three-quarter-length skirt, which

hangs from just above the hips down to the ankles. It is so clinging that at the bottom it is only just wide enough for the wearer to put one foot in front of the other and walk with small steps. So one is enclosed in the skirt as in a sheath. It is pleated from top to bottom, in very small pleats, so neatly that it is impossible to see the seams. These pleats are so strongly made and give the *saya* such elasticity, that I have seen *sayas* that had lasted for fifteen years and which were still pliant enough to show off the figure and allow freedom of movement.

The *manto* is also stylishly pleated, but is made in very light material, and would be unlikely to last as long as the skirt, nor could the pleating stand so long the continual movements of the wearer and the dampness of her breath. Society ladies wear a *saya* of black satin; women of fashion also have them in whimsical colors—purple, brown, green, dark blue, or striped—but never in pale colours, because these are preferred by the "ladies of the street". The *manto* is always black, enveloping the whole of the upper part of the body, leaving only one eye uncovered. The ladies of Lima wear a tight blouse only the sleeves of which are visible. These may be short or long, and are in a rich material: velvet, coloured satin or tulle; but most women have bare arms in all seasons. Their footwear is most elegant and attractive, pretty shoes in coloured-embroidered satin; when they are of one colour only, the ribbons are in a contrasting colour. They wear open-work silk stockings of various colours, with richly embroidered clocks. Spanish women are always remarkable for the richness and elegance of the shoes they wear, but those of Lima do it so charmingly that they really excel. They wear their hair parted in the middle; it falls in two perfectly made plaits ending in a large ribbon bow. This fashion however is not universal. Some wear it curled à la Ninon, falling in long wavy locks on to their bosoms, which, according to the custom of the country, they almost always leave bare. For the last few years, the fashion of wearing large crêpe-de-chine shawls has been introduced. This has made their costume more decent by veiling in its folds the bare flesh and the too clearly visible curves. Yet another touch of luxury that they go in for is a very fine linen handkerchief edged with lace. How graceful, how intoxicating they look, these beautiful ladies of Lima, in their lustrous black *sayas* gleaming in the sun,

---

1   Author's note: The satin is imported from Europe. Before the discovery of Peru, the garment was made with a local woollen fabric. Only poor women now use that cloth.

showing off the true figures of some, and the false ones of others—but even the latter are so well contrived that it is impossible to imagine any deceit! How gracefully they move their shoulders, when they pull the *manto* so that it conceals the entire face, after letting a passing glimpse of it be seen! How lithe and supple are their figures, and how they swing and ripple as they walk! How pretty are those small feet of theirs, and what a pity that they are just a little bit too fat!

A lady of Lima is not the same woman when she changes her *saya* for a pretty Parisian dress: one looks in vain for the seductive creature in a *saya* that one met only that morning at St Mary's church. This is why all foreign men in Lima go to church; not to hear the monks sink the divine service, but to admire these unique woman in their national costume. Everything about them is full of seductiveness: their poses are as delightful as their walk, and when they are kneeling, they bend their heads roguishly, allowing a view of their pretty bracelet-covered arms whilst their fingers, resplendent with rings, run over their rosary with voluptuous agility and they cast furtive glances which are calculated to turn ardour into rapture.

Many foreign men have described to me the magical effect that the sight of these women has often produced on them. An adventurous spirit had made them face countless dangers in the firm conviction that they would make their fortunes on these far shores. The ladies of Lima seemed to be the priestesses of this hope, or rather these men felt the that they had reached Mahomet's paradise, and that God had led them to an enchanted land is compensation for the pains of a long crossing and as recompense for their courage. Such fantasies do not seem surprising when one witnesses how many follies and extravagances foreigners commit for the sake of the ladies of Lima. Their heads are completely turned. They become obsessed with the desire to see the ladies' faces, which are carefully concealed, and this makes the men follow them with avid curiosity. But one must have long experience of *sayas* to follow one successfully, for they all look alike. It needs great concentration not to lose sight of the charming quarry in the crowd; she dodges to and fro like a serpent in the grass; she glides out of sight. I defy the loveliest English girl, with her blonde hair, her eyes which reflect the heavens, her complexion of lilies and roses, to compete with a pretty lady

from Lima in a *saya*! I equally defy the most seductive Frenchwoman, with her pretty little mouth half-open, her witty eyes, her elegant figure, her playful manner and all the subtlety of her coquetry, to compete with a pretty lady from Lima in her *saya*! Without fear of contradiction, I can say that the ladies of Lima so dressed would be proclaimed the queens of this earth, if it were only a question of shapeliness, and of the magnetism of the eye to ensure the sway that women are called upon to have over man; but though beauty beguiles the senses, it needs the inspiration that comes from the soul, a moral force, and the talents of the mind to prolong its reign. God has endowed women with more loving, more devoted hearts than men; and if, as there is no doubt, it is by love and devotion that we honour the Creator, woman is incontestably superior to man; but she must cultivate her intelligence and above all become mistress of herself in order to preserve this superiority. It is only in this way that she will be able to exercise all the influence that God intended when he gave her those qualities of the heart; but when she misunderstands her mission, and instead of being guide and inspiration of man, his mortal persuader, she only tries to charm him, to be the mistress of his senses, her influence will vanish with the desires she has provoked. And so it is that when these enchantresses, who have never had any interest in higher things, eventually, after electrifying the imagination of the young foreigners, reveal themselves as they are: blasé, their minds without culture and their souls without nobility, clearly loving only money; then the spell woven by their charm is immediately broken.

Yet the ladies of Lima do dominate men, because they are superior to the men in intelligence and moral fibre. The cultural phase which the country has reached is still far behind ours in Europe. There is in the whole of Peru no institution for the education of either sex. Intelligence has to develop on its own resources. Thus the pre-eminence of the women of Lima over the men, which exists in spite of the fact they are morally speaking inferior to those in Europe, must be due to the superior intelligence that God has given them. But their costume has been a major additional influence that they enjoy. If they were ever to abandon this costume without changing in other ways, if they could no longer rely on its powers of seduction and yet had not developed the quality of caring for the happiness and improvement of others—and up till now they have been unconscious of the need for such a quality—it is quite certain that they would immediately lose their dominant position. They would descend into a very lowly status, into as miserable a position as any human can occupy. They would no longer be able to indulge in the incessant activity made possible by being able to pass incognito, and would become the prey of boredom, without any means of raising themselves above the generally despised condition of creatures whose only resource comes from the pleasures of the senses. To demonstrate the truth of this, I shall give a short sketch of the customs of Lima society, from which the reader can judge for himself.

As I have already said, the *saya* is the national costume: all the women wear it, whatever their social class; it is respected, and as much a part of the country's heritage as the veil of Muslim women in the Orient. Throughout the year, the women of Lima walk in the streets in this disguise, and anyone who dared to remove from a woman in a *saya* the *manto* which completely hides her face, except for one eye, would suffer public indignation and severe punishment. It is accepted that a woman can *go out alone*; most are accompanied by a negress, but this is not essential. The costume so alters a woman's appearance, and even her voice, which becomes muffled because the mouth is covered, that unless there is something obvious about her, like being very tall or very short, with a limp or a hump, it is impossible to recognise her. I think I can leave it to the reader to imagine the consequences of this continual state of disguise, sanctioned by time and custom, and permitted or at least tolerated by the law. A lady of Lima wears a French-style négligé at breakfast with her husband, her hair done up just like our Parisian ladies. If she wants to go out, she puts on her *saya*—no corset is needed, since the belt sufficiently supports the figure—lets her hair down, "covers" herself,[2] that is to say, she wraps herself in her *manto*, and sets off wherever she pleases to go. She may meet her husband in the street, and he will not

recognise her[3]: she may give him the eye, simper, make provocative remarks, start up a conversation, accept the offer of ices, fruit, cakes, fix a rendezvous with him, leave him—only to start another conversation with a passing officer. She can allow this new adventure to go on as far as she wishes, without ever taking off her *manto*. She pays calls on her women friends, and returns home for dinner. Her husband does not ask where she has been, because he knows perfectly well that if she needs to conceal the truth she will lie to him, and as he has no means of preventing this, he takes the wisest course, and does not worry his head about it. So the ladies go unaccompanied to the theatre, to the bullfight, to public meetings, to the ball, to the promenade, to church, and to pay calls on their friends, and this is perfectly acceptable. If they meet anyone they wish to talk to, they do so, then leave them and remain free and independent in the crowd, much more so than the men, whose faces are uncovered. This costume has the great advantage of being economical, very clean and comfortable, always ready for use without any need of the slightest attention.

There is another practice which I must not omit: when the ladies of Lima wish to make their disguise even more impenetrable, they put on an old *saya*, all unpleated, torn and ragged, an old *manto* and an old blouse; but those who wish it to be known that they nevertheless belong to good society wear good shoes and take one of their finest handkerchiefs. Such a disguise, considered quite "correct," is called *disfrazar*. A *disfrazada* is held to be completely respectable; for that reason, one never addresses a word to her, and only approaches with caution. It would be out of place and even "unfair" to follow her. It is rightly assumed that since she has "disguised" herself, she must have "important reasons" for doing so, and therefore one ought not to take it upon one's self to pry into her activities.

After what has been said about the costume and customs of the women of Lima, it will be evident that their mentality will be quite different from that of European women who, from childhood, are slaves to

---

2   Translator's note: The author here gives the word *tapoda* as the Spanish expression for covering the face with the *manto*. I have been unable to trace this word; *taparse* is the normal expression.

3   Author's note: A number of husbands assured me that they did not recognise their wives when they met them.

the laws, customs, prejudices, and fashions—in fact to everything; whilst in her *saya*, a woman of Lima is free, enjoys her independence and has that self-confidence which is born of the ability to act according to the needs of one's personality. The woman of Lima, of whatever social class, is always *herself*; she never undergoes constraint of any sort. As a girl, she escapes from parental control through the freedom bestowed on her by her dress; when she marries, she does not take her husband's name, keeps her own and is always mistress of her own home. When she tires of that, she puts on her *saya* and goes out, just like a man taking up his hat and going where he will. In everything she does, she has the same freedom as he. In any intimate relations they may have, be they frivolous or serious, they always maintain their dignity, although their behavior in this respect is indeed very different from ours. Like all women they judge the strength of the love that they inspire by the extent of the sacrifices made for them; but because Peru, ever since it was discovered, has only attracted Europeans to come so far simply on account of the gold to be found there, and because gold and only gold, not talent or virtue, has been the standard of value and the motive of every action, and has alone been the gateway to success, the ladies of Lima, quite logically, look for proofs of love only in the amount of gold they are given: the value of the offering determines their view of the sincerity of the lover; and their vanity is satisfied to the extent of the sum or the worth of the valuables that they have received. When one wants to give an indication of how much Señor So-and-so loved Señora Such-and-such, one invariably says something like: "He used to give her bags and bags of gold; he would buy her the most expensive gifts he could find; he completely ruined himself for her." Just as we should say: "He killed himself for her." A rich woman will always take her lover's

money, even if it means giving it to her Negresses if she can't spend it herself. She considers it a "proof" of his love, the "only thing" that can "convince her that she is loved." Vanity makes travelers conceal this state of things, and when they talk of the ladies of Lima and the success they have had with them, they make no boast of the fact that they had cost them a small fortune, down to the final parting present. Such customs are very strange, but true. I have seen a number of society ladies wearing men's rings, chains, and watches.

The ladies of Lima spend little time on household matters, but as they are very attractive, this is enough to keep things in order. They have a pronounced taste for politics and intrigue. It is through their efforts that their husbands, their sons or other men who interest them, get public appointments: to achieve their ends, the women will overcome all obstacles and suffer all indignities. The men keep out of such business, and rightly so: they would not be nearly so good at it. The women love amusements and parties: they seek company, and play for high stakes, smoke cigars and ride horseback, not in the English fashion but wearing wide trousers like a man. They adore sea bathing and swim very well. As for the social talents, they pluck the guitar, sing rather badly (though a few are good musicians) and dance, quite delightfully, the national dances. They are generally without education, never read and are ignorant of what is going on in the rest of the world. They have much natural wit and understanding, good memories and are surprisingly intelligent.

I have depicted the women of Lima just as they are, not in the way they have been described by some other travelers. It wasn't easy for me, because the warm welcome and hospitality they gave me filled me with gratitude. But as a conscientious traveler I have felt obliged to tell the whole truth.

STUDY QUESTIONS

1. How does Tristan describe the clothing worn by women in Lima, notably the *manto* and *saya*?
2. Why does Tristan associate these garments with female freedom? Are you convinced by her arguments?

FRANCES CALDERON DE LA BARCA

4.7 DOMESTIC SERVANTS IN MEXICO, 1843

Frances Calderon de la Barca was a Scottish writer who became the wife of the Spanish ambassador to Mexico. During her two-year residence in Mexico between 1839 and 1841, Calderon wrote a series of letters to her friend William H. Prescott, a prominent historian. A collection of fifty-four of these letters was published as a book in 1843, in what became one of the most influential travel accounts of nineteenth-century Latin America. In this excerpt, Calderon describes the challenges of working with the domestic servants who were ubiquitous in Mexican households. Domestic service was one of the most commonly available jobs for the urban working classes, especially for women, yet because this work took place in the privacy of individual homes it is difficult for historians to uncover information about servant lives. While Calderon's account takes a condescending and dismissive tone, it is nevertheless revealing as to the conditions and experiences of indigenous and mestizo servants who worked in upper-class Mexican households.

LETTER THE NINTEENTH

June 3rd.

You ask me to tell you how I find Mexican servants. Hitherto I had avoided the ungrateful theme, from very weariness of it. The badness of the servants, is an unfailing source of complaint even amongst Mexicans; much more so amongst foreigners, especially on their first arrival. We hear of their addiction to stealing, their laziness, drunkenness, dirtiness, with a host of other vices. That these complaints are frequently just, there can be no doubt, but the evil might be remedied to a great extent. In the first place servants are constantly taken without being required to bring a recommendation from their last place; and in the next, recommendations are constantly given, whether from indolence or mistaken kindness, to servants who do not deserve them. A servant who has lived in a dozen different houses, staying about a month in each, is not thought the worse of on that account. As the love of finery is inherent in them all, even more so than in other daughters of Eve, a girl will go to service merely to earn sufficient to buy herself an embroidered chemise; and if, in addition to this, she can pick up a pair of small old satin shoes, she will tell you she is tired of working, and going home to rest, *"para descansar"* So little is necessary, when one can contentedly live on tortillas and chile, sleep on a mat, and dress in rags!

A decent old woman, who came to the house to wash shortly after our arrival in this country, and left us at the end of the month, *"para descansar."* Soon after, she used to come with her six children, they and herself all in rags, and beg the gardener to give her any *odds and ends* of vegetables he could spare. My maid asked her, why, being so poor, she had left a good place, where she got twelve dollars a month. "Jesus!" said she, "if you only knew the pleasure of doing nothing."

Source: http://digital.library.upenn.edu/women/calderon/mexico/mexico.html#XIX

I wished to bring up a little girl as a servant, having her taught to read, sew, etc. A child of twelve years old, one of a large family, who subsisted upon charity, was procured for me; and I promised her mother that she should be taught to read, taken regularly to church, and instructed in all kinds of work. She was rather pretty, and very intelligent, though extremely indolent; and though she had no stockings, would consent to wear nothing but dirty white satin shoes, too short for her foot. Once a week, her mother, a tall, slatternly woman, with long tangled hair, and a cigar in her mouth, used to come to visit her, accompanied by a friend, a friend's friend, and a train of girls, her daughters. The housekeeper would give them some dinner, after which they would all light their cigars, and, together with the little Josefita, sit, and howl, and bemoan themselves, crying and lamenting her sad fate in being obliged to go out to service. After these visits, Josefita was fit for nothing. If desired to sew, she would sit looking so miserable, and doing so little, that it seemed better to allow her to leave her work alone. Then, tolerably contented, she would sit on a mat, doing nothing, her hands folded, and her eyes fixed on vacancy.

According to promise, I took her several times to see her mother, but one day being occupied, I sent her alone in the carriage, with charge to the servants to bring her safely back. In the evening she returned, accompanied by the whole family, all crying and howling; "For the love of the Most Holy Virgin, Señora mia! Por la purissima concepcion!" etc., etc., etc. I asked what had happened, and after much difficulty discovered that their horror was occasioned by my having sent her alone in the carriage It happened that the Countess S— was in the drawing-room, and to her I related the cause of the uproar. To my astonishment, she assured me that the woman was in this instance right, and that it was very dangerous to send a girl of twelve years of age from one street to another, in the power of the coachman and footman. Finding from such good authority that this was the case, I begged the woman to be contented with seeing her daughter once a month, when, if she could not come herself, I would send her under proper protection. She agreed; but one day having given Josefita permission to spend the night at her mother's, I received next morning a very

dirty note, nearly illegible, which, after calling down the protection of the Virgin upon me, concluded–"but with much sorrow I must take my child from the most illustrious protection of your excellency, for she needs to rest herself, (es preciso que descanse,) and is tired for the present of working." The woman then returned to beg, which she considered infinitely less degrading.

Against this nearly universal indolence and indifference to earning money, the heads of families have to contend; as also against thieving and dirtiness; yet I think the remedy much easier than it appears. If on the one hand, no one were to receive a servant into their house, without respectable references, especially from their last place, and if their having remained one year in the same house were considered necessary to their being received into another, unless from some peculiar circumstances, and if on the other hand it were considered as unjust and dangerous, as it really is, to recommend a servant who has been guilty of stealing, as being "*muy honrado,*" very honest, some improvement might soon take place.

A porter was recommended to us as "muy honrado," not from his last place, but from one before. He was a well-dressed, sad-looking individual; and at the same time we took his wife as washerwoman, and his brother as valet to our attaché, thus having the whole family under our roof, wisely taking it for granted that he being recommended as particularly honest, his relations were "all honourable men." An English lady happened to call on me, and a short time after I went to return her visit; when she informed me that the person who had opened the door for her was a notorious thief; whom the police had long been in search of; that she had feared sending a servant to warn us of our danger, lest guessing the purport of her message, he might rob the house before leaving it. We said nothing to the man that evening, but he looked paler and more miserable than usual, probably foreseeing what would be the result of Mrs. —'s visit. The next morning C—n sent for him and dismissed him, giving him a month's wages, that he might not be tempted to steal from immediate want. His face grew perfectly livid, but he made no remark. In half an hour he returned and begged to speak with C—n. He confessed that the crime of which he concluded he was accused, he had in fact committed; that he had been tempted to a gambling house, while he had in his pocket a large sum of money belonging to his master. After losing his own money, he tried his fortune with what was not his own, lost the whole sum, then pawned a valuable shawl worth several hundred dollars, with which also he had been entrusted, and having lost everything, in despair made his escape from Mexico. He remained in concealment for some time, till hearing that we wanted a porter, he ventured to present himself to the housekeeper with his former certificate. He declared himself thoroughly repentant—that this was his first, and would be his last crime—but who can trust the good resolutions of a gambler! We were obliged to send him away, especially as the other servants already had some suspicions concerning him; and everything stolen in the house would in future have been attributed to him. The gentleman who had recommended him afterwards confessed that he always had strong suspicions of this man's honesty, and knew him to be so determined a gambler, that he had pawned all he possessed, even his wife's clothes, to obtain money for that purpose. Now as a porter in Mexico has pretty much at his disposal the property and even the lives of the whole family, it is certainly most blameable to recommend to that situation a man whose honesty is more than doubtful. We afterwards procured two soldiers from the *Invalidos*, old Spaniards, to act in that capacity, who had no other foiblesse but that of being constantly drunk. We at length found two others, who only got tipsy alternately, so that we considered ourselves very well off.

We had a long series of *galopinas*, kitchen-maids, and the only one who brought a first-rate character with her, robbed the housekeeper. The money, however, was recovered, and was found to have been placed by the girl in the hands of a rich and apparently respectable coachmaker. He refunded it to the rightful owner, and the galopina was punished by a month's imprisonment, which he should have shared with her. One of the most disagreeable customs of the women servants, is that of wearing their long hair hanging down at its full length, matted, uncombed, and always in the way. I cannot imagine how the Mexican ladies, who complain of this, permit it. Flowing hair sounds very picturesque, but when it is very dirty, and suspended over the soup, it is not a pretty picture.

The reboso, in itself graceful and convenient, has the disadvantage of being the greatest cloak for all untidiness, uncombed hair and raggedness, that ever was invented. Even in the better classes, it occasions much indolence in the toilet, but in the common people, its effect is overwhelming. When the reboso drops off, or is displaced by chance, we see what they would be without it! As for the sarape, it is both convenient and graceful, especially on horseback, but though Indian in its origin, the custom of covering the lower part of the face with it, is taken from the Spanish cloak; and the opportunity which both sarape and reboso afford for concealing large knives about the person, as also for enveloping both face and figure so as to be scarcely recognizable, is no doubt the cause of the many murders which take place amongst the lower orders, in moments of excitement and drunkenness. If they had not these knives at hand, their rage would probably cool, or a fair fight would finish the matter, and if they could not wear these knives concealed, I presume they would be prohibited from carrying them.

As for taking a woman-cook in Mexico, one must have strong nerves and a good appetite to eat what she dresses, however palatable, after having seen her. One look at her flowing locks, one glance at her reboso, *et c'est fini.* And yet the Mexican servants have their good qualities, and are a thousand times preferable to the foreign servants one finds in Mexico, especially the French. Bringing them with you is a dangerous experiment. In ten days they begin to fancy themselves ladies and gentlemen—the men have *Don* tacked to their name; and they either marry and set up shops, or become unbearably insolent. A tolerable French cook may occasionally be had, but you must pay his services their weight in gold, and wink at his extortions and robberies. There are one or two French *restaurans*, who will send you in a very good dinner at an extravagant price: and it is common in foreign houses, especially amongst the English, to adopt this plan whenever they give a large entertainment.

The Mexican servants have some never-failing good qualities. They are the perfection of civility—humble, obliging, excessively good-tempered, and very easily attached to those with whom they live; and if that *rara avis*, a good Mexican housekeeper, can be found, and that such may be met with I from experience can testify, then the troubles of the *ménage* rest upon her shoulders, and accustomed as she is to the amiable weaknesses of her *compatriotes*, she is neither surprised nor disturbed by them.

As for wages, a good porter has from fifteen to twenty dollars per month; a coachman from twenty to thirty—many houses keep two or even three coachmen, one who drives from the box, one who rides postilion, and a third for emergencies. Our friend —, who has many horses, mules, and carriages, has four; and pays forty dollars per month to his head coachman; the others in proportion. A French cook has about thirty dollars—a housekeeper from twelve to fifteen; a major-domo about twenty or more; a footman six or seven; galopine and chambermaid five or six; a gardener from twelve to fifteen. Sewing-girls have about three reals per diem. Porter, coachmen, and gardener, have their wives and families in the house, which would be an annoyance, were the houses not so large. The men-servants generally are much cleaner and better dressed than the women.

One circumstance is remarkable; that, dirty as the women-servants are, and notwithstanding the enormous size of Mexican houses, and Mexican families, the houses themselves are, generally speaking, the perfection of cleanliness. This must be due either to a good housekeeper, which is rarely to be found, or to the care taken by the mistress of the house herself. That private houses should have this advantage over churches and theatres, only proves that ladies know how to manage these matters better than gentlemen, so that one is inclined to wish *à la Martineau*, that the Mexican police were entirely composed of old women.

STUDY QUESTIONS

1. What types of language does Calderon use to describe domestic servants? What does this reveal about elite prejudices toward the lower classes?

2. What can we learn from Calderon's account about the day-to-day work life of domestic servants in Mexico?

3. What insight does her account provide as to how domestic servants felt about their work? Was service seen as a desirable profession? How did servants resist the demands of their employers?

CHAPTER 5

PROGRESS AND MODERNIZATION
The Elite's Strategy, 1870–1929

JUAN BAUTISTA ALBERDI

5.1 IMMIGRATION AS A MEANS OF PROGRESS, 1853

Juan Bautista Alberdi was an Argentine intellectual whose writings on immigration shaped a whole generation of political thought and policy in Latin America. Alberdi believed foreign immigrants were central to regional development, essential to bringing the cultural values of hard work and discipline that would prompt economic progress. His focus on the centrality of immigration is epitomized by his famous dictum, "To govern is to populate." In this excerpt, Alberdi lays out what he sees as the connection between Europe and civilization, arguing that foreign immigration could change Argentina for the better.

How and in what form will the reviving spirit of European civilization come to our land? Just as it always has come. Europe will bring us its fresh spirit, its work habits, and its civilized ways with the immigrants it sends us.

By the customs later communicated to our inhabitants, every European who comes to our shores brings us more civilization than a great many books of philosophy. Perfection that one cannot see, touch, or feel is poorly understood. An industrious worker is the most edifying of instruction manuals.

Do we want to plant and nourish the qualities of English liberty, French culture, and the industriousness of men from Europe and the United States? Then let us bring the living exemplars of these attributes to our shores and let those qualities take root here.

Do we want orderly, disciplined, energetic work habits to prevail in South America? Then let us fill our country with people who have a profound grasp of such habits. Those who are well acquainted with industrial Europe will soon form industrial South America. The plant of civilization is not propagated from seed (except very slowly). Rather, it is like a vineyard that takes root and spreads through its offshoots.

This is the only way that our America, uninhabited today, will become prosperous in a short time. To try to change without outside help is an extremely slow process. If we want to see our provinces be successful

Source: Gabriela Nouzeilles and Graciela Montaldo (eds.) *The Argentina Reader* (Durham, NC: Duke University Press, 2002), pp. 95–101. Translated by Patricia Owen Steiner

in short order, let us bring people from Europe whose good working habits are already well established.

Without large populations there is no flowering of culture, there is no substantial progress, everything is wretched and small. This is what happens to nations of only a half million inhabitants because of their limited population. They remain provinces and villages, and everything of theirs will always bear the stamp of a puny provincialism.

Important advice to men of South American countries. Primary schools, high schools, universities, are, by themselves alone, very poor means of progress without large manufacturing enterprises that are the fruits of great numbers of men.

Population—a South American necessity that affects all other needs—is the critical measure of the capacity of our governments. The minister of state who does not double his state's population in ten years is inept and has wasted his time on bagatelles and trifles. He does not deserve the recognition of his country.

If we were to take the ragged homeless from Chile, our gauchos, the half-breeds from Bolivia—the basic elements of our masses—and let them experience all the transformations of our best system of instruction, we would not in one hundred years have made any of them into an English laborer who works, spends, and lives in a dignified and comfortable manner. Or try giving a million inhabitants (the average population of these republics) the best education possible, on as enlightened a level as the Swiss canton of Geneva or as the most cultured province in France. Would we then have a great and flourishing state? Certainly not: we are talking about a million people in a territory suitable for 50 million. Can they be anything more than a miserable population?

But so goes the argument: by educating our masses, we will have order; having order, population from overseas will come to our continent.

I tell you now that you are turning upside down the way progress works. You will not have order, or education for the general public, unless it is through the influence of immigrants who have firmly established patterns of order and good education.

Multiply our population of serious people, and you will see that foolish agitators (with their plans for frivolous revolts) will be unsuccessful and that

they will become isolated from a world absorbed by concerns of real consequence.

How to achieve all this? More easily than by wasting millions on futile, trifling attempts to make endless improvements.

Foreign treaties: Sign treaties with foreigners in which you guarantee to inspect their natural rights to hold property, their civil rights, their safety, the right to acquire wealth, and their freedom of movement. Such treaties will prove to be the most beautiful key to progress for those countries that choose to stimulate their growth through immigration. For such legal guarantees to be inviolable and lasting, sign treaties for an indefinite and very prolonged length of time. Don't be afraid to commit yourself to European order and culture. . . .

If there is the risk that immigration might introduce a barbarism or tyranny that would threaten us, don't be so afraid that you forsake the future of our industry and civilization. Fear of treaties is a bad habit left over from the early days of our Revolution. It is an old principle, outdated and misguided—a poorly executed imitation of the foreign policy that Washington counseled for the United States under circumstances and for motives that were totally different from those that we face. . . .

Plan for immigration: Spontaneous immigration is the source of true and great immigration. Our governments should promote it, not by piecemeal concessions of land fit only for bears, not in fallacious and usurious contract (which hurt the immigrants more than they hurt the country being populated not by mere handfuls of men or individual arrangements to do business with some influential speculator. That is all false, the face of sterile immigration. Only by the great, large-scale, disinterested system that gave birth to California in four years, by the lavish extension of freedom, and by concessions can we persuade foreigners to forsake their own country and instead inhabit ours. We must try to make life and business here easier for them by eliminating restrictive measures so that they will achieve their legal objectives and their useful aspirations.

The United States is such an advanced country because it is now, and has been continually, composed of people from Europe. From the very beginning it received tremendous waves of European immigration. Those who believe that progress in the United States dates only from the time of independence deceive themselves. Under the colonial system, European immigration was as great and continuous as it was after independence. Legislators for the states tended wisely to promote immigration. One of the reasons for the perpetual disagreement of the United States with England was that England wanted to place barriers or difficulties in the way of this immigration, which they feared would turn its colonies into a colossus. Motives to settle in the United States are invoked in the colonists' Declaration of Independence. Take a look at that document, and then ask yourselves if mounting numbers of foreigners prevented the United States from the winning its independence or from creating a great and powerful nation.

Religious tolerance: If you would like to have moral, religious settlers, don't encourage atheism. If you want families with their own individual ways, with their own special customs, then respect their religion and the tenets of their creeds. Reduced to Catholicism to the exclusion of other beliefs, Spanish American is a lonely and silent monastery. This is a fatal dilemma: either remain exclusively Catholic and sparsely populated; or populate and prosper by being tolerant in religious matters. To attract Anglo-Saxon peoples and settlers from Sweden and Switzerland and then to deny them to exercise their religious beliefs is a form of hypocritical liberalism.

This is literally true: to exclude dissident religious sects from South America is to exclude the English, the Germans, the Swiss, North Americans who are not Catholics, that is to say, to exclude those settlers whom this continent needs most. To bring them here without their religion is to leave them without the features that help make them what they are. If people are not able to practice their beliefs, there is a real risk that they will become atheists.

Some intended policies violate common sense; one of these is to want population, families, and constructive mores and yet to make it difficult for settlers who are not Catholics to get married. To do so is to form an alliance between morality and prostitution. Since you are not able to destroy the invincible affinity of the sexes, what do you do about giving legitimacy to natural unions? Do you want to multiply concubines instead of wives, to destine our women to become the laughingstock of foreigners? To have babies born in America from such unions and be disadvantaged from the start is to fill our entire continent with gauchos and prostitutes. You would only promote sickness and impiety. This cannot be attempted in the name of Catholicism without insulting the magnificence of our noble church, a church that is capable of associating itself with all human progress. . . .

Inland immigration: Until now, European immigrants have settled along the coast, and from this fact comes the cultural superiority of the South American littoral over the interior provinces. . . .

The best way to introduce Europeans into the interior of our continent on a scale powerful enough to work a prodigious change in just a few years is by railroads, by navigable rivers, and by engaging in free trade. Europe comes to these distant regions on the wings of commerce and industry and is seeking the richness that our continent offers. Wealth, like population, like culture, is impossible when the means of communication are difficult, limited, and costly.

Wealth comes to our continent because of the opportunity offered by the ocean. Stretch out the ocean until it reaches the interior of this continent, by using steam engines on the land and on rivers, and you will have the interior as full of European immigrants as the coast is now.

Railroads: The railroad is the means of properly righting what colonizing Spain located upside down on this continent. She placed the heads of our states where the feet should be. To satisfy her aims of isolation and monopoly, that system made sense; for our expansion now, and for our commercial freedom, it is fatal. It is necessary to bring capital to our shores, to take the coast to our continent's interior. The railroad and the electric telegraph, which diminish space, bring about this marvel better than all the tycoons in the land. Railroads bring reforms and change the most difficult of situations, without either decrees or riots.

Railroads will unify the Argentine Republic better than all the congresses ever could. Congresses will then be able to declare the Republic one and indivisible. But, without a railroad system that extends to its remotest extremes, our country will always remain divisible and divided, despite all its legislative decrees. . . .

Without such powerful means of transportation you will not be able to bring to our provinces the kind of European stimulation that today regenerates our coastal regions. Immigrants are or will be to the local life of our territories what the great arteries are to the lower extremes of the human body, fountains of life. The Spaniards know this to be so; in the last years of their dominion over this continent they were seriously occupied with the construction of an interoceanic railroad across the Andes and the Argentine desert. Rivadavia was also deeply concerned by this same need and entertained the possibility of building a railroad.

Why do we regard as an impossible "utopia" the creation of a roadway that in another time preoccupied the Spanish government, so positive and parsimonious in its great works of improvements? . . .

Do we have insufficient capital for these enterprises? Then treat foreign capital as if it were our very own. Surround foreign capitalists with immunity from taxes and regulations, and give them privileges so that their money will be at home in our land.

South America needs capital as much as it needs population. An immigrant without funds is a soldier without weapons. Make pesos flow into these countries of future wealth and current poverty. But the peso too is an emigrant that demands many concessions and privileges. Grant foreign investors what they require; investment capital is the sure arm of progress for our countries. It is the secret on which the United States and Holland put such high value in order to give magic impetus to their industry and commerce. . . .

Interior navigation: Our great rivers, those moving paths, as Pascal called them, are another means of bringing the civilizing ways of European immigrants to the inner reaches of our continent. But rivers that are not navigated are like ones that do not exist. To keep them as the exclusive domain of our bands of impoverished and indigent peoples is to keep them unnavigable. For these rivers to fulfill their God-given destiny of populating the interior of this continent, we must establish the law of the seas, that is, waters where there is absolute freedom. God has not made our rivers great (like the Mediterranean Sea) just to be navigated by one family.

Proclaim the freedom of our waters. And, so that this may be permanent, so that the unstable hands of our governments do not take back today what they agreed to yesterday, sign perpetual treaties of free navigation. . . .

Do not be afraid either that our national identity will be compromised by the effect of numerous foreigners or that the national character will disappear. Such fear is meanspirited and preoccupied. A good deal of foreign blood has flowed in defense of South American independence. Montevideo, defended by foreigners, has deserved the name of New Troy. Valparaiso, made up of people who immigrated from other countries, is the luxurious Star of Chile. Of all nations, England has been the most conquered; all nations have tread on her soil and mixed their blood and race with hers. England is the product of all possible cross-breeding of castes, and, for just that reason, the English are the most perfect of men, and their nationality is so pronounced that it makes you believe that the common man is one integrated race.

Do not fear, then, the confusion of races and tongues. From Babel, from the chaos, there will emerge, some bright, fine day, the South American nationality. Our soil adopts men, it attracts and assimilates them and makes our land theirs. The emigrant is a colonist; he leaves the mother country for the country of his adoption. It was two thousand years ago that the words that form the motto of this century were first spoken: "Ubi patria, ubi bene." . . .

Victory will bring us laurels, but the laurel is a sterile plant for South America. A sprig of peace, which is golden, not in the language of poets, but in the language of economists, would be of more value. The epoch of heroes has passed; we are today entering into the age of good sense. The model of national greatness is not Napoléon; it is Washington. Washington represents, not military triumphs, but prosperity, exaltation, organization, and peace. He is the hero of the orderliness of freedom par excellence. . . .

To reduce a great mass of men to an eighth of its size in two hours by firing a cannon—that is the heroism of the past. In contrast, to multiply a small population in just a few days—that is the heroism of the modern statesman. The magnificence of creation in place of the savage magnitude of extermination. The population census will provide the measure of the accomplishment of the South American ministers of state.

STUDY QUESTIONS

1. Why does Alberdi describe Latin America as "uninhabited"? Is this an accurate description? Who might this formulation marginalize?
2. How does the connection between immigration and economic growth manifest itself according to Alberdi? What kinds of infrastructural changes will immigration support and how?
3. Are the Argentine masses capable of transformation in his opinion? Why or why not?

5.2 THE CUBA COMMISSION REPORT ON CHINESE INDENTURED WORKERS OF 1876

Many of the immigrants who came to Latin America in the nineteenth century were not the white Europeans desired by intellectuals like Juan Bautista Alberdi, but instead indentured Chinese workers (known at the time as "Coolies"). Chinese indentureship was especially common in Peru and Cuba. Between 1847 and 1880, approximately 125,000 Chinese indentured workers were taken to Cuba, while around 95,000 went to Peru. Work conditions were harsh, especially in Cuba, where Chinese indentured workers labored alongside African slaves. Death rates were high, and more than half of workers did not survive the term of their eight-year contracts. In 1873, the government of China sent an imperial mission to Cuba to investigate living and working conditions for indentured migrants. Hundreds of Chinese workers presented their testimony to the commission, allowing us to understand the experiences of ordinary indentured workers in their own words. This document presents an excerpt from the report published in 1876, and provides shocking evidence of the level of violence and brutality suffered by Chinese migrants in Cuba.

Some Employers are cruel by nature and harsh to the employed: others are kindly and treat Coolies well; what remarkable cases illustrate each side, and what is the general state of the relations between Employers and Employed?

When a master treats a servant well and gives no cause for complaint or accusation, there is nothing in his action which can result in any record of instances of it being preserved. On the other hand the cruelty and harshness of an employer aided by his administrator and overseers, the maiming of limbs, and the infliction of fatal injuries, though they may not generally be noticed or punished by the officials, cannot be effectually suppressed, and force themselves prominently before the eyes of all.

Thus Lai A-ssŭ deposes. "I recollect, the year before last a Chinese was murdered, and that his body was cast into the sea. It was found by the guards, and was recognized as that of a workman in the sugar warehouse. This however was denied by our employer, and no further

Source: Denise Helly, *The Cuba Commission Report: A Hidden History of the Chinese in Cuba. The Original Language Text of 1876* (John Hopkins University Press, 1993), pp. 66–69.

action was taken by the officials. Last year also, in the 7th month, a native of the Hoyüen district, by name A Erh, was killed. The authorities on this occasion sent for us to give testimony. Our master denied his guilt, and imputed the crime to an overseer, a negro, and the latter was in consequence imprisoned. At the same time another native of Hoyüen, who had declared that he had witnessed the commission of the act by the master himself, was sold away to the mountains. Our master also continually urged the negroes to beat us; he used to say, 'If one were killed, two others could be bought.'" Fan Ssǔ-'ho deposes, "the black overseers ever strike us, whenever they see us, whether we are working or not; and the administrator also beats us. I saw Ch'ên A- ssǔ struck dead simply for pushing with a bundle of cane against an overseer. It was then alleged, that he had hanged himself." Lü A-chên deposes, "the overseers were negroes, and though I committed no offence I was constantly flogged. I have seen men beaten to death, the bodies being afterwards buried, and no report being made to the authorities." Hsieh A-shêng deposes, "with me were a native of Sinning, by the name Ch'ên, and a native of K'aip'ing, by name Liang. The administrator accused them of cutting grass slowly, and directing four men to hold them in a prostrate position, inflicted, with a whip, a flogging which almost killed them. The first afterwards hanged himself, and the second drowned himself. The local officials visited the plantation but instituted no proper investigation, and I and my companions were prevented by our ignorance of the language from laying before them a statement of these crimes." Lo A-êrh deposes, "I and my uncle Lo Nan-shao were both sold to a railway company. An overseer with an iron bar wounded my uncle so severely that he died in half a month. I preferred a charge before the officials, and the overseer was arrested, but he was released after a month's confinement and no other punishment was imposed." 'Hu A-'hua deposes, "I heard that when Lin A-têng was murdered his body was placed in a chamber and examined by the officials, and that the overseer was imprisoned." Hsieh A-'hou deposes, "four men out of a gang of 30 newly arrived, died in the hospital four hours after they had entered it, on account of alleged sickness. Upon this 20 men laid before the authorities a charge of murder, and at the request of the administrator an official of

low rank visited the estate. I, acting as interpreter, translated the evidence of two witnesses who declared that sickness had been the cause of death. On the following day other officials continued the enquiry. All were present, and on a question being put as to the prior existence of sickness, the general answer was that the men had not been ill. The officer of low rank then declared that, on the previous occasion, I had interpreted incorrectly, and I was placed in prison. I was subsequently released on my master's bail. Liang A-kuang deposes, "with me was a Cantonese, by name A-liu. A little more than a month after arrival, being unable to endure the cruelties, he hanged himself. The official visited the estate for the purpose of making an inquiry, but our employer was rich and no further action ensued. In Cuba the officials are at the orders of the rich." Wang Mu-chiu deposes, "finding labour too arduous, I made a complaint to the officials, and the latter recommended my master to be less exacting, and to supply me with sufficient food. He assented, but when he had brought me back he forced me to work with chained feet during seven months." 'Huang Shih-jung deposed, "I was a witness of the sufferings of 'Huang A-kuang. Drive by the hardships he had run away. He was captured, placed in chains, and so severely flogged that the blood and flesh dropped down from him. He then, still in irons, was forced to labour, and being deprived of food, in hunger at some sugar-cane. This was observed by the administrator, who again flogged him and on the same evening hanged himself. Twenty of us preferred a complaint to the officials, declaring that we were unwilling to return to the plantation, but the master arranged that 12 should be brought back under guard, the remaining 8 being, on the advice of the authorities, sold to other plantations." Lin Ho deposes, "a native of the Shuntêh district, By name Li Tê, had worked on the plantation nine years, and possessed 72 ounces of gold, which he handed for safe custody to an overseer. The latter, aided by a negro, murdered him when in the field. The body was buried, and no report was ever made to the authorities." 'Huang A-tê deposes, "last year I saw the murder of a native Hiang-shan. An official visited the estate in order to examine the body, but never arrested the offender. The latter was a negro, and of this fact our master was aware, but he simply inflicted on him a slight chastisement, and the matter was then considered terminated. Negroes indeed receive better usage than the Chinese." Hu A-ssŭ deposes, "a native of Sinhwei, by name A-fêng, was murdered by the negroes. The body was buried and no report was made to the officials." Chang Luan deposes, "I saw the administrator flog a native of Tung-kwan, by name Mêng, so severely that his whole body was lacerated; chains also were attached to his feet. The latter hanged himself. The officials visited the estate, and entered into conversation with the administrator, but no questions were addressed to us." Yeh A-ling deposes, "in the 10th year of T'ungchih, a negro murdered a Chinese. The negro was a great favourite of our master, and the dead body was removed and buried. Certain Chinese having discovered the place of burial, our master induced the authorities to chastise them. He also intimated that they had committed the crime, and they were in consequence tried and eight men were sentenced to imprisonment." Ch'ên Lin-shan deposes, "as, after the completion of our contract term, the administrator flogged us with great severity, we all, 30 in number, became much discontented. On information being given to him of our having expressed indignation at his cruelty he placed more than 10 in irons, and having bribed the authorities, procured the presence of certain of the guards, who shot four. One of the four was a native of the district of Kaoming, by name Li A-ch'I, one was a native of the Kaoyao district, by name A-chao, one was a native of the prefecture of Hweichow, by name Li Kêng-yu, and the fourth was a native of the Sinhwei disctrict, and was named A-hsing."

The following instances of injuries were verified by personal inspection Scars of old wounds on the bodies of:—

Yüan A-Ts'ung	Liang A-lin
Tsêng Jung-Ch'ing	Lo A-chi
Wên A-chao	'Ho 'Hai
Li A-'hou	Lin Chao-chin
Liu A-chi	Chung Shêng
Ch'ên A-'hung	Kao A-lun
Li A-k'ai	Han Ch'ing-to
Liang A-'hung	T'an Lien-chin
Mo A-hsün	Liu A-t'ing
Ho A-hsien	Chang Shih-chên

Liang A-kuei	Hung A-i
Yen A-yu	

Scars on the heads of:—

Ch'ü A-ping	MiuYang-chiao
Shên T'ai-kao	Ch'ên A-shên

Scars on the head and face of:—

Chu Ts'ai-fang

Scars on the head and arms of:—

'Ho A-fa

Scars from wounds self-inflicted in the hope of death, on the throats of:

Huang A-ping
Lin Lun mei
Ch'ü Tan-k'o

Actual wounds on the bodies of:—

Wu A-chi'n
Lan A-mu

Actual wounds on the heads of:—

Chang ShêngYu A-t'ien

Actual wounds on the face of:—

Wu A-fang

Actual wounds on the chest of:—

Ch'ên Chung hsiu

Actual wounds on the legs and thighs of:—

Wang Ta-chêng	Ch'ên I-yu
Ts'ai A-lu	Ch'ü Chieh-k'ang
Lin Tzŭ yu	Li A-lü

The loss of the left ear by Liang A-yu, deliberately cut off by his master.

The loss of a portion of one ear by Huang A-shêng.

The loss of sight by Li A-ta, the disease of the eyes having commenced immediately after a flogging, during which 200 blows were administered.

The injury caused to one eye of Liang A-'hua.

The loss of two teeth of Ch'ên P'ie-ch'ang.

The fracture of the arm of the *hsiu-ts'ai* Ch'ên Shao-yen, of Li A-'hui. Yuan Al-shau and Ch'ên A-'hai.

The maiming of the right hand of Lo Kuan-hsiu by a blow from a knife between the thumb and forefinger.

The loss of four fingers by Liu A-lin, deliberately cut off.

The fracture of the fingers and toes of Li 'Hung and Li 'Ho.

The fracture of one leg of Lu Shêng-pao.

The loss of the use of one ankle by Wu A-kuang, the result of wearing fetters.

The maimed condition of the feet of Hsü A-fên, from the same cause.

STUDY QUESTIONS

1. Historians have emphasized the parallels between indentureship and slavery. To what extent does this comparison hold based on the evidence presented in the Commission Report?
2. What does the violence inflicted on Chinese workers tell us about elite attitudes toward labor in late nineteenth-century Cuba?

PASCUAL COÑA

5.3 A MAPUCHE CHIEFTAN REMEMBERS "PACIFICATION," 1930

One of the key nationalist discourses of the late nineteenth century was the need to secure the frontier and make land that was on the margins of national territory, such as densely forested tropical zones or plains areas, economically productive. This had deep significance for indigenous peoples who occupied these territories. In the Southern Cone, governments in Chile and Argentina launched all out wars of "pacification" in the 1880s, aimed at gaining control of Mapuche land. This document presents the reflections of Pascual Coña, a Mapuche lonko (chieftan), on the Chilean military offensive of 1883, which followed a major Mapuche uprising. Coña's testimony was recorded by a Capuchin missionary in the 1920s, decades after the war ended. Coña describes the cross-border alliances formed between Argentine and Chilean Mapuche, and explains how some Mapuche groups allied themselves with the invading Chilean military. It also underlines the devastating impact of the war on Mapuche communities.

The ancient Mapuche people mightily detested the foreigners. We have nothing in common with these foreigners; they belong to another race. Sometimes caciques who were neighbors of the *huincas* [non-Mapuches, Spaniards, or Chileans] launched raids against them; they fought and were defeated. Hatred against the foreigners grew with every battle.

Owing to the great aversion toward the huincas, every part of the indigenous world had been plotting to rise up against them. The first order by the

Source: Elizabeth Quay Hutchison, Thomas Miller Klubock, Nara B. Milanich, and Peter Winn (eds.) *The Chile Reader: History, Culture, Politics* (Durham, NC: Duke University Press, 2014), pp. 206–209. Translated by Ryan Judge and John White

Pehuenche caciques (Argentines) was given in a message to the Chilean chief Neculmán de Boroa. The message stated that they were ready for war in Chile, such as the Pehuenches had prepared in Argentina. In addition, a knotted cord was sent that indicated when the general malon would begin.

When the indigenous Argentine messenger arrived, he stated: "The chiefs Chaihuenque, Namuncura, Foyel, and Ancatrir have ordered me to visit the nobles of Chile. This is the reason for my arrival here. My chief orders me to say to you, the chiefs of Chile, the following: 'Alas, the huincas are there. The indigenous Argentines will rise up and finish the foreigners off; that you do the same with yours, that you also attack them; united we are going to make war against them.' In addition, take this knotted cord and adhere to the rebellion decidedly because the huincas are abominable." They gave me this order to tell the message to Neculmán. . . .

In this way news of the war was propagated everywhere; Colihuinca's messenger went with his knotted strings from cacique to cacique.

Pascual Painemilla de Rauquenhue and Pascal Paillalef de Alma were not advised [about the uprising]. They were in favor of the huincas; that is why the [cacique planning the uprising] wanted them dead.

All those who had received notice of the rebellion untied a knot each day. When the last day came, they called for general meetings of all the principal caciques.

When the meetings had already finished . . . the subject came to the attention of certain Chileans. So five men went to advise the Mapuches who were against the malon. . . . They went to address the cacique Colihuinca.

Upon hearing about their arrival the cacique Marimán, who was holding a meeting, sent some men to bring them to him. At night while they slept in Colihuinca's camp, they were captured. They were all taken prisoner and taken to where the Mapuches were meeting. Marimán and his followers were pleased, saying "we have already captured the victims, today we will celebrate a *nguillatún* [ceremonial assembly]." . . .

While in Toltén, Painemilla received a message from Calfupán relating the following: "You have been saved, I began the alarm when they [the Mapuches in rebellion] were still in view, but they have gone away. They demanded that I ally myself with them. Colihuinca,

Painecur, Huichal, and Carmona, the leaders of the mob, stated: 'You must help us, we are going to assault the town of Toltén.' I refused them and said: "if you want to be defeated then walk alone if you believe you are strong enough to conquer the soldiers.' They had many weapons so I did not dare." Because of these words fear of the leaders of the rebellion took over and they retreated.

The messenger also told us: when the rebellion arrived at Boca-Budi, the chief Paincur of Pichihuenque killed the Chilean José Maria López. Both men and several women were traveling down the river in a canoe when the warriors advanced from each riverbank, invaded the boat, and murdered the men. They did not kill the women, however; these fled to Toltén, as I found afterward.

When the caciques who were in rebellion withdrew, the followers of Calfupán pursued them. . . . The rebels were intimidated and retreated running. Calfupán's people were amused by their fear and intensified the persecution; they took the horses of some; killed one Mapuche; and, took five others prisoner. They took these captives, natives of Mañiu, to Toltén. Much later, the captives were set free.

With this the insurrection ended. It never arrived in Toltén. The chiefs returned to their huts and remained peaceful.

We stayed in Toltén for five days before returning to the land of Rauguenhue. What the other insurgents did in other regions I do not know nor can I tell. I can only say that much later in Nehuentúe, on the other side of Cautín, the Chilean Severino Ibáñez was killed.

After remaining in the house for two days, a message arrived from Painemilla that said: "You should come, we are meeting in Toltén on horseback and met with Chief Painemilla who pledged in the meeting to unite a great number of men, according to the orders of Governor Pascual López in Toltén. One hundred or so of us gathered there, the precise number I do not know. We are armed with spears. Ten of the Chileans carried firearms and I myself carried a shotgun.

Then we began to march to make war in turn against the mutinous Mapuche rebels. We went along the north bank of the river Toltén, passing by Peñehue, and arrive at Puculón. After massing together, we settled ourselves in the great mountains called Puqueno for a rest.

While in that place, we met an Indian who was asking for a pardon for his part of the raid. Later, the Chilean Juan Peña said: "This bad Indian subject assaulted us in Peñehue." If memory serves me correctly, he told us that he had killed his mother and stolen her possessions. "Today you will die," Juan Peña said. He went alongside the Mapuche, took out his gun and fired it. The gun did not discharge. Then, he asked for the shotgun from Juan Aburto, one of the Chileans. Juan Peña fired the gun. The Indian fell to the ground and died instantly.

In addition, Chief Painequeu came to surrender. Juan Peña said again: "These people have invaded Peñehue and I will kill them too." But this time Painemilla did not permit it so Painequeu escaped. . . .

We stayed in the mountains for a long while. Unexpectedly, we encountered fugitives, women, and a few other men. The women stayed with us but cried from fear believing that we were going to kill them. We did not. However, we asked that they give us their silver articles, including the spurs and stirrups that they had brought in great supply. We gave some of our warriors this task and the others gathered the cows and mares that we had.

We returned later to our old camp in Liuco. Half of the booty was handed over to Painemilla. The other half we buried. Painemilla gathered the lot of silver, filled a sack, and watched over it.

A few days ago we left for Quilaco. There we met with Pelquimán, son of Neculmán. In the time his father, he led a great multitude of fighters armed with lances forming Mapuche raiders.

As Neculmán had never realized his goal of defeating the Chileans in Toltén, he sent a message to Imperial, protectorate of Pancho Jaramillo, in order to display his concern. The first half of the message told the Governor: "I did not take part in the rebellion of the caciques, that is why you cannot blame me, my Governor. If you wish, I am ready to help in the retaliation against the chief that started the insurrection."

The Governor agreed and answered Neculmán: "What is done is done. I presume that you are without fault. Punish all those caciques and their fighters and do not get involved in any new conspiracies."

In light of this response, Neculmán put his fighters under the command of his son Pelquimán who would lead the attack. Pelquimán and his armed fighters grouped along a low ridge. We marched the same way and prepared for the attack. But in the end Pelquimán succumbed to the threats, affably greeted Painemilla, and began negotiations. They conversed for a time and we separated. I do not know anything more about the events during the attack.

After the attack, the poor Mapuches no longer possessed houses as they had been reduced to ashes. They remained in a very lamentable state. Thus the insurrection ended. We returned to the land of Rauquenhue never to leave again. We lived there in complete tranquility. We heard that the Chileans of other regions did not tire of hunting down the unfortunate Mapuches.

The chiefs Huichal, Colihuinca, and Juanito Millahuinca addressed themselves to the Governor to ask for a treaty. They brought their saddlebags full of silver objects as requested. But the Governor took the tokens of silver and made shackles for the chiefs. When they were released from prison, they were taken under guard to Boca-Budi. From most accounts it would have been just because these chiefs were the most to blame, especially Colihuinca who had surrendered five Chileans to those who ripped out their live hearts over there on the other side of Carahue.

Marimán, who had killed those men, did not surrender. He fled and remained hidden. Marimán was included in the pardon under the amnesty for the Mapuches that was declared later. . . . When he left his hiding place, he traveled for pleasure and reveled in his friendly relations with the authorities, more than before.

It's been heard said that in Nehuentúe, on the other side of the Cautín River, there was a Chilean by the name of Patricio Rojas. This monster took the Mapuches prisoner and locked them in a hut. Then he set fire to the hut and exterminated the Indians in the flames.

Such was the progress of the Indian uprising in the coastal region. The unfortunate Mapuches went from living in bad conditions to even worse. They had not taken much property from the Chileans, whereas a number of Chileans enriched themselves thanks to the livestock they pillaged from the Mapuches.

STUDY QUESTIONS

1. How did the Mapuche view Chileans, according to Coña?
2. How does Coña's narrative deepen our understanding of indigenous politics, including the existence of intracommunity rivalries and factions?
3. What do we learn about the significance of the war for the Mapuche people?

TERESA GONZÁLEZ DE FANNING

5.4 CONCERNING THE EDUCATION OF WOMEN, 1898

Teresa González de Fanning was a Peruvian writer and intellectual who played a critical role in the promotion of education for women. She founded the Liceo Fanning, one of the first women's colleges in Latin America, to promote scientific education and career preparation for women. Her extensive writings on women's education emphasized the centrality of women's intellectual development to national progress. This excerpt comes from a speech given by González to an audience of elite women in the aftermath of Peru's defeat in the War of the Pacific, and suggests that women's education should be central to the rebuilding of national morale.

As the principal of a girls' school, I have been able to observe the defects from which the education of women suffers in our country; and I am going to take the liberty of pointing out the most significant ones. I hope that the illustrious ladies who make up this respectable audience will take note of my observations and will correct, if they find them just, the dark blemishes which darken the moral beauty of the Peruvian woman.

Nations, like individuals, are exposed to terrible commotions, both in their physical and moral natures. These commotions consume their vital sap and their vigor and endanger their existence. The last war has been for Peru one of those terrible cataclysms that shook the social edifice.

In addition to the loss of so many of its good offspring, a loss that will never be felt enough or mourned enough, a profound malaise has come over the nation, almost a total unhinging of society that alarms the thinkers and the patriots. It seems that defeat, taking away the laurels to which we were entitled—given the justice of our cause—also has taken away our confidence in the highest expectations of the country as well as the energy necessary to realize them.

Dismay and skepticism have taken the place of the faith that multiplies our strength.... But where will the impulse which will lift this prostrated society, which will restore faith to the faithless, and which will resuscitate this Lazarus, come from?

Source: Gertrude M. Yeager (ed.) *Confronting Change, Challenging Tradition: Women in Latin American History*, Jaguar Books on Latin America, Number 7 (Wilmington, Delaware: Scholarly Resources Inc. Imprint), pp. 30–39.

It will seem to you a great audacity that I, small among the lesser ones, will dare to point out a remedy to such a tremendous malady, and that I would raise my voice in this sanctuary of knowledge, in the presence of such eminent patricians, philosophers, and statesmen. But the wisdom of history has shown us how many times. Providence has made us of feeble instruments to realize its loftiest goals.

Ladies and gentlemen, forgive, then, my audacity; excuse it in the name of the good intention that guides me, and allow me to ask you: Do you want to regenerate society? Do you want Peru to rise up powerful and vigorous, supported by its citizens who will enrich it with their virtue and make it occupy the place that it deserves among nations? Well, if you want it, then educate women. As long as there are mothers who do not understand the magnitude of their mission, you will not have citizens who will be able to lift the motherland from the cruel prostration to which it has been reduced by its maladies. And their influence is so significant that you must observe that always, behind a great man, you will find a great woman—call her mother, wife, or sister—who has assisted and encouraged him along the way.

The family is to the state what the waves are to the sea, the roots to the tree, the molecules to the body. Do away with the family and the state will disappear. Thus, it is mandatory that its regeneration should begin with the family. Educate the woman, raise her moral level to make her understand that she is the priestess of good, the worker of the future, and, like a sound wave, her harmonious echo will reverberate in the family and in society, and Peru will be saved.

For many centuries, woman has been the pariah of society. She was considered an agent of the evil genius, an inferior being; it was even doubted that she had a soul, and, consequently, she was found to be the annex of man.

In the ancient countries the birth of a son was a happy event worthy of being celebrated with canticles and solemn ceremonies; yet, the birth of a daughter was the total opposite—it was a curse of affliction and opprobrium of her parents.

In India, according to the sacred book of the Hindu, the woman who only gave birth to girls could be repudiated by her husband. In enlightened Athens, the father to whom a daughter was born manifested his sorrow by hanging on the door of his house a fleece of wool instead of the olive wreath with which he so happily would announce the birth of a son.

The humiliations suffered by a woman at birth were only the prelude to what was to come for the rest of her life, living like a serf, always subject to her father, to her husband, and even to her sons. The day of emancipation never dawned for her.

The Gospel, that wise code of love and fraternity, repaired that secular injustice, replacing woman's dignity as the companion of man, where she had been placed by the Creator. But it is not enough to have broken the chains of the serf to complete her redemption; it is necessary for her to learn the duties that her position demands.

Much has been done in this sense. The most illustrious thinkers of this and the past centuries have given the matter a great deal of thought. The philosopher from Geneva [Rousseau] states in his *Emile*: "Men will always be whatever women want; whoever desires to see great and virtuous men must educate women about greatness and beauty." A noteworthy contemporary writer has said: "The spirit of a people, as well as its traditions, its preoccupations, its virtues, and, better yet, the civilization of humankind—they all rest in the maternal breast."

But why accumulate quotations to convince you of a truth that exists in everybody's conscience? Fortunately, the time when women are considered almost like pieces of furniture has passed. Aside from the barest social rudiments, women were taught the duties of housekeeping when it was thought that the pen would be a dangerous instrument in their hands. An odd aberration made ignorance the safeguard of their innocence.

The time of obscurantism has passed, and today the culture of nations is measured by the degree of the prestige enjoyed by women. Witness to this is the Great American Republic, where not only are they regarded with particular respect, but also they find the same opportunity as men for acquiring knowledge.

Peru has followed this civilizing current. As soon as it joined the ranks of the independent nations, it quickly created schools which, without distinction, admitted both sexes to receive an education.

The large number of matrons and young women who exercise the career of the teacher reflects women's response to this call. Despite the fact that due to a lamentable oversight they have been denied access to higher education, they, nevertheless, by their own efforts are widening their sphere of influence.

Thus, we see that some of them have learned telegraphy, and they are rendering useful services in the government offices. We also see that another of our compatriots, after an excellent study of law, has petitioned Congress to authorize her to receive the degree of doctor of law, while yet another has undertaken a higher education for the purpose of studying the science of Hippocrates [medicine].

All this proves, then, that a positive step has been taken concerning women's instruction. However, you know well, ladies and gentlemen, that we cannot confuse instruction with education, and the latter, which we know is the most important, has followed a wrong path, which has led us astray from our objectives in educating our children. This objective we will say, making use of the expression of a well-learned French writer [Descartes], must not be other than to shape men or women: that is, rational creatures, subservient to duty, lovers of truth who will make full use of their faculties to accomplish their own perfection and be of use to the rest of the people.

Unfortunately, this is not the perspective from which most of our matrons have decided to educate the children that heaven has placed under their maternal aegis. Instead, many of them (this is painful to admit) are not even aware of their important mission, nor do they propose a determined objective for their children. They love their children very much, but their love is expressed in a condescendence that becomes outright weakness because of an excess of pernicious indulgence concerning its physical and spiritual development. Let us demonstrate this.

Hygiene prescribes that a child must receive, methodically and regularly, healthy and substantial nutriment, that excessive spices and stimulating beverages, spirits or alcohol, must be avoided and instead they should be given water and milk as prescribed by nature. The child must also enjoy the fresh morning air and do adequate exercise to develop muscles.

Is this done? Certainly not.

In times past it was accustomed that the children would go to sleep at sundown and would get up at sunrise; today, they stay up like adults, they get up late, feeling lazy and still half asleep, they come to the table where they refuse to eat and do not agree to eat unless they are cajoled and spoiled, and then, they only eat little bits. Because their mothers love them so much, their wishes are granted. Later they will make up for it by eating sweets and unwholesome treats. The result of this is weak, sickly children whose development will later resent this noxious practice which is already contributing to the degeneration of our race.

If we pass from the physical to spiritual education, the soul is saddened by the spectacle presented by our youth. Children who have not even reached adolescence exhibit the vices of old people. What can a country [expect] from a generation that enters life under such deplorable auspices?

Do not let it be said that we exaggerate the malady, because it is found in the churches as well as on the streets, in the classroom as well as at home. Many believe that children up to the age of seven or eight are unconscious beings who must be abandoned to their own devices because they are not responsible for their acts; to proceed otherwise would be to oppress [them] and to deprive them of the joys of childhood. It is claimed that the day will soon come when they will have to go to school, and with that they will have to be subject to a strict discipline. There the teacher will correct the defects derived from the natural disturbances of childhood.

Whoever thinks this way is making a grievous error. The soul of a child is a blank book, where it is up to the father and, more especially, up to the mother to write the first pages, sketching in the process the general outline of the work. When the principles are sound, the job of the teacher is easy and fruitful. On good soil, the good seed will produce a fresh, vigorous plant which will produce abundant fruit. The opposite is like building on sand.

Education must begin with life, and it is the mother, we insist, who is called to fulfill such a delicate mission. It is she who must shape the men of tomorrow, the future citizens, and those who must succeed them in the august priestliness of motherhood. Even when the child is in diapers and his halting tongue cannot express his thoughts without the help of mimicry, he already harbors little passions that time will ripen. The child is susceptible to wrath and envy, to revenge and jealousy. It is human nature which its vices and virtues in germinal form. These are potential assets that, well combined, will produce a felicitous result. That is the task placed on the mother by nature. She must work so all the notes of the instrument will harmonize to produce a perfect combination.

Through example and perseverance, she must modify bad inclinations and strengthen good tendencies; she must be firm and energetic, without being harsh, sweet and benevolent, without being weak. How can it be expected of a child, whose mirror is his mother, to love the truth if he notices that his mother does not do it? How can he be peaceful and tolerant if he receives examples of impatience and wrath? And how many times, instead of correcting bad inclinations, they are unwittingly fomented! How many times is the child incited to revenge, to anger, to lie, and to deceive?

How many times have we seen the case of the child who commits a small, mischievous act and is candidly told, "Is it not true, my little child, that it was So and So who did that?" The child, full of satisfaction, will hurry to answer in the affirmative. Thus, he receives his first lesson as to how one can avoid telling the truth for one's own benefit. Other times, it happens that he hits himself, and then he is asked to beat the object which he hit; he is allowed to savor the forbidden taste of revenge.

Children raised this way become used not to respect what belongs to others and to impose on others their despotic will. This way they are transformed into petty tyrants whose heavy yoke becomes unbearable when time erases the mirth of childlike grace.

A good education for women must have, at its base, religion, morality, and home economics. By a religious education, we understand the practice of a pure and simple Gospel morality, not the exaggerations that exalt the impressionable imagination of the youth and produce those mystical occurrences which are manifestations of more intemperate fanaticism than of sincere piety. This separates them

from society as if from a danger, and often it weakens the family ties that for the common benefit must be strengthened more and more every day. "In the spiritual world, as in the world of matter," says Jules Simon, "there is no progress whose cost is not too high, if it attacks, even slightly, the sacred ties of the family."

Applying this thought to religious education, we can say that if this education attacks the sacred bastion of the family, rendering it apart instead of bringing it together, it has surely deviated from the path prescribed by the Divine Master. The woman must be the sun of her home, she must vivify and stimulate it. In order to do this, she must possess a quality that is innate in her heart, something that mothers must cultivate with particular solicitude: we are talking about *abnegation*.

An egoist man is antipathetic; an egoist woman is a repulsive being, sort of a phenomenon outside the natural order. It is so much a characteristic of a woman to sacrifice herself for the benefit of her people, to spread happiness and comfort around her, to suffer as long as she alleviates the suffering of those close to her, to be the tutelary and providential angel to her children.

Her mission is to console, and she is never more beautiful or angelical than when she sacrifices her pleasure and even her necessary rest in favor of her people. The one who is not ready to sacrifice to fulfill these duties of elementary and sublime Christian charity does this because the poisonous plant of egoism germinates in her soul. To avoid egoism from taking root in the heart of her daughters, those who want to educate them well will never work too much.

A vice that has become infiltrated among us, just as a virus is infiltrated in blood, is the passion of luxury. Young girls enjoy silk and lace in a frightening way. Used to these things from birth, they [silk and lace] become every day more and more of a necessity. What they now demand from their parents will be later demanded from their husbands.

A very discreet lady used to say that "every silk dress means one less boyfriend for the girls." In effect, a young man of modest means who only enjoys a small income cannot take on the ominous burden of setting up a home and keep up the trend to which this woman is used. Some brave souls, who can only see the present, have taken this dangerous road; however, they have soon fallen like the fabled Icarus, and they have seen their jewels and their rich furnishings pass to the hands of the best bidder.

Others, more prudent, or perhaps more depraved, run away from marriages as if from cholera, and instead they create clandestine unions, harming in this manner public morals. The statistical registers furnish depressing numbers about this fact; of the number of children born, the illegitimate children exceed by far the number of legitimate ones. We do not believe that luxury is the only cause generating this occurrence, but it is definitely one of the main reasons.

It is true that in many cases luxury is more apparent than real. It is true that many young women, through dint of hard work and ingenuity, know how to fix themselves up and how to transform, at little cost, their clothes, giving them an air of elegant novelty. For these we only have applause and congratulations, [but,] unfortunately, they are not the majority.

Ordinarily, those fanatical worshippers of luxury and fashion lack even the most essential notion of home economics. We mothers know that they cannot even conceive of how to fix a dress without going to the dressmaker. They, of course, are incapable of adhering to a budget; and, not having enough with their regular income, they must pawn their possessions, with the subsequent loss of the pawned object and the economic instability that this accrues, thus setting the stage for the ruin of the family. Domestic peace cannot resist this hard test. On the contrary, this originates such profound harm that even considering it is frightening. Let us agree that a bad education is at the root of this problem.

We have said it before and we repeat it now: the mother must be the friend and adviser to her daughter, who must hold no secrets from her. Young girls' secrets can be guessed: when the fruit is ready, it tends to come off the tree that supports it. The magical word, hidden impulse that agitates her mind and excites her nervous system, is *love*.

Mothers, do not pretend to go against it, but try to direct it. Steam compressed in excess can blow up the machine; well channeled, it can work wonders. Avoid for your daughters the hidden and precocious escapades, [for] they corrupt the heart and hold a thousand dangers. Let them find through you that they must find a twin soul, a person who will complement their being, for it is a legitimate aspiration, and you will help with your advice.

If you manage to gain their trust, you will save yourselves much grief, and they will avoid many dangers. You will war with the street pirates, that corrupting plague, that leprosy of society that invades avenues and even the divine temples, lying in wait for the innocent. Make them look at love not as the fascinating and romantic mirage that their dreamy fantasy presents to them but as the transcendental act that will decide the happiness or the wretchedness of their whole life. They must not consider themselves the idol that a passionate husband adores perennially but the loving and discreet companion who, with her solicitous and affectionate behavior, will win his love and will make the home thrive.

Prepare them above all so they can face the storms of life. Women do not always get married, and when they get married, because of some predetermined order, they almost always outlive their husbands. In one case or the other, what will be their fate if they do not know how to keep their fortune, if they have it, or to earn a living if they don't?

This is an emergency that must worry parents. Do not raise girls who will grow old without growing up. Educate rational beings, capable of fending for themselves, and capable of facing all types of eventualities. Do not be satisfied with the fact that your daughters know a language halfway, or how to play music, or how to embroider. Put yourself in the situation where they must appeal to their knowledge to take care of their needs. It is a lifesaver which those who cross the stormy sea of life must not lack.

Woman is accused of being frivolous, which does not take into consideration that frivolity is not in her spirit but in the incomplete and superficial education that she receives. For lack of adequate sustenance, her activities and her intelligence are misused in futilities, not unlike the badly prepared vine which is covered with dense foliage, but, instead of the desired fruit, it produces only a few poor clusters of grapes.

STUDY QUESTIONS

1. What connections does González de Fanning draw between the War of the Pacific and the need for women's education? How effective are her arguments?
2. What types of discourses about motherhood are used to argue for women's education? Why does González de Fanning think education will make women more effective mothers, and why is this important? In what other ways will educational opportunities benefit women's lives?
3. What pedagogical elements does she believe should be at the heart of women's education?

FREDERICK UPHAM ADAMS

5.5 THE UNITED FRUIT COMPANY AND THE BANANA INDUSTRY, 1914

American companies played a key role in the massive expansion of agro-export industries in late nineteenth-century and early twentieth-century Latin America, bringing industrial production to tropical zones and creating enclave sectors that were under near-total corporate control. The most prominent of these American agricultural corporations was the United Fruit Company (UFCO). In this excerpt from *Conquest of the Tropics*, a book-length overview of the development of the Central American banana industry first published in 1914, the popular American writer Frederick Upham Adams provides gives a glowing account of the role of the UFCO in bringing bananas to the American consumer and advancing economic prosperity. Adams's travels through Central American banana plantations were sponsored by the UFCO, and his positive vision of the company has been critiqued by more recent generations of historians who have emphasized the brutal labor practices that underpinned the UFCO's economic model.

It is a peculiar and mysterious trait of a considerable portion of the people of the United States that they know little and seem to care little about their national neighbors to the tropical south. This is a regrettable, expensive, and inexcusable fault. Our insular indifference concerning the sentiments, problems, and aspirations of the southern peoples on this continent is construed by them to imply contempt. This has engendered in most of Latin America a feeling of resentment, suspicion, and unfriendliness toward the United States. It certainly is not an asset to acquire and retain the ill-will of those who should be allies with us in ties of friendly intercourse.

The plain truth of the matter is that we have over-cultivated and over-expressed an attitude of self-sufficiency. We are so sure that the United States is the greatest country in the world that we are inclined at times to act as if it were the only country in the world. Some of us are so narrow that we find it impossible to understand why a citizen of the United States cares to live or dares to invest a dollar outside of the confines of this native country. The broad spirit of initiative and enterprise recognizes no national lines.

The commercial conquest by Europe of the tropics of Africa, Asia, and the islands of the Pacific will be recounted by future historians as the monumental

Source: Frederick Upham Adams, *Conquest of the Tropics: The Story of the Creative Enterprises Conducted by the United Fruit Company* (Garden City, New York: Doubleday, Page & Company, 1914), pp. 354–356.

achievement of this age. That development is still in progress. It consists in applying the methods of a high civilization and scientific industry to great tropical sections which have remained undeveloped.

There is one dominant reason why the American tropics have not participated in the stupendous progress of all other tropical sections, and that reason is this: Instability of their governmental conditions has stopped the capital and the enterprise of the world from undertaking the development of their wonderful tropic resources. For this state of affairs the United States is largely to blame. Our national sins are not those of commission, but of omission. We have paid no attention to the welfare of our tropical neighbors for the purely selfish and ignorant reason that we did not consider the matter worth our while.

It has not yet dawned on our political leaders that our tropics are a great but unused asset. We are so accustomed to the careless or wilful destruction of forests and other of our own natural resources that it is a matter of slight interest to us whether our tropical neighbors make a specialty of anarchy or of productive peace. We will one day learn, as financiers already have learned at their bitter cost, that each civilized nation shares in the prosperity or distress of all other nations. We of the United States pay our share of the losses in the periods of lawlessness which blight Mexico and other tropical republics. The revolution, equally with the hurricane which destroys crops in the adjacent tropics, adds to the cost of living of the dwellers in every city, village, and section in the United States. On the other hand, any enterprise or any statesmanship which increases the productivity of these tropical sections adds directly to the assets and welfare of all of the people of the United States.

The United States is and always will be the chief market for the agricultural products of these tropical nations. The United States should supply to them in return the innumerable much needed products of its factories and mills, but even the share of this trade which we now hold will be lost unless we meet this situation with intelligence and sympathy.

. . . There has been inculcated in the public mind an impression that the American who ventures into the tropics is either a fool or knave. It has openly been affirmed by the public men of influence that American citizens have no rights which tropical nations are bound to respect or our Government obligated to protect. If an individual attains in the tropics a measure of success after great risks and hardships, and despite absolute lack of sympathy or support from his home Government or his home people, he is likely to be rewarded with the insinuation that he has "exploited" the tropics and its natives.

It is high time that the sober, thoughtful, and just majority of the America people called a halt on this discrimination against the pioneers in the development of the tropics bisected by the Panama Canal. The day has arrived when we have the choice of accepting and profiting by a legitimate opportunity, or of neglecting it and reaping thereby a harvest of misfortune and a loss of national prestige.

Every American citizen should in this connection know, consider, and profit by the history of the inception and development of the United Fruit Company. It is a story of the peaceful and honorable conquest of a portion of the American tropics, and one of which every citizen should be proud. It is a record of a monumental constructive work performed amid surroundings so difficult that the plain narrative seems more like a romance than the account of deeds actually performed.

. . . The banana, as an article of import and consumption in the United States, is purely a product of what I designate as the Machine. Jefferson and Franklin never had a chance to eat a banana. There did not exist the machinery of production and distribution by which it was possible to raise bananas in commercial quantities in the tropics and transport them to Philadelphia, New York, and Boston and deliver them to our ancestors in an edible condition. Bananas might as well have been solely a product of Mars so far as the people of the temperate zones were concerned.

The mass of the people who lived in the United States in 1870 were as unfamiliar with bananas as they were with electric lights and automobiles. It was known to them that bananas grew in the tropics, but the Machine had not yet been constructed which commercially merged New York, Chicago, and San Francisco with the fertile valleys of Costa Rica and Colombia. If a famine had occurred in the United States in the years prior to the birth of the Age of Invention, it would have been practically impossible to have levied on the fruits of the tropics.

But there is another and equally important reason why the banana could not have been transported from its native tropics and offered at retail prices which would have placed it at the command of the consuming public. There were no industrial enterprises with a capital and a scope fitted to undertake the huge task of producing and importing bananas. Industrial production was still on a small scale, practically local. The revolution which made industry national and international in its scope had not yet occurred. . . .

I retain a fairly vivid recollection of eating my first banana. It was in 1876, and I, then a youngster, was visiting the Centennial Exposition in Philadelphia with my father as guide and treasurer. When a young man, my father had spent some time in the tropical sections of Central America and the West Indies, and I had often heard him talk of revelling in bananas and other fruits of those then fever-stricken districts.

On the afternoon of the day when I encountered my first imported banana we had visited the horticultural department of the great exposition, and there was then pointed out to me one of the leading attractions of that exhibit, a scrubby banana tree from beneath whose fronds actually grew a diminutive bunch of bananas. My recollection is that this was a part of the government exhibit. In any event it was surrounded by a crowd of spectators, most of whom would have been delighted to have plucked a banana, a strip of bark, or even a bit of the earth which surrounded its roots n the huge box which served that purpose. The craze for the collection of "souvenirs," regardless of property rights or possible damage, was then already in vogue, though it had not sunk its victims to such deplorable depths of peculation as at present.

An attendant restrained the bolder of those who longed to touch or dissect this banana tree which was doing its feeble best under artificial conditions far removed from its native habitat. To my young and impressionable mind this was the most romantic of all the innumerable things I had seen in any of the vast buildings. It was the tangible, living, and expressive symbol of the far-distant and mysterious tropics. I had seen pictures of banana trees in text and Sunday-school books, and I had derived from them the pleasing but— as I have since learned—inaccurate information that the fortunate natives of the tropics have nothing to do but roam the flowery glades and live on bananas. I

had no difficulty in picturing such natives lounging beneath the small banana tree now before me, and I conjured from my imagination a boa constrictor emerging from the surrounding jungle and making away with a swarthy savage who was about to pluck his evening meal from the ripened bunch of bananas.

I presume my father was the only one there who had ever seen bananas growing in the tropics. He explained to me the difference between this hot-house product and that of the warm and humid coast lands near the equator, and as he talked the throng gathered about him and asked questions.

The "long arm of coincidence," as literary experts term it, was extended to me that day. On the same evening we took a walk along one of the business streets of Philadelphia. My father was fond of fruits, and he paused at a store and we looked over the tempting array. He was about to buy some peaches, when his attention was diverted to a basket containing small, cylindrical objects wrapped in tin foil.

"What are those?" he asked of the clerk, taking one from the basket and looking at it curiously.

"Bananas," proudly replied the salesman. "Bananas just imported from South America. They are a great luxury, sir, and this is the only place in Philadelphia which handles them."

"Bananas in tin foil!" exclaimed my father. "I presume most of your customers think they grow that way?"

"They are a novelty, sir, and only our best customers call for them. May I wrap up some for you?"

"How much are they?"

"Ten cents apiece, or six for half a dollar."

"That is more money than the native who raised them could earn in a month," laughed my father. "I will take half a dollar's worth."

Back in the room in our hotel I stripped the tin foil from one of them and revealed a substance which looked like the bananas I had seen that afternoon, save that this one was nearly black and the growing ones were green. I was about to bite into the skin when my father interfered and removed the peel, looked at the interior critically and rather doubtfully, tasted it, and gave it to me.

"It is not very good, but it is a banana," he said, peeling one for himself. "How do you like it?"

I assured him that it was delicious, but I presume that the novelty of the thing gave my taste a zest and the fruit a flavor not justified by its condition. Two of the six bananas were in such an advanced stage of decay that they were rejected, but we shared the others. They were small bananas, and it will have taken three of them to make the bulk of one of the delicious yellow bananas now at the cheap command of practically every consumer in the United States.

Thus in 1876 we paid about twenty times the present retail price of bananas, considering the bulk alone. The bananas which we bought and ate as a curiosity would now be condemned by the first food inspector who took a glance at them, but I suffered no harm and fell into pleasant dreams of tropics through which I roamed and ate lavishly of bananas which drooped from graceful trees and asked me to pick them.

We lived in Illinois and it was a number of years before I ever had a chance to see or eat another banana. . . .

In the thirty years which followed this experience I read and heard considerable about bananas. It was not until the middle eighties that we of the Middle West became fairly familiar with the banana as a fruit. The price still made it a luxury, and it occupied the relative position now held by the grapefruit and other tropical or subtropical products which have established their places in our ever-increasing national menu. . . .

The banana will never enjoy the popularity it deserves until the people of the temperate zones learn to know when it is ripe, and learn to not eat it in its raw state. There is popular delusion that the banana has ripened when it turns from its original green to a golden yellow, and those thus deluded decline to touch this fruit when dark spots appear in the yellow skin of the banana.

The banana is not fully ripe when it is yellow. This change from green to yellow is the first outward appearance of a chemical process incidental to the ripening process. Not until a considerable portion of the skin has turned to a deep brown has this ripening process sufficiently developed to give the fruit its greatest value as a delicious and a healthful food. A writer in a recent number of the *Journal of the American Medical Association* brought this fact out clearly when he said:

"The dictum that fruits should be eaten 'in their season' finds its limitations as regards variety in the temperate zones at certain periods of the year. There is, however, one fruit which is readily available fresh in the American markets at practically all seasons. It is unfortunate that an article of diet which meets nutritive requirements so well and so easily obtainable at reasonable cost as the banana should be the subject of so much misunderstanding among both physicians and laymen. For, despite the fact that over 40,000,000 bunches are reported to have been brought to the United States last year, it is popularly stated in many quarters that the banana is difficult of digestion and may gave rise to alimentary distress.

"The fruit is brought to our northern markets green, and is ripened by artificial heat. The color of the peel gives evidence of the degree of ripeness. The green banana contains, in the part exclusive of the skin, about 1.5 per cent of protein and 20 to 25 per cent of carbohydrate, almost entirely starch. In the ripe banana with the yellow-brown peel the edible part contains somewhat less carbohydrate; but that which remains is now almost entirely in the form of soluble sugars. Broadly speaking, then, the ripe banana is about one-fifth sugar; the green, one-fifth starch.

"Inasmuch as bananas are commonly eaten uncooked, it is obvious that more or less raw starch will be ingested if the fruit is not ripe, i.e., if the skin has not begun to shrivel and darken. No one would advise the use of uncooked potatoes; yet many people eschew a thoroughly ripe banana in the belief that this wholesome fruit is 'rotten' when the skin becomes darkened, whereas they eagerly eat the yellow-green starch-bearing fruit at its stage of incomplete ripeness."

It is entirely different matter when the green or semi-ripe banana is cooked. The application of heat renders the pulp nutritious and readily digestible, and the tropical natives prepare many delicious dishes by baking green bananas in ashes.

The *Magazine of the Housewives' League* discusses the food value of bananas entertainingly in a recent article, from which the following extracts are selected:

"The food value of the banana, long known in tropical countries, has within the past twenty years begun to be more highly appreciated by the masses of the northern countries, and the following facts, collated from the authoritative sources, will indicate the progress made by science and commerce in familiarizing the people living outside of tropical countries with its value as a foodstuff.

"From a sanitary point of view, the banana is superior to many other fruits. Exposed on stands on the street, in fruit stores and otherwise, by reason of the fact that it is always first peeled to get at the edible portion, it escapes all forms of germ life communications either by the air or contact with polluted substances. The skin of the fresh apple is generally eaten, with the risk of dirt and disease, by the ordinary people. Cooked the baked apple is open to the same objection—and the same facts apply to many other forms of fruit in a greater or less degree.

"For further comparison, the following table has been prepared by the Government:

	Bananas	Porterhouse Steak
Price per pound	.07 cents	25.00 cents
Cost of 100 calories	23.30 cents	22.50 cents
Energy—		
Total weight of food material	1.43 lbs.	.40 lbs.
Fuel value, calories	429.00 lbs.	444.00 lbs.

"This table indicates that the most strenuous form of labor can be supported by a banana diet equally as well as by the highest class meat diet. It is a well-established fact that in the States of Parana and Santa Catarina, Brazil, the entire population subsists exclusively on bananas as a good, and coffee as a drink; and these sections are famous for the strength and endurance of their laboring classes.

HOW TO COOK BANANAS

As has been explained, the banana should not be eaten raw until its yellow peel is mottled with brown. It is then not only readily digestible but delicious. On account of its natural protection from contamination, it has well been said that "The banana was put up and sealed by nature in a germ-proof package," and so long as that package is intact the banana itself furnishes absolute guarantee that it is a pure food.

Professional chefs and amateur cooks are constantly finding new ways to cook bananas. Here are a few recipes which have attained wide popularity:

BANANA FRITTERS

One-half cup of flour, one-quarter cup of cold water, one egg beaten, one-fourth teaspoon of melted butter, one pinch of baking powder.

Beat the yolk of the egg; add the water, and stir in the flour; add the salt, baking powder, and melted butter, then the white of the egg whipped to a stiff froth.

Put sliced bananas into this batter and fry. About three or four slices should be incorporated in each fritter. When done, dredge with powdered sugar and serve hot.

FRIED BANANAS

Select firm and rather slender fruit; peel and cut into sections about three inches long. Fry in hot butter, and, as the bananas cook, sprinkle with a little sugar, and roll about carefully in the frying pan until a light brown all over. Dish, pouring over any butter and sugar remaining in the pan. Serve very hot.

BANANA CROQUETTES

Peel the bananas, cut into short lengths, round the cut edges, dip in beaten egg, roll in sifted crumbs, and fry until tender and brown. Serve hot with any kind of roast meat.

BANANAS WITH BACON OR HAM

Prepare fruit as above. Cook in the same manner, using bacon or ham fat in place of butter, and serve on the platter with broiled bacon or ham. This dish, with a salad, makes an exceedingly good luncheon.

GELATINE OF BANANAS

Make a lemon, an orange or wine jelly, according to the rule for the kind of gelatine used. Mould this with sliced bananas only, or with oranges, white grapes, a few figs cut up, nuts, or any mixture liked.

Turn out and serve with whipped cream.

BANANA SHORTCAKE

When berries or fresh peaches are out of season, use sliced bananas between and on top of layers of shortcake.

Add the fruit the moment before serving, as the heat will discolor the fruit if allowed to stand after slicing when uncooked.

SPICED BANANAS

Stir gently thick slices of bananas in a syrup flavored with cinnamon, cloves, and a very little mace.

BANANA LOAF

Take a small loaf of sponge cake or angel food, and cut a well in the centre. Fill with sliced bananas and heap with whipped cream sweetened to taste.

BANANA CAKE

Bake a sponge cake or a plain cup cake in two layers.

Just before serving, put freshly sliced bananas between and on top of the layers of cake. Cover the top thickly with whipped cream and serve at the table in wedge-shaped pieces.

BANANA ICE CREAM

One quart of cream. One cup of sugar, pulp of five or six bananas, juice of one lemon, a pinch of salt.

Heat the cream with three-fourths of the sugar. Let it cool. Peel the bananas, split and remove the seeds and dark spots; rub through a sieve; add salt, lemon juice, and the fourth of a cup of sugar. Mix with the chilled cream and freeze at once.

BANANA BAVARIAN CREAM

One pint of cooked banana pulp sweetened, one-half box of granulated gelatine, one-half pint of cold water, one pint of cream.

Stew ripe bananas in a little water until there is a pint of pulp. Sweeten to taste. Soak the gelatine in the cold water. When thoroughly dissolved, beat through the pulp and stand in cracked ice, and stir until it begins to thicken.

Add the cream whipped very stiff, and a cup of chopped nuts. Put in a mould to harden. To serve, turn on a platter, surrounded with whipped cream, dotted with maraschino cherries.

Thus we see that the banana is a fruit, a food, a drink, a breakfast dish, a dessert, a confection, and a medicine. It shares with bread the distinction of a staff of life, and is a welcome addition to the menu of the affluent.

Created into an industry by the men who founded and who have made of the United Fruit Company a mighty enterprise, the banana has bequeathed to the United States a vast extension of its commerce, and has pointed the sure and honorable way for the further peaceful conquest of the American tropics. It already has taken a place as a fixture in our social economy, but it is destined to a much higher rank in the future as a factor in promoting the health, happiness, and prosperity of hundreds of millions of people who were strangers to this tropical fruit-food only a short generation ago. The United Fruit Company is more than a corporation. It is an institution, an American institution founded by certain of its citizens and conducted with a broadness of policy and an industrial statesmanship which lift it out of the class of mere money making profit and hunting corporations. It is doing for the American tropics and the American people what the Hudson Bay Company did for the British Empire in the frozen north of Canada. It has awakened the slumbering nations bordering on the Caribbean with the quickening tonic of Yankee enterprise. It has proved to the world that these tropics can be converted from a harassing liability into an asset of stupendous value, and it has solved for the world the problem of transforming deadly swamps and jungles to gardens on which can be raised the food products demanded to keep pace with the ever-increasing hunger of the city-house multitudes.

STUDY QUESTIONS

1. What does Adams see as the economic benefit of the development of tropical agriculture to the United States and Central America respectively?
2. Why does Adams have such strong memories of his first taste of a banana? How does the romanticization of bananas help us understand US neoimperialism in Latin America?
3. What can we learn about UFCO marketing efforts in the United States from the nutritional information and banana recipes Adams provides?

WEST INDIAN STRIKE COMMITTEE, LIMÓN, COSTA RICA

5.6 NOTICE TO WEST INDIAN FARMERS!

The creation of enclave economies in the tropical zones of Central America was accompanied by extensive migration from the British West Indies. American companies preferred English-speaking workers, while the scientific racism that was dominant in this period held that Black people were the best suited to manual labor in tropical environments. The United Fruit Company (UFCO) imported large numbers of British Caribbean workers to their plantations in Cuba and Central America, developing a system of ethnic differentiation—using workers from different ethnic backgrounds for different types of tasks—to undermine labor solidarity. In the Costa Rican province of Limòn, one of the earliest UFCO enclaves, Jamaican workers came to form a noteworthy middle class in the early twentieth century through a system of sharecropping that allowed some West Indians to serve as peasant smallholders who grew their own bananas and sold them to the UFCO. This set them apart from the mestizo and indigenous Costa Ricans and Panamanians who formed the bulk of the plantation workers on UFCO estates. This flyer was produced by a West Indian leadership committee during one of the many labor strikes against the UFCO in the 1920s and 1930s. It highlights the tensions that formed between different labor groups and the way in which the UFCO was able to play workers against each other to the company's own advantage.

NOTICE

—TO—

WEST INDIAN FARMERS!

Fellow Country Men;
Greeting:—

We beg to call your attention to the movement now on foot, that if you allow yourselves to be intimidated by self-seeking people, who are against the colour people and refuse to cut the fruit from your farms, we are the ones who will suffer, our wives and children will starve.

Remember for years we have been working in harmony with the Co. and they have always treated us right, now is the time for us to prove that we are no cowards, your fruit is your own property. Allow no one to prevent you from cutting same for delivery to the Co. Awake your own interest. This is not a strike, but a dangerous movement to destroy the Banana industry of Costa Rica.

Remember brothers, if there is no fruit there will be no jobs for any of us. The Co. can send their ships to other countries to obtain fruit, whilst yours will rot on the farm and everybody will suffer.

If we have no Bananas, there will be no ships, no machine shop, no trains, no commissaries and everything will be at a stand-still.

The Government has offered you protection. This movement is only to scare you. Don't be afraid to cut your fruit.

THE WEST INDIAN COMMITTEE
Express Priority
(Archivo Nacional de Costa Rica)

Source: Archivo Nacional de Costa Rica.

STUDY QUESTIONS

1. What arguments does the flyer use to suggest that the strike is against the interests of the West Indian community?
2. Try and read "between the lines" of the source to find windows into the wider context in which it was produced. Is there evidence, for example, of UFCO influence in the creation of the flyer? Do we see any cracks in the unity of the West Indian community vis-à-vis the strike?

CHANNING ARNOLD AND FREDERICK J. TABOR FROST

5.7 MAYAN WORKERS IN YUCATAN, MEXICO, 1909

The period under the dictatorship of Porfirio Diaz in Mexico (1876–1911) was one of political repression and frenzied economic growth. These twin currents had devastating impacts on worker rights and working conditions, especially for indigenous peoples. Some of the most notorious abuses were to be found in the Yucatan region, where indigenous Mayans were forced into debt servitude and subjected to corporal punishment. In this excerpt the British travel writers Channing Arnold and Frederick Frost present their observations of a visit by Porfirio Diaz to henequen plantations in Yucatan in 1909. Henequen is an agave plant, used to make rope, twine and paper, and was intensively produced on large plantations in this period.

The Indian harvest is about our Christmas time, and the labourers troop into the milpas, wicker baskets slung on their brown backs, and pick the cobs, dropping them over their shoulders into the baskets. Milpas are seldom of any great size, and the harvester usually carries his load back to the hacienda when he returns thither for his first real meal of the day, which he takes between ten and eleven. His menu is of the simplest, monotonously the same from year end to year end; just that fare upon which his lowlier ancestors toiled in the sun to build pyramid and temple. Black beans, always black beans; sometimes crushed into a purple-black pulp, sometimes frizzled in lard, sometimes with a thin vegetable soup, the stock,—pork, peppers, garlic, and a slice or two of pumpkin gourd. To this staple dish of frijoles there is very seldom added any meat save when he has been able to bag a chachalaka on his tramp to the milpas or a hacienda pig has been killed. Tortillas and coffee, not always the latter, complete his meal. Before the hour of noon he is back at his work till about five, when his day's labour is over.

There is no hardship in all this. It is just the simple life his race has always lived, and that which the average Mayan always would wish to live. There would be no hardship if—and it is a large, large IF—the patient toiler were a free man. The Yucatecans have a cruel proverb, *"Los Indios no oigan sino por las nalgas"* ("The Indians can hear only with their backs"). The Spanish

Source: Channing Arnold and Frederick J. Tabor Frost, *The American Egypt: A Record of Travel in Yucatan* (London: Hutchinson and Co, 1909), pp. 324–333.

half-breeds have taken a race once noble enough and broken them on the wheel of a tyranny so brutal that the heart of them is dead. The relations between the two peoples is ostensibly that of master and servant; but Yucatan is rotten with a foul slavery—the fouler and blacker because of its hypocrisy and pretence.

The peonage system of Spanish America, as specious and treacherous a plan as was ever devised for race-degradation, is that by which a farm labourer is legally bound to work for the land-owner, if in debt to him, until that debt is paid. Nothing could sound fairer: nothing could lend itself better to the blackest abuse. In Yucatan every Indian peon is in debt to his Yucatecan master. Why? Because every Indian is a spendthrift? Not at all; but because the master's interest is to get him and keep him in debt. This is done in two ways. The plantation-slave must buy the necessaries of his humble life at the plantation store, where care is taken to charge such prices as are beyond his humble earnings of sixpence a day. Thus he is always in debt to the farm; and if an Indian is discovered to be scraping together the few dollars he owes, the books of the hacienda are "cooked,"—yes, deliberately "cooked,"—and when he presents himself before the magistrate to pay his debt, say, of twenty dollars (£2) the hacienda can show scored against him a debt of fifty dollars. The Indian pleads that he does not owe it. The haciendado-court smiles. The word of an Indian cannot prevail against the Señor's books, it murmurs sweetly, and back to his slave-work the miserable peon must go, first to be cruelly flogged to teach him that freedom is not for such as he, and that struggle as he may he will never escape the cruel master who under law as at present administered in Yucatan has a complete a disposal of his body as of one of the pigs which root around in the hacienda yard.

It is only by a comparison of the law of debt in Yucatan for a white man, as the Yucatecans love to call themselves, that one can realise how wickedly unjust all this is, and how deliberate is the conspiracy to keep the Indian in a bondage which spells fortune to his master. For the Yucatecan debtor there appears to be no punishment and no means of compelling him to pay. Here is a case in point. To a store in Merida comes a Yucatecan who, falsely representing himself as employed by one of the richest of Meridan merchant-houses, gets a typewriting machine valued at two hundred and twenty-five dollars, on credit. He goes off with it, and at once sells it. For thus obtaining money by false pretences he is not punished, nor can the defrauded shopkeeper recover his goods or their value except by tedious process which will cost him more than he has already lost, even if he wins the day. Now, had this thief been an Indian, he could have been instantly arrested, his debt sold by the shopman to any haciendado, and the fellow would have become a slave for life. Thus is law meted out by the Yucatecan conspirators.

The Yucatecan millionaires are very sensitive on the question of slavery, and well they may be: for their record is as black as Legree's in *Uncle Tom's Cabin*. You have but to mention the word "slavery," and they begin a lot of cringing apologetics as to the comforts of Indians' lives, the care taken of them, and the fatherly relations existing between the haciendado and his slaves. Very *fatherly* indeed, as we shall shortly demonstrate! They take just so much care of the Indians as reasonably prudent men always take of their live stock; so much and no more.

We have spoken earlier of the recent visit paid to the country by President Diaz. It was the first time during the whole of his long reign that the great man had troubled himself about the limestone peninsula which forms the furthermost eastern part of his dominions, and the trembling Yucatecans looked to the bolts of the cupboard in which the family skeleton was hidden, and they were not over-satisfied with those bolts. They had new locks made and new and thicker doors fixed so that august presidential ears should not be offended by the rattling of those most unfortunate bones. With their teeth chattering, they hastened to put their house in order and sweep and garnish it, for they knew quite well that the eyes into which they had to throw dust were eyes which could see further than most eyes. It was all the fault of a snobbish governor. Many a henequen lord must have cursed the self-importance of their parvenu chief which had induced in him such discontent with the Spartan-like simplicity of his rule at Merida that he must needs wish to entertain presidential guests and bask in the sunshine of the mighty Diaz's approval. Dias, they knew very well, cared little or nothing for Indians *qua* Indians. But Diaz care immensely about the fair name of Mexico, which they knew they had done for years all they could to besmirch. Would he see the skeleton through the fatal door? If money and bribery were of any avail, those slave-owners would see to it that their terrible ruler should be fooled. But they had to calculate on more than his natural perspicacity. There was much reason to believe that ugly rumors had reached Mexico City of the slavery rife in the Yucatan, and that the President's visit was not unconnected with these. That skeleton must be cemented into its cupboard with the cement of millions of dollars if necessary.

Well, the President came. Never were there such junketings: night was turned into day; roadways were garlanded; gargantuan feasts were served. Lucullus never entertained Caesar with more gorgeous banquets than the henequen lords of Merida spread before Diaz. Small fortunes were spent on single meals. One luncheon party cost 50,000 dollars: a dinner cost 60,000, and so on. The official report of the reception reads like a piece out of the *Arabian Nights*. In their eagerness to keep that skeleton in its cupboard some of the haciendados actually mortgaged their estates. One of the most notable of the entertainments provided was that of a luncheon at a hacienda ninety miles south-east of the city of Merida. At the station where the President alighted for the drive to the farm, the roadway was strewn with flowers. Triumphal arches of flowers and laurels, of henequen, and one built of oranges surmounted by the national flag, spanned the route. The farm-workers lined the avenue of nearly two miles to the house, waving flags and strewing the road with flowers, while a *feu-de-joie* of signal rockets was fired on his alighting from his carriage. He then made a tour of the farm. Having inspected the henequen machinery he (we quote from the official report) "visited the hospital of the finca, and the large chapel where the Catholic labourers worshipped; the gardens and the beautiful orchard of fruit trees; and during his tour of inspection he honoured several labourers by visiting their huts thatched with palm-leaf and standing in their own grounds well cultivated by the occupants. More than two hundred such houses constitute the beautiful village of this hacienda, which breathes an atmosphere of general happiness. Without doubt a beautiful spectacle is offered to the visitor to this lovely finca with its straight roads, its pretty village clustering round the central building surrounded by gardens of flower and fruit trees."

At the luncheon the President in the course of his speech said:—"Only can a visitor here realise the energy and perseverance which, continued through so many years, has resulted in all I have seen. Some writers who do not know this country, who have not seen, as I have, the labourers, have declared Yucatan to be disgraced with slavery. Their statements are the grossest calumny, as is proved by the very faces of the labourers, by their tranquil happiness. He who is a slave necessarily looks very different from those labourers I have seen in Yucatan." The prolonged cheers and measureless enthusiasm evoked by these words (one can understand how the conspirators chuckled at the success of their efforts at deception) were agreeably interrupted by the appearance of an old Indian, who made a speech of welcome in his own language, presenting a bouquet of wild flowers and a photographic album filled with views of the hacienda. It is not necessary to quote the fulsome stuff which had been placed in the mouth of the poor old man by his master. It is simply a string of meaningless compliments which ends with these words: "We kiss your hands; we hope that you may live many years for the good of Mexico and her States, among which is proud to reckon itself the ancient and indomitable [surely a pathetic adjective under the circumstances] land of the Mayans." Well may the official report say that "it is only justice to declare that the preparations of the feast and the decorations of the finca showed that the proprietor had been anxious to prepare everything with the most extraordinary magnificence."

This feast was a gigantic fraud, a colossally impertinent fake from start to finish. Preparations indeed! That is the exact word to describe the lavish entertainments of Mexico's ruler here and elsewhere in Yucatan. Tens of thousands of dollars were lavished to guard the haciendados' secrets. In this particular case the huts of the Indian labourers which the President visited were "fake" huts. They had been, every one of them, if not actually built for the occasion, cleaned, whitewashed, and metamorphosed beyond recognition. They had been furnished with American bentwood furniture. Every Indian matron had been given a sewing-machine; every Indian lass had been trimmed out with finery and in some cases, it is said, actually provided with European hats. The model village round which the President was escorted was the fraud of a day; no sooner was his back turned than to the shops of Merida were returned sewing-machines, furniture, hats and everything, and the Indians relapsed again into that simplicity of furnitureless life which they probably cordially preferred.

We are not quoting the "faking" of this village as an example of hardship dealt out to the Indians, but as a proof of the ludicrous efforts made by those whose fortunes have been and are being built on slave labour to hide the truth from General Diaz. As for the poor old Mayan who addressed him, and as for the deputations of whip-drilled Indians who were paraded before him to express their untold happiness and loyalty, they very well knew that they had got to do exactly what they were told to do. We are not exaggerating when we state that it would have cost any Indian his life to have even attempted to make General Diaz aware of the truth. No Indian throughout civilised Yucatan could have been found to make the attempt. For nothing is sadder than the lack of all manliness and spirit which characterises the average Indian workman. It is the story of the Russian moujik over again. There is no combination or loyalty to each other among the hacienda Indians; and this is what makes possible what we are about to relate.

If the hardship of the Indians' lot was merely slavery, it might be argued that there were slender grounds for our indictment. Slavery may under certain circumstances be far from an evil, where the backward condition of a race is such as to justify its temporary existence, and where the slave-owner can be trusted. But the slave-owner can very seldom be trusted, and he certainly cannot be in Yucatan. It is no exaggeration to say that the enslavement of the Indians of Yucatan never has had, never can have, justification. Conceived in an unholy alliance between the Church and brute force, it has grown with the centuries into a race-degradation which has as its only objects the increasing of the millions of the slave-owners and the gratification of their foul lusts. The social condition of Yucatan to-day represents as infamous a conspiracy to exploit and prostitute a whole race as the history of the world affords. Yucatan is governed by a group of millionaire monopolists whose interests are identical, banded together to deny all justice to the Indians, who, if need be, are treated in a way an Englishman would blush to treat his dog. "The Indians hear only with their backs." Yes, but the ill-treatment of the poor wretches often does not end with a whipping: it ends in murder. We will give particulars of some cases.

Some years ago an Indian was thrashed to death on the estate of the brother of a high official in Yucatan. The body was easily disposed of, buried at night like a dog's. But some of his fellow-workmen talked, it seems, and news of the crime found its way to the capital. There a young lawyer, Perez Escofee, indignant at the report, took a solicitor down to the hacienda and got from some of the Indians affidavits as to their knowledge of the murder. Armed with these he published the facts in the Merida newspaper, demanding an investigation. The haciendado concerned sent his solicitor down and obtained from the very Indians sworn contrary statements. On these Perez, his adviser, and the editor who had had the courage to publish Escofee's first appeal, were arrested and thrown into prison. That is three years and more ago, and Escofee and his lawyer were still in Merida prison without trial at the time of our visit, if our information be correct. The haciendado's family dares not allow, and has so far proved powerful enough to prevent, a trial. The third man was liberated owing to very influential friends who threatened exposure if he were not released.

Another loathsome case was that of the beating to death of an Indian girl of eleven by her old Yucatecan mistress. The poor child had been guilty of some trifling disobedience, and the murderess, having plenty of money, had no difficulty in getting an order for burial, the death being announced as due to pneumonia. The truth would never have come out but for the prattling of the granddaughter of this human beast who, child-like, told some neighbors. Yucatecan mistresses beat their Indian servants mercilessly for slight faults; but it will scarcely seem credible to English readers that Yucatecans are so lost to all sense of manliness that they, too, are often guilty of the basest cruelty towards the women servants. We heard of one case where a Yucatecan, because the Indian girl was a little late in bringing him his early breakfast of milk and bread, threw in her face the jug of boiling milk, and beat her over the head with the long stick of crusty roll till she was unconscious. For such cowardly curs there is no punishment. In this case the poor girl confessed to a friend that for days she had murder in her heart, and this feeling of revenge worried her so that at last she went to the priest for advice. That worthy told her she must be docile: that she must submit herself in all things to her master. This is really the worst feature of the conspiracy to degrade the Indians, the part the Church plays. The priests back up the haciendados in everything because it is from them they get their money.

Another outrageous case was that in which a very rich Yucatecan was concerned. Because his Indian driver did not go quick enough to please him, he thrashed him into unconsciousness in the street, and afterwards had him put in prison on some trumped-up charge for six months. This case, however, was so public, that the family found it necessary to come to terms with the injured man.

It would not be at all true to say that the Indians are often beaten to death. Labour is far too scarce in Yucatan. A perfect network of regulations and laws are in force on all the haciendas to keep the Indians. The unfortunate wretches are absolutely essential to the fortune-getting of the Yucatecans, and are far too precious to be recklessly killed off. The haciendas are regarded as excellent breeding grounds for new generations of slaves. Thus a rule is that no Indian of either sex shall marry off the hacienda. The real truth is that the Indians are nothing but cattle, and just as much the property of their masters as the heifers in a farm-yard in England belong to the farmer. To a friend of ours an Indian came, saying he owed his master one hundred dollars, and begging that his debt might be paid and the he might come to work for him. Well, our friend agreed to pay his debt. Then round comes the master to say that the man really owed him three hundred and forty dollars—which of course was a lie, to be supported, if need be, by forged entries in the hacienda books. He further says he will not accept payment, as he wishes to get the man back and whip him publicly to make an example of him. The man said he would rather die than go back; and it ended by the master, fearful lest the slave should kill himself,

selling him for his debt to another haciendado, who, in turn, would get all the work he could get out of the poor devil. Thus, though there is no open slave market in Merida, these cowardly slave-owners traffic in their slaves at their own free will, and there is literally no escape for the Indians.

There are three reasons for the continuance of this cruel system. First, the prostitution of the Church to the haciendados. Superstitious to a degree remarkable even among the many semi-civilised peoples who have been victimised by Catholicism, the Mayans look to their priests as semi-divinities whose word is law; and a debauched priesthood, eager to make friends with the Mammon of Unrighteousness, and themselves unscrupulous in self-indulgence, greedily support slavery.

Secondly, the lack of loyalty among the Indians to each other. This is the natural effect of the centuries of oppression which they have endured. All the manliness of the race, all the spirit and nobility of a nature which wrung a tribute even from Spanish historians, have been effectually crushed out of them. This is indeed the saddest side of it all. The Yucatecan bullies have done their work so well that if the Indians of all the haciendas could be asked whether they were contented, a large majority, possibly almost all, would alphabetically declare themselves content. They are like prisoners who have been so long in the gloom of a dungeon that they would be actually terrified of the sunshine.

And thirdly, the water supply is an enormous auxiliary in the maintaining of the present disgraceful state of affairs. As we have said, there are no rivers in Yucatan, and the only water available is that obtained from the cenotes or wells attached to the haciendas. Practically you may say that the whole water supply of the country is in the hands of the landlords. To leave one farm would only mean going to another for the miserable serf. Each haciendado helps every other in keeping the slaves on the places. Thus, turn where he may, the Indian has no refuge but the woods, from which he would be hunted with dogs just as Mrs. Beecher Stowe has told us was always done in the South.

He submits to his fate; but hard as we have shown that to be, there is worse to be told. A slave, with a wage which is a mockery, a pittance, given really to make more plausible the case of his master, he must see his daughters submit to a systematic tyranny of lust which is really so base that it is difficult to write of it in calm language. Here in Yucatan every sexual horror which is the story of the South in the 'sixties horrified the world is reproduced, cloaked by the foulest hypocrisy. The Indian from her childhood up is the prey of the haciendado and his sons. From their foul clutches she cannot escape. If her father had, poor devil, any scruples left, he must stifle them or be prepared to risk his life by objecting. As a matter of fact, so immoral and degraded have almost all the hacienda Indians become, that objections to this *droit du Seigneur*, this *Jus Primae Noctis*, are almost unheard of. We are not writing without weighing our words carefully when we say that there are farms in plenty where the slave-owner demands as part of his serfs' obligations the right to every lass as soon as she enters on womanhood, sometimes much before. He demands it, and he does what he will with these children, for they are usually little else; and there is no remedy for the parents.

Inconceivable cynicism is the attitude of all Yucatecans towards sexual excesses. The young sons of fourteen and upwards are not restrained from, indeed they are often actually encouraged by fathers and even mothers in, indulging their boyish passions at the expense of the little Indian slave-girls. It is no answer to say, as some Yucatecans do, that the girls are in very many cases more than willing victims of their boy-lovers. Yucatecan lads are notably handsome, and even maids of the cold North would find it hard to withstand their wooing. It remains the fact that these youthful Don Juans in many cases do not woo at all. They command; and the girl-child must go at night to the boy's room or be cruelly beaten by him till she surrenders. If she plucked up courage to complain to her mistress, she would be simply laughed at. She is but a little slave-girl. What better fate could she ask for herself than to have thus early attracted the notice of the lad who will some day be her owner? And if a child results, why, it is but one more hacienda baby, brought up with the rest. No one cares; and if it be a girl, why then in the fullness of years it will most probably attract the notice of its own father, who by that time will have inherited the estates. The girl would not know, and dare not disobey if she did; and it is quite certain the man by that time would have ruined so many Indian girls that he would be past any sensitiveness where his self-gratifications were concerned. It is possible that the reader will by this time be willing to acquit us of any unfairness of which we may have seemed guilty in Chapter IV., when we divided the population of so-called civilised Yucatan into "Savages" and "Slaves."

As a rule it may be said that the Yucatecan is a benevolent master. It pays him better to be so, and every Yucatecan's one rule in life is to do what pays him. Indeed there is really no reason for him to be harsh. The average Indian is as submissive as a well-whipped hound, creeping up after a thrashing to kiss his master's hand. This Stephens actually witnessed, and the miserable slaves are always made to do it. He seldom disobeys: he works uncomplainingly all his life for no pay; and he breeds pretty daughters for his lord's gratification. The Yucatecan would indeed be hard to please if he quarrelled with such an exemplary beast of burden. And the habit of submission learnt through centuries of tyranny has affected the Mayan women. They exhibit a complacency towards their Yucatecan lovers which suggests, what alas! cannot be denied, that chastity means little to them to-day.

STUDY QUESTIONS

1. How is President Diaz received during his visit to Yucatan? How does Diaz present the conditions he encounters?
2. Why do Arnold and Frost argue that the visit is a fraud? How reliable are their observations?
3. What can we learn from the source about the experience of Mayan workers on Mexican haciendas in this period?

W. E. HARDENBURG

5.8 ABUSES IN THE PERUVIAN RUBBER INDUSTRY, 1912

The Amazonian Rubber Boom gave rise to appalling abuses of indigenous peoples. The boom occurred in reaction to the invention of rubber tires for the newly created motor car. Rubber trees grew wild in the Amazon, but indigenous knowledge was needed to find and access the latex within the trees. In this isolated environment, foreign corporations used violent tactics to coerce indigenous labor. The most notorious of these rubber corporations was the Peruvian Amazon Rubber Company, owned by a Peruvian trader named Julio Cesar Arana and financed by British merchants on the London stock exchange. In 1909 the American engineer Walter Hardenberg wrote an exposé of the labor tactics used by the Aranas, accusing them of enslaving the indigenous peoples and subjecting them to corporal and capital punishment, as well as sexual abuse. Hardenburg's account was borne out in a 1910 investigation by the British Consulate, led by Sir Roger Casement, and historians and anthropologists now refer to the Peruvian Amazon Rubber Company as having perpetrated a genocide against the Bora, Witote, and Andoke people. This excerpt comes from a 1912 book published by Hardenburg about his experiences in the Peruvian Amazon. The book was widely read in Britain and the United States and the publicity led to criminal proceedings against the Board of Directors of the Peruvian Amazon Company in London.

Another edifying spectacle that we witnessed was the condition of the poor Indians who loaded and unloaded the vessels that stopped at the port. There were from fifty to sixty of these unfortunates, so weak, debilitated, and scarred that many of them could hardly walk. It was a pitiful sight to see almost protruding through their skins, and all branded with the infamous *marca de Arana*,[1] staggering up the steep hill, carrying upon their doubled backs enormous weights of merchandise for the consumption of their miserable oppressors. Occasionally one of these unfortunate victims of Peruvian "civilisation" would fall under his load, only to be kicked up on his feet and forced to continue his stern labours by the brutal "boss."

I noticed the food they received, which was given to them once a day at noon; it consisted of a handful of *farina* and a tin of sardines—when there were any—for each group of four Indians, nothing more. And this was to sustain them for twenty-four hours, sixteen of which were spent at the hardest kind of labour!

But what was still more pitiful was to see the sick and dying lie about the house and out in the adjacent woods, unable to move and without any one to aid

---

1   The scars on their backs from floggings, called so after Julia C. Arana, the organiser and chief stock-holder of the Peruvian Amazon Company.

Source: a) W. E. Hardenburg, *The Putumayo: The Devil's Paradise: Travels in the Peruvian Amazon Region and an Account of the Atrocities Committed upon the Indians Therein* (London: T. Fisher Unwin; Adelphi Terrace, Leipsic: Inselstrasse, 1912), pp. 180–186; b) Chained Indian Rubber Gatherers in the Stocks: On the Putumayo River; frontispiece; c) An Incident of the Putumayo, p. 53; d) A Huitoto Indian Rubber Gatherer, p. 152.

them in their agony. These poor wretches, without remedies, without food, were exposed to the burning rays of the vertical sun and the cold rains and heavy dews of early morning until death released them from their sufferings. Then their companions carried their cold corpses—many of them in an almost complete putrefaction—to the river, and the yellow, turbid waters of the Caraparaná closed silently over them.

Another sad sight was the large number of involuntary concubines who pined—in melancholy sufferings—in the interior of the house. This band of unfortunates was composed of some thirteen young girls, who varied in age from nine to sixteen years, and these poor innocents—too young to be called women—were the helpless victims of Loayza and the other chief officials of the Peruvian Amazon Company's El Encanto branch, who violated these tender children without the slightest compunction, and when they tired of them either murdered them or flogged them and sent them back to their tribes.

Let us now take a glance at the system pursued by this "civilising company" in the exploitation of the products of this region—that is, the exploitation of the rubber and of the Indians. This system I afterwards ascertained to be as follows:—

The whole region under the control of this criminal syndicate is divided up into two departments, the chief centres of which are El Encanto and La Chorrera. El Encanto is the headquarters of all the sections of the Caraparaná and the right bank of the Putumayo, while La Chorrera is the capital of the sections of the Igaraparaná and those distributed between that river and the Caquetá. As already stated, the superintendent of El Encanto is Loayza, while that of La Chorrera is the celebrated Victor Macedo.

It is to these two centres that all the products are sent periodically on the backs of Indians, by canoe, or in small launches. Once here, it is shipped to Iquitos about every three months. At each of these centres all books are kept and all payments to the employees are made. The superintendents have the power of hiring and discharging all the men employed under them, and their slightest whim is law.

These two departments, as already hinted, are subdivided into sections, at the head of which are placed chiefs, under the instructions of the superintendents. Each chief has under his control a number of *racionales*, varying from five to eighty, whose business is to direct the Indians and force them to work. The chief of the section keeps a list of all the Indians resident in his section, and assigns to each worker—in some sections this term includes women and children—the number of kilos of rubber that he must deliver every ten days.

Armed with *machetes*, the Indians penetrate the depths of the forest, gashing frightfully every rubber-tree they can find, frequently cutting them so much and so deep, in their frantic efforts to extract the last drop of milk, that vast numbers of the trees die annually. The milk runs down the trunk of the tree and dries there. A few days afterwards the Indians return, and, gathering up the strings of rubber, place them in baskets, which they carry to their huts on their backs.

Here, in order to remove some of the pieces of wood, dry leaves, chunks of bark, sand, and other impurities, the Indians place the rubber in a *quebrada* and beat it well with clubs; in this way a few of the many foreign matters are removed and the rubber is made more compact. It is then wound up in big rolls, and, exposed to the air and the light, it soon becomes of a dull, blackish colour, and is ready for delivery.

At the expiration of the ten days the slaves start out with their loads upon their backs, accompanied by their women and children, who help them to carry the rubber. When they reach the sectionhouse, the rubber is weighed in the presence of the chief of the section and his armed subordinates. The Indians know by experience what the needle of the balance should mark, and when it indicates that they have delivered the full amount they leap about and laugh with pleasure. When it does not, they throw themselves face downwards on the ground, and in this attitude await their punishment.

As the rubber gets scarcer and scarcer the aborigines, in order to be able to deliver the full amount of rubber demanded from them, and thus to escape flagellations and tortures, frequently adulterate the rubber-milk with that of various other trees, in this way still further lowering the quality of the Putumayo rubber; for, as already remarked, all that produced in this section is what is technically known as *jebe débil*.

It will be easily seen that such a system—a system of organised robbery—of collection of rubber is likely to lend itself to abuse in a country where every man is a law unto himself, and there is absolutely no check upon the exercise of his most brutal instincts and passions. The probability of such abuse is increased immensely when—as in the present case—the earnings of the employees are made dependent on results, for Loayza, Macedo, and the chiefs of sections are paid, not salaries but commissions on the amount of rubber produced.

Thus it is to their advantage to extract the greatest amount of rubber in the least possible space of time, and to do this the Indians must either be paid or punished. If paid, the payment must be great enough to tempt a placid, indolent Indian to continuous exertion; if punished, the punishment must be severe enough to extract from his fears what cannot be obtained from an appeal to his cupidity. As the "civilising company" apparently does not believe in paying for what it can obtain otherwise, the rule of terror has been adopted throughout the company's dominions. Those who have studied the history of the Congo will see here precisely the same conditions which produced such lamentable results in the Belgian companies' sphere of operations. It would be strange indeed if, under such a system, some sort of abuse did not take place, and I am in possession of definite documentary evidence which, I think, justifies me in making the following statements as to the results of this system:—

1. The pacific Indians of the Putumayo are forced to work day and night at the extraction of rubber, without the slightest remuneration except the food necessary to keep them alive.

2. They are kept in the most complete nakedness, many of them not even possessing the biblical fig-leaf.

3. They are robbed of their crops, their women, and their children to satisfy the voracity, lasciviousness, and avarice of this company and its employees, who live on their food and violate their women.

4. They are sold wholesale and retail in Iquitos, at prices that range from £20 to £40 each.

5. They are flogged inhumanly until their bones are laid bare, and great raw sores cover them.

6. They are given no medical treatment, but are left to die, eaten by maggots, when they serve as food for the chiefs' dogs.

7. They are castrated and mutilated, and their ears, fingers, arms, and legs are cut off.

8. They are tortured by means of fire and water, and by tying them up, crucified head down.

9. Their houses and crops are burned and destroyed wantonly and for amusement.

10. They are cut to pieces and dismembered with knives, axes, and *machetes*.

11. Their children are grasped by the feet and their heads are dashed against trees and walls until their brains fly out.

12. Their old folk are killed when they are no longer able to work for the company.

13. Men, women, and children are shot to provide amusement for the employees or to celebrate the *sábado de Gloria*, or, in preference to this, they are burned with kerosene so that the employees may enjoy their desperate agony.

This is indeed a horrible indictment, and may seem incredible to many. On the other hand, we all know the inhuman atrocities of the Congo, and it seems reasonable to suppose that the conditions that have made that region so notorious do not fail to produce precisely similar results in the vast and isolated region of the Putumayo. In addition to this, during my subsequent investigations in Iquitos I obtained from a number of eye-witnesses accounts[2] of many of the abominable outrages that take place here hourly, and these, with my own observations, are the basis for the indictment.

---

2   Many of these have recently been published in *Truth*. —AUTHOR.

STUDY QUESTIONS

1. What economic and political forces account for the brutal treatment of indigenous rubber workers in the Putumayo, according to Hardenburg?
2. What role does sexual exploitation of indigenous women play in upholding this labor system?
3. The photos taken by Hardenburg became iconic images of the horrors underpinning the Amazonian rubber trade. What insight can we gain into indigenous people's experiences of this system by analyzing the three photos included here?

CHAPTER 6

WORLDS CONNECTING:
Latin America in an Imperial Age

THEODORE ROOSEVELT

6.1 THE PLATT AMENDMENT, 1902

The Platt Amendment was first passed by the US Congress in 1901 as part of the Army Appropriations Bill that provided the conditions for US withdrawal from Cuba following the Spanish-American War. It was signed into the Cuban Constitution by Theodore Roosevelt in 1902 as part of Cuba's formal establishment as an independent republic. The Platt Amendment served to enshrine Cuban political dependency on the United States by creating the constitutional basis for ongoing US military intervention, and by placing limits on the types of policies that could be implemented by the Cuban government.

Whereas the Congress of the United States of America, by an Act approved March 2, 1901, provided as follows:

Provided further, That in fulfillment of the declaration contained in the joint resolution approved April twentieth, eighteen hundred and ninety-eight, entitled "For the recognition of the independence of the people of Cuba, demanding that the Government of Spain relinquish its authority and government in the island of Cuba, and withdraw its land and naval forces from Cuba and Cuban waters, and directing the President of the United States to use the land and naval forces of the United States to carry these resolutions into effect," the President is hereby authorized to "leave the government and control of the island of Cuba to its people" so soon as a government shall have been established in said island under a constitution which, either as a part thereof or in an ordinance appended thereto, shall define the future relations of the United States with Cuba, substantially as follows:

"I. That the government of Cuba shall never enter into any treaty or other compact with any foreign power or powers which will impair or tend to impair the independence of Cuba, nor in any manner authorize or permit any foreign power or powers to obtain by colonization or for military or naval purposes or otherwise, lodgement in or control over any portion of said island."

"II. That said government shall not assume or contract any public debt, to pay the interest upon which, and to make reasonable sinking fund provision for the ultimate discharge of which, the ordinary revenues of

Source: Transcript of Platt Agreement (1903); https://www.ourdocuments.gov/doc.php?flash=false&doc=55&page=transcript

the island, after defraying the current expenses of government shall be inadequate."

"III. That the government of Cuba consents that the United States may exercise the right to intervene for the preservation of Cuban independence, the maintenance of a government adequate for the protection of life, property, and individual liberty, and for discharging the obligations with respect to Cuba imposed by the treaty of Paris on the United States, now to be assumed and undertaken by the government of Cuba."

"IV. That all Acts of the United States in Cuba during its military occupancy thereof are ratified and validated, and all lawful rights acquired thereunder shall be maintained and protected."

"V. That the government of Cuba will execute, and as far as necessary extend, the plans already devised or other plans to be mutually agreed upon, for the sanitation of the cities of the island, to the end that a recurrence of epidemic and infectious diseases may be prevented, thereby assuring protection to the people and commerce of Cuba, as well as to the commerce of the southern ports of the United States and the people residing therein."

"VI. That the Isle of Pines shall be omitted from the proposed constitutional boundaries of Cuba, the title thereto being left to future adjustment by treaty."

"VII. That to enable to the United States to maintain the independence of Cuba, and to protect the people thereof, as well as for its own defense, the government of Cuba will sell or lease to the United States lands necessary for coaling or naval stations at certain specified points to be agreed upon with the President of the United States."

"VIII. That by way of further assurance the government of Cuba will embody the foregoing provisions in a permanent treaty with the United States."

STUDY QUESTIONS

1. To what extent was the Platt Amendment at odds with Cuban national sovereignty? Are there particular clauses that are especially noteworthy in terms of limiting the autonomy of the Cuban government?
2. What did the United States hope to achieve in Cuba by insisting on these constitutional provisions?

PHILIPPE BUNAU-VARILLA

6.2 THE UNITED STATES AND PANAMANIAN INDEPENDENCE, 1914

The construction of the Panama Canal was one of the most important, yet controversial, outcomes of US intervention in Latin America in the early twentieth century. The Panama Canal represented a truly astonishing engineering feat and was key to the emergence of the United States as a global superpower. The canal gave the United States control of the only direct passageway

Source: Philippe Bunau-Varilla, *Panama: The Creation, Destruction, and Resurrection* (Ann Arbor: University of Michigan Library, 1914), pp. 302–303, 334–339. Courtesy of University of Michigan Library. All rights reserved. Reproduced by permission.

between the Atlantic and Pacific Ocean, while US success where so many other projects had failed enhanced American international prestige considerably. Yet the acquisition of the Canal was controversial. At the beginning of negotiations, the Canal belonged to Colombia, but when the treaty governing the project ran into trouble, the United States supported Panama in declaring independence from Colombia, with President Roosevelt sending gunboats to prevent Colombia from suppressing the independence movement with military force. An instrumental figure in Panama's independence movement was Phillipe Bunau-Varilla, who had served as chief engineer of an earlier French effort to build a canal, and who became Panama's ambassador to the United States following independence. In this excerpt from his autobiography, published ten years after Panamanian independence, Bunau-Varilla shares his reflections on his role in the outbreak of the movement, denying claims that his advocacy for US intervention was based on personal financial motives.

A grave question of conscience confronted me. "Had I the moral right to take part in a revolution and to encourage its development?" My answer was: "Yes."

"Yes, because I had twice warned President [of Colombia Jose Manuel] Marroquin in November 1902 and in June 1903, of the grave risks to which its anti-canal policy exposed Colombia.

"Yes, because I had again notified these risks to the Vice-President of the [Colombian] Senate, General Nel Ospina, in August 1903.

"Yes, because Colombia was obviously prosecuting a policy of piracy aiming at the destruction of the precious work of Frenchmen.

"Yes, because this great enterprise was placed in one of those ill-defined moral zones where politics tyrannise over law and violate justice with impunity.

"Yes, because in the absence of law, and in presence of arbitrary political action, every man has the right to oppose another political action in order to bring about the triumph of justice."

I certainly had the moral right to annul, by political action at Panama, the fatal effect which political action at Bogota [the capital of Colombia] was bound to have on the gigantic French interests of which I was the sole defender.

The only objection that could have been made, might have been that I had taken the Colombians unawares. But I had four times individually or publicly shown to Bogota the consequences of its policy!

Colombia had refused to pay the slightest heed. She had declared war against law and justice. Nothing remained but to carry on the war. It was for me a cruel duty, but it was my duty.

My conscience could not reproach me if I backed the revolution and took the leadership of those who were disposed to risk their lives in defence of their country's interests.

I exposed myself to the violent attacks of the Colombians, but I assured the existence of the work which, later on, was to flood their country with prosperity. I should have to remain exposed for many years to mad accusations, but the day would come when Colombia herself would render me justice to recognise that had been actuated by concern for her superior interest. Meanwhile I was sure to be approved by the civilised world. . . .

HELP ARRIVES FROM THE UNITED STATES

The 2nd of November [1903] passed without any news. On the third day expired the last day of the period of one week which I had fixed for the revolution, after the arrival of [Manuel] Amador at Panama.

Deeply disturbed by this silence I went on the morning of the 3rd to the offices of M. Lindo. I wanted to prepare with his ordinary code a dispatch [to Panama] which my conventional code did not allow me to send on account of its incompleteness. I wished to make a supreme appeal to the energy and courage of the people of the Isthmus. . . .

As I left the building to go to the telegraph office, a newsboy ran up to me and offered me the *Evening Telegram*. I bought it, and cast a glance at it.

It announced the landing of General [Juan] Tovar, and of the Colombian troops the very same morning at Colon [a Panama port city], as well as the arrival on the previous evening of the [US ship] *Nashville*. Nothing more—not a word of the slightest revolutionary movement.

Everything seemed to be irretrievably lost. . . .

I spend the whole afternoon in a state of profound dejection. My dear wife tried to comfort and encourage me in this infinite sorrow. Finally, she prevailed on me to dominate my grief and to go with her to dine. . . .

When I returned to the Waldorf Astoria at about 10 o'clock that evening a telegram was handed to me. It was in plain language, and signed by Amador. It ran thus:

"*Proclamada Independencia del Istmo sin sangre.* [Independence of the Isthmus proclaimed without bloodshed]—Amador."

The life of the great undertaking had been saved at the very moment when it seemed to be destroyed for ever.

What had taken place?

The rumour of the arrival of the American man of war that I had announced had promptly leaked out and spread all over the Isthmus.

From the morning of the 2nd November, all the inhabitants of Colon were looking towards Kingston [Jamaica], hoping for the appearance of the ship symbolising American protection.

As the hours passed disappointment gradually invaded all hearts.

Towards nightfall despair was general, when suddenly a light smoke arose in the direction of the north-east.

This was a ray of hope! If it were the liberator?

Little by little the smoke thickened, the ship emerged above the horizon and soon the Star-Spangled Banner dominated the Bay of Colon.

A burst of delirious enthusiasm shook the whole Isthmus.

It was really true! Bunau-Varilla had effectively obtained for the unfortunate country the protection of the powerful Republic!

At this moment without one word having been uttered the Revolution was accomplished in the hearts of all. The *régime* of Colombian tyranny was over!

A BLOODLESS REVOLUTION

The people were so intoxicated with joy, that serious business was postponed until the following day.

Instead of supplying the wharves of Colon with an armed force to prevent a possible landing of the Colombian troops, nothing was done.

This would have entailed the immediate interference of the American cruiser, and prevented a landing which would have provoked disorder. But the confederates had forgotten this detail in their blind happiness.

It happened that this arrival of the Colombian troops, which they had invented in order to justify the dispatch, *Press steamer Colon*, took place the very same day they had announced.

In the morning of the 3rd November, General Tovar arrived quietly with about 500 soldiers.

It was the news which the *Evening Telegram* had brought to me.

This unexpected event awoke the confederates. The employees of the Panama Railroad availed themselves of various technical pretexts to delay the formation of a special train required for the troops.

General Tovar took the train for Panama, leaving his troops behind him at Colon.

Meanwhile the patriotic excitement determined by the arrival of the *Nashville* was steadily gaining on the entire population as well as garrison of Panama.

The aged Dr. Amador [who became the first president of Panama] gave the example. He went to the barracks, and started the whole movement by having General Tovar and his officers arrested by General [Esteban] Huertas, Commander of the Panama garrison.

The Independent Republic of Panama was immediately proclaimed.

The revolution had been made without shedding a drop of blood. It was due to the unanimous explosion of a whole nation, which refused to be stifled by the policy of Bogota.

But as it happens with nations depressed by long military oppression this explosion had taken place only when the people felt they were no longer alone.

This revolution, which it would have been so easy to accomplish from the 27th of October when there were no obstacles in the way, was accomplished in face of the dreaded troops of the tyrant.

If these troops had arrived twenty-four hours earlier nobody would have made a move.

But they had landed twelve hours after the symbolic arrival of the *Nashville* had fired in all hearts the spark of hope, and thus restored general self-confidence. People had seen therein the extended hand of the powerful neighbor Republic. And this proof of friendship had made all hearts beat more quickly and raised everybody's courage.

The Republic of Panama had therefore been born; and it had sprung from a legitimate revolt against the most intolerable oppression.

THE REVOLUTION WAS NOT FOMENTED BY THE UNITED STATES

Colombia can say to-day that the Republic of Panama was born owing to American protection. This is true if the word protection is understood as expressing solidarity between the mighty and the weak in the defence of common and legitimate interests. It was not born from a conspiracy fomented by the American authorities. It developed out of the simultaneous and parallel, but distinct, movement in two separate spheres of the same aspiration, the completion of the Panama Canal. Everyone on remained in his proper place and acted his legitimate part.

Mr. [US president Theodore] Roosevelt avoided, during the first revolutionary attempts, anything which could resemble collusion. The abandonment of Amador by those who had promised him everything is the obvious demonstration that the American Government had refused to lend itself to anything of a compromising character.

The action of President Roosevelt was as correct as it was active and resolute. . . .

The claim of Colombia is, and will remain, untenable, because she herself forfeited her right by her policy.

Her rights challenged superior rights: the right of a nation to exist; the right of humanity to circulate.

She violated the very basis of her sovereign rights, namely, the duty of the sovereign to protect his subjects.

With a stroke of the pen [that is, the refusal to ratify a treaty with the United States for purchase of canal rights] she condemned the whole of the population of one of her provinces to destruction.

With a stroke of the pen she challenged the whole of humanity which had a pre-eminent right of way across the Isthmus.

With a stroke of the pen she cynically announced her will to confiscate from the French share and bond holders all that still remained from the wreck of the great enterprise.

With a stroke of the pen she disavowed her contract for the extension of the term of the French concession, on the pretext that certain formalities had not been fulfilled, whereas through her own fault, it was a physical impossibility to fulfill them.

These are the violations of superior rights which made the revolution of Panama the most legitimate of protests against tyranny. . . .

THE REACTION IN AMERICA

On the day following, November 2, was published [in the *New York Sun*] the admirable article of which I give the following extracts.

Colombia Before The World To-Day

The Congress at Bogota adjourned on Saturday without having ratified the Canal Treaty negotiated by the Colombian Government with ours. The end of the session opens no hopeful path toward an agreement hereafter, with these same politicians or their successors. As all the world knows, the terms of compensation offered by the United States in the Treaty were liberal beyond precedent; the contemptuous rejection of these terms by the [US] Congress, after their acceptance as satisfactory by the representatives of Colombia in the preliminary process, has had no explanation that is respectable, and but one explanation that is credible. That is blackmail; attempted blackmail of the French owners of the canal property, because it was believed at Bogota that they would submit rather than lose the opportunity to sell for forty millions; attempted blackmail of the United States, because it was believed at Bogota that this rich and enterprising nation would pay to the very limit of tropical avarice rather than give up its project or take the alternative to the vastly inferior route through Nicaragua. . . .

The attitude of Colombia as an obstructionist for extortion is the same toward the whole civilised world as it is toward the United States in particular. That Government is trying to block the mightiest enterprise ever undertaken for the common benefit of the globe's commerce. Colombia's duty to the world is repudiated along with her obligations to the United States. She is neither entitled to the sympathy and moral support of any great power, nor likely to receive such sympathy and support.

STUDY QUESTIONS

1. What does Bunau-Varilla present as the key motivations for Panamanian independence from Colombia? What role does he attribute to the United States in this process?
2. Why does Bunau-Varilla emphasize American public opinion in his discussion of the responses to Panamanian independence?

6.3 CARTOONS DEPICTING U.S. RACIAL STEREOTYPES TOWARD LATIN AMERICA, 1899–1904

Political cartoons are some of the most revealing sources about American attitudes toward Latin America during the high point of imperialist intervention and highlight especially the racial stereotypes and assumptions that infused US policy in the region.

The first image displayed here, titled "School Begins" was created by the cartoonist Louis Darlymple and published in the popular satirical magazine *Puck* in 1899. The image shows Uncle Sam teaching a group of students including those labeled "Cuba" and "Puerto Rico," and the caption reads: "Uncle Sam (to his new class in Civilization) *Now, children,* you've got to learn these lessons whether you want to or not! But just take a look at the class ahead of you, and remember that, in a little while, you will feel as glad to be here as they are!"

The second cartoon was published in The *St. Paul Pioneer Press* in 1904. It shows Uncle Sam looking out of the window at "San Domingo" (representing the Dominican Republic) having a temper tantrum. The caption reads: "Maybe I'll have to bring the boy into the house to keep him quiet."

The third cartoon was published in *The Chicago Inter-Ocean* in 1905. It shows Uncle Sam holding "Puerto Rico" by the hand while a boy representing Cuba plays with guns and weapons across the river. The caption reads: "To think that bad boy came close to being your brother."

Source: School Begins; Courtesy of the Library of Congress (LOC-DIG-ppmsca-28668) / Uncle Sam to Porto Rico; John L. Johnson, *Latin America in Caricature* (University of Texas Press, 1980), p. 45 / Uncle Sam "Maybe I'll have to bring the boy into the house to keep him quiet"; *The St. Paul Pioneer Press*, 1904. Taken from *Latin America in Caricature* by John J. Johnson (University of Texas Press, 1980), p. 71.

STUDY QUESTIONS

1. What are some of the commonalities in the ways these different cartoons depict Latin American nations? What assumptions about the region underpin the images?
2. What are some of the most notable ways in which racial ideas infuse the cartoons? How do depictions of racial difference connect to depictions of economic themes?
3. What political actions do the cartoonists seek to recommend to their audience?

JOSÉ MARTÍ

6.4 THE TRUTH ABOUT THE UNITED STATES, 1894

José Martí was an iconic Cuban intellectual and one of the most influential figures in the Cuban struggle for independence. His writings form some of the most significant examples of Latin American cultural resistance to the United States. Martí was strongly anti-imperialist, and was alarmed by US attitudes toward Cuba, which he warned could lead to annexation. He was also fervently opposed to the racial thinking that dominated the era, and argued for a "raceless" nationalism, in which all Cubans would be equal regardless of race. He also challenged the race-based international hierarchies that positioned Europe and the United States as culturally superior to Latin America. Martí was intimately familiar with the United States: between 1880 and 1894 he lived and traveled in the United States for long stretches at a time, attempting to raise support for independence within the Cuban émigré communities in Tampa and New York. During this period he wrote a series of newspaper articles about his experiences living in the United States and what they revealed about the meaning of US dominance. This is an excerpt from one of his most famous articles, first published in *Patria*, a New York-based newspaper for Cuban exiles, on March 23, 1894.

In Our America it is vital to know the truth about the United States. We should not exaggerate its faults purposely, out of a desire to deny it all virtue, nor should these faults be concealed or proclaimed as virtues. There are no races; there are only the various modifications of man in details of form and habits, according to the conditions of climate and history in which he lives, which do not alter the identical and the essential. Superficial men—who have not explored human problems very thoroughly, or who cannot see from the heights of impartiality how all nations are boiling in the same stew pot, and how one finds in the structure and fabric of them all the same permanent duel between constructive unselfishness and iniquitous hate—are prone to amuse themselves by finding substantial variety between the egotistical Saxon and the egotistical Latin, the generous Saxon and the generous Latin, the Saxon bureaucrat and the Latin bureaucrat. Both Latins and Saxons are equally capable of having virtues and defects; what does vary is the peculiar outcome of the different historical groups. In a nation of English, Dutch and Germans of similar background, no matter what their disagreements, perhaps fatal, brought upon them by the original separations between nobility and the common man who founded that nation together, and by the inevitable—and in the human species innate—hostility of greed and vanity brought about by aristocracies confronted with the law and self-denial revealed to them, one cannot explain the confusion of political customs and the melting pot of nations in which the *conquistador*'s needs permitted the native population to live. With parricidal blindness the privileged class spawned by the Europeans is still barring the way to those frightened and diverse peoples.

A nation of strapping young men from the North, bred over the centuries to the sea and the snow and

Source: José Martí, "The Truth about the United States," *Inside the Monster: Writings on the United States and American Imperialism*. Edited and with an introduction by Philip S. Foner. (New York: Monthly Review Press, 1975), pp. 49–54.

the virility aided by the perpetual defense of local free-dom, cannot be like a tropical isle, docile and smil-ing, where the famished outgrowth of a backward and war-minded European people, descendants of a coarse and uncultured tribe, divided by hatred for an accom-modating submission to rebellious virtue, work under contract for a government that practices political piracy. And also working under contract are those simple but vigorous Africans, whether vilified or rancorous, who from a frightful slavery and a sublime war have entered into citizenship with those who bought and sold them, and who, thanks to the dead of that sublime war, today greet as equals the ones who used to make them dance to the lash. Concerning the differences between Latins and Saxons, and the only way that comparisons can be drawn, one must study the conditions they may have shared. It is a fact that in those Southern states of the American Union where there were Negro slaves, those Negroes were predominantly as arrogant, shift-less, helpless and merciless as the sons of Cuba would be under conditions of slavery. It is supinely ignorant and slightly infantile and blameworthy to refer to the United States and to the real or apparent conquests of one or more of its territories as one total nation, equally free and definitely conquered. Such a United States is a fraud and a delusion. Between the shanties of Dakota and the virile and barbaric nation in process of growth there, and the cities of the East—sprawling, privileged, well-bred, sensual and unjust—lies an entire world. From the stone houses and the majestic freedom north of Schenectady, to the dismal resort of stilts south of St. Petersburg, lies another entire world. The clean and concerned people of the North are worlds apart from the choleric, poverty-stricken, broken, bitter, lack-luster, loafing Southern shop keepers sitting on their cracker barrels. What the honest man should observe is precisely that it was not only impossible to fuse the elements of diverse tendency and origin out of which the United States was created, within a period of three centuries of life in common or of one century of politi-cal awareness, but that compulsory social intercourse exacerbates and accentuates their principal differences and turns the unnatural federation into a harsh state of violent conquest. It is a quality of lesser people and of incompetent and gnawing envy, this pricking holes in manifest greatness and plainly denying it for some defect or other, or this going to great lengths of prediction, like someone brushing a speck of dust off the sun. But it is a matter of certification rather than of prophecy for anyone who observes how, in the United States, the reasons for unity are weakening, not so-lidifying; how the various localities are dividing and irritating national politics, not uniting with it; how democracy is being corrupted and diminished, not strengthened and saved from the hatred and wretch-edness of monarchies. Hatred and misery are posing a threat and being reborn, and the man who keeps this to himself instead of speaking out is not complying with his duty. He is not complying with his duty as a man, the obligation of knowing the truth and spread-ing it; nor with his duty as a good American who sees the continent's peace and glory secure only in the frank and free development of its various native entities. As a son of Our America he is not fulfilling his obligations to prevent the peoples of Spanish blood from falling under the counsel of the smirking toga and the skittish interest, whether through ignorance or disillusionment or impatience, in the immoral and enervating servitude of a damaged and alien civilization. In Our America it is imperative to know the truth about the United States.

Wrongs must be abhorred, whether or not they are ours. The good must not be hated merely because it is not ours. But it is worthless and irrational and cowardly for inefficient or inferior people to aspire to reach the stability of a foreign nation by roads other than those which brought security and order to the envied nation, through individual effort and the ad-aptation of human freedom to the forms required by the particular constitution of that nation. With some people, an excessive love for the North is the unwise, but easily explained, expression of such a lively and vehement desire for progress that they are blind to the fact that ideas, like trees, must come from deep roots and compatible soil in order to develop a firm footing and prosper, and that a newborn baby is not given the wisdom and maturity of age merely because one glues on its smooth face a mustache and a pair of side burns. Monsters are created that way, not Nations. They have to live of themselves, and sweat through the heat. With other people, their Yankee mania is the innocent result of an occasional little leap of pleasure, much as a man judges the inner spirit of a home, and the souls who pray or die therein, by the smiles and luxury in the front parlor, or by the champagne and carnations on the banquet table. One must suffer, starve, work, love and study, even in vain, but with one's own individual courage and freedom. One must keep watch with the poor, weep with the destitute, abhor the brutality of wealth, live in both mansion and tenement, in the school's reception hall and in its vestibule, in the gilt and jasper theater box and in the cold, bare wings. In this way a man can form opinions, with glimmers of reason, about the authoritarian and envious Republic and the growing materialism of the United States. With other posthumous weaklings of Second Empire literary dandyism, or the false skeptics under whose mask of indifference there generally beats a heart of gold, the fashion is to scorn the indigenous, and more so. They cannot imagine greater elegance than to drink to the foreigner's breeches and ideas, and to strut over the globe, proud as the pompom tail of the fondled lap dog. With still others it is like a subtle aristocracy which, publicly showing a preference for the fair-skinned as a natural and proper thing to do, tries to conceal its own humble half-breed origins, unaware that when one man brands another as a bastard, it is always a sign of his own illegitimacy. There is no more certain announcement of a woman's sins than when she shows contempt for sinners. It matters not whether the reason is impatience for freedom or the fear of it, moral sloth or a laughable aristocracy, political idealism or a recently acquired ingenuity—it is surely appropriate, and even urgent, to put before Our America the entire American truth, about the Saxon as well as the Latin, so that too much faith in foreign virtue will not weaken us in our formative years with an unmotivated and baneful distrust of what is ours. In a single war, the War of Secession, more concerned with whether the North or the South would predominate in the Republic than with abolishing slavery, the United States lost more men per capita than were lost in the same amount of time by all the Spanish republics of America put together, and its sons had been living

under republicanism for three centuries in a country whose elements were less hostile than in any other.

More men were lost in the United States Civil War than in Mexico to victorious Chile in the naturally slow process of putting upon the surface of the New World, with nothing but the enterprise of popular instinct and the rhetorical apostolate of a glorious minority, the remote peoples of widespread nuclei and contrary races, where the rule of Spain had left all the rage and hypocrisy of theocracy, and all the indolence and suspicions of a prolonged servitude. From the standpoint of justice and a legitimate social science it should be recognized that, in relation to the ready compliance of the one and the obstacles of the other, the North American character has gone downhill since the winning of independence, and is today less human and virile; whereas the Spanish-American character today is in all ways superior, in spite of its confusion and fatigue, to what it was when it began to emerge from the disorganized mass of grasping clergy, unskilled ideologists and ignorant or savage Indians. And to aid in the understanding of political reality in America, and to accompany or correct with the calm force of fact, the ill-advised praise (pernicious when carried to extremes) of the North American character and political life, *Patria* is inaugurating, with today's issue, a permanent section devoted to "Notes on the United States." In it, we will print articles faithfully translated from the country's earliest newspapers, without editorial comment or changes. We will print no accounts of events revealing the crimes or accidental faults, possible in all nations, where none but the wretched spirit finds sustenance and contentment, but rather those structural qualities which, for their constancy and authority, demonstrate two useful truths to Our America: the crude, uneven and decadent character of the United States, and the continuous existence there of all the violence, discord, immorality and disorder blamed upon the peoples of Spanish America.

STUDY QUESTIONS

1. What does Martí see as the essence of "the truth" about the United States? Who is the "Our America" who must learn this truth?
2. What arguments does Martí use to challenge the idea that North Americans and Latin Americans are inherently different in their cultural behavior and characteristics?

FANNY CHAMBERS GOOCH INGLEHART

6.5 *FACE TO FACE WITH THE MEXICANS*

Fanny Chambers was an American women who spent seven years in the 1870s and 1880s living in Mexico with her husband. She decided to write a travel memoir specifically to help Americans understand Mexico. The full title of her book was Face to Face with the Mexicans: The Domestic Life, Educational, Social and Business Ways, Statesmanship and Literature, Legendary and General History of the Mexican People, as seen and studied by an American woman during her seven years of intercourse with them. Yet Chambers's accounts of her travels and her experiences in her Mexican home are also deeply revealing of the assumptions and stereotypes that Americans brought to their interactions with Mexicans. This excerpt focuses on the relations between Chambers and her domestic staff and underlines the cultural differences between American and Mexican understandings of domestic work.

CHAPTER III: NO ES COSTUMBRE

We were overshadowed by the dome of a magnificent cathedral, the exterior of which was embellished with life-sized statues of saints. The interior presented a costly display of tinted walls, jeweled and bedecked images, and gilded altars. Its mammoth tower had loomed grimly under the suns and stars of a hundred years, and the solidity of its perfect masonry has so far defied the encroachments of time.

The city of our adoption boasted an Alameda, where the air was redolent of the odor of the rose and violet, and made musical with the tinkling of fountains; and where could be seen the "beauty and chivalry" of a civilization three centuries old, taking the evening air.

Plazas beautified with flowers, shrubs, and trees, upon which neither money nor pains had been spared, lent a further charm. Stores were at hand wherein could be purchased fabrics of costly texture, as well as rare jewels—in fact, a fair share of the elegant superfluities of life; and yet in the midst of so much civilization, so much art, so much luxury of a certain kind, so much wealth, I found to my dismay, upon investigation, that I was a least fifty miles from an available broom!

Imagine the dilemma, you famously neat housekeepers of the United States! A house with floors of pounded dirt, tile, brick, and cement, and no broom to be had for money, though, I am pleased to add, one was finally obtained for love. My generous little Mexican neighbor and friend, Pomposita, taking pity on my despair, gave me one—which enabled me to return the half-worn borrowed broom of another friend.

Owing to the exorbitant demands of the customhouse, such humble though necessary articles were not then imported: and the untutored sons of La Republica manufactured them on haciendas, from materials crude beyond imagination.

Once or twice a year long strings of *burros* may be seen, wending their way solemnly through the streets; girt about with a burden of the most wonderful brooms.

These brooms were of two varieties; one had handles as knotty and unwieldy as the thorny *mesquite*, while the other was still more primitive in design, and looked like old field Virginia sedge grass tied up in bundles. They were retailed by men who carried them through the streets on their backs.

Source: Fanny Chambers Good Inglehart, *Face to Face with the Mexicans* (New York: Fords, Howard, and Hulbert, 1887) pp. 84–96.

For the rude character of their brooms, however, the manufacturers are not to blame, but the sterility of the country, and the failure of nature to provide suitable vegetable growths.

Every housekeeper takes advantage of the advent of the *escobero* (broom-maker), to lay in a stock of brooms sufficient to last until his next visit. It was two months before an opportunity of buying a broom, even from a "wandering Bavarian," was afforded me, and during that time I came to regard Doña Pomosita's gift as the apple of my eye.

"*Mer-ca-ran las es-co-bas!*" One morning a new sound assailed my ears, as it came up the street, gathering force and volume the nearer it approached. I heard it over and over without divining its meaning. But at last a man entered our portal and in a tone that made my hair stand on end and with a vim that almost shook the house, he screamed—"*Es-co-Bas, Señ-o-ra!*"—drawing each word out as long as a broom-handle, then rolling it into a low hum, which finally died into a whispered—"Will you buy some brooms?" Had he known my disposition and special fondness for broom-handles—without reference to my household need—he would have brought them to me directly, dispensing with his car-splitting medley—to a woman for three months without a broom!

On ascertaining that the *escobero* would not visit the city again for some time, I bought his entire stock, and laid them up with prudent foresight, against the possibility of another broom famine.

With a genuine American spirit, I concluded to have a general house-cleaning, and, equipped with these wonderful brooms, with Pancho's assistance the work began. The first place demanding attention was the immense parlor, with its floor of solid cement. Pancho began to sweep, but the more he swept, the worse it looked—ringed, streaked, and striped with dust. I thought he was not using his best efforts, so with a will, I took the broom and made several vigorous strokes, but to my amazement, it looked worse than ever. In my despair a friend came in, who comprehended the situation at a glance, and explained that floors of that kind could not be cleaned with a broom; that *amoli*—the root of the *ixtli* (eastly)—soap-root—applied with a wet cloth, was the medium of renovation.

The *amoli* was first macerated and soaked for some time in water. A portion of the liquid was taken in one vessel and clear water in another. The cleansing was done in small squares, the rubbing all in one direction. The effect was magical—my dingy floor being restored to its original rich Indian red.

Now and then, while on his knees, rubbing away with might and main, Pancho would throw his eyes up at me with a peculiar expression of despair, while he muttered in undertone: "*No es costumbre de los mosos lavar los suclos*" ("It is not customary for mozos to wash floors").

Insatiable curiosity is the birthright of the poor of Mexico, and on this remarkable day they gathered about the windows until not another one could find room—talking to Pancho, who looked as if already under sentence for an infraction of the criminal code. They made strange motions with their fingers, exclaiming at the same time: "*Es una verguenza el mozo hacer tales cosas!*" ("It is a shame for mozo to do such things!") Others replied by saying: "*Es un insulto!*" ("It is an insult!"), while others took up the argument of the case by saying: "*Por supuesto que si*" ("Why, of course it is"). But all this did not cause Pancho to give me a rude look or an impertinent word.

The floor now looked red and shiny, the windows were clear and glistening, and the six hair-cloth chairs stood grimly along the wall, in deference to the custom. My little friend took her departure, and Pancho moved lamely about, as if stiffened by his arduous labor.

In all my housekeeping experiences nothing ever occurred which for novelty was comparable to the events of that morning. I felt sure that when Mother Noah descended from Mount Ararat, and assumed the responsibilities of housekeeping—or more properly tent-keeping—on the damp plain, however embarrassing the limitation of her equipments may have been, she was at least spared the provocation of a scornful and wondering audience, greeting her efforts on every side with that now unendurable remark, "*No es costumbre.*"

I afterward learned the cause of the commotion, when it transpired that such services as floor-cleaning are performed, not by the *mozo*, but by a servant hired for the occasion, outside the household.

In a few moments my *lavandera*—washerwoman—entered, accompanied by her two pretty, shy little girls. Having complimented the fresh appearance of the house,—Pancho now and then explaining what he had done,—she informed me that the following day would be the *dia de santo*—saint's day—of one of her bright-eyed *chiquitas*, and *"hay costumbre"* ("there is a custom") of receiving tokens on these days from interested friends. Acting upon this hint, I went to my bedroom, followed by Juana and the *niñas*, who displayed great surprise at every step. My red and yellow covered beds they tapped and talked to as if they had been animate things, calling them, *"camas bonitas, coloradas y amarillas!"* ("pretty beds, red and yellow!")

I turned the bright blankets over, that they might see the springs, and the sight utterly overcame them. Their astonishment at the revelation of such mysterious and luxurious appendages made them regard me with mingled awe, astonishment, and suspicion. The mother struck the springs with her fists, and as the sound rang out and vibrated, the children retreated hastily, shaking with alarm.

Wishing to conform to the customs, and remembering Juana's hint, I unlocked my "Saratoga." The *chiquitas* stood aside, fearing, I suppose, that from the trunk some frightful apparition might spring forth. When the lid went back they exclaimed: *"Valgame Dios!"* (Help me, God"), and crossed themselves hastily, as if to be prepared for the worst. I invited them to come near, at the same time opening a compartment filled with bright flowers and ribbons.

This was a magnet they could not resist, and overcoming their fears, they came and stood close to the trunk, now and then touching the pretty things I exhibited to their wondering eyes. I gave each of them a gay ribbon, and while they were talking delightedly and caressing the pretty trifles, by some mischance the fastening of the upper tray lost its hold. Down it came with a crash—being still heavily packed—and away went the children, screaming and crying, one taking one direction, the other another.

We went in pursuit of them, and when found, one was crouching down in the court-yard under a rose-bush, while the other stood in terror behind the heavy parlor door. Both were shaking, their teeth chattering, while they muttered something about *"el diablo! el diablo!"*

By this time I understood the line which people of this class in Mexico unflinchingly draw between their own humble station and mine, yet I felt moved to treat the frightened children with the same hospitality which in my own land would have proved soothing under similar circumstances. Acting upon

this inspiration, I went quickly and brought a basin of water to wash their tear-stained faces. to my utter surprise, they exclaimed in the same breath: *"No lo permit!"* ("We cannot permit it!") *"No es costumbre."*

The mother approached me with an expression of deep concern and seriousness in her eyes, and with her forefinger raised in gentle admonition. Looking me earnestly in the face, she began moving her finger slowly from side to side directly before my eyes, saying: *"Oiga, Señorita, sepa V. que en esta tierra, cuando nosotros los Mexicanos"* (referring of course to her own class) *"tenemos el catarro"* (emphasizing the last word on G sharp), *"nunca nos lavamos las caras"* ("Listen to me, my good lady, in this country, when we have the catarrh (meaning a bad cold), we never put water on our faces").

"Why not?" I asked.

"Porque no estamos acostumbradas, y por ell clima, sale más mala la enfermedad" ("Because we are not accustomed to it, and on account of the climate, the sickness is made worse").

Thus ended the dialogue. But the children did not hold me responsible for their fright, and bade me a kindly *adios*, promising to return again, a promise fulfilled every week, but on no account would they ever venture near *that* trunk again.

Pancho was determined to give to us and our belongings, as far as possible, the exterior appearance of the *"costumbres."* On entering my room after a little absence, one day, I found him straining every nerve and panting for breath. He had made a low bench, and was trying to place my Saratoga on it, but his strength was not equal to the task. The explanation came voluntarily that, on account of the *animalitos*, it was customary for families to keep trunks on benches or tables. I soon found the *animalitos* had referenced to the various bugs and scorpions which infest the houses, and all trunks were really kept as Pancho said.

As time passed, Pancho constituted himself our instructor and guide in every matter possible, including both diet and health. He warned us against the evil effects of walking out in the sun after ten o'clock in the morning, and especially enjoined upon us not to drink water or wash our faces on returning, as catarrh and headache would be sure to follow. Supposing this only the superstition of an ignorant servant, I took a special delight in taking just such walks, and violating these rules, but every time I paid the forfeit in a cold and headache, according to prediction. I was now satisfied that Pancho was not only wise as a serpent and harmless as a dove, blest with a keen eye of discrimination, but also a first-class health officer, and in the movement of his forefinger lay tomes of reason and good sense. But I had soon to discover that he would have no infringement of his privileges; and, come what would, he was determined to have his *pilon* in the market.

The servants who came and went often warned me that under no consideration must I go to market, but this was one of my home customs, and I could see no reason for its discontinuance. The system of giving the *pilon* (fee) to the servants, by merchants and market-people, as I already knew, would be a stumbling-block in my way. I had discussed in Pancho's presence my determination to go regularly, when I fancied I saw a strange light come into his eyes, which soon explained itself. He came humbly before me, in a short time, hat in hand, his face bearing the sorrowful, woe-begone look of one in the depths of an overwhelming calamity, saying, that a cart had run over his grandmother, and he would have to leave. He had been so kind and considerate in every way—never tiring of any task he had to perform—and so faithful, that I would prove my sympathy and good will to him by an extra sum—outside his wages—which might be a blessing, and aid in restoring his aged grandmother. He walked off, as if distressed beyond measure, at the same time assuring me that he would send his *comadrita* (little godmother of his children) and her husband, who would serve me well.

They came, but it was unfortunate for Pancho. The woman was an inveterate talker, and soon informed me that she was not the *comadrita* of his children; nor had a cart run over his grandmother; in fact, he had none, as she had died before Pancho was born. This was a new phase of the subject, but I was not long in solving the enigma. He had been goaded long enough by my American methods, he had become the butt of ridicule from his friends, and now he would assert himself.

However well he was treated in our house, to be called upon to surrender the most precious boon of all his *"costumbres"* —the market fees—never! But to wound my feelings in leaving was far from his wishes, so he shrewdly planned and carried out the tragic story of the mishap to his grandmother.

The *comadrita* introduced herself with chastened dignity as Jesusita Lopez; but with head loftily erect, and an air of much consequence, informed me that the name of her *marido*—(husband)—was Don Juan Bautista (John the Baptist), *servidores de V.*—("your obedient servants").

She smiled at every word, a way she had of assuring me of her delight in being allowed to serve me, but at the same time, glanced ominously at the cooking-stove. The smile lengthened into a broad grin when Don Juan Bautista came in sight; in her eyes he was "kingdoms, principalities, and powers." Together they examined the stove—talking in undertone—stooping low and scrutinizing every compartment. At last Don Juan Bautista arose, and turning to me said, "Jesusita cannot cook on this *máquina Americana*" (American machine).

"Why?" I asked. He straightened himself up to the highest point, half on tip toe, at the same time nodding his head, and pointing his forefinger at Jesusita, emphatically replied:

"Because it will give her disease of the liver—*como siempre*—as always, with the servants here."

On going to the kitchen a little later, I was surprised to see the gentle Jesusita seated in the middle of the floor, by a charcoal fire, with all my pottery vessels in a heap beside her. Meats, vegetables, and water were all at hand, and she was busily engaged in preparations for dinner. I told her to come and see how well she could cook on the American machine, but she only answered, *"No es constumbre"*; besides, "Don Juan Bautista said it would give her the *cufermedad*, or sickness, before mentioned—and no man knew more than he"—which meant I should use my own machine.

I called upon Don Juan Bautista to go with me to market, when he at once entered into a lengthy discourse about ladies going to such places; that the *jente decente* (people of pedigree) never did such things; that "the people in the streets and markets would talk much and say many things." But of this I had already had a foretaste.

I was about to lead the way through the big door, when Jesusita came forward and laid her soft hand upon me, saying: "Señora, *do* not go; Juan knows better than you about such business. In this country ladies like you send the *mozo*." But I was proof against her persuasive eloquence. To surrender my entire nationality and individuality was not possible for a good American.

The pair talked aside in low undertone, which I watched with feigned indifference and half-closed eyes. Jesusita glanced commiseratively at me, as if she had used her best efforts to no purpose; but Don Juan Bautista threw his most determined and unrelenting expression upon me, as if to say: "Well, she has had enough warning; now the responsibility rests on her own shoulders!"

He looked back at Jesusita as he stepped from the door, nodding his head—"Well,—I will go; but she will wish she had not gone!"

In the market Juan Bautista never left me for a moment, inspecting closely everything I bought—now and then throwing in a word when he thought I was paying too much. He counted every cent as fast as I paid it out, and noted every article placed in the basket. I had nearly completed my purchases, and was talking to a woman about the prospect of butter—regretting the difficulty of getting it,—when she leaned across the table, waggling that tireless forefinger at me, saying, *"En este tiempo ya no hay, no es costumbre"* ("At this time of the year there is none"), Juan Bautista chiming in (with the interminable waggle of his forefinger also), *"No! no hay!"* ("No, indeed, there is none").

The last purchase was made, and I was about closing my purse, when glancing up, I saw Juan Bautista's great merciless eyes fixed upon me, while he said in a firm voice: "But, *mi pilon*, Señora!" This is the custom of the country. If you stay at home, I get my *pilon* from the merchants and market people; if you come—I must have it any how. A wrangle was impossible, and handing him *dos reales* (twenty-five cents), I went home a far wiser woman.

Jesusita looked proudly upon the towering form of Juan Bautista as he entered the portal—basket in one hand, *dos reales* in the other. Not a word was spoken between them, but looks told volumes. *She* knew what

Juan could do, and *he* had proved to her his ability to cope with the stranger from any part of the world. To myself I confessed that in Don Juan Bautista I had found a foeman worthy of my steel.

I asked him to light the fire in the stove and I would make another effort to instruct Jesusita in its management. He went about it, while I withdrew for a few moments to my room. Very soon I noticed that the house was full of smoke. Supposing it to be on fire, I ran to the kitchen, which was in a dense fog, but no fire visible. Nor was Jesusita or Don Juan Bautista to be found. The cause of the smoke was soon discovered. He had built the fire in the oven, and closed the doors!

I clapped my hands for them, according to custom; but they came not. I then found them sitting in the shady court; Jesusita's right arm lay confidingly on Juan Bautista's big left shoulder, as she looked up entreatingly at the harsh countenance of the arbiter of her fate.

I gleaned from their conversation that she wished to remain, but her *marido* was evidently bent on going. On my approach they rose politely, and Juan Bautista delivered the valedictory, assuring me in pleasant terms of their good will; and it was not the *pilon* business—*that* had been settled—but the certainty that Jesusita's health would be injured by using the cooking-stove decided him.

He said they would go to their *"pobre casa"*—I knew they had none; then gathering up their goods and chattels, with the unvarying politeness of the country, *"Hasta otro vista"* ("Until I see you again"), *Vaya V. con Dios!* ("May God be with you!"), they stepped lightly over the threshold—looked-up and down the street, uncertain which way to go—then out they went into the great busy world. Thus disappeared forever from my sight Pancho's *comadrita*.

STUDY QUESTIONS

1. What are some of the main differences between Mexican and American ideals and expectations about work within the home? How do these differences reflect ideas about class, ethnicity, and gender?

2. How does Chambers define the "American spirit"? How is this idea interpreted and responded to by the Mexican workers she encounters?

LUISA CAPETILLO

6.6 MEN'S OPINION ABOUT WOMEN AND MY OWN, 1916

Luisa Capetillo (1879–1922) was one of the most important female leaders to emerge from the Latin American labor movement. A Puerto Rican feminist and anarchist, she became radicalized while working as a lector, or reader, in a US-owned tobacco factory, and became one of the most important union organizers on the island. Capetillo was a truly transnational figure: she traveled extensively between Cuba, Puerto Rico, the Dominican Republic, and the United States, working to organize Cuban, Dominican, and Puerto Rican tobacco workers in New York and Tampa as well as in the Caribbean islands, and standing in solidarity with strikers. Capetillo pushed forcefully for women's rights. She called for women's right to vote and insisted on women's right to dress as they pleased. She was jailed in 1919 for wearing trousers in public. Capetillo was a well-published and influential author who published op-ed essays under the header "Mi Opinión" (My Opinion) in a range of radical labor publications. In this piece from 1916, Capetillo challenges the dominant male perspective on the abilities of women.

MEN'S OPINION ABOUT WOMEN, AND MY OWN

Women should always be women! Women's work is her home! She should not be *macho*! Mend socks and shorts! Doze under the comforting lamplight knitting socks! Who asked for their opinion? Who asked them to get involved in politics or dare to run for office? That cannot be allowed! Haven't we already let them enter the sacred halls to become lawyers and doctors? Well, they're not satisfied. Now they want to become judges, mayors, chiefs of police or legislators. Is that why we let them study, so that they can push us aside, dare to take over our jobs and surpass us? I don't know how these women can forget how weak and indiscreet they are by nature. You can't trust them or teach them anything, because immediately, they want to take over. But how can women imitate man? She can't, because she's inferior. Even Mother Nature condemns her to seclusion during childbirth and breast-feeding.

That's how men talk and that's their conception of women, forgetting all about their wives, mothers and daughters. But you don't have to be afraid that everything will be lost, or that these arguments will disturb the peace of the home, because a woman doesn't stop being a woman just because she's involved in politics or expresses her opinion, or becomes a legislator or a detective. A woman will always be a woman, whether she's a good or bad mother, whether she has a husband or lover. She's a woman, not only when she's powdered and wearing lace and ribbons, just like a man doesn't stop being a man when he learns to cook, mend, sweep and sew. How many men do that! Women do not pretend to be superior to men; at least that's not their intention. They will, however, surpass men by their acts and the fulfillment of their duties.

The immense majority of women do not smoke or get drunk. And this is one of the qualities that will

Source: Norma Valle-Ferrer, *Luisa Capetillo: Pioneer Puerto Rican Feminist* (New York: Peter Lang, 2006), pp. 76–77.

make them superior in all human endeavors. So it isn't women's intention to imitate men, especially not their faults, but maybe their strengths and virtues. The other day I read that a young woman applied for the job of a steamboat stoker, and later the boss said, "She did a better job, and besides, she doesn't drink whiskey."

All this will benefit the human race. Women are preferred as nurses since men are really not good at it. Women will be preferred as doctors because of their values and the way they are. They will heal for love in order not to see suffering. Women will be preferred as lawyers because of their insight and persuasive skills.

They will be preferred as legislators because their laws will correct the abuses against the unhappy workers and the wretched poor. Women will be preferred in politics because they will not sell themselves and they will keep their word. All of this, in general terms, and with few exceptions. Women will not invade the gambling dens, nor will drunkenness cause them to mistreat their husbands and children. Women don't want to invade men's terrain, where they would acquire their vices and abuses. A woman will always be a mother even if she doesn't have children. She will try to correct everything that might harm future generations.

STUDY QUESTIONS

1. What types of argument does Capetillo use to argue that women should be allowed to participate in the same range of economic and political activities as men? To what extent do her arguments differ from those of European and American feminists writing in the same era? Is Capetillo arguing for equality with men, or something else?

2. To what extent does Capetillo's emphasis on women's nurturing and moral characteristics reflect specifically Latin American ideals about women and motherhood?

6.7 PHOTOS OF BELTERRA AND FORDLANDIA, 1931–1945

Fordlandia was one of the most ambitious, yet least successful, American colonization projects in tropical Latin America. Henry Ford sought to establish rubber plantations in Amazonian Brazil that would provide the raw materials for the automobile tires needed by his car factories in Michigan and allow him to cut production costs by controlling his supply of materials. Following the social engineering ideology that underpinned his other business interests, he sought to explicitly recreate the American suburbs in Brazil, in order to impose order on the Amazonian tropics. Fordlandia was designed around a grid-like street system lined with American-style homes, and all worker needs were to be provided by the Ford Corporation, including recreational facilities, a hospital, a dentist's

Source: From the Collections of The Henry Ford. Gift of Ford Motor Company.

office, and a school that provided its students with pencils, books, and uniforms. Ford saw this work as bringing civilization, insisting that his aim was not to make money but to help develop and modernize Brazil. The Brazilian government granted Ford near total authority over the land he purchased in the state of Para, and the project took the idea of an American corporate enclave to a new level. However, the project failed: most of the rubber trees planted did not take root, and those that did suffered from blight. An internationally renowned botanist brought in to help insisted the only solution was the creation of a second plant, Belterra, on a separate location, but this also failed to thrive. By the end of World War II the project had quietly faded and Ford's grandson sold the land back to the Brazilian government in 1945 for a fraction of what he had paid, while the American residents returned home to the United States.

These images from the Henry Ford Archive showcase the ambition of Ford's modernization project, the challenging conditions faced by workers, and Ford's long reach beyond the economic and into the cultural realm. They include: a photo of workers clearing the jungle in 1934; the sawmill and power house at Fordlandia in 1932; the Fordlandia dancehall; schoolchildren sitting in front of the Henry Ford School in Belterra 1940; workers bringing a patient to the Henry Ford Hospital in 1931; Fordlandia houses in 1933; the Golf course at Fordlandia in 1941; a shoe store in Fordlandia in 1938; houses on Riverside Avenue in Fordlandia in 1933; and boy scouts boxing at the golf course in 1945.

STUDY QUESTIONS

1. What do the photos tell us about the successes and challenges of Henry Ford's project to replicate the American suburbs in Amazonian Brazil?

2. What can we learn from the photos about life in Fordlandia and Belterra? The photos mainly document the experiences of American expatriates—what do they reveal about Brazilian and indigenous peoples at the sites?

CHAPTER 7

PROGRESS AND ITS DISCONTENTS, 1880–1920

EUCILDES DA CUNHA

7.1 *REBELLION IN THE BACKLANDS*, 1902

Rebellion in the Backlands is one of the classics of Brazilian literature. It provides a first-hand account of the Brazilian military's brutal response to a late nineteenth-century uprising in Canudos, an isolated backland area in the state of Bahia. The uprising pitted a religious sect of approximately seven thousand people, commanded by a messianic leader, Antonio Conselheiro, against the Brazilian government, whose authority the sect rejected. Most of the rebels were impoverished sertanejos (residents of the backlands) of mixed European-African descent. The war ended in what now many would label a genocide: the near total annihilation and massacre of the peasant rebels and the death of more than ten thousand people. Eucildes da Cunha was a journalist with a background as a former army officer and military engineer, who was assigned to cover the army's campaign against the Canudos uprising by Brazil's largest newspaper. His book describing and contextualizing what he witnessed was published in 1902 and is considered a sociological masterpiece and a crucial work in understanding the development of Brazilian national identity. Da Cunha was deeply influenced by the pseudoscientific racial theories of the era, yet his work is of critical importance in that it represented the first serious attempt to explore the expansiveness of Brazilian identity and to critically examine the Brazilian population and landscape. In his sympathy with the rebel peasants, da Cunha challenged the logic of modernization and progress that identified the interior of Brazil and its nonwhite population with backwardness and questioned the moral dynamics of dominant discourses of development. The following excerpts are taken from two parts of the book. The first reflects on the role ethnic miscegenation had played in shaping the physiology and character of the backland peasants. The second describes the final, brutal confrontation between the Brazilian army and the rebels at Canudos.

Source: John Charles Chasteen, *Born in Blood and Fire: Latin American Voices* (New York: W. W. Norton & Company, Inc., 2011), pp. 144–150. Translated by Samuel Putnam

Indian blood naturally predominated in the backlands populations that formed along the middle reaches of the great São Francisco River. After their initial mixture, these populations then evolved in isolation from the rest of Brazil, conserving the traditions of the past during three centuries, right now to our own day. Whoever travels through those backlands today will observe a notable homogeneity among the people who populate them. The physical characteristics of sertanejo populations vary only slightly, displaying a stable racial type that contrasts at a glance from the highly variable racial mixtures of our Atlantic coastal region. On the coast there is no single, modal type, and one encounters all shades of skin color according to the particular ancestry of each individual, whereas the backland populations seem produced from a single mold, exhibiting an athletic build, straight or wavy hair, and a narrow range of complexions indication a well-amalgamated combination of European, Indian, and African ancestry. The sertanejos likewise share the same mental and moral makeup, the same vices and the same virtues. This uniformity is truly impressive and indicates that the northern backlander has undeniably become a stable and fully formed ethnic and racial type.

Here some parenthetical considerations are in order. A mixture of highly divergent races is, in the majority of cases, prejudicial. Extreme miscegenation leads to the developmental regression, and the *mestiço*[1] lacks both the physical vitality of his non-European ancestors and the intellectual vigor of the European ones. Racially mixed populations may exhibit a certain brilliance of mind, but they are almost always erratic and unstable. We should not possess unity of race, and it is possible that we shall never possess it. The backlands population offers reason for optimism, however: more stable, more robust physically and therefore more capable of superior moral and mental development. Let

us conclude this unappealing parenthetical digression, however, and proceed to a direct consideration of the unique figure presented by our backward fellow countryman, the sertanejo.

The sertanejo's gait is gangly, sinuous, swaying, and loose-jointed. His slouching posture aggravates the effect and gives him a beaten-down hair of humility. When standing, he invariably slumps against a nearby wall or doorway. When on horseback, if he stops to exchange a couple of words with someone he knows, he slips his weight into the stirrup on a single side and reclines against the saddle. When walking, even when walking rapidly, he does not advance firmly in a straight line, but rather, meanders in a manner reminiscent of backland trails. And whenever he stops on foot for any reason, to roll and light a cigarette, for example, he immediately drops—and drops is precisely the word—into a squatting position and sits on his heels, where he can remain for long period perfectly balanced and on his two big toes, with a charming but also slightly ridiculous ease.

The sertanejo has a characteristic air of fatigue expressed in his invincible sluggishness, her perennial lack of muscular vitality, his lazy speech, his awkward gestures, his unsteady gait, his constant tendency to immobility, even in the languid cadence of the songs he habitually sings.

But this air of fatigue is entirely misleading, and nothing is more surprising than seeing it suddenly vanish. The sartanejo's apparently rickety organism undergoes a complete transmutation in an instant whenever anything requires that he unleash his slumbering energies. The man is transfigured. Swiftly, he straightens up and his movements and profile take on entirely new contours. His head, now firmly erect atop his powerful shoulders, flashes with a fearless and piercing gaze. A charge of energy courses through his nervous system, galvanizing his formerly relaxed body, and from the awkward rustic figure of the backlands emerges a potent bronze titan endowed with extraordinary force and agility.

In his normally indolent posture on horseback, the sertanejo rides along behind his herd of cattle, swaying gently in the saddle almost as if he were lying in the hammock where he spends most of his time at home. But let some steer stray into the tangled scrub

---

1   SOURCE: adapted from Euclides da Cunha, *Os sertões* (Rio de Janeiro: Laemmert, 1903). Pp. 558–91, 593–94, 615–16. Portuguese *mestiço* is mostly equivalent to Spanish *mestizo*, although *mestiço* refers to any race mixture, whereas *mestizo* generally refers only to Spanish and indigenous mixtures. Da Cunha's discussion of degeneration in race mixture goes on for pages. Only the key points are represented here [Translator's note.]

some distance up the trail, the horseman suddenly digs his spurs into the flanks of his mount, and off they go, like a shot. Nothing can stop the sertanejo in hot pursuit. Gullies, ravines, dry riverbeds lined by thick and thorny brush do not even slow him down. Anywhere a frightened steer can go, a mounted sertanejo can follow. Leaning forward, glued to his horse's back, his legs clamped to the animal's sides, rider and horse become one, a powerful centaur. Now they burst into a clearing, now they plunge one more into the undergrowth, galloping at full speed. Now the rider twists his body to dodge low boughs, now he leaps off his mount with acrobatic ease to avoid collision with a tree trunk that would otherwise send him sprawling, but, holding firmly to his horse's mane the whole time, he returns to the saddle with a single bound, and all this at an undiminished gallop.

No sooner has the unruly steer been retrieved, however, than the sertanejo slouches once again in the saddle, and sways along with the inert appearance of a semi-invalid. . . .

At dawn on the first of October 1897, the artillery began to prepare for the army's final assault on the rebellious settlement of Canudos. The artillery barrage consisted of converging fire from a semicircle of cannon on the high ground surrounding the cluster of poor huts that remained. The barrage lasted merely forty-eight minutes, but the effect was annihilating. The aim of the guns had been carefully calibrated the night before and they simply could not miss the immobile target. The army was determined to teach the impenitent rebels a fulminating, implacable lesson with a final bayonet charge. So, to eliminate any obstacles to the advancing soldiers, the artillery pulverized and leveled everything on the ground over which the assault would pass.

The tortured stretch of territory was visibly transformed under the withering fire. Roofs caved in, crushing the people huddled in tiny rooms underneath them, walls of mud-daub construction exploded in a rain of splinters and clods, and here and there amid the cluster of crumbling dwellings, tongues of flame licked out, isolated at first, then quickly joining together in a major conflagration. Above the flames, explosive artillery shells arched across the overcast sky of that luminous morning, and not one failed to deliver its deadly payload. They exploded in the ruins of the church, in the town square, on the roofs of the houses, or sometimes passed through the roofs and exploded inside. They exploded in the twisting alleyways, blowing rubbish everywhere. The guns ranged back and forth across what remained of Canudos, demolishing it house by house.

No screams were heard, meanwhile, no one was seen fleeing, nothing. And when the last shot was fired, when thunderous noise finally ceased altogether, the quiet of the stricken settlement gave the impression that the population had somehow inexplicably fled. There was a brief silence, then a bugle sounded atop Favela Hill, and the assault began.

By prior arrangement, the waiting troops sprang forward from three points to converge on the ruined church. Most were invisible as they advanced through the alleyways or along the bottom of the dry streambed. Only one battalion, the Fourth Infantry, was visible to the other combatants, who watched it march forward in quick step and close formation, bayonets at the ready, all the way to the entrance of the town square. It was the first time that an army unit had managed to get there intact.

The Fourth Infantry entered the square in heroic style. But within a few steps the formation started to break apart, instantly off balance. Some soldiers dropped to the ground, as if to take up sheltered firing positions behind the wreckage of the ruined church. Some could be seen scattering backwards, others, charging forward. Dispersed groups milled about in confusion. And then, in the air that still hung silent over Canudos, rose a dull rumble as if from an underground explosion.

The sertanejos were coming to life, suddenly and surprisingly, as always, barring the way to the aggressor with theatrical glory. The Fourth Infantry, which was now absorbing the full fire of the ambush, was brought to a halt, and so were the Twenty-Ninth and Thirty-Ninth Infantry, just arriving. All prearranged maneuvers were now abandoned. Rather than converging on the church, the various battalions fragmented as the troops sought shelter in narrow alleyways.

For almost an hour, the army units that watched from the hilltops around the settlement could detect nothing more happening in the square below; other than the mounting din of distant shouting and rifle fire, a muddled uproar punctuated only by constant, successive, muffled, and anguished bugle calls. The two attacking brigades simply vanished, completely swallowed up by the jumble of splintered houses around the square. Nor did the sertanejos appear, as one might have expected, running toward the square. Assaulted from three directions, the sertanejos were hypothetically to be driven together toward the massed formations of bayonets that were supposed to be waiting for them. But the army's plan had failed totally, and that failure spelled defeat. Encountering unexpected resistance, the troops had stopped and entrenched themselves defensively in a manner entirely contrary to their assigned mission. And now, spilling out of the maze of huts and smoking rubble around the square, the sertanejos descended invisibly on the soldiers who were pinned down there.

Shortly before nine o'clock, the beleaguered army units were encouraged by an illusion of victory. Several reserve battalions reached the square, and one of their members managed to unfurl a Brazilian flag and spread it out on a remaining wall of the ruined church by tucking its corners into the cracks. Dozens of bugles sounded a tribute, and thousands of throats joined them, shouting "Long Live the Republic!"

Surprised, the sertanejos ceased firing, and the square was filled for the first time with jubilant troops. Many spectators, including three generals who had been watching from a safe distance, poured down the slope to join them in square. Hats and swords waved in the air as the joyful soldiers abandoned their positions in a delirious tumult and ran to embrace one another in celebration.

The cruel struggle had finally ended, or so it seemed.

Then, just as the generals began to fight their way through the noisy throng, they were startled to hear bullets began to whine loudly just about their heads. The battle was on again, and the square was suddenly swept clean once more.

And, returning in disarray to their sheltered positions, slipping down along the high banks of the dry streambed, crouching and running for cover wherever they could find it in the grip of sudden terror, bitterly disappointed, feeling singularly cheated by the disappearance of the victory that had appeared so imminent, mocked again by the sertanejos in the very moment when they had thought them vanquished at last, the would-be victors began to understand that the final

battle was not going to be over until it had devoured them all, one by one. Their six thousand modern rifles, their six thousand sabers would not be enough. The blows of twelve thousand arms, the stamp of twelve thousand boot heels, untold numbers of shrapnel-producing shells, all the executions, all the destruction by fire, thirst, and starvation, all the ten months of fighting with its pulverization of the settlement during a hundred days of continuous cannonading under the impassive, clear blue skies of Canudos, all the devastation of its churches, with their altars thrown down and their holy images reduced to ashes—all this had been to no avail. To no avail had they attempted to extinguish the ardent religious vision, consoling and powerful, that had called the settlement into existence.

Other measures would be required to deal with an enemy so impervious to the most violent and destructive forces of nature. Fortunately, the army had foreseen the need for such measures and provided itself with dozens of dynamite bombs. Dynamite filled the need precisely. Somehow, the sertanejos had inverted the usual psychology of warfare. Their reverses only stiffened their resolve. Hunger made them stronger. Defeat made them as hard as rocks.

It made perfect sense. The army's final assault had struck solid rock, the bedrock of our nationality and our race.[2] Dynamite, therefore, was precisely the thing. Its use was appropriate and necessary. It was a consecration.

The firing ceased, and an anguished silence descended on the firing line as the dynamite was deployed. Then, a convulsive earth tremor shook the settlement and radiated out toward the overlooking hills with their encampments and artillery batteries. Seismic shocks rippled across the ground as the last standing fragments of church walls, like rows of jagged teeth, finally tottered and fell, as roof after roof was blown into the air, creating a low-hanging cumulus

---

2   Readers who have followed my logic and evidence concerning our national genesis, and thus recognize our unfortunate current lack of racial unity, will appreciate the significance of my having identified a remarkably stable ethnic subtype in the sertanejo population. It is only natural that, once I accepted the bold and inspiring conjecture that we in Brazil are destined to achieve racial unity eventually, I should have identified the sturdy backlander as the physical nucleus of our future development, the veritable bedrock of our race. [Author's note].

cloud of dust. Terrified shrieks were heard in the brief intervals between the thunderous explosions that rocked the earth. Now, it seemed, the end had indeed come as the very last bit of Canudos was blasted apart.

Outside of the zone of destruction, the troops waited for the flaming thundercloud to subside in order to renew their definitive assault.

But they would have to wait still longer. Rather than advancing, they found themselves reeling back as, incredibly, incomprehensibly, the smoldering rubble began to spit bullets at them once more. The would-be attackers had to dive for shelter. Barely did they glimpse, amid the smoke and flames, the movement of a few figures, women carrying children or pulling them along by the hand deeper into the collapsed rubble figures fleeing randomly or writhing on the ground, their clothes on fire. And other figures, coming at them through the smoke, leaping over flames, making no attempt now to hide, standing up on the few remaining rooftops: the last defenders of Canudos. Their faces and naked torsos singed and smudged, boldly, suicidally, on they came. . . .

STUDY QUESTIONS

1. To what extent does da Cunha's writing challenge or reinforce the dominant scientific racism of the period?
2. How does da Cunha characterize the final military encounter between the Brazilian military and the Canudos rebels? How does this relate to his vision of Brazilian national identity?

JOSÉ ENRIQUE RODÓ

7.2 ARIEL, 1900

Ariel is one of the most enduring pieces of the Latin American canon. José Enrique Rodó was a Uruguayan literary scholar whose masterwork, first published in 1900, drew on characters from Shakespeare's *The Tempest* to argue for the moral and aesthetic superiority of Latin America over the United States and to map out a plan for Latin American cultural development. The book was wildly popular with the Latin American literary classes, and became the foundation for a new generation's cultural nationalism. In this excerpt, Rodó introduces the character of Prospero, who leads the reader through a seminar that explores the different cultural forces at play in turn-of-the-century Latin America, in which he counterposes the vibrancy of Ariel (who serves as a metaphor for Latin America) against the moribund materialism of Caliban (identified with the United States.) For Rodó, the greatest danger of the modern era was the threat of utilitarianism, in which material development becomes an end of its own and spiritual and moral values are sidelined. The essay explores these threats and lays out a vision for an authentically Latin American vision of modernity.

Translated by F. J. Stimson
Source: José Enrique Rodó, Ariel (translated by F. J. Stimson [J. S. of Dale]), (Boston and New York: Houghton Mifflin Comany, The Riverside Press Cambridge, 1922), pp. 31–33, 40–45, 70–73, 94–95, 98–101.

That afternoon, at the end of a year of classes, the wise magician of Shakespeare's *Tempest,* often called Prospero, was bidding his young disciples farewell, gathering them about him one last time.

The students were already present in the large classroom in which an exquisite yet austere décor honored in every fastidious detail the presence of Prospero's books, his faithful companions. An exquisite bronze of *The Tempest's* Ariel, like the presiding spirit of that serene atmosphere, dominated the room. It was the teacher's custom to sit beside this statue, and this is why he had come to be called Prospero, the magician who in the play is attended and served by the fanciful figure depicted by the sculptor. Perhaps, however, an even deeper reason and meaning for the name lay in the master's teaching and character.

Shakespeare's ethereal Ariel symbolizes the noble, soaring aspect of the human spirit. He represents the superiority of reason and feeling over the base impulses of irrationality. He is generous enthusiasm, elevated and unselfish motivation in all actions, spirituality in culture, vivacity and grace in intelligence. Ariel is the ideal toward which human selection ascends, the force that wields life's eternal chisel, effacing from aspiring mankind the clinging vestiges of Caliban, the play's symbol of brutal sensuality.

The regal statue represented the "airy spirit" at the very moment when Prospero's magic sets him free, the instant he is about to take wing and vanish in a flash of light. Wings unfolded; gossamer, floating robes damascened by the caress of sunlight on bronze; wide brow uplifted; lips half-parted in a serene smile—everything in Ariel's pose perfectly anticipated the graceful beginnings of flight. Happily, the inspired artist who formed his image in solid sculpture hand also preserved his angelic appearance and ideal airiness.

Deep in thought, Prospero stroked the statue's brow. Then he seated the young men about him and in a firm voice—a *masterful* voice capable of seizing an idea and implanting it deep within the listener's mind with all the penetrating illumination of a beam of light, the incisive ring of chisel on marble, or the life-infusing touch of brush upon canvas or sculpting wave upon sand—he began to speak, surrounded by his affectionate and attentive students.

Here beside the statue that has daily witnessed our friendly gatherings—from which I have tried to remove any unwelcome austerity—I am going to speak with you one last time, so that our farewell may be the seal stamped on a covenant of emotions and ideas.

I call upon Ariel to be my numen, so that my words will be the most subtle and most persuasive I have ever spoken. I believe that to address the young on any noble and elevated subject is a kind of sacred discourse. I also believe that a young mind is hospitable soil in which the seed of a single timely word will quickly yield immortal fruit.

It is my wish to collaborate on but one page of the agenda that you will draw up in your innermost being and shape with your personal moral character and strength while preparing to breathe the free air of action. This individual agenda—which sometimes may be formulated or written but sometimes is revealed only during the course of action itself—is always to be found in the spirit of those groups and peoples who rise above the multitudes. If, when referring to the philosophy of individual choice, Goethe could say with such profundity that the only man worthy of liberty and life is the man capable of winning them for himself with each new day, can it not also be said—with even greater truth—that the honor of each generation requires it to win liberty and life through its increasing intellectual activity, its own particular efforts, its faith in resolutely expressing the ideal, and its place in the evolution of ideas?

As you earn yours, you must begin by recognizing in yourselves a first article of faith. The youth you are now living is a form of power; it is you who must employ it. And it is a treasure: it is you who must invest it. Cherish that treasure, that power, never lose your burning pride in it, and use it well. I agree with Ernest Renan: "Youth is the discovery of a boundless horizon: Life." This discovery of unexplored worlds must then be completed with the manly strength that conquers them. And no spectacle can be imagined that is more likely to excite both the interest of the thinker and the inspiration of the artist than that of a generation marching toward its future, eager for action, heads high, smiles revealing a haughty disdain for the possibility of disillusion, hearts inspired by visions of bountiful and remote lands, like the Cipango and El Dorado of the heroic chronicles of the Conquistadors.

From the rebirth of human hopes, from the eternal promise that the future will bring the realization of all that is good, the soul awakening to life acquires its beauty—an ineffable beauty composed, like the dawn in Victor Hugo's *Contemplations*, of a "vestige of dream and beginning of thought."

The fact that. . . . I believe that I see everywhere the need for a revitalization, for a revelation of new strengths. I believe that America is in great need of her youth. This is why I am addressing myself to you. This is why I am so extraordinarily interested in your moral orientation. The energy of your word and your example can combine the living strength of the past with the work of the future.

Let us speak, then, of how to assess the life that lies before you.

The many vocations available to you will dictate that you travel in diverse directions and will determine a different temperament and distinctive aptitude in each of you. Some among you will be men of science, others artists, still others men of action. The profound awareness of the fundamental unity of our natures, however, must take precedence over the predilections that bind each of us to our different ways of life. This unity demands that the primary aim of each individual should be to live an unblemished and exemplary life in which nobility and selflessness are communicated before any other faculty. More compelling than professional and cultural variation is our individual responsibility to contribute to the common destiny of rational beings. "There is one profession, which is that of being *man*," was Guyau's profound observation. And Renan, in his assessment of unequal and undeveloped civilizations, reminds us that the goal of man cannot be exclusively to learn, or feel, or imagine, but, rather, to be truly and wholly *human*. This is the ideal of perfection toward which each of us must channel his energies, with the hope that as one individual he may represent the species in miniature.

Aspire, then, to develop to the fullest possible measure the totality of your being—not merely one aspect of it. Do not shrug your shoulders before any noble or creative manifestation of human nature under the pretext that your individuality and preferences bind you to a different one. When you cannot be a participant, you can be an attentive spectator. There is a certain false and vulgarized concept that conceives of education as totally subordinate to a utilitarian end. Such utilitarianism, with its attendant premature specialization, mutilates spiritual integrity and tends to suppress from learning all that is selfless and ideal. This process does not sufficiently take into account the danger of preparing for the future narrow minds that because they can see no reality other than the most immediate will live in icy isolation, separated from others in the same society who have chosen different ways of life.

The fact that each of us must dedicate himself to a specific activity, to a single mode in our culture, does not in any way prevent our hearing the symphony of the spirit and realizing the common destiny of all rational beings. That single activity, that specific cultural mode, will be but one basic note in the harmony of the whole. The famous assertion by the slave of antiquity, "I am a man, nothing human is alien to me," is an eternal truth that will resonate forever in our consciousness. Our capacity to understand must be limited only by our inability to comprehend narrow minds. To be incapable of seeing that Nature has more than one face, that humans have a variety of ideas and interests, is to live in a shadowy dreamworld penetrated by a single ray of light. When intolerance and exclusivity are born of the tyranny that can be imposed by inspiration, or of the obsessiveness that can result from even the most ideal and selfless project, they may be justified—even deserving of sympathy. When, however, intolerance arises from vulgarity, when it attests the limitations of a mind incapable of reflecting more than a partial appearance of things, then intolerance becomes the most abominable of inferiorities.

Unhappily, it is the civilizations that have achieved a whole and refined culture that the danger of spiritual limitation is most real and leads to the most dreaded consequences. In fact, to the degree that culture advances, the law of evolution, manifesting itself in society as in nature to be a growing tendency toward heterogeneity, seems to require a corresponding limitation in individual aptitudes and the inclination to restrict more severely each individual's field of action. While it is a necessary condition to progress, the development of specialization brings with it visible disadvantages, which are not limited to narrowing the horizon of individual intelligences and which inevitably falsify our concept of the world. Specialization, because of the great diversity of individual preferences and habits, is also damaging to a sense of solidarity. . . .

This disjunction of which I have spoken is as damaging to the *aesthetic* of the social structure as it is to its solidarity. The incomparable beauty of Athens, the longevity of the model this goddess of a city bequeathed to us, were owing to a concept of life based on the total harmony of all human faculties and the mutual agreement that all energies should be directed toward glory and power of mankind. Athens knew how to exalt both the ideal and the real, reason and instinct, the forces of the spirit and those of the body. It sculpted all four faces of the soul. Every free Athenian drew around himself a perfect circle to contain his actions, and no disturbing impulse was allowed to impinge upon the graceful proportions within that sphere. The Greek was an athlete and an animated sculpture in the Gymnasium; a citizen of the Pnyx; a debater and intellectual in the Forum. He exercised his will in a broad range of activities, and his intellect in many creative endeavors. This is why Macaulay argued that one day of public life in Attica offered a more brilliant program of instruction than any we draw up in our modern institutions. And from that free and unique flowering of fully developed human nature was born the *Greek miracle*—an inimitable blend of activity and serenity: the spring of the human spirit; a sparkling moment in history.

In our times, the increasing complexity of our civilization would seem to preclude any serious thought of recapturing the harmony possible only in an age of grace and simplicity. But within the complexity of our culture, within the progressive diversity of characters, skills, and values that is the inescapable consequence of progress, it is still reasonable to hope that all human beings may be aware of the fundamental ideas and sentiments that ensure the harmony of life—the *spiritual concerns* to which no rational human being may remain indifferent.

When a sense of materialism and comfort dominates a society as energetically as it does today, the effects of the narrow mind and the single-faceted culture are particularly calamitous for the diffusion of ideals. Although venerated by those who denote their noblest energy to it, for the vast majority of others the ideal remains a remote and perhaps not-even-suspected area of life. All manner of selfless meditation, ideal contemplation, and individual tranquility in which the daily struggle of the utilitarian yields briefly to the serenity that comes from the more elevated gaze of reason are in contemporary society unknown to millions of otherwise civilized and cultivated individuals whose education or habits reduce them to the automatism of strictly materialistic activities. Yes, this kind of servitude must be the most dismal and opprobrious of all moral damnations. I exhort you to defend yourselves, to be militant in preventing your spirit from being mutilated by the tyranny of a single, or a self-interested, objective. Never devote more than a part of yourselves to utility, or to passion. Even within material servitude, the inner self, the self of reason and sentiment, may remain free. Do not, then, use the excuse of commitment to work or responsibilities to justify the enslavement of your spirit. . . .

The inextricably linked concepts of utilitarianism as a concept of human destiny and egalitarian mediocrity as a norm for social relationships compose the formula for what Europe has tended to call the spirit of *Americanism*. It is impossible to ponder either inspiration for social conduct, or to compare them with their opposites, without their inevitable association with the formidable and productive democracy to our North. Its display of prosperity and power is dazzling testimony to the efficacy of its institutions and to the guidance of its concepts. If it has been said that "utilitarianism" is the word for the spirit of the English, then the United States can be considered the embodiment of the word. And the Gospel of that word is spread everywhere through the good graces of its material miracles. Spanish America is not, in this regard, entirely a land of heathens. That powerful federation is effecting a kind of moral conquest among us. Admiration for its greatness and power is making impressive inroads in the minds of our leaders, and perhaps even more, in the impressionable minds of the masses, who are awed by its incontrovertible victories. And from admiring to imitating is an easy step. A psychologist will say that admiration and conviction are passive modes of imitation. . . . Common sense and experience should in themselves be enough to establish this simple relationship. We imitate what we believe to be superior or prestigious. And this is why the vision of an America de-Latinized of its own will, without threat of conquest, and reconstituted in the image and likeness of the North, now looms in the nightmares of many who are genuinely concerned about our future. This vision is the impetus behind an abundance of similar carefully thought-out designs and explains the continuous flow of proposals for innovation and reform. We have our *USA-mania*. It must be limited by the boundaries our reason and sentiment jointly dictate.

When I speak of boundaries, I do not suggest absolute negation. I am well aware that we find our inspirations, our enlightenment, our teachings, in the example of the strong; nor am I unaware that intelligent attention to external events is singularly fruitful in the case of a people still in the process of forming its national entity. I am similarly aware that by persevering in the educational process we hope to modulate the elements of society that must be adapted to new exigencies of civilization and new opportunities in life, thus balancing the forces of heritage and custom with that of innovation. I do not, however, see what is to be gained from denaturalizing the character—the *personality*—of a nation, from imposing and identification with a foreign model, while sacrificing irreplaceable uniqueness. Nor do I see anything to be gained from the ingenuous belief that identity can somehow be achieved through artificial and improvised imitation. . . . In a social structure, as in literature and art, forced imitation will merely distort the configuration of the model. The misapprehension of those who believe they have reproduced the character of a human collectivity in its essence, the living strength of its spirit, as well as the secret of its triumphs and prosperity, and have exactly reproduced the mechanism of its institutions and the external form of its customs, is reminiscent of the delusion of naïve students who believe they have achieved the genius of their master when they have merely copied his style and characteristics.

In such a futile effort there is, furthermore, an inexpressible ignobility. . . . Protecting our *internal* independence—independence of personality and independence of judgment—is a basic form of self-respect. Treatises on ethics often comment on one of Cicero's moral precepts, according to which one of our responsibilities as human beings is zealously to protect the uniqueness of our personal character—whatever in it that is different and formative—while always respecting Nature's primary impulse: that the order and harmony of the world are based on the broad distribution of her gifts. The truth of this precept would seem

even greater when applied to the character of human societies. Perhaps you will hear it said that there is no distinctive mark or characteristic of the present ordering of our peoples that is worth struggling to maintain. What may perhaps be lacking in our collective character is a sharply defined "personality." But in lieu of an absolutely distinct and autonomous particularity, we Latin Americans have a heritage of race, a great ethnic tradition, to maintain, a sacred place in the pages of history that depends upon us for its continuation. Cosmopolitanism, which we must respect as a compelling requisite in our formation, includes fidelity both to the past and to the formative role that the genius of our race must play in recasting the American of tomorrow.

. . . .

Everything in our contemporary America that is devoted to the dissemination and defense of selfless spiritual idealism—art, science, morality, religious sincerity, a politics of ideas—must emphasize its unswerving faith in the future. The past belonged entirely to the arm that wages battle; the present, almost completely to the rugged arm that levels and constructs; the future—a future whose proximity is directly related to the degree of will and thought of those who desire it—offers both stability and ambience for the development of the best qualities of the soul.

Can you envision it, this America we dream of? Hospitable to the world of the spirit, which is not limited to the throngs that flock to seek shelter in her. Pensive, without lessening her aptitude for action. Serene and firm, in spite of her generous enthusiasms. Resplendent, with the charm of an incipient, calm purpose that recalls the expression on a child's face when the germ of a troubled thought begins to disturb its captivating grace. Hold this America in your thoughts. The honor of your future history depends on your having constantly before the eyes of your soul the vision of this regenerated America, filtered down from above upon the realities of the present, like the sun's rays that penetrate the vast rose window of a Gothic nave to cast their warm glow upon somber walls. If you are not to be the founders, you will be the immediate precursors. Future rolls of glory will laud the memory of precursors. . . .

It is not in the name of death, as Hartmann would have it, but in the name of life itself, and hope, that

I call upon you to dedicate a portion of your soul to the work of the future. In making this plea, I have taken my inspiration from the gentle and serene image of Ariel. The beneficent spirit that Shakespeare—perhaps with the divine unawareness frequent in inspired institutions—imbued with such high symbolism is clearly represented in the statue, his ideals magnificently translated by art into line and contour. Ariel is reason and noble sentiment. Ariel is the sublime instinct for perfectibility, by virtue of which human clay—the *miserable clay* of which Arimanes' spirits spoke to Manfred—is exalted and converted into a creature that lives in the glow of Ariel's light: the center of the universe. Ariel is for Nature the crowning achievement of her labors, the last figure in the ascending chain, the spiritual flame. A triumphant Ariel signifies idealism and order in life; noble inspiration in thought; selflessness in morality; good taste in art; heroism in action; delicacy in customs. He is the eponymous hero in the epic of the species. He is the immortal protagonist: his presence inspired the earliest feeble efforts of rationalism in the first prehistoric man when for the first time he bowed his dark brow to chip at rock or trace a crude image on the bones of the reindeer; his wings fanned the sacred bonfire that the primitive Aryan, progenitor of civilized peoples, friend of light, ignited in the mysterious jungles of the Ganges in order to forge with his divine fire the scepter of human majesty. In the later evolution of superior races, Ariel's dazzling light shines above souls that have surpassed the natural limits of humankind, above heroes of thought and fantasy, as well as those of action and sacrifice, above Plato on the promontory of Sunium, as well as above St. Francis of Assisi in the solitude of Monte della Verna. Ariel's irresistible strength is fueled by the ascendant movement of life. Conquered a thousand times over by the indomitable rebellion of Caliban, inhibited by victorious barbarism, asphyxiated in the smoke of battles, his transparent wings stained by contact with the "eternal dunghill of Job," Ariel rebounds, immortal; Ariel recovers his youth and beauty and responds with agility to Prospero's call, to the call of all those who love him and invoke him in reality. At times his beneficent empire reaches even those who deny him and ignore him. He often directs the blind forces of evil and barbarism so that, like others, they will contribute to the work of good. Ariel will pass through human history, humming, as in Shakespeare's drama, his melodious song to animate those who labor and those who struggle, until the fulfillment of the unknown plan permits him—in the same way that in the drama he is liberated from Prospero's service—to break his material bonds and return forever to the center of his divine fire.

I want you to remember my words, but even more, I beseech you to cherish the indelible memory of my statue of Ariel. I want the airy and graceful image of this bronze to be imprinted forever in the innermost recesses of your mind. I remember that once while enjoying a coin collection in a museum my attention was captured by the legend on an ancient coin: the word *Hope*, nearly effaced from the faded gold. As I gazed at that worn inscription, I pondered what its influence might have been. Who knows what noble and active role in forming the character and affecting the lives of human generations we could attribute to that simple theme's working its insistent suggestion upon those who held it in their hands? Who knows, as it circulated from hand to hand, how much fading joy was renewed, how many generous plans brought to fruition, how many evil proposals thwarted, when men's gaze fell upon the inspiring word incised, like a graphic cry, on the metallic disc. May this image of Ariel—imprinted upon your hearts—play the same imperceptible but decisive role in your own lives. In darkest hours of discouragement, may it revive in your consciousness an enthusiasm for the wavering ideal and restore to your heart the ardor of lost hope. Once affirmed in the bastion of your inner being, Ariel will go forth in the conquest of souls. I see him, far in the future, smiling upon you with gratitude from above as your spirit fades into the shadows. I have faith in your will, in your strength, even as I have faith in the will and strength of those to whom you will give life, to whom you will transmit your work. Often I am transported by the dream that one day may be a reality: that the Andes, soaring high above our America, may be carved to form the pedestal for this statue, the immutable altar for its veneration.

These were the words of Prospero. After pressing the master's hand with filial affection, the youthful disciples drifted away. His gently spoken words, like the lament of ringing crystal, lingered in the air. It was last hour of the day. A ray from the dying sun penetrated the room, pierced the shadows, and fell upon the bronze brow of the statue, seeming to strike a restless spark of life in Ariel's exalted eyes. Lingering in the gloom, the beam of light suggested the gaze the spirit, captive in the bronze, cast upon the departing youths. They left in silent unanimity, each absorbed in serious thought—the delicate distillation of meditation that a saint exquisitely compared to the slow and gentle fall of dewdrops upon the fleece of a lamb. When their harsh encounter with the throng brought them back to the surrounding reality, it was night. A warm, serene summer night. The grace and quietude the night spilled upon the earth from its ebony urn triumphed over the rudeness of man's accomplishments. Only the presence of the multitude forbade ecstasy. A warm breeze rippled the evening air with languid and delicious abandon, like wine trembling in the goblet of a bacchant. The shadows cast no darkness on the pure night sky, but painted its blue with a shade that seemed to reflect a pensive serenity. In that cobalt sky, great stars sparkled amid an infinite retinue: Aldebaran, girded with purple; Syrius, like the cup of nielloed silver calyx upturned above the world; the Southern Cross, whose open arms extend across our America as if in defense of one last hope. . . .

It was then, following the prolonged silence, that the youngest of the group, the one they called "Enjolras" on account of his resemblance to Hugo's pensive character, pointed to the meandering human flock, and then to the radiant beauty of the night:

"As I watch the passing throng, I notice that although people are not gazing at them. Something is descending from above upon these indifferent masses, dark as newly turned earth. The scintillation of the stars is like the movement of the sower's hands."

STUDY QUESTIONS

1. Who is the intended audience for Rodó's essay? How does the audience impact the radicalism of Rodó's vision?
2. What can we learn from the excerpt about why Rodó was so uncomfortable with utilitarianism and materialism as the foundation of modernity? In what ways did *Ariel* challenge these commodified values?

EMILIANO ZAPATA

7.3 THE PLAN OF AYALA, 1911

Emiliano Zapata was a leading figure in the Mexican Revolution. His Plan of Ayala was central to the radicalization of the revolution and the shift toward peasant-oriented politics. In the Plan of Ayala, Zapata denounces President Francisco Madero and accuses him of betraying the values of the revolution. Most significantly, Zapata lays out a vision for significant land reform, including the nationalization of large estates and their redistribution among peasants and indigenous communities. The plan enshrined Zapata as the most important peasant leader in the South of Mexico and ushered in a critical new phase in revolutionary politics in which the peasantry broke decisively with urban elites. The document would become something of a sacred text in the Zapatista movement.

Source: Gilbert M. Joseph and Timothy J. Henderson (eds.), *The Mexico Reader: History, Culture, Politics* (Durham, NC: Duke University Press, 2002), pp. 339–343.

Liberating Plan of the sons of the State of Morelos, affiliated with the Insurgent Army which defends the fulfillment of the Plan of San Luis, with the reforms that it believes necessary to increase the welfare of the Mexican Fatherland.

The undersigned, constituted into a Revolutionary Junta to sustain and carry out the promises made to the country by the Revolution of 20 November 1910, solemnly declare before the civilized world which sits in judgement on us, and before the Nation to which we belong and which we love, the propositions we have formulated to do away with the tyranny that oppresses us and to redeem the Fatherland from the dictatorships that are imposed upon us, which are outlined in the following plan:

1. Taking into consideration that the Mexican people, led by don Francisco I. Madero, went out to shed their blood to reconquer liberties and vindicate their rights which had been trampled upon, and not so that one man could seize power, violating the sacred principles that he swore to defend with the slogan "Effective Suffrage and No Reelection," thereby insulting the faith, cause and liberties of the people; taking into consideration that the man to whom we refer is don Francisco I. Madero, the same who initiated the aforementioned revolution, who imposed his will and influence as a governmental norm upon the Provisional Government of the ex-president of the Republic, licenciado Francisco León de la Barra, causing with these deed much bloodshed and many misfortunes to the fatherland in a cunning and ridiculous fashion, having no goals to satisfy apart from his own personal ambitions, his boundless instincts for tyranny, and his profound disrespect for the fulfillment of the preexisting laws emanating from the immortal Constitution of 1857, written with the revolutionary blood of Ayutla.

Taking into account that the so-called chief of the Liberating Revolution of Mexico, don Francisco I. Madero, due to his great weakness and lack of integrity, did not bring to a happy conclusion the Revolution that he began with the help of God and of the people, since he left intact the majority of the governing powers and corrupt elements of oppression from the dictatorial Government of Porfirio Díaz, which are not and can never in any way be representative of the National sovereignty, and that, being terrible enemies of ourselves and of the principles that we defend, are causing the ills of the country and opening new wounds in the breast of the Fatherland, making it drink its own blood; taking also into account that the aforementioned don Francisco I. Madero, current president of the Republic, tried to avoid fulfilling the promises he made to the Nation in the Plan of San Luis Potosí,. . . nullifying, persecuting, imprisoning, or killing the revolutionary elements who helped him to occupy the high post of president of the Republic, by means of false promises and numerous intrigues against the Nation.

Taking into consideration that the oft-mentioned Francisco I. Madero has tried to silence with the brute force of bayonets and to drown in blood the people who ask, solicit, or demand the fulfillment of the promises of the Revolution, calling them bandits and rebels, condemning them to a war of extermination, without conceding or granting any of the guarantees that reason, justice, and the law prescribe; taking equally into account that the president of the Republic, Francisco I. Madero, has made of Effective Suffrage a bloody mockery by imposing, against the will of the people, the licenciado José María Suárez as Vice-President of the Republic, imposing also the governors of the States, designating such men as the so-called general Ambrosio Figueroa, cruel tyrant of the people of Morelos; and entering into collaboration with the científico party, feudal hacendados and oppressive caciques, enemies of the Revolution he proclaimed, with the aim of forging new chains and continuing the mould of a new dictatorship more opprobrious and more terrible than that of Porfirio Díaz; so it has become patently clear that he has undermined the sovereignty of the States, mocking the laws with no respect for life or interests, as has happened in the state of Morelos and other states, bringing us to the most horrific anarchy registered in contemporary history. Due to these considerations, we declare Francisco I. Madero incapable of realizing the promises of the revolution of which he was instigator, because he has betrayed all of his principles, mocking the will of the people in his rise to power; he is incapable of governing and because he has no respect for the law and for the justice of the people, and is a traitor to the Fatherland, humiliating the Mexicans by blood and fire because they wish for freedom and an end to the pandering to científicos, hacendados and caciques who enslave us; today we continue the Revolution begun by [Madero], and will carry on until we defeat the dictatorial powers that exist.

2. Francisco I. Madero is disavowed as Chief of the Revolution and as President of the Republic for the reasons expressed above. We shall bring about the overthrow of this functionary.

3. We recognize as Chief of the Liberating Revolution General Pascual Orozco, second of the caudillo don Francisco I. Madero, and in case he does not accept this delicate post, we shall recognize as chief of the Revolution General Emiliano Zapata.

4. The Revolutionary Junta of the State of Morelos manifests to the Nation, under formal protest, that it adopts the Plan of San Luis Potosí as its own, with the additions that shall be expressed below, for the benefit of the oppressed peoples, and it will make itself the defender of the principles that they defend until victory or death.

5. The Revolutionary Junta of the State of Morelos will not admit transactions or agreements until it has brought about the defeat of the dictatorial elements of Porfirio Díaz and of Francisco I. Madero, for the Nation is tired of false men and traitors who make promises like liberators, and upon attaining power forget those promises and become tyrants.

6. As an additional part of our plan, we make it known: that the lands, forests and waters that have been usurped by the hacendados, científicos or caciques in the shadow of venal justice, will henceforth enter into the possession of the villages or of citizens who have titles corresponding to those properties, and who have been despoiled through the bad faith of our oppressors, and they shall maintain that possession with weapon in hand, and the usurpers who believe they have rights to those lands will be heard by the special tribunals that will be established upon the triumph of the Revolution.

7. In view of the fact that the immense majority of Mexican villages and citizens own no more land than that which they tread upon, and are unable in any way to better their social condition or dedicate themselves to industry or agriculture, because the lands, forests, and waters are monopolized in only a few hands; for this reason, we expropriate without previous indemnization one third of those monopolies from the powerful proprietors, to the end that the villages and citizens of Mexico should obtain ejidos, colonias, and fundos legales for the villages, or fields for sowing or laboring, and this shall correct the lack of prosperity and increase the well-being of the Mexicans.

8. The hacendados, científicos or caciques who directly or indirectly oppose the present Plan, shall have their properties nationalized and two thirds of those properties shall be given as indemnizations of war, pensions to widows and orphans of the victims who are killed in the struggles surrounding the present Plan.

9. In order to execute the procedures respecting the aforementioned properties, the laws of disamortization and nationalization shall be applied, as convenient; for our norm and example shall be the laws put into effect by the immortal Juárez against ecclesiastical properties, which chastised the despots and conservatives who have always wanted to impose upon us the ignominious yoke of oppression and backwardness.

10. The insurgent military chiefs of the Republic who rose up in arms to the voice of don Francisco I. Madero in order to defend the Plan of San Luis Potosí, and who now forcefully oppose the present Plan, will be judged traitors to the cause that they defended and to the Fatherland, for presently many of them, in order to placate the tyrants, or for a fistful of coins, or owing to schemes or bribes, are shedding the blood of their brothers who demand the fulfillment of the promises that were made to the nation by don Francisco I. Madero.

11. The expenses of war will be appropriated according to article XI of the Plan of San Luis Potosí, and all of the procedures employed in the Revolution that we undertake will be in accordance with the same instructions that are set out in the mentioned Plan.

12. Once the Revolution that we are making has triumphed, a junta of the principle revolutionary chiefs of the different States will name or designate an interim President of the Republic, who will convoke elections for the organization of federal powers.

13. The principal revolutionary chiefs of each State, in council, shall designate the governor of the State, and this high functionary will convoke the

elections for the proper organization of public powers, with the aim of avoiding forced appointments that bring misfortune to the people, like the well-known appointment of Ambrosio Figueroa in the State of Morelos and others, who condemn us to the precipice of bloody conflicts sustained by the dictator Madero and the circle of científicos and hacendados who have suggested this to him,

14. If President Madero and the rest of the dictatorial elements of the current and old regime want to avoid the immense misfortunes that afflict the fatherland, and if they possess true sentiments of love for it, they must immediately renounce the posts they occupy, and by doing so they shall in some way staunch the grievous wounds that have opened in the breast of the Fatherland, and if they do not do so, upon their heads shall fall the blood and anathema of our brothers.

15. Mexicans: consider the deviousness and bad faith of a man who is shedding blood in a scandalous manner, because he is incapable of governing; consider that his system of Government is tying up the fatherland and trampling upon our institutions with the brute force of bayonets; so that the very weapons we took up to bring him to Power, we now turn against him for failing to keep his promises to the Mexican people and for having betrayed the Revolution he began; we are not personalists, we are partisans of principles and not of men!

Mexican people, support this Plan with weapons in your hands, and bring prosperity and welfare to the Fatherland.

Liberty, Justice, and Law. Ayala, State of Morelos, November 25, 1911

General in chief, Emiliano Zapata; signatures.

STUDY QUESTIONS

1. What does Zapata see as the commonalities between President Madero and Porfirio Diaz? What does this characterization tell us about the tensions between elite and peasant priorities?
2. Why does Zapata see land reform as so essential? What changes will land reform usher in?

7.4 THE MEXICAN CONSTITUTION OF 1917

The Constitution of 1917 represented the formalization and institutionalization of the Mexican Revolution. It is still in effect today. The Constitutional Convention held in the city of Santiago de Querétaro was presided over by President Carranza, but the majority of the delegates were educated middle-class professionals who were more radical than their leader, and the convention pushed firmly toward social justice. Although many of its provisions were never fully enforced, the constitution became a model for progressive political movements around the world. Two of the most notable clauses of the constitution are Article 3 and Article 123, each replicated here. Article 3 provided for the full separation of Church and State and guaranteed the right to a secular education. Article 123 articulated the rights of workers, providing for overtime pay and maternity leave and enshrining the right of labor to organize and strike.

Source: English Translation of the New Mexican Constitution, Effective from May 5th 1917.

. . . Art. 3—Instruction is free; but that imparted in the official schools as also the primary, intermediate and higher instruction imparted in private establishments, must be laical. No religious body, nor a minister of any religious sect, will be allowed to establish or direct schools of primary education. Private primary schools may only be established under official supervision. In the official schools primary instruction will be imparted gratis. . . .

Art. 123—The Congress of the Union and the State Legislatures will make laws relative to labor with regard to the needs of each part of the Republic, and in conformity with the following principles, which shall govern the labor of workmen, journeymen, employees, domestic servants and artisans, and in general every contract of labor,

I. Eight hours will be the maximum limit of a day's work.

II. The maximum limit of night work shall be seven hours. Unhealthy and dangerous occupations are forbidden to women in general and to children under sixteen years of age. Night work in industrial concerns is also forbidden to women and to children under sixteen years of age; nor may they work in commercial establishments after ten o'clock at night.

III. For children over twelve and under sixteen years of age the maximum limit of a day's work shall be six hours. The labor of children under twelve years of age may not be the object of a contract.

IV. Each workman will enjoy at least one day's rest for every six days worked.

V. During the three months immediately preceding childbirth women shall not perform any work requiring a considerable physical effort; during the month following childbirth they shall enjoy a rest with their wages or salary paid in full, and retaining their employment and the rights they may have acquired under their contracts. During the time of lactation they will enjoy two daily extraordinary periods of rest of one half hour each in order to nurse their children.

VI. The minimum wage paid a workman will be that considered sufficient, taking into consideration the conditions prevailing in the respective region of the country, to supply the normal needs of life of the workman, his education and his lawful pleasures, considered as the head of a family. In all agricultural, commercial, manufacturing or mining enterprises, the workman will have a right to share in the profits in the manner adjusted by clause IX of this Article.

VII. The same wage must be paid for the same work, regardless of sex or nationality.

VIII. The minimum wage is exempt from attachment, recompense or discount.

IX. The fixing of the minimum wage and the profit-sharing mentioned in clause VI shall be done by special commissions appointed in each community and subordinated to the Central Board of Conciliation to be established in each State.

X. Wages must be paid in legal currency and not in merchandise, orders, counters or any other representative sign as a substitute for money.

XI. When for extraordinary circumstances it becomes necessary to increase the hours of work, the overtime shall be paid for at the rate of one hundred percent more than the rate fixed for regular time. In no case may the overtime exceed three hours daily, nor continue for more than three consecutive days; no women of any age nor boys under sixteen years of age may be allowed to work overtime.

XII. In all agricultural, industrial, mining or other class of work, employers are obligated to furnish their workmen with comfortable and sanitary habitations, for which they may charge rents not exceeding one half of one per cent of the assessed value of the property. Schools, hospitals and other services necessary to the community should also be established by them. In the case of factories located within the bounds of inhabited places, where they employ more than one hundred persons, the first condition mentioned above must be complied with.

XIII. In addition, in these labor centers when their population exceeds two hundred inhabitants, a space of land of not less than five thousand square meters shall be set aside for the construction of public markets, and buildings designed for municipal purposes and places of amusement. The establishment of saloons and gambling houses is prohibited in such labor centers.

XIV. Employers are held responsible for labor accidents and diseases caused by the work done; therefore, employers must pay the corresponding indemnity according to whether death or temporary or permanent disability has ensued, in accordance with the provisions of the law. This responsibility shall hold good even though the employer has contracted for the work through a labor agent.

XV. Employers are obligated to observe in the installation of their establishments all the precepts of law regarding hygiene and sanitation, and to adopt adequate measures to prevent accidents from the use of machinery, tools and materials of work as also to organize the work in such a manner as to assure the greatest guarantee possible for the health and lives of the workmen, compatible with the nature of the business under penalties which the law will establish.

XVI. Both the workmen and the employers shall have a right to unite for the defense of their respective interests, forming syndicates, unions, etc.

XVII. The laws will recognize the right of workmen and employers to strike and to suspend work.

XVIII. Strikes shall be lawful when their object is to secure a balance between the various factors of production, and to harmonize the rights of capital and labor. In Public service, the workmen must give ten days notice in advance of declaring the strike to the Board of Conciliation and Arbitration. Strikes may only be considered unlawful when the majority of the strikers resort to acts of violence against persons or property, or in case of war when the strikers belong to institutions and services dependent on the Government. Employees of military manufacturing establishments of the Federal Government are not included in the provisions of this clause inasmuch as they are a branch of the national army.

XIX. Suspensions of work shall only be lawful when the excess of production renders it necessary to close down in order to maintain prices above the cost of production, and when previously approved by the Board of Conciliation and Arbitration.

XX. Differences or conflicts between capital and labor shall be submitted for settlement to a Board of Conciliation and Arbitration consisting of an equal number of representatives of the employers and workmen, of one representative of the Government.

XXI. If the employer refuses to submit his difference to arbitration or to accept the decision of the Board, the labor contract shall be considered as terminated, and the employer must indemnify the workmen by the payment of three months' wages, in addition to any liability incurred by reason of the dispute. If the workmen reject the decision of the Board the contract will be considered to have terminated.

XXII. The employer who discharges a workman without just cause or for being a member of a union or syndicate, or for having taken part in a lawful strike, must at the option of the laborer either perform the contract or indemnify the workman by the payment of three months' salary. He will also have the same obligation if the workman leaves his employ on account of lack of good faith on the part of the employer, or of mistreatment either as to his own person or that of his wife, parents, children, brothers or sisters. The employer may not evade this responsibility when the mistreatment is committed by subordinates or agents acting with his consent or knowledge.

XXIII. Credits in favor of workmen for salaries or wages accrued during the past year, or other indemnities shall be given preference over any other claims in cases of execution proceedings or bankruptcy.

XXIV. The debts contracted by workmen in favor of their employers or of the associates, subordinates or agents of their employers, can only be charged against the workmen themselves, and in no case nor for any reason collected from the members of their families, nor shall such debts be collected by taking more than the entire wages of the workmen for any one month.

XXV. No charge may be made for securing work for workmen by municipal offices, employment bureaus or other public or private agencies.

XXVI. Every contract between a Mexican and a foreign employer must be legalized before a competent municipal authority and vised by the Consul of the country to which the workman wishes to go, with the understanding that in addition to the usual clauses, it is clearly specified that the cost of repatriation of the laborer will be for the cost of the foreign employer.

XXVII. The following stipulations will be null and void and not binding on the contracting parties, even though included in the contract: (a) Those which provide for an inhuman day's work on account of it notorious excessiveness, in view of the nature of the work. (b) Those providing a wage which in the judgment of the Board of Conciliation and Arbitration is not remunerative. (c) Those which provide a period of more than one week before wages are paid. (d) Those which assign places of amusement, eating houses, cafes, tavern, saloons or shops for the payment of wages, unless employees of such establishments are the ones Involved. (e) Those which involve a direct or indirect obligation to purchase articles of consumption in specified shops or places. (f) Those which permit retaining wages by way of fines. (g) Those constituting a renunciation on the part of the workmen of the indemnities to which he may be entitled because of labor accidents, diseases contracted from the work, damages occasioned by nonperformance of the contract, or for discharge from the work. (h) All other stipulations which imply the waiver by the workman of some right vested in him by the labor laws.

XXVIII. The laws shall determine what property constitutes the family estate, which goods shall be inalienable and may not be mortgaged, nor attached, and may bequeathed and inherited by means of simplified formalities of the succession proceedings.

XXIX. There will be considered of social utility: Institutions of popular insurance for old age, sickness, life, lack of employment, accident, and others of a similar character; therefore, both the Federal and State Governments will encourage the organization of such institutions, to instill and inculcate habits of thrift.

XXX. The cooperative associations for the construction of cheap and sanitary habitations for workmen are likewise to be considered of public utility, when these properties are intended to be acquired in ownership by the workmen within specified periods.

STUDY QUESTIONS

1. Why was education given such a central role in the constitution?
2. What are some of the most striking rights granted to workers by the 1917 constitution?
3. What do these rights reveal about the role of organized labor in the Mexican revolution?

ALFONSINA STORNI

7.5 AN OLD STORY, 1919

The spread of democratization and modernization did not lead to equal rights for women. In this essay, first published in the literary journal *La Nota* in 1919, the Argentine poet Alfonsina Storni reflects on the importance of feminism and laments its limited impact on progressive thought in the male-dominated intellectual circles of Buenos Aires. Storni was one of the most significant first-wave feminists in Latin America, and she advocated fervently for women's political rights and sexual autonomy. A single mother, Storni achieved great career success, winning multiple literary prizes for her work, before committing suicide in 1938 at the age of forty-six.

AN OLD STORY

There was a time when I had no intention of writing a serious word about feminism. It seemed to me that to talk about an accomplished fact was a waste of time.

But then I came across an article by Carlos Gutiérrez Larreta entitled "Women's Committees," which appeared in the previous issue of this journal. It has snapped me out of my torpor and is inducing me to commit the millionth foolish act of my life.

I believe that my kind friend has written the article just the way he usually recites his certainly magnificent madrigals and sonnets.

He has smoked two or three Turkish cigarettes, read his favorite poets, and then taken a few brightly colored billiard balls and caromed them around with a gold pen.

These caroms are his article.

But in the life of the brilliant little billiard balls the writer plays with are weighty worlds, and the billiard cue that moves them is subject to formidable laws. As we contemplate the implications of these laws our whole being trembles; our faces fall, our tears flow, and we are suddenly saddened and confused by this inescapable, inexplicable thing.

Only by making a carefree game cunning can one speak of feminism in terms of chivalrous pardon for feminine mischievousness.

I believe that feminism deserves much more than flippant gallantry because it is as important as a complete collective transformation.

I would even dare assert that so-called feminism is nothing more than man's managerial failure to achieve by legal means the necessary equilibrium of human happiness.

If every chief of state and every head of the family were capable of knowing, and then satisfying, all the needs of the people under them, there would be an end to all modern problems, including the now-famous problem of feminism.

But life is not an equation perceived by the eyes of man. However much one looks ahead, one will never see the intimate spiritual depths of each individual whose longings, unsatisfied, become the very struggle required for evolution.

Of this permanent discontent, of this third, of this expectation, of this endless movement eternity is made.

To say man is superior to woman, woman is equal to man, etc. seems to me no more than words, words, words.

To speak of feminism and to separate it from everything like an isolated entity, with no relationship and merely as an arbitrary expression of feminine caprice, seems utter nonsense to me.

Source: Gabriela Nouzeilles and Craciela Montaldo (eds.), *The Argentina Reader* (Durham, NC: Duke University Press, 2002), pp. 254–258. Translated by Patricia Owen Steiner

To think that "woman wants this despite the fact that we are advising her otherwise" is not to think at all.

What does woman want?

Are thoughts and collective aspirations like mushrooms that sprout up whenever or wherever they feel like it?

Did men dictate that nails would emerge from their fingers?

To poke fun at feminism, for example, seems to me as curious as to poke fun at a finger because it ends in a nail. To arrive at what we call *feminism*, humanity has followed a process as exact as the one that an embryo follows to become a fruit or that a fruit follows to transform its elements from an embryo, each in their successive steps.

There is as much truth in the embryo as in the stem, in the stem as in the leaves, in the leaves as in the flower or any other stage of its development.

Clearly we have the right to express an opinion about which moment of that transformation appears to us to be more harmonious, more complete.

The writer we mentioned finds that the [ancient] Greeks, such exalted beings, had no feminism.

But this does not have to be the reason for the sublimity of Greece. By following such criteria we would come to believe that it was enough for a population not to have feminism for it to demonstrate its equilibrium.

I could point out to him that the Middle Ages, which did not have feminism, is an example of a barbarous period characterized by its humiliation of feminine dignity under the pretext of a stupid chastity and a religion that was as depressing as it was avaricious.

But in truth we have nothing in the past that can enlighten us about a movement like the present one, the fruit of our own days.

If the time in which we live is compared to some luminous periods of the past, such as [ancient] Greece, for example, it is seen as a setback, and we cannot attribute this setback to feminism.

On the contrary, feminism stems from this setback by seeking for "its" support, "its" ray of light, in troubled waters where nothing is visible. And, for that seeking, women want to use their own eyes.

Let me make myself clear: Catholic dogma is bankrupt; civilization is bankrupt; everything that has been built up in the last twenty centuries is crashing down with a deafening roar, its balance destroyed, its center of gravity out of kilter.

Men, after repeating the same old things for a long time, are bored with themselves and are demanding new actions, new words, new life.

This is as old as the sun.

We go now from unity to the parts.

Power is distributed, knowledge is distributed, responsibility is distributed. Man does not know what awaits him when he loses his protectorate, but he wants to free himself from it. Today every human cell wants to feel responsibility.

To disperse, to separate, to divide.

This is what things say.

Nonexistent or ineffectual dogma, a hard economic life, imperfect justice—for whom is woman now waiting? What holy word or perception of human justice leads her to accept the idea that she always comes out the loser, without daring to say, "I want to try doing this for myself"?

I understand perfect submission when the hand directing one's life is perfect, when that hand has taken care of and foreseen everything, for then obedience is sweet, slavery a pleasure.

But, while everything is changing and an infinity of laws and customs from earlier times are being modified, a group of women, protected by neither state nor man, are taking up the struggle against the new laws and customs.

These are the women who have had to earn their own living, those who are in a position to talk about the bunches of flowers that masculine piety tosses at their feet lest their delicate soles get hurt.

In the struggle for existence there is no truce, no sex, no pity, no flowers. Oh, poet! It's every man for himself. The first one gets the prize, and often the one arriving second, if he's stronger, snatches it away.

At least that's the pattern I personally experienced in my hard apprenticeship.

It is in great part this ruthless aspect of life that has broken woman's submission and that now tries her will, tries her ideas, tries her personality.

She doesn't part company with man, but she has stopped believing in the divine mission that dogma assigned him.

She doesn't turn against man, for, as she struggles, she thinks about her son, a man. But she distrusts the state's protection, she distrusts man's justice, and she tends, as I said before, to exercise her responsibility.

It is true that this way of living separates her somewhat from her instincts, but who says that instinct is an end and not simply a means?

Isn't it perhaps true that choice is one of the capabilities that characterizes humankind?

Only the egotism of the species can lead man to believe that he is the one uniquely qualified to make choices. I firmly believe that feminism today is a question of justice.

This way of thinking to which woman aspires, in fact, goes hand in hand with the condition of being born free that belongs to both woman and man—the right to exercise free will.

Naturally, in the course of developing her general abilities, woman will do as many foolish things as man has done, and goes right along doing, despite his long experience in directing affairs.

I believe also that perfection is unattainable and that woman and man, as they try to reach it, will both make the same kind of mistakes that have already been made.

But in the feminine exercise of this aspiration to responsibility there is no other justification than the unknown law that governs us, the law that has provided man with all his downfalls and consequently with all the changes through which he manages to survive.

None of us knows where this movement we call *feminism* is heading, but nothing will detain it.

Meanwhile, before long, women will obtain the suppression of the laws and concepts that have shameful impact on feminine dignity, laws that a number of stalwart women have already rendered null. To transform words like *shame, pardon,* and *error* into *right of the woman, right of the mother,* and *right of the human being* will be one of the inevitable and invaluable triumphs of feminism.

As for the rest, woman's increased development implies a refinement of her femininity, a greater spiritual grace, a harmony that is restored only by controlled instincts.

This may seem a contradiction to my earlier paragraph, but it is not.

Instinct controlled by clear, conscious reasoning is a very different thing from instinct harshly suffocated because of dogma. Putting instincts in proper balance will be another of feminism's victories.

And if Christ, according to my kind friend Gutiérrez Larreta, had woman mapped out for a different direction, he will see, once again, that neither women nor men now succeed—nor ever will succeed—in comprehending that direction. For, although it may be opportune to present myths in articles and essays, these myths are ultimately indigestible for humankind because humankind is so weak, so trusting in an infinite divine goodness that, despite all the gospels, allows mankind to kill, rob, or commit "rosy, silky little sins," in the words of Rubén Darío, who, without Christ's permission, must have been quite a feminist. . . .

STUDY QUESTIONS

1. Why is feminism relevant to men as well as women, according to Storni?
2. What types of rights does Storni see as especially important to the advancement of women?

7.6 CUBAN TOURISM MATERIALS, 1920s

During the 1920s tourism boomed in Cuba. The island was marketed to wealthy Americans as a place to escape the cold weather and to enjoy drinking, gambling, and other pursuits outlawed in the United States during prohibition. Havana in particular became a major destination for North American tourists, fueled by the imagination of entrepreneurs like Milton Hershey, who turned his sugar business into a tourist attraction. The following materials are postcards and other promotional materials created during the Cuban tourist boom. They include a 1920 postcard of the Hershey Estates, a 1922 postcard of the Havana Carnival, and a 1925 postcard of the San Souci Bar. Also presented are the cover of the *Havana Journal* from July 1927 depicting the Malecon of Havana (the main seaside promenade); images of embroidered handkerchiefs sold to tourists; and the cover of the sheet music for Irving Berlin's 1919 hit song "I'll See You in Cuba."

Habana: Comparsa de Carnaval. Carnival Season

Source: Taken from the Viki Gold Levi Cuban Materials Collection in the Wolfsonian Digital Images Catalog at FIU, http://www.wolfsonian.org/research-library/research-at-the-museum/special-collections-and-archives/the-vicki-gold-levi-collection

STUDY QUESTIONS

1. What are the key elements of Cuban culture being marketed to American tourists in these materials? What role did Cuban people play in the images being presented?
2. What types of insights do these visual materials provide about the impact of tourism on Cuban society in the 1920s?

CHAPTER 8

THE DEPRESSION AND AUTHORITARIAN POPULISTS, 1930–1950

FRANKLIN DELANO ROOSEVELT
8.1 THE GOOD NEIGHBOR POLICY, 1933

In the 1930s President Franklin D. Roosevelt sought to articulate a new version of foreign policy with regards to US–Latin American relations, one that would be less interventionist and that would seek to build reciprocal exchanges with the region. Roosevelt's vision became known as the "Good Neighbor Policy" and led to the termination of the US occupation of Nicaragua and Haiti and the annulment of the Platt Amendment. This speech was given by Roosevelt to the Governing Board of the Pan-American Union in Washington, DC, on April 12, 1933, to celebrate "Pan-American Day" and is considered one of the earliest and fullest articulations of the Good Neighbor Policy.

THE PRESIDENT BEGINS TO CARRY OUT THE GOOD-NEIGHBOR POLICY. APRIL 12, 1933

Address of the President before the Special Session of the Governing Board of the Pan-American Union on the occasion of the celebration of "Pan-American Day," Washington.

I rejoice in this opportunity to participate in the celebration of "Pan-American Day" and to extend on behalf of the people of the United States a fraternal greeting to our sister American Republics. The celebration of "Pan-American Day" in this building, dedicated to international good-will and cooperation, exemplifies a unity of thought and purpose among the peoples of this hemisphere. It is a manifestation of the common ideal of mutual helpfulness, sympathetic understanding and spiritual solidarity.

There is inspiration in the thought that on this day the attention of the citizens of the twenty-one Republics of America is focused on the common ties—historical, cultural, economic, and social—which bind them to one another. Common ideals and a community of interest, together with a spirit of cooperation, have led to the realization that the well-being of one Nation depends in large measure upon the well-being of its neighbors. It is upon these foundations that Pan Americanism has been built.

Source: *The Public Papers and Addresses of Franklin D. Roosevelt with a Special Introduction and Explanatory Notes by President Roosevelt, Volume Two: The Year of Crisis, 1933* (New York: Random House, 1938), pp. 129–131

This celebration commemorates a movement based upon the policy of fraternal cooperation. In my Inaugural Address I stated that I would "dedicate this Nation to the policy of the good neighbor—the neighbor who resolutely respects himself and, because he does so, respects the rights of others—the neighbor who respects his obligations and respects the sanctity of his agreements in and with a world of neighbors." Never before has the significance of the words "good neighbor" been so manifest in international relations. Never have the need and benefit of neighborly cooperation in every form of human activity been so evident as they are today.

Friendship among Nations, as among individuals, calls for constructive efforts to muster the forces of humanity in order that the atmosphere of close understanding and cooperation may be cultivated. It involves mutual obligations and responsibilities, for it is only by sympathetic respect for the rights of others and a scrupulous fulfillment of the corresponding obligations by each member of the community that a true fraternity can be maintained.

The essential qualities of a true Pan Americanism must be the same as those which constitute a good neighbor, namely, a mutual understanding, and, through such understanding, a sympathetic appreciation of the other's point of view. It is only in this manner that we can hope to build up a system of which confidence, friendship and good-will are the cornerstones.

In this spirit the people of every Republic on our continent are coming to a deep understanding of the fact that the Monroe Doctrine, of which so much has been written and spoken for more than a century, was and is directed at the maintenance of independence by the peoples of the continent. It was aimed and is aimed against the acquisition in any manner of the control of additional territory in this hemisphere by any non-American power.

Hand in hand with this Pan-American doctrine of continental self-defense, the peoples of the American Republics understand more clearly, with the passing years, that the independence of each Republic must recognize the independence of every other Republic. Each one of us must grow by an advancement of civilization and social well-being and not by the acquisition of territory at the expense of any neighbor.

In this spirit of mutual understanding and of cooperation on this continent you and I cannot fail to be disturbed by any armed strife between neighbors. I do not hesitate to say to you, the distinguished members of the Governing Board of the Pan-American Union, that I regard existing conflicts between four of our sister Republics as a backward step.

Your Americanism and mine must be a structure built of confidence, cemented by a sympathy which recognizes only equality and fraternity. It finds its source and being in the hearts of men and dwells in the temple of intellect.

We all of us have peculiar problems, and, to speak frankly, the interest of our own citizens must, in each instance, come first. But it is equally true that it is of vital importance to every Nation of this Continent that the American Governments, individually, take, without further delay, such action as may be possible to abolish all unnecessary and artificial barriers and restrictions which now hamper the healthy flow of trade between the peoples of the American Republics.

I am glad to deliver this message to you, Gentlemen of the Governing Board of the Pan-American Union, for I look upon the Union as the outward expression of the spiritual unity of the Americas. It is to this unity which must be courageous and vital in its element that humanity must look for one of the great stabilizing influences in world affairs.

STUDY QUESTIONS

1. What are the obligations of a good neighbor, according to Roosevelt?
2. What connections does Roosevelt draw between Pan-Americanism and the Monroe Doctrine?

LÁZARO CÁRDENAS

8.2 MESSAGE TO THE MEXICAN NATION ON THE OIL QUESTION, 1938

In 1938, Mexican President Lázaro Cárdenas announced the nationalization of foreign-owned oil companies. In this speech introducing the new policy, Cárdenas insists that in accordance with the Constitution of 1917, all mineral and oil reserves found within Mexico belong to the nation. The oil expropriation was wildly popular in Mexico and consolidated popular support for Cárdenas, however, it led to tensions and economic boycotts from the United States, Britain, and the Netherlands, whose oil companies were significantly impacted.

In refusing to comply with the mandates of the Nation's judicial institutions which, through the supreme Court, condemned them on every count to pay their workers the judgment in the economic suit which they themselves brought before the judicial tribunals by reason of their inconformity with the resolutions of the Labor Tribunal, the oil companies have adopted a position which obliges the Executive of the Union to seek among the recourses of our legislation an efficacious means of definitely preventing, now and in the future, the annulment or the attempted annulment of judicial decisions at the simple will of one or both of the parties to a dispute by means of a declaration of insolvency, as is being attempted in the present case, with the result that the dispute is brought back to the very question that has already been judicially decided. It must be realized that such action would destroy the social norms governing the equilibrium of all the inhabitants of a nation, as well as that of their activities, and would establish a precedent for future proceedings to which industries of any description established in Mexico, and which might become involved in disputes with their workers, could resort, were they free to maneuver with impunity to evade their obligations or

reparation of the wrongs occasioned by their methods and their obstinacy.

Furthermore, notwithstanding the Government's serenity and the considerations shown them, the oil companies have persisted in carrying on, inside and outside the boundaries of the country, an adroit undercover campaign with which the Federal Executive two months ago taxed one of the managers of the said companies and which he did not deny; this campaign has now been productive of the results they sought: serious injury to the Nation's economic interests, with the purpose of annulling by these means the legal pronouncements of the Mexican authorities.

Under these circumstances, merely to carry out the procedure of the execution of the judgment stipulated by our laws would not be sufficient to reduce the oil companies to obedience, for the withdrawal of their funds in anticipation of the verdict of the High Tribunal that sentenced them prevents this procedure from being either practical or efficacious; moreover, to place attachments on oil production, or on plant and equipment, or even on oil fields, would imply interminable legal proceedings that would only prolong a situation which decorum demands be immediately

Source: Lázaro Cárdenas, "The President's Message to the Nation," March 18, 1938, *Mexico's Oil: A Compilation of Official Documents in the Conflict of Economic Order in the Petroleum Industry, with an Introduction Summarizing its Causes and Consequences* (Mexico City: Government of Mexico, 1940)

settled, and would also imply the necessity of overcoming the obstacles which the companies would certainly raise in the path of the normal productive process and of the immediate sale of the oil produced, and which would render difficult the coexistence of the part of the industry affected with the part that would undoubtedly remain free and in the hands of the companies themselves.

In this situation, of itself sufficiently delicate, the Public Power would find itself beset by the social interest of the Nation, which would be severely affected, for a fuel production insufficient for the various activities of the country, among which must be considered some as important as transportation, or a total absence of production, or even an oil production made more expensive by the difficulties, would within a short time necessarily give rise to a crisis incompatible not only with the progress but with the peace itself of the Nation; it would paralyze banking activity and commercial interchange in many of its chief aspects; public works, or general interest to the country, would become little short of impossible; and the existence of the Government itself would be gravely endangered, for with the loss of the State's economic power, its political power would also be lost and chaos would ensue.

It is thus evident that the problem placed before the Executive Power of the Nation by the refusal of the oil companies to comply with the verdict of the highest Judicial Tribunal is not merely a simple case of execution of judgment, but a concrete situation demanding urgent solution. It is demanded by the interests of the working class in all the industries of the country; it is demanded by the public interest of all Mexicans, as well as of the foreigners residing in the Republic, who require peace and the fuel which is the life-blood of their activities; and it is demanded by the very sovereignty of the Nation, which would otherwise be left at the mercy of the maneuvers of foreign capitalists who, forgetful of the fact that they had previously organized themselves into Mexican companies, in accordance with Mexican laws, are now attempting to evade the mandates and responsibilities imposed upon them by the country's authorities.

This is a clear and evident case obliging the Government to apply the existing Expropriation Act, not merely for the purpose of bringing the oil companies

to obedience and submission, but because, in view of the rupture of the contracts between the companies and their workers pursuant to a decision of the labor authorities, an immediate paralysis of the oil industry is imminent, implying incalculable damage to all other industry and to the general economy of the country. . . .

The Government has already taken suitable steps to maintain the constructive activities now going forward throughout the Republic, and for that purpose it asks the people only for its full confidence and backing in whatever dispositions the Government may be obliged to adopt.

Nevertheless, we shall, if necessary, sacrifice all the constructive projects on which the Nation has embarked during the term of this Administration in order to cope with the financial obligations imposed upon us by the application of the Expropriation Act to such vast interests; and although the subsoil of the country will give us considerable economic resources with which to meet the obligation of indemnization which we have contracted, we must be prepared for the possibility of our individual economy also suffering the indispensable readjustments, even to the point, should the Bank of Mexico deem it necessary, of modifying the present exchange rate of our currency, so that the whole country may be able to count on sufficient currency and resources with which to consolidate this act of profound and essential economic liberation of Mexico. . . .

And, finally, as the fear may arise among the interests now in bitter conflict in the field of international affairs that a deviation of raw materials fundamentally necessary to the struggle in which the most powerful nations are engaged might result from the consummation of this act of national sovereignty and dignity, we wish to state that our petroleum operations will not depart a single inch from the moral solidarity maintained by Mexico with the democratic nations, whom we wish to assure that the expropriation now decreed has as its only purpose the elimination of obstacles erected by groups who do not understand the evolutionary needs of all peoples and who would themselves have no compunction in selling Mexican oil to the highest bidder, without taking into account the consequences of such action to the popular masses and the nations in conflict.

STUDY QUESTIONS

1. To what factors does Cárdenas attribute the decision to expropriate the oil reserves?
2. What impact will the nationalization of oil have on the Mexican economy, according to Cárdenas?

8.3 A LANDOWNERS ACCOUNT OF PEASANT UPRISING IN EL SALVADOR, 1932

In 1932, El Salvador was rocked by political violence, in a series of events whose causes have been the source of extensive historical debate. In January 1932, thousands of mostly indigenous peasants rose up in a coordinated rebellion throughout western El Salvador. Armed mostly with machetes, they attacked army barracks and municipal offices in around a dozen towns. They managed to hold six of the smaller towns for about three days, occupying the homes of elites and places of governance. During the rebellion, around one hundred people were killed. The Salvadorian army quickly retaliated, but their response went far beyond simply taking back control from the peasant rebels. Instead, they embarked on a scorched-earth campaign in which as many as thirty thousand people were murdered in the space of two weeks. In towns that had been taken by rebels, peasants were gathered into municipal plazas by the army and machine-gunned en masse, while paramilitary lynch mobs roamed the countryside executing anyone rumored to have been involved. The mass killing is now known as *"La Matanza"*: simply, the massacre. Some scholars have labeled it an ethnocidal genocide, as most of those killed were indigenous, while the perpetrators were those who identified as mixed-race ladinos. Others have seen it as a precursor to Cold War purges of communism, as the peasant rebels were identified by the military as communists. Few original sources for either the peasant rebellion or the mass killing that followed have survived—most of the rebels were illiterate and were killed before they could pass their stories into oral tradition, while the military government is suspected of having systematically destroyed documents related to the massacre. The excerpt below provides a landowner's account of the peasant uprising that preceded the massacre. It was published in *Diario de Santa Ana*, the major regional newspaper for western El Salvador, shortly after the rebellion, and provides insight into the fears of wealthy Ladinos, as well as their desire for vengeance. As such, it illuminates the attitudes that helped fuel the massacre. Note that while the author identifies the rebels as communists, historians are less clear that the peasant rebels were motivated by Marxist-Leninist philosophies and a desire to achieve political revolution.

An honorable resident of Juayúa, with whom I had the opportunity to converse, offered me a newspaper clipping, which contained the account that one of the hacienda owners from that region gave of the activities of the communists in those days. This account was published in the *Diario de Santa Ana*, in the edition of Monday, February 1, 1932.

It reads as follows:

"I never imagined, not even for a second, what communism could be capable of in our popular

Source: Héctor Lindo-Fuentes, Erik Ching, and Rafael Lara-Martinez, *Remembering a Massacre in El Salvador: The Insurrection of 1932, Roque Dalton, and the Politics of Historical Memory* (Albuquerque: University of New Mexico Press, 2007), pp. 333–337.

masses, which constitute some ninety-five percent of the inhabitants here.

"Neither you, nor anyone who lives in the towns, in the cities, and feels defended by the agents of order, can have even a slight idea of how we have felt here, in decisive moments, upon finding ourselves alone, absolutely alone, in the hands and at the mercy of the masses, of the kind that was no more than a horde of enraged savages, with demonic impulses, who were loudly jeering the Ladino, jeering the boss and brandishing their machetes, thirsting for robbery, thirsting for any thievery imaginable."

THEY SAY THEY DID NOT GET INVOLVED . . .

"Fortunately for those of us who live in the countryside, the horde set off first for the villages, and while there enjoyed themselves by engaging in ignominy, true pillage, shameful acts, robberies, outrages and every sort of thievery; the armed forces came and were able to repel the barbarous movement a little, in order to later combat it efficaciously. Otherwise, at this hour when I am writing to you, I would be in the ground, and with me so many others who have committed no other crime than living here, engaged in cultivating the land. There is not a single Indian who is not an affiliate of devastating communism. One or another who stayed at home, was waiting for the final notice in order to join the ranks. Good farmhands whom I had considered loyal and whom we had treated as part of the family here, were the first to join up and lend their contingent to the dark cause. And these people have such nerve that now that they seem rather vanquished by the activities of the government, which ended up annihilating them, those same ones who just a short time ago were making attempts on our lives and on all we possess, are the ones who are now seeking protection and swearing that they belonged to us and that they did not get involved.

They want to dodge the danger. But that punishment is being exacted! And it should continue as it has begun, with a strong hand, forcefully, executing the leaders and every participant, in order to see if they manage to finish off the plague."

THEY WANTED TO MAKE 'MINCEMEAT' OF HIM . . .

"They passed by here with the great mob, on the night of Saturday the 23rd, those who attacked Nahuizalco,

and with no time to make mincemeat of me, since their presence was urgently required at Nahuizalco; they made do with shouting blasphemies and pointing me out as one of the first who should fall into their hands. In the mob, in the immense confused multitude, they were all there: close to two hundred farmhands of mine, of my neighbors and of my brothers. Those men whom we had thought to be humble, honorable, who have been receiving favors of every kind on our part, to whom we grant land for their crops without charging them any ground rent; who we have paid with religious punctuality. Their wage, which, although small, as is always paid in this country, is a wage in conformity with their abilities, since they are incapable of earning more; some of them barely able to do their job, and others who had to be led out by the hand, in order to teach them to do basic chores, because of the idlers they are, they do not take pains to become efficient nor to better themselves at anything. And they, who carry the germ of roguish blood, who are of a constitution inferior to ours, who are of a conquered race, it only takes a little to inflame their infernal passions against the Ladino, at whom they point, because they hate us and they will always latently hate us. An extremely grave, extremely dangerous error was made with them in granting them citizens' rights. This was enormously bad for the country. They were told that they were free, that the nation also belonged to them, and that they had the full right to elect their leaders and to rule. And they understand that to say leaders and to rule is exactly the same as engaging in robbery, theft, scandal, the destruction of property, etcetera, and killing their employers."

DEPICTING SCENES OF JUAYÚA

"The example is there in Juayúa. None of you has the slightest idea of what occurred there in my hometown. It was shameful, horrifying, it sets one's nerves on end, and I do not want to bring it all up. Society girls were grinding corn and making tortillas for the bandits, and afterward. . . . they committed upon them all that a barbarian, an assassin, or a villain might harbor in his poisoned breast against a Ladino girl, an honorable young lady. They broke down doors with machetes and then lit off rockets and bombs, just for the fun of it. They dragged, they beat. They cruelly and barbarously killed, mutilating him alive, he who had a big heart, a heart of progress and civilization for Juayúa. I am referring to the unfortunate Emilio Redaelli. And if they did not kill more of the 'bourgeois' people, as they say, it was because that would come last, turning themselves first to robbery and then to killing the rich, in order to take over their houses and live in them: such was one of the most salient points in their plan for governing."

THEY WERE ON THE BRINK OF DYING

"Once the town of Nahuizalco was sacked, on the night of Saturday the 25th, they came toward Tajcuiluilán on Sunday morning, two-hundred strong, and from there they headed to El Canelo and neighboring estates, to have their way with our lives and our property. They jeered us and unsheathed their knives."

"I, who always felt I could dispose of ten Indians in a row, they with their machetes and I with my revolver and fifty bullets; I, who have not trembled before these wicked men, because I saw them as humble little lambs when they were looking good, and I felt I had the rogues under the might of my arm if our might be measured; when I made out that throng, the mob of two hundred that was coming after me, I had to mount my horse and I broke into a dizzying race over rocky ground and precipices, tearing apart fences, until I joined up with a brother of mine on his hacienda. . . .

"Luckily, before getting to my property, the mob was turned back in order to reinforce Nahuizalco since in those instants the government troops were arriving and they wanted to repel the force that had been constituted. That saved us. Although a few still did come and made off with many things of personal use that they found on their way."

'YOU SHOULD HAVE SEEN THEM IN ACTION . . . !'

"We want the plague exterminated at the roots; otherwise, it will sprout forth with greater determination, now experts and less foolish, because in new attempts they will pitch themselves against the lives of everyone, first, and finally slit our throats. We need the strong hand of the government, without asking advice from anybody, because there are pious people who preach forgiveness because they have not yet had their lives hanging by a thread. They did well in North America to do away with them; by shooting them first, before they impeded the development of progress in that nation; first they killed the Indians because the Indians will never have good sentiments toward anything. We, here, have been treating them as family, with every consideration, and now you have seen them in action! They have ferocious instincts."

THE ONLY CRY: SILENCE . . . !

"A nephew of mine tells that he saw from the window of his house when one of those gentle farmhands who was so awfully good before, shouted, 'Silence!' at the poor widow of Colonel Vaquero, who upon identifying the body of her ill-fated husband, killed by machete blows, the night of the event, broke into tears out of the natural grief of her lacerated heart. 'Silence!' the gentle farmhand shouted at her, unsheathing his machete, and ordering the widow to remove herself, and to not even sob, while they put the body of the commander of Juayúa cut down in his prime, in a coffin in order to go bury him. 'Silence!' another one of these gentle ones screamed at Mrs. Maria de Math, because upon seeing that they were dragging Mr. Emilio Redaelli, already moribund, she shouted from her window, 'Poor Mr. Emilio!' 'Silence!' the gentle one shouted, and grabbing her by the hand led her to the jail, and many entreaties and implorations were needed in order to get them to give her back her freedom."

STUDY QUESTIONS

1. How does the account describe the actions of the rebels? What strategies does the author use to push the government to intervene in suppressing the rebellion?
2. The document is written before *La Matanza* occurred. How useful is it for understanding the rationale behind the mass killings that would follow it? What evidence do you see of a desire for vengeance?

8.4 EYEWITNESSES TO THE HAITIAN GENOCIDE OF 1937

General Rafael Trujillo came to power in the Dominican Republic in 1930 following a military coup and a fraudulent election, and quickly established a repressive and authoritarian state system. One of the key platforms of his regime was "deafricanization," and Trujillo followed an aggressive policy of *anti-haitianismo* (anti-Haitianism) in an effort to establish the Dominican Republic as a "white" nation, in contrast to the black Haitian nation on the other side of the border. This policy reached its apogee in 1937 in a massacre of approximately twenty thousand Haitian immigrants by the Dominican army. This document presents the testimony of two survivors of the genocide, who shared their stories as part of an oral history project.

· · ·

ANONYMOUS MAN IN OUANAMINTHE

At the time of the massacre, I was a child, so I wasn't at risk. When the massacre started, I was at school; I went to a religious school. The fathers had a choir for all the children who sang; and they had a group of kids who knew how to sing, and I was always singing with the Fathers. When the massacre started, the children were in school, and I was at choir. And October 7th, the day of the patron saint festival at Dajabon, the Fathers took us over there, since the frontier was free to cross, and no one was afraid to cross the border at that time. So the Fathers took us to go to mass there, so that we could sing in the choir at mass there. And while we were in the church, I saw a band of Dominican military who were milling about outside while we were in church. Since we were children, we didn't understand anything. What happened then was that the military wanted to kill people that very day—they actually wanted to take people from the church and kill them! What happened was that the Fathers, who were foreign (they were French), I think the Fathers weren't pleased at all with this? (pa rapo), they didn't want it to happen, and yet when it became night, around six PM, around that time, they started killing people anyway. They starting killing people around six o'clock, while people starting crying out for help, people starting running, they came wounded, they crossed the massacre river, they all came wounded, they killed a lot of people. A lot of people who were saved came here. And so, this is how I came to Dosmond colony. When people started arriving, the Vincent government rounded up people in the Dominican Republic; the war began with a lot of people dead, a lot of Haitians were taken when war came to the frontier. They finished killing people after one week, a week later. The Vincent government sent for the rest of the Haitians. Then Trujillo sent his men to gather and haul out the rest of the Haitians left behind; they brought war to the border. In Ounaminthe, when you looked at the river, it was completely a sea of people and donkeys—it was completely full!—Because many of the people—in fact most of the Haitians on the Dominican side—were afraid to live the Dominican Republic any more. They were forced to leave although they didn't have a place to go to in Haiti since they had never lived there. When they arrived in Haiti, they were homeless refugees. So the government had to make colonies for them because Desmond was a big savanna, a place where I knew everyone by name. My father has a beautiful garden in the savanna. It really

Source: Lauren Derby and Richard Turits, "Temwayai Kout Kouto, 1937: Eyewitnesses to the Genocide," in Cecile Accilien, Jessica Adams, and Elmide Méléance (eds.) *Revolutionary Freedoms: A History of Survival, Strength and Imagination in Haiti* (Educa Vision, Inc, 2006)

was a savanna—there weren't any houses at all, nothing like it. The place was a desert. Before the massacre, in the frontier, although there were two sides, the people were one, united. All the tradesmen in Dajabon—all the cobblers and tailors—they were all Haitian. And even today there are Haitians all over Ouanaminthe, even though they still die today, there are still Haitian children there today, crossing the border daily. Haitian children, even if they were born in Dajabon, they still went to school in Haiti, every morning they would cross the border to go to school, every afternoon they would return; their parents lived in Dajabon, but they came to school here. Haitians have always lived the French system of education, and the Catholic schools. Even the Dominicans love the French language, and the French language helps them to speak Kreyol a lot.

IRELIA PIERRE, DOSMOND/OUNAMINTHE

I was born in the Dominican Republic. When the massacre broke out, I was very small. I remember that I had been in school awhile. The day of my brother's marriage, after the service was over, a Dominican arrived at the reception. The reception was the morning that the massacre broke out, and people started fleeing. That night we hid. The next morning when we woke up, some of the older people said "Be careful if you go out"; so we stayed at home. Everyone came to my grandparent's house. They said they were going to Haiti because a revolution had broken out, and that they were killing Haitians. They all slept at my grandparents. During the night, a woman said to me, "You come with me to my house." I said, "No, I'm going to stay with my mother—I can't leave her here." So we went out to the garden where my mother was working, and she cut some bananas and put them in her bag. I carried a tree branch. Suddenly, I looked over and saw a lot of Guardia [Dominican military] getting off their horses, and I heard them say, "There's one over there in the garden," then they entered the garden and killed the girl. When I saw that, I ran. It was night. While I was running, I saw an uncle of mine, who took me into his house to protect me. When I arrived at his house I was terrified. They didn't let me sleep; they took me to another place. That morning at four AM they all took their bags and we started to march towards Haiti. While we were walking, some Dominicans told us to be careful and not go through Dajabon, but to pass around it, since they were killing people there. When we arrived

at the Dajabon savanna, we saw Guardia. When we saw him I said, "Mama, we're going to die, we're going to die!" She told me to be quiet. Then the guardia said "esta preso, esta preso!" [that one's arrested!]. After that they had us all stand in the sun in the savanna. When we said we were thirsty, they said they would give us water soon. While we watched, we saw one Guardia on a horse who had a rope to tie up people. When he saw that if he tied up too many people they started to run, he began to kill them and throw them in a hole. He killed everyone; I was the only one who was saved. They thought I was dead because they had given me a lot of machete blows. I was awash in blood—all the blood in my heart. After all these tribulations, it's thanks to God that I didn't die. They killed them all in front of me; they tied them up, and after they killed them, they threw them down. I was small when I lived through all of this, but I remember it all too clearly. I remember calling out after the Guardia had left, "Mama!", but she was dead; "Papa!", but he was dead; they died one after another. I was left alone in the savanna without anything to eat or drink. . . . There were a lot of small children who were thrown up in the air and stabbed with a bayonet, and then placed on top of their mothers. They killed my entire family, my mother, my father. We were twenty-eight—all were killed. I was the only one to survive that I knew of. After they finished cutting me up, it was a group of older men who had come from Haiti who found me on the ground in the sand along the banks of the Massacre River. They picked me up and returned me to Haiti. They brought me to Ouanaminthe, but they didn't take me in—they said they couldn't take care of me so they said they would send me to Cap Haitian; when I arrived there, there would be people there to take care of me. [Most of the massacre victims were sent to a hospital in Cap Haitian, where they were attended by the Catholic Church.] I spent a month in bed in the hospital, after which time they sent me to live in Ouanaminthe. When I arrived here, I didn't have any family to receive me, so I went back to Cap again. I stayed under the auspices of the state. After about a year, they sent me back to Ouanaminthe again, at which time I lived there with some other foreigners. God gave me the strength to survive. Now I am married and have four children, but my entire family died during the massacre. Both my mother and father were born in the Dominican Republic. We lived in Loma de Cabrera. My father worked in agriculture, growing manioc, peanuts, rice on his own land—land that he had bought. He had ten karo [a Haitian peasant unit of land measurement] of land. He also kept some cattle, pigs, chickens, and goats. We grew enough food to feed the family (we never bought food at the market) but also to sell. I used to go to the market with my mother where we sold everything— peas, rice, bananas, corn. I only spoke Kreyol since we lived among the Haitians. I hardly spoke Spanish at all. There were some Dominicans in the area where we lived, but not many; there were mostly Haitians. There were both marriages between Haitians and Dominicans, as well as concubinage. There were no problems that I remember between Haitians and Dominicans— for example, no jealousy for Haitian land. The first problem was the massacre. . . .

STUDY QUESTIONS

1. What can we learn from the testimonies about Haitian-Dominican relations prior to the massacre? How connected were the two groups? Was the massacre expected?
2. What challenges do historians face in using personal testimonies collected several decades after an event? How might these challenges shape the way we should interpret these two eyewitness accounts?

JOANA DE MASI ZERO

8.5 LIFE OF A FACTORY WORKER UNDER VARGAS, 1930s

Getúlio Várgas was a populist leader who led Brazil as president for eighteen years, first from 1934 to 1945, and again from 1951 until his suicide in 1954. He was one of the most prominent of a wave of populists who rose to power in Latin America in the 1930s on nationalist platforms that emphasized industrialization and social welfare. Vargas ruled in an authoritarian manner, suspending elections and dissolving Congress and concentrating power in the Executive. Yet he also pushed through changes in economic and social policy that earned him great popularity among the working classes, who nicknamed him "Father of the Poor." Among the core basis of Vargas supporters were factory workers. The factory worker Joana de Masi Zero, a daughter of Italian immigrants, joined the ranks of millions of urban Brazilians who loved Vargas in spite of his flaws. In this excerpt, she explains how the social reforms Vargas pushed into law improved her life.

My name is Joana de Masi Zero. I was born in São Paulo on October 23, 1916, in the district of Mooca. In those days, Mooca wasn't like it is today. There were houses, you could walk around. There wasn't much movement, although the streetcar passed by Ipanema Street. . . . you catch it and were downtown in ten minutes.

We lived on Guarapuava Street. The houses there were simple, like all of the ones on old streets, close together. Ours was a duplex, with large rooms with

Source: Robert M. Levine and John J. Crocitti (eds.), *The Brazil Reader: History, Culture, Politics* (Durham, NC: Duke University Press, 1999)

high ceilings. The privy was outside. Later on, we built one inside, but the old outhouse remained in use, too. Our yard was ample, with many plants, including guavas, oranges, and even a pear tree. We kept chickens in the back of the yard. We also had Angora cats, who jumped over the wall and ran around everywhere, but they didn't get close to the chickens. . . .

My sister Carmela and I stayed by the front door; when neighbors passed by we would chat with them. My mother didn't let us go out alone because we were girls and it could be dangerous. When Carmela and I and our friends did go out we all would hold hands; sometimes we walked singing. I only went through primary school. It was a good school; I started when I was eight. In those days, you started then and went until you were twelve.

I studied in a private school, Sete de Setembro, and then went on to another. My sister Carmela and I finished, but our older sister had to stop and go to work. In school, boys and girls had separate classes. No one mixed in those days, even during recess. The boys stayed on one side and the girls on the other. The school yard was divided so that no one could have contact with anyone from the other group. They entered on the left side and we on the right. The boys' teachers were very energetic. Boys are more rebellious; sometimes the teachers punished the boys right in the corridor. We wore uniforms. On regular days, we had blouses with the school emblem embroidered on it. On special days, we wore uniforms of white linen, pleated skirts, and white blouses. We wore white pants for physical education. . . . Everyone was neat and well groomed.

We studied many things: Portuguese grammar, arithmetic, history, geography, science, sewing, singing, gymnastics, everything. We studied four hours each day, from eight to noon. . . .

My family worked hard. My father was a textile supervisor. In those days, they earned a good living. . . . 200 *mil-réis* a month in 1920. This was good money. Salaries weren't meager, like today. You could buy what you needed at home. My mother even saved a bit. We built our house and paid it off fairly quickly, but then my father had an accident and died. He was handling a machine when it injured him. He hung on for a month. On his death certificate it said he died of pneumonia, because he couldn't breathe. My mother wanted to give him medicine against infection, but he refused, saying, "I'm not going to take anything!" He said his blood was good, that he didn't need anything. I was five when my father died. My grandfather came to live with us, but he died, too. Only the women remained, my mother, my grandmother, and we three sisters.

The house was my mother's, but the rest? For food and clothing we had to work. First, my mother went to work in a chicken coop; later, she started to sew men's clothing at home. My oldest sister started working when she was a girl. She was the first, when she was twelve. Then I went to work, and finally Carmela. At first, she stayed home, doing chores: she would prepare lunch and keep house. My older sister worked in a textile factory, going from one to another. It was she who taught Carmela how to do textile work. My first job was sewing carpets by hand. I was twelve. I worked for a year and a half. It was in a private house, and they hired girls to work. Then I went to a factory, the Santa Madalena, on Bresser Street. When I went to work there my mother had to get me a work permit because I was still a minor, fourteen years of age. Actually, I was younger; I started in July, but my birthday was in October. Only then I worked legally. Only my sisters and I left school. Our other friends continued because their parents could afford it. . . . When I was fifteen, I moved to a more difficult machine in the factory. You earned more. . . . forty-five *mil-réis* a month if you produced up to your daily quota.

I went from factory to factory. . . . finding different jobs. . . . I worked in one factory for twenty-five years. Getúlio was president. Many people said that he was a dictator, but he did many things for us workers. His labor laws were good. There were no strikes, at least never at places where I was working. Sometimes, to avoid strikes, the bosses dismissed us early, saying to us: "You go home; we're going to stop the machines so we won't have any fights at the door." They meant with the militants. All the laws we have today were thanks to [Vargas]. . . . The first minimum wage was forty *mil-réis* a month. Then they started to withhold payments for pensions—three *mil-réis* a month. Everyone paid whether they wanted to or not. It was taken out of your pay envelope. Later, this system changed for the worse; retirement paid almost nothing. Every time the politicians changed the laws they took more from us. Getúlio's time was good; later, I don't know. We earned well and prices didn't go up. You went out to buy milk, for example, and the price was always the same. We didn't live in luxury; we made our own clothes—we knew how to sew—we were well dressed, we had money to go to the movies every week, sometimes twice. We ate well, we lived well. They say he was a dictator, but for us he was good.

But when the factory moved to Mooca, with new machinery, production didn't go well. We earned little at the beginning . . . our salaries were affected. But then the law required that the employers give raises of 35 percent. My employer said that he couldn't, that he couldn't even pay 5 percent more. . . . He didn't even want to negotiate. We went to the union, and the union officials took our case. Unions worked well then, at least ours did. It had a lawyer who worked for it, Dr. Paranhos. We could talk to him about any problem we had. The complaint took more or less a year to be decided, and in the end we won. So the boss left

Mooca and moved the factory to Vila Maria, because he wanted to cheat us. He hired others and paid them less. On the whole, though, our bosses were decent, human. They came to visit; my mother invited them into the living room. They always asked about how my mother was.

When Getúlio died it was like a death in the family. People were sad. No one talked; everyone was quiet. It was a really sorrowful day, especially for the workers. Things were closed for, I think, three days.

I retired when I turned sixty-five. The first month I earned the same as I had made when I was working, and after that, for a while as well. Then they began to take a little here and there, and the government took more and more, and now I earn almost nothing.

STUDY QUESTIONS

1. How did the death of Joana's father impact her family? What does her story tell us about the absence of social policy in this period?
2. What benefits does Joana argue Vargas brought to factory workers? What evidence does she use to support her claim that Vargas was good for working people?

MAGDA PORTAL

8.6 PROLETARIAN SONG

Magda Portal was a Peruvian author, poet, and political activist. She played a key role in the vanguard literary movement of the 1930s, and was one of the founders of the Peruvian political party APRA (Popular Revolutionary Alliance for America). *Proletarian Song*, one of Portal's best-known poems, highlights how poetry was used by leftist intellectuals to articulate progressive political values.

Proletarian Song
"Life belongs to the lucky"
dawns in the scrawled slogans of the street
morning wheels over the asphalt
of screeching hot earth

Trees at the city outskirts
salute the worker
with branches tossed
by the gaiety of the vagabond wind
the great libertarian

Source: Kathleen Weaver, *Peruvian Rebel: The World of Magda Portal, with a Selection of Her Poems* (University Park: Pennsylvania State University Press, 2010), pp. 194–197.

Like pain a shadow tracks
the silhouette of a man
entering the broad
factory doorway
inside: the human pant of machines
pulleys groan
under the weight of human thought
balconies onto eternity
eyes follow the constructive labor
the entire factory is
one surging mechanism

a titanic organism
powered by "the marvelous motor"
of the brains of 100 united men
the beautiful spectacle of mind
and muscle in action
sweat decorates their faces
like a smile
playing on lips
tense with concentration
the factory is all things

STUDY QUESTIONS

1. How does the poem represent the urban working classes? What types of descriptive imagery stands out to you as you read?
2. What do we learn from the poem about the role of proletarian imagery within interwar revolutionary politics?

EVA PERÓN
8.7 *IN MY OWN WORDS*, 1952

Eva Perón, better known as Evita, was one of the most iconic figures of the mid-twentieth century. The second wife of Juan Perón, she was a former actress who came from an impoverished and illegitimate background to become the First Lady of Argentina. Her glamour and beauty, as well as her own class origins, played a critical role in helping Perón build a lasting connection with the *descamisados*, the urban masses who formed his key support base. Evita played an important role in Perón's first administration, running the Ministries of Labor and Health, providing charitable support for the poor through her Eva Perón Foundation, and pushing for women's right to vote and heading the women's wing of the Peronist party. She was well known for delivering passionate speeches that praised Perón and the *descamisadas*. In 1952, Evita died after an extended private battle with ovarian cancer. The following is an excerpt from her "deathbed manuscript," a series of letters and observations she dictated to aides while sick. Perón read parts of the manuscript at her funeral, but it was then lost until the 1980s, and there are debates among historians about how much was the work of posthumous ghostwriters. Nevertheless, the document remains important as a window into how Evita served to legitimize and advance Peronism.

Source: Laura Dail, *In My Own Words* (New York, NY: The New Press, 2005), p. 49–58.

MY MESSAGE

Recently, in the hours of my illness, I have thought often of this message from my heart.

I love the *descamisados*, the women, the workers of my people too much, and, by extension, I love all the world's exploited people, condemned to death by imperialisms and the privileges of land ownership, too much . . .

The suffering of the poor, the humble, the great pain of so much of humanity without sun and without sky hurts me too much to keep quiet. . . .

My Message is for them: for my people and for all of humanity's people.

I no longer want to explain my life or my work.

I no longer seek praise. I couldn't care less about the hatred or the praise of men who belong to the race of exploiters.

I want to incite the people. I want to ignite them with the fire of my heart. I want to tell them the truth that a humble woman from the country—the first woman of the people who would not let herself be dazzled by power or glory—learned in the world of those who rule and govern humanity's people.

I want to tell them the truth that no one has ever spoken, because no one was able to follow the farce the way I did, to learn the whole truth.

Because no one who left the people to take my path ever went back. They were dazzled by the marvelous fantasy of power, and they remained there to enjoy the lie.

I, too, wore all the honors of glory, of vanity, and of power. I let myself be adorned by the finest jewels on earth. Every country of the world paid homage to me, in some respect. Everything that the clique of men with whom I happened to live—as the wife of an extraordinary president—wanted to offer me, I accepted, with a smile, "using my face" to guard my heart. But smiling, in the middle of the farce, I learned the truth of all their lies.

I can now say how much they lie, all that they deceive, everything they pretend, because I know men in their greatness and in their misery. Often, I have had before my eyes, at the same time, as if to compare them face to face, the misery of greatness and the greatness of misery.

I would not let the soul I brought from the street be yanked away. . . . That is why I was never seduced by the grandeur of power, and I could see their misery; and that is why I never forgot my people's misery and why I could see their greatness.

I now know all the truths and all the lies of the world.

I have to tell them to the people from where I came. And I have to tell them to all the deceived people of humankind: to the workers, the women, the humble *descamisados* of my Nation, and all the *descamisados* on earth—to the infinite race of the people!—as a message from my heart.

I HAD TO FLY WITH HIM

In *My Mission in Life*, with my paltry words, I talked about the wonderful day of my existence when I met Perón.

He was already at battle.

I remember it as if I could see him now, with his sparkling eyes, his head held high, his clean smile, his words lit from the first in his heart.

From the first moment, I saw the shadow of his enemies, stalking him like vultures from above or like vicious snakes from the beaten earth.

I thought Perón was too much alone, overly confident in the winning power of his ideals, believing the first thing anyone said as if it were his own generous and clean, sincere, and honorable words. I was not drawn by his stature or the honors of his position—even less by his military stripes.

From the first moment, I saw his heart . . . and on top of the pedestal of his heart, the mast of his ideals holding the flag of his Nation and his People close to the sky.

I saw his immense solitude, like the solitude of the condor, like that of the highest peaks, like the solitude of stars in the immenseness of infinity.

And in spite of my smallness, I decided to accompany him.

To follow him, to be with him, I would have been, would have done anything—anything but change the course of his destiny!

That was when I told him one day, "I am prepared to follow you, wherever you go."

Little by little, I took on his battles, too.

Sometimes because his enemies provoked me. Other times because I was outraged by their treachery and their lies.

I had decided to follow Perón, but I was not resigned to follow him from a distance, knowing that he was surrounded by enemies and ambitious men, who disguised themselves with friendly words—and by friends who didn't feel even the head of the shadow of his ideals.

I wanted to spend the days and nights of his life with him, in the peace of his rests, and in the battles of his fight.

I already knew that, like a condor, he was flying high and alone . . . and yet I had to fly with him!

I admit that in the beginning I did not realize the magnitude of my decision. . . . I thought I could help Perón with my affection as a woman, with the company of my heart smitten by his person and his cause . . . but nothing more! I thought my task was to fill his loneliness with the joy and enthusiasm of my youth.

MY COLONEL

And so we embarked upon our journey, happy and joyful in the midst of the battle.

One day he confessed that I, his little *"giovinota,"* as he often called me, was the only loyal and sincere companion of his life.

Never had my smallness pained me as it did that day! And I decided I would do the impossible to be a better companion to him.

I remember asking him to be my teacher. In the respites of his fight, he would teach me a little of as much as I could learn.

I liked to read by his side. We started with Plutarch's *The Parallel Lives* and then moved on to *The Complete Letters of Lord Chesterfield to his son Stanhope.* In a short time, he taught me a little of the languages he knew: English, Italian, French.

Without realizing it, I was also learning, from his conversations, the history of Napoleon, of Alexander, and of all of history's great men.

And that is how he taught me to view our own history differently.

With him, I learned to read the panorama of domestic and international political questions. He often spoke to me of his dreams and his hopes, his grand ideals.

Nestled in a corner of my Colonel's life, it strikes me that I was like a bouquet of flowers in his house. I never attempted to be more than that.

However . . . , the battle that broke out around Perón was too harsh, his enemies very strong, his loneliness almost infinite, and my love too great for me to resign myself to being nothing more than a touch of joy on "my Colonel's" path.

THE FIRST SHADOWS

Most of the men around Perón at that time considered me nothing but a simple opportunist.

They were mediocre, in the end . . . unlike me with my soul burning, they had not been able to feel the fire of Perón, of his greatness and of his goodness, of his dreams and of his ideals.

They thought I was "calculating" with Perón, because they were measuring with the paltry yardstick of their souls.

I got to know them close up, one by one. Later, almost every one of them betrayed Perón. Some in October of 1945; others later . . . , and I had the pleasure of insulting them to their faces, denouncing out loud the disloyalty and dishonor with which they proceeded, of fighting them until proving the hypocrisy of their actions and intentions.

I remained alone next to "my Colonel" until they took him prisoner.

From those days on, I distrusted upper-class friends and men of honor. And I clung blindly to the humble men and women of my people who, without so much "honor" and without so many "titles" or "privileges," know how to risk their lives for a man, for a cause, for an ideal . . . for a simple feeling from the heart!

Those first great disappointments made me see my path clearly.

But I could not believe in anything or anyone who wasn't of his people.

Since then I have told him countless times in every tone of voice so that he'll never forget it, how, with so many words, the men who generally surround a president feign their honor and loyalty.

The peoples of the earth should not just elect the man who will lead them. They should know how to protect him from their enemies, who lurk in the antechambers of every government.

On behalf of my people, I protected Perón, and I ejected their enemies from the antechambers—sometimes with a smile and other times with the harsh words of the truth I spoke in their faces with all the indignation of my rebelliousness.

THE PEOPLE'S ENEMIES

The people's enemies were and remain Perón's enemies.

I have seen them approach him with every kind of malice and lie.

I want to denounce them definitively.

Because they will be the eternal enemies of Perón and of the people, here and every place in the world where the flag of justice and liberty is raised. We have defeated them, but they belong to a race that will never die definitely.

In our blood, we all have the seeds of selfishness that could turn us into enemies of the people and its cause.

We must squash it wherever it springs up . . . if we want the world one day to reach the bright noonday of the people. And if we do not want the night to fall again over their victory.

Perón's enemies . . . I have seen them up close and personal.

I never remained in the rearguard of his battles.

I was in the front line of combat, fighting the short days and the long nights of my zeal, infinite like the thirst of my heart. And I carried out two tasks—I don't know which was more worthy of a small life like mine, but my life in the end—one, to fight for the rights of my people, and the other, to watch Perón's back.

In this double duty, immense for me, armed with nothing but my ardent heart, I met the enemies of Perón and my people.

They are the same!

Yes! I never saw anyone from our race—the race of the people—fighting against Perón.

But I did see the others.

Sometimes I've seen them cold and insensitive. I swear with all the force of my fanaticism that they always revolted me. I have felt them cold like toads or snakes. The only thing that moves them is envy. There is no need to fear them. The envy of toads could never conceal the song of nightingales!

But we must move them off the road.

They cannot be near the people or the men whom the people elect to lead them.

And they definitely cannot be the leaders of the people.

The leaders of the people must be fanatics for the people.

If not, they grow dizzy at the top—and they do not return!

And I've seen them, too, with the dizziness of the heights of power.

FANATICS

Only fanatics—who are idealists and partisan—do not give up. The cold and indifferent should not serve the people, because they cannot even if they want to.

To serve the people, one has to be prepared for anything—including death.

The cold do not die for a cause, but only by accident. Fanatics do.

I like fanatics and all of history's fanaticisms. I like the heroes, the saints, the martyrs, whatever the cause and reason behind the fanaticism.

Fanaticism turns life into a permanent and heroic process of dying; but it is the only way that life can defeat death.

That is why I am a fanatic. I would give my life for Perón and for the people . . . because I am sure that only by giving it will I win the right to live in them for all of eternity. And fanatical is how I want the women of my people, the workers and the *descamisados* to be.

Fanaticism is the only force that God gave the heart to win its battles.

It is the great strength of the people: the only one that its enemies do not have, because they have abolished from the world everything that smacks of the heart.

That is why we will defeat them. They have money, privilege, hierarchy, power, and wealth . . . , but they can never be fanatics . . . because they have no heart. We do.

They cannot be idealists because ideas have their roots in intelligence, but ideals have their foundation in the heart.

They cannot be fanatics because shadows cannot see themselves in the mirror of the sun.

Face to face, they, with all the strength in the world, and we, with our fanaticism, we will always prevail.

We must convince ourselves once and for all. The world will belong to the people if the people decide to ignite the sacred fire of our fanaticism, but igniting ourselves means burning, ignoring the siren of the mediocre, ignoring the imbeciles who speak to us of prudence.

Those who speak of sweetness and of love forget that Christ said, "I have come to bring fire over the earth and what I most want is that it burn!"

He gave us a divine example of fanaticism.

Next to him, what are the eternal preachers of mediocrity?

STUDY QUESTIONS

1. How does Evita use her own story of social mobility to connect to draw broader arguments about the class significance of Perón's government? How convincing are her claims?
2. How does Evita depict her relationship with Juan Perón? What does this reveal about the gendered power dynamics she had to navigate to succeed in her role?
3. What does Evita mean when she repeatedly describes herself as a "fanatic"? How significant is this terminology to understanding populist politics in Argentina?

RAÚL PREBISCH

8.8 A NEW ECONOMIC MODEL FOR LATIN AMERICA, 1950

Conventional economic development strategies in Latin America were based on the theory of comparative advantage: that tropical regions could produce crops and raw materials more cheaply than other areas and could thus achieve economic growth most efficiently by selling their agricultural products to industrialized nations and importing industrial goods in return. The Argentine economist Raúl Prebisch turned this theory on its head. Prebisch emphasized the power structures that underpinned trading institutions and agreements, and argued that the global economy was divided into "center" (the modern industrialized economies) and "periphery" (the producers of primary raw materials), with trading agreements systematically benefiting the center at the expense of the periphery. Therefore economic development could not be achieved simply through sale of agricultural products. This insight became the foundation of the new "structuralist" school of economic thought and was the precursor to dependency theory and import-substitution industrialization (ISI). In 1950 Prebisch was appointed as executive director of the Economic Commission for Latin America (ECLA or CEPAL), a UN agency. This is an excerpt from the first and most influential policy paper he issued through ECLA, *The Economic Development of Latin America and Its Principle Problems*.

Source: Economic Commission for Latin America, *The Economic Development of Latin America and Its Principal Problems* (Lake Success, NY: United Nations Department of Economic Affairs, 1950), pp. 1–8.

In Latin America, reality is undermining the out-dated schema of the international division of labour, which achieved great importance in the nineteenth century and, as a theoretical concept, continued to exert considerable influence until very recently.

Under that schema, the specific task that fell in Latin America, as part of the periphery of the world economic system, was that of producing food and raw materials for the great industrial centres.

There was no place within it for the industrialization of the new countries. It is nevertheless being forced upon them by events. Two world wars in a single generation and a great economic crisis between them have shown the Latin-American countries their opportunities, clearly pointing the way to industrial activity.

The academic discussion, however, is far from ended. In economics, ideologies usually tend either to lag behind events or to outlive them. It is true that the reasoning on the economic advantages of the international division of labour is theoretically sound, but it is usually forgotten that it is based upon an assumption which has been conclusively proved by false facts. According to this assumption, the benefits of technical progress tend to be distributed alike over the whole community, either by the lowering of prices or the corresponding raising of incomes. The countries producing raw materials obtain their share of these benefits through international exchange, and therefore have no need to industrialize. If they were to do so, their lesser efficiency would result in their losing the conventional advantages of such exchange.

The flaw in this assumption is that of generalizing from the particular. If by "the community" only the great industrial countries are meant, it is indeed true that the benefits of technical progress are gradually distributed among all social groups and classes. If, however, the concept of the community is extended to include the periphery of the world economy, a serious error is implicit in the generalization. The enormous benefits that derive from increased productivity have not reached the periphery in a measure comparable to that obtained by the peoples of the great industrial countries. Hence, the outstanding difference between the standards of living of the masses of the former and the latter and the manifest discrepancies between their respective abilities to accumulate capital, since the margin of saving depends primarily on increased productivity.

Thus there exists an obvious disequilibrium, a fact which, whatever its explanation or justification, destroys the basic premise underlying the schema of the international division of labour.

Hence, the fundamental significance of the industrialization of the new countries. Industrialization is not an end in itself, but the principal means at the disposal of those countries of obtaining a share of the benefits of technical progress and of progressively raising the standard of living of the masses.

The Latin-American countries are thus faced with an immense general problem, embracing a series of minor ones which must be defined before embarking on the long task of research and practical measures which will be necessary if there is a firm intention to solve the problems.

It would be premature, in this initial report, to draw conclusions that would have only the doubtful value of an improvisation. Admittedly much remains to be done in the Latin-American countries, both in learning the facts and in their proper theoretical interpretation. Though many of the problems of these countries are similar, no common effort has ever been made to even examine and elucidate them. It is not surprising, therefore, that the studies published on the economy of Latin-American countries often reflect the points of view of the experience of the great centres of the world economy. Those studies cannot be expected to solve problems of direct concern to Latin America. The case of the Latin-American countries must therefore be presented clearly, so that their interests, aspirations and opportunities, bearing in mind, of course, the individual differences and characteristics, may be adequately integrated within the general framework of international economic co-operation.

The task ahead is thus considerable and the responsibility heavy. To deal with it methodically, it would be necessary to begin with a preliminary examination of the principal problems as a whole, at the same time bringing out certain general considerations suggested by direct contact with the economic life of Latin America. Such is the purpose of this report.

The industrialization of Latin America is not incompatible with the efficient development of primary production. On the contrary, the availability of the best capital equipment and the prompt adoption of new techniques are essential if the development of industry is to fulfill the social objective of raising the standard of living. The same is true of the mechanization of agriculture. Primary products must be exported to allow for the importation of the considerable quantity of capital goods needed.

The more active Latin America's foreign trade, the greater the possibility of increasing productivity by means of intensive capital formation. The solution does not lie in growth at the expense of foreign trade, but in knowing how to extract, from continually growing foreign trade, the elements that will promote economic development.

If reasoning does not suffice to convince us of the close tie between economic development and foreign trade, a few facts relating to the situation today will make it evident. The economic activity and level of employment in the majority of the Latin-American countries are considerably higher than before the war. This high level of employment entails increased imports of consumer goods, both non-durable and durable, besides those of raw materials and capital goods, and very often exports are insufficient to provide for them.

This is evident in the case of imports and other items payable in dollars. There are already well-known cases of scarcity of that currency in certain countries, despite the fact that the amount of dollars supplied by the United States to the rest of the world in payment of its own imports was considerable. In relation to its national income, however, the import coefficient of the United States has, after a persistent decline, arrived at a very low level (not over 3 per cent). It is, therefore, not surprising that, notwithstanding the high income level of the United States, the dollar resources thus made available to the Latin-American countries seem insufficient to pay for the imports needed for their intensive development.

It is true that as the European economy recovers, trade with that continent can profitably be increased, but Europe will not supply Latin America with more dollars unless the United States increases its import coefficient for European goods.

This, then, is the core of the problem. It is obvious that if the above-mentioned coefficient is not raised, Latin America will be compelled to divert its purchases from the United States to those countries which provide the exchange to pay for them. Such a solution is certainly very dubious, since it often means the purchase of more expensive or unsuitable goods.

It would be deplorable to fall back on measures of that kind when a basic solution might be found. It is sometimes thought that, by reason of the enormous productive capacity of the United States, that country could not increase its import coefficient for the purpose of providing the basic solution to this world problem. Such a conclusion cannot be substantiated without a prior analysis of the factors that have caused the United States steadily to reduce its import coefficient. These factors are aggravated by unemployment, but can be overcome when it does not exist. One can understand that it is of vital importance, both to Latin America and the rest of the world, that the United States achieve its aim of maintaining a high level of employment.

It cannot be denied that the economic development of certain Latin-American countries and their rapid assimilation of modern technology, in so far as they can utilize it, depend to a very large extent upon foreign investment. The implications involved render the problem far from simple. The negative factors include the failure to meet foreign financial commitments during the great depression of the nineteen thirties, a failure which, it is generally agreed, must not be allowed to happen again. Fundamentally the problem is the same as that referred to in the preceding paragraph. The servicing of these foreign investments, unless new investments are made, must be paid for by means of exports in the same currency and, if these do not show a corresponding increase, in time the same difficulties will arise again. They will be the greater if exports fall violently. The question thus arises whether, pending that basic solution, it would not be wiser to direct investments toward such productive activities as would, through direct or indirect reduction of dollar imports, permit the regular servicing of foreign obligations.

Here one must beware of dogmatic generalizations. To assume that the meeting of foreign commitments and the proper functioning of the monetary system depend upon nothing more than a decision to obey certain rules of the game is to fall into an error involving serious consequences. Even when the gold standard was in operation in the great centres, the countries of the Latin-American periphery had great difficulty in maintaining it, and their monetary troubles frequently provoked condemnation from abroad. The more recent experiences of the large countries have brought a better understanding of some aspects of the situation. Great Britain, between the two wards, encountered difficulties somewhat similar to those which arose and continue to arise in the Latin-American countries, which have never taken kindly to the rigidity of the gold standard. That experience doubtless helps to bring about a better understanding of the phenomena of the periphery.

The gold standard has ceased to function, as in the past, and the management of currency has become even more complex in the periphery. Can all these complications be overcome by a strict application of sound rules of monetary behavior? Sound rules for these countries are still in the making. Here there arises another vital problem; that of utilizing individual and collective experience to find a means of harmoniously fitting monetary action into a policy of regular and intensive economic development.

Let this not be interpreted as meaning that the classic teachings are of no value. If they do not provide positive rules, they at least show what cannot be done without impairing the stability of the currency. The extremes to which inflation has gone in Latin America show that monetary policy was not based upon these teachings, since some of the larger Latin-American countries increased circulation to a greater extent than did those countries which had to meet enormous war expenditure.

There is yet another aspect of the problem of dollar shortage. It is true that, as already stated, a high level of employment increases imports. But it is also a fact that an excessive monetary expansion has often unduly increased the pressure on the balance of payments, thus leading to the use of foreign exchange for purposes not always compatible with economic development.

These facts must be taken into account in an objective analysis of the effects of the inflationary increase on the process of capitalization. It must, however, be admitted that, in most of the Latin-American countries, voluntary savings are not sufficient to cover the most urgent capital needs. In any case, monetary expansion does not bring about an increase in the foreign exchange reserves necessary for the importation of capital goods; it merely redistributes income. It must now be determined whether it has led to a more active capital formation.

The point is a decisive one. The raising of the standard of living of the masses ultimately depends on the existence of a considerable amount of capital per man employed in the industry, transport and primary production, and on the ability to use it well.

Consequently, the Latin-American countries need to accumulate an enormous amount of capital. Several have already shown their capacity to save to the extent of being able to finance a large part of their industrial investments through their own efforts. Even in this case, which is exceptional, capital formation has to overcome a strong tendency towards certain types of consumption which are often incompatible with intensive capitalization.

Nevertheless, it does not appear essential to restrict the individual consumption of the bulk of the population, which, on the whole, is too low, in order to accumulate the capital required for industrialization and for the technical improvement of agriculture. An immediate increase in productivity per man could be brought about by well-directed foreign investments added to present savings. Once this initial improvement has been accomplished, a considerable part of the increased production can be devoted to capital formation rather than to inopportune consumption.

How are sufficient increases in productivity to be achieved? The experience of recent years is instructive. With some exceptions, the rise in employment necessitated by industrial development was made possible by the use of men who technical progress had displaced from primary production and other occupations, especially certain comparatively poorly paid types of personal services, and by the employment of women. The industrial employment of the unemployed, or ill-employed, has thus meant a considerable improvement in productivity and, consequently, where other factors have not brought about a general lowering of productive efficiency, a net increase in national income.

The great scope for technical progress in the field of primary production, even in those countries where it has already been considerable, together with the perfecting of existing industries, could contribute, to national income, a net increase that would provide an ever-increasing margin of saving.

All this, however, especially in so far as it is desired to reduce the need for foreign investments, presupposes a far greater initial capitalization than is usually possible with the type of consumption of certain sectors of the community, or the high proportion of national income absorbed, in some countries, by fiscal expenditure, which makes no direct or indirect contribution to national productivity.

It is, in fact, a demonstration of the latent conflict existing in these countries between the desire to assimilate, quickly, ways of life which the technically more advanced countries adopted step by step as their productivity increased, and the need for capitalization without which this increase in productivity could not be achieved.

For the very reason that capital is scarce, and the need for it great, its use should be subjected to a strict standard of efficacy which has not been easy to maintain, especially where industries have developed to meet an emergency. There is, however, still time to correct certain deviations and, above all, to avoid them in the future.

In order to achieve this, the purpose of industrialization must be clearly defined. If industrialization is considered to be the means of attaining an autarchic ideal in which economic considerations are of secondary importance, any industry that can produce substitutes for imports is justifiable. If, however, the aim is to increase the measurable well-being of the masses, the limits beyond which more intensive industrialization might mean a decrease in productivity must be borne in mind.

Formerly, before the great depression, development in Latin-American countries was stimulated from abroad by the constant increase of exports. There is no reason to suppose, at least at present, that this will again occur to the same extent, except under very exceptional circumstances. These countries no longer have an alternative between vigorous growth along those lines and internal expansion through industrialization. Industrialization has become the most important means of expansion.

This does not mean, however, that primary exports must be sacrificed to further industrial development. Exports not only provide the foreign exchange with which to buy the imports necessary for economic development, but their value usually includes a high proportion of land rent, which does not involve any collective cost. If productivity in agriculture can be increased by technical progress, and if, at the same time, real wages can be raised by industrialization and adequate social legislation, the disequilibrium between incomes at the centres and the periphery can gradually be corrected without detriment to that essential economic activity.

This is one of the limits of industrialization which must be carefully considered in plans of development.

Another concerns the optimum size of industrial enterprises. It is generally found in Latin-American countries that the same industries are being attempted on both sides of the same frontier. This tends to diminish productive efficiency and so militates against fulfilling the social task to be accomplished. The defect is a serious one, which the nineteenth century was able to attenuate considerably. When Great Britain proved, with facts, the advantages of industry, other countries followed suit. Industrial development, however spurred by active competition, tended towards certain characteristic types of specialization which encouraged profitable trade between the various countries. Specialization furthered technical progress and the latter made possible higher incomes. Here, unlike the case of industrial countries by comparison with those producing primary products, the classic advantages of the division of labour between countries that are equal, or nearly so, followed.

The possibility of losing a considerable proportion of the benefits of technical progress through an excessive division of markets thus constitutes another factor limiting the industrial expansion of these countries. Far from being unsurmountable, however, it is a factor which could be removed with mutual benefit by a wise policy of economic interdependence.

Anti-cyclical policies must be included in any programmes for economic development if there is to be an attempt, from a social point of view, to raise real income. The spread of the cyclical fluctuations of the large centres to the Latin-American periphery means a considerable loss of income to these countries. If this could be avoided, it would simplify the problem of capital information. Attempts have been made to evolve an anti-cyclical policy, but it must be admitted that, as yet, but little light has been thrown on this subject. Furthermore, the present dwindling of metallic reserves of several countries means that, in the event of a recession originating abroad, they would not only be without a plan of defense but would lack means of their own to carry out the measures demanded by the circumstances.

STUDY QUESTIONS

1. What is Prebisch's primary critique of the international division of labor?
2. What strategies must Latin American countries prioritize to ensure economic development? What role should industrialization play in the regional economy? What challenges would the region face in making this shift?

CHAPTER 9

THE CHALLENGES OF MODERNITY, 1930–1950

AUGUSTO SANDINO

9.1 TO ABOLISH THE MONROE DOCTRINE, 1933

Augusto Sandino was a Nicaraguan revolutionary who led guerrilla resistance against the US occupation of Nicaragua between 1927 and 1933 and became an iconic figure associated with Latin American anti-imperialism. Sandino was assassinated by the National Guard troops of Anastasio Somoza in 1934, and his name and image would become the symbol of resistance to Somoza's subsequent forty-year dictatorship. This excerpt is from a 1933 proclamation in which he called for all the nations of Central America to unite in fighting the United States and to reject the logic of the Monroe Doctrine which underpinned US economic and political intervention in the region.

Well then, deeply convinced that the grotesque yankee imperialism, day by day is infiltrating the domestic and foreign policy of Central America, turning our cowardly leaders into mummies—the vibrating spirit of the Indohispanic race becomes at this time the Autonomist Army of Central America to save its racial dignity, flinging militarily, politically and economically away from its territory the Wall Street bankers, even if to do this we will have to leave our bodies dead, lying face up towards the sun.

The Autonomist Army of Central America declares abolished the farcical Monroe Doctrine and by the same declaration annuls the right that said doctrine pretends to have to enmesh itself cowardly in the political life, domestic and foreign, of the Indohispanic republics.

We do not protest against the magnitude of the intervention, but simply against intervention. The United States has gotten into the affairs of Nicaragua for many years. We cannot rely on their promise that someday they will leave from here.

STUDY QUESTIONS

1. How does Sandino characterize the consequences of US intervention in Nicaragua?
2. Why does Sandino see military resistance as key to opposing US interests?

Source: "To Abolish the Monroe Doctrine: Proclamation from Augusto César Sandino," Nicaragua National Archives.

PEDRO CAMPOS ALBIZU

9.2 PUERTO RICAN NATIONALISM, 1936

Pedro Campos Albizu was the leading figure in the Puerto Rican Independence movement and was the president of the Puerto Rican Nationalist Party from 1930 until his death in 1965, facing multiple periods of imprisonment for his political activism. The statement excerpted here was given to the press in 1936, following his indictment for sedition. It lays out the core principles of the Puerto Rican nationalist movement.

The republic was founded sixty-eight years ago. When on September 23, 1868, our ancestors proclaimed our independence from Spain, they solemnly affirmed that the revolution was founded on no complaint against our motherland.

Puerto Rico was rich in name and in reality. Our Christian heritage had created a model family and a solid society. The nation was in the vanguard of modern civilizations.

Great men in all fields of human conquest brought honor to the land of their birth. Privileged intellects like Stahl and Tanguis in the natural sciences; Morel Campos, the musical genius; Oller and Campeches, masters of painting; great thinkers like Hostos; poets inspired by pure spirituality like Gautier Benitez; great seamen like Admiral Ramon Power; fighters for the freedom of the new world like Marshal Valero and General Rius Rivera; noble statesmen and patriots like Betances; and spiritual leaders of a generous, hospitable and peaceful nation like Bishop Arizmendi.

It was these prestigious figures from among the legions of great men and women of a nation who, for three centuries, served as a foundation for the expansion of Christian civilization in the Americas.

It must not be forgotten that an expedition from Puerto Rico under the command of Ponce de León planted the cross on the North American continent in 1531, a hundred years before the founding of Jamestown, Virginia.

The founders of the republic in 1868 fought only for the principle that no nation shall be master over the destiny of another nation.

This principle is the basis of international law and universal civilization and cannot be violated under any pretext.

It is the principle of human dignity formulated so that it applies to the family of nations.

Spain, the motherland, the founding hidalgo of modern universal civilization, recognized this fundamental principle of international relations as our forefathers of 1868 explained it, and conceded to Puerto Rico the Autonomous Magna Carta by virtue of which relations between Spain and Puerto Rico were to be regulated through treaties, thus recognizing our country as a sovereign, free, and independent nation.

This recognition of our place in the family of free nations was irrevocable and binding on all powers and could never be placed at the mercy of the vicissitudes of our motherland's or any other wars.

The Treaty of Paris, imposed by force on Spain by the United States on April 11, 1899, is null and void

Source: Manuel Maldonado-Denis (ed.) *La Conciencia nacional puertorriqueña*, (Mexico City: Siglo Veintiuno Editores, 1972); Translated: for marxists.org by Mitchell Abidor; CopyLeft: Creative Commons (Attribute & ShareAlike) marxists.org 2012. Declaration made to representatives of the Associated Press.

as pertains to Puerto Rico. For this reason, the military intervention of the United States in our fatherland is simply one of the most brutal and abusive acts perpetrated in contemporary history.

We demand the withdrawal of the armed forces of the United States from our soil as the natural and legitimate defense of Puerto Rican independence.

We are not as fortunate as our forefathers of 1868. They fought for the pure principle of national sovereignty. They had no complaint against the motherland, Spain.

We must make demands against the United States of North America, such as indemnification for the enormous damages systematically and cold-bloodedly perpetrated against a peaceful and defenseless nation.

Puerto Rico's favorable commercial balance during the thirty-five years of North American military intervention is approximately $400,000,000. According to this imposing figure, Puerto Rico should be one of the planet's richest and prosperous countries. In fact, poverty is our patrimony. This money is in the power of the citizens of continental North America.

If we calculate conservatively the financial value of the commercial monopoly forcibly imposed on us by the United States by virtue of which we are forced to sell our merchandise to the North Americans at the price they set, and add what we must pay for North American merchandise at whatever price the North Americans want to impose on us, we arrive at a figure of no less than $50,000,000.

The result of this pitiless exploitation and the abuses perpetrated against our nation are made evident through the universal poverty, the illnesses and the elevated mortality rates of our population, the highest in the Americas.

Seventy-six per cent of our national wealth is in the hands of a few North American corporations for whose benefit alone the present military government is maintained.

A stupid assault has been made on our Christian social order in a brutal effort to dissolve our family structure and destroy the morality of a noble race, imposing via governmental agencies the spread of prostitution under the deceitful banner of birth control; the ridiculous effort to destroy our Hispanic civilization with a system of public education used in the United States to enslave the masses; the mad arrogance of claiming to spiritually guide a nation whose soul was forged in the purest Christianity: these are our most serious complaints.

In Puerto Rico the United States of America is confronting face to face the spirit of Lexington, of Zaragoza, of Ayacucho.

The present imperial policies by which they want to dissolve nationalism through terror and assassination is a provocation and an act of imperialist foolishness aimed at satisfying a handful of North American corporations.

The people of the United States, if they have not become totally insensitive to the principles that allowed them to be a free nation, must show common sense, must be guided solely by their national interests.

This national interest is guaranteed to respect Puerto Rico's independence.

These are the aspirations of Puerto Rican nationalism.

STUDY QUESTIONS

1. What historical examples does Campos Albizu use to underline the importance of national sovereignty?
2. How has US economic and political intervention impacted Puerto Rico in his opinion? Who does he say American policies are designed to benefit?

JOSÉ VASCONCELOS

9.3 *THE COSMIC RACE*, 1925

José Vasconcelos was one of the intellectual leaders of the Mexican Revolution, and held a variety of important roles in cultural institutions, including serving as minister for education and director of the National Library. In *The Cosmic Race*, his most important and influential work, Vasconcelos challenges the scientific racism that had dominated the late nineteenth and early twentieth century, and argues that Latin America's history of race mixture had allowed for the creation of a new kind of hybridity that would advance humanity. His work is considered the foundational text for the ideology of mestizaje—the celebration of Latin American race mixture and the elevation of the mestizo as a symbol of national and regional identities.

Greece laid the foundations of Western or European civilization; the white civilization that, upon expanding, reached the forgotten shores of the American continent in order to consummate the task of re-civilization and re-population. Thus we have the four stages and the four racial trunks: the Black, the Indian, the Mongol, and the White. The latter, after organizing itself in Europe, has become the invader of the world, and has considered itself destined to rule, as did each of the previous races during their time of power. It is clear that domination by the whites will also be temporary, but their mission is to serve as a bridge. The white race has brought the world to a state in which all human types and cultures will be able to fuse with each other. The civilization developed and organized in our times by the whites has set the moral and material basis for the union of all men into a fifth universal race, the fruit of all the previous ones and amelioration of everything past. . . .

From the start, from the time of the discovery and the conquest, it was the Castilians and the British (or the Latins and the Anglo-Saxons, if we include the Portuguese, on one side, and the Dutch, on the other) the ones who accomplished the task of beginning a new period of history by conquering and populating the new hemisphere. Although they may have thought of themselves simply as colonizers, as carriers of culture, in reality, they were establishing the basis for a period of general and definitive transformation. The so-called Latins, well endowed with genius and courage, seized the best regions, the ones they thought were the richest, while the English had to be satisfied with what was left to them by a more capable people. Neither Spain nor Portugal allowed the Anglo-Saxons to come near their domains, and I do not mean for reasons of war, but not even to take part in commerce. Latin predominance was unquestionable at the beginning. No one would have suspected at the time of the Papal arbitration which divided the New World between Spain and Portugal that, a few centuries later, the New World would no longer be Spanish nor Portuguese but English. No one would have imagined that the humble colonists of the Hudson and the Delaware, so peaceful and diligent, would go on taking over, step by step, the best and largest expansions of land, until they formed a republic which today constitutes one of the largest empires in History.

Source: José Vasconcelos, *The Cosmic Race*. © 1979 California State University, Los Angeles (English Edition) Afterword © 1997 The Johns Hopkins University Press. All rights reserved.
First Spanish edition published 1925, © Herederos de Jose Vasconcelos. Bilingual edition originally published by the Department of Chicano Studies, California State University, Los Angeles, 1979. Johns Hopkins Paperbacks edition, 1997.

Our age became, and continues to be, a conflict of Latinism against Anglo-Saxonism; a conflict of institutions, aims and ideals. . . .

Let us recognize that it was a disgrace not to have proceeded with the cohesion demonstrated by those to the north, that prodigious race which we are accustomed to lavish with insults only because they have won each hand at the secular fight. They triumph because they join to their practical talents the clear vision of a great destiny. They keep present the intuition of a definite historical mission, while we get lost in the labyrinth of verbal chimeras. It seems as if God Himself guided the steps of the Anglo-Saxon cause, while we kill each other on account of dogma or declare ourselves atheists. How those mighty empire builders must laugh at our groundless arrogance and Latin vanity! They do not clutter their mind with the Ciceronian weight of phraseology, nor have they in their blood the contradictory instincts of a mixture of dissimilar races, *but they committed the sin of destroying those races, while we assimilated them, and this gives us new rights and hopes for a mission without precedent in History.*

For this reason, adverse obstacles do not move us to surrender, for we vaguely feel that they will help us to discover our way. Precisely in our differences, we find the way. If we simply imitate, we lose. If we discover and create, we shall overcome. The advantage of our tradition is that it has greater facility of sympathy towards strangers. This implies that our civilization, with all defects, may be the chosen one to assimilate and to transform mankind into a new type; that within our civilization, the warp, the multiple and rich plasma of future humanity is thus being prepared. This mandate from History is first noticed in that abundance of love that allowed the Spaniard to create a new race with the Indian and the Black, profusely spreading white ancestry through the soldier who begat a native family, and Occidental culture through the doctrine and example of the missionaries who placed the Indians in condition to enter into the new stage, the stage of world One. Spanish colonization created mixed races, this signals its character, fixes its responsibility, and defines its future. The English kept on mixing only with the whites and annihilated the natives. Even today, they continue to annihilate them in a sordid and economic fight, more efficient yet than armed conquest. This

proves their limitation and is indication of their decadence. The situation is equivalent, in a larger scale, to the incestuous marriages of the pharaohs which undermined the virtues of the race; and it contradicts the ulterior goals of History to attain the fusion of peoples and cultures. To build an English world and to exterminate the red man, so that Northern Europe could be renovated all over an America made up with pure whites, is no more than a repetition of the triumphant process of a conquering race. This was already attempted by the red man and by all strong and homogeneous races, but it does not solve the human problem. America was not kept in reserve for five thousand years for such a petty goal. The purpose of the new and ancient continent is much more important. Its predestination obeys the design of constituting the cradle of a fifth race into which all nations will fuse with each other to replace the four races that have been forging History apart from each other. The dispersion will come to an end on American soil; unity will be consummated there by the triumph of fecund love and the improvement of all the human races. In this fashion, the synthetic race that shall gather all the treasures of History in order to give expression to universal desire shall be created.

The so-called Latin peoples, because they have been more faithful to their divine mission in America, are the ones called upon to consummate this mission. Such fidelity to the occult design is the guarantee of our triumph. . . .

Thus, what no one even thought of doing on the Anglo-Saxon area of the continent was done on the Latin side. In the north, the contrary thesis continued to prevail: The confessed or tacit intention of cleaning the earth of Indians, Mongolians or Blacks, for the greater glory and fortune of the Whites. In fact, since that time, the systems which, continuing to the present, have placed the two civilizations on opposing sociological fields were very well defined. The one wants exclusive dominion by the Whites, while the other is shaping a new race, a synthetic race that aspires to engulf and to express everything human in forms of constant improvement. If it were necessary to adduce proof, it would be sufficient to observe the increasing and spontaneous mixing which operates among all peoples in all of the Latin continent; in contrast with the inflexible line that separates the Blacks from the

Whites in the United States, and the laws, each time more rigorous, for the exclusion of the Japanese and Chinese from California.

The so-called Latins insist on not taking the ethnic factor too much into account for their sexual relations, perhaps because from the beginning they are not, properly speaking, Latins but a conglomeration of different types and races. Whatever opinions one may express in this respect, and whatever repugnance caused by prejudice one may harbor, the truth is that the mixture of races has taken place and continues to be consummated. It is in this fusion of ethnic stocks that we should look for the fundamental characteristic of Ibero-American idiosyncrasy. It may happen sometimes and, in fact, it has already happened, that economic competition may force us to close our doors, as is done by the Anglo-Saxons, to an unrestrained influx of Asians. But, in doing so, we obey reasons of economic order. We recognize that it is not fair that people like the Chinese, who, under the saintly guidance of Confucian morality multiply like mice, should come to degrade the human condition precisely at the moment when we begin to understand that intelligence serves to refrain and regulate the lower zoological instincts, which are contrary to a truly religious conception of life. If we reject the Chinese, it is because man, as he progresses, multiplies less, and feels the horror of numbers, for the same reason that he has begun to value quality. In the United States, Asians are rejected because of the same fear of physical overflow, characteristic of superior stocks; but also because Americans simply do not like Asians, even despise them, and would be incapable of intermarriage with them. The ladies of San Francisco have refused to dance with officials of the Japanese Navy, who are men as clean, intelligent, and, in their way, as handsome as those of any other navy in the world. Yet, these ladies will never understand that a Japanese may be handsome. Nor is it easy to convince the Anglo-Saxon that if the yellow and the black races have their characteristic smell, the Whites, for a foreigner, also have theirs, even though we may not be aware of it. In Latin America, the repulsion of one blood that confronts another strange blood also exists, but infinitely more attenuated. There, a thousand bridges are available for the sincere and cordial fusion of all races. The ethnic barricading of those to the north in contrast to the much more open sympathy of those to the south is the most important factor, and at the same time, the most favorable to us, if one reflects even superficially upon the future, because it will be seen immediately that we belong to tomorrow, while the Anglo-Saxons are gradually becoming more a part of yesterday. The Yankees will end up building the last great empire of a single race, the final empire of White supremacy. Meanwhile, we will continue to suffer the vast chaos of an ethnic stock in formation, contaminated by the fermentation of all types, but secure of the avatar into a better race. In Spanish America, Nature will no longer repeat one of her partial attempts. This time, the race that will come out of the forgotten Atlantis will no longer be a race of a single color or of particular features. The future race will not be a fifth, or a sixth race, destined to prevail over its ancestors. What is going to emerge out there is the definitive race, the synthetical race, the integral race, made up of the genius and the blood of all peoples and, for that reason, more capable of true brotherhood and of a truly universal vision.

In order to come near this sublime purpose, it is necessary to keep on creating, so to speak, the cellular tissue which will serve as the flesh and support of this new biological formation. In order to create that Protean, malleable, profound, ethereal, and essential tissue, it will be necessary for the Ibero-American race to permeate itself with its mission and embrace it as a mysticism. . . .

How different the sounds of the Ibero-American development [from that of the Anglo—Saxons]! They resemble the profound scherzo of a deep and infinite symphony: voices that bring accents from Atlantis; depths contained in the pupil of the red man, who knew so much, so many thousand years ago, and now seems to have forgotten everything. His soul resembles the old Mayan *cenote* of green waters, laying deep and still, in the middle of the forest, for so many centuries since, that not even its legend remains any more. This infinite quietude is stirred with the drop put in our blood by the Black, eager for sensual joy, intoxicated with dances and unbridled lust. There also appears the Mongol, with the mystery of his slanted eyes that see everything according to a strange angle, and discover I know not what folds and newer dimensions. The clear mind of the White, that resembles his skin and his dreams, also intervenes. Judaic striae hidden within the Castilian blood since the days of the cruel expulsion now reveal themselves, along with Arabian melancholy, as a remainder of the sickly Muslim sensuality. Who has not a little of all this, or does not wish to have all? There is the Hindu, who also will come, who has already arrived by way of the spirit, and although he is the last one to arrive, be seems the closest relative. . . . So many races that have come and others that will come. In this manner, a sensitive and ample heart will be taking shape within us; a heart that embraces and contains everything and is moved with sympathy, but, full of vigor, imposes new laws upon the world. . . .

Now that we have expressed the theory of the formation of the future Ibero-American race, and the manner in which it will be able to take advantage of the environment in which it lives, only the third factor of the transformation which is taking place in our continent remains to be considered: The spiritual factor, which has to direct and consummate this extraordinary enterprise. Some may think, perhaps, that the fusion of the different contemporary races into a new race that will fulfill and surpass all the others is going to be a repugnant process of anarchic hybridization. By comparison, the English practice of marrying only within the same stock may be seen as an ideal of refinement and purity. The primitive Aryans from Hindustan attempted precisely that English system, in order to keep themselves from mixing with the colored races. However, since those dark races possessed a wisdom necessary to complement that of the blond invaders, the true Hindu culture was not produced until after the centuries had completed the mixture, in spite of all written prohibitions. Furthermore, the fateful mixture was useful not only for cultural reasons, but because the physical specimen itself needs to be renovated in its kin. North Americans have held very firmly to their resolution to maintain a pure stock, the reason being that they are faced with the Blacks, who are like the opposite pole,

like the antithesis of the elements *to* be mixed. In the Ibero-American world, the problem does not present itself in such crude terms. We have very few Blacks, and a large part of them is already becoming a mulatto population. The Indian is a good bridge for racial mixing. Besides, the warm climate is propitious for the interaction and gathering of all peoples. On the other hand, and this is essential, interbreeding will no longer obey reasons of simple proximity as occurred in the beginning when the white colonist *took* an indian or black woman because there were no others at hand. In the future, as social conditions keep improving, the mixture of bloods will become gradually more spontaneous, *to* the *point* that interbreeding will no longer be the result of simple necessity but of personal *taste* or, at least, of curiosity. Spiritual motivation, in *this* manner, will increasingly superimpose itself upon the contingencies of the merely physical. By spiritual motivation, we should understand, rather than reflective thinking, the faculty of personal *taste* that directs the mysterious selection of one particular person out of the multitude. . . .

We have the duty to formulate the basis of a new civilization, and for that very reason, it is necessary that we keep in mind the fact that civilizations cannot be repeated, neither in form nor in content. The theory of ethnic superiority has been simply a means of combat, common to all fighting peoples, but the battle that we must wage is so important that it does not admit any false trickery. We do not claim that we are, nor that we shall become, the first race of the world or the most illustrious, the strongest and the most handsome. Our purpose is even higher and more difficult to attain than temporary selection. . . .

We in America shall arrive, before any other part of the world, at the creation of a new race fashioned out of the treasures of all the previous ones: The final race, the cosmic race.

STUDY QUESTIONS

1. What are the key differences Vasconcelos elucidates between attitudes toward race and race mixture in Anglo-Saxon and Latin civilizations?
2. What evidence does Vasconcelos use to support his argument that race mixture is the future of humanity? How does he connect this argument to different regional histories?
3. Are all groups seen as equal contributors to the mixed-race culture? Can you see any residues of scientific racism embedded within Vasconcelos's thinking?

JOSÉ CARLOS MARIÁTEGUI

9.4 ON THE INDIGENOUS PROBLEM, 1928

The Peruvian intellectual José Carlos Mariátegui was one of the most influential Latin American socialists of the interwar period. He founded two influential Marxist journals and established the Peruvian Socialist Party. He believed that Latin American socialism must be fully grounded in local conditions, and as such he was deeply interested in indigenous rights. His writings on the challenges facing Peruvian indigenous people are considered foundational to indigenista philosophy—a school of thought that encouraged the revalorization of the indigenous heritage of Latin America. Yet Mariátegui also insisted that indigenous people themselves must participate directly in any economic and political strategies intended to change their situation, and that white and mestizo intellectuals should not just write about Indians but also work with them in solidarity. This is an excerpt from an essay originally published in 1928 in the journal *Labor* (founded by Mariátegui).

ON THE INDIGENOUS PROBLEM:
BRIEF HISTORICAL REVIEW

The population of the Inca empire, according to conservative estimates, was at least ten million. Some people place it at twelve or even fifteen million. The conquest was, more than anything, a terrible carnage. The Spanish conquerors, with their small numbers, could not impose their domination, but only managed to terrorize the Indigenous population. The invaders' guns and horses, which were regarded as supernatural beings, created a superstitious impression. The political and economic organization of the colony, which came after the conquest, continued the extermination of the Indigenous race. The viceroyalty established a system of brutal exploitation. Spanish greed for precious metals led to an economic activity directed toward mines that, under the Incas, had been worked on very small scale because the Indians, who were largely an agricultural people, did not use iron and only used gold and silver as ornaments. In order to work the mines and *obrajes* (sweatshops) where weaving was done, the Spanish established a system of forced labor that decimated the population. This was not only a state of servitude, as might have been the case had the Spanish limited the exploitation to the use of land and retained the agricultural character of the country, but was in large part a state of slavery. Humanitarian and civilizing voices called for the king of Spain to defend the Indians. More than anyone, Father Bartolomé de Las Casas stood out in their defense. The Laws of the Indies were inspired by the purpose of protecting the Indians. It recognized their traditional organization into communities. But in reality the Indians continued to be at the mercy of a ruthless feudalism that destroyed the Inca economy and society without replacing it with something that could increase production. The tendency of the Spanish to settle on the coast drove away so many aboriginals from the region that it resulted in a lack of workers. The viceroyalty wanted to solve this problem through the importation of African slaves. These people were appropriate to the climate and challenges of the hot valleys and plains of the coast and, in contrast, inappropriate for work in the mines in the cold sierra highlands. The African slave reinforced the Spanish domination that in spite of the Indigenous depopulation was still outnumbered

Source: *José Carlos Mariátegui: An Anthology.* Edited and Translated by Harry E. Vanden and Marc Becker. (New York: Monthly Review Press, 2011).

by the Indians who, though subjugated, remained a hostile enemy. Blacks were devoted to domestic service and other jobs. Whites easily mixed with blacks, producing a mixture of a type characteristic of the coastal population that has greater adherence to the Spanish and resists Indigenous influences.

The independence revolution was not, as is known, an Indigenous movement. It was a movement of and for the benefit of *creoles* and even Spanish living in the colonies. But it took advantage of the support of the Indigenous masses. Furthermore, as illustrated by the Pumachus, some Indians played an important role in its development. The liberal program of the revolution logically included the redemption of its egalitarian principles. And so, among the first acts of the republic, were several laws and decrees in favor of the Indians. They ordered the distribution of land, the abolition of forced labor, and so on. But the revolution in Peru did not bring in a new ruling class, and all of these provisions remained on paper without a government capacity to carry them out. The colony's landholding aristocracy, the owner of power, retained their feudal rights over land and, therefore, over the Indians. All provisions apparently designed to protect them have not been able to do anything against feudalism even today.

The viceroyalty seems less to blame than the republic. The full responsibility for the misery and depression of the Indians originally belongs to the viceroyalty. But in those inquisitorial days, a great Christian voice, that of Fray [Friar] Bartolomé de Las Casas, vigorously defended the Indians against the brutal methods of the colonizers. There has never been as stubborn and effective an advocate of the aboriginal race during the republic.

While the viceroyalty was a medieval and foreign regime, the republic is formally a Peruvian and liberal regime. The republic, therefore, had a duty the viceroyalty did not have. The republic has the responsibility to raise the status of the Indian. And contrary to this duty, the republic has impoverished the Indians. It has compounded their depression and exasperated their misery. The republic has meant for the Indians the ascent of a new ruling class that has systematically taken their lands. In a race based on customs and an agricultural soul, as with the Indigenous race, this dispossession has constituted a cause for their material

and moral dissolution. Land has always been the joy of the Indians. Indians are wed to the land. They feel that "life comes from the earth" and returns to the earth. For this reason, Indians can be indifferent to everything except the possession of the land, which by their hands and through their encouragement is religiously fruitful. *Creole* feudalism has behaved, in this respect, worse than Spanish feudalism. Overall, the Spanish *encomendero* often had some of the noble habits of feudal lords. The *creole encomendero* has all the defects of a commoner and none of the virtues of a gentleman. The servitude of the Indian, in short, has not decreased under the republic. All uprisings, all of the Indian unrest, have been drowned in blood. Indian demands have always been met with a military response. The silence of the puna[1] afterward guards the tragic secret of these responses. In the end, the republic restored, under the title of the road labor draft, the system of *mitas*.

In addition, the republic is also responsible for the lethargic and weak energies of the race. The cause of the redemption of the Indians became under the republic a demagogic speculation of some strongmen. *Creole* parties have signed up for their program. And thus the Indians lost their will to fight for their demands.

In the highlands, the region mostly inhabited by the Indians, the most barbaric and omnipotent feudalism remains largely unchanged. The domination of the earth in the hands of the *gamonales*, the fate of the Indigenous race, falls to an extreme level of depression and ignorance. In addition to farming, which is carried out on a very primitive level, the Peruvian highlands also have another economic activity: mining, almost entirely in the hands of two large U.S. companies. Wages are regulated in the mines, but the pay is negligible, there is almost no defense for the lives of the workers, and labor laws governing accidents are ignored. The system of *enganche*, which through false promises enslaves workers, put the Indians at the mercy of these capitalist companies. The misery of agrarian feudalism is so great that Indians prefer the lot offered by the mines.

The spread of socialist ideas in Peru has resulted in a strong movement reflecting Indigenous demands. The new Peruvian generation knows that Peru's progress will be fictitious, or at least will not be Peruvian, if it does not benefit the Peruvian masses, four-fifths of whom are Indigenous and peasant. This same trend is evident in art and in national literature in which there is a growing appreciation of Indigenous forms and affairs, which before had been depreciated by the dominance of a Spanish colonial spirit and mentality. *Indigenista* literature seems to fulfill the same role of Mujika literature in pre-revolutionary Russia. Indians themselves are beginning to show signs of a new consciousness. Relationships between various Indigenous settlements which before were out of contact because of great distances grow day by day. The regular meeting of Indigenous congresses that are sponsored by the government initiated these linkages, but as the nature of their demands became revolutionary they were denatured as advanced elements were excluded and the representation was made apocryphal. *Indigenista* currents press for official action. For the first time the government has been forced to accept and proclaim *indigenista* views, and has decreed some measures that do not touch *gamonal* interests and are ineffective because of this. For the first time the Indigenous problem, which disappears in the face of ruling-class rhetoric, is posed in its social and economic terms and is identified more than anything as a land problem. Every day more evidence underscores the conviction that this problem cannot find its solution in a humanitarian formula. It cannot be the result of a philanthropic movement. The patronage of Indigenous chieftains and phony lawyers are a mockery. Leagues of the type of the former Pro-Indigenous Association provide a voice clamoring in the wilderness. The Pro-Indigenous Association did not arrive in time to become a movement. Their action was gradually reduced to the generous, selfless, noble, personal actions of Pedro S. Zulen and Dora Mayer. As an experiment, the Pro-Indigenous Association served

to contrast, to measure, the moral callousness of a generation and an era.[2]

The solution to the problem of the Indian must be a social solution. It must be worked out by the Indians themselves. This concept leads to seeing the meeting of Indigenous congresses as a historical fact. The Indigenous congresses, misled in recent years by bureaucratic tendencies, have not yet formed a program, but their first meetings indicated a route for Indians in different regions. The Indians lack a national organization. Their protests have always been regional. This has contributed in large part to their defeat. Four million people, conscious of their numbers, do not despair of their future. These same four million people, though they are nothing more than an inorganic mass, a dispersed crowd, are unable to decide its historical course.

Carlos Mariátegui wrote this "Brief Historical Review" at the request of the Tass News Agency in New York, and it was translated and published as "The New Peru," in *The Nation* 128 (January 16, 1929). It was reprinted in *Labor* (Year I, No.1, 1928) with the title "On the Indian Problem: Brief Historical Review." An editorial note from Mariátegui preceded it indicating that these notes "in a sense complement a chapter on 'The Problem of Indian' in *Seven Interpretative Essays on Peruvian Reality*." For this reason, the editors of *Obras Completas* added it to this essay beginning with the third edition, April 1952.

Source: Jose Carlos Mariátegui, "Sobre el problema indigena," *Labor: Quincenario de información e ideas* 1/1 (November 10, 1928): 6.

1. Cold, desolate highland region.
2. The Asociación Pro-Indígena (Pro-Indigenous Association) was a moderate Peruvian association dedicated to advancing Indigenous rights. It operated in the first part of the twentieth century.

STUDY QUESTIONS

1. How does Mariátegui explain the subordinated status of the Peruvian indigenous people? Which historical and contemporary forces are to blame for this in his opinion?
2. How does Mariátegui's Marxist philosophy shape his arguments about the needs of indigenous people?

GILBERTO FREYRE

9.5 *THE MASTERS AND THE SLAVES*, 1933

Gilberto Freyre was a Brazilian sociologist whose 1933 book *The Masters and the Slaves* was one of the definitive works of early twentieth-century Brazilian thought. It was widely read across Latin America and also shaped perceptions about Brazilian race relations in Europe and the United States. Freyre's work explored the history of race mixture in Brazil, which he saw as rooted in fluid racial relations during the period of slavery, and argued for the positive cultural influence of the African heritage. Freyre's work challenged the assumptions of scientific racism and provided a foundation for the projection of Brazil as a nation of racial harmony—an ideology that is often referred to as "racial democracy." Yet it has subsequently been critiqued for its romanticization of slavery and for the hierarchical thinking embedded within it.

This essay is the first of a series in which I have undertaken to study the formation and disintegration of patriarchal society in Brazil, a society that grew up around the first sugar-mills or sugar plantations established by Europeans in our country, in the sixteenth century. It was upon this basis that the society in question developed: the production of sugar by means of a socio-economic system that represented, in a way, a revival of European feudalism in the American tropics. In the nineteenth century the system was to undergo an alteration that was not so much one of form or sociological characteristics as of economic content or cultural substance, through the substitution of coffee for sugar as the mainstay of the regime.

Sociologically matured through an experience of three centuries, the tropical feudalism of Brazil has conditioned the expression of life and culture and the relations of man with nature in this part of the Americas down to our own time, and its disintegration is a process that today may still be studied in a living form; for its survivals constitute the most typical elements of the Brazilian landscape, physical as well as social.

The majority of our countrymen are the near descendants either of masters or of slaves, and many of them have sprung from the union of slave-owners with slave women. The visiting foreigner cannot be said to have seen Brazil unless he has been in the old Big House of some sugar or coffee plantation, with what is left of its family silver, its rosewood, its porcelain, its ancestral portraits, its garden, its slave quarters, and its chapel filled with images of the saints and the mortal remains of former inmates. These Big Houses, slave quarters, and plantation chapels blend harmoniously with the fields of sugar-cane, the coffee groves, the palm trees, the mangoes, the breadfruit trees; with the hills and plains, the tropical or semitropical forest, the rivers and waterfalls; with the horse-teams of the former masters and the oxen that were the companions in labor of the slaves. They likewise blend with those descendants of the white or near-white masters and of the Negro, mulatto, or *cafuso*[1] slaves who out of inertia have remained

---

1   Offspring of Indian and Negro. (Translator.)

Source: Gilberto Freyre, *The Masters and the Slaves [Casa-Grande & Senzala]: A Study in the Development of Brazilian Civilization.* Translated from the Portuguese by Samuel Putnam. [Second English-Language Edition, Revised.] Introduction to the paperback edition by David H. P. Maybury-Lewis. University Of California Press.

rooted in these old places where their grandfathers held aristocratic sway or engaged in servile toil.

So perfect is this fusion that, even though they are now all but lifeless, these old elements, or mere fragments, of the patriarchal regime in Brazil are still the best integrated of any with their environment and, to all appearances, the best adapted to the climate. As a result, the curious observer of today has the impression that they have grown up together fraternally, and that, rather than being mutually hostile by reason of their antagonisms, they complement one another with their differences. Men, animals, houses, vegetables, techniques, values, symbols, some of remote derivation, others native—all of these today, now that the conflict between modes of life and the at times bitter clash of interests have subsided, tend to form one of the most harmonious unions of culture with nature and of one culture with another that the lands of this hemisphere have ever known.

If we speak of a union of cultures, it is for the reason that the most diverse ethnic factors have contributed to this picture, bringing with them cultural heritages that were widely different and even opposed: the Portuguese "old Christian,"[2] the Jew, the Spaniard, the Dutch, the French, the Negro, the Amerindian, the descendant of the Moor. As for the Jew, there is evidence to the effect that he was one of the most active agents in the winning of a market for the sugar-producers of Brazil, a function that, during the first century of colonization, he fulfilled to the great advantage of this part of the Americas. He would appear to have been the most efficient of those technicians responsible for setting up the first sugar-mills. The history of patriarchal society in Brazil is, for this reason, inseparable from the history of the Jew in America. In speaking of his economic activity in the post-Columbian world, the fact should be stressed that among the Portuguese of the continent theological hatreds and violent racial antipathies or prejudices were rarely manifested. The same is true of the relations between whites and blacks: those hatreds due to class or caste, extended, and at times disguised, in the form of race hatred, such as marked the

history of other slave-holding areas in the Americas, were seldom carried to any such extreme in Brazil. The absence of violent rancors due to race constitutes one of the peculiarities of the feudal system in the tropics, a system that, in a manner of speaking, had been softened by the hot climate and by the effects of a miscegenation that tended to dissolve such prejudices. This was the system that, in our country, grew up around the sugar-mills and, later, the coffee plantations.

To be sure, the social distance between masters and slaves under this system, corresponding to differences in color, was an enormous one, the whites being really or officially the masters and the blacks really or officially the slaves.[3] The Portuguese, however, were a people who had experienced the rule of the Moors, a dark-skinned race but one that was superior to the white race in various aspects of its moral and material culture; and accordingly, though they themselves might be white and even of a pronounced blond type, they had long since formed the habit of discovering in colored peoples—or, as "old Christians," in the people of Israel and Mohammedans as well—persons, human beings, who were brothers, creatures and children of God with whom it was possible to fraternize, and with whom, as a matter of fact, their forebears had had fraternal relations. And all of this, from the very first years of colonization, tended to mitigate the system. It was this habit that led the Portuguese readily to adopt the foodstuffs, standards of feminine beauty, and modes of life of peoples that by other Europeans were looked upon as being absolutely inferior; and to this liberal attitude certain students of the subject have given the name "Lusitania~Franciscanism."[4]

It is a known fact that in some of the best Portuguese families at the time of the colonization of Brazil there was Jewish, Moorish, or Indian blood, and this in no way detracted from the prestige of the families in question when these strains were of socially illustrious

---

2   As distinguished from the "new-Christian," the latter being a euphemism for a Jew who had accepted Christian baptism, the implication being, frequently, that he still clung to his old faith. (Translator.)

3   The color line between master and slave, as is brought out later (see p. xxi-xxii), was far from being always distinct. The master might be a *brancarão*, or light-skinned mulatto, and the slave very often was partly white. (Translator.)

4   The allusion, of course, is to the teachings or general attitude of St. Francis of Assisi and the Franciscan Order. (Translator.)

origin. The same thing happened in America, where one of the first Brazilian colonists, a man of noble birth, was married to the daughter of an Indian chief. They had many descendants who became outstanding figures among the agrarian aristocracy and in the field of politics, literature, the magistracy, and the colonial clergy, a state of affairs that continued under the Empire and down to our own day. It was one of these descendants who became South America's first Cardinal.

It thereby becomes possible to interpret the formation of Brazilian society in the light of a "synthetic principle"—to make use of an expression consecrated by usage—such as, perhaps, could not be applied with alike degree of appropriateness to any other society. So viewed, our social history, despite the grievous and persisting imprint left upon it by the experiences of feudal economic system, is undergoing a process whose direction is that of a broad democratization of interhuman relationships, of interpersonal relations, of relations between groups and between regions. The fact of the matter is that miscegenation and the interpenetration of cultures—chiefly European, Amerindian, and African culture—together with the possibilities and opportunities for rising in the social scale that in the past have been open to slaves, individuals of the colored races and even heretics: the possibility and the opportunity of becoming free men and in the official sense, whites and Christians (if not theologically sound, at any rate sociologically valid ones)—the fact is that all these things, from an early period, have tended to mollify the interclass and interracial antagonisms developed under an aristocratic economy.

Accepting this interpretation of Brazilian history as a march toward social democracy, a march that has on various occasions been interrupted and frequently has been disturbed and rendered difficult we are unable to conceive of a society with tendencies more opposed to those of the Germanic *Weltanschauung*. What we have here is a society whose national direction is inspired not by the blood-stream of families, much less that of a race, as the expression of a biological reality, nor, on the other hand, by an all-powerful State or Church; it is, rather, one of diverse ethnic origins with varying cultural heritages which a feudal economic system maintained throughout whole centuries a relative degree of order, without being able, meanwhile, to

destroy the potential of the subordinated cultures by bringing about the triumph of the master-class culture to the exclusion of the others.

The sentiment of nationality in the Brazilian has been deeply affected by the fact that the feudal system did not here permit of a State that was wholly dominant or a Church that was omnipotent, as well as by the circumstance of miscegenation as practiced under the wing of that system and at the same time practiced against it, thus rendering less easy the absolute identification of the ruling class with the pure or quasi-pure European stock of the principal conquerors, the Portuguese. The result is a national sentiment tempered by a sympathy for the foreigner that is so broad as to become, practically, universalism. It would, indeed, be impossible to conceive of a people marching onward toward social democracy that in place of being universal in its tendencies should be narrowly exclusive or ethnocentric.

It would, truly enough, be ridiculous to pretend that the long period, ever since colonial times, during which a large part of Brazil had lived under a system of feudal organization had predisposed its people to the practice of political democracy, which recently underwent a crisis among us under a dictatorship that was at once near-fascist[5] in its ideology and Brazilian and paternalistic in fact. The major effort that is being put forth by the apologists of the present dictator is in the direction of popularizing him as the "Father" of his people, the "Father" of the workers or of the poor. It seems to me, meanwhile, that no student of Luso-American society can fad to recognize the fact that—as a consequence of the weakness rather than the virtue of the slave-holders and landowners—what I have here called Brazilian feudalism was in reality a combination of aristocracy, democracy, and even anarchy. And this union of opposites would appear to be serving as the basis for the development in Brazil of a society that is democratic in its ethnic, social, and cultural composition and, at the same time, aristocratic in its cult of superior individuals and superior families, and in the tolerance that it accords to differing personalities.

Hence a certain fondness that the Brazilian has for honoring differences. In Brazil individuals of the most widely varied social origins and personalities, differing

---

5   *"Para-fascirta"* is Freyre's word. (Translator.)

likewise in race or religion, or by the fact that some are the descendants of Negro slaves while others are of white European or *caboclo*[6] ancestry, have risen to the highest positions. Some have been the sons of black women, like the one-time Archbishop of Mariana, Dom Silverio. Another, like the ex-Chancellor Lauro Muller, may be the son of an impoverished German immigrant. Still another may be the son of a non-Portuguese Jew, like David Campista, who was for some time Minister of Finance, and who in 1910 was practically President of the Republic. The most divergent types, in short, have been the object of the Brazilian's admiration and of his confidence. We Brazilians—and this, paradoxical as it may appear, is due to the effect of our "feudalism," which was at once aristocratic, democratic, and anarchistic in tendency—do not possess that cult of uniformity and horror of individual, family, and regional differences which are the accompaniments of the equalitarian spirit throughout so large a part of English-speaking America.

There are men in the public life of our country today, descendants of old and feudal families, of whom everyone knows just what service to the nation or to the community is to be expected, so marked are the characteristics and the differences of each one of these families. The Andradas of Sao Paulo, for example, are known for their stern idealism; the Calmons are noted for their suavity and spirit of conciliation; the Prados are realistic conservatives, the Mendes de Almeidas conservative idealists. This, to cite but a few. Yet such is our respect for individual differences that no one would be surprised to see a Prado a Communist leader in politics or a Mendes de Almeida a Surrealist in poetry or in art. We have seen the son of one old feudal family embarking for India and turning fakir; another, in Paris, became an airplane-inventor; a third, back in the days of slavery, became an abolitionist agitator; a fourth was a Protestant leader and terribly antipapist. And none of these was regarded as a madman. On the contrary, all were admired by their fellow countrymen; for the latter love and esteem those individuals who stand out by reason of their superior talents, knowledge, or virtue.

One word more, with regard to the title of the present essay in the original. That title does not mean that I have undertaken to trace the history of domestic architecture in patriarchal Brazil, with added commentaries of a sociological nature. The two expressions that make up the title—the Portuguese *casa-grande* (that is, big house or mansion in English) and the African *senzala* (slave quarters)—have here a symbolic intention, the purpose being to suggest the cultural antagonism and social distance between masters and slaves, whites and blacks, Europeans and Africans, as marked by the residence of each group in Brazil from the sixteenth to the nineteenth century. An antagonism and a distance that conditioned the evolvement of the patriarchal agrarian or, simply, the feudal complex[7] in Portuguese America, and which were in their turn conditioned by other influences: that of the physical environment and those deriving from the antecedents of the Portuguese colonizer, of the Negro, and of the native or *caboclo*. Without for a moment forgetting the fact that the antagonism and distance of which we are speaking had their force broken by the interpenetration of cultures and by miscegenation—the democratizing factors of a society that otherwise would have remained divided into two irreconcilable groups—we cannot view with indifference the aristocratic effect of those interpersonal and interregional relations symbolized by the Big-House-and-Slave-Quarters complex in the history of Brazilian society and Brazilian culture.

Availing myself, then, of this symbolism (which since the first appearance of this essay, in 1933, has been utilized by other students of our history, sociology, and economy), my purpose has been to "evoke that clear-cut image" which, as a distinguished Hispanic-American historian—a disciple, it may be, of Hans Freyer—observed not so long ago is the recourse open to historical sociologists, confronted as they often are with the impossibility of reducing "the characteristics of a historical process to the precision of a concept," or of subjecting them to "hard and fast limitations."

GILBERTO FREYRE
Recife, July 1945

---

6   American Indian or Indian-white mixture. (Translator.)

7   The author employs this term in the sociological sense; see p. 133, note 171. (Translator.)

STUDY QUESTIONS

1. What role does slavery play in shaping Brazilian race relations, according to Freyre? How does his portrayal of slavery fit with the documents you viewed in chapter 4 of this volume?
2. What role does African heritage play in Brazilian national identity, according to Freyre? Are his views about African culture largely positive or negative?

NICOLÁS GUILLÉN

9.6 SON NUMBER 6, 1947

Nicolás Guillén was a Cuban poet and one of the defining figures associated with *Afro-Cubanismo*, a cultural movement that celebrated Cuba's African heritage. His work dealt with African themes and recreated African song and dance rhythms in literary form; situating these traditions at the heart of Cuban culture. This poem comes from Guillén's 1947 collection *El son entero*, and is based on the rhythms of the popular Afro-Cuban dance, the *son*.

Son Number 6

I'm Yoruba, crying out Yoruba
Lucumí.
Since I'm Yoruba from Cuba,
I want my lament of Yoruba to touch Cuba
the joyful weeping Yoruba
that comes out of me.

I'm Yoruba
I keep singing
and crying.
When not Yoruba
I am Congo, Mandinga, or Carabalí.
Listen my friends, to my *"son"* which begins like this:

Here is the riddle
of all my hopes:
what's mine is yours,
what's yours is mine;
all the blood
shaping a river.

The silk-cotton tree, tree with its crown;
father, the father with his son;
the tortoise in its shell.
Let the heart-warming *"son"* break out,
and our people dance,
heart close to heart,
glasses clinking together
water on water with rum!
I'm Yoruba, I'm Lucumí,
Mandinga, Congo, Carabalí.
Listen my friends, to the *"son"* that goes like this:

We've come together from far away,
young ones and old,
blacks and whites, moving together;
one is a leader, the other a follower,
all moving together;
San Berenito and one who's obeying
all moving together;
Blacks and Whites from far away,

Source: Nicolas Guillén, "Son Number 6" ["Son Número 6", 1947], *Yoruba from Cuba: Selected Poems* (Leeds, UK: Peepal Tree, 2005) pp. 66–69.

all moving together;
Santa María and one who's obeying
all moving together;
all pulling together, Santa María,
San Berenito, all pulling together,
all moving together, San Berenito,
San Berenito, Santa María.
Santa María, San Berenito,
everyone pulling together!

I'm Yoruba, I'm Lucumí
Mandinga, Congo, Carabalí.

Listen my friends, to my "*son*" which ends like this:
Come out Mulatto,
walk on free,
tell the white man he can't leave . . .
Nobody breaks away from here;
look and don't stop,
listen and don't wait
drink and don't stop
eat and don't wait,
live and don't hold back
our people's "*son*" will never end!

STUDY QUESTIONS

1. How is Cuba's African heritage represented within the poem? How is this heritage connected to Cuban nationalism more broadly?
2. Guillén's work is often described by scholars as encapsulating a "poetic mestizaje"—the blending of European and African traditions. What elements within this poem reflect this syncretic approach?

ALICIA MOREAU DE JUSTO

9.7 THE CIVIL EMANCIPATION OF WOMEN, 1919

Alicia Moreau de Justo was one of the leading figures in the early feminist movement in Argentina. In 1918, she cofounded the National Feminist Union in Argentina, bringing together women's rights activists from various traditions. She worked collaboratively with women's leaders from other parts of Latin America, most notably forming an intellectual partnership with Paulina Luisi in Uruguay. In this excerpt from an essay published in the journal *Humanidad Nueva*, she argues for the need for changes in women's legal status, including the right to suffrage. Although women did not get the vote in Argentina until 1947, Moreau's ideas and activism played a critical role in advancing women's rights.

The emancipation of woman is not so much the result of the law, as it is the formulation of customs. Not simply following the evolution of customs, but sometimes intervening as a disturbing element, it impresses the new spirit upon the past, which cannot always agree with the present. This causes a situation to arise, more or less intensely felt, more or less consciously interpreted, when the inequality between that which

Source: Alicia Moreau de Justo, "The Civil Emancipation of Women." Published in *Humanidad Nueva*.

the law establishes and that which marks the new social order is too pronounced. This gives birth to reforms born of a strength by those who love progress and are capable of understanding it, as well as being sufficiently independent to suppress the consecrated fetters. It tends to suppress inequality and to modernize the law, imposing regulations on the oppressor. . . .

The situation of the Argentine woman in society has been modified profoundly in the last quarter of a century, and especially in the last ten years. Living in intimate unity with the people of Europe, she has penetrated into the broad fields of industry, agriculture, commerce, science, literature and arts; her activities have constantly increased and the situation created by the war has accentuated this in such a manner that the most retiring spirits have been brought to the front. He who studies this gradual ascent of woman towards a more widely recognized position in the more civilized European countries, recognizes the positiveness, I might almost say, inevitability, with which this movement makes progress as all movements do which are the evolution of a people.

United as we are to European nations and penetrated by them, we cannot escape the social transformation which has taken place. Not only should their machinery and merchandise reach us, but also their ideals, their aspirations. . . . Though there may still exist the marked inequality of a town lost in the pampas fifty years ago, without electric lights and cinematographs, the moral progress is most extraordinary. . . . It is difficult to determine the exact mental type of the actual Argentine woman, as there exist, not only the marked differences created by the economic situations of life, but the differences of education and surroundings. . . . And we must also consider the influence which the nationality of the ancestors exercised. This prevents us from uniting in one and the same description the Argentine descendants from natives and from those descended from Italians, French and Russians, who have lived for some time in this country. But without considering all the differences which exist, we can point out two types, not determined by the mental differences of each type, but by the differences they represent, to our way of thinking, as two stages of evolution in the Argentine woman.

In the first place there exists the type which we may call the Spanish Colonial. She is the direct descendant of the woman born in the home which the historians have described, which was formed by the union of the Spaniard and the aborigines, a home ruled absolutely by the father. "All the family is constituted for his benefit!" says Dr. Juan Augustin C. Garcia. "The father disposes almost absolutely of the person of his children. He can pawn them and sell them in case of necessity. The property acquired by a son, with the son's money or with that of his parents, belongs to the father; the son's income from property acquired, i.e., inherited from his mother or secured by his efforts in commerce or industry, during the father's lifetime, belongs exclusively to the father; because, with the exception of special cases, the son's emancipation depends entirely upon the will of his father." If such was the situation of the law accorded for the son, the continuer of the family, the inheritor of the name, it is easy to imagine what would be the position of the daughter. "The mother occupied an inferior situation. In all prerogatives she was considered competent only in the case of the death of the father, to give her consent to the marriage of her children under 25 years of age. She has a part in the earnings of the conjugal partnership, but she is not her husband's inheritor except in the so-called marital fourth". . . . Under these conditions and without any other horizon, the life of women was spoken of carelessly. Women were almost always hard working, but intellectually a cipher, because of the deadening action of a society which judged that it was dangerous for the honesty and repose of a home, if women should know how to read and write. Yet it was woman, who was fully capable of understanding and associating herself with the great · collective movements, of sharing the aspirations of noble men, and rising to the point of heroic abnegation, when the hour arrived for the great struggle for the independence of her country.

This Colonial home, strongly dominated by religious beliefs, moulded by archaic prejudices, was impregnated by a spirit so Spanish that it caused men at one and the same time to treat woman with gallantry and yet depreciate her value, to praise her grace and beauty and to belittle her weakness and ignorance, to fight duels for her at the merest suspicion that might offend a lady, and yet permit himself to greet any woman who crossed his path with insolence and audaciousness; which permitted a father to speak of his children as two sons and one female. Her concepts of the value of women will cause Spain perhaps, to be the last of all European countries to solve the problem for women, in spite of the brilliant personalities she has always had.

Though present day conditions have left their impress on this home, this ancient spirit still exists in many Argentine households. To many Argentines the woman continues to be the eternal minor, a being incapable and weak, who always accepts the strength of the masculine arm. She has not a determined value as an individual. She has only a specific value derived from her sex; she is not a personality in whom may exist a vocation, an ideal aspiration, she is a woman—beautiful—gracious—sometimes capable of creating in man a condition which will induce him to found a new family. It is the idea of Rousseau: "Woman was made to please man. That he ought to please her in his turn is not such an immediate necessity—it merely lies in his power. He pleases by the mere fact of his strength." There are in woman, according to this, only two great virtues which are to determine her lot: beauty and fecundity, and the only object for her existence—matrimony.

The life of this feminine type may thus be divided into two stages, the first is the stage before marriage; while it lasts, she lives from the work of her father or brother, as incapable of any activity except in the participation of some work or society, in a state of intellectual inertia and the fear of free activity. . . . If she reaches the second stage of matrimony and leaves the parasitic life which, if it had not been changed by marriage would have been prolonged into the type of the *solterona* or old maid, continuing to live at the expense of her parents or on the generosity of the legislature, which because of a supposed or real ancestor has conceded her a pension. (This applies to widows also.). . . . The second type, the fat, respectable woman of tradition, whose time is employed between the care of her family and religious and social duties. Do not speak to her of scientific, social, political or artistic Questions, she is ignorant of them. Do not speak to her of that which as a mother ought to interest her above all things, the education of her children. In all this as in all things, she will follow the current. . . . This type of Spanish Colonial woman has been modified and now tends to disappear, especially from the great centers which are in direct communication with modem thought, and are putting away the *cheripa* and the cowhide boots.

Another woman tends to replace her, whom we may call the European Argentine, descended from the homes transplanted by the current of immigration, a horizon enlarged by labor, frequently rude, it is true, but making it impossible to depreciate her work, which Agustin Alvarez speaks of as the fruit of our Spanish inheritance. This second type we may designate as expressing the beginning of a greater freedom of thought and independence of action. In this home, which differs from the first, in form and reality, in the daily contact with men who think and feel along different lines, she cannot accept the limitations which hamper or check the individual. And if some deplore this lack of familiar and social tradition, nevertheless they see in it the support of the moral ideals, which guide the lives of men and create new forces, permitting our democracy to extract from them sufficient benefits and idealism, to create new moral types which can substitute the old family ideals.

In this European Argentine home, woman has a greater individual value. Her own personality has a more defined character. Her youth is not wasted in the hope of becoming married, for she participates in the social activities. It is this woman who fills almost all our normal, professional and secondary schools, and they contribute as workers and teachers to the national greatness. Great is the distance which separates us from the surroundings, in which the Spanish Colonial type dominates, in which woman, who is not of the very poor, hides her work as an object of shame, impressed upon her by dire necessity. . . . Far from the surroundings which, through the merest shade of distinction, impose a shame between the necessity of working and the shame imposed by the seal of immodesty and dishonesty.

Today we are penetrated by the spirit of European and American civilization which exalts the creative forces and dignifies work, making the conditions of a social parasite a stigma. It is these women, who, under the impulse of new economic and social conditions, demand each day with greater energy and decision their share of labor and social responsibility.

There exists in the Republic according to the census of 1914: 174,893 women who work in trades, commerce and the liberal professions. This figure represents 22 per cent of the total workers above the age of fourteen. The director of the census, Señor Alberto Martinez, comments upon this fact in a praiseworthy manner. "We ought to mention it as true national progress. The grade of independence which woman has achieved in society, the application she makes of her intelligence in her activities, as well as the respect and consideration which surround her for this, are eloquent signs of the advancement of culture."

There exist I said, 714,893 women whose work is distributed as follows.

Buenos Aires, Federal Capital		194,517
Province of Buenos Aires		101,243
"	" Santa Fe	46,039
"	" Cordoba	69,755
"	" Corrientes	41,779
"	" Santiago del Estero	49,530
"	" Tucuman	41,603
"	" Entre Rios	36,413
"	" San Luis	16,487
"	" Mendoza	19,008
"	" San Juan	8,866
"	" Catamarca	16,322
"	" La Rioja	14,590
"	" Salta	22,950
"	" Jujuy	15,642
"	" National Territories	20,104

These 714,893 women are distributed in the following occupations:

Industrial Manual Arts	252,999	under a total of		841,337
Personal Service	182,711	"	" "	" 218,619
Agriculture and Stock Raising	41,578	"	" "	" 529,866
Commerce	21,217	"	" "	" 293,646
Instruction and Education	43,640	"	" "	" 83,184
Women Directors and Teachers	21,961	and Men Teachers and Directórs 6,505		
Sanitary Professions	4,368	"	" "	" 14,763
Public Administration	6,279	"	" "	" 108,852
Fine Arts	1,799	"	" "	" 14,192
Letters and Sciences	915	" "	" "	" 8,809

This large number is not alone the result of her own desires, but the result of our social and economic pressure. The increased necessity, the possibility to acquire the products of industries, which make life more comfortable and agreeable, while prices are going higher, impels many a woman to look for the means of maintaining herself and her family. . . . Her horizon no longer limited by a hothouse atmosphere and the narrow surroundings of the home, forces her to enter into contact with the social scale to which she belongs, and prevents her remaining separate or indifferent to the problems which agitate the social state in which she lives. She has a social value and marriage ceases to be for her her only object, the only honorable means of earning her livelihood. This turns marriage into the loving, moral aspiration to which she feels herself drawn by the normal development of her life. I know very well that this type of woman whom I have tried to describe, the product of the transformation which is being realized in our midst, is subject to much criticism, and I do not pretend to make her an ideal being, any more than man is an ideal being. They are both children of the same circumstances. . . .

Woman, the product of the new surroundings will replace the Spanish Colonial type in spite of resistance, born of lack of understanding. For the same spirit will bring her forward with surety, which today replaces superstition and error, by investigation and analysis. . . . If then, this is the evident march of events. . . .we have to follow the march of those who precede us, who are teachers in the work of civilization. Nothing is more logical than that we should come to understand what it is that hinders, what it is that oppresses us. It is in fact only injustice which engenders pain and discomfort. . . . Law, conceived, wrought and completed by man, ought to follow the evolution of the social life, instead of responding only to the past and becoming an obstacle, giving privileges and awakening the spirit of rebellion. Unfortunately, among the countries which do not feel this lack of harmony between the old laws and the new, is our country. Happy are those, capable of modifying in behalf of the present, and even more of the future; which show themselves as capable of suppressing that which oppresses and retards; making law a justice, something more than vain words.

STUDY QUESTIONS

1. What are the three types of women Moreau identifies as existing in Argentina in the early decades of the twentieth century? What factors account for their differences?
2. What relationships does Moreau draw between women's work outside the home and women's legal status?

FRIDA KAHLO

9.8 SELF PORTRAIT ALONG THE BORDER LINE BETWEEN MEXICO AND THE UNITED STATES, 1932

Frida Kahlo was a Mexican painter, whose work drew on indigenous and folk art traditions to explore themes of identity, gender, race, and class in Mexican society. Kahlo was especially well known for her self-portraits, which were often magical realist in nature, and drew heavily on pre-Columbian and Catholic iconographies. Kahlo was married to the Mexican muralist Diego Rivera, who became internationally famous in the decades following the Mexican Revolution, and she spent the 1920s and 1930s traveling with him as he worked on commissions in Mexico and the United States. Kahlo created this painting while in Detroit as Rivera painted a mural for the Detroit Institute of Arts. Her painting depicts herself standing on the border line, with the sun and moon shining on depictions of the rich and ancient culture of Mexico on the one side, and the industrial pollution of the United States obscuring the American flag on the other. Kahlo is shown standing on a stone bearing the inscription: "Carmen Rivera painted her portrait in 1932"—a reference to the way in which in the United States she was seen simply as Rivera's wife who dabbled in painting, not an artist in her own right.

Source: https://www.fridakahlo.org/self-portrait-along-the-boarder-line.jsp

STUDY QUESTIONS

1. How does the painting depict Kahlo's feelings toward Mexico and the United States? What insights can we gain from the painting about postrevolutionary Mexican nationalism?
2. Frida Kahlo's work is often celebrated as feminist and proindigenous in nature. Can you see elements of these philosophies in this painting?

CHAPTER 10

REVOLUTION AND REFORM IN LATIN AMERICA, 1950–1980

10.1 BOLIVIAN LEGISLATIVE DECREE NO. 03464 RELATIVE TO AGRARIAN REFORM, AUGUST 2, 1953

Land reform was at the heart of debates over social inequality in mid-twentieth-century Latin America. The most significant land reform occurred in Bolivia, following the 1952 uprising that brought the Movimiento Nationalista Revolutionario (MNR) to power. The revolution followed a failed election in which the winning party, led by MNR leader Victor Paz Estenssorro, had been prevented from coming into office by a military junta. One of the first acts of the MNR government was to pass this Agrarian Reform Bill. The law was aimed primarily at breaking up large agricultural estates and redistributing land via compensated expropriation to the largely indigenous peasantry. At the time of the bill, 92 percent of all cultivable land was held by the wealthiest 6 percent of Bolivians, while the remaining 94 percent of the population had access to only the remaining 8 percent of land. As a result, the MNR viewed land reform as essential to economic development as well as social justice. Over the next fifteen years 45 percent of peasant families would gain access to an average of twenty hectares of land.

BOLIVIA: LEGISLATIVE DECREE NO. 03464 RELATIVE TO AGRARIAN REFORM

August 2, 1953 (FAO translation)

1. The soil, the sub-soil and the waters of the territory of the Republic shall belong by original right to the Bolivian Nation.

2. The state shall recognise and guarantee private agrarian property where it serves a purpose benefiting the national community: it shall plan, regulate, supervise and organise the exercise thereof and shall promote the equitable distribution of the land in order to ensure the economic and cultural liberty and welfare of the Bolivian population. . . .

4. Considered as State domains shall be uncultivated lands reverting thereto owing to lapse of concession or for some other reason, vacant lands outside the urban radius of population centres, lands belonging to the

Source: Kenneth L. Karst and Keith S. Rosenn, *Law and Development in Latin America: A Case Book* (Berkeley: University of California Press, 1975).

organs and self-administering bodies of the States, forest lands under Government control and all property considered to be of such character under legislation in force.

5. Private agrarian property is that which is acknowledged and granted to natural or juridical persons in order that they shall exercise their right in accordance with the civil laws and the conditions of this Legislative Decree. The State recognises only those forms of private agrarian property enumerated in the following Articles.

6. The farm-house plot has the function of a rural residence, inadequate to satisfy the needs of a family.

7. The small property is that worked by the peasant and his family personally, the produce of which enables them reasonably to satisfy their needs. The personal labour of the peasant does not exclude the collaboration of possible assistants for certain tasks.

8. The medium property is that having an area larger than the small property as defined above, which while lacking the characteristics of the capitalist agricultural undertaking, is operated with the assistance of paid workers or with the aid of technical and mechanical equipment, the bulk of its produce being intended for the market.

9. The Indian community property is that acknowledged as such under legislation in force, on behalf of certain social groups of Indians.

10. The co-operative agrarian property is:

   a) That property granted to farmers forming a co-operative association for the purpose of acquiring the land, putting it in order, cultivating it and settling thereon;

   b) The lands of small and medium property owners, contributed for the establishment of the registered capital of the co-operative;

   c) Lands of peasants who have received grants of land belonging to former latifundia and who have formed a co-operative society for their cultivation;

   d) Lands belonging to agricultural co-operative societies under any other title not included in the foregoing paragraphs.

11. The agricultural undertaking shall be characterised by the investment of supplementary capital on a large scale, a system of paid labour and the use of up-to-date technical methods, exception being made

as regards the latter in the case of areas with an uneven terrain. The determination of these factors in detail shall be governed by special regulations.

12. The State does not recognise the latifundium which is a rural property of large area varying according to its geographical situation, either undeveloped or substantially under-developed, by the diffuse field-cropping system with the use of obsolete implements and methods resulting in the waste of human effort, or by the imposition of lease rent; it is also characterised as regards the use of the land in the inter-Andean zone by the grant of parcels, small plots *(pegujales)*, allotments *(sayañas)*, part holdings and other equivalent forms, so that its profitability owing to the disequilibrium [among] the factors of production, is fundamentally dependent upon the extra yield which is contributed by the peasants in their capacity of servants or tenant-farmers and which is taken by the landowner as rent in the form of service, thus constituting a system of feudal oppression reflected in agricultural backwardness and a low standard of living and culture of the peasant population. . . .

29. This Legislative Decree establishes the bases for the achievement of economic and political democracy in the rural area by the designation and grant of lands affected thereby as established under its provisions.

30. The latifundium shall be abolished. The possession of large corporative agrarian property or of other forms of large-scale concentration of land by private persons and by bodies which, by their legal structure, hinder its equitable distribution among the rural population, shall not be permitted.

31. Industrial capital investment in rural areas, for example in grain and sugar mills, cold storage plants and other forms of enterprise for manufacturing production shall be considered as beneficial wherever such enterprise exists side by side with medium and small properties and purchases their products at a fair price without arrogating to itself large areas of land. Large-scale capital investment which acquires extensive areas of land for itself shall be considered harmful, because besides retaining the source of wealth, it monopolizes the market and eliminates the independent farmer by unfair competition.

32. The small property is not affected by this Legislative Decree. . . .

33. The medium holding is not affected. It may, however, in exceptional cases, be affected in respect of those areas owned by farmers (allotments, small plots, etc.) the possession of which is assumed by the workers, without prejudice to the grant of land in other zones, to the extent of the minimum area of the small property. Where these areas, which are inalienable, become vacant by the departure of those workers to whom land has been granted, they shall be consolidated on behalf of the medium property holder to the extent of the maximum area of the medium property, subject to the requirement that compensation small be made for the improvements carried out by the worker.

34. Landed property defined as a latifundium in accordance with Article 12 shall be affected by this Legislative Decree to the extent of its entire area.

35. For the purposes of the preceding Article, property whereon the owner has invested capital in modern agricultural methods and machinery and which is worked by him personally or by his closest relatives shall not be considered as a latifundium.

In those regions where the topography of the cultivable land hinders the use of machinery, only the personal labour of the owner or of his closest relatives shall be stipulated.

This type of property as well as those properties having the characteristics referred to in Article 8 shall be reduced to the dimensions of the medium property with all the rights and duties devolving upon the owner of medium property.

36. The agricultural undertaking [which] on the date of proclamation of this Legislative Decree employs the mixed system of colonization and wage-payment shall not be affected if it has been ascertained that an amount of supplementary capital has been invested which is at least double that of the land capital and that up-to-date cultivation techniques have been employed thereon.

STUDY QUESTIONS

1. What differences does the legislation draw between large, medium, and small landholdings in terms of state-recognized property rights?
2. What rationale does the law give for breaking up *latifundia* (very large estates)? What economic benefits would this change generate?

CAROLINA MARIA DE JESUS

10.2 *CHILD OF THE DARK*, 1960

The extreme levels of poverty experienced by many urban Latin Americans became the subject of increased public and policy attention in the 1960s. One of the critical works in drawing attention to the plight of slum dwellers was the diary of Carolina Maria de Jesus, an Afro-Brazilian writer and single mother who lived in a favela in a house she built herself out of plywood and cardboard, and who supported her three children in part by scavenging paper and tin cans from a rubbish heap. In her diary, she recorded the challenges of her day-to-day life, as well as the problems faced by those around her, often denouncing the political and economic elites whose leadership failures she saw as contributing to her situation. De Jesus's diary was published in 1960 after a chance encounter

Source: Carolina Maria de Jesus, *Child of the Dark.* (London: Penguin, 1962).

with a Brazilian journalist, who serialized it in a major newspaper. The book became the most successful in Brazilian publishing history, and was a best seller in North America and Europe, helping Carolina achieve her dream of leaving the favela. The diary is a critically important historical source, providing a rare firsthand window into the intimate life of a woman seeking to lift her family out of desperate poverty.

July 15, 1955 The birthday of my daughter Vera Eunice. I wanted to buy a pair of shoes for her, but the price of food keeps us from realizing our desires. Actually we are slaves to the cost of living. I found a pair of shoes in the garbage, washed them, and patched them for her to wear.

I didn't have one cent to buy bread. So I washed three bottles and traded them to Arnaldo. He kept the bottles and gave me bread. Then I went to sell my paper. I received 65 cruzeiros. I spent 20 cruzeiros for meat. I got one kilo of ham and one kilo of sugar and spent six cruzeiros on cheese. And the money was gone.

I was ill all day. I thought I had a cold. At night my chest pained me. I started to cough. I decided not to go out at night to look for paper. I searched for my son João. He was at Felisberto de Carvalho Street near the market. A bus had knocked a boy into the sidewalk and a crowd ·gathered. João was in the middle of it all. I poked him a couple of times and within five minutes he was home.

I washed the children, put them to bed, then washed myself and went to bed. I waited until 11:00 for a certain someone. He didn't come. I took an aspirin and laid down again. When I awoke the sun was sliding in space. My daughter Vera Eunice said: "Go get some water, Mother!"

July 16 I got up and obeyed Vera Eunice. I went to get the water. I made coffee. I told the children that I didn't have any bread, that they would have to drink their coffee plain and eat meat with *farinha*.[1] I was feeling ill and decided to cure myself. I stuck my finger down my throat twice, vomited, and knew I was under the evil eye. The upset feeling left and I went to Senhor Manuel, carrying some cans to sell. Everything that I find in the

garbage I sell. He gave me 13 cruzeiros. I kept thinking that I had to buy bread, soap, and milk for Vera Eunice. The 13 cruzeiros wouldn't make it. I returned home, or rather to my shack, nervous and exhausted. I thought of the worrisome life that I led. Carrying paper, washing clothes for the children, staying in the street all day long. Yet I'm always lacking things, Vera doesn't have shoes and she doesn't like to go barefoot. For at least two years I've wanted to buy a meat grinder. And a sewing machine.

I came home and made lunch for the two boys. Rice, beans, and meat, and I'm going out to look for paper. I left the children, told them to play in the yard and not go into the street, because the terrible neighbors I have won't leave my children alone. I was feeling ill and wished I could lie down. But the poor don't rest nor are they permitted the pleasure of relaxation. I was nervous inside, cursing my luck. I collected two sacks full of paper. Afterward I went back and gathered up some scrap metal, some cans, and some kindling wood. As I walked I thought—when I return to the favela there is going to be something new. Maybe Dona Rosa or the insolent Angel Mary fought with my children. I found Vera Eunice sleeping and the boys playing in the street. I thought: it's 2:00. Maybe I'm going to get through this day without anything happening. João told me that the truck that gives out money was here to give out food. I took a sack and hurried out. It was the leader of the Spiritist Center at 103 Vergueiro Street. I got two kilos of rice, two of beans, and two kilos of macaroni. I was happy. The truck went away. The nervousness that I had inside left me. I took advantage of my calmness to read. I picked up a magazine and sat on the grass, letting the rays of the sun warm me as I read a story. I wrote a note and gave it to my boy João to take to Senhor Arnaldo to

---

1   *Farinha:* a coarse wheat flour.

buy soap, two aspirins, and some bread. Then I put water on the stove to make coffee. João came back saying he had lost the aspirins. I went back with him to look. We didn't find them.

When I came home there was a crowd at my door. Children and women claiming Jose Carlos had thrown stones at their houses. They wanted me to punish him.

July 17 Sunday A marvelous day. The sky was blue without one cloud. The sun was warm. I got out of bed at 6:30 and went to get water. I only had one piece of bread and three cruzeiros. I gave a small piece to each child and put the beans, that I got yesterday from the Spiritist Center, on the fire. Then I went to wash clothes. When I returned from the river the beans were cooked. The children asked for bread. I gave the three cruzeiros to João to go and buy some. Today it was Nair Mathias who started an argument with my children. Silvia and her husband have begun an open-air spectacle. He is hitting her and I'm disgusted because the children are present. They heard words of the lowest kind. Oh, if I could move from here to a more decent neighborhood!

I went to Dona Florela to ask for a piece of garlic. I went to Dona Analia and got exactly what I expected:

"I don't have any!"

I went to collect my clothes. Dona Aparecida asked me:

"Are you pregnant?"

"No, Senhora," I replied-gently.

I cursed her under my breath. If I am pregnant it's not your business. I can't stand these favela women, they want to know everything. Their tongues are like chicken. feet. Scratching at everything. The rumor is circulating that I am pregnant! If I am, I don't know about it! . . .

July 18 I got up at 7. Happy and content. Weariness would be here soon enough. I went to the junk dealer and received 60 cruzeiros. I passed by Arnaldo, bought bread, milk, paid what I owed him, and still had enough to buy Vera some chocolate. I returned to a Hell. I opened the door and threw the children outside. Dona Rosa, as soon as she saw my boy Jose Carlos, started to fight with him. She didn't want the boy to come near her shack. She ran out with a stick to hit him. A woman of 48 years fighting with a child! At times, after I leave, she comes to my window and throws a filled chamber pot onto the children. When I return I find the pillows dirty and the children fetid. She hates me. She says that the handsome and distinguished men prefer me and that I make more money than she does.

Dona Cecilia appeared. She came to punish my children. I threw a right at her and she stepped back. I told her:

"There are women that say they know how to raise children, but some have children in jails listed as delinquents."

She went away. Then came that bitch Angel Mary. I said: -"

"I was fighting with the banknotes, now the small change is arriving. I don't go to anybody's door, and you people who come to my door only bore me. I never bother anyone's children or come to your shack shouting against your kids. And don't think that yours are saints; it's just that I tolerate them."

Dona Silvia came to complain about my children. That they were badly educated. I don't look for defects in children. Neither in mine nor in others. I know that a child is not born with sense. When I speak with a child I use pleasant words. What infuriates me is that the parents come to my door to disrupt my rare moments of inner tranquility. But when they upset me, I write. I know how to dominate my impulses. I only had two years of schooling, but I got enough to form my character. The only thing that does not exist in the favela is friendship.

Then came the fishmonger Senhor Antonio Lira and he gave me some fish. I started preparing lunch. The women went away, leaving me in peace for today. They had put on their show. My door is actually a theater. All children throw stones, but my boys are the scapegoats. They gossip that I'm not married, but I'm happier than they are. They have husbands but they are forced to beg. They are supported by charity organizations.

My kids are not kept alive by the church's bread. I take on all kinds of work to keep them. And those women have to beg or even steal. At night when they are begging I peacefully sit in my shack listening to Viennese waltzes. While their husbands break the boards of the shack, I and my children sleep peacefully. I don't envy the married women of the favelas who lead lives like Indian slaves.

I never got married and I'm not unhappy. Those who wanted to marry me were mean and the conditions they imposed on me were horrible.

Take Maria José, better known as Zefa, who lives in shack number nine on "B" Street. She is an alcoholic and when she is pregnant she drinks to excess. The children are born and they die before they reach two months. She hates me because my children thrive and I have a radio. One day she asked to borrow my radio. I told her I wouldn't loan it, and as she didn't have any children, she could work and buy one. But it is well known that people who are given to the vice of drink never buy anything. Not even clothes. Drunks don't prosper. Sometimes she throws water on my children. She claims I never punish my kids. I'm not given to violence. Jose Carlos said:

"Don't be sad, Mama. Our Lady of Aparecida[2] will help you, and when I grow up I'll buy a brick house for you."

I went to collect paper and stayed away from the house an hour. When I returned I saw several people at the riverbank. There was a man unconscious from alcohol and the worthless men of the favela were cleaning out his pockets. They stole his money and tore up his documents. It is 5 P.M. Now Senhor Heitor turns on the light. And I, I have to wash the children so they can go to bed, for I have to go out. I need money to pay the light bill. That's the way it is here. Person doesn't use the lights but must pay for them. I left and went to collect paper. I walked fast because it was late. I met a woman complaining about her married life. I listened but said nothing. I tied up the sacks, put the tin cans that I found in another sack, and went home. When I arrived I turned on the radio to see what time it was. It was 11:55. I heated some food, read, undressed, and laid down. Sleep came soon. . . .

What an ordeal it is to search for paper. I have to carry my daughter Vera Eunice. She is only two years old and doesn't like to stay at home. I put the sack on my head and carried her in my arms. I bore the weight of the sack on my head and the weight of Vera Eunice in my arms. Sometimes it makes me angry. Then I get ahold of myself. She's not guilty because she's in the world.

---

2   *Our Lady of Aparercida: a carved image of the Virgin Mary that legend says appeared in a grotto, and has become the patron saint of Brazil.*

I reflected: I've got to be tolerant with my children. They don't have anyone in the world but me. How sad is the condition of a woman alone without a man at home.

Here all the women pick on me. They say that I talk too well and that I know how to attract men. When I'm nervous I don't like to argue. I prefer to write. Every day I write. I sit in the yard and write.

I can't go looking for paper. Vera Eunice doesn't want to sleep and neither does Jose Carlos. Silvia and her husband are quarreling. They've got nine children but don't respect them. Every day they fight.

I sold the paper and got 140 cruzeiros. I worked too hard and felt ill. I took some Dr. Ross's "Pills of Life" for my liver and lay down. When I was sleeping I was awakened by the voice of Antonio Andrade arguing with his wife. . . .

May 2, 1958 I'm not lazy. There are times when I try to keep up my diary. But then I think it's not worth it and figure I'm wasting my time.

I've made a promise to myself. I want to treat people that I know with more consideration. I want to have a pleasant smile for children and the employed.

I received a summons to appear at 8 P.M. at police station number 12. I spent the day looking for paper. At night my feet pained me so I couldn't walk. It started to rain. I went to the station and took José Carlos with me. The summons was for him. José Carlos is nine years old.

May 3 I went to the market at Carlos de Campos Street looking for any old thing. I got a lot of greens. But it didn't help much, for I've got no cooking fat. The children are upset because there's nothing to eat.

May 6 In the morning I went for water. I made João carry it. I was happy, then I received another summons. I was inspired yesterday and my verses were so pretty, I forgot to go to the station. It was 11:00 when I remembered the invitation from the illustrious lieutenant of the 12th precinct.

My advice to would-be politicians is that people do not tolerate hunger. It's necessary to know hunger to know how to describe it.

May 9 I looked for paper but I didn't like it. Then I thought: I'll pretend that I'm dreaming.

May 10 I went to the police station and talked to the lieutenant. What a pleasant man! If I had known he was going to be so pleasant, I'd have gone on the first summons. The lieutenant was interested in my boys' education. He said the favelas have an unhealthy atmosphere where the people have more chance to go wrong than to become useful to state and country. I thought: if he knows this why doesn't he make a report and send it to the politicians? To Janio Quadros, Kubitschek,[3] and Dr. Adhemar de Barros? Now he tells me this, I a poor garbage collector. I can't even solve my own problems.

Brazil needs to be led by a person who has known hunger. Hunger is also a teacher.

Who has gone hungry learns to think of the future and of the children.

May 11 Today is Mother's Day. The sky is blue and white. It seems that even nature wants to pay homage to the mothers who feel unhappy because they can't realize the desires of their children.

The sun keeps climbing. Today it's not going to rain. Today is our day.

Dona Teresinha came to visit me. She gave me 15 cruzeiros and said it was for Vera to go to the circus. But I'm going to use the money to buy bread tomorrow because I only have four cruzeiros.

Yesterday I got half a pig's head at the slaughterhouse. We ate the meat and saved the bones. Today I put the bones on to boil and into the broth I put some potatoes. My children are always hungry. When they are starving they aren't so fussy about what they eat.

Night came. The stars are hidden. The shack is filled with mosquitoes. I lit a page from a newspaper and ran it over the walls. This is the way the favela dwellers kill mosquitoes.

May 13 At dawn it was raining. Today is a nice day for me, it's the anniversary of the Abolition. The day we celebrate the freeing of the slaves. In the jails the Negroes were the scapegoats. But now the whites are more educated and don't treat us any more with contempt. May God enlighten the whites so that the Negroes may have a happier life.

It continued to rain and I only have beans and salt. The rain is strong but even so I sent the boys to school. I'm writing until the rain goes away so I can go to Senhor Manuel and sell scrap. With that money I'm going to buy rice and sausage. The rain has stopped for a while. I'm going out.

I feel so sorry for my children. When they see the things to eat that I come home with they shout:

"Viva Mama!"

Their outbursts please me. But I've lost the habit of smiling. Ten minutes later they want more food. I sent João to ask Dona Ida for a little pork fat. She didn't have any. I sent her a note:

"Dona Ida, I beg you to help me get a little pork fat, so I can make soup for the children. Today it's raining and I can't go looking for paper. Thank you, Carolina."

It rained and got colder. Winter had arrived and in winter people eat more. Vera asked for food, and I didn't have any. It was the same old show. I had two cruzeiros and wanted to buy a little flour to make a *virado*.[4] I went to ask Dona Alice for a little pork. She gave me pork and rice. It was 9 at night when we ate.

And that is the way on May 13, 1958, I fought against the real slavery-hunger! . . .

When I arrived from the Palace that is the city, my children ran to tell me that they had found some macaroni in the garbage. As the food supply was low I cooked some of the macaroni with beans. And my son João said to me:

"Uh, huh. You told me we weren't going to eat any more things from the garbage."

It was the first time I had failed to keep my word. I said:

"I had faith in President Kubitschek."

"You had faith, and now you don't have it any more?"

"No, my son, democracy is losing its followers. In our country everything is weakening. The money is weak. Democracy is weak and the politicians are very weak. Everything that is weak dies one day."

The politicians know that I am a poetess. And that a poet will even face death when he sees his people oppressed.

May 21 I spent a horrible night. I dreamt I lived in a decent house that had a bathroom, kitchen, pantry, and even a maid's room. I was going to celebrate the birthday of my daughter Vera Eunice. I went and bought some small pots that I had wanted for a long time. Because I was able to buy. I sat at the table to eat. The tablecloth was white as a lily. I ate a steak,

---

3 Juscelino Kubitschek: President of Brazil from 1956 to 1961.

4 *Virado:* a dish of black beans, manioc flour, pork, and eggs.

bread and butter, fried potatoes, and a salad. When I reached for another steak I woke up. What bitter reality! I don't live in the city. I live in the favela. In the mud on the banks of the Tiete River. And with only nine cruzeiros. I don't even have sugar, because yesterday after I went out the children ate what little I had.

Who must be a leader is he who has the ability. He who has pity and friendship for the people. Those who govern our country are those who have money, who don't know what hunger is, or pain or poverty. If the majority revolt, what can the minority do? I am on the side of the poor, who are an arm. An undernourished arm. We must free the country of the profiteering politicians.

Yesterday I ate that macaroni from the garbage with fear of death, because in 1953 I sold scrap over there in Zinho. There was a pretty little black boy. He also went to sell scrap in Zinho. He was young and said that those who should look for paper were the old. One day I was collecting scrap when I stopped at Born Jardim Avenue. Someone had thrown meat into the garbage, and he was picking out the pieces.

He told me:

"Take some, Carolina. It's still fit to eat."

He gave me some, and so as not to hurt his feelings, I accepted. I tried to convince him not to eat that meat, or the hard bread gnawed by the rats. He told me no, because it was two days since he had eaten. He made a fire and roasted the meat. His hunger was so great that he couldn't wait for the meat to cook. He heated it and ate. So as not to remember that scene, I left thinking: I'm going to pretend I wasn't there. This can't be real in a rich country like mine. I was disgusted with that Social Service that had been created to readjust the maladjusted, but took no notice of we marginal people. I sold the scrap at Zinho and returned to Silo Paulo's backyard, the favela.

The next day I found that little black boy dead. His toes were spread apart. The space must have been eight inches between them. He had blown up as if made out of rubber. His toes looked like a fan. He had no documents. He was buried like any other "Joe." Nobody tried to find out his name. The marginal people don't have names.

Once every four years the politicians change without solving the problem of hunger that has its headquarters in the favela and its branch offices in the workers' homes.

When I went to get water I saw a poor woman collapse near the pump because last night she slept without dinner. She was undernourished. The doctors that we have in politics know this.

I found a sweet potato and a carrot in the garbage. When I got back to the favela my boys were gnawing on a piece of hard bread. I thought: for them to eat this bread, they need electric teeth.

I don't have any lard. I put meat on the fire with some tomatoes that I found at the Peixe canning factory. I put in the carrot and the sweet potato and water. As soon as it was boiling, I put in the macaroni that the boys found in the garbage. The favelados are the few who are convinced that in order to live; they must imitate the vultures. I don't see any help from the Social Service regarding the favelados. Tomorrow I'm not going to have bread. I'm going to cook a sweet potato.

May 22 Today I'm sad. I'm nervous. I don't know if I should start crying or start running until I fall unconscious. At dawn it was raining. I couldn't go out to get any money. I spent the day writing. I cooked the macaroni and I'll warm it up again for the children. I cooked the potatoes and they ate them. I have a few tin cans and a little scrap that I'm going to sell to Senhor Manuel. When João came home from school I sent him to sell the scrap. He got 13 cruzeiros. He bought a glass of mineral water: two cruzeiros. I was furious with him. Where had he seen a favelado with such highborn tastes?

The children eat a lot of bread. They like soft bread but when they don't have it, they eat hard bread.

Hard is the bread that we eat. Hard is the bed on which we sleep. Hard is the life of the favelado.

STUDY QUESTIONS

1. What are some of the strategies Carolina uses to find money to feed her children? How does she feel about the work she undertakes?
2. What do we learn from the account about the tensions and conflicts between the people who live in the favelas? What factors fuel these conflicts?
3. How does the poverty Carolina lives in shape her view of Brazilian politics?

ABDIAS DO NASCIMENTO

10.3 THE MYTH OF RACIAL DEMOCRACY, 1968

The Afro-Brazilian intellectual Abdias do Nascimento emerged in the 1960s as one of the most important leaders of the movement for black rights in Brazil. Nascimento was pushed into exile by the Brazilian military government in 1964 and subsequently held academic positions in Nigeria and the United States. Nascimento was a fervent critic of the state ideology of "racial democracy," which held that the history of race mixing in Brazil meant there was little racism or racial inequality. Nascimento engaged with the transnational black power movement, and was a correspondent of Martin Luther King Jr. and James Baldwin. This piece was first published in the Brazilian journal Cadernos Brasileiros in 1968 as part of a special edition commemorating the eightieth anniversary of the 1888 "Golden Law," which abolished slavery and emancipated the enslaved in Brazil. Nascimento emphasizes the continued impact of slavery on the life chances of Afro-Brazilians, decades after emancipation.

Now that eighty years have passed since the abolition of slavery in Brazil, it is opportune to look objectively at the results of the law of May 13, 1888. Are the descendants of African slaves really free? Where do Brazilian blacks really stand in relation to citizens of other racial origins, at all levels of national life?

More than ten years ago, a reporter from a prominent Rio de Janeiro magazine asked various persons of color to respond to these questions. But the interviews were never published, although the questions obviously remain valid and hold the same significance, because since then nothing has changed in the way blacks live in this country.

The abolitionist campaign stopped abruptly in 1888. . . . Abolition was a façade: juridical, theoretical, abstract. The ex-slaves were driven to the brink of starvation; they found only disease, unemployment, complete misery. Not only the elites, but all of Brazilian society closed the avenues through which blacks might have survived; they shut off the possibility of a decent, dignified life for the ex-slaves. They created a fabric of slogans about equality and racial democracy that has served to assuage the bad national conscience. Abroad, it presents our country as a model of racial coexistence; internally, the myth is used to keep blacks tricked and docile.

There was a phase during which the condition of blacks awakened the interest of scholars, especially in the Northeast. But although sincere, the intellectuals dealt with black culture as ethnographic material for their literary and academic exercises . . . [when, instead], the situation of blacks cried out for urgent practical action to improve radically their horrible existence. . . .

It is a characteristic of our racial democracy myth that it accurately defines a "pathology of normality. . . ." There is no exaggeration here. We remember that Brazilians of dark pigmentation number nearly thirty million. Certain apostles of "whitening" would like to see the extinction of the Negro as an easy way to resolve the problem. . . . The white portion, or the less-Negro population, would continue to monopolize political power, economic power, access to schools, and to well-being, thanks to the legacy of the wretched "Golden Law," which Antonio Callado has correctly dubbed, "The Law of White Magic." Under the law of white magic, the black is as free as any other Brazilian. In practice—without any white or black magic—the

Source: Taken from Abdias do Nascimento, "The Myth of Racial Democracy," in Robert M. Levine and John J. Crocitti (eds.) *The Brazil Reader: History, Culture, Politics* (Durham: Duke University Press, 1999), pp. 379–381.

Negro is simply this: a racial pariah consigned to the status of a subaltern.

Why should the Negro be the only one to pay for the onus of our "racial paradise"? I stand corrected. The Indian, as well, has been treated in the same way. According to a study by the federal government itself, practices to liquidate indigenous peoples have been employed in the [current] decade of the 1960s. Another mask yanked off the face of our vaunted Brazilian humanism, tempered with compassion and Christian spirit. . . .

It is imperative for human dignity and a civic duty for Brazilians to struggle—blacks and whites—to transform the concept of racial democracy into reality. The Negro should organize to take up the promise deeded to him by history. This should be done without messianism, without hatred or resentment, but firmly and steadfastly in pursuit of the just place to which we are entitled. The Negro should create pressure groups, instruments for direct action. In the process, we will encounter our qualified leaders. Only through dynamic organization will the Negro obtain equality of opportunity and the status of a better life . . . not only for Brazilian blacks, but for all Brazilian people.

Naturally, anything directed against the status quo runs risks. But Negroes run risks from the instant of their birth. Do not fear the label of "black racist," because the product of intimidation is docility. It is enough for us to know that our cause has integrity, and follow our conscience as democrats and humanists. Our historical experience shows us that antiracist racism is the only path capable of extinguishing the differences between races.

STUDY QUESTIONS

1. What does Nascimento mean when he says abolition was "a facade"?
2. What changes need to be made for the ideal of "racial democracy" to become a reality for Afro-Brazilians according to Nascimento?

FIDEL CASTRO

10.4 HISTORY WILL ABSOLVE ME, 1953

"History Will Absolve Me" is perhaps Fidel Castro's most famous speech, and it serves as a foundational document for understanding the Cuban Revolution. It was delivered by Castro in 1953, when he was on trial for his role in leading the attack on the Moncada Barracks, in which Castro and other young student rebels had attempted to overthrow the regime of Fulgencio Batista. Castro was sentenced to fifteen years' imprisonment for his role in the attacks (later commuted in 1955, when the Moncada prisoners were granted amnesty in exchange for exile) and wrote up his speech, which was smuggled out of the prison in matchboxes and published and disseminated. The speech took place before Castro became a Marxist, and it positioned the July 26 movement as the inheritors of José Martí's vision for a fully independent Cuba. It calls for a series of moderate, nationalist reforms, including land redistribution. The speech served to enshrine Castro as the intellectual leader and key figurehead of the anti-Batista movement.

Source: Andrew Paul Booth and Brian Baggins, *History Will Absolve Me*, trans. Pedro Álvarez Tabío and Andrew Paul Booth (La Habana, Cuba: Editorial de Ciencias Sociales, 1975); online version—1997, Castro Internet Archive (marxists.org), 2001.

. . . Why were we sure of the people's support? When we speak of the people we are not talking about those who live in comfort, the conservative elements of the nation, who welcome any repressive regime, any dictatorship, any despotism, prostrating themselves before the masters of the moment until they grind their foreheads into the ground. When we speak of struggle and we mention the people we mean the vast unredeemed masses, those to whom everyone makes promises and who are deceived by all; we mean the people who yearn for a better, more dignified and more just nation; who are moved by ancestral aspirations to justice, for they have suffered injustice and mockery generation after generation; those who long for great and wise changes in all aspects of their life; people who, to attain those changes, are ready to give even the very last breath they have when they believe in something or in someone, especially when they believe in themselves. The first condition of sincerity and good faith in any endeavor is to do precisely what nobody else ever does, that is, to speak with absolute clarity, without fear. The demagogues and professional politicians who manage to perform the miracle of being right about everything and of pleasing everyone are, necessarily, deceiving everyone about everything. The revolutionaries must proclaim their ideas courageously, define their principles and express their intentions so that no one is deceived, neither friend nor foe.

In terms of struggle, when we talk about people we're talking about the six hundred thousand Cubans without work, who want to earn their daily bread honestly without having to emigrate from their homeland in search of a livelihood; the five hundred thousand farm laborers who live in miserable shacks, who work four months of the year and starve the rest, sharing their misery with their children, who don't have an inch of land to till and whose existence would move any heart not made of stone; the four hundred thousand industrial workers and laborers whose retirement funds have been embezzled, whose benefits are being taken away, whose homes are wretched quarters, whose salaries pass from the hands of the boss to those of the moneylender, whose future is a pay reduction and dismissal, whose life is endless work and whose only rest is the tomb; the one hundred thousand small farmers who live and die working land that is not theirs, looking at it with the sadness of Moses gazing at the promised land, to die without ever owning it, who like feudal serfs have to pay for the use of their parcel of land by giving up a portion of its produce, who cannot love it, improve it, beautify it nor plant a cedar or an orange tree on it because they never know when a sheriff will come with the rural guard to evict them from it; the thirty thousand teachers and professors who are so devoted, dedicated and so necessary to the better destiny of future generations and who are so badly treated and paid; the twenty thousand small business men weighed down by debts, ruined by the crisis and harangued by a plague of grafting and venal officials; the ten thousand young professional people: doctors, engineers, lawyers, veterinarians, school teachers, dentists, pharmacists, newspapermen, painters, sculptors, . etc., who finish school with their degrees anxious to work and full of hope, only to find themselves at a dead end, all doors closed to them, and where no ears hear their clamor or supplication. These are the people, the ones who know misfortune and, therefore, are capable of fighting with limitless courage! To these people whose desperate roads through life have been paved with the bricks of betrayal and false promises, we were not going to say: "We will give you . . . but rather: "Here it is, now fight for it with everything you have, so that liberty and happiness may be yours!"

The five revolutionary laws that would have been proclaimed immediately after the capture of the Moncada Barracks and would have been broadcast to the nation by radio must be included in the indictment. . . .

The first revolutionary law would have returned power to the people and proclaimed the 1940 Constitution the Supreme Law of the State until such time as the people should decide to modify or change it. And in order to effect its implementation and punish those who violated it—there being no electoral organization to carry this out—the revolutionary movement, as the circumstantial incarnation of this sovereignty, the only source of legitimate power, would have assumed all the faculties inherent therein, except that of modifying the Constitution itself: in other words, it would have assumed the legislative, executive and judicial powers.

This attitude could not be clearer nor more free of vacillation and sterile charlatanry. A government acclaimed by the mass of rebel people would be vested with every power, everything necessary in order to proceed with the effective implementation of popular will and real justice. From that moment, the Judicial Power—which since March 10th had placed itself against and outside the Constitution—would cease to exist and we would proceed to its immediate and total reform before it would once again assume the power granted it by the Supreme Law of the Republic. Without these previous measures, a return to legality by putting its custody back into the hands that have crippled the system so dishonorably would constitute a fraud, a deceit, one more betrayal.

The second revolutionary law would give non-mortgageable and non-transferable ownership of the land to all tenant and subtenant farmers, lessees, share croppers and squatters who hold parcels of five caballerias of land or less, and the State would indemnify the former owners on the basis of the rental which they would have received for these parcels over a period of ten years.

The third revolutionary law would have granted workers and employees the right to share 30% of the profits of all the large industrial, mercantile and mining enterprises, including the sugar mills. The strictly agricultural enterprises would be exempt in consideration of other agrarian laws which would be put into effect.

The fourth revolutionary law would have granted all sugar planters the right to share 55% of sugar production and a minimum quota of forty thousand arrobas for all small tenant farmers who have been established for three years or more.

The fifth revolutionary law would have ordered the confiscation of all holdings and ill-gotten gains of those who had committed frauds during previous regimes, as well as the holdings and ill-gotten gains of all their legates and heirs. To implement this, special courts with full powers would gain access to all records of all corporations registered or operating in this country, in order to investigate concealed funds of illegal origin, and to request that foreign governments extradite persons and attach holdings rightfully belonging to the Cuban people. Half of the property recovered would be used to subsidize retirement funds for workers and the other half would be used for hospitals, asylums and charitable organizations.

Furthermore, it was declared that the Cuban policy in the Americas would be one of close solidarity with the democratic peoples of this continent, and that all those politically persecuted by bloody tyrannies oppressing our sister nations would find generous asylum, brotherhood and bread in the land of Marti; not the persecution, hunger and treason they find today. Cuba should be the bulwark of liberty and not a shameful link in the chain of despotism.

These laws would have been proclaimed immediately. As soon as the upheaval ended and prior to a detailed and far reaching study, they would have been followed by another series of laws and fundamental measures, such as the Agrarian Reform, the Integral Educational Reform, nationalization of the electric power trust and the telephone trust, refund to the people of the illegal and repressive rates these companies have charged, and payment to the treasury of all taxes brazenly evaded in the past.

All these laws and others would be based on the exact compliance of two essential articles of our Constitution: one of them orders the outlawing of large estates, indicating the maximum area of land any one person or entity may own for each type of agricultural enterprise, by adopting measures which would tend to revert the land to the Cubans. The other categorically orders the State to use all means at its disposal to provide employment to all those who lack it and to ensure a decent livelihood to each manual or intellectual laborer. None of these laws can be called unconstitutional. The first popularly elected government would have to respect them, not only because of moral obligations to the nation, but because when people achieve something they have yearned for throughout generations, no force in the world is capable of taking it away again.

The problem of the land, the problem of industrialization, the problem of housing, the problem of unemployment, the problem of education and the problem of the people's health: these are the six problems we would take immediate steps to solve, along with restoration of civil liberties and political democracy.

This exposition may seem cold and theoretical if one does not know the shocking and tragic conditions of the country with regard to these six problems, along with the most humiliating political oppression.

Eighty-five per cent of the small farmers in Cuba pay rent and live under constant threat of being evicted from the land they till. More than half of our most productive land is in the hands of foreigners. In Oriente, the largest province, the lands of the United Fruit Company and the West Indian Company link the northern and southern coasts. There are two hundred thousand peasant families who do not have a single acre of land to till to provide food for their starving children. On the other hand, nearly three hundred thousand caballerias of cultivable land owned by powerful interests remain uncultivated. If Cuba is above all an agricultural State, if its population is largely rural, if the city depends on these rural areas, if the people from our countryside won our war of independence, if our nation's greatness and prosperity depend on a healthy and vigorous rural population that loves the land and knows how to work it, if this population depends on a State that protects and guides it, then how can the present state of affairs be allowed to continue?

Except for a few food, lumber and textile industries, Cuba continues to be primarily a producer of raw materials. We export sugar to import candy, we export hides to import shoes, we export iron to import plows. . . . Everyone agrees with the urgent need to industrialize the nation, that we need steel industries, paper and chemical industries, that we must improve our cattle and grain production, the technology and processing in our food industry in order to defend ourselves against the ruinous competition from Europe in cheese products, condensed milk, liquors and edible oils, and the United States in canned goods; that we need cargo ships; that tourism should be an enormous source of revenue. But the capitalists insist that the workers remain under the yoke. The State sits back with its arms crossed and industrialization can wait forever.

Just as serious or even worse is the housing problem. There are two hundred thousand huts and hovels in Cuba; four hundred thousand families in the countryside and in the cities live cramped in huts and tenements without even the minimum sanitary requirements; two million two hundred thousand of our urban population pay rents which absorb between one fifth and one third of their incomes; and two million eight hundred thousand of our rural and suburban population lack electricity. We have the same situation here: if the State proposes the lowering of rents, landlords threaten to freeze all construction; if the State does not interfere, construction goes on so long as landlords get high rents; otherwise they would not lay a single brick even though the rest of the population had to live totally exposed to the elements. The utilities monopoly is no better; they extend lines as far as it is profitable and beyond that point they don't care if people have to live in darkness for the rest of

their lives. The State sits back with its arms crossed and the people have neither homes nor electricity.

Our educational system is perfectly compatible with everything I've just mentioned. Where the peasant doesn't own the land, what need is there for agricultural schools? Where there is no industry, what need is there for technical or vocational schools? Everything follows the same absurd logic; if we don't have one thing we can't have the other. In any small European country there are more than 200 technological and vocational schools; in Cuba only six such schools exist, and their graduates have no jobs for their skills. The little rural schoolhouses are attended by a mere half of the school age children—barefooted, half-naked and undernourished—and frequently the teacher must buy necessary school materials from his own salary. Is this the way to make a nation great?

Only death can liberate one from so much misery. In this respect, however, the State is most helpful—in providing early death for the people. Ninety per cent of the children in the countryside are consumed by parasites which filter through their bare feet from the ground they walk on. Society is moved to compassion when it hears of the kidnapping or murder of one child, but it is indifferent to the mass murder of so many thousands of children who die every year from lack of facilities, agonizing with pain. Their innocent eyes, death already shining in them, seem to look into some vague infinity as if entreating forgiveness for human selfishness, as if asking God to stay His wrath. And when the head of a family works only four months a year, with what can he purchase clothing and medicine for his children? They will grow up with rickets, with not a single good tooth in their mouths by the time they reach thirty; they will have heard ten million speeches and will finally die of misery and deception. Public hospitals, which are always full, accept only patients recommended by some powerful politician who, in return, demands the votes of the unfortunate one and his family so that Cuba may continue forever in the same or worse condition.

With this background, is it not understandable that from May to December over a million persons are jobless and that Cuba, with a population of five and a half million, has a greater number of unemployed than France or Italy with a population of forty million each?

When you try a defendant for robbery, Honorable Judges, do you ask him how long he has been unemployed? Do you ask him how many children he has, which days of the week he ate and which he didn't, do you investigate his social context at all? You just send him to jail without further thought. But those who burn warehouses and stores to collect insurance do not go to jail, even though a few human beings may have gone up in flames. The insured have money to hire lawyers and bribe judges. You imprison the poor wretch who steals because he is hungry; but none of the hundreds who steal millions from the Government has ever spent a night in jail. You dine with them at the end of the year in some elegant club and they enjoy your respect. In Cuba, when a government official becomes a millionaire overnight and enters the fraternity of the rich, he could very well be greeted with the words of that opulent character out of Balzac—Taillefer—who in his toast to the young heir to an enormous fortune, said: "Gentlemen, let us drink to the power of gold! Mr. Valentine, a millionaire six times over, has just ascended the throne. He is king, can do everything, is above everyone, as all the rich are. Henceforth, equality before the law, established by the Constitution, will be a myth for him; for he will not be subject to laws: the laws will be subject to him. There are no courts nor are there sentences for millionaires."

The nation's future, the solutions to its problems, cannot continue to depend on the selfish interests of a dozen big businessmen nor on the cold calculations of profits that ten or twelve magnates draw up in their air-conditioned offices. The country cannot continue begging on its knees for miracles from a few golden calves, like the Biblical one destroyed by the prophet's fury. Golden calves cannot perform miracles of any kind. The problems of the Republic can be solved only if we dedicate ourselves to fight for it with the same energy, honesty and patriotism our liberators had when they founded it. Statesmen like Carlos Saladrigas, whose statesmanship consists of preserving the status quo and mouthing phrases like "absolute freedom of enterprise," "guarantees to investment capital" and "law of supply and demand," will not solve these problems. Those ministers can chat away in a Fifth Avenue mansion until not even the dust of the bones of those whose problems require immediate solution remains. In this present-day world, social problems are not solved by spontaneous generation.

A revolutionary government backed by the people and with the respect of the nation, after cleansing the different institutions of all venal and corrupt officials, would proceed immediately to the country's industrialization, mobilizing all inactive capital, currently estimated at about 1.5 billion pesos, through the National Bank and the Agricultural and Industrial Development Bank, and submitting this mammoth task to experts and men of absolute competence totally removed from all political machines for study, direction, planning and realization.

After settling the one hundred thousand small farmers as owners on the land which they previously rented, a revolutionary government would immediately proceed to settle the land problem. First, as set forth in the Constitution, it would establish the maximum amount of land to be held by each type of agricultural enterprise and would acquire the excess acreage by expropriation, recovery of swampland, planting of large nurseries, and reserving of zones for reforestation. Secondly, it would distribute the remaining land among peasant families with priority given to the larger ones, and would promote agricultural cooperatives for communal use of expensive equipment, freezing plants and unified professional technical management of farming and cattle raising. Finally, it would provide resources, equipment, protection and useful guidance to the peasants.

A revolutionary government would solve the housing problem by cutting all rents in half, by providing tax exemptions on homes inhabited by the owners; by tripling taxes on rented homes; by tearing down hovels and replacing them with modern apartment buildings; and by financing housing all over the island on a scale heretofore unheard of, with the criterion that, just as each rural family should possess its own tract of land, each city family should own its own house or apartment. There is plenty of building material and more than enough manpower to make a decent home for every Cuban. But if we continue to wait for the golden calf, a thousand years will have gone by and the problem will remain the same. On the other hand, today possibilities of taking electricity to the most isolated areas on the island are greater than ever. The use of nuclear energy in this field is now a reality and will greatly reduce the cost of producing electricity.

With these three projects and reforms, the problem of unemployment would automatically disappear and the task of improving public health and fighting against disease would become much less difficult.

Finally, a revolutionary government would undertake the integral reform of the educational system, bringing it into line with the projects just mentioned with the idea of educating those generations which will have the privilege of living in a happier land. Do not forget the words of the Apostle: "A grave mistake is being made in Latin America: in countries that live almost completely from the produce of the land, men are being educated exclusively for urban life and are not trained for farm life." "The happiest country is the one which has best educated its sons, both in the instruction of thought and the direction of their feelings." "An educated country will always be strong and free."

The soul of education, however, is the teacher, and in Cuba the teaching profession is miserably underpaid. Despite this, no one is more dedicated than the Cuban teacher. Who among us has not learned his three Rs in the little public schoolhouse? It is time we stopped paying pittances to these young men and women who are entrusted with the sacred task of teaching our youth. No teacher should earn less than 200 pesos, no secondary teacher should make less than 350 pesos, if they are to devote themselves exclusively to their high calling without suffering want. What is more, all rural teachers should have free use of the various systems of transportation; and, at least once every five years, all teachers should enjoy a sabbatical leave of six months with pay so they may attend special refresher courses at home or abroad to keep abreast of the latest developments in their field. In this way, the curriculum and the teaching system can be easily improved. Where will the money be found for all this? When there is an end to the embezzlement of government funds, when public officials stop taking graft from the large companies that owe taxes to the State, when the enormous resources of the country are brought into full use, when we no longer buy tanks, bombers and guns for this country (which has no frontiers to defend and where these instruments of war, now being purchased, are used against the people), when there is more interest in educating the people than in killing them there will be more than enough money.

Cuba could easily provide for a population three times as great as it has now, so there is no excuse for the abject poverty of a single one of its present inhabitants. The markets should be overflowing with produce, pantries should be full, all hands should be working. This is not an inconceivable thought. What is inconceivable is that anyone should go to bed hungry while there is a single inch of unproductive land; that children should die for lack of medical attention; what is inconceivable is that 30% of our farm people cannot write their names and that 99% of them know nothing of Cuba's history. What is inconceivable is that the majority of our rural people are now living in worse circumstances than the Indians Columbus discovered in the fairest land that human eyes had ever seen.

To those who would call me a dreamer, I quote the words of Marti: "A true man does not seek the path where advantage lies, but rather the path where duty lies, and this is the only practical man, whose dream of today will be the law of tomorrow, because he who has looked back on the essential course of history and has seen flaming and bleeding peoples seethe in the cauldron of the ages knows that, without a single exception, the future lies on the side of duty. . . .

I know that imprisonment will be harder for me than it has ever been for anyone, filled with cowardly threats and hideous cruelty. But I do not fear prison, as I do not fear the fury of the miserable tyrant who took the lives of 70 of my comrades. Condemn me. It does not matter. History will absolve me.

STUDY QUESTIONS

1. What are the "five revolutionary laws" Castro claims his July 26 movement would have passed if they had been successful in taking power from Batista? Why are these changes so necessary, according to Castro?
2. What are the six problems Castro identifies as being at the heart of Cuba's political and economic situation? Who are the Cubans most affected by these problems?
3. What role does the imagery and ideology of José Martí play in legitimizing Castro's arguments in this speech?

CHE GUEVARA

10.5 *SOCIALISM AND MAN IN CUBA, 1965*

Che Guevara achieved his controversial status as a global revolutionary icon for his role as a guerrilla leader. Yet Guevara was also one of the most important thinkers associated with Latin American socialism, and in his voluminous writings worked to adapt Marxist theory to Latin American realities. This is an excerpt from one of his most famous and influential texts, in which Guevara reflects on the challenges associated with the transition from capitalism to socialism. Written at a moment when the Soviet model of a planned economy was gaining dominance in Cuba, Guevara argued that economic planning should move away from production and consumption goals, and focus instead on creating a "new man" who would be motivated by moral, not material, rewards. Only a shift in cognitive thinking would allow for a true break from capitalism and capitalist values.

In capitalist society individuals are controlled by a pitiless law usually beyond their comprehension. The alienated human specimen is tied to society as a whole by an invisible umbilical cord: the law of value. This law acts upon all aspects of one's life, shaping its course and destiny. The laws of capitalism, which are blind and are invisible to ordinary people, act upon the individual without he or she being aware of it. One sees only the vastness of a seemingly infinite horizon ahead. That is how it is painted by capitalist propagandists who purport to draw a lesson from the example of Rockefeller—whether or not it is true—about the possibilities of individual success. The amount of poverty and suffering required for a Rockefeller to emerge, and the amount of depravity entailed in the accumulation of a fortune of such magnitude, are left out of the picture, and it is not always possible for the popular forces to expose this clearly. . . .

In any case, the road to success is portrayed as beset with perils—perils that, it would seem, an individual with the proper qualities can overcome to attain the goal. The reward is seen in the distance;

the way is lonely. Furthermore, it is a contest among wolves. One can win only at the cost of the failure of others. . . .

I would now like to try to define the individual, the actor in this strange and moving drama of the building of socialism, in a dual existence as a unique being and as a member of society.

I think the place to start is to recognize the individual's quality of incompleteness, of being an unfinished product. The vestiges of the past are brought into the present in one's consciousness, and a continual labor is necessary to eradicate them. The process is two-sided. On the one hand, society acts through direct and indirect education; on the other, the individual submits to a conscious process of self-education. The new society in formation has to compete fiercely with the past. This past makes itself felt not only in one's consciousness—in which the residue of an education systematically oriented toward isolating the individual still weighs heavily—but also through the very character of this transition period in which commodity relations still persist. The commodity is the economic cell of capitalist society. So long as it exists its effects will

Source: Che Guevara, *Socialism and Man in Cuba*. Written: March, 1965. First Published: March 12, 1965, under the title, "From Algiers, for Marcha. The Cuban Revolution Today."
Source: *The Che Reader* (Ocean Press, 2005). Translated: See also: Alternate Translation Transcription/Markup: Ocean Press/ Brian Baggins. Copyright: © 2005 Aleida March, Che Guevara Studies Center and Ocean Press.

make themselves felt in the organization of production and, consequently, in consciousness.

Marx outlined the transition period as resulting from the explosive transformation of the capitalist system destroyed by its own contradictions. In historical reality, however, we have seen that some countries that were weak limbs on the tree of imperialism were torn off first—a phenomenon foreseen by Lenin.

In these countries, capitalism had developed sufficiently to make its effects felt by the people in one way or another. But it was not capitalism's internal contradictions that, having exhausted all possibilities, caused the system to explode. The struggle for liberation from a foreign oppressor; the misery caused by external events such as war, whose consequences privileged classes place on the backs of the exploited; liberation movements aimed at overthrowing neo-colonial regimes—these are the usual factors in unleashing this kind of explosion. Conscious action does the rest. A complete education for social labor has not yet taken place in these countries, and wealth is far from being within the reach of the masses through the simple process of appropriation. Underdevelopment, on the one hand, and the usual flight of capital, on the other, make a rapid transition without sacrifices impossible. There remains a long way to go in constructing the economic base, and the temptation is very great to follow the beaten track of material interest as the lever with which to accelerate development.

There is the danger that the forest will not be seen for the trees. The pipe dream that socialism can be achieved with the help of the dull instruments left to us by capitalism (the commodity as the economic cell, profitability, individual material interest as a lever, etc.) can lead into a blind alley. When you wind up there after having traveled a long distance with many crossroads, it is hard to figure out just where you took the wrong turn. Meanwhile, the economic foundation that has been laid has done its work of undermining the development of consciousness. To build communism it is necessary, simultaneous with the new material foundations, to build the new man and woman. . . .

That is why it is very important to choose the right instrument for mobilizing the masses. Basically, this instrument must be moral in character, without neglecting, however, a correct use of the material incentive—especially of a social character.

As I have already said, in moments of great peril it is easy to muster a powerful response with moral incentives. Retaining their effectiveness, however, requires the development of a consciousness in which there is a new scale of values. Society as a whole must be converted into a gigantic school.

In rough outline this phenomenon is similar to the process by which capitalist consciousness was formed in its initial period. Capitalism uses force, but it also educates people in the system. Direct propaganda is carried out by those entrusted with explaining the inevitability of class society, either through some theory of divine origin or a mechanical theory of natural law. This lulls the masses, since they see themselves as being oppressed by an evil against which it is impossible to struggle.

Next comes hope of improvement—and in this, capitalism differed from the earlier caste systems, which offered no way out. For some people, the principle of the caste system will remain in effect: The reward for the obedient is to be transported after death to some fabulous other world where, according to the old beliefs, good people are rewarded. For other people there is this innovation: class divisions are determined by fate, but individuals can rise out of their class through work, initiative, etc. This process, and the myth of the self-made man, has to be profoundly hypocritical: it is the self-serving demonstration that a lie is the truth.

In our case, direct education acquires a much greater importance. The explanation is convincing because it is true; no subterfuge is needed. It is carried on by the state's educational apparatus as a function of general, technical and ideological education through such agencies as the Ministry of Education and the party's informational apparatus. Education takes hold among the masses and the foreseen new attitude tends to become a habit. The masses continue to make it their own and to influence those who have not yet educated themselves. This is the indirect form of educating the masses, as powerful as the other, structured, one. . . .

But the process is a conscious one. Individuals continually feel the impact of the new social power and perceive that they do not entirely measure up to its standards. Under the pressure of indirect education, they try to adjust themselves to a situation that they feel is right and that their own lack of development had prevented them from reaching previously. They educate themselves.

In this period of the building of socialism we can see the new man and woman being born. The image is not yet completely finished—it never will be, since the process goes forward hand in hand with the development of new economic forms. . . .

They no longer travel completely alone over lost roads toward distant aspirations. They follow their vanguard, consisting of the party, the advanced workers, the advanced individuals who walk in unity with the masses and in close communion with them. The vanguard has its eyes fixed on the future and its reward, but this is not a vision of reward for the individual. The prize is the new society in which individuals will have different characteristics: the society of communist human beings.

The road is long and full of difficulties. At times we lose our way and must turn back. At other times we go too fast and separate ourselves from the masses. Sometimes we go too slow and feel the hot breath of those treading at our heels. In our zeal as revolutionaries we try to move ahead as fast as possible, clearing the way. But we know we must draw our nourishment from the mass and that it can advance more rapidly only if we inspire it by our example.

Despite the importance given to moral incentives, the fact that there remains a division into two main groups (excluding, of course, the minority that for one reason or another does not participate in the building of socialism) indicates the relative lack of development of social consciousness. The vanguard group is ideologically more advanced than the mass; the latter understands the new values, but not sufficiently. While among the former there has been a qualitative change that enables them to make sacrifices in their capacity as an advance guard, the latter see only part of the picture and must be subject to incentives and pressures of a certain intensity. This is the dictatorship of the proletariat operating not only on the defeated class but also on individuals of the victorious class.

All of this means that for total success a series of mechanisms, of revolutionary institutions, is needed. Along with the image of the multitudes marching toward the future comes the concept of institutionalization as a harmonious set of channels, steps, restraints and well-oiled mechanisms which facilitate the advance, which facilitate the natural selection of those destined to march in the vanguard, and which bestow rewards on those who fulfill their duties and punishments on those who commit a crime against the society that is being built. . . .

This institutionalization of the revolution has not yet been achieved. We are looking for something new that will permit a complete identification between the government and the community in its entirety, something appropriate to the special conditions of the building of socialism, while avoiding at all costs transplanting the commonplaces of bourgeois democracy— such as legislative chambers, for example—into the society in formation.

Some experiments aimed at the gradual institutionalization of the revolution have been made, but without undue haste. The greatest brake has been our fear lest any appearance of formality might separate us from the masses and from the individual, which might make us lose sight of the ultimate and most important revolutionary aspiration: to see human beings liberated from their alienation.

Despite the lack of institutions, which must be overcome gradually, the masses are now making history as a conscious collective of individuals fighting for the same cause. The individual under socialism, despite apparent standardization, is more complete. Despite the lack of a perfect mechanism for it, the opportunities for self expression and making oneself felt in the social organism are infinitely greater.

It is still necessary to deepen conscious participation, individual and collective, in all the structures of management and production, and to link this to the idea of the need for technical and ideological education, so that the individual will realize that these processes are closely interdependent and their advancement is parallel. In this way the individual will reach total consciousness as a social being, which is equivalent to the full realization as a human creature, once the chains of alienation are broken. This will be translated concretely into the reconquering of one's true nature through liberated labor, and the expression of one's own human condition through culture and art. . . .

In order to develop a new culture, work must acquire a new status. Human beings-as-commodities cease to exist, and a system is installed that establishes a quota for the fulfillment of one's social duty. The means of production belong to society, and the machine is merely the trench where duty is performed. A person begins to become free from thinking of the annoying fact that one needs to work to satisfy one's animal needs. Individuals start to see themselves reflected in their work and to understand their full stature as human beings through the object created, through the work accomplished. Work no longer entails surrendering a part of one's being in the form of labor power sold, which no longer belongs to the individual, but becomes an expression of oneself, a contribution to the common life in which one is reflected, the fulfillment of one's social duty.

We are doing everything possible to give work this new status as a social duty and to link it on the one hand with the development of technology, which will create the conditions for greater freedom, and on the other hand with voluntary work based on the Marxist appreciation that one truly reaches a full human condition when no longer compelled to produce by the physical necessity to sell oneself as a commodity. Of course, there are still coercive aspects to work, even when it is voluntary. We have not transformed all the coercion that surrounds us into conditioned reflexes of a social character and, in many cases, is still produced under the pressures of one's environment. (Fidel calls this moral compulsion.) There is still a need to undergo a complete spiritual rebirth in one's attitude toward one's own work, freed from the direct pressure of the social environment, though linked to it by new habits. That will be communism. The change in consciousness does not take place automatically, just as change in the economy does not take place automatically. The alterations are slow and not rhythmic; there are periods of acceleration, periods that are slower, and even retrogressions. . . .

At the risk of seeming ridiculous, let me say that the true revolutionary is guided by great feelings of love. It is impossible to think of a genuine revolutionary lacking this quality. Perhaps it is one of the great dramas of the leader that he or she must combine a passionate spirit with a cold intelligence and make painful decisions without flinching. Our vanguard revolutionaries must idealize this love of the people, of the most sacred causes, and make it one and indivisible. They cannot descend, with small doses of daily affection, to the level where ordinary people put their love into practice.

The leaders of the revolution have children just beginning to talk, who are not learning to say "daddy";

their wives, too, must be part of the general sacrifice of their lives in order to take the revolution to its destiny. The circle of their friends is limited strictly to the circle of comrades in the revolution. There is no life outside of it.

In these circumstances one must have a large dose of humanity, a large dose of a sense of justice and truth in order to avoid dogmatic extremes, cold scholasticism, or an isolation from the masses. We must strive every day so that this love of living humanity is transformed into actual deeds, into acts that serve as examples, as a moving force.

The revolutionary, the ideological motor force of the revolution within the party, is consumed by this uninterrupted activity that comes to an end only with death, unless the construction of socialism is accomplished on a world scale. If one's revolutionary zeal is blunted when the most urgent tasks have been accomplished on a local scale and one forgets about proletarian internationalism, the revolution one leads will cease to be a driving force and sink into a comfortable drowsiness that imperialism, our irreconcilable enemy, will utilize to gain ground. Proletarian internationalism is a duty, but it is also a revolutionary necessity. This is the way we educate our people. . . .

Allow me to draw some conclusions:

We socialists are freer because we are more fulfilled; we are more fulfilled because we are freer.

The skeleton of our complete freedom is already formed. The flesh and the clothing are lacking; we will create them.

Our freedom and its daily sustenance are paid for in blood and sacrifice. Our sacrifice is a conscious one: an installment paid on the freedom that we are building.

The road is long and, in part, unknown. We recognize our limitations. We will make the human being of the 21st century—we, ourselves. We will forge ourselves in daily action, creating a new man and woman with a new technology.

Individuals play a role in mobilizing and leading the masses insofar as they embody the highest virtues and aspirations of the people and do not wander from the path.

Clearing the way is the vanguard group, the best among the good, the party.

The basic clay of our work is the youth; we place our hope in it and prepare it to take the banner from our hands. . . .

STUDY QUESTIONS

1. What are the differences between the ways in which capitalist and socialist systems understand the value and role of a human being, according to Guevara?
2. What role does the individual have to play in the transition to socialism?

RÉGIS DEBRAY

10.6 *CONVERSATIONS WITH ALLENDE, 1972*

Salvador Allende was elected President of Chile in 1970, becoming the first Marxist leader to be democratically elected to power in Latin America. Allende's Popular Unity government sought to find a route to socialism through the established political system, rather than by overthrowing existing structures, as occurred in the Cuban Revolution. In this interview, Allende discusses the Popular Unity Program and the challenges it faced with the French intellectual and revolutionary Régis Debray. Debray was deeply committed to Latin American revolution and had fought alongside Che Guevara in Bolivia. The interview took place over a series of meetings, just a few months into Allende's government.

DEBRAY: Let us now discuss the current situation in Chile. With Frei, reformism ended, it failed. With you in government, the Chilean people has chosen the road of revolution, but what is revolution? It is the transfer of power from one class to another. Revolution is the destruction of the machinery of the bourgeois State and the replacement of it by another, and none of this has happened here. What is happening then?

ALLENDE: Excuse me, comrade, let's deal with the question in stages. Indeed, the people of Chile chose the road of revolution and we have not forgotten a fundamental principle of Marxism: the class struggle. During the electoral campaign we said that the purpose of our struggle was to change the regime, the system. That we sought to form a government in order to obtain the power to carry out the revolutionary transformation

which Chile needs, to break the nation's economic, political, cultural and trade union dependency. And you say nothing has happened here? What country do you think you're in? But wait, look Regis. During the few months we've been in power, we've–

DEBRAY: Done a lot of things.

ALLENDE: Yes, we've done quite a lot. We have been able to do them because behind them there is the tradition of the Chilean working class which began its struggle at the beginning of the last century and emerged as a force to be reckoned with during this century. In 1909, the Federación Obrera (Workers' Federation) was founded in Chile. It was originally a mutual aid organization, but in 1919, with a new programme, it set itself the objective of abolishing the capitalist regime. You must take into account the fighting tradition

Source: Régis Debray, "Conversations with Allende," *The Chilean Revolution*, (Random House, 1972), pp. 81–93.

of the Chilean working class. There have been stages in its development when its interests have coincided with those of the petty bourgeoisie. You must also remember that in Chile there are parties, drawn from the masses, which genuinely represent the ideology of the working class. At present, the people are in government, and from this position they are struggling to gain power through the programme of the Popular Unity, implemented by a vanguard composed of two Marxist parties, the Socialists and the Communists, two parties of bourgeois popular extraction, the Radicals and the Social Democrats, and two movements of similar background, the Christian Movement (MAPU) and the Independent Popular Alliance (API). In addition, the government can count on the support of the working class organized through the Single Workers' Union. This is a working-class government because the predominant ideology is that of the working class. The interests of the exploiting class are not represented in the Government—on the contrary, there are wage-earners in the Cabinet, four of them workmen. Through this Government, the majority of the people will replace the minority which has been in power until now. As for the bourgeois State at the present moment, we are seeking to overcome it. To overthrow it!

DEBRAY: But bourgeois democracy remains intact here. You, in fact, hold the executive power.

ALLENDE : Yes.

DEBRAY: But not legislative or judicial power; nor the apparatus of police power. Legality, the Institutions, these were not the work of the proletariat; the bourgeoisie formulated the Constitution to suit its own ends.

ALLENDE: Of course, but listen for a moment, we'll get to that later. What did we say during the electoral campaign? We said that if it was difficult, although not impossible, to win the election, the stage between victory and taking Government was going to be very difficult, and it would be yet more difficult to build, because we were blazing a new trail, for Chile, opened by Chileans, for our country. And we said that we would take advantage of what openings there are in the present Constitution to open the way to the new Constitution, the people's Constitution. Why? Because in Chile we

can do it. If we put forward a bill and Congress rejects it, we invoke the plebiscite. I'll give you an example: we propose that there should be no longer two houses in Congress, the proposal is rejected by Congress, we hold a referendum and win. Hence the end of the two house system, and we now have to go to a single house, as we had proposed. And who are the people going to elect to this house? Its representatives, I would presume. If we put into practice what we have said, and carry on with what we are doing. . . .

DEBRAY: And one has to admit one thing, comrade. Since the elections, you have won many votes, or rather supporters and allies among the people.

ALLENDE: I believe so.

DEBRAY: I'm told so by a number of people. The Popular Unity is broadening its support socially. It is interesting that instead of the traditional loss of support of a "Government of the left" once it has got into power, in this case, support is growing. Do you envisage a time when there will be a genuinely popular revolutionary majority?

ALLENDE: Look. We haven't been around long enough to show a loss of support, but of one thing I am sure, yes, and that is that our adversaries on the right, and even a lot of people on the left, mind you, first of all didn't believe we would win, and then they didn't think we would carry out what we had said we'd do. Then, we hit back hard at reaction. Persistently. We hit them, they don't recover, and we let them have it again. For example, the Constitutional Reform for nationalizing copper. Think of the CUT-Government agreement; think of the creation of the National Peasant Council, the expropriation of an important textile company in Concepcion, the nationalization of steel, the nationalization of coal, the Bill to nationalize the banks. Now then, Regis, are we or are we not seeking the path which leads to Socialism. No wonder the people are behind us, supporting us. Look, I'm going to Valparaiso this afternoon. Come with me.

DEBRAY: With pleasure.

ALLENDE: There's a public meeting, and you'll be able to see how the people respond.

DEBRAY: I know you are on exceptionally good terms with the masses.

ALLENDE: The people have grasped the importance of the measures we have taken. In addition to the basic socioeconomic measures, we had an immediate programme for improving the living conditions of the workers. We are the first Government to fulfil its election promises. For example, a major problem is malnutrition in infants. We proposed to give half a litre of free milk to every child, and this we are doing. We have eliminated the various types of loaf of bread and enforced a standard size to eliminate price juggling. Bread is part of the staple diet of the people. Chile is a country which suffers from high inflation—in 1969 it was one of the ten countries with the highest rates of inflation—and readjustment of incomes, on an annual basis at least, applicable to salary and wage earners has to be introduced. The Popular Front Government, which inherited a rate of inflation of 35%, must regulate incomes by law in 1971. This time the Bill we have submitted to Congress is not a traditional one; the object is to facilitate economic development. Not only are we seeking to restore the lost purchasing power to the working class, but we are aiming to stimulate demand in order to accelerate internal economic development, which was impeded by the bourgeois Christian Democrat Government. Don't be frightened, we haven't forgotten that we are making our way towards Socialism.

DEBRAY: No. I realize that there are special circumstances in Chile and that it was necessary to proceed in this way. The important thing is that things are moving and a lot of progress has been made in two months. But I come back to my earlier question, comrade Allende; the workers behind you have voted you into office, but if I ask you how and when you are going to win real power, what is your answer?

ALLENDE: My answer is that we shall have real power when copper and steel are under our control, when saltpetre is genuinely under our control, when we have put far-reaching Land Reform measures into effect, when we control imports and exports through the State, when we have collectivized a major portion of our national production. I say "a major portion" because in our programme we announced frankly to the nation that

there would be three sectors in the economy: nationalized industry, a mixed sector and the private sector. Now then, if these things—affirming our national sovereignty, recovering our basic wealth and attacking monopolies—do not lead to Socialism, I don't know what does. But there will be no further doubt as to whether we hold real power as soon as Chile becomes an economically independent country. Hence our basic, most vital, principle is one of anti-imperialism, as a first step towards the making of structural changes. Hence the most important bill we have to get through is the one to nationalize copper, Chile's fundamental source of wealth. What do you think?

DEBRAY: Yes, it is. Undoubtedly, at the moment the main emphasis of your activities, the main battle front, is concerned with the economic infrastructure. To understand this, one only has to remember that this Continent has a long history of pseudo-socialist phraseology and populist demagogy which is renowned for its failure to deal effectively with the economic and financial bases on which the capitalist system is built. But the problem of Socialism cannot be simplified into a problem of ownership of means of production. You, comrade President, know better than I that nationalization in itself means little. "It remains to be seen whether nationalization can be converted from a mere legislative act on the part of the State into a genuine process of socialization, real and effective control and management by the State— and this does not only depend on the will, but also on the general development of productive resources. The class nature of the State which nationalizes the means of production remains to be seen. It remains to be seen whether the relationships of power and authority between the men in those centres of production actually change once the workers have theoretically become the owners of the factories or the land where they work." You know Lenin's slogan: "Socialism equals electrification plus the Soviets." We could change the terms which don't apply to the Chile of today, but could we now discuss the "Soviet" as well as the "electrification" aspect, "men" as well as "things'. . . ?

ALLENDE: It is true that if one views the problem from the point of view of building the socialist society, once one has got over the decisive and very absorbing current problems of the Constitution and securing power for the people and the destruction of the economic bases of monopolistic capitalism, other problems begin to come to the fore. As you rightly point out, the problems of the control and growth of socialized productive resources and the new relationships between the men inside and outside production need to be dealt with. With regard to the first problem, you have to realize that one of the outstanding features of Chilean capitalism has been its strongly monopolistic character, although the productive structure on which it is based is quite weak. In industry, for example, less than 3% of our companies control more than half of our industrial resources: capital, volume of sales, profits, etc. . . . Into the bargain, most of these firms, and most of those in other sectors, are dominated by a clique of no more than fifty industrial, commercial and financial groups. Well now, in Chile there is a long tradition of State intervention in economic activities, along capitalist lines of course. Any number of State-controlled undertakings, control of prices and supplies, partial or total control of foreign trade, etc. . . . Thus, from this point of view, we find ourselves already approaching socialism through the antechamber of State monopolies and State capitalism. The essential thing is to change the socio-economic content of their management. To this end, we must expropriate the means of production which are still in private hands. To quite some extent, the infrastructure for productive resources and their control has been prepared.

DEBRAY: But how will the new social relationship be established in this context?

ALLENDE: As for relations between men, and the possible and desirable forms they may take, you are well aware that this subject has been discussed fully in the Socialist countries and that various standards have been adopted or tried out in practice. We are aware that the subject has not been closed, and without any doubt no one can claim dogmatically that they have "found *the* solution"; we must draw upon our own experience, which in turn springs from the historical and social

contradictions which have given rise to our socialist revolution. Of course, there are certain elements which are derived from the experience of other countries, which are more or less common to many of them: the creation of a new system of values in which the social character of human activity is underlined; reassessment of work as the essential human function; reduction of the impulses stimulating self-interest and individualism to a minimum. In the meantime, we can show that in practice the management of the concerns in which the State has intervened, or which it has expropriated, is now in the hands of Workers' Committees in each factory, headed by a manager appointed by the State. Their objective is no longer to make profits, but to meet the present and future needs of the people. As State ownership progresses, the planned means towards this end will be strengthened.

DEBRAY: Comrade President, as a Marxist, you are well aware that no social class relinquishes power with good grace. We know that the people are not yet in power, but at least they are in office and to an outside observer it would seem that the change of Government took place in a very civilized and stylish manner. For example, I recently came across a copy of *Le Monde* in which I read, and I quote: "For the first time in history, in Chile, Marxism is settling comfortably into the seat hitherto occupied by the bourgeois democrats." Have things really been as easy as that? Have the gentlemen of the previous government really been as benevolent as all that towards the Government of Popular Unity?

ALLENDE: I think there is a slightly distorted impression with regard to the resistance put up by the reactionaries to our succeeding in office. During the elections, they used every means available. Already in 1958 and 1964, they used lies, calumny and slander, dirty anti-communism, and in 1970, it was worse still. Well, they were wrong, not us. Such was their insolence that they thought they could win a three horse race. We won, but I must tell you, Regis—as I told the people, and as I was saying to you only a moment ago—it is difficult, but not impossible to win. Let me enlarge on this. We beat them by playing to their own rules. Our tactics were right, theirs were wrong. But I said at the time to the people: "between 3 September and 4 November, Chile is going to feel like a football being kicked about by a Pele." I expressed it like that so that the people could understand. *Le Monde* can say what it likes, but the facts in Chile were very different. From 4 September, the day on which I was elected President, till 3 November, the date on which I assumed office, I was not a man preparing to take over government, I felt more like a Director of Public Prosecutions.

DEBRAY: But wasn't this job being done by someone from the previous Government?

ALLENDE: Obviously, there was a Director of Public Prosecutions, but he had no interest in protecting the legal system which had conferred power on the Popular Unity. I warned this official, in good time, that a powerful textile industrialist had arranged for a bomb to be planted in his house in order to justify his leaving Chile with his money. The Chief of Police did nothing, and the bomb went off. Following our public protests and denouncements, the people implicated in this plot were arrested but the magistrate at the hearing set them free. They were members of an ultra-reactionary political party, and they fled the country. To help you understand this case, I should point out that the first phase of this conspiracy on the part of the enemies of Chile and its working class was a campaign of alarmism designed to provoke panic in the weaker sectors. The plan was that the fear instilled in our weaker friends would spread and thus the next phase of the plot could be put in train. I should add that this was an organized conspiracy. Some of the conspirators made some spectacular withdrawals from the banks, which caused thousands of anxious citizens to draw their money from the savings centres. The radio and press media spoke in terms of the "danger of Marxism," and the Minister of Finance of the outgoing Government, instead of pacifying those who were really worried by the campaign of alarmist rumours, made a speech calculated to intensify the false impression of chaos in the country. It was in this climate that the second phase of the conspiracy was put into effect—the bombing of public buildings and monuments, private houses, offices, etc. . . . Santiago's international airport was on the point of being blown up.

DEBRAY: Was this the first time such a situation had existed in Chile?

ALLENDE: But I've only told you the beginning of it. They invented an organization which was supposed to be responsible for the attacks; of course, it was described as a revolutionary organization. The idea was to blame us for the attacks. Members of the reactionary conspiracy assassinated a uniformed policeman who was on guard duty in a public building, and fired on another, who was seriously wounded; he was on patrol at the entrance of a foreign embassy. Two attempts were made on my life, but failed thanks to the watchfulness of my personal guard of revolutionary comrades.

DEBRAY: And the Commander-in-Chief of the Army was killed instead?

ALLENDE: I was the intended victim. Tragically, they killed the Commander-in-Chief of the Army because he refused to take part in the reactionary conspiracy. The conspirators hoped that the crime would be laid at the door of the political body I represented and that the armed forces, particularly the army, would react politically to prevent the decision of the people bringing us into office from being implemented. However, Army Intelligence found evidence which points to the origins of the assassins.

DEBRAY: Did you feel there was a possibility of civil war? Could you see it coming? Were you afraid of it? How close were you?

ALLENDE: Yes, the assassination of General Rene Schneider proved how close we were. Had the reactionaries kidnapped the Commander-in-Chief of the Army, we would undoubtedly have been on the verge of civil war. They continued to provoke the armed forces in an attempt to get them to overthrow Congress. Don't forget that the criminal attack occurred forty-eight hours before Parliament met for a Plenary Session to sanction the presidential election results constitutionally. By this stage, the Popular Unity already had the Parliamentary votes to ratify the victory won in the election of 4 September, so that the unconstitutional manoeuvre which consisted of a letter sent by the defeated presidential candidate, Jorge Alessandri, was forestalled. Having lost all possibility of defeating the Popular Unity legally, the conspirators went outside bourgeois law. What could the people do? We had to defend ourselves.

DEBRAY: So the outward appearance of the bourgeoisie conducting a clean, democratic campaign does not fit the facts? Was there resistance against allowing you to assume the Presidency?

ALLENDE: Probably, if not on a personal level, certainly from the existing regime as a whole. It stands to reason that it should be so—you, as a Marxist, know that as well as I do, Regis.

DEBRAY: The reactionaries defended to the last; they exhausted every possibility . . .

ALLENDE: Not every possibility, no, because they are still active . . .

DEBRAY: Yes, this is to be expected. This leads me to a question which well . . . may or may not be of interest. Why for the first time, as President of Chile, have you been obliged to resort to a personal political guard?

ALLENDE: I turned for protection, as you say, to a group of comrades because I had no confidence in the Political Police of the bourgeoisie. I knew that the Director of Public Prosecutions was doing nothing to find the people responsible for the attack. Worse still, I was quite sure that he knew who one of them was. So I had to seek other means of safety, not for my own life, but for what I represented. This is why I am accompanied by these young comrades, each one a proven revolutionary, each one a militant volunteer, and they take care of my personal safety.

DEBRAY: Didn't you feel protected by the Government before?

ALLENDE: No. As I have told you, the top police officials were political puppets.

DEBRAY: Is it true that there was an attack on members of your family in front of your house and that you had to come out to defend them with a gun in your hand because the Government had "forgotten" to allocate Carabineros to guard you?

ALLENDE: What I can say is that I had every confidence as to how the armed forces would behave. As for the Carabineros, you have to remember that they take their orders from the Government, through the Minister of the Interior. Also, at the time of one of the attacks on my home, there was only one policeman on guard at the door, and he didn't have orders to shoot. The gang that attacked was large, so I had to come out shooting to frighten them away.

DEBRAY: What significance is there for you in the fact that, in order to get through the first phases of the so-called "peaceful process," you had to resort to men and methods who have little to do with this line to ensure your personal safety?

ALLENDE: It's a question of form; the objective is the same, even if the tactics are different. You know that today in Uruguay, the Tupamaros, who have nothing to do with the Socialist Party or the Communist Party are working towards the possibility of a broad-based unity in Uruguay. You also know that here there was almost a confrontation between the MIR and the Communist Party as a result of the university elections in Concepcion,18 and I stepped in and helped to stop it happening.

DEBRAY: Precisely, and since this is your role, that of unifier of the parties of the left, catalyst of the popular forces, it occurs to one that your enemies inside and outside the country would have good reason to eliminate you at present. If this came about, what do you think would happen?

ALLENDE: The notion that history is based on personalities is a common delusion among the bourgeois class. The reactionary forces encourage this belief, and try to turn it to their political advantage; it is one of their favourite tactics to resort to methods of this kind, but we have an answer to this in the awareness of the people. I believe that although this would apparently be the easiest course for the reactionaries, the consequences of such an act would in fact be even worse for them. This is not to say that my presence contains them, but, without a shadow of doubt, if this happened, it would be quite evident that the reactionaries are no longer prepared to play to the rules which they themselves invented. They can lay no accusations at my door—all the civil liberties have been maintained: freedom to hold meetings, freedom of opinion, freedom of the press, etc. . . . The social process is not going to disappear because one of its leaders disappears. It may be delayed or prolonged, but in the long run, it can't be stopped. In the case of Chile, if they assassinate me, the people will carry on, they will follow their course, with the difference perhaps that things will be much harder, much more violent, because it would be a very clear and objective lesson for the masses showing .them that these people stop at nothing. And I have accounted for this possibility; I don't lay myself open to it, I don't offer opportunities, but at the same time, I don't think about the possibility of this happening all the time.

DEBRAY: If they go outside the law, will you also go outside the law? If they hit out, will you hit back?

ALLENDE: If they deal us an illegal blow? We'll return it a hundredfold, you can be sure of that. . . .

STUDY QUESTIONS

1. How does Allende define revolution? What steps is his government taking to achieve revolutionary transformation? What impact did he hope these changes would have on the structures of the Chilean economy and political system?
2. What challenges did Allende identify as most difficult to overcome?
3. What was Debray's attitude toward Chilean socialism? What do his responses reveal about transnational linkages in Latin American revolutionary movements?

GUSTAVO GUTIERREZ

10.7 *A THEOLOGY OF LIBERATION*, 1971

The Peruvian priest Gustavo Gutierrez is one of the most important theologians of the twentieth century. He is one of the intellectual founders of liberation theology, a philosophy that interpreted biblical scripture through the lens of Marxist theory, and that insisted the Catholic Church needed to focus its efforts on the poor and work toward the transformation of political and economic structures that maintained and supported poverty. *A Theology of Liberation* was Gutierrez's seminal work, and was first published in Peru in 1971. In this excerpt, Gutierrez grapples with the biblical meaning of poverty and lays out his arguments in support of a "preferential option for the poor."

Source: *A Theology of Liberation: History, Politics and Salvation/Gustavo Gutiérrez*. Translated and edited by Sister Caridad Inda and John Eagleson (Maryknoll, New York: Orbis, 1988), pp. 162–173.

For some years now we have seen in the Church a recovery of a more authentic and radical witness of poverty. At first this occurred within various recently founded religious communities. It quickly went beyond the narrow limits of "religious poverty," however, raising challenges and questions in other sectors of the Church. Poverty has become one of the central themes of contemporary Christian spirituality and indeed has become a controversial question. From the concern to imitate more faithfully the poor Christ, there has spontaneously emerged a critical and militant attitude regarding the countersign that the Church as a whole presents in the matter of poverty.

Those who showed this concern—with John XXIII at the head—knocked insistently at the doors of Vatican II. In an important message in preparation for the opening of the Council, John opened up a fertile perspective saying, "In dealing with the underdeveloped countries, the Church presents herself as she is and as she wants to be—as the Church of all men and especially the Church of the poor. Indeed, from the first session of the Council the theme of poverty was very much in the air. Later there was even a "Schema 14," which on the issue of poverty went beyond "Schema 13" (the draft for *Gaudium et spes*). The final results of the Council, however, did not correspond to the expectations. The documents allude several times to poverty, but it is not one of the major thrusts.

Later, *Populorum progressio* is somewhat more concrete and clear with regard to various questions related to poverty. But it will remain for the Church on a continent of misery and injustice to give the theme of poverty its proper importance: *the authenticity of the preaching of the Gospel message depends on this witness.*

The theme of poverty has been dealt with in recent years, especially in the field of spirituality. In the contemporary world, fascinated by a wealth and power established upon the plunder and exploitation of the great majorities, poverty appeared as an inescapable precondition to sanctity. Therefore the greatest efforts were to meditate on the Biblical texts which recall the poverty of Christ and thus to identify with Christ in this witness.

More recently a properly theological reflection on poverty has been undertaken, based on ever richer and more precise exegetical studies. From these first attempts there stands out clearly one rather surprising result: poverty is a notion which has received very little theological treatment and in spite of everything is still quite unclear. Lines of interpretation overlap; various exegeses still carry weight today, even though they were developed in very different contexts which no longer exist; certain aspects of the theme function as static compartments which prevent a grasp of its overall meaning. All this has led us onto slippery terrain on which we have tried to maneuver more by intuition than by clear and well-formulated ideas.

AMBIGUITIES IN THE TERM "POVERTY"

Poverty is an equivocal term. But the ambiguity of the term does nothing more than express the ambiguity of the notions themselves which are involved. To try to clarify what we understand by *poverty*, we must clear the path and examine some of the sources of the ambiguity. This will also permit us to indicate the meaning we will give to various expressions which we will use later.

The term *poverty* designates in the first place *material poverty*, that is, the lack of economic goods necessary for a human life worthy of the name. In this sense poverty is considered degrading and is rejected by the conscience of contemporary persons. Even those who are not—or do not wish to be—aware of the root causes of this poverty believe that it should be struggled against. Christians, however, often have a tendency to give material poverty a positive value, considering it almost a human and religious ideal. It is seen as austerity and indifference to the things of this world and a precondition for a life in conformity with the Gospel. This interpretation would mean that the demands of Christianity are at cross purposes to the great aspirations of persons today who want to free themselves from subjection to nature, to eliminate the exploitation of some persons by others, and to create prosperity for everyone. The double and contradictory meaning of *poverty* implied here gives rise to the imposition of one language on another and is a frequent source of ambiguities. The matter becomes even more complex if we take into consideration that the concept of material poverty is in constant evolution. Not having access to certain cultural, social, and political values, for example, is today part of the poverty that persons hope to abolish. Would material poverty as an "ideal" of Christian life also include lacking these things?

On the other hand, poverty has often been thought of and experienced by Christians as part of the condition—seen with a certain fatalism—of marginated peoples, "the poor," who are an object of our mercy. But things are no longer like this. Social classes, nations, and entire continents are becoming aware of their poverty, and when they see its root causes, they rebel against it. The contemporary phenomenon is a collective poverty that leads those who suffer from it to forge bonds of solidarity among themselves and to organize in the struggle against the conditions they are in and against those who benefit from these conditions.

What we mean by material poverty is a subhuman situation. As we shall see later, the Bible also considers it this way. Concretely, to be poor means to die of hunger, to be illiterate, to be exploited by others, not to know that you are being exploited, not to know that you are a person. It is in relation to this poverty—material and cultural, collective and militant—that evangelical poverty will have to define itself.

The notion of *spiritual poverty* is even less clear. Often it is seen simply as an interior attitude of unattachment to the goods of this world. The poor, therefore, are not so much the ones who have no material goods; rather it is they who are not attached to them—even if they do possess them. This point of view allows for the case of the rich person who is spiritually poor as well as for the poor person who is rich at heart. These are extreme cases that distract attention toward the exceptional and the accessory. Claiming to be based on the Beatitude of Matthew concerning "the poor in spirit," this approach in the long run leads to comforting and tranquilizing conclusions.

This spiritualistic perspective rapidly leads to dead ends and to affirmations that the interior attitude must necessarily be incarnated in a testimony of material poverty. But if this is so, questions arise: What poverty is being spoken of? The poverty that the contemporary conscience considers subhuman? Is it in this way that spiritual poverty should be incarnated? Some answer that it is not necessary to go to such extremes, and they attempt to distinguish between destitution and

poverty. The witness involves living poverty, not destitution. But then, as we have said, we are not referring to poverty as it is lived and perceived today, but rather to a different kind of poverty, abstract and made according to the specifications of our spiritual poverty. This is to play with words—and with persons.

The distinction between evangelical counsels and precepts creates other ambiguities. According to it, evangelical poverty would be a counsel appropriate to a particular vocation and not a precept obligatory for all Christians. This distinction kept evangelical poverty confined incommunicado for a long time within the narrow limits of religious life, which focuses on "the evangelical counsels." Today the distinction is only another source of misunderstandings.

Because of all these ambiguities and uncertainties we have been unable to proceed on solid ground; we have wandered along an unsure path where it is difficult to advance and easy to wander. We have also fallen into very vague terminology and a kind of sentimentalism which in the last analysis justifies the status quo. In situations like the present one in Latin America this is especially serious. We see the danger, for example, in various commentaries on the writings of Bossuet regarding "the eminent dignity of the poor in the Church"; or in symbolism like that which considers the hunger of the poor as "the image of the human soul hungering for God"; or even in the expression "the Church of the poor," which—in spite of the indisputable purity of intention of John XXIII—is susceptible to an interpretation smacking of paternalism.

Clarification is needed. In the following pages we will attempt to sketch at least the broad outlines. We will try to keep in mind that—as one spiritual writer has said—the first form of poverty is to renounce the idea we have of poverty.

BIBLICAL MEANING OF POVERTY

Poverty is a central theme both in the Old and the New Testaments. It is treated both briefly and profoundly; it describes social situations and expresses spiritual experiences communicated only with difficulty; it defines personal attitudes, a whole people's attitude before God, and the relationships of persons with each other. It is possible, nevertheless, to try to unravel the knots and to clear the horizon by following the two major lines of thought that seem to stand out: poverty as a scandalous condition and poverty as spiritual childhood. The notion of evangelical poverty will be illuminated by a comparison of these two perspectives.

POVERTY: A SCANDALOUS CONDITION

In the Bible poverty is a scandalous condition inimical to human dignity and therefore contrary to the will of God. This rejection of poverty is seen very clearly in the vocabulary used. . . .

Indigent, weak, bent over, wretched are terms which well express a degrading human situation. These terms already insinuate a protest. They are not limited to description; they take a stand. This stand is made explicit in the vigorous rejection of poverty. The climate in which poverty is described is one of indignation. And it is with the same indignation that the cause of poverty is indicated: the injustice of oppressors. . . .

Poverty is not caused by fate; it is caused by the actions of those whom the prophet condemns:

> These are the words of the Lord:
> For crime after crime of Israel
> I will grant them no reprieve
> because they sell the innocent for silver
> and the destitute for a pair of shoes.
> They grind the heads of the poor into the earth
> and thrust the humble out of their way
> [Amos 2:6–7].

There are poor because some are victims of others. "Shame on you," it says in Isaiah,

> you who make unjust laws
> and publish burdensome decrees,
> depriving the poor of justice,
> robbing the weakest of my people of their rights,
> despoiling the widow and plundering the
> orphan [10:1–2].

The prophets condemn every kind of abuse, every form of keeping the poor in poverty or of creating new poor. They are not merely allusions to situations; the finger is pointed at those who are to blame. Fraudulent commerce and exploitation are condemned (Hos. 12:8;

Amos 8:5; Mic. 6:10–11; Isa. 3:14; Jer. 5:27; 6:12), as well as the hoarding of lands (Mic. 2:1–3; Ezek. 22:29; Hab. 2:5–6), dishonest courts (Amos 5:7; Jer. 22:13–17; Mic. 3:9-11; Isa. 5:23, 10:1–2), the violence of the ruling classes (2 Kings 23:30, 35; Amos 4:1; Mic. 3:1–2; 6:12; Jer. 22:13–17), slavery (Neh. 5:1–5; Amos 2:6; 8:6), unjust taxes (Amos 4:1; 5:11–12), and unjust functionaries (Amos 5:7; Jer. 5:28). In the New Testament oppression by the rich is also condemned, especially in Luke (6:24–25; 12:13–21; 16:19--31; 18:18–26) and in the Letter of James (2:5–9; 4:13–17; 5:16).

But it is not simply a matter of denouncing poverty. The Bible speaks of positive and concrete measures to prevent poverty from becoming established among the People of God. In Leviticus and Deuteronomy there is very detailed legislation designed to prevent the accumulation of wealth and the consequent exploitation. It is said, for example, that what remains in the fields after the harvest and the gathering of olives and grapes should not be collected; it is for the alien, the orphan, and the widow (Deut. 24:19–21; Lev. 19:9–10). Even more, the fields should not be harvested to the very edge so that something remains for the poor and the aliens (Lev. 23:22). The Sabbath, the day of the Lord, has a social significance; it is a day of rest for the slave and the alien (Exod. 23:12; Deut. 5:14). The triennial tithe is not to be carried to the temple; rather it is for the alien, the orphan, and the widow (Deut. 14:28–29; 26:12). Interest on loans is forbidden (Exod. 22:25; Lev. 25:35–37; Deut. 23:20). Other important measures include the Sabbath year and the jubilee year. Every seven years the fields will be left to lie fallow "to provide food for the poor of your people" (Exod. 23:11; Lev. 25:2–7), although it is recognized that this duty is not always fulfilled (Lev. 26:34–35). After seven years the slaves were to regain their freedom (Exod. 21:2–6) and debts were to be pardoned (Deut. 15:1–18). This is also the meaning of the jubilee year of Lev. 25:10ff. "It was," writes de Vaux, "a general emancipation . . . of all the inhabitants of the land. The fields lay fallow: every man re-entered his ancestral property, i.e. the fields and houses which had been alienated returned to their original owners.

Behind these texts we can see three principal reasons for this vigorous repudiation of poverty. In the first place, poverty contradicts the very meaning of *the Mosaic religion.* Moses led his people out of the slavery, exploitation, and alienation of Egypt so that they might inhabit a land where they could live with human dignity. . . .

The rejection of the exploitation of some by others is found in the very roots of the people of Israel. God is the only owner of the land given to people (Lev. 25:23, 38); God is the one Lord who saves the people from servitude and will not allow them to be subjected to it again (Deut. 5:15; 16:22; Lev. 25:42; 26:13). And thus Deuteronomy speaks of "the ideal of a brotherhood where there was no poverty." In their rejection of poverty, the prophets, who were heirs to the Mosaic ideal, referred to the past, to the origins of the people; there they sought the inspiration for the construction of a just society. To accept poverty and injustice is to fall back into the conditions of servitude which existed before the liberation from Egypt. It is to retrogress.

The second reason for the repudiation of the state of slavery and exploitation of the Jewish people in Egypt is that it goes against *the mandate of Genesis* (1:26; 2:15). Humankind is created in the image and likeness of God and is destined to dominate the earth. Humankind fulfills itself only by transforming nature and thus entering into relationships with other persons. Only in this way do persons come to a full consciousness of themselves as subjects of creative freedom which is realized through work. The exploitation and injustice implicit in poverty make work into something servile and dehumanizing. Alienated work, instead of liberating persons, enslaves them even more. And so it is that when just treatment is asked for the poor, the slaves, and the aliens, it is recalled that Israel also was alien and enslaved in Egypt (Exod. 22:21–23; 23:9; Deut. 10:19; Lev. 19:34).

And finally, humankind not only has been made in the image and likeness of God; it is also *the sacrament of God.*... The other reasons for the Biblical rejection of poverty have their roots here: to oppress the poor is to offend God; to know God is to work justice among human beings. We meet God in our encounter with other persons; what is done for others is done for the Lord.

In a word, the existence of poverty represents a sundering both of solidarity among persons and also of communion with God. Poverty is an expression of a sin, that is, of a negation of love. It is therefore incompatible with the coming of the Kingdom of God, a Kingdom of love and justice.

Poverty is an evil, a scandalous condition, which in our times has taken on enormous proportions. To eliminate it is to bring closer the moment of seeing God face to face, in union with other persons.

POVERTY: SPIRITUAL CHILDHOOD

There is a second line of thinking concerning poverty in the Bible. The poor person is the "client" of Yahweh; poverty is "the ability to welcome God, an openness to God, a willingness to be used by God, a humility before God. . . .

Spiritual poverty finds its highest expression in the Beatitudes of the New Testament. . . . The poverty which is called "blessed" in Matt. 5:1 ("Blessed are the poor in spirit") is spiritual poverty as understood since the time of Zephaniah: to be totally at the disposition of the Lord. This is the precondition for being able to receive the Word of God. It has, therefore, the same meaning as the gospel theme of spiritual childhood. God's communication with us is a gift of love; to receive this gift it is necessary to be poor, a spiritual child. This poverty has no direct relationship to wealth; in the first instance it is not a question of indifference to the goods of this world. It goes deeper than that; it means to have no other sustenance than the will of God. This is the attitude of Christ. Indeed, it is to him that all the Beatitudes fundamentally refer.

In *Luke's* version ("Blessed are you poor" [6:20]) we are faced with greater problems of interpretation. Attempts to resolve these difficulties follow two different lines of thinking. Luke is the evangelist who is most sensitive to social realities. In his Gospel as well as in Acts the themes of material poverty, of goods held in common, and of the condemnation of the rich are frequently treated. This has naturally led to thinking that the poor whom he blesses are the opposite of the rich whom he condemns; the poor would be those who lack what they need. In this case the poverty that he speaks of in the first Beatitude would be *material poverty.*

But this interpretation presents a twofold difficulty. It would lead to the canonization of a social class. The poor would be the privileged of the Kingdom, even to the point of having their access to it assured, not by any choice on their part but by a socio-economic situation which had been imposed on them. Some commentators insist that this would not be evangelical and would be contrary to the intentions of Luke. On the opposite extreme within this interpretation are those who claim to avoid this difficulty and yet preserve the concrete sociological meaning of poverty in Luke. Situating themselves in the perspective of wisdom literature, they say that the first Beatitude opposes the present world to the world beyond; the sufferings of today will be compensated for in the future life. Extraterrestrial salvation is the absolute value which makes the present life insignificant. But this point of view implies purely and simply that Luke is sacralizing misery and injustice and is therefore preaching resignation to it.

Because of these impasses, an explanation is sought from another perspective: Matthew's. Like Matthew, Luke would be referring to *spiritual poverty* or to openness to God. As a concession to the social context of Luke there is in this interpretation an emphasis on real poverty insofar as it is "a privileged path . . . towards poverty of soul."

This second line of interpretation seems to us to minimize the sense of Luke's text. Indeed, it is impossible to avoid the concrete and "material" meaning which the term *poor* has for this evangelist. It refers first of all to those who live in a social situation characterized by a lack of the goods of this world and even by misery and indigence. Even further, it refers to a marginated social group, with connotations of oppression and lack of liberty.

All this leads us to retrace our steps and to reconsider the difficulties—which we have recalled above—in explaining the text of Luke as referring to the materially poor.

"Blessed are you poor for yours is the Kingdom of God" does not mean, it seems to us: "Accept your poverty because later this injustice will be compensated for in the Kingdom of God." If we believe that the Kingdom of God is a gift which is received in history, and if we believe, as the eschatological promises—so charged with human and historical content—indicate to us, that the Kingdom of God necessarily implies the reestablishment of justice in this world, then we must believe that Christ says that the poor are blessed *because* the Kingdom of God has begun: "The time has come; the Kingdom of God is upon you" (Mark 1:15). In other words, the elimination of the exploitation and poverty that prevent the poor from being fully human has begun; a Kingdom of justice which goes even beyond what they could have hoped for has begun. They are blessed because the coming of the Kingdom will put an end to their poverty by creating a world of fellowship. They are blessed because the Messiah will open the eyes of the blind and will give bread to the hungry. Situated in a prophetic perspective, the text in Luke uses the term *poor* in the tradition of the first major line of thought we have studied: poverty is an evil and therefore incompatible with the Kingdom of God, which has come in its fullness into history and embraces the totality of human existence.

AN ATTEMPT AT SYNTHESIS: SOLIDARITY AND PROTEST

Material poverty is a scandalous condition. Spiritual poverty is an attitude of openness to God and spiritual childhood. Having clarified these two meanings of the term *poverty* we have cleared the path and can now move forward towards a better understanding of the Christian witness of poverty. We turn now to a third meaning of the term: poverty as a commitment of solidarity and protest.

We have laid aside the first two meanings. The first is subtly deceptive; the second partial and insufficient. In the first place, if *material poverty* is something to be rejected, as the Bible vigorously insists, then a witness of poverty cannot make of it a Christian ideal. This would be to aspire to a condition which is recognized as degrading to persons. It would be, moreover, to move against the current of history. It would be to oppose any idea of the domination of nature by humans and the consequent and progressive creation of better conditions of life. And finally, but not least seriously, it would be to justify, even if involuntarily, the injustice and exploitation which is the cause of poverty.

On the other hand, our analysis of the Biblical texts concerning *spiritual poverty* has helped us to see that it is not directly or in the first instance an interior detachment from the goods of this world, a spiritual attitude which becomes authentic by incarnating itself in material poverty. Spiritual poverty is something more complete and profound. It is above all total availability to the Lord. Its relationship to the use or ownership of economic goods is inescapable, but secondary and partial. Spiritual childhood—an ability to receive, not a passive acceptance—defines the total posture of human existence before God, persons, and things.

How are we therefore to understand the evangelical meaning of the witness of a real, material, concrete poverty? *Lumen gentium* invites us to look for the deepest meaning of Christian poverty *in Christ*: "Just as Christ carried out the work of redemption in poverty and under oppression, so the Church is called to follow the same path in communicating to others the fruits of salvation. Christ Jesus, though He was by nature God . . . emptied himself, taking the nature of a slave (Phil. 2:6), and being rich, he became poor (2 Cor. 8:9) for our sakes. Thus, although the Church needs human resources to carry out her mission, she is not set up to seek earthly glory, but to proclaim humility and self-sacrifice, even by her own example" (no. 8). The Incarnation is an act of love. Christ became human, died, and rose from the dead to set us free so that we might enjoy freedom (Gal. 5:1). To die and to rise again with Christ is to vanquish death and to enter into a new life (cf. Rom. 6:1–11). The cross and the resurrection are the seal of our liberty.

The taking on of the servile and sinful human condition, as foretold in Second Isaiah, is presented by Paul as an act of voluntary impoverishment: "For you know how generous our Lord Jesus Christ has been: He was rich, yet for your sake he became poor, so that through his poverty you might become rich" (2 Cor. 8:9). This is the humiliation of Christ, his *kenosis* (Phil. 2:6–11). But he does not take on the human sinful condition and its consequences to idealize it. It is rather because of love for and solidarity with others who suffer in it. It is to redeem them from their sin and to enrich them with his poverty. It is to struggle against human selfishness and everything that divides persons and allows that there be rich and poor, possessors and dispossessed, oppressors and oppressed.

Poverty is an act of love and liberation. It has a redemptive value. If the ultimate cause of human exploitation and alienation is selfishness, the deepest reason for voluntary poverty is love of neighbor. Christian poverty has meaning only as a commitment of solidarity with the poor, with those who suffer misery and injustice. The commitment is to witness to the evil which has resulted from sin and is a breach of communion. It is not a question of idealizing poverty, but rather of taking it on as it is—an evil—to protest against it and to struggle to abolish it. As Ricoeur says, you cannot really be with the poor unless you are struggling against poverty. Because of this solidarity—which must manifest itself in specific action, a style of life, a break with one's social class—one can also help the poor and exploited to become aware of their exploitation and seek liberation from it. Christian poverty, an expression of love, is solidarity *with the poor* and is a protest *against* poverty. This is the concrete, contemporary meaning of the witness of poverty. It is a poverty lived not for its own sake, but rather as an authentic imitation of Christ; it is a poverty which means taking on the sinful human condition to liberate humankind from sin and all its consequences.

Luke presents the community of goods in the early Church as an ideal. "All whose faith had drawn them together held everything in common" (Acts 2:44); "not a man of them claimed any of his possessions as his own, but everything was held in common" (Acts 4:33). They did this with a profound unity, one "in heart and soul" (ibid.). But as J. Dupont correctly points out, this was not a question of erecting poverty as an ideal, but rather of seeing to it that there were no poor: "They had never a needy person among them, because all who had property in land or houses sold it, brought the proceeds of the sale, and laid the money at the feet of the apostles; it was then distributed to any who stood in need" (Acts 4:34–35). The meaning of the community of goods is clear: to eliminate poverty because of love of the poor person. Dupont rightly concludes, "If goods are held in common, it is not therefore in order to become poor for love of an ideal of poverty; rather it is so that there will be no poor. The ideal pursued is, once again, charity, a true love for the poor."

We must pay special attention to the words we use. The term *poor* might seem not only vague and churchy, but also somewhat sentimental and aseptic. The "poor" person today is the oppressed one, the one marginated from society, the member of the proletariat struggling for the most basic rights; the exploited and plundered social class, the country struggling for its liberation. In today's world the solidarity and protest of which we are speaking have an evident and inevitable "political" character insofar as they imply liberation. To be with the oppressed is to be against the oppressor. In our times and on our continent to be in solidarity with the "poor," understood in this way, means to run personal risks-even to put one's life in danger. Many Christians—and non-Christians—who are committed to the Latin American revolutionary process are running these risks. And so there are emerging new ways of living poverty which are different from the classic "renunciation of the goods of this world."

Only by rejecting poverty and by making itself poor in order to protest against it can the Church preach something that is uniquely its own: "spiritual poverty," that is, the openness of humankind and history to the future promised by God. Only in this way will the Church be able to fulfill authentically—and with any possibility of being listened to—its prophetic function of denouncing every human injustice. And only in this way will it be able to preach the word which liberates, the word of genuine fellowship.

Only authentic solidarity with the poor and a real protest against the poverty of our time can provide the concrete, vital context necessary for a theological discussion of poverty. The absence of a sufficient commitment to the poor, the marginated, and the exploited is perhaps the fundamental reason why we have no solid contemporary reflection on the witness of poverty.

For the Latin American Church especially, this witness is an inescapable and much-needed sign of the authenticity of its mission.

STUDY QUESTIONS:

1. What differences does Gutierrez elucidate between material and spiritual poverty?
2. What arguments does Gutierrez use to insist that the Church must engage in struggle for social and economic change? What implications does this have for the political role of the Catholic Church?

CAMILO TORRES

10.8 MESSAGE TO CHRISTIANS, 1965

Camilo Torres was one of the most noteworthy Liberation Theology priests. He took up arms to fight for socialist revolution with the guerrilla movement Colombian National Liberation Army (ELN) and died in combat in 1966. The study of sociology played in key role in the development of Torres's revolutionary consciousness: he studied at the Catholic University of Leuven in Belgium and was a cofounder of the Department of Sociology at the National University of Colombia before being dismissed for his radicalism and support of student activism. Torres wrote extensively about the connections between Marxism and Christianity. In this excerpt from a newspaper editorial published shortly after he joined the ELN, Torres outlines his belief that to commitment to social revolution was essential to truly follow the path of Jesus Christ.

Source: John Gerassi (ed.) *Revolutionary Priest: The Complete Writings & Messages of Camilo Torres* (New York: Vintage Books, a Division of Random House).

MESSAGE TO CHRISTIANS

The convulsions caused by the political, religious, and social events of recent times may have sown a great deal of confusion among Colombian Christians. At this decisive moment in our history, we Christians must take a firm stand on the essential bases of our religion.

In Catholicism the main thing is love for one's fellow man: " . . . he who loves his fellow man has fulfilled the Law" (Romans 13:8). For this love to be genuine, it must seek to be effective. If beneficence, alms, the few tuition-free schools, the few housing projects—in general, what is known as "charity"—do not succeed in feeding the hungry majority, clothing the naked, or teaching the unschooled masses, we must seek effective means to achieve the well-being of these majorities. These means will not be sought by the privileged minorities who hold power, because such effective means generally force the minorities to sacrifice their privileges. For example, employment could be increased by investing the capital now leaving Colombia in dollars in the creation of new job opportunities here in the country. But, due to the virtually daily devaluation of the Colombian peso, those with money and power are never going to prohibit currency exportation, because it frees them from devaluation.

Thus, power must be taken from the privileged minorities and given to the poor majorities. If this is done rapidly, it constitutes the essential characteristic of a revolution. The revolution can be a peaceful one if the minorities refrain from violent resistance. Revolution is, therefore, the way to obtain a government that will feed the hungry, clothe the naked, and teach the unschooled. Revolution will produce a government that carries out works of charity, of love for one's fellows—not for only a few but for the majority of our fellow men. This is why the revolution is not only permissible but obligatory for those Christians who see it as the only effective and far-reaching way to make the love of all people a reality. It is true that "there exists no authority except from God" (Romans 13:1). But St. Thomas teaches that it is the people who concretely have the right to authority.

When the existing authority is against the people, it is not legitimate, and we call it a tyranny. We Christians can and must fight against tyranny. The present government is tyrannical because it receives the support of only twenty percent of the voters and because its decisions emanate from the privileged minorities.

The temporal defects of the church must not shock us. The church is human. The important thing is to believe that it is also divine and that if we Christians fulfill our obligation to love our fellow man, we are thereby strengthening the church.

I have given up the duties and privileges of the clergy, but I have not ceased to be a priest. I believe that I have given myself to the revolution out of love for my fellow man. I have ceased to say Mass to practice love for my fellow man in the temporal, economic, and social spheres. When my fellow man has nothing against me, when he has carried out the revolution, then I will return to offering Mass, God permitting. I think that in this way I follow Christ's injunction: "Therefore, if thou art offering thy gift at the altar, and there rememberest that thy brother has anything against thee, leave thy gift before the altar and go first to be reconciled to thy brother, and then come and offer thy gift" (Matthew 5:23–24). After the revolution we Colombians will be aware that we are establishing a system oriented toward the love of our neighbor. The struggle is long; let us begin now.

STUDY QUESTIONS

1. Why is revolution in Colombia so essential to living in true accordance with Christianity according to Torres? On what basis does Torres separate Christian principles from the structure of the Catholic Church?
2. In what ways does sociological theory inform Torres's argument that poverty is inconsistent with Christianity?
3. What are the implications of Torres's writings for our understanding of the relationship between Christianity and Marxism?

10.9 THE PUERTO RICAN WOMAN: OBJECT OF POPULATION CONTROL, 1976

In the United States and Europe, second-wave feminism was deeply intertwined with support for birth control and family planning. In contrast, in many parts of Latin America, reproductive politics were more complicated, and birth control was often viewed as advancing US imperialism, a reflection of US policy concern with population growth in the developing world. In Puerto Rico, in particular, many feminists were openly hostile to birth control initiatives, as a result of controversial US medical experimentation with the contraceptive pill and intrauterine devices in the island from the 1940s through the 1970s. This excerpt comes from a resolution presented by a group of Puerto Rican feminists at the International Tribunal of Crimes Against Women, a UN conference held in Brussels in 1976.

We present before the INTERNATIONAL TRIBUNAL OF CRIMES AGAINST WOMEN the case of the women of Puerto Rico.

WE ACCUSE the United States of America, a state by which our country is dominated.

WE ACCUSE, simultaneously, their intermediaries on the island, and the exploitative economic interests that both represent:

FIRST: they denied us the right to use our bodies, using us as objects for their population control plans without the least respect for our integrity as human beings.

SECOND: they experimented on us Puerto Rican women with drugs that are still in an experimental stage as if we were guinea pigs or laboratory animals.

THIRD: they sterilized 35 percent of the female population of reproductive age.

FOURTH: they burdened Puerto Rican women with the sole responsibility for population control, at the same time benefitting from and perpetuating machista values in our society.

FIFTH: they assured the interests of great economic powers at the expense of women

SIXTH: they united the cultural premise of the Puerto Rican people that the women is solely responsible for procreation [and] the belief that the excess population is the direct cause of poverty, directing as a result all methods of birth control to the use of women.

STUDY QUESTIONS

1. What arguments do these women use to support their assertion that the history of birth control in Puerto Rico represented an international crime against women?
2. Why does birth control perpetuate male-dominated, or *machista* values, according to this resolution?
3. What alternative development strategies does the resolution argue would be more advantageous to women than the expansion of birth control?

Source: "The Puerto Rican Woman: Object of Population Control," Presentation of Mujer Integrante Ahora to the International Tribunal of Crimes Against Women, Brussels, March 1976. In *Documentos del feminismo en Puerto Rico: Fascimiles de la historia* (University of Puerto Rico Press, 2001), pp. 296–306.
Translation: Nicola Foote.

CHAPTER 11

COUNTERREVOLUTION IN LATIN AMERICA, 1960–1980

11.1 MEMORANDUM OF CONVERSATION, BY THE ASSISTANT SECRETARY OF STATE FOR INTER-AMERICAN AFFAIRS (CABOT)

US intervention in Guatemala in 1954 represents one of the most notorious and consequential moments of Cold War US–Latin American relations. It occurred in response to a major land reform program initiated in 1952 by President Jacobo Arbenz. Notably, Arbenz was a democratically elected and moderate leftist, but his commitment to redistribution of land led to US allegations that the regime was in fact communist and would sponsor the spread of communism and Soviet influence throughout Latin America. Tensions between Arbenz and the US government were further heightened by the impact of land reform on the United Fruit Company (UFCO, the dominant banana company, operating today as Chiquita). Uncultivated land held by the UFCO was expropriated and compensated based on the value the company had claimed in their tax returns. Yet the UFCO claimed that their land was worth more, and company officials pushed the US government to intervene on their behalf. This UFCO pressure played a key role in pushing forward the 1954 CIA-sponsored coup that deposed Arbenz and ushered in decades of military repression in Guatemala. This memorandum recounts a conversation between the Guatemalan ambassador to the United States and the American assistant secretary of state for Inter-American Affairs. It provides important contextualization for the intervention.

SUBJECT

Farewell Call on President by Guatemalan Ambassador In a briefing memorandum for the President concerning Ambassador Toriello's visit, dated Jan. 15, 1954, Under Secretary of State Smith stated in part the following:

"Last month President Arbenz told Ambassador Peurifoy Guatemalan Communists are 'honest,' follow Guatemalan not Soviet interests, and visit Moscow to study Marxism, not to get instructions. Guatemalan Communists are in fact disciplined agents of international Communism, preaching authentic

Source: National Archives and Records Administration, RG 59, Central File 611.14/1-1654. Confidential. https://2001-2009. state.gov/r/pa/ho/frus/ike/iv/20210.htm

Soviet-dictated doctrine and openly affiliated with numerous international Communist labor and front groups.

"We have repeatedly expressed deep concern to the Guatemalan Government because it plays the Communist game. Our relations are further disturbed because of the merciless hounding of American companies there by tax and labor demands, strikes, and, in the case of the United Fruit Company, inadequately compensated seizures of land under a Communist-administered Agrarian Reform Law." (Eisenhower Library, Eisenhower Papers, Whitman File, International Series, "Guatemala")

PARTICIPANTS
The President
Señor Dr. Don Guillermo Toriello,
Ambassador of Guatemala
Mr. John M. Cabot, Assistant Secretary

The Guatemalan Ambassador called on the President to say farewell before returning to Guatemala to become Foreign Minister.

Following an exchange of courtesies, the President made a reference to relations between the United States and Guatemala. The Ambassador seized on this to peddle to the President his oft-told tale of how Guatemala is a victim of "calumny." He said there were communists in Guatemala but they occupied only a few insignificant positions in the Government. Guatemala had always suffered from dictators but since 1944 it had had a democratic government which was undertaking much needed reforms, notably the agrarian reform.

The President said we had no wish to dominate any country. We regarded our Latin neighbors as sovereign equals, and did not try to interfere in their affairs. In consequence they had always been independent. We hated communism. The President contrasted the status of our neighbors with that of Poland and Czechoslovakia and the Baltic states. Soviet communism was the worst dictatorship the world had ever known, and we were determined to block the international communist conspiracy. We certainly had the impression that the Guatemalan Government was infiltrated with communists, and we couldn't cooperate with a Government which openly favored communists.

The Guatemalan Ambassador pleaded for greater cooperation. The armed forces had not been infiltrated, yet they couldn't get ammunition. The Guatemalan airline couldn't get a permanent contract. The effect of all this was to help the communists. If we helped the Guatemalans more, they would soon get rid of the communists.

The President said that we really couldn't help a government which was openly playing ball with communists. The people of the United States hated communism and if we helped them there would be a coup against him (this laughingly).

The Ambassador said that the real question was not that of communists in the Guatemalan Government, but of the monopolistic position of the United Fruit in the country. The Ambassador brought out a little map of Guatemala to show the United Fruit's stranglehold on ports, railways, etc. He went into his usual discreetly distorted indictment of the United Fruit and insisted that this, and not communism in the Government, was the source of the difficulties in relations between the United States and Guatemala. He also brought out two scrapbooks of anti-Guatemalan articles published in the U.S. press.

The President said that we certainly wanted no more than justice for any American companies operating in Guatemala. We would be agreeable to having an international tribunal decide what the rights of the controversy were. Moreover, we realized that contracts made many years ago were subject to revision under changing circumstances.

The Ambassador continued to harp on the line that the United Fruit, and not the few Guatemalan communists, were the source of our difficulties in relations. Mr. Cabot interjected that avowed communists occupied key positions in the National Agrarian Department, the official press and radio, and other government agencies, and that the highest officials of the Guatemalan Government were openly supporting them and listening to their advice.

The Ambassador continued to press his argument with skill. He particularly mentioned that Sullivan & Cromwell, the Secretary of State's former firm, represented the United Fruit. The President by this point had risen to indicate the interview was ended. Mr. Cabot, thinking the Ambassador had charged that he had stock in the United Fruit, pointed out that this was untrue.

The President asked about the charges against the United Fruit. Mr. Cabot said there were certainly two sides to that question. The Ambassador said that they paid no taxes, just one cent per stem on bananas. He also mentioned that no immediate compensation had been given for the United Fruit lands seized. The President suggested that perhaps this could be settled by an international judgment, perhaps headed by a Latin American. Mr. Cabot pointed out that we had proposed action along these lines, but Guatemala considered this a matter of sovereignty.

The entire conversation, which lasted half an hour, was in personally friendly terms. The Ambassador presented his case very persuasively—with skillful emphasis and suppression. The President made a very able and convincing exposition of our thesis that the issue is communism in the Guatemalan Government, not the United Fruit question, and that the latter can be decided by international decision.

STUDY QUESTIONS

1. What are the differences between the way in which Guatemalan and US officials understand and represent the issues surrounding the United Fruit Company operations in Guatemala?
2. What evidence does the memorandum provide of the mindset of top-ranking US officials in the run-up to the coup of 1954? How clearly are their intentions to intervene telegraphed to Guatemalan leaders? What is the central basis for American concern about Guatemalan politics?

ERNESTO CARDENAL

11.2 SOMOZA UNVEILS SOMOZA'S STATUE OF SOMOZA AT THE SOMOZA STADIUM, 1961

Ernesto Cardenal (b. 1925) is a Nicaraguan poet, Catholic priest, and political leader. His widely read and influential poetry is notable for its advancement of revolutionary ideals and values and its fervent anti-imperialism. In the 1950s, Cardenal was involved in an armed uprising against the Somoza dictatorship. He became an active member of the Sandinista National Liberation Front (FLSN) when it was formed in 1961, later serving as minister of culture in the Sandinista government. This poem was written while Cardenal was studying theology in exile from Nicaragua. It provides a strong critique of the cult of personality that underpinned Somoza's dictatorship.

It's not that I think the people raised this statue
   to me,
because I know better than you that I ordered it
   myself.

Nor that I have any illusions about passing with it
   into posterity
because I know the people will one day tear it
   down.

Source: "Somoza Unveils Somoza's Statue of Somoza at the Somoza Stadium," by Ernesto Cardenal. Taken from: The Art Divas (http://www.theartdivas.com/). Blog of Rabih Alameddine, http://www.theartdivas.com/2016/11/somoza-unveils-somozas-statue-of-somoza.html. Translated by Donald Walsh.

Nor that I wished to erect to myself in life
the monument you'll not erect to me in death:

I put up this statue just because I know you'll
hate it.

STUDY QUESTIONS

1. What strategies does Cardenal use in his poem to criticize the Somoza regime? How effective is the poem at presenting a political argument?
2. What insight can we gain from the poem provide as to why the Somoza regime—in common with other authoritarian regimes in Latin America—would be so hostile to cultural and literary activists?

JOHN F. KENNEDY

11.3 THE ALLIANCE FOR PROGRESS, 1961

One of the most notable foreign policy initiatives of John F. Kennedy's brief presidency was his effort to establish more positive collaborative relationships between the United States and Latin America. Responding to concerns about the radicalization of the left in Latin America in the aftermath of the Cuban Revolution, Kennedy proposed a Ten-Year Plan of sustained US investment to stimulate economic growth and promote democracy in the region, which he envisaged as a "Marshall Plan" for Latin America. The main rationale for the program was to stem the spread of communism in Latin America through moderate reforms that would allow a wider range of Latin American people to have a stake in capitalist development. Through the Alliance for Progress, Kennedy promised billions of dollars in foreign aid and corporate investment to improve education, land use, healthcare, and infrastructure. The speech excerpted here was delivered by Kennedy at a White House Reception for Members of Congress and the Diplomatic Corps of the Latin American Republics in March 1961 and lays out the parameters and rationale for the program.

March 13, 1961

It is a great pleasure for Mrs. Kennedy and for me, for the Vice President and Mrs. Johnson, and for the Members of Congress, to welcome the Ambassadorial Corps of our Hemisphere, our long time friends, to the White House today. One hundred and thirty-nine years ago this week the United States, stirred by the heroic struggle of its fellow Americans, urged the independence and recognition of the new Latin American Republics. It was then, at the dawn of freedom throughout this hemisphere, that Bolivar spoke of his desire to see the Americas fashioned into the greatest region in the world, "greatest," he said,

Source: "John F. Kennedy Speeches: Address at a White House Reception for Members of Congress and for the Diplomatic Corps of the Latin American Republics, March 13, 1961," John F. Kennedy Presidential Library & Museum. https://www.jfklibrary.org/Research/Research-Aids/JFK-Speeches/Latin-American-Diplomats-Washington-DC_19610313.aspx

"not so much by virtue of her area and her wealth, as by her freedom and her glory."

Never in the long history of our hemisphere has this dream been nearer to fulfillment, and never has it been in greater danger.

The genius of our scientists has given us the tools to bring abundance to our land, strength to our industry, and knowledge to our people. For the first time we have the capacity to strike off the remaining bonds of poverty and ignorance—to free our people for the spiritual and intellectual fulfillment which has always been the goal of our civilization.

Yet at this very moment of maximum opportunity, we confront the same forces which have imperiled America throughout its history—the alien forces which once again seek to impose the despotisms of the Old World on the people of the New.

I have asked you to come here today so that I might discuss these challenges and these dangers.

We meet together as firm and ancient friends, united by history and experience and by our determination to advance the values of American civilization. For this New World of ours is not a mere accident of geography. Our continents are bound together by a common history, the endless exploration of new frontiers. Our nations are the product of a common struggle, the revolt from colonial rule. And our people share a common heritage, the quest for the dignity and the freedom of man.

The revolutions which gave us birth ignited, in the words of Thomas Paine, "a spark never to be extinguished." And across vast, turbulent continents these American ideals still stir man's struggle for national independence and individual freedom. But as we welcome the spread of the American Revolution to other lands, we must also remember that our own struggle—the revolution which began in Philadelphia in 1776, and In Caracas in 1811—is not yet finished. Our hemisphere's mission is not yet completed. For our unfulfilled task is to demonstrate to the entire world that man's unsatisfied aspiration for economic progress and social justice can best be achieved by free men working within a framework of democratic institutions. If we can do this in our own hemisphere, and for our own people, we may yet realize the prophecy of the great Mexican patriot, Benito Juarez, that "democracy is the destiny of future humanity."

As a citizen of the United States let me be the first to admit that we North Americans have not always grasped the significance of this common mission, just as it is also true that many in your own countries have not fully understood the urgency of the need to lift people from poverty and ignorance and despair. But we must turn from these mistakes—from the failures and the misunderstandings of the past to a future full of peril, but bright with hope.

Throughout Latin America, a continent rich in resources and in the spiritual and cultural achievements of its people, millions of men and women suffer the daily degradations of poverty and hunger. They lack decent shelter or protection from disease. Their children are deprived of the education or the jobs which are the gateway to a better life. And each day the problems grow more urgent. Population growth is outpacing economic growth—low living standards are further endangered and discontent—the discontent of a people who know that abundance and the tools of progress are at last within their reach—that discontent is growing. In the words of Jose Figueres, "once dormant peoples are struggling upward toward the sun, toward a better life."

If we are to meet a problem so staggering in its dimensions, our approach must itself be equally bold—an approach consistent with the majestic concept of Operation Pan America. Therefore I have called on all people of the hemisphere to join In a new Alliance for Progress—Alianza para Progreso—a vast cooperative effort, unparalleled in magnitude and nobility of purpose, to satisfy the basic needs of the American people for homes, work and land, health and schools—techo, trabajo y tierra, salud y escuela.

First, I propose that the American Republics begin on a vast new Ten Year Plan for the Americas, a plan to transform the 1960's into a historic decade of democratic progress.

These 10 years will be the years of maximum progress–maximum effort, the years when the greatest obstacles must be overcome, the years when the need for assistance will be the greatest.

And if we are successful, if our effort is bold enough and determined enough, then the close of this decade will mark the beginning of a new era in the American experience. The living standards of every American family will be on the rise, basic education will be available to all, hunger will be a forgotten ex-perience, the need for massive outside help will have passed, most nations will have entered a period of self-sustaining growth, and though there will be still much to do, every American Republic will be the master of its own revolution and its own hope and progress.

Let me stress that only the most determined efforts of the American nations themselves can bring suc-cess to this effort. They, and they alone, can mobilize their resources, enlist the energies of their people, and modify their social patterns so that all, and not just a privileged few, share in the fruits of growth. If this effort is made, then outside assistance will give vital impetus to progress; without it, no amount of help will advance the welfare of the people.

Thus if the countries of Latin America are ready to do their part, and I am sure they are, then I believe the United States, for its part, should help provide resources of a scope and magnitude sufficient to make this bold development plan a success—just as we helped to pro-vide, against equal odds nearly, the resources adequate to help rebuild the economies of Western Europe. For only an effort of towering dimensions can ensure ful-fillment of our plan for a decade of progress.

Secondly, I will shortly request a ministerial meeting of the Inter-American Economic and Social Council, a meeting at which we can begin the massive planning effort which will be at the heart of the Alliance for Progress.

For if our Alliance is to succeed, each Latin nation must formulate long-range plans for its own devel-opment, plans which establish targets and priorities, ensure monetary stability, establish the machinery for vital social change, stimulate private activity and initia-tive, and provide for a maximum national effort. These plans will be the foundation of our development effort, and the basis for the allocation of outside resources.

A greatly strengthened IA-ECOSOC working With the Economic Commission for Latin America and the Inter-American Development Bank, can assemble the leading economists and experts of the hemisphere to help each country develop its own development plan—and provide a continuing review of economic progress in this hemisphere.

Third, I have this evening signed a request to the Congress for $500 million as a first step in fulfilling

the Act of Bogotá. This is the first large-scale inter-American effort, instituted by my predecessor President Eisenhower, to attack the social barriers which block economic progress. The money will be used to combat illiteracy, improve the productivity and use of their land, wipe out disease, attack archaic tax and land tenure structures, provide educational opportunities, and offer a broad range of projects designed to make the benefits of increasing abundance available to all. We will begin to commit these funds as soon as they are appropriated.

Fourth, we must support all economic integration which is a genuine step toward larger markets and greater competitive opportunity. The fragmentation of Latin American economies is a serious barrier to in-dustrial growth. Projects such as the Central American common market and free trade areas in South America can help to remove these obstacles.

Fifth, the United States is ready to cooperate in serious, case-by-case examinations of commodity market problems. Frequent violent changes in com-modity prices seriously injure the economies of many Latin American countries, draining their resources and stultifying their growth. Together we must find practi-cal methods of bringing an end to this pattern.

Sixth, we will immediately step up our Food for Peace emergency program, help establish food re-serves in areas of recurrent drought, help provide school lunches for children, and offer feed grains for use in rural development. For hungry men and women cannot wait for economic discussions or diplomatic meetings—their need is urgent—and their hunger rests heavily on the conscience of their fellow men.

Seventh, all the people of the hemisphere must be allowed to share in the expanding wonders of science—wonders which have captured man's imagination, chal-lenged the powers of his mind, and given him the tools for rapid progress. I invite Latin American scientists to work with us in new projects in fields such as medicine and agriculture, physics and astronomy, and desalini-zation, to help plan for regional research laboratories in these and other fields, and to strengthen coopera-tion between American universities and laboratories.

We also intend to expand our science teacher training programs to include Latin American instruc-tors, to assist in establishing such programs in other American countries, and translate and make available revolutionary new teaching materials in physics, chemistry, biology, and mathematics, so that the young of all nations may contribute their skills to the advance of science.

Eighth, we must rapidly expand the training of those needed to man the economies of rapidly developing countries. This means expanded technical training programs, for which the Peace Corps, for example, will be available when needed. It also means assistance to Latin American universities, graduate schools, and research institutes.

We welcome proposals in Central America for intimate cooperation in higher education—cooperation which can achieve a regional effort or increased effectiveness and excellence. We are ready to help fill the gap in trained manpower, realizing that our ultimate goal must be a basic education for all who wish to learn.

Ninth, we reaffirm our pledge to come to the defense of any American nation whose independence is endangered. As its confidence in the collective security system of the OAS spreads, it will be possible to devote to constructive use a major share of those resources now spent on the instruments of war. Even now, as the government of Chile has said, the time has come to take the first steps toward sensible limitations of arms. And the new generation of military leaders has shown an increasing awareness that armies cannot only defend their countries—they can, as we have learned through our own Corps of Engineers, they can help to build them.

Tenth, we invite our friends in Latin America to contribute to the enrichment of life and culture in the United States. We need teachers of your literature and history and tradition, opportunities for our young people to study in your universities, access to your music, your art, and the thought of your great philosophers. For we know we have much to learn.

In this way you can help bring a fuller spiritual and intellectual life to the people of the United States—and contribute to understanding and mutual respect among the nations of the hemisphere.

With steps such as these, we propose to complete the revolution of the Americas, to build a hemisphere where all men can hope for a suitable standard of living, and all can live out their lives in dignity and in freedom.

To achieve this goal political freedom must accompany material progress. Our Alliance for Progress is an alliance of free governments, and it must work to eliminate tyranny from a hemisphere in which it has no rightful place. Therefore let us express our special friendship to the people of Cuba and the Dominican Republic—and the hope they will soon rejoin, the society of free men, uniting with us in common effort.

This political freedom must be accompanied by social change. For unless necessary social reforms, including land and tax reform, are freely made—unless we broaden the opportunity for all of our people—unless the great mass of Americans share in increasing prosperity—then our alliance, our revolution, our dream, and our freedom will fail. But we call for social change by free men, change in the spirit of Washington and Jefferson, of Bolivar and San Martin and Martin—not change which seeks to impose on men tyrannies which we cast out a century and a half ago. Our motto is what it has always been—progress yes, tyranny no—progreso si, tirania no!

But our greatest challenge comes from within—the task of creating an American civilization where spiritual and cultural values are strengthened by an ever-broadening base of material advance—where, within the rich diversity of its own traditions, each nation is free to follow its own path towards progress.

The completion of our task will, of course, require the efforts of all governments of our hemisphere. But the efforts of governments alone will never be enough. In the end, the people must choose and the people must help themselves.

And so I say to the men and women of the Americas—to the campesino in the fields, to the obrero in the cities, to the estudiante in the schools—prepare your mind and heart for the task ahead—call forth your strength and let each devote his energies to the betterment of all, so that your children and our children in this hemisphere can find an ever richer and a freer life.

Let us once again transform the American continent into a vast crucible of revolutionary ideas and efforts—a tribute to the power of the creative energies of free men and women—an example to all the world that liberty and progress walk hand in hand. Let us once again awaken our American revolution until it guides the struggle of people everywhere—not with an imperialism of force or fear—but the rule of courage and freedom and hope for the future of man.

STUDY QUESTIONS

1. Why does Kennedy see widespread poverty as a threat to democracy in Latin America? What examples does he use to bolster his argument?
2. Why is Latin American development essential to the future of the United States, according to Kennedy?
3. What are the most urgent problems Kennedy intended the Alliance for Progress to solve? What are the potential weaknesses of the solutions he proposes?

11.4 THE BRAZILIAN CONSTITUTION OF 1967

In 1964 the democratically elected left-wing government of João Goulart was overthrown in a military coup supported by the United States. A military junta was established to run the country, and would remain in power until 1985. The rationale for the imposition of military rule was that "internal enemies" and "subversives" (communist guerrillas) threatened the national security of Brazil. The military government would commit widespread human rights abuses, including the torture and extrajudicial murder of alleged dissidents, in the name of extirpating leftist radicalism. Notably, the repressive tactics pursued by the Brazilian military regime were enshrined in legal codes: rather than acting outside of legal norms, the junta simply changed laws and the constitution to support the tactics they deployed. This strategy of legalization of state repression can be seen most notably in the 1967 Constitution, which gave the armed forces extraordinary powers and significantly restricted the civil and political rights of the citizenry.

EXCERPTS FROM THE 1967 BRAZILIAN CONSTITUTION

National Organization—The Union's Jurisdiction

Art. 8—It behooves the union . . .

III—to decree a state of siege . . .

VII—to organize and maintain the federal police for the purpose of providing . . .

> c) investigation of penal violations against national security, political and social order, or detrimental to the union's property, services, and interests, as well as other violations, the

practice of which has interstate repercussions and requires uniform suppression, as provided by law;

> d) censorship of public entertainment . . .

Political Rights

Art. 142—The electors shall be Brazilians of more than eighteen years of age, registered in accordance with the law.

Par. I—Registration and voting are obligatory for Brazilians of both sexes, saving the exceptions established by law . . .

Source: "Excerpts from the 1967 Brazilian Constitution," courtesy of the Embassy of Brazil, Washington, DC, 1968.

Par. 3—The following may not register as electors:

a) the illiterate;
b) those who do not know how to express themselves in the national language;
c) those who have been deprived, temporarily or permanently, of political rights.

Art. 143—Suffrage is universal, and the vote is direct and secret, saving in the cases provided in this Constitution; proportional representation of the political parties is assured in the form the law may establish.

Art. 144—Besides the cases provided in this Constitution, political rights:

I—shall be suspended:

a) for absolute civil incapacity;
b) by reason of criminal conviction, while its effects shall last . . .

II—shall be lost . . .

b) for a refusal, based on religious, philosophical, or political conviction, to perform a duty or service imposed on Brazilians in general . . .

Par. 1—In the cases of item no. II of this Article, the loss of political rights determines the loss of elective mandate, and public office or function; and the suspension of these rights, in the cases provided in this Article, entails the suspension of elective mandate, public office, or function, for as long as the causes that determined the loss shall last.

Par. 2—The suspension or loss of political rights shall be decreed by the president of the republic in the cases of Article 141, I and II, and of this Article, no. II, "b" and "c"; and, in the others, by a judicial sentence, ample defense being always assured to the defendant. State of Siege

Art. 152—The president of the republic may decree a state of siege in case of:

I—grave disturbance or [dis]order, or threat of its outbreak . . .

Par. I—The decree of martial law shall specify the regions to be included, appoint the persons entrusted with its execution, and the norms to be observed.

Par. 2—Martial law authorizes the following coercive measures:

a) obligation to live in a given locality;

b) detention in buildings not destined for persons accused of common crimes;
c) search and arrest in homes;
d) suspension of the freedom of assembly and of that of association;
e) censorship of correspondence, of the press, of telecommunications, and public entertainment;
f) temporary use and occupation of the property of autonomous government enterprises, mixed-economy companies, or concessionaires of public services, as well as the suspension of the exercise of an office, function, or employment in these entities.

Par. 3—In order to preserve the integrity and independence of the country, the free working of the powers and the practice of the institutions, when they are gravely threatened by factors of subversion or corruption, the president of the republic, after hearing the National Security Council, may take other measures established in law.

Art. 153—The duration of martial law, except in the case of war, shall not be greater than sixty days and may be extended for an equal length of time.

Par. I—In any event, the president of the republic shall submit his act to the National Congress, together with its justification, within five days.

Par. 2—If the National Congress is not assembled, it shall be immediately convened by the president of the Federal Senate.

Art. 154—While martial law is in effect, and without prejudice to other measures provided in Article 151, the National Congress may also, by means of law, determine the suspension of constitutional guarantees.

Sole Par.—During martial law, the immunities of federal deputies and senators may be suspended, by secret vote of two-thirds of the members of the house to which the congressman belongs.

Art. 155—Martial law ending, its effects shall cease and the president of the republic, within thirty days, shall send a message to the National Congress with a justification of the measures adopted.

Art. 156—The nonobservance of any of the provisions relative to martial law shall render the constraint illegal and shall allow victims thereof to appeal to the judicial power.

STUDY QUESTIONS

1. In what ways were political rights limited by the 1967 constitution? How were these restrictions connected to the war on radicalism?
2. What extraordinary powers did the military government grant itself through the decree relating to a state of siege? To what extent did these powers facilitate human rights abuses?

ELENA PONIATOWSKA

11.5 *MASSACRE IN MEXICO, 1971*

Elena Poniatowska (b. 1932) is a French-born Mexican journalist and writer who rose to prominence as a social critic and testimonial author in the 1960s. *Massacre in Mexico* is one of her most famous and important works, and provides a deep investigative account of the Tlateloco Massacre of October 2, 1968, in which hundreds of student protesters were killed by the Mexican military and police in a plaza in a residential neighborhood of Mexico City. The massacre occurred just ten days before the opening of the Mexico City Summer Olympic Games, and the Mexican government sought to suppress news of the massacre, insisting that only a small number of people had been killed, and blaming protesters for the violence. Poniatowska's work was crucial in providing a counternarrative: she interviewed hundreds of eyewitnesses in the immediate aftermath and the months that followed, and published their in-depth testimonies. The excerpts presented here include testimonies from student participants in the protest; residents of the apartment buildings surrounding the plaza who were witnesses to the massacre and whose homes were invaded by police; and mothers of students who were missing after the protest and who had to search for their bodies in city morgues.

. . . . I couldn't understand why the crowd kept heading back toward where the men in the white gloves were shooting at them. Meche and I hid there behind a pillar watching the crowd coming toward us, shouting and moaning, being fired on, running away in the opposite direction, and then immediately coming back our way again, falling to the ground, running away again, and then coming back and falling to the ground again. The whole thing just didn't make sense: whatever were they doing? A whole great crowd was running first in one direction and then another: they'd run away and then head back our way again, and more of them would fall on the

ground. I thought they should all have sense enough to keep away from the men who were shooting at them, but they kept coming back. I found out later that they were also being shot at from the other side of the Plaza.

Margarita Nolasco, anthropologist

The Army units approached from all directions and encircled the crowd in a pincers movement, and in just a few moments all the exits were blocked off. From up there on the fourth floor of the Chihuahua building, where the speakers' platform had been set up, we couldn't see what the Army was up to and we couldn't

Source: Elena Poniatowska, *Massacre in Mexico*, Reprint edition (Columbia: University of Missouri Press, 1991), pp. 212–214, 219–228, 248, 268, 295–299.

understand why the crowd was panicking. The two helicopters that had been hovering over the Plaza almost from the very beginning of the meeting had suddenly started making very hostile maneuvers, flying lower and lower in tighter and tighter circles just above the heads of the crowd, and then they had launched two flares, a green one first and then a red one; when the second one went off the panic started, and we members of the Committee did our best to stop it: none of us there on the speakers' stand could see that the Army troops below us were advancing across the Plaza. When they found themselves confronted by a wall of bayonets, the crowd halted and immediately drew back; then we saw a great wave of people start running toward the other side of the Plaza; but there were Army troops on the other side of the Plaza too; and as we stood watching from up there on the speakers' stand, we saw the whole crowd head in another direction. That was the last thing we saw down below, for at that moment the fourth floor was taken over by the Olimpia Battalion. Even though we had no idea why the crowd had panicked and was running first in one direction and then in the other, those of us who had remained there at the microphone till the very last found ourselves looking down the barrels of machine guns when we turned around. The balcony had been occupied by the Olimpia Battalion and we were ordered to put our hands up and face the wall, and given strict orders not to turn around in the direction of the Plaza; if we so much as moved a muscle, they hit us over the head or in the ribs with their rifle butts. Once the trap they had set snapped shut, the collective murder began.

Gilberta Guevara Niebla, of the CNH

There was nothing we could do but keep running. They were firing at us from all directions. We ran six or eight feet, keeping under cover, and then ten or twelve feet out in the open. Rifle fire sounds very much like a jet taking off. There was nothing to do but keep running. We heard the display windows of the shops on the ground floor of the Chihuahua building shatter, and we suddenly decided we ought to make a run for the stairway. As I stood down there, babbling all sorts of nonsense, I also suddenly remembered all my many friends and comrades at the meeting and got terrible cramps in my stomach. I remembered names, faces. As I reached this stairway that the people from the CNH who were going to speak had been going up and down all during the afternoon, I met Margarita and Meche, who said to me in the most despairing tone of voice, "Maria Alicia, our children are up there on the fourth floor!"

For the first time I had the feeling I might be able to do something useful amid all this confusion and suffering, despite my sense of utter helplessness, and I said to them, "I'll go up there with you."

The youngster who had saved my life—by leaping on me and throwing me to the floor there on the speakers' stand when they first started shooting at us—went upstairs with us: he was my armor, my cape, my shield. I have no idea who he was. I have a photographic memory, but I can't remember his face at all. . . . . The three of us started up the stairs, and on the first landing we met another youngster. I had seen him on the speakers' stand there on the fourth floor of the Chihuahua building, too, talking with various Movement people as though he knew them very well. I remember him particularly because he'd apparently been wounded in the right wrist and had a white handkerchief wrapped around his hand.

"Don't leave, *señora*, it'll all be over soon," he said to me.

I was about to go downstairs again, because I'd spied some girl friends of mine down on the esplanade. But the boy took me by the arm and very solicitously helped me up the stairs. I was touched by this courageous behavior on the part of yet another student hero, and went upstairs with him.

Then Mercedes shouted, *"Señor,* my children are there upstairs!"

Margarita shouted that her children were up there too, and I stopped there on the stairs and looked at the youngster escorting me, thinking that the courage of those kids is really incredible sometimes. Many hours later, I discovered that my escort was one of the assassins guarding the stairway so that none of the CNH people would escape. He took us back downstairs then, and I remember that we were caught up in a whole crowd of people and shoved to the corner of the Chihuahua building, and that meanwhile there was a steady hail of bullets from the buildings.

A girl came by shouting, "You murderers, you murderers!" I took her in my arms and tried to calm her down, but she kept screaming, louder and louder, until finally the youngster behind me grabbed hold of her and started shaking her. I noticed then that her ear had been shot off and her head was bleeding. The people in the crowd kept piling one on top of another, seeking shelter from the rain of bullets; we were all right on each other's necks, and I felt as though I were caught in the middle of a riot or squeezed in a sardine can.

I stood there staring at the tips of the coffee-colored shoes of some woman. Several rounds of machine-gun bullets suddenly raked the spot where we were standing, and I saw one bullet land just a few inches from that woman's shoe. All she said was, "Oh, my goodness!" and another voice answered, "Make a run for it. If you stay here you'll be even worse off; you're sure to get hurt here." We all started running again and just then I spied a red Datsun with a young girl at the wheel. She'd been shot, and I saw her collapse on top of the steering wheel; the horn kept blowing and blowing. . . . The youngster kept saying, "Don't look, don't look." We ran on toward one of the buildings behind Chihuahua. . . .

Maria Alicia Martinez Medrano, nursery-school director

I tugged at my brother's arm. "Julio, what's the matter?" I asked him. I tugged at his arm again; his eyes were half closed and there was a very sad look in them. And I heard him murmur the words "I think . . ."

My mind was a total blank. The tremendous crush of people screaming in panic made it hard for me to hear what he was saying. I thought later that if I'd known, if I'd realized that Julio was dying, I would have done something absolutely crazy right then and there.

Later some of the soldiers who had been shooting at the buildings around the Plaza came over to us. The smell of gunpowder was unbearable. Little by little people made room for me so I could kneel down beside Julio.

"Julio, Julio, answer me, little brother," I said to him. "He must be wounded," one woman said to me. "Loosen his belt."

When I loosened it, I could feel a great big wound. I found out later at the hospital that he had three bullet wounds: one in the stomach, one in the neck, and another in the leg. He was dying.

Diana Salmerón de Contreras

"Hey, little brother, what's the matter? Answer me, little brother. . . ."

Diana Salmerón de Contreras

The hail of bullets being fired at the Chihuahua building became so intense that around seven p.m. a large section of the building caught on fire.

The fire burned for a long time. All the floors from the tenth to the thirteenth were enveloped in flames, and many families were forced to leave the unit, amid the heavy gunfire, carrying their children in their arms and risking their lives. We also saw many others struck by bullets fall to the ground.

Jorge Aviles R., in a story entitled "Serious Fighting for Hours between Terrorists and RSoldiers," El Universal, October 3, 1968

"Little brother, speak to me. . . . Please, somebody get him a stretcher! . . . I'm right here, Julio. . . . Soldier, a / stretcher for somebody who's been wounded. . . . What's the matter, little brother? . . . . Answer me, little brother. . . . A stretcher! . . .

Diana Salmerón de Contreras

A number of dead bodies lying in the Plaza de las Tres Culturas. Dozens of wounded. Hysterical women with their children in their arms. Shattered windows. Burned-out apartments. The outer doors of the buildings destroyed. Water pipes in a number of buildings broken. Water leaking all over many of them. Yet the shooting went on and on.

News story entitled "Terrible Gun Battle in Tlatelolco. The Number of Dead Not Yet Determined and Dozens Wounded," Excelsior, October 3, 1968

Now that I'd managed to get to Julio and we were together again, I could raise my head and look around. The very first thing I noticed was all the people lying on the ground; the entire Plaza was covered with the bodies of the living and the dead, all lying side by side. The second thing I noticed was that my kid brother had been riddled with bullets.

Diana Salmerón de Contreras

This reporter was caught in the crowd near the Secretariat of Foreign Relations. A few steps away a woman fell to the ground—she had either been wounded or had fainted dead away. A couple of youngsters tried to go to her rescue, but the soldiers stopped them.

Felix Fuentes, in a news story entitled "It All Began at 6:30 p.m.," La Prensa, October 3, 1968

"Soldier, please have somebody bring a stretcher!"

"Shut up and stop pestering me or you'll be needing two of them!" was the only reply I got from this "heroic Johnny," as our president calls the soldiers in the ranks.

Just then a med student hurried over and said to this "heroic Johnny," "That boy there ought to be taken to the hospital right away!"

"Shut your trap, you son of a bitch," the soldier answered.

Everyone standing around watching began shouting in chorus, "A stretcher, a stretcher, a stretcher!"

A couple of people made a makeshift stretcher out of some lengths of pipe and an overcoat. But the med student who helped us was arrested.

Diana Salmerón de Contreras

In a few minutes the whole thing became a scene straight out of hell. The gunfire was deafening. The bullets were shattering the windows of the apartments and shards of glass were flying all over, and the terror-stricken families inside were desperately trying to protect their youngest children.

Jorge Aviles R., in "Serious Fighting for Hours Between Terrorists and Soldiers"

Lucianito is there upstairs!

Elvira B. de Concheiro, mother of a family

"Please let me go with him—I'm his sister!" I begged. They gave me permission to leave the Plaza with the stretcher-bearers. I climbed into the Army ambulance with my brother.

Diana Salmerón de Contreras

PEOPLE-UNITE-PEOPLE-UNITE-PEOPLE-UNITE

Chant at demonstrations

Why don't you answer me, *hermanito*?

Diana Salmerón de Contreras

Everything was a blur—I don't know if it was because I was crying or because it had started to rain. I watched the massacre through this curtain of rain, but everything was fuzzy and blurred, like when I develop my negatives and the image begins to appear in the emulsion. . . . I couldn't see a thing. My nose was running, but I just snuffled and went on shooting pictures,

though I couldn't see a thing: the lens of my camera was spattered with raindrops, spattered with tears. . . .

Mary McCallen, press photographer

[As they started lining us up against the wall of the church] I saw two of my pals from *Excelsior* there, a reporter and a press photographer. They'd grabbed Jaime Gonzalez's camera away from him. The reporter was saying, "I'm a journalist," but one of the soldiers answered, "Very pleased to meet you, but I couldn't care less whether you're a journalist or not; just stand over there against the wall." They'd slashed Jaime Gonzalez's hand with a bayonet to get his camera away from him.

Raúl Hernández, press photographer, in a story entitled "The Gun Battle as the Press Photographers Saw It," La Prensa, *October 3, 1968*

Before I climbed into the Army ambulance, a "student" whom I'd seen at UNAM came up to me and said, "Your handbag, please . . .""

"What do you want it for?" I asked.

The soldier who was with me was surprised too: "Who are *you*?" he asked him. But then he noticed a white handkerchief or something in the fake student's hand and said to him, "Oh, you're one of *them*, are you?"

The guy was an undercover agent posing as a student. I handed him my purse, and he searched through it and then gave it back to me. I have no idea to this day why he asked me for it.

They took my brother to the hospital then, and I waited there for hours to find out how the operation had gone. A male nurse kept coming in every so often, and one time he asked the women who were there waiting it out, just as I was, "Which one of you was with a boy in a blue suit?"

"He was with me . . .I came here with a boy in a blue suit," I said.

They took me to identify Julio's body and sign the necessary papers.

When we held the wake for Julio, I was deeply touched by his fellow students' loyalty to him and their concern for us. All the boys from Vocational 1 came to the house the minute they heard the tragic news of his death. They had taken up a collection and offered us some five hundred pesos. My sister told them we didn't really need the money, and would prefer that they use it for the Movement. "No," they all said. "The way we see it your brother is the Movement. We'd like you to accept the money."

Julio was fifteen years old, a student Vocational 1, the school out by the Tlatelolco housing unit. That was the second political meeting he'd ever gone to. He had asked me to go with him that day. The first meeting we went to together was the big Silent Demonstration. Julio was my only brother.

Diana Salmerón de Contreras

"You little fool, you! How could you have been so stupid as to hold on to that collection box? Why didn't you get rid of it downstairs?"

And the girl, still half dazed, answered, with simply unbelievable naïveté, "You mean I should have thrown it away? Oh, I couldn't have done that—it's money that belongs to the CNH! It's their money—I couldn't possibly have thrown it away!"

We took the CNH label off the Mobil Oil can she'd been collecting the money in, opened it, and took the money out of it.

"Oh, no, don't do that! . . .that money belongs to the Movement. . . . It's money for the CNH—how can you possibly take it?" she moaned.

"Listen, it doesn't matter who the money belongs to. I promise I'll keep it for you and give it back to the Movement later. . . ."

And despite her protests, we emptied the can. Most of the coins in it were twenty-céntimo pieces[1]; as I remember, there were fourteen pesos altogether. Amid this terrible massacre, the bullets flying in all directions, the building on fire, the leaking gas mains, the broken water mains, the ambulance sirens that set our teeth on edge, the only thing that had mattered to this young girl was hanging onto her CNH collection box. We also set a match to her movement handbills, because she simply didn't realize what trouble she'd be in if she were found with leaflets like that in her possession.

We heard someone inserting a key in the lock on the bathroom door and turning it.

"They've gone, *senora*!" a voice said. It was my mother's helper.

Mercedes Olivera de Vazquez, anthropologist

Ambulances from the Red and Green Cross and from the Central Military Hospital began to enter Tlatelolco, approaching along several streets at once. They did not arrive until after eight-thirty.

According to reliable witnesses, the Army troops continued to attack any group of more than ten persons, charging them with fixed bayonets.

A journalist from AMEX[2] reports that around seven p.m. he saw a student fall to the ground upon being hit by a rifle bullet fired by one of the soldiers, whereupon the soldier finished him off by stabbing him to death with his bayonet. This particular incident occurred on the corner of Allende and Nonoalco.

Margarita Garcia Flores, press secretary, UNAM

Around five that morning, the entire family started organizing. My husband began making the rounds of the various offices of the Attorney General, Pepe went to all the police stations, Chelo and I went to the Red and Green Cross hospitals and all the other hospitals and morgues where there were dead or wounded. The twins, Ruben and Rogelio, went off to work, waiting for us to get in touch with them the minute we had any news.

At the Red Cross hospital, they asked me if I was brave enough to go down to the morgue in the basement. (The Red Cross hospital is on Ejercito Nacional, opposite Sears.) I replied, "Don't you think a mother is automatically brave enough to do a thing like that?"

One of the hospital employees went down with me in the elevator. My daughter didn't go in with me: "Wait here for me outside, Chelo," I told her. Once inside the morgue, the hospital employee pressed a switch and began to pull the drawers out. In the first one he pulled out there was the corpse of a youngster about sixteen years old; his skin had already turned a deep purple. Since part of his face was missing, I tried to identify him by looking at his teeth and seeing if he had any moles on his face, since all my children have them. The only thing left of this cadaver's face was the jawbone and a couple of teeth. When I saw this youngster's dead body, I was sure it was Pichi, because every one of the corpses I saw seemed to be one of my children; every dead body I saw seemed to be one of my boys; but in order to make sure I opened whatever was

---

1   *A coin worth about one and one half cents. (Translator's note.)*

2   *A Mexican news agency. (Translator's note.)*

left of their lips and looked at their teeth, and none of them was Pichi, because there is a big gap between my son's front teeth and the teeth of all these corpses were very close together, and my oldest son has gold caps on his. . . . They produced other corpses that had been brought in from Tlatelolco, but none of them was Pichi. Lots of them were women's bodies, but I didn't pay much attention to them because what I was looking for was bodies of dead boys. I only remember one of the women's bodies—a woman about forty-five years with henna hair, dressed in an orange blouse.

We went upstairs again, and I asked the hospital attendant where he thought we should look next.

"Go over to the emergency clinic at Balbuena," he told us.

On the way over there Chelo and I didn't say one word to each other. The only ones they'd brought there to the clinic were people who'd been wounded; they wouldn't let me in to see them, and none of them fit the description I gave. I was absolutely beside myself, and asked again where else they might have taken people who'd been injured. They said that a number of them had been taken to Rubén Leñero Hospital, but that they would refuse to answer any questions there because everyone who had been brought to Leñero was under arrest. I found out later that they'd taken fifty-eight students who had been wounded there, but none of the dead.

I gave an official from the Public Prosecutor's office photos of my sons and he came back after a while and said to me, "No, they aren't here. None of the ones we have here look like these photographs you've given me."

People were going all over the city searching for their dead or wounded. I went to the headquarters of the Third Police Precinct in Lagunilla then. When I arrived, the streets were full of smoke, as though there were a heavy fog, because they'd set a bus on fire and it was producing great clouds of smoke.

I asked the cops there if I could go inside the police station, and one of them said it was okay: "Go on in if you want to, it'll teach you a lesson." They'd made everybody who wanted to go in form a line, so we walked over and stood in it. They were admitting people in groups of five.

"Wait for me out here, Chelo, don't go in," I said to my daughter.

When they let me in, I walked down a hall and was ushered into a room that was freezing cold—it seemed even colder than the one at the Red Cross hospital. The first thing I saw in there were seven corpses of youngsters about twelve to fifteen years old, but these particular bodies had already been identified. That's why they'd been separated from the rest. Since these seven bodies were the only ones I noticed at first, I thought they were the only ones there, but then I began looking around the room and saw three stone slabs with three dead bodies of railway workers on them, with their heads half blown off by dum-dum bullets. I realized they were railway workers because they had bandanas around their necks and were dressed in coarse blue cotton work shirts. The other corpses were underneath them. The first one I caught sight of was a woman about to give birth: the fetus's head was showing because the bullets had ripped her belly all to pieces.

Later I asked Cosme, my husband, "How come her belly was ripped apart like that?"

"Because they were dum-dum bullets," he answered.

A little farther on I saw the body of the Olympic Games hostess, a very pretty girl with long dark hair, lying there with a peaceful expression on her face. Her whole bosom was bare, like a flower that had opened, and I thought to myself that she must surely be even colder than I was, so I took my sweater off and put it over her. She was naked from the waist up and it made me feel bad seeing her lying there with her breasts exposed like that, so that everybody could see. There were other dead bodies there—twelve more of them—all railway workers, piled up one on top of the other, and I asked the policeman, "How come there are only railway workers' bodies here? What about the students who were killed?"

"They didn't bring any of them here," he answered.

"Well, where are they then?"

"You might take a look out at Military Camp 1."

And when I asked there in the police station how I could get to Military Camp 1, a lieutenant colonel told me, "It's no use going out there, *señora*. They won't tell you a thing. It's no use trying out there."

I was really in a state when I left the police station, because it had all been such a terrible experience. I walked and walked, and it all seemed like a nightmare that had made me break out in a cold sweat. I walked on and on down the entire length of the Paseo de la Reforma, hugging the walls. I wasn't even aware of Chelo walking along there beside me. We didn't say one word to each other. She didn't ask me one question. We turned off the Reforma then and headed home. The others came back then, one by one.

"I haven't found out a thing," Cosme reported.

"I couldn't find out a single thing," my son Pepe reported.

It was two weeks before I had any word at all. I remember that I sat for hours at a time at the window waiting. I felt sick to my stomach the whole time. I was as limp as a dishrag and felt as though I were at the end of my rope. And I'm a strong woman. For two weeks I never sat down to a meal, I was so upset. I hardly ate a bite, really; I just drank liquids every once in a while. We never sat down together at the table from then on. Two weeks later I found out that Pichi had been in cell block H in Lecumberri, and I went to pick him up the day they let him out because they couldn't prove the charges against him. We found out where Eduardo was when my son Rogelio got word at the place where he worked that he was in Military Camp 1. He was alive! I was terribly distraught, I admit, but it would have been hard not to be upset. When they transferred Eduardo to Lecumberri, his fiancée and I went to see him.

They would only let one of us into cell block H to see him, and said to me, "You go in, *senora.*"

Everything that all of us had been through made me very brave, because when I saw Eduardo stumbling down the stairway from his cell block like a mole, clinging to the banisters, and only recognizing me because he could hear my voice as I shouted to him "Eduardo, over here! I'm over here!"—well, it's something I'll never forget. He had to crawl downstairs like that, clutching the banister, because they'd beaten him within an inch of his life and he'd lost his glasses. All he had to guide him was my voice. He's had to wear glasses for the last four years and can hardly see without them; they're glasses with a very strong correction, with thick thick lenses—that's why everybody calls him Owl-Eyes.

The whole thing made me terribly depressed, and I began writing a great many poems to give vent to my feelings. Read this one, for instance:

PRISON BARS

Move the prison bars even closer together
As close as you possibly can
Because however close together you place them
You will never be able
To trap the desire for freedom behind them.
And I suggest that you also
Erect bars shutting out the sky
So that people's thoughts cannot escape
And cause you trouble.

One morning when I read in the papers that Díaz Ordaz was going to have an operation on his eye, I wrote an epigram for the occasion:

The doctors are doing their best
To give light to a person who plunges others in
    darkness.
Wouldn't it be more proper
To give him a little dose of hemlock?

I am going to hand my poems over to you—not so that you'll try to get them published or anything like that, but just to see what you think of them. Write my name down, go ahead, write it down; after all the things I've been through, could anything worse possibly happen to me? What more can they do to me now that they've got my son there behind prison bars?

Celia Espinoza de Valle, grade-school teacher,
mother of a family

They brought several bodies to Military Camp 1. A friend of mine who's also an accountant went to claim his mother's body, and they told him they'd give it to him on one condition: he would have to sign a statement that his mother was a dangerous agitator. He signed everything they asked him to. Everything. His mother was a little old lady who had been there at Tlatelolco by the sheerest chance.

Maria de la Paz Figueroa, public accountant

STUDY QUESTIONS

1. What do the testimonies Poniatowska presents reveal about the nature and goals of state violence against civilian protesters? Was the violence expected? Do we learn anything about the motivations of the police and military?

2. Why are these firsthand testimonies important? To what extent do they challenge state authoritarianism? Are there difficulties for historians in working with this type of testimonial source?

11.6 SCHOOL OF THE AMERICAS "STUDY MANUAL," 1982

The US Army School of the Americas (SOA) was a training facility for Latin American military and police personnel. It was first established in 1946 in the Panama Canal Zone but was moved to Fort Bragg, Georgia, in 1984 as part of the Panama Canal renegotiation treaty. During the period in which guerrilla movements proliferated in Latin America, the US government invested heavily in expanding the scale of SOA operations in an effort to suppress the spread of communist guerrilla armies through intensive training in counterinsurgency tactics. By 2000, when the institute underwent a change in name and mission, the School of the Americas had trained approximately sixty thousand military and police officers from across Latin America. The study manual excerpted here dealt specifically with the detection and suppression of antigovernment political and military activity and was used to teach military intelligence strategies. The manual was used in the school between 1982 and 1991 and was written by US intelligence officers. It was based on US Army documents produced in the 1960s, as well as updated versions of earlier study manuals and lesson plans from the 1970s. In addition to being given to military students at the SOA, copies of the manual were distributed directly to military officers in Colombia, Ecuador, El Salvador, Guatemala, and Peru. This study manual—along with others used by the School—were declassified in 1996 as part of a Congressional investigation into CIA collusion with the Guatemalan military in human rights abuses. Evidence that the study manuals included reference to execution and torture of dissidents led to widespread criticism of the School, prompting a change of name and mandate in 2000. The US Department of Defense responded to criticisms of School teachings by noting that in 1992 they had conducted an internal investigation of the study manuals and ordered all copies destroyed (with the exception of an archival copy of each volume) because they contained "objectionable and questionable material." The passages flagged by the Department of Defense internal review are italicized in the translated excerpt presented here.

A School of the Americas "Study Manual"
The U.S. Department of Defense

The purpose of this chapter is to present the procedures one must follow in the recruitment and utilization of the personnel needed to gather intelligence for the government. . . .

We can define "employee" as that person who lends services in exchange for remuneration or compensation. Because insurrectionary movements can emerge in different zones of economic, political, and geographic influence, the government cannot depend only upon information given voluntarily by loyal citizens or on *information obtained involuntarily from insurgents who have been captured.* Some incentive must exist in order to assure the continued supply of information to the government. Consequently, it is necessary to disseminate throughout all segments of society informers whose services can be paid for. An employee is that person who can provide useful intelligence information in exchange for some

Source: Robert H. Holden and Eric Zolov (eds.) *Latin America and the United States: A Documentary History* (New York: Oxford University Press), pp. 313–316.

compensation, whether it is monetary or of another nature. This person might be a village peasant, a cell member of the insurgent organization, or a person in charge of propaganda.

The informers should be dispersed in all places considered important, in every mass organization, regardless of its size, and in every place where there might appear any outbreak of insurrection. . . .

In planning operations it is very important to realize that even when one does not perceive any guerrilla activity, an insurrectionary movement might be in gestation. Every countermeasure that is focused solely on guerrilla activity without taking into consideration the secret organization and the great preparation necessary before the outbreak of violence is destined to fail.

The mere elimination of the guerrillas will not alter in any way the basic organization of the insurgents. If one is to achieve permanent victory, internal defense operations must be planned with the goal of attacking the insurgent organization before the guerrillas can initiate their operations, an attack that encompasses both the secret subversive elements and the military wing once the movement begins its second phase. . . .

During the initial phases, the insurgents are feverishly occupied with the formation of front organizations and the infiltration of institutions with large numbers of people. We have already seen how a relatively small number of people can manage to control an organization by means of infiltration and rigged elections. The government can learn about insurgent activity within these organizations in a timely way by distributing its employees in every organization suspected of being of interest to the insurgent group. Among the principal organizations of this type are political parties, unions, and student and youth groups. Since the insurgents' tactics follow a continuously repeated pattern, the government's employees can warn about their behavior. . . .

The insurgents will necessarily have to make contacts with certain people in the local area like merchants and vendors in order to obtain supplies and other goods. When they can be persuaded to become government employees, these merchants can help to identify the liaisons used by the insurgents in these operations. . . .

Insurrection is an evil which cannot be tolerated. A secret organization can be identified and made use of. However, a CI [counterintelligence] agent must know how and where to look in order to locate the foci of insurrection, and therefore must have the necessary information. The agent must also know the characteristic weaknesses of the insurgent organization and how to proceed in order to take advantage of them. . . .

Probably the most common motives for mercenaries is the desire for profit. Often the potential employee already has a job, but wishes to enhance his earnings. Even when money is the commonly used medium for transactions, the individual may ask to be paid with certain goods that are difficult to obtain. . . .

The possibilities of finding people disposed to collaborate with the government in an area where an insurrectionary movement is developing are immense. *Specific individuals, organizations, and commercial firms should be targeted for infiltration by employees of the government, with the goal of gaining information about the guerrillas.* . . .

A vital part of this program is the educational system established for indoctrinating and compensating government employees who become informers when approached by guerrillas seeking to recruit them. *The CI agent might arrange for the arrest or detention of the employee's relatives, jail the employee,* or *give him a beating as part of the plan for placing the employee within the guerrilla organization.* Of course, [the CI agent] will have to plan all of these demonstrations carefully, and utilize them at the exact moment in order to bolster the assertions of the employee. . . .

The CI agent can increase the value of the employee by destroying the guerrilla organizational structure that surrounds the employee. *This can be done by means of arrests, executions,* or *raids, making sure not to expose the employee as the source of information.* If the employee is one of the few survivors, he could become the key member of a new or different guerrilla organization. In this situation, the employee's reputation might be reinforced by fabricating stories, documents, and witnesses that would not only be credible, but difficult to refute, given that few guerrillas will have survived. . . .

There are other methods of providing outside help with the goal of assuring the promotion of an employee [within a guerrilla organization]. One method is through the influence of an employee higher up in the guerrilla organization; another is by eliminating a potential guerrilla rival. . . .

It is much more difficult to locate an employee in an area or an organization after the guerrillas have seized control. The CI agent can place an employee beforehand, during, or after the guerrillas have gained control of an area; however, the earlier it is done, the better the chances are for success. . . .

STUDY QUESTIONS

1. What techniques does the manual recommend for combatting guerrilla units? Is there discussion of how these strategies might impact civilians?
2. To what extent are the counterinsurgency techniques outlined in the manual at odds with international norms and legislation regarding human rights?

11.7 THE CALL TO THE MARCH OF EMPTY POTS AND PANS, 1971

The March of the Empty Pots and Pans is the name given to a series of protests by conservative Chilean women against Salvador Allende's government. Allende's election ushered in a period of tremendous economic and political instability in Chile. Price controls and wage increases were introduced by the government in the hope of improving conditions for workers, but these also led to inflation as well as shortages of essential foodstuffs. The first March of the Empty Pots and Pans took place in December of 1971, during the state visit of Fidel Castro to Chile. More than five thousand women took to the streets banging on cooking pots and pans to protest the food shortages that were resulting from the economic reforms. These marches would continue for the next two years, and formed the foundation of a large-scale opposition movement against Allende, which would ultimately contribute to the military coup of 1973. This document is the original call to action issued by the organizers of the first women's march in November 1971, as they prepared for the Castro visit, and lays out the motivations behind the planned protest.

The gravity of the situation facing our country has forced us to call upon all the women of Chile. We, more than anyone, are living the profound drama that our country has suffered for the past year.

When Allende assumed the presidency, we analyzed the conditions that made it possible for him to become the president of Chile. We were confident that he would secure our democratic lifestyle, respect our rights, and [that] the security of those unalterable principles—guaranteed by the Constitution—would be jealously guarded by he who assumed control of the nation.

Source: Margaret Power, *Right-Wing Women in Chile: Feminine Power and the Struggle against Allende 1964–1973* (University Park: Pennsylvania State University Press, 2001).

Time has shown us that this security is illusory. We have witnessed how hate has been sown, [along with] the lack of respect for authority and those values that for us are fundamental: personal honor and physical safety.

Sectarianism and the arrogance of government officials have filled us with concern for the future of the fatherland and of our children.

Even our most important values are threatened; an evangelical church was burned, and a pastor was attacked simply because he opposed totalitarian ideas and attitudes.

The government's attempts to control all the media, the radio, television, magazines, newspapers, is serious. As part of this, [we see] the [government's] maneuvers to control the supply of paper through the nationalization of the Compania Manufacturera de Papeles y Cartones. We know that if this were to happen, only those who support the government will receive paper.

They promised land to those who work it and workers' participation in the factories. The opposite has happened: the peasants do not have land and the state has taken over the factories.

The worst abuses have taken place in the University of Chile, where the rector, Edgardo Boeninger, is the victim of an infamous campaign of insults simply because he demands respect for man's most sacred values.

We all live the drama caused by the lack of food. We are not inventing false campaigns to attack the government. Daily we see that there is no meat, chicken, milk, noodles, and other essential items, and when we do find these products, we have to pay prices that are far beyond our resources. For these reasons we make this fervent call to all Chilean women, so that once and for all, we can have our say [on the issue of] the future of Chile and our children.

We will gather on Wednesday, December 1st, 6:00 P.M., Plaza Italia, in the March of Chilean Women.

STUDY QUESTIONS

1. What are the factors that motivate the women's march according to the document?
2. To what extent are gendered ideals concerning womanhood and motherhood embedded within the call to action? How might gender norms have impacted the success of the protest?

PETER WINN

11.8 DIARY OF A COUP, 1973

Peter Winn is a well-known historian of Latin America. In 1973, as a young researcher and journalist with a new PhD, he was present in Chile as the military coup against Allende unfolded. In this excerpt he uses extracts from his diary to provide an eyewitness account of the events of September 11, 1973. Winn was a supporter of the Allende government. He had been given advance notice that a coup was being planned, but was still shocked by the turn of events. His account captures the violence of the day and its impact on civilians, as well as the deep foreboding and uncertainty that accompanied the coup.

Source: Elizabeth Quay Hutchinson, Thomas Miller Klubock, Nara B. Milanich, and Peter Winn (eds.)*The Chile Reader: History, Culture, Politics* (Durham and London: Duke University Press, 2014), pp. 443–449.

During the September 11 military intervention, the fifth coup attempted that year, civilians gathered to observe and wonder at the spectacle, even as troops were dispatched to universities, workplaces, and private homes throughout the country, arresting, torturing, and sometimes executing former government officials and Allende supporters. Winn's testimony reflects the jarring realization—common among many Chileans—of the radical change portended by the events unfolding before them. Like other foreigners who had come to live in Chile to witness Popular Unity's experiment in democratic revolution, Winn shared in the culture of fear created by the military's unrelenting and systematic attack on the civilian population, although unlike the US citizen Charles Horman, a journalist whose murder was the basis for the Costa-Gavras film *Missing*, he lived to tell about it. The arrest and disappearance of foreigners in the days following the coup sparked some of the earliest criticisms of the military regime by foreign governments, although the US Embassy in Chile refused to investigate or protest the disappearance of their own citizens as a result of military violence. In this essay, the historian Peter Winn quotes from his own diary to provide an eyewitness account of the 1973 military coup as it developed in downtown Santiago.

I awoke at dawn on that gray and chilly late winter day, after a night of too little sleep, filled with dreams of foreboding, and left my house early in the morning to get to the downtown offices of Identificaciones before they opened in order to get my Chilean resident ID Card. I had been there the Friday before, but there were so many people on line to get their safe conducts to leave the country that I had waited in vain to be seen.

One of them was Andre Gunder Frank, the leftist intellectual and adviser to the MIR, the Revolutionary Left Movement, who gave me the incredulous look reserved for fools and madmen when I told him what I was there for. "Don't you know that there is going to be a rightist military coup?" he said pointedly. I had just been told by the head of Allende's Foreign Press Office that it would be on September 12th.

"Yes," I said, trying to sound brave and principled, "but I'm staying." So, I scoped out where the staircase was closest to the office where I needed to go and which outside door to enter to get there fast. When the doors opened on September 11, I was first on line outside the ID card office. The young woman who had not been able to assist me the day before smiled at me and said she would call me in five minutes. But when she returned a few minutes later it was with a worried look on her face and a hurried statement that she would not be able to process my request—or anyone else's— that day, that her office—which had scarcely opened, was about to close for the day. Something in her voice

stopped me. "Why?" I asked. "Is something wrong?" Her response was so classically Chilean that I have to use her words: "Me parece que hay un problemita en La Moneda"—"It seems as if there is a little problem at the presidential palace."

This was it. I raced down the stairs and out the door heading for the Plaza de la Constitución. Next door to the offices of Identificaciones were the offices of Investigaciones, the Chilean FBI, the one security service that Allende had been able to staff with his loyalists. As I passed its doorway two detectives sprinted out carrying submachine guns and heading for a squad car. I asked them if anything had happened. One shouted over his shoulder—"No. . . todavía"— "No . . . not yet." I walked rapidly to the Foreign Press Office—which overlooked the presidential palace and Constitution Plaza. The head of the office was not there, but my friend his assistant was. I asked what was happening. "It seems that there is an uprising of the armed forces," he replied. "All of them?" I asked. "No," he said. "Just the Army, the Navy and the Air Force." That was not as crazy a statement as it sounds. It meant that the Carabineros, the militarized national police, the second largest force in Chile, with bases in every city, town, and village in Chile, was still loyal to the Allende government. If that remained true, a resistance to the coup could be mounted. I went to the window and saw the Carabinero buses disgorging dozens of uniformed police with heavy machine guns to take up defensive positions around La Moneda, joined by *tanquetas*, the light tanks of the Carabineros.

The telephone rang and my friend picked it up: "Sí, sí, sí . . ." I heard him say disconsolately. He put down the phone and turned to me. "And now the Carabineros," he said sadly. I looked out the window and saw the tanquetas begin to leave the square and the Carabineros pick up their machine guns and get back on the bus leaving the presidential palace all but unguarded. "Where is Allende?" I asked. "He is inside La Moneda. He has said that he will only leave feet first."

It was just after 9 A.M., and they had orders to lock the doors and the building. I was welcome to stay if I wanted to, I was told. I debated for a minute. The office had a great view of the presidential palace and the square in front of it. I would be able to see perfectly whatever happened. But I remembered the Swedish photographer who was shot and killed in a similar window during the *tancazo* armored regiment mutiny.[1] Moreover, if the coup succeeded, I would be in effect a prisoner in what its leaders would consider enemy territory. Most of all, I did not like the idea of being shut up, unable to leave no matter what happened.

So, I thanked him and wished him luck and dashed out of the building just as its front gates were being locked. I decided to watch what happened from the far corner of the square, so that I would not have to cross it to retreat towards my building roughly a mile away. It was 9:30 and there was a small crowd of people, most of them workers from suddenly closed government offices milling around in the street. Most of them were Allende supporters who were hoping for loyal troops who would rescue the government, as had happened in the tancazo two months before.

Suddenly Carabineros arrived and began to push the crowd back from the square. I took out my journalist credentials and tried to talk with them, but the look of rage with which they regarded me—and the civilians around me—stopped me. "This is going to be a very different coup than people expected," I thought.

Close to 10 A.M. army tanks suddenly arrived in front of La Moneda and one took up position at the corner of the square near us, its gun turret facing away from the presidential palace. The crowd cheered, thinking that it was there to defend Allende. Then, slowly, its gun turret wheeled and aimed at the presidential palace. There was first stunned silence and then an audible gasp. We were standing near a shopping arcade. The Carabineros told everyone to go into the arcade, whose gates would be pulled shut and locked.

There they would be safe from the fighting. I considered it but rejected the image. It looked too much like being shut up in a jail. I decided to take my chances out on the street. Weeks later I learned that after the coup, people inside the arcade were taken to the National Stadium for interrogation and some of them disappeared forever.

A few minutes after ten, however, it looked like a bad decision. The tanks started firing on La Moneda and suddenly there were bullets everywhere, raining down from the government office buildings where the Socialist Youth were posted as snipers to defend the presidential palace. The corner was untenable. There were people lying wounded around me. I made my way back down Morandé Street hugging the walls to the next doorway, where I took refuge behind its neo-classical columns.

In back of me, the tanks and machine guns were firing away, but in front of us the street was alive with sniper bullets. There seemed no escape. Opposite were the offices of *El Mercurio*, the leading rightist newspaper. From its second floor window a telescopic sight suddenly appeared pointing at me. There was nowhere for me to hide. If it was a gun, I was dead. I watched transfixed as the sight slowly swiveled and faced the presidential palace, revealing a camera with a long telephoto lens. I breathed a sigh of relief.

Then the firing stopped, as suddenly as it had begun. People came out from their hiding places, at first gingerly and then with greater confidence, as if it was all over. It was a symbolic corner, with the Congress building and the court building. They gathered in between these two symbols of Chile's constitutional democracy and being Allende's Chile, they began to argue: who was responsible? Was it the Left? Was it the Right? Was it the Center? Was it the United States? I listened with a sense of prophetic nostalgia, thinking to myself: "This may be the last public political debate that you will hear in Chile for a very long time." But I also noticed that the

---

1   On June 29, 1973, a tank regiment of the Chilean army surrounded La Moneda but was repelled by forces loyal to Commander Carlos Prats.

debate in front of me was getting more and more ac-rimonious. Then, just when I thought it would come to blows—itself emblematic of the political polariza-tion in Chile by September 11, 1973—the firing started again, and the antagonists all took refuge under the newspapers and magazines representing Left, Center, and Right hanging down from the newspaper kiosk at the corner, itself a symbol of the political pluralism and free press that was about to disappear.

The bullets were all around me now. A man stand-ing next to me got hit and I decided it was time to leave. I began to run down Morandé Street, along the side of the Congress, when suddenly I was stopped by what seemed to be a red puddle in the middle of the street—it was a pool of blood. . . . I began to run again, faster this time. As I passed the street where the headquarters of the Communist Party and the CUT (Central Unica de Trabajadores) labor confederation were located, I saw the Carabinero tanquetas firing away. Shots rang out near me and the tanqueta wheeled and began to fire in my direction. I ducked around the corner and kept running until I reached the old market close to the river. As I emerged from behind an overturned fruit cart, I saw them: there all along the broad boulevard of the Parque Forestal along the River Mapocho was the army, two regiments' worth . . . with tanks and ma-chine guns. The soldiers seemed very young, conscripts of 17 or 18—and they were very nervous. If I had been afraid that the Carabineros near the Plaza would kill us civilians out of rage, here I was concerned that they could kill me out of nervousness and inexperience.

They were herding civilians across the river, out-side of their battle station perimeter. I crossed the bridge near the Mapocho railway station and turned east toward my apartment and the Plaza Italia. More and more people were crowding Costanera Avenue as buses were stopped and their riders were forced into the street at gunpoint, many of them with their hands over their heads out of fear, like refugees from some war movie. Manicured men in business suits, together with down and out beggars and street peddlers.

But for the first time, the firing seemed distant. I stopped to rest and looked back across the river toward the downtown battle zone that I had just escaped. Someone had a transistor radio tuned to the military warning that they would bomb the presidential palace

if Allende would not surrender. The young woman next to me began to cry. I assumed that she was an Allende supporter, but I was mistaken. She was mostly apolitical, she explained, but leaning toward the Right. She had voted for the rightist candidate Jorge Alessan-dri in 1970 and said to me: "Two days before I would have been happy to see Allende hanging from a lamp-post, but this—the Chilean military attacking the pres-idential palace, the symbol of Chilean democracy, this should not happen. This is not the Chilean way." The sky was getting darker, with a hint of rain. "El cielo no querrá ver lo que pasará,"—"Heaven doesn't want to see what is going to happen," she said.

I decided that I had to try and return to my apart-ment while I still could. I asked a young soldier where I could cross. He motioned to a bridge upriver near Es-tados Unidos Street. It took me past the old U.S. Con-sulate. . . . I headed down a little side street toward the Alameda, the main thoroughfare that I had to cross to reach my apartment in the Torres San Borja complex, opposite what would become the headquarters of the military regime. I passed a group of worried but deter-mined men coming out of a doorway with a Social-ist Party banner. Two of them had pistols tucked into their belts. I overheard them making plans for what they would do when the troops arrived. I stole a last glance at their tense, sad faces, at a determination born more out of desperation than optimism. . . .

I turned the corner toward the Alameda passing by the headquarters of the neo-fascist Patria y Liber-tad and the Communist "Comité de Pobladores Sin Casa"—opposite poles of a Chilean pluralism. . . . I expected sniper fire, but there was none. The Alam-eda, normally a raucous river of traffic, was empty and silent. I crossed with surprising ease and made my way to my building opposite the Marcoleta market. Near its entrance was a crowd of people downing liter bot-tles of milk from an abandoned stand, as if they were chugging beers, looking at each other and laughing as if they had shared an illicit pleasure, but their laughs bordered on hysteria.

I made it to my building and took the elevator to my apartment on the 19th floor, finally safe, feeling myself a privileged foreigner in that security. I turned on the radio in time to hear the final threat to bomb the presidential palace. I got my camera out in time to track the Hawker Hunter jets streaking toward La Moneda with my telephoto lens, wishing it was a telescopic sight instead, squeezing the trigger over and over again, but to no avail. In the near distance I heard the sound of the impact of their rockets. From my window I could see black smoke billowing from the presidential palace. . . .

I took out my tape recorder and began to record the military announcements. There would be an indefinite curfew. . . . Then came the shock: a list of leftist leaders who would turn themselves in to the nearest military post or police station. It was a strange list, including many people I knew who were moderates in the Allende government, people who posed no threat to the military coup. . . . This list was followed by another, a list of foreigners who were also to turn themselves in at once. . . . Andre Gunder Frank's name was on the list. I breathed a silent prayer that he had left the country in time. Then, in a moment of terror, I suddenly realized that if other innocuous people were on the wanted list, mine might be there too. . . . I might not be safe after all. . . . It was a terrifying realization which brought home to me the new Chile that was about to be born. . . .

Phone calls began to come in, from friends and Chileans who saw me as a foreign journalist who could get the word out. Not to despair [they said] . . . loyal troops were on the way . . . recently retired General Prats was leading them. . . . loyal provincial commanders in the north were still holding out—all of them false rumors or wishful thinking. . . .

By nightfall, phone calls brought truer but grimmer tidings—Allende's death in the ruins of La Moneda, the triumph of the coup throughout the country. Outside my window, fighting continued. The city was blacked out, and from my window high over Santiago,

I could see the helicopter gunships home in on leftist factories and shantytowns, a horrific lightshow of headlights and tracer bullets lighting up the darkened city sky. I slept fitfully, awakened at 4 A.M. by a loud bomb explosion. In the distance something large was on fire. I couldn't sleep.

The firing went on all the following day, along with reports of the targets attacked—the Pedagógico, the leftist education school of the University of Chile; the Sumar textile factory, the working-class districts of San Miguel, the "Red County," the shantytowns near the Cordillera. That night the Armed Forces commanders, the new Junta de Gobierno, appeared on television for the first time. Each one addressed the nation in turn. Pinochet was the most enigmatic, terse and anti-Marxist, but vague, as if he hadn't thought about what he would say or wanted to do. The most scarily rightist was the Air Force commander Gustavo Leigh, who talked of "the struggle to excise the Marxist cancer from the Chilean body politick and of the need to reverse the preceding 50 years of Chilean history"—i.e., not just the three years of Allende's road to socialism, but also the Alliance for Progress reforms of the Christian Democratic government of the 1960s, the welfare state and labor reforms of the Popular Front of the 1930s, even Arturo Alessandri's introduction of mass democratic politics of the 1920s. Clearly this was not going to be a "soft coup," a brief period of military rule to calm things down and then return power to the civilian political leaders as in the past.

Later that night I was awakened by the sound of animals roaring in agony. It was the lions in the zoo across the river, who had not been fed for two days. It seemed to me that they were expressing what too many Chileans felt that night, that they were symbolic of a nation in agony.

STUDY QUESTIONS

1. What are the reactions of the civilians Winn encounters to the military coup? To what extent do their perspectives vary based on political allegiance? Were any of the interactions between civilians and the military surprising? Why or why not?

2. How vulnerable was Winn himself during the coup and in the days that followed? What can we learn from his reactions to the creation of the "wanted list" by the military?

MARIA AND MATTHEW POSNER

11.9 TESTIMONIES OF THE MOTHERS OF THE PLAZA DEL MAYO, 1996

The Mothers of the Plaza del Mayo represents one of the most celebrated and important grassroots political movements in modern Latin American history. Formed by mothers whose children had been disappeared by the Argentine military government, the group played a key role in drawing international attention to the human rights abuses perpetrated by the military junta. The mothers had encountered each other while looking for their children, and starting in April 1977 they began to hold weekly protests in the central public plaza in Buenos Aires, wearing white scarves on their heads to denote their status as mothers, and holding up photos of their missing sons and daughters. As their movement began to attract international attention—notably during the 1978 World Cup hosted in Argentina—three of the early leaders of the movement were themselves disappeared by the military government. The movement continues to exist today and still holds regular rallies in the Plaza in memory of those who died. The group has partnered with forensic researchers to identify the remains of bodies using DNA analysis, and worked with a sister organization, The Grandmothers of the Plaza del Mayo, to gain accountability for the military's trafficking in the babies of disappeared pregnant women and to identify children adopted by military officials. In this excerpt from an interview conducted shortly after the transition to civilian rule, Marta Vázquez, a member of the Mothers of the Plaza del Mayo, describes the life of her disappeared daughter, Maria Marta Vázquez de Lugones, and reflects on what her daughter's abduction meant for her own life and how it shaped her political activism.

MARTA VÁZQUEZ, MOTHER OF MARÍA MARTA VÁZQUEZ DE LUGONES, 23 YEARS OLD, ABDUCTED WITH HER HUSBAND CÉSAR AMADEO LUGONES, 26 YEARS OLD, ON MAY 14, 1976

MARÍA MARTA MADE ME GO TO THE SHANTYTOWN . . .

Before, I used to think that I understood my daughter, and now I realize I didn't, in spite of the fact that I took part in her work. Many times—I don't know whether it was because I saw her working so hard, imbued with that love she had for others, especially children—I would sometimes selfishly think that she was risking her health and her life, because, like her friends, she didn't use a timetable to go to the shantytown if they needed her. She would stay at night keeping the children company if their mother was at the hospital taking care of another little brother. Other times she and her friends would go to the hospital to help out; they saved several little ones, because when they realized that a child was dying, they would pick it up and rush it to the hospital. They also saved a little one who had fallen down a well. Listen, they've done incredible things. I used to see her arriving home overwhelmed because of all that was happening over there. She lived it, she suffered, it made her sick.

Source: Matilde Mellibovsky, *Circle of Love over Death: Testimonies of the Mothers of the Plaza de Mayo*, translated by Maria Proser and Matthew Proser (Willimantic, CT: Curbstone Press), pp. 90–102.

I remember telling her once—to see if she would react and change a bit: "But María Marta, this is impossible, I can't accept your leading this kind of life, worrying so much about those children when you should come first . . ."

I know I was hard, harder than my feelings, to see if I could get her to change a bit.

And I'll never forget the look she gave me, her eyes opened wide, as if amazed, while she told me: "Mother, how can you be so insensitive!"

I knew the shantytown in Lower Flores, the area called Belen, where María Marta used to work. There was a very humble shack where two or three priests lived: Father Ricciardelli, Father Vernazza and others who left later. In one of the rooms a little school had been organized to help the children with their homework and to teach them. Since they often lacked teachers, María Marta took me there many times to teach. There was an almost blind nun, Sister Luisa, who lived there—devoted to the children.

And between María Marta, her husband, and the rest of the group that worked in the little school in Belen, they built a child-care facility where Sister Luisa looked after many children so that their mothers could work. The girls would go off and on to help, and I also went once or twice. The little school stayed open until they destroyed it with a bulldozer. But the church, now called the Mother of the People, remains, and Father Ricciardelli is still there.

MY FAMILY

María Marta is the only one of my children who is a girl. José María (we call him Perucho) and I are the parents of six children. Five boys and María Marta, who is the fourth. I will never forget the day our only girl was born, one of the happiest days of my life. Because after three males, I was expecting another male child, so when the doctor told me "it's a girl," I kept looking at him and could not believe it.

She has been extraordinary from a very young age. Because of José María's occupation—he is a diplomat—we have lived mostly outside the country. We came back to Buenos Aires, where María Marta did her fifth year at the school of Our Lady of Mercy, and there she met Mónica Mignone, with whom she became best friends. They disappeared on the same day. Both of them had chosen to become psychology teachers and went together to Salvador University. They were very close, they worked in the same shantytown. When María Marta started studying at the Mercy School, she began by going to the South with the Sisters to do mission work.

The second time she went South, to Lake Puelo, she met César Lugones, who would become her husband.

They disappeared together, on the very same night. César was doing the same kind of work María Marta did. He was also a very aware kid, and he had worked from a very young age with Sister Luisa in the shantytown. They met at the Association of Christian Youths, preparing for the trip and readying all they had to take. By the second year, or maybe the third, they were already an integral part of that group of kids. It was a mixed group, and they got married the following year. Once married, they kept living the same kind of life because both of them were so very dedicated. They gave so much of themselves . . . . One of the things I remember is that if one of their companions lost his job, César would ask him to write articles for the magazine for which he used to work so that he could earn something. That's the way both of them were.

When they were kidnapped, María Marta was 23 and César 26 years old, and even worse, César was convalescing from a lung operation. He had been very sick; it was a miracle he had been saved.

He had hardly started to work and was being very careful about himself. I remember that he would sit in the sun at Chacabuco Park, across the street from where they lived. From the first moment of his disappearance, we feared for his health. How innocent we were, thinking that the children were going to return and worrying that perhaps he would not be able to stand the incarceration because of his health.

María Marta and César were Catholic militants. I'll just tell you that they were good friends with several priests, and that on the day they got married, five officiated at their marriage rites.

It was a beautiful ceremony. They got married in the Euskalechea College Chapel and the children of the shantytown went with their guitars and sang all the songs.

María Marta and César always sang in the village with them, because I assure you, both of those kids lived in the village. It was their life; they organized a soccer club and pilgrimages to Luján.

THEY LEFT US SUCH A GREAT EXAMPLE OF A LIFE WELL-LIVED. . . .

Really, confronted with such great pain and sorrow for the loss we have suffered, the fact that these two kids have left us so much, such a great example of a life well-lived, so many lessons, gives me a feeling of happiness inside when I think about it. And that is what gives me strength, it is something that has opened the way for me to do the task we have performed with the Mothers and to go forward. Because if somebody had told me more than ten years ago that I was going to do what I have, I would have never believed myself capable of it.

And you know, another thing I can't forget is the last day I saw my daughter. María Marta disappeared with César on May 14th at dawn. They went after her at her place. But I was living in Mexico at the time with Perucho where he was on a diplomatic mission at the Argentinian Embassy. And we had come back in March, 1976 for our son Carlos' wedding. We stayed until April 8. April 8, 1976 was the last day, but no, exactly on the 7th, because I traveled on the 8th.

On the 14th they disappeared, on May 14th. They went looking for them at three in the morning. It was an operation that started at eleven in the evening because on the same night they took six of their friends, six or seven, I can't remember now. And they began at eleven in the evening at the house of one of them, at one a.m. at another's, at three a.m. at our children's, who lived in a small apartment across from the park. The only witness was the doorman. They dragged him out violently, they ordered him to open the door and then they screamed at him to leave, but he hid behind the staircase and remained listening and watching. Several of the men stayed downstairs in the entrance hall and some others went up to the apartment. And the doorman says that after a good while they came down and told those who were left on watch downstairs: We didn't find anything." And others stayed in the cars. The doorman assures us that one of them in the cars wore a Uniform. After a while, he saw them brought down and taken out already tied up. The doorman's testimony is the only thing we've been left with; it was he who saw them when he opened the door, who managed to see somebody wearing a uniform outside in the car, in a sort of van, while the rest were all in civilian clothes, fully armed. The

apartment was turned upside-down. They took away many things. The key disappeared, no one could go in until forty-eight hours later, and, when this was possible, the apartment door was opened, whereas on the first day her brothers had been unable to get in. . . .

Emilio and Chela's family (Mónica Mignone's parents) talked to my sons and told them about Mónica. My children went to María Marta's place but there was no one there by then, so we don't know if the ransacking that took place in the apartment happened on the same night, or if they came back afterwards to take away the things.

When she lived at home, María Marta was always rebuking me for being obsessed with neatness and cleanliness.

She was always telling me: "Mom, how important is all this? What's the sense of it? Why do you worry so much about it? No, it's not important! . . . . and at that time I was annoyed. And when she was no longer here, after she disappeared—it's something that until even today, after ten years—when I am about to clean a piece of furniture, when I am about to dust, I remember her words and I tell myself. "She was so right! Why do I worry about these material things when there are so many other things that have a much larger meaning." I have learnt from my daughter to be less superficial, that we can use our time in other ways but, regrettably, now when she is no longer here.

My children are all tall, rather lean. She was the opposite, the *only* one who wasn't tall. She had ash-blond hair, blue eyes, and had a tendency to put on weight. She had wide hips, from Perucho's side. Her nose was like mine, a little bit aquiline. As for her personality, she was cheerful. And being a tremendously responsible girl, she never gave us any trouble, not while in primary or secondary school, nor at the university, never, never anything. She was always very independent, and wherever she was she was a bit of a leader.

She always studied in religious schools. When she was at Our Lady of Belén during her fourth year in high school, the Sisters called me, very annoyed. I didn't know what was going on. When María Marta saw an injustice, she didn't keep her mouth shut about it. Small though she was, she had character.

They had had exams and they had included subjects which *they* hadn't studied the whole year. She didn't remain silent, and she stirred up all the mothers. Everyone complained and the vice-principal called us, furious, and us: "This cannot be! This girl is too independent!"

Now, looking at her photograph when she was six years and we were living in Chile, I see that in spite of her there was already in her *eyes* a maturity, a sweetness, there was something that was . . .ethereal, there was something that was the way she was. And that is the memory that has stayed with us.

Now I look at it, I can look at it. And I feel so much love, something very special. At the beginning, do you know? When I was alone and looked at it, I would start crying like a mad woman. I couldn't stand it, I hugged the photo. True, I would embrace it and cry out and begNow time has taught me that there is another way of living and going forward.

MYSELF, SEARCHING

They disappeared on May 14 at three in the morning, and our sons, Carlos, a lawyer, and Rafael, who is today an agricultural engineer, called us on the phone at dawn on the 15th. Perucho didn't travel for fifteen days because Carlos said to him: "Dad, don't come, we are going to take care of it." And after fifteen days of fruitless attempts, he called asking for one of us to come.

Perucho came and because of the position he held, spent two months trying to get something done at the highest levels; Emilio Mignone went too. . . .

They tried to move everything, everything, everything: the Church, everything they could think of, and . . .nothing. He came back disheartened, feeling like an old rag. He hadn't managed to get any information. And I tell you that we had good friends in the Army, but there was no one who would tell him this is the way it is, or this isn't the way it is, or anything. After two or three days, these friends blotted themselves off the map, or they promised a lot but did nothing, they started to refuse us . . . and all of our friends, childhood friends, my family's old friends, families we were friends with, they disappeared, they ignored us, terrible!

That's when, after two months, in October, José María, dismissed from his job, returned to the country. We think this was due to the situation too. In November he stopped working for the diplomatic service and started making inquiries and began to act. During the first

year, 1977, and for a long time after, there was always somebody at our place, waiting for her to come back.

Eight or ten months had already gone by since her disappearance. Perucho kept on making inquiries, filing requests, along with Emilio and Chela Mignone.

And one day I stood before my husband (he was used to my always being at home) and I told him: "I'm going with you, I want to go." And so I started to participate in all the inquiries and interviews.

One day Emilio advised us to start going to the interviews by ourselves. And I remember the first time that Chela and I went by ourselves. We went to the Navy Department to see someone on a high level. Like everybody else, he falsely told us that nothing was going on, that they could not give us any information, that they didn't know anything. They thought that we were naive, that we didn't realize what was going on. I continued with this work along with Perucho until May, 1977 more or less. Then Chela let me know that there was a group of Mothers who met in the Plaza de Mayo on Thursdays at three o'clock in the afternoon. So I went to the Mothers of the Plaza de Mayo. Azucena was there, who indisputably had great drive and was very decisive and gave us ideas which we went along with. And so we began to take action together. We'd go to different sites, to Army regiments, to Army Command #1, stand at the entrance door—we'd take turns.

The way my husband came to accept my activity so fully was admirable. He accompanied us a lot, and even when he didn't participate in the circle, most of the time he was at the Plaza. Our husbands were afraid of what could happen to us there.

And I will never forget August, 1977, the first time they detained some of us. It was Marta, Aurora Morea, and myself. This is how it happened: on that day a special security force came to suppress activities in the Plaza. They saw us walking in a circle and they dispersed us very quickly. They would disperse us and we'd separate, get together again, and come back to re-establish the circle around the pyramid. And they'd get very irritated because we weren't going away. We'd leave for a little while and come back. We repeated this trick over and over again for many years: we'd get back together and then get back in a circle. That time, one of the first, when we were coming back, the patrolmen were standing on the Hipólito y Rigoyen side of the Plaza, and we saw that they had one of the Mothers by the side of the patrol vehicle. I remember that I lowered my voice and told Mrs. Morea: "We're not leaving, look, there is a Mother by the patrol wagon, let's see what's going on." And we went around the circle moving towards the patrol vehicle. There were three patrolmen together, and they had her standing next to one of them, and the minute we approached, they got her into the vehicle. Then we walked by them, looked and asked what was going on. They told us very harshly that we didn't have any business there, that we had to leave. I will never forget the expression of the one who was giving the orders, an officer in fatigues. His eyes looked as if they were on fire, and he was shouting at us in an outraged voice: "You don't need to be here! You have to leave!" Mrs. Morea answered by telling him that this was a public Plaza, that it belonged to everybody, that there was no reason for her to leave. And he screamed at her: "Get into the patrol car!" "Very well," she told him. And she looked at me and I told him: "And me too"; and so the three of us got into the patrol wagon. And that was the first time they detained somebody at the Plaza.

They only had us for a few hours because my husband was at the Plaza, so Azucena and the other Mothers ran towards him. At that time Ruiz Palacios was the Home Affairs sub-secretary, under Harguindeguy, and he had received us twice. So at the door of the Government Palace, the women found Perucho, who had an audience with Ruiz Palacio. They told him that there were problems, that a woman had been detained. "How? who? and Marta?" "She's one of them," they told him. He became desperate, stirred up the whole Secretariat, got to Ruiz Palacios' office and in two or three hours they gave the order to free us. But while we were at Police Station No.3, many more detained people arrived, about twenty journalists and people who were going by.

And they kept all the detainees for hours. When my husband got to the Station, the order came from the Ministry to free me, but he said: "No, my wife was detained together with other women. If you don't let all of them leave, she won't leave." And so all three of us who had been arrested were freed, and we waited outside. After two or three hours, everybody started coming out. The men were kept longer.

That's how, without even realizing it, I started to struggle and work with the Mothers, and the group started to develop, to unify, to fight, and without any

planning, to confront the dictatorship—which at that time was so horrendous. And for us going to the Plaza every Thursday became a need. It didn't matter how we were feeling because I will tell you, every Thursday, before going to the Plaza, when I woke up and remembered what day it was, my stomach started to ache. This nervous feeling was something so overwhelming that I couldn't find any peace. But it was simply a matter of getting onto the Plaza, and that seemed to calm me down, to fill me with an unknown strength. When I was confronted and was told no, I pushed on, and I fought on two or three occasions. How I did it, I don't know.

We knew that they were listening on our phone lines, that we were being watched all of the time, but also that what we were doing was something that was not against the law, that it was human, that is was legal, that we didn't have anything to hide. And so we kept on marching ahead, talking to each other on the phone. When we wanted to say that we had a meeting, we'd say: "We're going to play canasta"; "We're going to sew." Others would say, "We're going to do some embroidering." And so it went on like this for a long time, until the Association of Mothers of the Plaza de Mayo was formed. Just the same, we kept on meeting in our houses until we had our first house on Uruguay Street. Then all the meetings took place there. The group had grown a lot.

The Mothers' group was incredible. When somebody new arrived, nobody—ever—would ask her who she was, or where she came from. Sometimes we had doubts about some people coming for the first time, but usually we recognized when they were working for the security services. Then we acted in such a way that they wouldn't come back—they felt exposed. And afterwards, since it was a group in which we leaned on each other, the strength that one of us lacked on a certain day, another had for that occasion. The other had words of consolation, for pushing us to keep on going, words of valor, of courage, and so we kept on. And I believe that all these small brushes that we had with the police and the security forces, instead of intimidating us, gave us more courage, mobilized us even more.

The forces of repression caused the disappearance of Azucena and the French nuns—for Sister Alicia also walked with us. They thought that we were going to stop gathering at the Plaza, but it didn't happen, we didn't get scared. I will never forget it, it was something so incredible. I met Esther Careaga, who marched with us, on Avenida de Mayo, across from the *La Prensa* newspaper office, and I asked her: "What are you doing here?" Her disappeared daughter had been freed. "Don't come any longer, you'll put yourself in danger." And her answer: "But this is something stronger than me. Even if it is only from this spot, I have to see you." She stayed at the edge of the Plaza border . . .she told us that she couldn't stop coming.

I believe that Azucena's disappearance made us stronger. I will never forget her last words to us. She disappeared when we were preparing the Open Letter with the names of eight hundred disappeared which came out on December 10, 1977 in the *La Prensa* daily. I remember we were checking the lists at the house of one of the Mothers, and she lifted her head, looked at us and said: "If something happens to me, you keep on, don't forget that." We spread her message. And we made good on it.

Preaching any ideology was something we did not allow. The only thing that moved us, always, has been the search for our children. All the actions we have undertaken were directed towards that goal. Even if during this period we failed to obtain the results we were seeking—our children's reappearance, alive—I believe we have obtained quite a bit. We have managed to spread the knowledge of the horror we have been living under for so many years, the massacre that's taken place, this genocide. We have let our country and the whole world know what has happened here. And I think this is quite a bit.

I can tell you that I began this fight and kept it up because of the support I got from my family because I don't know if I would have been able to do it alone. My husband always backed me up, and so did my sons. The way they pushed me to continue was really incredible. They thought that our way of doing things, disorganized, you might say, was the factor that made it hard to wipe us out, because if they had wanted to

they could have done it. It is possible that they didn't attach importance to us, that they didn't believe we were going to achieve what we achieved.

Many times I wanted to stop. I felt embittered, tired: "You have to go on, you have to go there," and if we had to travel, with all the sacrifice of leaving the family behind, I would go because my family pushed me to go. And I believe that the same thing happened to many of the Mothers. My sons adored their sister.

Understanding what has happened cost us very dearly, and I would say that until a very short time ago, we were still waiting for our children. Because of what they have taught us, I now think that the model of their lives, their sacrifice, hasn't been in vain. Because all the children, not just mine, were alike. I'd talk to another of the Mothers and her son seemed to be my son. They have taken away the best of our young people, and that cannot be forgotten, that has to be remembered always. This marvelous sacrifice of youth has to remain forever in our memories. To achieve this, above all so that we learn that this can never be repeated, so that our young people enjoy the right to live in peace and in freedom, we Mothers keep on fighting and will always fight.

But I don't want to close my testimony without telling about the last image I have of my daughter. On May 7, 1976, María Marta and Cesar came to say good-bye at my parents' house because they were unable to go to Ezeiza Airport on the following day. And when they were already in the elevator, I told them: "Children, be careful, don't work so hard, don't be so open . . . ." And she, with her angelical smile, looked at me from the back of the elevator and answered: "But Mom! What are you thinking of! Why do you worry so much?" And she told me this with a great smile. That was the last thing that María Marta said to me. And I watched her slowly descend in the elevator shaft. And thus she disappeared from our lives, as if the earth had swallowed her up.

STUDY QUESTIONS

1. How does Marta characterize her daughter María? What types of political activity was María engaged in that led the military government to target her?
2. How did Marta become connected with the Mothers of the Plaza del Mayo? How did participation in this movement change her own political and personal identity?

CHAPTER 12

THE LATE COLD WAR IN LATIN AMERICA, 1970s–1990

MARGARET RANDALL

12.1 *SANDINO'S DAUGHTERS: TESTIMONIES OF NICARAGUAN WOMEN IN STRUGGLE*, 1981

The military leadership role played by women was one of the most notable features of the Sandinista National Liberation Front (FSLN) that came to power in Nicaragua in 1979 following a decade-long revolutionary war. The level of women's involvement in the Sandinista guerrilla movement was unprecedented in world history: approximately 30 percent of all troops in the revolutionary army were women, and many women held military command roles. The FSLN promoted gender equality as a core part of its platform, helping to attract women supporters. The following is an excerpt from an interview with Monica Baltodano and her mother, Zulema, which was conducted in 1980 by Margaret Randall, an American-born writer and activist who was deeply involved in revolutionary political movements in Latin America. Monica Baltodano joined the guerrilla movement in 1973 at the age of eighteen, and in 1977 was jailed and tortured by the Somoza regime. After her release she played a key role in the final stages of the revolution, leading a battalion of seven thousand during the final military offensive on Managua. During the period of revolutionary government, Baltodano served as minister for regional affairs. She later became a critic of the FLSN under the leadership of Daniel Ortega—in part over his conservative position on gender issues—and subsequently separated from the party, becoming active in other left-wing political causes.

MONICA: I was born in Leon on August 14, the day of the little *griteria*.[1] Both my parents came from working class families. My father's mother was a domestic worker who got involved with her boss—or, I should say, the boss got involved with her. And my mother is the daughter of a carpenter and his wife. When I was born my father was a law student. My mother had a small shop.

---

1   *Griteria* is a popular religious festival.

Source: Margaret Randall, *Sandino's Daughters: Testimonies of Nicaraguan Women in Struggle*, edited by Lynda Yanz (New Brunswick: Rutgers University Press, 1995), pp. 59–68, 70–76.

She put my dad through law school, working long, hard days in the shop. She had four children during that period.

ZULEMA: I identified with the struggle from the time I was very young. I knew that things had to change one day. I didn't know how, but I was aware that we lived in a time of injustice and that we had to rebel. I used to have arguments with my husband. Sometimes Monica or our younger daughter Amparita didn't agree with their grades so I would say, "If they don't agree, they have a right to go and complain. It is their right." I was like that. During the school sit-ins, I spent many nights at the school. My husband never backed us, never gave his support. That created problems between us and eventually led to our separation.

I have nine children. Or I should say, had nine children, one died in the war. I had two sons and seven daughters. Monica was the first to get involved. By her third year of high school she was already participating in school activities for grievances, for the political prisoners, in the teachers strike, the milk strike, and others. She was only thirteen then. . .

MONICA: I'm the third in our family. We were nine altogether, one after another, with a year or a year-and-a-half difference between us. My dad began working with a cotton farmer and then became one himself, in Leon. At that point, for a very short period, my dad had money. Cotton is a very treacherous way to make a living. One day you're rich and the next you're out on the street. That's exactly what happened to us. My dad went bankrupt when the Black Hill erupted and destroyed the surrounding plantations (ours included).

From then on we were poor—but it was a contradictory kind of poverty. We studied in Catholic schools, the two boys in La Salle and the seven girls in La Pureza. We were poor but attended a rich kids' school. It was awful. In those places you are indoctrinated into a completely traditional, archaic class mentality. All of us hated it. That was our life until my mom separated from my dad and we came to Managua looking for a way to survive.

I had always been a humanitarian, slightly different from my classmates and others in my family. When I was a child I wanted to be a missionary and go to Africa or some place like that. I think many comrades started off like that. Even before I was involved in anything I used to put a political emphasis on the social research nuns assigned, to show that the causes of poverty were in the system and not spiritual phenomena. Then in my fourth year of high school I started my political activity. I worked on the campaign to free Doris Tijerino from prison. That's the first demonstration I remember going to. I made posters and everything; I was so excited. My friends were shocked by my activities.

In 1970, the year of the teachers strike, I was invited to Managua to attend a course on group dynamics called "Faith and Joy." It was an important experience for me. Some of the people in the course were very political and challenged the rest of us. They talked about the need to change the structure, the system. They said that poverty has social roots and doesn't come about as a result of the intrinsic evil of mankind. They were more radical than most of the people I'd met up till then.

At the end of that school year the students held a big meeting. We decided not to spend the vacation fooling around and instead to study and organize. For three months we helped build the Christian movement in our area.

ZULEMA: We moved to Managua in 1972. Monica had already graduated. She continued her involvement in the Christian movement in Managua. By then Monica was active in what they called self-examination. She worked with people in the slum neighborhoods. By that point the Christian movement was beginning to worry the authorities and was forced to start taking security precautions.

MONICA: I was a believer. I remember how, during the school sit-in, we went every day to the chapel to pray to the Virgin to make the authorities release the prisoners. The basic issue which distinguished us from the comrades we called "communist" was whether or not liberation would require armed struggle. The priests used to say that when you got to the university, radicals there turned you on to Marxism. To avoid our being converted to Marxism the priests promoted

a highly social Christianity which was supposedly not in contradiction with social activism.
According to the priests, we had to carry the voice
of Christianity to the campus, and offer proof of
Christian testimony.

I remember a Christian meeting we organized
in 1972. A member of the FSLN spoke to us about
Nicaraguan history. He gave it an interpretation
I was totally unfamiliar with, that is, a Marxist
interpretation. That was an important turning
point for me. I was still a Christian when I entered
university but I had stopped believing in all the
trappings. I wanted nothing to do with rosaries or
masses or anything. I still believed in God, but a
God removed from the Church. . . .

My mother was very influential in my becoming a revolutionary. In high school I defended the
idea of a peaceful road to liberation. My mom
would argue with me. She'd say, "No, at my age
I'm convinced that we'll only win through armed
struggles. . . . ""I would argue against her and
then my comrades—some of whom were in the
Revolutionary Students Front (FER)—would say,
"the woman's right." I'd get furious. But it was she
who thought like that at first. Afterwards, when
I began thinking seriously about armed struggle,
she drew back a little. When she saw me getting in
deeper and deeper, she backtracked even further.
She may have held her earlier convictions but she
feared what might happen to her daughter. . . .

ZULEMA: With Monica active in the FER, my daughter
Amparita participating, and the youngest starting
to take part—let me tell you, what I felt most
was fear. Deep inside I knew that what they were
fighting for was just, yet I felt tremendous fear.
Sometimes I tried to get Monica to abandon the
struggle. I would say that I didn't believe in the
triumph of the Revolution. It was taking so long.
By then things had calmed down again. Victory
was nowhere in sight. I didn't even read the
pamphlets they brought to the house. I just
didn't read them. I remember one girl used to
invite me to see plays; once we saw Gorki's
Mother. I went and it was all nice, but that was
the extent of my participation.

We mothers saw the experiences of other
mothers. So many dead sons and daughters. Their

deaths seemed senseless. All the Nicaraguan
people felt the same way, really. Everyone called
them "the crazy kids" going off to meet their
death. "How will they ever be able to compete
with the Guard when the Guard is armed to the
teeth?" We were convinced of that. They were
right in protesting but we didn't believe they
could win. Each of us thought our children would
just be more martyrs.

I started to get more active around the time
of the earthquake in 1973. When the earthquake
struck, a group of us were occupying the Managua
cathedral. There were about 40 of us from Leon.
We were protesting the commercialization of
Christmas. After the earthquake we returned to
Leon. Monica joined the rescue and to help
make ends meet I opened a boarding house.
Monica was at university then so of course the
boarders she brought home were activists. So
many people lived in the house during that
period. I began to get more and more involved
myself, by helping them. . . .

There were many instances of kids being
stuck in jail and then their parents or teachers
would have to fight to get them out. Monica got
into something like that. She was at a rally in
Guadalupe and they picked her up and another
comrade at about nine at night. She was only
kept for about half an hour, but they opened a
file on her and started following her. I remember
that "Chele" Auilera, a notorious guard, followed
her a lot. From that time on they didn't lose
sight of the two corners of our house. We were
always watched. . . .

MONICA: I joined the FER in 1972. The earthquake
was in December and in early 1973 I was recruited by the FSLN. I think I always wanted to
be a revolutionary. I remember men would say
things to me like: "When we get married, I'll get
you your own car and you won't have to
work. . . . etc. etc." By the next day I would be
saying "no way!" I couldn't even consider that
kind of life.

It was a time when there was a lot of discussion and debate about the role of women in the
struggle. At an early point women in the Christian
movement were more conscious than many in the

FER. There were always scores of women in the Christian movement and they participated on the basis of a strong conviction. Later when the FSLN began working in the Christian movement the fact that the women involved were really strong and had a high level of consciousness had an effect on the FSLN.

The problem of male chauvinism was evident among comrades in the FER and FSLN. Some men harboured distinctly sexist attitudes toward women. They believed that women were for domestic tasks alone and that we shouldn't go beyond being messengers. There were a lot of arguments. Some comrades were open to dealing with sexism while others remained closed. Some said women were no good in the mountains, that they were only good "for screwing," that they created conflicts—sexual conflicts. But there were also men with very good positions. Carlos Fonseca, for example, was a solid comrade on this issue. It's been a long struggle! We won those battles through discussions and by women comrades demonstrating their ability and their resistance.

By 1974 I was underground. I was in the countryside, between Telica and El Sauce. I was arrested in July of 1977. . . .

ZULEMA: We mothers have a thing about our kids, you know. We get to thinking one is more intelligent, or another is happier. . . . So I began reading the pamphlets in an effort to find out why, even though they were intelligent, they had chosen this road, the road to death. And I assure you, it helped being more politically aware. It helped later when I had to bear up under the hard blows I received. If I hadn't been clear politically I might have reacted the way many mothers did. Some are still resentful. It's their lack of political consciousness. . . .

When Monica went underground I went six months without news—nothing. She did leave instructions for some friends to visit me to explain the situation. By that point I had made up my mind that this was the way it was going to have to be but I still doubted that they would win. The truth is that a lot of people were dying.

There were so many people killed or taken prisoner and put through the military courts. . . .

While we were living in Linda Vista, Monica wrote me that she was pregnant. That really frightened me. One day a woman came by and started asking me questions about myself. I was suspicious and afraid, but when she came back four days later, she brought Monica and her son. Monica had sent her to check out the house. They came with the baby and a small box of clothes. Monica stayed for the day and then left late in the afternoon. She left her son with me. He was crying when she left. She had nursed him for three months and now I had to bottle-feed him. That visit was only the second time I'd seen Monica since she'd gone underground.

After that I started getting letters more frequently—naturally, there was a baby in the picture now. She told me to name him Pancasan.[2] That scared me; people were bound to be suspicious. We told people he was my other daughter's child, but giving him that name. . . . My husband said, "Are you kidding? That's crazy!" and I even said "I'm going to name him Bayardo." But that night I kept thinking about it and decided no, what if my daughter dies and I haven't even given her the pleasure of naming her son. I registered him as Pancasan. . . .

I continued to get more involved. They sent me word that my daughter didn't have enough food, that she didn't even have salt, so I started sending her things every month or two. I joined with other comrades—Santos Buitrago[3] and other women—to help the prisoners. At first we were

---

2   "Pancasan" refers to a guerrilla experience in August 1967 in which a great many of the strongest members of the FSLN were killed in ambush. In spite of the military failure, the Pancasan experience is considered a political landmark in the struggle.

3   Santos Buitrago is Julio Buitrago's mother. Julio was the FSLN leader who was killed when the house he was in was surrounded on July 15, 1969, in Managua. After the death of her son, Santos Buitrago became one of the leading figures of the mothers' movement.

very timid about it and hardly did a thing. Once we were assigned to find safehouses and people who would donate money to the struggle. At one point I had five people, each giving 100 *cordobas* a month.

When the baby was seven months old Monica was taken prisoner in Matagalpa. She was held there for three months and then the jury pardoned her. There were no charges against her. At first they scheduled her release for October 17. That turned out to be the same day as the incident at San Carlos, in Masaya, where several militants died. I don't know if they had planned to let her out or not but they took advantage of the San Carlos incident to keep her in jail. They sent her to Managua where she was held another six months.

After Monica was arrested I didn't care if the whole world knew I was a revolutionary. I became fully involved. We formed the Committee of Relatives of the Political Prisoners. I worked to defend her with all my might. If they even lifted a finger against her I went to *La Prensa* or to the radio and made public what was happening. I was no longer afraid, nothing mattered.

MONICA: When I was arrested I was working in Esteli. I was in charge of the North and travelled frequently to Jinotega, Matagalpa. . . . That day we were going to a meeting in Matagalpa and I guess someone started tailing us after we left Sebaco. A jeep and a red Cherokee caught up with us. They started shooting and were shooting to kill. I don't know how the three of us managed to get out alive. I leaped out and ran away from the highway into the fields. I walked a whole day. Finally I had to ask a peasant for directions. He betrayed me and I was captured in Dario. I was in jail for nine months.

They didn't give me the electric shocks so many other women received. They just beat me. But the worst part of being in jail was the cell itself. The stench was so bad you couldn't sleep. They tied you to the wall and you had to sleep like that. The experience toughens you. They say it prepares you to break and finally talk, but actually it helps you grow.

There many other comrades in the Central Jail in Managua when I arrived. They spoke to me through a little hole they'd made with a fork. They worked on it till you could see through it and use it like a telephone. I proposed we carve a big hole from the little one so we could move from cell to cell. We learned all that in there. We learned how to protest, to scream, to demand sun. They treated us even worse than the men prisoners. The men comrades had a collective kitchen, ping-pong tables, a television set. . . . we had nothing. We were stuck in tiny cells all day; we barely managed to keep sane. We began throwing ourselves against the walls, and since the Central Jail was visited by people the authorities didn't want seeing such spectacles, we finally got them to give us sun, longer visiting hours, and other concessions. We never did get conjugal visits like the men.

ZULEMA: The entire time Monica was in jail we fought so they would give the political prisoners sun and visiting hours. I carried out letters signed by all the women; we got them out in the lids of fruit jars. Alesio Gutierrez, the head of the prison, said to me one day, "How did this letter get out of here?" I told him some guard brought it out. "Some guard we gave 20 *cordobas* to," I said. I took the letter, signed by all the prisoners, to *La Prensa*. We learned how to take advantage of that. . . .

That's how the time went by, six months of planning, fighting and participating. We also worked with the women who were organizing the occupation of the United Nations office. That sit-in also included relatives of missing peasants. It was a great experience. Eight of us went, four from Managua and four peasant women. There was also another comrade, Cela, the coordinator.

The action was a protest. We women with political prisoners had no illusions that the prisoners would be released as a result of the protest. Our major objective was to mobilize and politicize the masses. . . .

When the time came for Monica's release, I went to *La Prensa* again. I argued with Alesio Gutierrez, the head of the prison, and demanded to know if they were really going to release her this time. There were all kinds of problems and delays, but finally they let her go. A rally was organized for her at the university. All the students were there to hear her speak. Afterwards they said we should all go down to the Red Cross where a group of women were on a hunger strike. I was afraid all over again. How was Monica going to go to a demonstration when she'd just been released from prison?

When the demonstration left and headed for the hunger strike we slipped away. The plan was to make sure we weren't followed. It worked. All the informers went to the demonstration. There was no one near our house. Monica went in alone, changed into a dark blouse and came out again. About two blocks away comrades were waiting for her. That's how she went underground again. So ended her prison life. I kept going to the jail. By this time I was signing in as the aunt of another woman, named Baltodano. . . .

MONICA: After I was released from prison I worked for a while in Carazo and then later was put in charge of the Capital. I had been in charge of the North Front, so it was only a matter of learning the particular situation in Managua.

You asked me if I ever had problems in leadership because I am a woman. I think I was rather lucky in that respect. For example, here in Managua I worked with Walter Mendoza and Ramon Cabrales. I worked with comrades who have the mentalities of new men. I don't think they even thought about the fact that I was a woman. Besides, I had prestige and a lot of experience. There were some difficulties with comrades who didn't know me. Where problems did arise, it was usually with sympathizers, not members of the Organization. This was particularly the case in the North; northerners have terrible problems with male chauvinism. They saw me as a woman and not as a leader so they didn't help me as much as they helped the men.

In fact, if you were living in a safehouse in the North you knew you had to help with the sweeping, the cooking and the dishes—if you were a woman. That was my experience. I also had tons

of letters to answer so I had to start at five in the morning and work until late at night. In the North we worked all day and only went onto the streets at night. Sometimes a male comrade might arrive and spend a whole day with us before heading for the mountains. He would have nothing to do all day and so could help with the dishes, but it was hard for the sympathizers to accept this. The comrade often understood but the woman of the house didn't. She would say, "How is a man going to help me?" One woman asked me, "How is it that you don't wash Bayardo's clothes if you're his wife?" . . . .

The final offensive here in Managua began sooner than we had planned. We even had problems transferring the weapons from the west side of the city to the east where we were going to stage the resistance. There were three of us on Managua's General Staff: Oswaldo Lacayo, Raul Venerio and me. What did I do in the insurrection here? I walked. I had to visit all the points of combat. Every day I went out walking and my feet swelled up like balloons. It was an enormous zone. I went back and forth—co-ordinating, doing political work, enforcing discipline among the people on the barricades.

After twelve days we had no more munitions. It was terrible to see the *compitas*.[4] Then came the decision for the retreat to Masaya. That retreat is historic, right? We had to leave with around 7,000 people, including civilians, children and militia. We divided into groups: the vanguard, the centre—where all the wounded were—followed by the rearguard.

We reached Masaya and then Carazo, where we stayed about a week. Later we went on to Granada. We went to Granada knowing that Somoza was going to resign that day. We had received the news while we were still in Masaya. We went through at dawn and fought the whole day. By nightfall we had surrounded an area known as La Polvora. I remember I even had a

---

4 *Compita* is the diminutive of *compa*, derived from *companero* or comrade. It's a term used in Nicaragua to identify a fellow revolutionary.

bath after that battle. Then the next step was ne-gotiating with the Guard. After cleaning up we headed out. I remember a woman asking me where I was going. "To the surrender," I replied. We approached the hospital, keeping a good distance from the guard post, moving up house by house. When we got closer to their headquarters and had ourselves positioned around the building, we got word that they wanted to surrender. One of the Guard came out draped in a flag and I went to talk to him. That dialogue is taped and filmed. At first he refused to speak to me because I was a woman!

ZULEMA: Toward the end, what happened was what was bound to happen. All my children left, every last one. They all became involved in the struggle. At home we lived more poorly, but we had a solid political consciousness. Then came the time to make bombs and harass the Guard. My two youngest children were assigned to make contact bombs. That was the last year, during the Carlos Fonseca memorial.[5] They made bombs and painted walls.

---

5   Carlos Fonseca, Commander-in-Chief of the Nicaraguan Revolution and a founding member of the FSLN, was killed in battle on November 8, 1976.

The paint for the slogans came from my house. My daughter Amparita was the most politically advanced and had a fair amount of responsibility. My son who had gone to study in Leon had also joined the Organization. Besides the two of them, another woman comrade came to stay in the house. They all did physical exercises in the house to keep in shape. And we prepared enormous quantities of food—rice and black beans, and *pinolillo*. I made gallons of *pinol*. That's what we lived on.

In our last house I didn't pay rent for five months. It belonged to a millionaire. That's the period we worked the hardest. We lived in four different houses that year. As soon as the Guard caught wind of us and began coming by we would move. We left no trace. Then the Guard would forget about us and we could go on working. In addition to *pinol*, there were arms, powder and bottles for Molotov cocktails at the house. . . .

Around that time I began sleeping alone in the house. Alone with Monica's boy. I said to my other kids, "If they capture me, they're going to get me alone. I'm old." All the kids went to sleep elsewhere. They came over during the day but didn't stay the night because that was when the raids were most likely to occur. They never did raid us.

STUDY QUESTIONS

1.   What were some of the gendered challenges Baltodano faced as she ascended to the role of guerrilla commander? How did her male comrades respond to her leadership?

2.   What role did Zulema play in supporting Monica in her political and military work? How did Monica's activism shape Zulema's politicization? To what extent did Monica's own transition to motherhood impact this mother–daughter dynamic?

MARIA DA SILVA MIGUEL

12.2 THE PEOPLE IS POET, 1990

In the latter stages of the Cold War, liberation theology became institutionalized in Latin America, coming to dominate local church hierarchies, especially in Brazil, where the Catholic Church became notably progressive, promoting lay participation in the faith through Base Ecclesiastical Communities (CEBs), and issuing documents defending the right of the masses to land, food and political participation. Through CEBs, many ordinary Brazilians were empowered to claim owner-ship of their own spiritual lives through Bible reading groups and lay pastoral associations and to take up leadership roles in their communities. This poem was written in 1990 by Maria da Silva Miguel—an Afro-Brazilian great-grandmother from a São Paulo favela, whose parents had been born into slavery—and was originally published in a national religious magazine. Through partici-pation in a CEB, Miguel had learned to read as an older adult, and she began writing poetry at the age of sixty-five, earning success as writer of songs for her church and for political movements, in-cluding the land rights movement and the women's movement. The poem reveals how the practice of liberation theology changed the interior, and not just the material, lives of the poor.

One day a woman cried. "I am a Warrior!"
and the echo of her voice was heard beyond the
    borders.
I am Woman—Mother and Warrior,
the stove is no longer my limit.
I am called queen of the home,
but I am greater than ocean and sea.
I am Mother, I give life,
I am a Woman, Pain.
I am a Warrior, a Bird—I sing!

I raise up my people and pull them out of slavery,
my name is Liberation!
Whoever wants to find me, I'm not only in the
    home,
I'm in the struggle, I'm a Warrior!
I am Black, I am Poor, I am Old and nearly Illiterate,
Everyone knows me—
I am the remnant who dreams of happiness and
    love
I am merely Maria Miguel!

STUDY QUESTIONS

1. What insights does the poem provide as to how liberation theology changed Maria da Silva Miguel's perception of herself and her own capabilities?
2. What does the poem reveal about the intersections between liberation theology and struggles for racial and gender equality?

Source: Maria da Silva Miguel, "The People Is Poet," in *The Struggle Is One: Voices and Visions of Liberation* (Albany: State University of New York Press, 1994).

VICTOR MONTEJO AND VICTOR PERERA

12.3 *TESTIMONY: DEATH OF A GUATEMALAN VILLAGE*, 1987

The military coup of 1982, which brought Efraín Ríos Montt to power in Guatemala, marked an intensification of the already decades long civil war in Guatemala, and would have devastating consequences for the Mayan indigenous population, tens of thousands of whom were killed in a state-sponsored genocide. Victor Montejo is a Jakaltek Maya, originally from Guatemala, who built a successful academic career in the United States and became an internationally recognized scholar and author. In his youth Montejo worked as a schoolteacher in a remote village named Tzalalá in the central highlands of Guatemala. In September 1982, he became an eyewitness to genocide when the village in which he worked was invaded by the military and many of the men and boys killed. The massacre occurred when a member of the village civil patrol—an informal militia created at the behest of the army to watch out for guerrillas—mistook an army detachment dressed in olive fatigues in place of their conventional uniforms for guerrillas and opened fire. The army accused the civil patrol of launching a guerrilla attack and killed all those involved, before entering the village and torturing the inhabitants in a quest for information. Montejo was arrested after being accused of supporting the guerrillas by a neighbor. He was later released and managed to flee the country. In this excerpt, Montejo recounts his interrogation by the Guatemalan military.

ACCUSATIONS

I remained seated under the eaves of the chapel, watching in consternation the captives who gazed vacantly at some undefined point in the horizon. Very close by, the commander scratched his buttocks with his nails, trying to loosen the trousers that pinched his overblown body.

The sergeant appeared with a soldier, holding in his hand a scrap of paper I recognized as a matchbook cover. He presented it to the commander with a show of gravity.

"What happened?" the lieutenant asked him.

"Well, he confessed."

"What did he say?"

"He gave a name. Here it is."

The sergeant handed him the matchbook cover and whispered in his ear, too softly for me to hear. The commander turned on me a fixed glare. I suspected nothing, but as he stood over me I had the sense that something bad was about to happen.

"You're the prof here, is that right?" the commander asked.

"Sí *mi comandante*, what can I do for you?"

My forthright reply set him aback. Without further commentary, he snapped at me: "Follow these men."

The sergeant and the soldier escorted me to my classroom, where they had taken the tall dark youth a while back so he would "tell some jokes."

They opened the door and pushed me inside, then closed it shut, leaving me entirely at their mercy.

Manuel lay face down on the floor, in a pool of blood, with his hands tied behind his back. His face looked grotesquely disfigured.

Source: Victor Montejo and Victor Perera, *Testimony: Death of a Guatemalan Village* (Willimantic, CT: Curbstone Press, 1995), pp. 41–47.

I sat down on one of the old desks of the class-room, showing neither fear nor nervousness. I knew that if I betrayed weakness I would lose any advantage I would have during the interrogation. I gathered up my strength and would not humble myself before these men, who regarded me like hungry wolves. I focussed my mind so I would not stumble over my own words or fall into the traps they were setting for me.

Six soldiers stood over me, pointing their black Galils at my head with malicious smiles on their lips. I turned aside to avoid their twisted scowls, with which they tried to intimidate me. A soldier approached from behind, ready to place a noose around my neck to choke me. I rose from my seat at once. If I allowed them to strike me at the outset without defending myself, I would lose my hard-won confidence. I stood up before he had a chance to collar me and looked into their eyes.

"Señores," I said in a firm voice, "I am no criminal for you to be assaulting me without reason. I ask to know what I am accused of, as I consider myself innocent."

"As innocent as the great whore," the sergeant called out. "Here is your accuser. You are a guerrilla, the same as your companion."

He addressed the tortured youth, shouting. "All right, you fucker—tell your companion what you confessed to us. Go on, wretch."

As he said this the sergeant began to kick him in the face, the head and the stomach. I almost broke down seeing the blows he gave Manuel. I've never been able to tolerate the sight of a suffering fellow being. Whenever my mother slaughters a hen for dinner or a fiesta I always turn aside so I won't have to see its neck twisted. Now that I beheld a human being tortured and bloodied. I felt a great heaviness and fear.

Despite his wretched state, Manuel turned his head toward me with difficulty and spoke with hatred, spitting out blood on the floor.

"Look brother, I heard your voice one night when two men came to threaten me, calling me a loud-mouth reactionary, and I am certain that you were one of them. I am sure I heard your voice."

As he finished speaking a soldier reached out one hand and punched me in the midsection, causing me to double over with pain. To avoid another blow, I sat down quickly on the old desk, as the sergeant said to me with gloating disdain:

"Now we have you and you can't get out of this one. You heard your own companion accuse you."

"That accusation has no validity." I said, with strained dignity. "Many people in this world have the same or similar voices, and this man who accused me falsely, is lying. I would never oppose the government—I am a schoolteacher and my salary is paid by the State. Let this young man tell you when he has seen me break any law. If he can accuse me of acting illegally and prove it, I am ready to pay the consequences; but if he can't, I plead with you to let me go because I assure you that I know nothing of these matters."

They began pummelling Manuel once again, shouting: "Speak up, shit-face, what else do you know about this two-bit schoolmaster?"

"I know nothing more." the beaten youth replied. "I only know that he accompanied the one who threatened me that night, and that he is a guerrilla."

I turned to Manuel and said. "Look. Manuel, don't accuse me falsely. It's better if you resign yourself. Better to die alone and without remorse than to drag others to their death. What will you gain by killing me?"

He replied with great effort. "Well, I want them to kill you, too. We can die together."

Manuel had been an easy-going sort, with a cheerful disposition. When we met in the streets he always greeted me, and we played soccer together now and then. He had the reputation in the village of being a loudmouth, which is why he may have been threatened by one of the men he mistook me for.

Disregarding his words, I entreated with him softly, while I prayed inside me for him to take back his accusation. And so that the soldiers would ask me no more questions, I hastily pointed out:

"You see, señores, he can prove nothing against me. And as a Christian, I know perfectly well it does no good to kill one another."

The sergeant stepped toward me in a rage. "Look, little schoolmaster son of *la chingada*. Don't you come off giving us any orders." And he struck me in the face with the knotted rope. But I remained unmoved, looking him directly in the eyes.

One of the soldiers who sat at a corner table got up and tried to calm down his fellows. "That's enough, boys. Stop behaving like such shits."

The sergeant dismissed him with a withering look and stood on top of Manuel, who remained face down on the floor, and began jumping up and down, coming down hard on his lungs and chest. Not satisfied with this, he kicked him once more on the left cheek until more blood flowed from his nose and mouth. The sergeant shouted like one demented:

"There will be no pity for these motherfuckers. They deserve to be kicked to death like this. Did you hear me, turd?" He went on taunting Manuel. "Where are your companions? And what else do you know about this little schoolmaster?"

Manuel did not utter another word, but could only whimper each time the sergeant kicked him savagely in the side. The commander walked in just then, and ordered the sergeant to take us out and place us with the other captives. They quickly picked up the bloodied Manuel, who could hardly stand, and pushed him out the door. I did not wait but walked directly behind the commander.

It was like emerging from a tunnel. I looked up with gratitude at the open sky, but my spirits fell on hearing the screams of the women who were shut up inside the chapel.

While I was being interrogated in the school, the lieutenant had ordered the beating of the other captives, and I saw they all had cracked lips and teeth stained with blood.

The commander kept on shouting and insisting they point out their companions, whose names did not appear on the list. The younger ones all kept quiet, even as they were beaten and screamed at. Their silence provoked the fury of the commander, who began firing his rifle crazily into the air.

The screams of the women in the chapel grew louder. Several of them, particularly the mothers of the captives, tried to get outside, but the guards threatened to crack their skulls open.

The commander kept up his inquisitorial questioning, but no one said a word. It was clear they did not know anything.

"Whichever of you speaks up will be spared." the commander said, and one of the bound captives

opened his mouth to speak. They grabbed him by the hair and lifted him to his feet.

"Finally, we have one willing to talk. Speak up, wretch." the commander roared furiously. "Who are your accomplices?"

The dazed man looked around him as if in a trance. He looked over the entire group, not knowing where to rest his eyes. Finally, he pointed somebody out. "That one—" he said, jabbing his finger at one of the civil defenders who still held his polished *garrote* in one hand. The defender began to shake, as two soldiers pulled him out of the group.

"No *señores*. I'm not anything," the man blubbered, "You are mistaken—"

His neighbors stepped forward to defend him.

"No, *señor comandante*. This man is one of the civil defenders who most incites us to battle the guerrillas. And he is one of the richest men in the community."

The lieutenant released the defender, who returned to his place looking white as a sheet.

I had not given much thought to my own situation until then. Only when they released the defender did I become aware that I had a rope around my neck. I stood in the center of the plaza like a thief or a murderer, exposed to the stares of the entire community, whose intentions toward me at the moment I could not tell. I felt like one condemned.

When one of the villagers I considered a friend walked past me. I addressed him in a soft voice. "Look, friend, do me the favor of speaking to the headman, so they will intercede for me. Let them say they know me as the schoolmaster of the Village, and they have not seen me engage in any subversive activities."

But this friend stepped backward as if it were the very devil speaking to him. All he said was, "I am afraid."

A while later one of the headmen who had spoken up for the defender came near, and I signalled to him to aid me in the same way, but he only replied with hand signals, opening his palm as though to say, "Wait."

I knew that answer was equivalent to a "No," and so I decided to remain quiet. I had no other recourse but to gaze up at the sky and go on praying for my captive friends, for my family and for myself.

It was now four in the afternoon. Every Friday by this time I would be with my family, playing with my children. But now I had fallen into the hands of these tyrants, and I feared I would never see my children again.

I did not want anyone to see my tears, and turned my face up toward the sky, which had clouded over. I called to mind my brother, who had been killed by the *kaibile*—he was the first innocent to have been cut down in my town by the machinegun bursts of the special army units. The idea took hold in my head that he was sitting in the clouds and looking down at me

with a reassuring smile. I thought also about my parents, and of the other brothers who were some distance away, unaware of what had befallen me.

I turned my back to the plaza and could not recognize the faces of my acquaintances. My vision was blurred by the tears that had sprung from my eyes; I looked at everyone as though in a dream. Wherever I looked, the men crouched and avoided my eyes, turning to one side.

STUDY QUESTIONS

1. What strategies did the army use to gain information from the villagers? From the account, do we gain any insight as to whether these strategies were effective?

2. Why did Montejo believe he had been accused of guerrilla activity by Manuel? What did Montejo's position in the community have in common with the other man accused of being a guerrilla during the interrogation?

RAYMOND BONNER

12.4 MASSACRE OF HUNDREDS REPORTED IN SALVADOR VILLAGE, 1982

The El Mozote Massacre took place in El Salvador On December 11 and 12, 1981, when the Salvadoran army killed more than eight hundred civilians—virtually all of the inhabitants of the village of El Mozote—including babies and children. The massacre was one of the worst abuses of the civil war and took place in a village that had been widely understood locally to be neutral in the conflict—occasionally selling supplies to guerrillas but not supporting recruitment. The *New York Times* article reproduced here was the first account of the massacre to be published in the international media. Its author, the journalist Raymond Bonner, had been smuggled to visit the site by guerrilla leaders roughly a month after the massacre occurred. The article immediately attracted controversy. The Salvadoran army and government denied the report and the Regan administration accused Bonner—a former Captain in the Marines and a Stanford JD—of bias and exaggeration. Conservative media accused the *New York Times* of seeking to influence an upcoming Congressional hearing on US involvement in the Salvadoran civil war, and the *Wall Street Journal* ran an op-ed accusing Bonner of being overly credulous in

Source: Raymond Bonner, "Massacre of Hundreds Reported in Salvador Village: Massacre Is Reported in a Salvadoran Village" Special to *The New York Times*. *New York Times* (1923–Current file); Jan 27, 1982; ProQuest Historical Newspapers: *The New York Times* with Index. Pg. A1

his reporting. Bonner was recalled to New York and subsequently left the Times. Yet forensic excavations carried out by Argentine investigators following the Salvadoran Peace Accords of 1992 confirmed Bonner's report that hundreds of civilians had been killed at El Mozote; and in 1993 a detailed article on the massacre and its subsequent cover-up was published by Mark Danner in the *New Yorker* (later to be expanded into a 1994 book) that upheld the veracity of Bonner's original account. In 2011 the Salvadoran government officially apologized for the massacre.

MOZOTE, El Salvador—From interviews with people who live in this small mountain village and surrounding hamlets, it is clear that a massacre of major proportions occurred here last month.

In some 20 mud brick huts here, this reporter saw the charred skulls and bones of dozens of bodies buried under burned-out roofs, beams and shuttered tiles. There were more along the trail leading through the hills into the village, and at the edge of a nearby cornfield were the remains of 14 young men, women and children.

733 VICTIMS LISTED

In separate interviews during a two-week period in the rebel-controlled northern part of Morazán Province, 13 peasants said that all these, their relatives and friends, had been killed by Government soldiers of the Atlacatl Battalion in a sweep in December.

The villagers have compiled a list of the names, ages and villages of 733 peasants, mostly children, women and old people, who they say were murdered by the Government soldiers. The Human Rights Commission of El Salvador, which works with the Roman Catholic Church, puts the number at 926.

A spokesman for the Salvadoran armed forces, Col. Alfonso Cotto, called the reports about "hundreds of civilians" being killed by Government soldiers "totally false." Those reports were fabricated by "subversives," he said.

"A GREAT MASSACRE"

It is not possible for an observer who was not present at the time of the massacre to determine independently how many people died or who killed them. In the interviews, the peasants said uniformed soldiers, some swooping in by helicopters, did the shooting. The rebels in this zone are not known to wear uniforms or use helicopters."

"It was a great massacre," 38-year-old Rufina Amaya told a visitor who traveled through the area with those who are fighting against the junta that now rules El Salvador. "They left nothing."

Somewhere amid the carnage were Mrs. Amaya's husband, who was blind, her 9-year-old son and three daughters, ages 5 years, 3 years and 8 months.

Mrs. Amaya said she heard her son scream: "Mama, they're killing me. They've killed my sister. They're going to kill me." She said that when the soldiers began gathering the women into a group. She escaped and hid behind some trees in back of the houses.

From Dec. 8 to Dec. 21, according to Salvadoran newspapers, soldiers from the Atlacatl Battalion took pan in a sweep through Mozote and the surrounding mountain villages as part of one of the largest search-and-destroy operations of the war against the leftist guerrillas who are fighting to overthrow the United States–supported junta. According to the villagers, no Americans accompanied the troops on the sweep.

Asked whether the Atlacatl Battalion had been involved in an operation in the northern mountainous region of Morazan in December, Col. Cotto said he could not provide specific details about military operations.

"We have been at war since 1979 against the subversives," he said. As part of that war, he said, air force and army units, including the Atlacatl Battalion, are continually conducting operations throughout the country.

280 CHILDREN REPORTED SLAIN

In Mozote, 280 of the 482 peasants killed, according to the list the villagers have prepared, were children under 14 years old. In Capilla, villagers say the soldiers murdered a father and his nine children, a mother and her five; in Cerro Pando, 87 adults and 62 children.

The Human Rights Commission has at other times also charged the army with killing large numbers of civilians during its operations. According to the commission, more than 100 were killed in the northern part of the province of Cabanas in November; 143, including 99 children under 16 years old, were said to have been killed in San Vicente in October, and about 300 in Usulutan in September.

Under banana trees at the edge of a cornfield near this village were 14 bodies. A child of about 5 or 6 years old was among the heap. Spent M-16 cartridges littered the dirt about 15 to 20 feet from the bodies. The rebels do have some M-16 rifles captured from army units, and they are standard issue for the Atlacatl Battalion.

A few peasants, handkerchiefs or oranges pressed against their noses to help block the stench, poked among the rubble for anything salvageable.

Up the mountain trail a short distance, 12 recently cut wood planks about 10 inches by three-eighths of an inch by 12 feet were propped against the trees. On the patio of the adobe hut, saws and crude homemade machetes and hammers were stained with blood.

Inside, five skulls were strewn among the smashed tiles. The men were carpenters, according to a boy who was working among beehives behind the mud hovel.

Mrs. Amaya said the first column of soldiers arrived in Mozote on foot about 6 P.M. Three times during the next 24 hours, she said, helicopters landed with more soldiers.

She said the soldiers told the villagers they were from the Atlacatl Battalion. "They said they wanted our weapons. But we said we didn't have any. That made them angry, and they started killing us."

Many of the peasants were shot while in their homes, but the soldiers dragged others from their houses and the church and put them in lines, women in one, men in another. Mrs. Amaya said. It was during this confusion that she managed to escape, she said.

She said about 25 young girls were separated from the other women and taken to the edge of the tiny village. She said she heard them screaming.

"We trusted the army," Mrs. Amaya said when asked why the villagers had not fled. She said that from October 1980 to August 1981, there had been a regular contingent of soldiers in Mozote, often from the National Guard. She said that they had not abused the peasants and that the villagers often fed them.

Rebel leaders in this region said Mozote was not considered a pro-rebel village. But the guerrillas did say that 3,000 of their supporters had fled the area when the army came in.

MEN AND BOYS FLED

When the soldiers and helicopters began arriving in the village of La Joya, the older boys and men fled, said 46-year-old Cesar Martinez.

"We didn't think they would kill children, women and old people, so they remained," he explained. But, he said, the soldiers killed his mother, his sister and his sister's two children, ages 5 and 8 years. He said that among the others the soldiers killed were a 70-year-old woman and another woman and her 3-day-old baby.

On the wall of one house, Mr. Martinez said the soldiers scrawled "the Atlacatl Battalion will return to kill the rest."

Sitting next to Mr. Martinez as he talked was 15-year-old Julio. Julio said his mother, father, 9-year-old brother and two sisters, ages 7 and 5 years, had been killed by the soldiers in La Joya. He said that when he heard the first shooting, he ran and hid in a gulley.

Julio said that he has returned to his village once since the massacre, to bury his family and two of his friends, ages 7 and 10 years.

WHETHER TO LEARN OR FIGHT

Julio has never been to school, and unlike many boys his age in this area, he had not been involved in the revolutionary movement. Now he is confused: He doesn't know whether to attend the school for children that is operated by the guerrillas or learn to use a rifle so "I can fight against the enemy," he said.

Another La Joya peasant, 39-year-old Gumersindo Lucas, said that before he fled with his wife, children and other relatives, he took his 62-year-old mother, who was too sick to walk, to a neighbor's house and hid her under some blankets. He said the soldiers shot her there and then burned the house.

Holding his half-naked chubby-cheeked 4-month-old daughter, who was wearing a red T-shirt and a tiny red bracelet, Mr. Lucas said that he had not sympathized with the rebels. Now, he said, "I want my wife and children to go to Honduras, but I am going to stay and fight."

Mrs. Amaya said she has not been able to return to Mozote since the massacre. "If I return, I will hear my children crying. . . . "

STUDY QUESTIONS

1. What are the main allegations laid out in Bonner's account in the *New York Times?*
2. What sources does Bonner use to substantiate his account? How reliable are these sources?

12.5 REPORT OF THE CHILEAN COMMISSION ON TRUTH AND RECONCILIATION: THE 1978–1990 PERIOD

Following the transition to civilian rule in Chile in 1990, a national commission was established to provide a bipartisan assessment of human rights abuses under the military regime. The following excerpt from the report examines police and military cover-ups of extrajudicial killings and disappearances during the period 1978–1990 in which the military regime was consolidated and institutionalized. The majority of the abuses documented here were attributed to the National Information Center (CNI)—the military secret police agency established by the Pinochet regime in 1977, which combined the equivalent functions of the CIA, FBI, and Secret Service in the United States.

. . . During the 1981–1989 period, disappearances were carried out in such a way that there are practically no witnesses who saw the events or the places where the victims were held. Executions. . . took place in different types of contexts:

* In some cases there really was a gun battle between the pursued and the pursuers, who were attempting either to arrest or kill their object. In some instances, those captured or wounded were then killed.
* In other cases, the activist being pursued was simply killed in an ambush, which was then presented as a gun battle.
* In a few instances there were other forms of execution, such as throat slitting, and kidnapping and execution with many shots to the head.

. . . Disposal of the body

The bodies of those said to have been killed in a gun battle—whether real or fictitious—were generally handed over to their relatives. In some other instances their bodies were left on different properties, along a

road, or in a swamp. There is no information about what may have happened to the remains of those who disappeared during this period.

. . . Methods for concealing the facts and issuing disinformation

From the case narratives presented here, one can discern a variety of procedures used after the fact to resolve difficulties over the illegality of the arrest and to prevent the victim from being identified, or more generally to conceal or distort what happened. CNI agents were so protective of one another that on a number of occasions when appearing in court they did not provide their real names but used assumed names or nicknames.

2. CASES

A. FICTITIOUS GUN BATTLES

During this period the official explanation for the deaths of left activists was continually that they had been killed in gun battles with members of security

Source: United States Institute of Peace (www.usip.org) "Report of the Chilean National Commission on Truth and Reconciliation."

agencies, primarily the CNI. This Commission has nonetheless been able to determine that a very large number of these gun battles never took place. The accounts given by officials were a way to evade government responsibility for these events.

We will now describe how those who were officially described as killed in gun battles were actually killed. Some people who were killed in genuine armed of the official report, the Commission has come to the conviction that Germán de Jesús Cortés was executed by CNI agents, and regards his death as a human rights violation for which government agents were responsible.

On August 2, 1980, Santiago RUBILAR SALAZAR, a company manager, was killed. He had left his house in Santiago on July 26 en route to Valparaiso, and was due to return two days later. He did not return. The day he was due to return his wife found that her house had been searched. CNI members arrested her and her brother-in-law, and took them to their headquarters on Calle Borgolio for interrogation about Rubilar's activities.

The official account was that Santiago Rubilar was killed August 2 in a gun battle with police as he was fleeing in a car. He was reported to have taken the car's owner and her son with him as hostages. In the course of events one policeman and the hostages were said to have been wounded. Rubilar was also said to be wanted for robbing the branch banks on Calle Santa Elena on July 28.

When an appeal for protection was initiated on Rubilar's behalf, the Ministry of Interior sent an exempt decree for his arrest. This decree proves that the official report is false. That decree was dated July 20, 1980, that is, before the bank robberies; it also mentions, in addition to Rubilar, the two people he was said to be holding as hostages as he was running away on August 2, 1980. In view of this evidence, the Commission has come to the conviction that Santiago Rubilar was executed by government agents in violation of his human rights.

On November 7, 1980, the MIR activists Rubén Eduardo ORTA JOPIA, an electrician, and Juan Ramón OLIVARES PEREZ, a worker, were killed in Santiago. According to the official account, at 1:20 A.M., CNI members are said to have halted a Citroneta that was driving along Avenida Domingo Santa Maria near the Vivaceta Bridge. The official account assumes that the two people in the car were trying to attack the CNI garrison which was nearby. They fired a burst of automatic weapons fire at the agents when they approached. The report also says that the car was carrying a variety of weapons.

However, the Commission received testimony indicating that CNI agents had arrested both of these people earlier that day. The story that they had tried to attack a CNI garrison while driving an old Citroneta, and that none of the agents were wounded by the burst of automatic weapons fire shot at them is implausible. The bodies, moreover, showed signs of torture. For all these reasons, the Commission has come to the conviction that Ruben Eduardo Orta and Juan Ramón Olivares were executed by CNI agents in violation of their human rights.

On January 18, 1981, Leandro Abraham ARRATIA REYES, 36, a photographer and CP activist, was killed. He had returned to Chile legally in October 1980. The official account stated that as CNI members were trying to arrest Leandro Arratia in the early morning, he resisted and climbed on top of a house at Calle Ricardo Santa Cruz No. 651 in the district of Santiago. The officers were forced to use their police weapons and shot him down. The Commission received statements by his relatives to the effect that early on the morning of January 14, 1981, security forces searched his house in the Conchali district. They demanded that he cooperate with them by identifying old friends and providing information on their activities. His relatives also say that on January 16, an individual came up to him while he was waiting for a bus. There was no further word on him until the official account.

In the judicial investigation, a CNI agent who was involved in the operation in which Arratia was killed said that he had been assigned to investigate his activities. Furthermore, the autopsy report says some of his bullet wounds came from being shot from behind, and hence it is at odds with the official version. Keeping in mind the previous accounts, Arratia's political activity, the search of his house, the surveillance over him, and other evidence gathered, the Commission has come to the conclusion that he was executed by CNI members in violation of his human rights.

NELTUME

In mid-1981, small farmers in the area of Neltume in the Tenth Region, reported that there was a guerrilla camp in the area. The guerrillas were MIR activists who had secretly returned to the country as part of what they called "Operation Return." They tried to set up a base in the Andes in southern Chile so that the leaders of their organization could later establish headquarters. With this information in hand, CNI agents dispatched from Santiago and members of the police and the army began an intensive operation.

In July 1981, members of the security forces discovered the camp, which was still being built. They seized a large amount of equipment and documentation. The guerrillas fled up into the mountains with agents in pursuit. In August the MIR decided to send two of its members down to the cities below to look for food and renew contacts with their fellow party members. CNI agents detected and caught them, however, and took them to Santiago. These prisoners revealed the site where they were to meet with their comrades and the password they were to use.

On September 13, 1981, agents used this information to kill Raúl Rodrigo OBREGON TORRES, a surveyor, when he came to the site to meet with his comrades. The Commission holds the conviction that he was executed, and that the agents utilized their knowledge of the meeting place and the password. Hence the official version which, like other similar reports, was spread through DINACOS reports claiming that people had been killed in gun battles, is false.

On September 17, security forces killed Pedro Juan YAÑEZ PALACIOS, an electrician's assistant who had become separated from the group because he was in poor physical condition due to the adverse weather they had to endure, and because one of his comrades had amputated his frozen and gangrenous foot. Hence the Commission came to the conviction that it is highly improbable that he would have offered resistance.

Around this time the group split, and three members went toward the area of Remeco Alto, to the house of a relative of one of them, in order to obtain food. The people in the house themselves alerted the soldiers to their presence. The soldiers caught them in their sleep and killed them. Patricio Alejandro CALFUQUIR HENRIQUEZ and Próspero del Carmen GUZMAN SOTO, both workers, were killed inside the house, which was completely destroyed by the shooting. José Eugenio MONSALVE SANDOVAL, also a worker, managed to flee a few yards from the house, but was caught and executed. The Commission has verified that none of these three people offered resistance before being killed. This all happened September 20, 1981.

On September 21, the two members of the groups who had been arrested at the outset, René Eduardo BRAVO AGUILERA and Julio César RIFFO FIGUEROA, both of whom were workers, were executed. They had been brought to the site of the operation from Santiago. The official statement issued by DINACOS does not say how they died nor does it acknowledge the fact that they had been previously arrested. Other CNI reports state that they were arrested but were killed when they tried to escape. That story is hardly credible given the military deployment and the tight security to which they must have been subjected. The omissions in the official statement only confirm this point.

Finally on November 28, 1981, soldiers executed Juan Angel OJEDA AGUAYO, a medical assistant, in Quebrada Honda. The Commission finds credible the account of an eyewitness to the events who says that there was no armed confrontation in this case either.

In considering these events, what was said in Part One, Chapter Two of this report should be kept in mind. The actions or intentions for which those killed may have been responsible and even considerations on the danger they represented must be clearly separated from the lawfulness or unlawfulness of the officials' actions in combating them. Of course governments cannot be expected to fail to combat an insurgency or to do so with inadequate means in order to comply with some standard of behavior. However, it is proper to demand that certain norms governing the use of force be observed under all circumstances.

Bearing this in mind, the Commission believes that in all of the Neltume events but one, the officials who had already arrested two of these people were in a position to apprehend the rest instead of killing them. Its participants may have seen Neltume as the beginning of a guerrilla struggle. However, given the ineptitude and poor condition of the MIR activists who were involved in this operation, and the vast superiority of government forces, it was actually more a police matter than one that was truly military. Since the rational alternative of arresting these people was present in each of these situations, it was not lawful to choose to execute them, let alone to kill people whom they already had physically in their power.

The only real gun battle involved Miguel CABRERA FERNANDEZ, a worker whom police found in Choshuenco and killed in a shoot out on October 16, 1981. The Commission believes he was killed in the gun battle, and that his human rights were not violated.

In view of the foregoing, the Commission believes all the other cases were executions in which the human rights of those killed were violated. . . .

B. OTHER EXECUTIONS

On March 18, 1978 the body of Jorge Lenin VERNAL HONORES, an active Socialist and former head of the housing department at the Pension Fund for Privately Employed Persons, was found. The DINA had held him under arrest in March and April of 1974. On March 16, 1978, he was again arrested at his home, and his dead body was found March 18.

The police report states that the body was found on the northern bank of the Mapocho River opposite Calle Barnechea. The autopsy report says the cause of death was asphyxiation due to being under water and encephalic cranial and spinomedular trauma. Further on it states that "the injuries could have been caused as the body was being pulled through the current or it could have another cause, especially the fracture of the spinal column." That report is contradicted by the report and map prepared for the judicial investigation, which make it clear that the body was found on Calle Barnechea, some meters away from the Mapocho River.

A number of other anomalies in that legal process suggest that government agents were involved in these events. Among them are the following:

* Falsified extrajudicial statements by relatives accompanied by police investigations purporting to show that Vernal was a habitual drunk; in the court they had to deny having made such statements.
* The fact that the police could not tell the judge the name of the officers who found the body since they had failed to register the information and it was impossible to check it.

* The speculation in the autopsy report and the report prepared by the investigative police Criminal Medical department propose contradictory hypotheses on what caused the injuries on his body. The former says that it could have been due to one or more blunt instruments or other devices or by the body being dragged through the water; the latter says it could have been a traffic accident and that he could then have fallen into the water.

Taking into account Jorge Vernal's political activism, the fact that he was being held under arrest when the events that cost his life took place, and the obstruction of the justice system, the Commission has come to the conviction that he was executed, that government agents can be presumed to have been responsible, and that his killing was a human rights violation.

On August 23, 1978, Alfonso Luis AROS PARDO, a taxi driver who was active in the Christian Left, was killed when he was held up, according to newspaper reports. His party work, the persecution that his relatives say he suffered, and the fact that when they received his body none of his valuable items such as a watch, a chain, and so forth had been taken, enable this Commission to reject the claim that it was a robbery and to state that Alfonso Aros was executed by government agents who were acting for political reasons in violation of his human rights.

On April 28, 1979, the body of José Aristeo AVILES MIRANDA, 72, a contractor who was not known to be politically active, was found in the Lampa district in front of the El Montijo estate in Renca. The previous day he had left his house in the Pudahuel district to do some errands. One of his sons had been held prisoner on Dawson Island after the military coup and had later gone into exile. The cause of the death of Jose Aviles according to the death certificate is cranial encephalic trauma. The press said it was an execution by the MIR and that the finding of the body had enabled the security services to trace a series of executions committed by that group.

The Commission has come to the conviction that Jose Aristeo Aviles was executed for political reasons in violation of his human rights but it does not have the evidence that would make it possible to identify who was responsible.

The Commission came to a similar conviction in the case of Arturo Ricardo NUÑEZ MUÑOZ, a MIR activist, who was arrested on May 17,1979, and whose body bearing two bullet wounds to the head appeared the next day in the area of Quilicura. As in the previous case the newspapers reported that "the MIR claimed that it assassinated one of its activists."

On June 23, 1979, Alberto Eugenio SALAZAR BRICEÑO, a former sailor, and Iris Yolanda VEGA BIZAMA, a merchant, both of whom were active in the MIR, were killed in Concepción by a bomb explosion. The official account said that they were trying to place a bomb at the Radio National station when it exploded on them. The public was told that ten persons whom the CNI accused of being part of the group that planned the operation were arrested. The results of the judicial process to which these events gave rise refutes this account. On June 11, 1980, all concerned were absolved since they could not be proven to have committed any crime. Meanwhile, the investigation into the deaths of these two men established that there were signs that they had been murdered, but there was no proof that would make it possible to accuse particular persons. In view of these conclusions, the Commission has come to the conviction that Alberto Salazar and Iris Vega were executed in violation of their human rights; and taking into account their political activity and the falsity of the official statement, it attributes their killing to government agents.

On August 13, 1979, Mario Daniel ACUÑA SEPULVEDA, a public employee who was active in the Socialist party, was killed in La Serena. According to the official account issued in a statement by the office of the regional intendant, there was an explosion on a piece of property that belonged to Acuna. The police alerted the CNI which went to search the property. When they identified themselves, someone inside the building threw a bomb and ran. They chased him through the yard but before they entered the house, a second explosion occurred inside and broke all the windows. They found Acuna dead in the bathroom and arrested another person.

This Commission has in its possession evidence enabling it to state that the above account is false. In the judicial process it was established that, contrary to the official account, it was a CNI agent who went to the police station in Tierras Blancas to report the supposed explosion and asked them to allow him to contact the CNI headquarters. Thus it was not the police who called the CNI. Furthermore, it is not likely that the only person to hear the explosion that precipitated matters should have been a CNI agent. Nor is it plausible that the operation should immediately move to Acuna's house, when it is clear that they had no proof that the explosion had occurred there.

The autopsy report notes the possibility that his death may have been the result of foul play. When an effort was made to consider this possibility by reexamining the body to check the condition of his hands and see whether it was he who had handled the explosive device, his hands mysteriously disappeared after the body was exhumed, and they could not be subjected to expert examination. The judge assigned to the judicial investigation declared himself incompetent when he determined that persons with military immunity were involved in these events.

The foregoing, combined with the fact that at that time members of the Socialist party did not advocate the use of violence, led the Commission to the conviction that Mario Acuna was executed by CNI agents.

C. SELECTIVE EXECUTIONS

Tucapel Francisco JIMENEZ ALFARO, a leader of the National Association of Public Employees who was a very important figure of the nationwide anti-government movement at that time, was stopped on February 25, 1982 in the taxi he was driving. He was taken to a secondary road 40 kilometers west of Santiago. There he was shot in the head and killed, and his throat was slit. The motive was not robbery, since he still had money on his person. He had been followed previously on a number of occasions, apparently by security agents, specifically members of the National Secretariat of Occupational and Sector Associations and the CNI. Subsequently there were a number of maneuvers aimed at covering up the crime and impeding the work of investigators. One person confessed to having committed the crime and then committed suicide; later however, it turned out that that person had been murdered, and the confession was false.

The Commission has come to the conviction that a crime was committed for political reasons, and that Tucapel Jimenez's human rights were violated. Although it cannot categorically state that government agents committed this crime, in weighing all the evidence, it honestly believes that the government is involved in his death, since even if the perpetrators were not government agents, they at least enjoyed government protection.

TRIPLE THROAT SLITTING

On March 18, 1985, at a time when a state of siege was in effect in the country, Santiago NATTINO ALLENDE, who worked in advertising and was a Communist but was not known to have any responsibilities in the party, was abducted in the street in the wealthy area of the city. Early the next morning Jose Manuel PARADA MALUENDA, who headed the department of analysis at the Vicariate of Solidarity, was abducted as he was taking his daughter to the Colegio Latinoamericano de Integracion. At the same time Manuel Leonidas GUER-RERO CEBALLO, who taught at the school and was a leader in the Association of Chilean Teachers (Agech), was abducted. He had been Jose Manuel Parada's friend for many years. . .

The kidnappers had an array of means at their disposal in these two operations. In the case of Santiago Nattino they said they were police and that they were arresting him because of economic problems. Witnesses say that a helicopter was involved in the other kidnapping and that traffic in the area was diverted. The cruelty of the action was made clear when a teacher who tried to stop it was shot point blank.

Connected to these two attacks was the abduction of Ramon Arriagada in February of that year. He had a degree in architecture. He was interrogated on the activities of Manuel Guerrero and Jose Parada. Both were involved in making an analysis of the structure and functioning of the Joint Command, on the basis of information obtained some time before from confessions of a former member.

The abduction was also connected to an operation against the Agech office at Londres No. 75 in the capital carried out on the night of March 28. Santiago Nattino received correspondence and had a telephone line at that location. Manuel Guerrero went there often because he was a leader of the organization. A number of teachers were taken out of the location and held in jail. The place where they were held was later discovered to be the DICOMCAR headquarters

on Calle Dieciocho. This was the same site that the Joint Command had previously used under the name of "the Company."

Despite a great deal of effort expended, there was no word about any of those who had been abducted until March 30, 1985, when their bodies were found with their throats slit along the road between Quilicura and the Pudahuel airport. This crime had a major impact in Chile and elsewhere, and led to an extensive judicial investigation. Government officials initially explained the crime as the result of an internal purge within the Communist party. However, on the basis of the facts recounted and those gathered in the judicial investigation, the Commission has come to the conviction that Manuel Guerrero, Jose Parada, and Santiago Nattino were executed by government agents because of their political involvement and hence in violation of their human rights. . . .

On August 2, 1980, Eduardo JARA ARAVENA, a journalism student and MIR activist, was killed. He and Cecilia Alzamora had been abducted together on July 23 at the corner of Calles Eliodoro Yanez and Los Leones. He was held prisoner along with other persons whom his captors, who identified themselves as members of the Avengers of Martyrs Commando Unit (COVEMA) connected to the killing of Colonel Roger Vergara. While he was held prisoner he was subjected to tortures, such as being beaten all over his body, and receiving electrical current and other torture, all of which produced obvious serious effects, such as deep gashes on his wrists, burns on his ankles and lips, and bruises on his forehead and nose. While in prison he was continually groaning from pain, but that only prompted those holding him to beat him further. The prisoners were frequently transferred and they were later able to identify some of the detention sites as investigative police buildings.

Their captors released Jara and Cecilia Alzamora on August 2 in the La Reina district. He was then taken to Emergency Clinic No. 4, and died there that same day. The Commission has come to the conviction that Eduardo Jara died of the torture he endured while under arrest and that at least members of the investigative police were involved in it, and thus it regards his death as a human rights violation for which government agents were responsible.

On October 18, 1984, Mario FERNANDEZ LOPEZ, 49, a truck owner who was active in the Christian Democrat party, died. CNI agents arrested him at his home in the city of Ovalle early on the morning of October 17. He was taken to CNI buildings in La Serena and tortured by agents. The next day he had to be taken to the emergency ward of the regional hospital in La Serena, but he was already dying. He died at 10:30 P.M. as a result of violent blows to the abdominal wall which caused a hypobolemic shock due to tissue damage, according to the autopsy report.

In response, the CNI made a public statement that, "On October 18, the prisoner suffered a nervous breakdown and lost control over himself because his terrorist and subversive activities had been discovered, and he beat himself against the prison furniture. No one else was involved. He injured himself in unspecified ways, thus making it advisable to transfer him to the regional hospital in La Serena because his heartbeat and breathing had stopped." In the court case, two CNI employees were accused of unnecessary violent actions leading to death. In view of the evidence gathered, the Commission has come to the conviction that Mario Hernandez died of the torture inflicted by CNI agents, and hence it does not regard the official report as truthful, and it regards these events as a human rights violation for which government agents were responsible.

On October 22, 1984, the body of Juan Antonio AGUIRRE BALLESTEROS, 23, a baker who was not politically active, was found. At about 5:45 a.m. on September 4, 1984, a day on which people were being called out to participate in a national protest against the military government, police arrested Aguirre and some friends of his as they were on their way to work at the corner of Calle Brangranza and Avenida Salvador Gutiérrez in Pudahuel. He was blindfolded and taken to a place where he was physically abused, according to testimony by people who were being held along with him. His body was found 51 days later at the Codegua marshlands in the area of La Leona in San Rafael de Melipilla. Officials have never acknowledged his arrest. Taking into account the evidence gathered, the Commission has come to the conviction that Juan Aguirre died of the torture to

which he was subjected by government agents, and that his body was thrown onto unused land to conceal what had happened; it regards his killing as a human rights violation for which government agents were responsible.

On February 22, 1985, Carlos GODOY ECHEGOYEN, a student who was active in the Socialist party, died. He was in Quintero together with other young Socialist party activists when police from the local police station arrested them and accused them of being involved in a guerrilla training school. The young people were interrogated and tortured at the Quintero police station and then transferred to Viria del Mar. Later they were taken back to Quintero, and members of DICOMCAR who had made a special trip from Santiago took charge of the operation. The young people were beaten and electrical current was applied to them. Godoy died as a result of this mistreatment on February 22, 1985. In their official report, the police said that the cause of death was a heart condition. Information in the hands of the Commission, including his prior medical records and the autopsy reports, leaves no room to doubt that Carlos Godoy's death was the result of torture that government agents had inflicted on him in violation of his human rights.

On June 24, 1989, police arrested Marcos QUEZADA YAÑEZ, 17, a student who was active in the Pro-Democracy party (PPD), on the street in Curacautin, and took him to the checkpoint. A few hours later he died as a result of "shock, probably from an electric current," according to the autopsy report. Taking into account the evidence gathered, the Commission has come to the conviction that Marcos Quezada did not commit suicide—and hence it rejects the official report—but that he died as a result of torture applied by government agents in violation of his human rights.

E. DISAPPEARANCES

. . . On December 15, 1977, police came looking for Pedro Gonzalo MILLAS MARQUEZ, who was frightened and tried to run away but was caught and arrested. Before his disappearance he had previously been harassed repeatedly by police from the police station in Lautaro because of his previous support for the Popular Unity government. There has been no further word on him since that day. The Commission came to the conviction that Pedro Millas disappeared at the hands of government agents who thus violated his human rights.

On January 23, 1978, at 3:45 P.M. the army subofficer Guillermo JORQUERA GUTIERREZ was arrested by police from the Fourteenth station in Santiago on Calle Bustos No. 2021, which is near the Venezuelan embassy in Chile. According to the police report, this subofficer was trying to seek asylum and in the process he abused a police officer but did not cause serious injury. A few hours later police officials handed Guillermo Jorquera over to the army intelligence directorate as prisoner. He was a well-known intelligence specialist who had worked for the DINA outside the country and in the Foreign Ministry. He had worked on intelligence and security matters in the Foreign Ministry while Carlos Guillermo Osorio Mardones was minister. Osorio Mardones's tragic death which occurred shortly before these events is regarded as relevant to the asylum attempt, arrest, and disappearance of Guillermo Jorquera.

High level army officials told the courts that he had been released the day he was arrested, and no charges were made, and the matter was not brought to either the court system or the military prosecutor's office. That claim is not credible when seen in the light of the accusations made against him the moment he was arrested and the fact that there has been no further word about him. In view of the foregoing, the Commission concluded that there is sufficient evidence to conclude that he disappeared at the hands of government agents in violation of his human rights.

In the early morning of February 8, 1978, members of the investigative police arrested Luis Rene CESPEDES CARO, at his home in the Angel Bueguefio shantytown in the La Cisterna district in Santiago. They also arrested his brother and two other persons. They were all taken to investigative police headquarters on Calle General Mackenna in Santiago. The others were released in the predawn hours, but Cespedes was not released and has been disappeared since then. The Commission came to the conviction that Luis Cespedes disappeared at the hands of government agents who thus violated his human rights.

In early March 1978, police from the checkpoint of the Zafiartu neighborhood in Chillan arrested Celindo del Carmen CATALAN ACUÑA in the Santa Elvira sector of the city. The youth's relatives observed him being arrested. Since then there has been no word on him. The Commission came to the conviction that Celindo Catalan disappeared at the hands of government agents who thus violated his human rights.

On February 20, 1980, police in Curicó arrested Fermin del Carmen MARTINEZ ROJAS and took him to the checkpoint at Barrio Norte in the city. Police officials told his relatives that he had been released that same day in order to get the money he needed for bail. This claim does not fit the usual way the police function in arrests, and does not explain why nothing further has been heard of Martinez. The Commission came to the conviction that Fermin Martinez disappeared at the hands of government agents who thus violated his human rights.

On November 15, 1981, at about 8:30 P.M. a group of ten young people were standing around on Avenida Departamental in Santiago when an investigative police van pulled up. Four civilians with automatic weapons got out and threatened to arrest them and take them away unless they left the area. One of the youths jokingly told the men that they would not all fit in the truck. The remark annoyed the police, and they responded by violently beating the young man and then arresting and taking away Hipolito ZUÑIGA ADASME and Pablo RODRIGUEZ LEAL. Both have been disappeared since then. The Commission came to the conviction that both of these people disappeared at the hands of government agents who thus violated their human rights.

On December 12, 1981, Oscar Elicer ROJAS CUELLAR, a MIR activist, was arrested in Santiago, very probably by CNI agents. He has been disappeared since then. After a war tribunal found him guilty in 1973, Oscar Rojas had been able to have his sentence reduced to exile. He served part of this punishment in exile in England. In 1980 he had returned to Chile clandestinely, since he was prohibited from entering the country. All the members of his MIR cell were killed in gun battles with the CNI, except for one survivor who is still in prison. CNI officials subjected this prisoner to exhaustive interrogation, including asking about Rojas' activities. That fact, taken in conjunction with other evidence on him, led this Commission to the conviction that he disappeared at the hands of government agents in violation of his human rights.

On December 20, 1984, Sergio Fernando RUIZ LAZO, a MIR leader who had secretly returned to Chile at the beginning of the month, was arrested in Santiago by CNI agents. Sergio Ruiz had been arrested by DINA agents in 1975 and was held prisoner at Villa Grimaldi, Cuatro Alamos, and Tres Alamos. He then lived with his family in exile in France. Officials had issued an exempt decree barring him from entering the country. Even though officials denied that he had been arrested, this Commission received information from witnesses and other evidence indicating that he was held prisoner at the CNI facility on Calle Borgono before he disappeared. The Commission came to the conviction that Sergio Ruiz disappeared at the hands of government agents who thus violated his human rights.

The adolescent Rubén Simón SOTO CABRERA disappeared on January 18, 1983 in Valparaiso. In light of the evidence it was able to examine, this Commission believes that agents of the security services can reasonably be assumed to have been responsible. In 1973 his father, Gustavo Soto Peredo, who was active in the Communist party, and his brother Gustavo Soto Cabrera, a MIR activist, were arrested and then disappeared. The Commission came to the conviction that Ruben Soto disappeared at the hands of government agents who thus violated his human rights.

FIVE DISAPPEARANCES IN SEPTEMBER 1987

On September 1, 1987 army colonel Carlos Carreño, an engineer at Famae [military weapons factory] was kidnapped from his home in the La Reina district in Santiago by an FPMR group. A few hours later a whole series of operations was conducted by the CNI and security forces who were working jointly and in collaboration with police personnel to locate him. Over the next few days house-to-house sweeps to locate the colonel were extended throughout the metropolitan area. In the course of these operations CNI agents arrested five young CP activists who appear to have been connected to the FPMR.

They were Jos' Julián PEÑA MALTES, an engineer who was arrested September 9, 1987; Julio Orlando MUÑOZ OTAROLA, a technician arrested on the street on September 9, 1987; Manuel Jesus SEPULVEDA SANCHEZ, who was arrested September 10, 1987 after leaving his house in Santiago at 7:00 P.M.; Alejandro Alberto PINOCHET ARENAS, an automobile mechanic, who was arrested in the street before witnesses in the course of a large operation on September 10, 1987; and Gonzalo Ivan FUENZALIDA NAVARRETE, a furniture maker, who was arrested September 9–10, 1987 (CNI agents had searched the house of his fiancée on September 3 and had first asked what his nickname was).

Even though officials and the head of the CNI denied that these people had been arrested, this Commission can only regard it as a certain and true fact, in view of their political activity, the circumstances of their arrest, what witnesses say about how the arrest was made in the one instance in which there are eyewitness accounts, and the overall context of the moment. The Commission came to the conviction that all these people disappeared at the hands of government agents or of people working for government agents who thus violated their human rights.

On the night of November 14, 1989, Héctor Segundo PACHECO AVENDAÑO was arrested in the Lo Herminda de la Victoria shantytown, in Cerro Navia. He was involved in a human rights working group in the chapel of Our Lady of Hope in the shantytown where he lived. On two previous occasions he had protested that he was being pursued by unidentified persons and that they were keeping the local parish under surveillance. The Commission came to the conviction that Hector Pacheco suffered a grave human rights violation, namely being arrested and then disappearing. It was not able to determine who was responsible for these actions, however.

STUDY QUESTIONS

1. What evidence do the report authors use to question prior official accounts and to certify that human rights abuses had taken place?
2. What are the commonalities, if any, in the backgrounds and experiences of the victims documented here?

12.6 THE CHIQUITA PAPERS: SEC DEPOSITION PAPERS DETAILING PAYMENTS TO GUERRILLA AND PARAMILITARY GROUPS, 1994

In 2007 Chiquita Brands, the world's largest supplier of bananas, was sentenced in the United States for funding an international terrorist group through their Colombian banana operations. The documents created during this conviction reveal that between 1989 and 1997—a period in which the civil war in Colombia intensified following the entrance of proceeds from narcotrafficking into the long-running conflict—Chiquita executives negotiated and delivered large cash payments totaling $1.7 million to illegal armed groups on both the left and the right in exchange for the protection of local employees. The company's legal team claimed this was the result of extortion and blackmail by militias, but the documents suggest a much more blurred line between extortion and the purchase of security services as a cost of doing business. Chiquita was convicted of funding the right-wing paramilitary group United Self-Defense Forces of Colombia (AUC), but their funding of left-wing guerrilla groups including the FARC and the ELN escaped sanction in US courts on a technicality, as those groups had not been declared international terrorist organizations by the US government at the time payments were made (they received this designation only in 1997). The declassified documents excerpted here are internal memos from within the Chiquita corporation dating to January 1994. They are taken from the records of the US Securities and Exchange Commission (SEC) investigation that led to the sentencing of Chiquita and were obtained by the National Security Archives at George Washington University via a Freedom of Information Act request.

SUBJECT: REPORTABLE PAYMENTS IN COLOMBIA AND MANAGER'S EXPENSE PAYMENTS

This memo documents my understanding of the Turbo and Santa Marta Divisions' transactions that are reportable on the Statement of Policies and Procedures and Manager's Expense summaries. Also, I will include my understanding of the Divisions' handling and reporting of payments for security purposes and payments to the respective trade association. This information is based on inquiries of local Management and through my observation of documents that were made available to me. This memo with attachments will constitute our working papers related to this area and the documentation of the work that we performed.

We limited the scope of our testing and the related procedures performed to disbursements and certain corporate compliance areas. . . . Our work primarily consisted of a disbursement sample, review of policies and procedures, and discussions with management, since this engagement constitutes a disbursement review. We did not perform detailed substantive testing of balance sheet values and compliance testing beyond the disbursement-related systems. Had we performed additional procedures or had we performed a complete audit of each of the aforementioned entities, other matters may have come to our attention that would have been reported in this memorandum and detailed in the related working papers.

Source: "The Chiquita Papers," National Security Archives, Briefing Book, No. 586. National Security Archive, Suite 701, Gelman Library, The George Washington University, Washington, DC.

MANAGER'S EXPENSE

I understand, based on my discussions with Management and based on my review of documents Management made available to me, that the Manager's Expense Account at both Divisions largely consists of guerilla extortion payments made by the Security Department through our intermediary or Security Consultant, Rene Osorio. I understand that the Security Consultant is our contact with the various guerrilla groups in both Divisions. Management in Santa Marta advised me that all extortion payments, referred to as "citizen security" currently handled through the Security Department, either [redacted] in Medellin, and recorded in the respective Division's accounting records in an account named "Gastos de Seguridad Ciudadana." I understand that these payments *are not supported by any receipt by any outside recipient* and are being expended as a Company expense. Totals of such payments were $110M at Turbo and $3M at Santa Marta for the period January 1, 1993 through October 25, 1993. These amounts have been expensed via the Manager's Expense Account in 1993.

The Turbo General Manager told me that the Guerilla Groups are used to supply security personnel at the various farms. This is *not* practiced at the Santa Marta Division. . . .

Through October 1993, the Divisions are in a loss position for financial and tax purposes of $2.3 million for Turbo and $6.1 million for Santa Marta. Therefore, local Management is not very concerned that they are expensing these payments without supporting documentation. Management believes that the loss situation the divisions are experiencing would mitigate the lack of documentation for the payments, in the event that the Divisions are audited by local tax authorities. . . .

I have included schedules (Exhibits II through IV) of the manager's expense accounts for both divisions for the period January through October 1993. I have agreed these to the general ledger activity and noted only two differences with a zero net effect. Both of the differences were at the Turbo Division, which I have documented on Exhibit II.

STATEMENT OF POLICIES
AND PROCEDURES DISCLOSURES

1. Based on discussions I had with each of the General Managers at both of the Divisions, the only reportable transactions to governments, governmental agencies, governmental employees, political parties, or political candidates that they were aware of are the donations totalling $1,441 at Turbo and $444 at Santa Marta for the period January 1, 1993 through October 25, 1993, as outlined in Exhibit I. I noted no other reportable transactions from my review of the entity. I discussed the nature of reportable payments with them. They seem to better understand and committed to properly report the payments that constitute a reportable transaction. These items were reported separately in our internal [illegible] response of [illegible] disbursements issued in March 1994.

TRADE ASSOCIATIONS

2. Both Divisions belong to trade associations that represent the respective areas in promoting the region's bananas, in improving the general infrastructure, and coordinating the facilitation of government services, and promoting overall safety in the region. The involvement in and influence over the association varies by Division. The Turbo Division appears to have some influence over their respective trade association, AUGURA. Management receives a budget and certain transaction details, such as information relating to facilitating payments and donations to the various entities. Whereas, the Santa Marta Division receives no such transaction information of budgets from its regional trade association, FUNDEBAN. Due to the influence and knowledge factors, the Turbo Division reports the governmental-related AUGURA payments made by the trade association on its quarterly Statement of Policy and Procedure disclosure (these started third quarter 1993); while the Santa Marta Division does not report governmental-related FUNDEBAN payments on its quarterly disclosure. The trade associations assess the Divisions $0.02 per box of exported fruit. The Divisions pay for both produced and associate producer–purchased fruit. Amounts assessed by such associations for the period January 1, 1993 through October 25, 1993 were approximately $106M at Turbo and $133M at Santa Marta.

In the event that you should have questions or comments regarding the aforementioned areas, please feel free to contact me.

STUDY QUESTIONS

1. Why are the payments to guerrillas—which are noted by the author of the memo to be illegal—being discussed internally by Chiquita Executives? What concerns do some local executives have about the payments?

2. What do the annotations on the memo reveal about the legal advice being given to Chiquita officials on this issue of security financing?

12.7 EL DIARIO INTERVIEWS CHAIRMAN GONZALO, 1988

Sendero Luminoso, or Shining Path, was a Maoist guerrilla movement that waged warfare against the Peruvian state from 1980 to 1992. It was first formed in the 1960s by Abimael Guzmán, a philosophy professor at the University of Ayacucho, who took the name Chairman Gonzalo. During the 1970s Shining Path developed support within the universities, but its power and support expanded significantly following the transition from military to civilian rule in 1980. Shining Path rejected democracy as a tool to oppress the masses and protect capitalism and instead proposed revolutionary warfare as a path toward a new society based on "true" communism. Gonzalo was deeply influenced by Chairman Mao, and promoted a vision in which, through violent struggle, revolutionaries would lead the peasantry in the creation of a new society. During the 1980s, Shining Path attracted great support from highland peasants as well as urban students, and by the mid-1980s controlled large swathes of the countryside as well as many poor urban barrios on the outskirts of Lima and other major cities. The group was responsible for many brutal acts of violence, killing as many as thirty-five thousand people. Their violence was met by the state and private militias, which also engaged in extrajudicial killings, with the result that a total of seventy thousand people were killed in the civil war, the majority of them peasants. In 1988—the height of the civil war—Gonzalo agreed to a major interview with the Shining Path newspaper *El Diario*. In this excerpt from the interview, Gonzalo discusses how Maoism shaped his philosophies and his strategic commitment to violence, and lays out the argument that Shining Path was fighting "the people's war."

EL DIARIO: How has the Party changed through the people's war?

CHAIRMAN GONZALO: First, and most important, the work leading up to the people's war helped us to come to understand Maoism as a new, third, and higher stage of Marxism. It has helped us develop the militarization of the Party and its concentric construction. Through the people's war, a People's

Source: "Interview with Chairman Gonzalo" (http://www.blythe.org/peru-pcp/docs_en/interv.htm).

Guerrilla Army has been forged. It was formed not long ago, in 1983.

The People's Guerrilla Army is important. It is the principal form of organization corresponding to the people's war which is the principal form of struggle. The People's Guerrilla Army which we have founded and which is developing vigorously, is being built based on Chairman Mao Tsetung's theories, and on a very important thesis of Lenin's concerning the people's militia. Lenin, concerned that the army could be usurped and used to bring about a restoration, held that a people's militia should assume the functions of the army, police and administration. This is an important thesis and the fact that Lenin was not able to put it into practice due to historical circumstances does not make it any less important and valid. It is so important that Chairman Mao himself paid a lot of attention to the task of developing a people's militia. So our army has these features and it was formed by taking those experiences into account. But, at the same time, it has its own specific features. We have a structure composed of three forces: a main force, a local force and a base force. We have no independent militia, because it exists in the ranks of the Army itself, which was formed according to this criteria. It was the above-mentioned principles which guided us, but we also think it's correct to say that the People's Guerrilla Army could not have been built in any other way given our concrete conditions. This army, all the same, has been able to act in every situation and can be readjusted and reorganized as necessary in the future.

Another thing that has come out of the people's war, its main achievement, is the New Power. We see the question of the New Power as being linked to the question of the united front, basing ourselves on what Chairman Mao said in his work "On New Democracy." We've also kept in mind the long and putrid experience with frontism in Peru where they've bastardized and continue to bastardize the united front, yesterday with the so-called "National Liberation Front" and today mainly with the self-proclaimed United Left and other monstrosities in formation like the much cackled-about "Socialist Convergence." In other words, we always take into account the principles

and concrete conditions of our reality. (That is why we don't understand why they call us dogmatists. In the final analysis, paper will put up with whatever is written on it.) This has led us to form the Revolutionary Front for the Defense of the People [Frente Revolucionario de Defensa del Pueblo (FRDP)—TRANS.]. Here is another point. We were the ones who formed the first front for the defense of the people in Ayacucho. Patria Roja appropriated this heroic example, but deformed it in creating their "FEDIP." Even the name is wrong. If this is a front for defense of the people, why doesn't it defend the interests of the people? We build the Revolutionary Front for the Defense of the People only in the countryside, and in the form of the People's Committees it becomes the basis of Power. And those People's Committees in an area form a Base Area, and all the Base Areas together we call the New Democratic People's Republic in formation. In the cities we have established the Revolutionary Movement for the Defense of the People which also serves to wage the people's war in the city, gather forces, undermine the reactionary order and develop the unity of class forces in preparation for the future insurrection.

Other changes have to do with the forging of cadre. Obviously war forges in a different way. It steels people, permits us to imbue ourselves more deeply with our ideology, and forge iron-like cadre who dare to challenge death, to snatch the laurels of victory from the clutches of death. Another change in the Party that we could point to, but on a different plane, has to do with the world revolution. The people's war has enabled the Party to demonstrate clearly how, by grasping Marxism-Leninism-Maoism, we can develop a people's war without being subordinate to any power, be it a superpower or any other power— how it's possible to rely on our own strength to carry forward people's war. All this has given the Party prestige on an international level that it never had before, and this is not vanity, far from it, it's just a simple fact, and it has also allowed us to serve the development of the world revolution as never before. In this way the Party, through the people's war, is fulfilling its role as the Communist Party of Peru.

EL DIARIO: How do the workers and peasants participate in the People's Guerrilla Army?

CHAIRMAN GONZALO: The peasantry, especially the poor peasants, are the main participants, as fighters and commanders at different levels in the People's Guerrilla Army. The workers participate in the same ways, although the percentage of workers at this time is insufficient.

EL DIARIO: Chairman, where has the New Power developed most, in the countryside or in the city?

CHAIRMAN GONZALO: We are developing the New Power only in the countryside. In the cities it will be developed in the final stage of the revolution. It is a question of the process of people's war. I think that when we analyze people's war we'll be able to deal with this point a little more.

EL DIARIO: Chairman, moving on a bit, the documents of the Communist Party establish you as the Leader of the Party and the revolution. What does this imply, and how is it different from the revisionist theory of the cult of the personality?

CHAIRMAN GONZALO: Here we must remember how Lenin saw the relationship between the masses, classes, the Party and leaders. We believe that the revolution, the Party, our class, generate leaders, a group of leaders. It has been like this in every revolution. If we think, for instance, about the October Revolution, we have Lenin, Stalin, Sverdlov and a few others, a small group. Similarly, in the Chinese revolution there's also a small group of leaders: Chairman Mao Tsetung, and his comrades Kang Sheng, Chiang Ching, Chang Chunchiao, among others. All revolutions are that way, including our own. We could not be an exception. Here it's not true that there is an exception to every rule because what we're talking about here is the operation of certain laws. All such processes have leaders, but they also have a leader who stands out above the rest or who leads the rest, in accordance with the conditions. Not all leaders can be viewed in exactly the same way. Marx is Marx, Lenin is Lenin, Chairman Mao is Chairman Mao. Each is unique, and no one is going to be just like them.

In our Party, revolution, and people's war, the proletariat, by a combination of necessity and historical chance, has brought forth a group of leaders. In Engels' view, it is necessity that generates leaders, and a top leader, but just who that is is determined by chance, by a set of specific conditions that come together at a particular place and time. In this way, in our case too, a leadership has been generated. This was first acknowledged in the Party at the Expanded National Conference of 1979. But this question involves another basic question that can't be overlooked and needs to be emphasized: there is no Leadership that does not base itself on a body of thought, no matter what its level of development may be. The reason that a certain person has come to speak as the Leader of the Party and the revolution, as the resolutions state, has to do with necessity and historical chance and, obviously, with Gonzalo Thought. None of us knows what the revolution and the Party will call on us to do, and when a specific task arises the only thing to do is assume the responsibility.

We have been acting in accordance with Lenin's view, which is correct. The cult of personality is a revisionist formulation. Lenin had warned us of the problem of negating leadership just as he emphasized the need for our class, the Party and the revolution to promote our own leaders, and more than that, top leaders, and a Leadership. There's a difference here that is worth emphasizing. A leader is someone who occupies a certain position, whereas a top leader and Leadership, as we understand it, represent the acknowledgment of Party and revolutionary authority acquired and proven in the course of arduous struggle—those who in theory and practice have shown they are capable of leading and guiding us toward victory and the attainment of the ideals of our class.

Khrushchev raised the issue of the cult of personality to oppose comrade Stalin. But as we all know, this was a pretext for attacking the dictatorship of the proletariat. Today, Gorbachev again raises the issue of the cult of personality, as did the Chinese revisionists Liu Shao-chi and Deng Xiaoping. It is therefore a revisionist thesis that in essence takes aim against the proletarian dictatorship and the leadership and leaders of the revolutionary process in order to cut off its head. In our case it aims specifically at robbing the people's war of its Leadership. We do not yet have a dictatorship of the proletariat, but we do have a New Power that is developing in accordance with the norms of new democracy, the joint dictatorship of the workers, peasants and progressives. In our case they seek to rob this process of leadership, and the reactionaries and those who serve them know very well why they do this, because it is not easy to generate revolutionary leaders and Leadership. And a people's war, like the one in this country, needs revolutionary leaders and Leadership, someone who represents the revolution and heads it, and a group capable of leading it uncompromisingly. In sum, the cult of the personality is a sinister revisionist formulation which has nothing to do with our concept of revolutionary leaders, which conforms with Leninism. . . .

EL DIARIO: Chairman, let's talk about the people's war now. What does violence mean to you, Chairman Gonzalo?

CHAIRMAN GONZALO: With regard to violence we start from the principle established by Chairman Mao Tsetung: violence, that is the need for revolutionary violence, is a universal law with no exception. Revolutionary violence is what allows us to resolve fundamental contradictions by means of an army, through people's war. Why do we start from Chairman Mao's thesis? Because we believe Mao reaffirmed Marxism on this question, establishing that there are no exceptions whatsoever to this law. What Marx held, that violence is the midwife of history, continues to be a totally valid and monumental contribution. Lenin expounded upon violence and spoke about Engels' panegyric praise of revolutionary violence, but it was the Chairman who told us that it was a universal law, without any exception. That's why we take his thesis as our starting point. This is an essential question of Marxism, because without revolutionary violence one class cannot replace another, an old order cannot be overthrown to create a new one—today a new order led by the proletariat through Communist Parties.

The problem of revolutionary violence is an issue that is more and more being put on the table for discussion, and therefore we communists and revolutionaries must reaffirm our

principles. The problem of revolutionary violence is how to actually carry it out with people's war. The way we see this question is that when Chairman Mao Tsetung established the theory of people's war and put it into practice, he provided the proletariat with its military line, with a military theory and practice that is universally valid and therefore applicable everywhere in accordance with the concrete conditions.

We see the problem of war this way: war has two aspects, destructive and constructive. Construction is the principal aspect. Not to see it this way undermines the revolution—weakens it. On the other hand, from the moment the people take up arms to overthrow the old order, from that moment, the reaction seeks to crush, destroy and annihilate the struggle, and it uses all the means at its disposal, including genocide. We have seen this in our country; we are seeing it now, and will continue to see it even more until the outmoded Peruvian State is demolished.

As for the so-called dirty war, I would like to simply point out that they claim that the reactionary armed forces learned this dirty war from us. This accusation clearly expresses a lack of understanding of revolution, and of what a people's war is. The reaction, through its armed forces and other repressive forces, seeks to carry out their objective of sweeping us away, of eliminating us. Why? Because we want to do the same to them—sweep them away and eliminate them as a class. Mariategui said that only by destroying, demolishing the old order could a new social order be brought into being. In the final analysis, we judge these problems in light of the basic principle of war established by Chairman Mao: the principle of annihilating the enemy's forces and preserving one's own forces. We know very well that the reaction has used, is using, and will continue to use genocide. On this we are absolutely clear. And consequently this raises the problem of the price we have to pay: in order to annihilate the enemy and to preserve, and even more to develop our own forces, we have to pay a price in war, a price in blood, the need to sacrifice a part for the triumph of the people's war.

As for terrorism, they claim we're terrorists. I would like to give the following answer so that everyone can think about it: has it or has it not been Yankee imperialism and particularly Reagan who has branded all revolutionary movements as terrorists, yes or no? This is how they attempt to discredit and isolate us in order to crush us. That is their dream. And it's not only Yankee imperialism and the other imperialist powers that combat so-called terrorism. So does social-imperialism and revisionism, and today Gorbachev himself proposes to unite with the struggle against terrorism. And it isn't by chance that at the VIIIth Congress of the Party of Labor of Albania Ramiz Alia dedicated himself to combatting terrorism as well with the pioneers of the people's revolutionary army! It is no longer a plot against some detested individual, no act of vengeance or desperation, no mere "intimidation"—no, it was a well thought-out and well prepared commencement of operations by a contingent of the revolutionary army. Fortunately, the time has passed when revolution was "made" by individual terrorists, because people were not revolutionary. The bomb has ceased to be the weapon of the solitary "bomb thrower," and is becoming an essential weapon of the people.

Lenin taught us that the times had changed, that the bomb had become a weapon of combat for our class, for the people, that what we're talking about is no longer a conspiracy, an isolated individual act, but the actions of a Party, with a plan, with a system, with an army. So, where is the imputed terrorism? It's pure slander.

Finally, we always have to remember that, especially in present-day war, it is precisely the reactionaries who use terrorism as one of their means of struggle, and it is, as has been proven repeatedly, one of the forms used on a daily basis by the armed forces of the Peruvian State. Considering all this, we can conclude that those whose reasoning is colored by desperation because the earth is trembling beneath their feet wish to charge us with terrorism in order to hide the people's war. But this people's war is so earthshaking that they themselves admit that it is of national dimensions and that it has become the principal problem facing the Peruvian State. What terrorism could do that? None. And moreover, they can no longer deny that a Communist Party is leading the people's war. And at this time some of them are beginning to reconsider; we shouldn't be too hasty in writing anyone off. There are those who could come forward. Others, like Del Prado, never.

EL DIARIO: What are some of the particularities of the people's war in Peru, and how does it differ from other struggles in the world, in Latin America, and from the Movimiento Revolucionario Tupac Amaru (MRTA)?

CHAIRMAN GONZALO: That's a good question. I thank you for asking it, because it gives us a chance to look at the Party's so-called "dogmatism" a bit more. There are even those who say that we incorrectly try to apply Chairman Mao in an era where he is no longer applicable. In short, they babble on so much that we feel perfectly justified asking whether they have any idea what they are talking about. This includes the much-decorated senator who is a specialist in violence.

People's war is universally applicable, in accordance with the character of the revolution and adapted to the specific conditions of each country. Otherwise, it cannot be carried out. In our case, the particularities are very dear. It is a struggle that is waged in the countryside and in the city, as was established as far back as 1968 in the plan for the people's war. Here we have a difference, a particularity: it is waged in the countryside and the city. This, we believe, has to do with our own specific conditions. Latin America, for instance, has cities which are proportionately larger than those on other continents. It is a reality of Latin America that can't be ignored. Just look at the capital of Peru, for example, which has a high percentage of the country's population. So, for us, the city could not be left aside, and the war had to be developed there as well. But the struggle in the countryside is principal, the struggle in the city a necessary complement. This is one particularity, there's another.

In the beginning of the people's war we confronted the police. That was the reality because only in December 1982 did the armed forces enter the war. This is not to say that they had not been used in a support role before then. They had, in

addition to their studying the process of our development. It is a particularity because we created a power vacuum in the countryside and we had to establish the New Power without having defeated large armed forces—because they hadn't come into the war. And when they did, when they came in, it was because we had established People's Power. That was the concrete political situation in the country. If we had applied the letter and not the spirit of Mao we would not have established the New Power and we would have been sitting, waiting for the armed forces to come in. We would have gotten bogged down. Another particularity was the structure of the army which I've already talked about.

All these are particularities. We have already spoken to the countryside and city, to how to carry out the war, to the army, to how the New Power arose; and the militarization of the Party itself is another particularity. These are specific things that correspond to our reality, to the application of Marxism-Leninism-Maoism, of Chairman Mao's theory on people's war, to the conditions in our country. Does this make us different from other struggles? Yes.

Why do we differ from others? Because we carry out people's war this makes us different from other struggles in Latin America. In Cuba, people's war was not carried out, but they also had their own particularities which they have intentionally forgotten. Before, they said Cuba was an exceptional case—Guevara said this—the fact that U.S. imperialism didn't take part. Later they forgot this. Aside from this, there was no Communist Party there to give leadership. These are questions of Cubanism and its five characteristics: an insufficient class differentiation which demanded that saviors save the oppressed; socialist revolution or a caricature of revolution; united front but without the national bourgeoisie; no need for Base Areas; and as noted, no need for a Party. What we are seeing in Latin America today is just the development of these same positions, only more and more at the service of social-imperialism and its contention with Yankee imperialism for world hegemony. We can see this clearly in Central America. The MRTA, the little that we know of it, falls into the same category.

Finally, another issue that makes us different—and forgive me if I'm insistent—concerns independence, self-reliance, and making our own decisions. Because others do not have these characteristics they are used as pawns, while we are not. And one far-reaching difference: we take Marxism-Leninism-Maoism as our guide, others do not. In sum, the greatest difference, the fundamental difference, is in the point of departure; ours is the ideology of Marxism-Leninism-Maoism, principally Maoism, applied to the specific conditions of our country, and I insist here again, that this is with clear particularities which show the falsehood of the so-called dogmatism they accuse us of—which they do at the behest of their masters.

STUDY QUESTIONS

1. What does Gonzalo mean by the concept of the "people's war"? What philosophical and political influences underpin his argument?
2. How does Gonzalo present and rationalize the need for violence? What do these ideas have in common with those of military regimes in Central and South America discussed elsewhere in this chapter?
3. How are peasants represented within Gonzalo's interview?

SILVIO RODRIGUEZ

12.8 SILVIO RODRIGUEZ SINGS OF THE SPECIAL PERIOD, 1990s

The collapse of the Soviet Union in 1989 generated severe economic and social problems in Cuba. The island had come to rely on Soviet subsidies, notably cheap oil, while the USSR had been the primary market for Cuban sugar and other exports. The United States responded to Cuba's loss of their primary trading partner by tightening the embargo via the Helmsburton Act, which placed trade sanctions on any nation that traded with Cuba. In response to the economic challenges generated by these changes, the Castro government declared Cuba to be in a Special Period in a Time of Peace, introducing food rationing, changing agricultural production, and outlawing private automobiles in favor of mass transit in order to conserve gasoline. Tourism was also reintroduced to the island in an effort to generate alternative revenues. Ordinary Cubans faced tremendous hardships during this time. Food shortages led to widespread malnutrition, power outages were common, and wait times for buses and other forms of transit increased significantly. Tourism introduced new types of inequality between those who had access to the dollar economy and those who did not, and a vast black market proliferated. Out-migration to the U.S. increased significantly, with many Cubans undertaking enormously risky (and illegal) journeys on rafts to seek greater economic opportunity. Silvio Rodriguez is one of Cuba's most popular and important folk-singers, whose work has documented the Cuban revolution through song since the 1960s. In the songs presented here he reflects on the challenges of the special period. In *Disillusionment* he reflects on the consequences of the reintroduction of tourism and other capitalist enterprises into the island; in *The Fool* he explores the pressures on Cubans–especially those like himself with an international profile-to defect overseas; in *The Fifties Club* he laments the rise of competition and materialism; and in *Flowers* he decries the resurgence of prostitution and sex trafficking in the island.

Disillusionment

Like coins
Disillusionment jingles its theme
Disillusionment.
With a red mouth
And big droopy breasts
Disillusionment
Smoking light tobacco
And exhaling alcohol
The owner of the bed embroidered
In underwear.

What frenzy in interrogation
What suicide in investigating
A brilliant fashion show
Disillusionment.

It opened a business
Reviving leisure
Disillusionment.
Like tourism
It invented the abyss
Disillusionment

Source: *The Cuba Reader: History, Culture, Politics*, eds. Aviva Chomsky, Barry Carr, and Pamela Maria Smorkaloff (Durham and London: Duke University Press, 2003), pp. 280–288.

It touched the diamond
And turned it to coal
And it planted a good-for-nothing
In the administration.

The Fool

To keep my icon from being smashed,
To save myself among the few and the odd ones,
To grant me a space in their Parnassus,
To give me a little corner in their altars,
they come to invite me to repent,
they come to invite me not to lose out,
they come to invite me to undefine myself,
they come to invite me to so much bullshit.
I can't say what the future is,
I've always been what I've been,
Only God, up there, is divine.
I will die just as I've lived.
I want to keep on betting on the lost cause,
I want to be with the left hand rather than right,
I want to make a Congress of the united,
I want to pray deeply an "our son."
They'll say that craziness has gone out of fashion,
They'll say that people are evil and don't deserve it,
but I'll leave with my mischievous dreams
(perhaps multiplying bread and fish).
I can't say what the future is,
I've always been what I've been,
Only God, up there, is divine.
I will die just as I've lived.

They say that I'll be dragged over the rocks
when the Revolution comes crashing down,
that they'll smash my hands and my mouth,
that they'll tear out my eyes and my tongue.
It may well be that I'm the child of foolishness,
the foolishness of what today seems foolish:
the foolishness of accepting one's enemy,
the foolishness of living without a price.
I can't say what the future is,
I've always been what I've been,
Only God, up there, is divine.
I will die just as I've lived.

The Fifties Club

I arrive at the club of the fifty-year-olds (1950s)
and one hand brings the bill

The sum (addition) calls my attention
    from back to my cradle
Every fire, every undertaking [with the implication
    of something you really *want* to do]
comes with a price tag next to it
    in spite of what has been paid.
I wonder what kind of business this is in
    which even desire becomes an object of
    consumption what will I do when the
    sun sends its bill?
But I keep turning my face to the east
and order another breakfast [using an
    Anglicism; that is, the word *order* isn't really
    used like that in Spanish] in spite of the cost
    of love.

Let debts and inflation come,
IOUs, fines, recessions.
Let the pickpocket try to grab the taste of my
    bolero.
Whoever the boss may be
Let him charge me diligently (that cruel hand will
    find out when I send him my bill).

Flowers

The night flowers of Fifth Avenue open
For those poor gentlemen who go to the hotel
Flowers that break in the darkness
Flowers of winks of complicity
Flowers whistling suicides
Flowers with a fatal aroma

What gardener has sown our Fifth Avenue
With such a precise nocturnal variety
What is their species, what is their country
What fancy fertilizer nourished their root
Giving them a wild tone
Where could their womb be?

Flowers that go through forbidden doors
Flowers that know what I'll never know
Flowers that string their dream of life
In garlands without faith
Flowers of sheets with eyes
Disposable flowers
Doorbells of desire
Flowers eating the leftovers of love

They sprout, they bounce, they explode
  on our Fifth Avenue
They are pulled up and depart with swift air
They say that a flower's job is hard

When its petals wither in the sun
Pale nocturnal flowers
Flowers of disillusionment.

STUDY QUESTIONS

1. What threats does Rodriguez see in the re-introduction of capitalist economic systems in the 1990s? What have these economic changes meant for the Cuban people, according to Rodriguez?
2. What insights do Rodriguez's songs provide into the cultural values of those who, like himself, remained committed to the Cuban Revolution?

CHAPTER 13

NEOLIBERALISM AND ITS DISCONTENTS, 1980–2015

FERNANDO HENRIQUE CARDOSO

13.1 INAUGURAL ADDRESS, 1995

The transition to democracy in Latin America was accompanied by an increased dominance of neo-liberal economic paradigms and policies. Nowhere better epitomized this interlocking shift than Brazil, where Fernando Henrique Cardoso—a distinguished Marxist scholar and one of the key Latin American intellectuals associated with the development of dependency theory—won the presidency in 1995 and enacted sweeping neoliberal economic reforms. Cardoso's government led a major privatization initiative in which a variety of state-run enterprises were denationalized and sold to private foreign companies—a direct reversal of his earlier academic work which had held that the power of foreign corporations led to economic dependency and underdevelopment in Latin America. In this excerpt from his inaugural speech, President Cardoso explains how his administration will move the country forward by embracing the free market system.

Your Excellencies, Deputies, Senior Officials of the Republic, Ladies and Gentlemen,

I have come to add my hope to the hope of all on this day that brings us together. Before giving voice to the president, however, allow me to speak as the citizen who made an obsession out of hope, as have so many other Brazilians. I belong to a generation that grew up lulled by the dream of a Brazil that would be at the same time democratic, developed, free, and fair. The flame of this dream was lit in the distant past. It was lit by the heroes of our independence; by the abolitionists; by the revolutionary "lieutenants" of the Old Republic.

This flame is the one I saw shining in the eyes of my father, Leonidas Cardoso, one of the generals in the campaign called "the oil is ours," just as it shone at the end of the empire in the eyes of my grandfather, an abolitionist and republican.

For the students such as I who threw all their enthusiasm into these struggles, oil and industrialization were our ticket to the modern, postwar world. They guaranteed a seat for Brazil in the car of technological progress, a car that was accelerating and threatened to leave us behind in the dust. For some time, during the presidency of Juscelino Kubitschek, the

Source: Robert M. Levine and John J. Crocitti (eds.) *The Brazil Reader: History, Culture, Politics* (Durham: Duke University Press, 1999), pp. 280–288.

future seemed to us to be very near. There was development. Brazil was becoming rapidly industrialized. Our democracy functioned, despite the fits and starts. And there were prospects of social progress. But history takes turns that confound us. The "golden years" of Juscelino Kubitschek ended on a note of heightened inflation and political tensions.

In their stead, we had the somber years that initially recouped growth, but that sacrificed freedom. These years brought progress, but only for the few. And then, not even that, merely the legacy—this time, shared by all—of an external debt that tied down the economy and an inflation rate that aggravated social ills during the decade of the eighties. And so I watched my children grow and saw my grandchildren appear, dreaming and struggling to decry the day in which development, freedom, and justice—justice, freedom, and development—would walk side by side throughout the land.

I never doubted that this day would come.

But I also never thought this day would find me in the office I enter today, chosen by a majority of my fellow citizens to lead the journey toward the Brazil of our dreams. Without arrogance, but with absolute conviction, I say to you: This country shall be a success story!

Not because of me, but because of all of us. Not just because of our dreams—our tremendous desire to see a successful Brazil—but because the time is now ripe and Brazil has all it needs to thrive.

We have recuperated what ought to be the most precious treasure of any people: our freedom. Peacefully, calmly, despite the bruises and scars that remain as a symbol to ensure that there will be no repetition of the violence, we turned the page on the authoritarianism that under many names and guises has undermined our republic since its foundation. For today's young people, who literally put on their war paint and took over the streets demanding decency from their representatives, and for the people of my generation as well, who learned the value of freedom when they lost it, democracy is an unchallengeable conquest. Nothing and no one shall make us give it up again. We have recovered our confidence in development.

It is no longer just a matter of hope. Nor is it a matter of euphoria for the two good years we just enjoyed. This year will be better. Next year will be better still. Today, there is no responsible specialist who forecasts anything but a long period of growth for Brazil. International conditions are favorable. The burden of our external debt no longer suffocates us. Here in Brazil, our economy is like a healthy plant after a long drought. The roots—the people and businesses that produce wealth—have resisted the rigors of stagnation and inflation. They have survived. They have emerged with greater strength after their travails. Our business community has proved to be capable of innovation, of retrofitting their factories and offices, of overcoming their difficulties.

Brazil's workers have proved to be capable of facing up to the hardships of arbitrary practices and recession, and the challenges of new technologies. They have reorganized their unions so as to be capable, as they are today, of demanding their rights and their fair share of the results of economic growth. The time has come to grow and blossom.

Even more important, today we know what the government must do to sustain the growth of the economy. And we shall do it. In fact, we are already doing it. When many doubted if we would be capable of putting our own house in order, we started off over the last two years to put that house in order. Without yielding a millimeter of our freedom, without breaking any agreements or harming any rights, we did away with superinflation.

We owe all of this not just to those who set a new course for the economy, but also to President Itamar Franco, who has earned the respect of Brazilians for his simplicity and honesty. At this moment in which he leaves office, surrounded by well-earned esteem, I thank Itamar Franco on behalf of the nation for the opportunities he has afforded us. By choosing me to succeed him, an absolute majority of Brazilians clearly opted for the continuation of the "Real" Plan, and for the structural reforms that are necessary to do away with the specter of inflation once and for all. As president, I shall dedicate myself to this task with all my energy, and I will count on the support of the Congress, the states, and all the community leaders of the nation. So, we have our freedom back. And we shall have development. What is missing is social justice.

This is the major challenge facing Brazil in the final days of the century. This will be the number one objective of my administration. Joaquim Nabuco, the premier advocate of abolitionism, thought of himself and his companions as having been delegated with a "mandate from the black race." Not a mandate from the slaves, since they did not have the means to demand their rights. But a mandate that the abolitionists took on even so, because they felt the horror of slavery in their hearts, and they understood that the shackles of slavery kept the entire country trapped in economic, social, and political backwardness.

We, too, feel horrified when we see our fellow citizens and—even if they aren't Brazilian—human beings by our side subjugated by hunger, disease, ignorance, violence. This must not go on! Just as was the case of abolitionism, the reform movement I represent is not against anyone. It does not seek to divide the nation. It seeks to unite the nation by rallying us round the prospect of a better future for all. But, in contrast to Nabuco, I am well aware of the fact that my mandate resulted from the free votes of my fellow citizens. From the majority, regardless of their social status. But my mandate also came, to a tremendous degree, from those that have been excluded; the humblest Brazilians who paid the bill of inflation without being able to defend themselves; those that are humiliated in hospital and social security lines; those that earn so little compared to all they give the country in factories, fields, stores, offices, hospitals, schools, on construction sites, streets and highways; those that clamor for justice because they are, in fact, aware of and willing to fight for their rights—it is, to a great degree, to all of them that owe my election.

I will govern for us all. But if it becomes necessary to do away with the privileges of the few to do justice to the vast majority of Brazilians, let there be no doubt: I will be on the side of the majority. In all tranquillity, as is my wont, but in all firmness. Always seeking the paths of dialogue and persuasion, but without shying away from the responsibility of decision making. Knowing that most Brazilians do not expect miracles, but will demand results from the government on a daily basis. Among other reasons, because Brazilians believe in Brazil again, and are in a hurry to see Brazil improve more and more.

It is also a satisfaction for us to see that interest regarding Brazil is increasing among other countries. Our efforts to consolidate democracy, adjust the economy, and attack social problems are monitored abroad with very high expectations. Today, everyone understands that our transition to democracy was slower and occasionally more difficult than that of other countries. This was because our transition was deeper and broader. We restored democratic freedoms and began overhauling our economy at the same time. For this very reason, we constructed a more solid foundation on which to build. We have the support of society for changes. Society knows what it wants and where we should go. Speedily, at the rapid pace of communications and the liberalization of the Brazilian economy, we leave behind xenophobic attitudes that are more accurately described as the effect than the cause of our relative closure in the past.

None of the above implies that we will renounce even a fraction of our sovereignty, nor neglect the means to guarantee it. As commander in chief of our armed forces, I shall be mindful of their needs in terms of modernization to ensure that the forces will reach operational levels in line with Brazil's strategic stature and international commitments. In this regard, I shall assign new tasks to the armed forces staff, going beyond their current responsibilities. And I shall order proposals to be presented on the basis of studies to be carried out in conjunction with the navy, army, and air force, in order to tailor the gradual adaptation of our defense forces to the demands of the future.

In the post–cold war world, the importance of countries such as Brazil no longer depends solely on military and strategic factors, but on domestic political stability, the general level of well-being, and the vital signs of the economy—the capacity to grow and create jobs, the technology base, our share of international trade—and also on clear, objective, and feasible diplomatic proposals.

For this very reason, the implementation of a consistent national development program should strengthen us in a growing manner on the world stage. Times are favorable for Brazil to seek more active participation within this context. We have a constant identity and a lasting set of values that will continue to be expressed by our foreign policy. Continuity means reliability in the international sphere. Sudden changes, unmindful of the long-term view, might satisfy short-term interests, but they do not forge the profile of a responsible state. Nevertheless, we should not be afraid to innovate when our interests and values indicate this option.

During a phase of radical transformations colored by the redefinition of the rules for political and economic comity among nations, we cannot turn our backs on the course of history out of mere nostalgia for a past seen through rose-colored glasses. We must, however, be mindful of the course that history is taking in order to influence the design of the new world order. The time has therefore come to update our discourse and activities abroad, in consideration of the changes in the international system and the new domestic consensus as to our objectives.

The time has come to openly discuss what Brazil's profile should be as a sovereign nation in this world in transformation; the debate should involve the Ministry of External Affairs, the Congress, academia, labor unions, the business community, and nongovernmental organizations. We will retire dated ideological dilemmas and outworn forms of confrontation, and face up to the new themes that impel cooperation and conflict among countries today: human rights and democracy; the environment and sustainable development; the broadened range of tasks relating to multilateralism and regionalization; dynamizing international trade, and overcoming protectionism and unilateralism. Other key themes are access to technology, efforts to ensure nonproliferation, and the struggle against the various manifestations of international crime.

We will take maximum advantage of Brazil's ubiquitous presence, both in political and economic terms. A presence that will allow us both to increase our participation in regional integration movements, beginning with Mercosul, as well as to explore the dynamism of unified Europe, NAFTA, the Asian-Pacific region. And we will also identify areas with new potential in terms of international relations, such as the postapartheid South Africa, not to mention countries such as China, Russia, and India, which because of their continental size, face problems similar to ours in the effort to ensure economic and social development.

I believe that Brazil has a place reserved for it among the countries on this planet that will do well during the next century and I am convinced that the only major obstacles that stand in our way are the result of our domestic imbalances—the extreme inequalities among regions and social groups. We know that the development of a country in today's world is not measured by the quantity of goods that it produces. The real degree of development is measured by the quality of care a country provides to its people. To its people and to its culture. In a world in which communications are global and instantaneous, and yet, in which the target groups are becoming fragmented and specialized, cultural identity holds nations together.

We Brazilians are an extremely homogenous people in cultural terms. Our regional differences are mere variations on a basic cultural theme, the result of a fusion of Western and Portuguese with African and Amerindian traditions. Our intellectuals, our artists, and our cultural agents are the genuine expression of our people. I want to acclaim them and provide them with the conditions that will allow them to become builders of citizenship. For citizenship means not just the right of the individual, but also the pride of being part of a country that has values and a style of its own.

The priorities that I put forth to the voters, and which were approved by the majority, are those that have direct repercussions on people's quality of life: employment, health, safety, education, food production. Job creation will come with the return of growth, but not automatically. This administration will be committed to specific programs and actions in this field. And we will throw ourselves heart and soul into the great challenge facing Brazil, and not just this or that region; facing us all, and not just those left on the sidelines—the challenge of decreasing inequalities until we have done away with them.

Providing access to hospitals and respect for those being helped, eliminating unnecessary delays, fighting waste and fraud, all these are factors that are just as indispensable to proper health care management as is the existence of sufficient funding. But health must be viewed—and so it shall be, under my administration—primarily as the prevention and not just the curing of diseases. A modern approach to health includes basic sanitation, mass vaccination campaigns, adequate food and sports for all.

The school must be the heart of the teaching process once again. Schools are not just the function of the teacher. A school is far more than that. It is a gathering place where the actions of parents, the solidarity of the social medium, the participation of students and teacher and proper administration are added together to train properly prepared citizens.

To make the great leap that will be required on the threshold of the new millennium, we can no longer co-exist with massive levels of illiteracy or functional illiteracy. It is a sorry illusion, indeed, to believe that the mere consumption of gadgets will make us "modern" even if our children continue to pass through our schools without absorbing the barest minimum of knowledge needed to keep up with modernity's rapid pace.

We have had enough of a situation in which we built ridiculously monumental schools, and then filled them with badly paid and badly trained teachers, as well as unmotivated students who were not materially or psychologically ready to take full advantage of their education.

To fully exercise our mandate to do away with destitution, we must also do away with spiritual impoverishment. Let the modern media help us in our task. Together with information and entertainment, let us engage our television networks in a true national crusade to rescue citizenship through education, beginning with a tremendous effort to provide literacy and cultural education.

My mission, beginning today, is to ensure that these priorities of our people will also be our government's priorities. This will demand a broad reorganization of our government machinery. The federal administrative system has deteriorated significantly after year upon year of excesses and fiscal difficulties. Patronage, corporativism, and corruption drain away the taxpayer's money before it reaches those who should be the legitimate beneficiaries of government activities, primarily in the social arena.

The congressional investigations and the decisive steps taken by President Itamar Franco's administration began to rid us of these parasites over the last two years. It will become necessary to stir up many hornet's nests before completing our housecleaning and providing the structural reforms that are so necessary if public services are to become efficient. This does not frighten me.

I know that I will have the support of the majority of our nation. And also the support of many employees who care deeply for the civil service. The most important support, in fact, is not the kind extended to the government or to the president as an individual. The most important support is the kind we give one another, as Brazilians, and the support we all give to Brazil.

This veritable social revolution, this revolution of people's mindsets, will only occur with the cooperation of all society. The administration has a key role to play, and I will see that this role is carried out. But without congressional approval of changes in the Constitution and our legislation—some of which I pointed out in my farewell speech to the Senate—and unless public opinion is mobilized, our good intentions will be stillborn phrases in speeches.

We must stitch together new ways for society to participate in the process of change. A fundamental share of this growing awareness, these demands on the part of our citizenry and the mobilization I have described, will depend on the mass media. Our media were a fundamental part of the redemocratization processes and they have also been key to the recuperation of morality in public life. Now a new and pivotal role has been reserved for them in the effort to mobilize everyone in the building of a fairer and better society; while maintaining their critical independence and their passion for the veracity of their information.

Once Brazilians have better access to information and are in a position to be more critical of the policies that are actually implemented than of the folklore surrounding so many aspects of daily life, once they are in a position to put events into proper perspective and demand greater consistency from actions rather than judge mere intentions, then Brazilians will be better prepared to exercise their citizenship. . . .

Let us ensure a decent life for our children, taking them off the streets where they have been abandoned, and above all, putting an end to the shameful massacres of children and youths. Let us vigorously guarantee equal rights to equals. To women, who form the majority of our people, and to whom the country owes both respect and opportunities for education and employment.

To the racial minorities and to some near-majority groups—primarily the blacks—who expect equality to be, more than a mere word, the portrait of a reality. To the Amerindian groups, some of them living witnesses of human archaeology and all of them witnesses of our diversity. Let us transform solidarity into the active ingredient of our citizenship in search of equality.

And our hope of seeing a free, prosperous, and fair Brazil shall beat ever more strongly in the breast of each Brazilian like a great truth. In conclusion to this speech, I wish to leave behind a heartfelt word of gratitude. To the people of my country, who with generosity, elected me to office during the very first round of voting. To the many who accompany me in our political struggles. To my family, who was capable of understanding the challenges of history.

To the Congress I served in up until today and which now swears me in, with the proclamation of the judiciary, as president of the republic. To the heads of state from countries that are our friends, and to the foreign delegations that honor us with their presence during this ceremony. To our guests. To all the citizens, men and women, of this Brazil of ours, once again I ask that you have much faith, much hope, much confidence, much love, and much work. And I call on you to change Brazil.

Thank you very much.

STUDY QUESTIONS

1. What is the connection between the market economy and political freedom, according to Cardoso?
2. What steps does Cardoso promise his administration will take to deal with poverty and social exclusions? To what extent are these policies entwined with his embrace of neoliberalism?

GARY S. BECKER

13.2 LATIN AMERICA OWES A LOT TO ITS CHICAGO BOYS, 1997

Gary S. Becker was an economist at the University of Chicago who achieved incredible influence in his academic field, as well as in international politics. One of the founding figures of the "Chicago School" of neoliberal economic theory, Becker won the Nobel Prize for Economic Sciences in 1992 as well as the US Presidential Medal of Freedom in 2007 for his work on the connection between social life and the market. Chicago-educated economists, including many who had worked directly with Becker, played a key role in the economic reforms enacted under Pinochet's military regime in Chile, becoming known as the "Chicago Boys." These economists held key roles in the Pinochet administration and implemented policies focused on deregulation, privatization, and the elimination of social programs. Their work has been controversial, generating intense debates among political scientists and economists as to the outcomes of the reforms they initiated, as well as over whether their support for a military government notorious for its human rights abuses can be considered morally acceptable. In this op-ed published in the influential American business magazine *Businessweek* in 1997, Becker argues that the "Chicago Boys" had received insufficient credit for their work in regenerating the Chilean economy.

Source: Gary S. Becker, "Latin America Owes a Lot to Its 'Chicago Boys,'" *Business Week*, June 9, 1997 (Bloomberg, L.P.).

On my first visit to South America in the early 1980s, I heard a candidate in the Colombian presidential elections attack the "Chicago boys." These were not remnants of Al Capone's gang, but Latin American economists educated in the department of economics of the University of Chicago. I was impressed that our former students were important enough to be discussed in a presidential election—and shocked that they were then apparently so unpopular.

Chicago boys generally advocated widespread deregulation, privatizations, and other free-market policies for closely controlled economies. They rose to fame as leaders of the early reforms initiated in Chile during the rule of General Augusto Pinochet. Chicagoans were attacked partly because central planning and government controls were still advocated by economists in that region.

The Chicago boys took a lot of heat for agreeing to work for Pinochet. Like most generals who seize power, he initially ran the economy as a centrally directed, military-type system. Only after this approach failed did he, in desperation, turn to the free-market policies advocated by the Chicagoans. In retrospect, their willingness to work for a cruel dictator and start a different economic approach was one of the best things that happened to Chile.

PARIAH NATION

In the past, Chile and other Latin nations did not have competitive capital, but a cozy system of monopoly capitalism, where high tariffs kept out more efficient foreign competition and where domestic companies received subsidized government loans and other favors. Unions liked the system, too, since they had rigid job-protection legislation and often controlled medical-insurance premiums and other profitable programs. The elderly received generous retirement and health benefits financed by heavy taxes on younger workers.

This system of providing political favors to powerful interest groups was highly inefficient and produced stagnant economies. After a bad start, the revolutionary economic reforms initiated in Chile caused that economy to boom beyond the wildest expectations even of their teachers in Chicago. Chile's annual growth in per

capita real income from 1985–96 averaged a remarkable 5%, far above the rest of Latin America.

Chile went from a pariah nation controlled by a dictator to an economic role model for the whole undeveloped world. Chile's performance then became still more impressive when the government was transformed into a democracy.

Other nations began to believe that free-market reforms could also help them. Chile's success especially grated on its large rival, Argentina. Decades of abysmal economic policies had reduced Argentina from among the top 10 nations in per capita income at the start of this century to about 75th.

ROCKY ROAD

In 1989, Argentina elected the Perónist Carlos Saúl Menem, and he continued the interventionist policies that nation had so long endured. But Menem quickly realized that these, too, were failing and asked Domingo Cavallo, a Harvard University–educated economist sympathetic to Chicago-style policies, to initiate a radical freeing of Argentina's economy. This ended the long period of stagnation, and the nation began to grow rapidly, even weathering the sharp recession in 1992 caused by Mexico's financial troubles. Cavallo was recently replaced by a Chicago graduate, Roque Fernandez, who continued the reform, which has generated violence in the provinces where unemployment is high.

Chile and Argentina were soon followed down the path of free-market policies by Mexico, Peru, Bolivia, and Colombia. Although the road has occasionally been rocky, these nations generally reversed their economic stagnation, began to grow more rapidly, raised living standards, and sharply increased exports. Meanwhile, countries like Brazil and Venezuela that have been slow to introduce reform experienced greater difficulties and grew more slowly.

Free-market reforms have not solved all the problems of Latin American societies. For example, a recent World Bank study documents that this region has greater economic inequality than other regions of the world, in good part because schooling and other human capital investments in the very poor have been inadequate.

Although unions and older business families accustomed to special privileges stand ready to promote the old mercantilist policies should Latin economies falter, the changes initiated by the Chicago boys in Chile have spurred an economic and political revolution in Latin America that is unlikely to be reversed. Their teachers are proud of their richly deserved glory.

STUDY QUESTIONS

1. What types of changes enacted by Chicago-trained economists in Chile and other South American countries does Becker see as especially significant?
2. What does Becker see as the connection between neoliberal economic reform and the shift from military to democratic rule?
3. Notably, Becker does not mention the human rights abuses committed by the Pinochet regime in his discussion of the economic changes enacted by the regime. How can we interpret this absence of attention?

13.3 SUPREME DECREE NO. 355: CREATION OF THE COMMISSION ON TRUTH AND RECONCILIATION, CHILE, APRIL 25, 1990

A key part of the transition from military to democratic rule in many Latin American countries was the establishment of Truth and Reconciliation committees designed to help heal national divides by uncovering the truth about human rights violations that had occurred under military rule. These commissions were viewed by civilian political leaders as essential to restoring trust in the government, and to overcoming divisions within national populations that had been deeply traumatized by the militarization and weaponization of political partisanship. This form of restorative justice was supported by the international community. The Chilean Commission on Truth and Reconciliation was established in 1990 by the first postmilitary President Patricio Alwyn. It was composed of an intentionally politically diverse group of leaders, including members of the Pinochet government; those who had been forced into exile; and members of anti-Pinochet political movements. The commission was tasked with creating as complete a picture as possible of the human rights abuses that occurred during the military dictatorship and providing recommendations about how these abuses should be compensated, as well as how such abuses could be prevented in the future. This excerpt provides the text of the original presidential decree that created the commission in April 1990.

Source: "Supreme Decree No. 355," Report of the Chilean National Commission on Truth and Reconciliation (Notre Dame, Indiana: University of Notre Dame Press, 1993), vol. I/II, Foreword, xxi–xxii, pp. 24, 26.

SUPREME DECREE NO. 355

Executive Branch
Ministry of Justice
Undersecretary of the Interior
Creation of the Commission on Truth and Reconciliation
Santiago, April 25, 1990.
The following decree was issued today:
No. 355. Considering:

1. That the moral conscience of the nation demands that the truth about the grave violations of human rights committed in our country between September 11, 1973 and March 11, 1990 be brought to light;

2. That only upon a foundation of truth will it be possible to meet the basic demands of justice and create the necessary conditions for achieving true national reconciliation;

3. That only the knowledge of the truth will restore the dignity of the victims in the public mind, allow their relatives and mourners to honor them fittingly, and in some measure make it possible to make amends for the damage done;

4. That the judiciary has the exclusive responsibility, in each particular case, to establish what crimes may have been committed, to identify those persons guilty and to apply the proper sanctions.

5. That the nature of such legal procedures makes it unlikely that the judiciary will quickly provide the country with an overall sense of what has happened;

6. That delaying the formation of a serious common awareness in this regard may potentially disrupt our life as a national community and militates against the yearning among Chileans to draw closer together in peace;

7. That without in any way affecting the responsibilities of the judiciary, it is the duty of the president as the person charged with governing and administering the state and the person responsible for promoting the common good of society to do all within his power to help bring this truth to light as quickly and effectively as possible;

8. That a conscientious report by highly respected people with moral authority in our country, who are to receive, gather, and analyze all the evidence given to them or that they can obtain on the most serious cases of human rights violations, will make it possible for national public opinion to come to a rational and well-grounded idea of what has happened and will offer the various branches of government information that will make it possible or easier to take the measures appropriate to each one;

In no case is the Commission to assume jurisdictional functions proper to the courts nor to interfere in cases already before the courts. Hence it will not have the power to take a position on whether particular individuals are legally responsible for the events that it is considering.

If while it is carrying out its functions the Commission receives evidence about actions that appear to be criminal, it will immediately submit it to the appropriate court.

Article Three:

The Commission is to be made up of the following persons:

Raúl Rettig Guissen, who will serve as president
Jaime Castillo Velasco
José Luis Cea Egaña
Mónica Jiménez de La Jara
Ricardo Martin Díaz
Laura Novoa Vásquez
Gonzalo Vial Correa
José Zalaquett Daher.

Article Four:

In order to carry out its assigned task the Commission is to:

1. Receive the evidence provided by alleged victims, their representatives, successors, or relatives within the time period and in the manner that the Commission itself will determine;

2. Gather and weigh the information that human rights organizations, Chilean and international, intergovernmental and non-governmental, may provide on their own initiative or upon request about matters within their competence;

3. Carry out as much investigation as it may determine suitable for accomplishing its task, including requesting reports, documents, or evidence from government authorities and agencies; and

4. Prepare a report on the basis of the evidence it has gathered in which it is to express the conclusions of the Commission with regard to the matters mentioned

in Article One in accord with the honest judgement and conscience of its members.

The report is to be presented to the president, who will then release it to the public, and will adopt the decisions or initiatives that he regards as appropriate. With the submission of its report the Commission will conclude its work and will automatically be dissolved.

STUDY QUESTIONS

1. What rationale does the decree provide for the formation of the commission?
2. What limits are placed on the power held by the commission?

EJERCITO ZAPATISTA DE LIBERACION NACIONAL

13.4 FIRST MESSAGE FROM LACANDON JUNGLE, 1994

The EZLN—often referred to as the Zapatistas—are a revolutionary militant group based in Chiapas, a province inhabited largely by indigenous Maya in the south of Mexico. Led by the former sociology and philosophy professor Subcomandante Marcos (since 2014 renamed Subcomandante Insurgente Galeano), the group is primarily composed of indigenous Mayans who seek greater control over local resources, especially land. Formed initially in 1983, the group gained international prominence in 1994, when they launched an armed insurrection against the Mexican government on the day the North American Free Trade Agreement (NAFTA) went into effect. The goal of the uprising was to instigate a nationwide rebellion against neoliberalism in Mexico, using the insurrection as a platform to call the world's attention to their opposition to NAFTA, which the Zapatistas believed would worsen the impoverishment of Chiapas. On the morning of January 1, 1994, an army of three thousand Zapatistas gained control of cities throughout Chiapas, but their victory was short-lived and the military quickly regained power. However, the armed insurrection continued on a smaller scale, and the group attracted significant international attention and support, emerging as a global touchstone for opposition to neoliberalism. The emergence of the Zapatista movement challenged the assumption that the end of the Cold War and the collapse of the Soviet Union would lead to the end of leftist revolutionary politics in Latin America. The First Declaration from the Lacandon Jungle, excerpted here, essentially serves as the foundational text for the Zapatista movement, and lays out its core political, military and social demands and goals.

Source: Ejercito Zapatista de Liberacion Nacional, "First Message from Lacandon Jungle", in *Vivan Los Zapatistas*, 1994.

EZLN's Declaration of War

"Today we say 'enough is enough!' (Ya Basta!)"

First Declaration from the Lacandon Jungle

EZLN's Declaration of War

TO THE PEOPLE OF MEXICO:

MEXICAN BROTHERS AND SISTERS:

We are a product of 500 years of struggle: first against slavery, then during the War of Independence against Spain led by insurgents, then to avoid being absorbed by North American imperialism, then to promulgate our constitution and expel the French empire from our soil, and later the dictatorship of Porfirio Diaz denied us the just application of the Reform laws and the people rebelled and leaders like Villa and Zapata emerged, poor men just like us. We have been denied the most elemental preparation so they can use us as cannon fodder and pillage the wealth of our country. They don't care that we have nothing, absolutely nothing, not even a roof over our heads, no land, no work, no health care, no food nor education. Nor are we able to freely and democratically elect our political representatives, nor is there independence from foreigners, nor is there peace nor justice for ourselves and our children.

But today, we say ENOUGH IS ENOUGH.

We are the inheritors of the true builders of our nation. The dispossessed, we are millions and we thereby call upon our brothers and sisters to join this struggle as the only path, so that we will not die of hunger due to the insatiable ambition of a 70 year dictatorship led by a clique of traitors that represent the most conservative and sell-out groups. They are the same ones that opposed Hidalgo and Morelos, the same ones that betrayed Vicente Guerrero, the same ones that sold half our country to the foreign invader, the same ones that imported a European prince to rule our country, the same ones that formed the "scientific" Porfirsta dictatorship, the same ones that opposed the Petroleum Expropriation, the same ones that massacred the railroad workers in 1958 and the students in 1968, the same ones the today take everything from us, absolutely everything.

To prevent the continuation of the above and as our last hope, after having tried to utilize all legal means based on our Constitution, we go to our Constitution, to apply Article 39 which says:

"National Sovereignty essentially and originally resides in the people. All political power emanates from the people and its purpose is to help the people. The people have, at all times, the inalienable right to alter or modify their form of government. "

Therefore, according to our constitution, we declare the following to the Mexican federal army, the pillar of the Mexican dictatorship that we suffer from, monopolized by a one-party system and led by Carlos Salinas de Gortari, the maximum and illegitimate federal executive that today holds power.

According to this Declaration of War, we ask that other powers of the nation advocate to restore the legitimacy and the stability of the nation by overthrowing the dictator. We also ask that international organizations and the International Red Cross watch over and regulate our battles, so that our efforts are carried out while still protecting our civilian population. We declare now and always that we are subject to the Geneva Accord, forming the EZLN as our fighting arm of our liberation struggle. We have the Mexican people on our side, we have the beloved tri-colored flag highly respected by our insurgent fighters. We use black and red in our uniform as our symbol of our working people on strike. Our flag carries the following letters, "EZLN," Zapatista National Liberation Army, and we always carry our flag into combat. Beforehand, we refuse any effort to disgrace our just cause by accusing us of being drug traffickers, drug guerrillas, thieves, or other names that might by used by our enemies. Our struggle follows the constitution which is held high by its call for justice and equality.

Therefore, according to this declaration of war, we give our military forces, the EZLN, the following orders:

First: Advance to the capital of the country, overcoming the Mexican federal army, protecting in our advance the civilian population and permitting the people in the liberated area the right to freely and democratically elect their own administrative authorities.

Second: Respect the lives of our prisoners and turn over all wounded to the International Red Cross.

Third: Initiate summary judgments against all soldiers of the Mexican federal army and the political police that have received training or have been paid by foreigners, accused of being traitors to our country, and against all those that have repressed and treated badly the civil population and robbed or stolen from or attempted crimes against the good of the people.

Fourth: Form new troops with all those Mexicans that show their interest in joining our struggle, including those that, being enemy soldiers, turn themselves in without having fought against us, and promise to take orders from the General Command of the Zapatista National Liberation Army.

Fifth: We ask for the unconditional surrender of the enemy's headquarters before we begin any combat to avoid any loss of lives.

Sixth: Suspend the robbery of our natural resources in the areas controlled by the EZLN.

To the People of Mexico: We, the men and women, full and free, are conscious that the war that we have declared is our last resort, but also a just one. The dictators are applying an undeclared genocidal war against our people for many years. Therefore we ask for your participation, your decision to support this plan that struggles for work, land, housing, food, health care, education, independence, freedom, democracy, justice and peace. We declare that we will not stop fighting until the basic demands of our people have been met by forming a government of our country that is free and democratic.

JOIN THE INSURGENT FORCES OF THE ZAPATISTA NATIONAL LIBERATION ARMY.

General Command of the EZLN

1993

STUDY QUESTIONS

1. How is the history of colonialism presented and deployed within the Zapatista message? How does this link to the core Zapatista slogan "Ya Basta!"—"enough!"?

2. What role does the international community play in the military demands outlined in the Declaration? How does this international focus connect to the protest against globalization embedded in the Zapatistas' economic message?

ALONSO SALAZAR

13.5 *BORN TO DIE IN MEDELLIN*, 1990

Beginning in the late 1970s, cocaine surged in international demand, fueling the rise of powerful drug cartels throughout Latin America. During the 1980s by far the most important was the Medellin Cartel run by Pablo Escobar. At the height of its operations, the Medellin Cartel supplied 90 percent of the global cocaine market and generated up to $100 million per day in profit. The consequences for the Colombian city of Medellin were profound. As the cartel gained near complete control of the city, violent conflict surged, and the city became the murder capital of the world, with young men especially impacted as both killers and murder victims. In this excerpt from his best-selling book, first published in 1990, the Colombian anthropologist Alonso Salazar talks with Antonio, a teenager who worked as a contract killer for the cartel, about his life and work. The interview was conducted while Antonio lay in a hospital bed having been shot in the stomach while boarding a bus. He died shortly after the interview was completed.

Source: Alonso Salazar, *Born to Die in Medellin*, trans. Nick Caistor (Colombia: CINEP, 1990), pp. 12–18.

ANTONIO

When I was a kid I used to get a bit of money using a home-made pistol. Then Lunar and Papucho—they're both dead now—let me have proper guns, so I started to steal and kill for real. You get violent because there are a lot of guys who want to tell you what to do, to take you over, just because you're a kid. You've got to keep your wits about you, to spread your own wings. That's what I did, and off I flew; anybody who got in my way paid for it.

I learned that lesson from my family. From the old woman, who's tough as nails. She's with me whatever I do. She might not look much, but she's always on my side. The only regret I have in quitting this earth is leaving her on her own. To know she might be all alone in her old age. She's fought hard all her life, and she doesn't deserve that.

My old man died about 14 years ago. He was a hard case too, and taught me a lot, but he was always at the bottle, and left us in the lurch. That was why I had to fend for myself, to help my ma and my brothers and sisters. (That's how I started in a gang—but also because it was something inside me, I was born with this violent streak.)

Lunar, the leader of the gang, was only a teenager but he was tough all right. He'd been in the business for years already. He lived in Bello for a while and knew the people from Los Monjes. He learned a lot from them, so when he came to live here he started up his own gang. He had a birthmark or *lunar* on his cheek, that's how he got the nickname. It was thanks to him and Papucho, the other leader, that I learned how to do things properly.

I'll never forget the first time I had to kill someone. I had already shot a few people, but I'd never seen death close up. It was in Copacabana, a small place near Medellín. We were breaking into a farmhouse one morning when the watchman suddenly appeared out of nowhere. I was behind a wall, he ran in front of me, I looked up and was so startled I emptied my revolver into him. He was stone dead. That was tough, I won't lie, it was tough for me to take. For two weeks I couldn't eat a thing because I saw his face even in my food . . . but after that it got easy. You learn to kill without it disturbing your sleep.

Now it's me who's the gang leader. Papucho was killed by the guys up on the hill there. They set a trap for him and he fell for it. They asked him to do a job for them, then shot him to pieces. A friend of his was behind it, who'd sold out. Lunar made me second-in-command because we understood each other almost without speaking—we didn't need words.

Lunar didn't last much longer; he was never one to back down from a fight, never a chicken. He really enjoyed life; he always said we were all playing extra time anyway. And he was enjoying himself when he died: he was at a dance about three blocks down the hill when they shot him three times in the back. He was on his own because he reckoned there were no skunks down there. The kid who shot him died almost before he could blink. We tracked him down that same night, and sent him on his trip to the stars.

After Lunar's death another wise guy thought he'd take over the gang. I had to get tough and show him who was boss. For being such a smart ass now he's pushing up the dirt as well. It's me who gives the orders round here, I say what we do and don't do. There were about fifty of us to begin with, but a lot of them have been killed or put inside, and others have grassed. There's only twenty of us real hard cases left. They're all teenagers, between 15 and 18. I'm the oldest. A lot get killed or caught, but more always want to join, to get some action.

Whenever anyone wants to join I ask around: "Who is this kid? Can I trust him?" Then I decide if he can join or not. They're all kids who see things as they are; they know they won't get anywhere by working or studying, but if they join us they'll have ready money. They join because they want to, not because we force them. We don't tell anybody they have to. Not all of them are really poor, some do it for their families, others because they want to live in style.

Before we finally choose someone we give him a test: to take something somewhere, to carry guns and to keep them hidden. Then finally we give them a job to do. If the kid shows he can do it, then he's one of us. But if he ever grasses on us, if he shoots his mouth off, if he gets out of line, then he's dead meat. Everyone understands that. Then again, we support each other all we can; "If you haven't got something and I have, take it, friend—as a gift, not a loan." We also help if someone's in trouble. We look after each other, but nobody can double-cross us.

We take good care of our guns, because they're hard to come by. The last kid I shot died because of that.

"Antonio, help me out will you brother? Lend me a gun for a job I have to do," he said to me.

"I'll let you have this .38, but be sure you give it back tomorrow; you know the rules."

I lent it to him because the kid had always been straight with us, but this time he wasn't. So I went to talk to him, and he came up with a really strange excuse. He said the law had taken it from him. I gave him another two days, and when he didn't show up I passed the death sentence. He knew he was a marked man, so he didn't make any attempt to hide. It was easy for me.

The thing is, it's hard to find guns. You either have to shoot a guy to get his, or buy them, and a good weapon costs. (We nearly always buy them from the police, and they sell us the ammo too.) I've also bought grenades from a retired army guy. We've had T-55s, 32-shot mini-Uzis, 9mm Ingrands, but we usually use sawn-off shotguns, pistols and revolvers. We're all good shots.

We practice late at night, two, three in the morning, in some woods over at Rionegro. We set up a line of bottles and fire at them. I smash the lot. You have to keep a steady hand when you're on a job, you only have one chance to kill someone, you can't afford to miss. You only have a few seconds so you have to know what you're doing: if the dummy doesn't die, you could. You have to know how to handle your weapon, to shoot straight, and how to make your get-away. We learn a lot from films. We get videos of people like Chuck Norris, Black Cobra, Commando, or Stallone, and watch how they handle their weapons, how they cover each other, how they get away. We watch the films and discuss tactics.

We learn to ride motor bikes on the hills round here. They're all souped up, really quick. Most of them are stolen; we buy papers for them for 20,000[1] pesos down at the traffic police. Our territory is from the bus terminal down to the school. People who don't mess with us have no problems, but anyone who tries to muscle in either gets out or dies. We help the people in our neighbourhood, they come to us and say: "we've got nothing to eat," so we help them and keep them happy. And when we've done a job that pays well, we make sure they get some. We look after them so that they're on our side. Whenever someone tries to move in on our territory, I personally go and kneecap them as a warning they should never come back.

Lots of kids in the neighbourhood want to be in a gang. All I tell them is if that's what they want to do they have to be serious about it, but I don't force them to join. Most of them start by stealing cars, then they save up to buy a shotgun, which is the cheapest weapon around. We give them cartridges so they can get started.

I reckon I've killed 13 people. That's 13 I've killed personally, I don't count those we've shot when we're out as a gang. If I die now, I'll die happy. Killing is our business really, we do other jobs, but mostly we're hired to kill people.

People from all sorts of places contract us: from Bellavista jail, from El Poblado, from Itagúi. People who don't want to show their faces, and take you on to get rid of their problem for them. I try to work out whether our client means business, if he can pay us. We charge according to who we have to hit: if he's important, we charge more. We're putting our lives, our freedom, our guns on the line. If we have to leave the city to deal with some big shot, our price is anything up to three million. Here in Medellín the lowest we go is half a million.

We don't care who we have to give it to, we know it has to be done, that's all there is to it. Whoever it may be: I have no allegiances. I'll drive the bike and gun anyone down—myself, no problem. Sometimes we don't even know who it is we have to kill. You hear later who the hit was, from the news on the radio. It's all the same to us, we've done our job, that's all.

Whenever I have to kill someone, all I think is: too bad for him he crossed my path. If their back is towards me, I call out, so I can make sure I've got the right guy, and when he turns round, I give it to him. I don't worry about it, I don't worry about running into the law, or that things will go wrong, nothing like that. (I only hope I don't kill a woman or a child in a shoot-out. If I'm going to kill, there has to be a reason for it.)

---

1   £1 = 545 pesos (1990).

Once we went out to a small town to deal with a local councillor. We don't usually know who is giving us the contract, but in this case it was more or less direct contact, and we realised that the guy who wanted him dead was the leader of a political party. We kept well away from him after that, because you can be the ones who end up paying. They can easily have you rubbed out as well to get rid of witnesses. We made a million on that job.

The week before, we went to the town to see the lie of the land. We were shown the client, we took a look at where the police were, worked out how to get out afterwards. On the Saturday, I went back with a girlfriend. She was carrying the weapon—a submachine gun—in her bag. We took a room in the best hotel, pretending we were a honeymoon couple. We took our time checking out the town, making sure nothing could go wrong.

On the Sunday, two of the gang stole a car in Medellín, and kept the owner in a room in Guayaquil until the job was done. One of them drove to the town and parked where we'd agreed, right on time. The councillor always liked to have a coffee in a corner bar after his meetings. My girlfriend showed up with the gun around two in the afternoon. I took it and waited for the action. Waiting like that really gets you down. You get real nervous. I've found a trick which always helps me: I get a bullet, take out the lead, and pour the gunpowder into a hot black coffee. I drink the lot, and that steadies my nerves.

At ten to six I left the hotel and sat waiting in the bar. It was a hot evening, and there were a lot of people on the street. I saw our car arrive and park a few metres away. The target came in a couple of minutes later. On the dot as promised.

It was beginning to get dark, which is always useful. I took another good look round to make sure there was nothing unusual going on, then paid for my drink. When the waiter was giving me my change, I pulled out the submachine gun and started firing. Everybody hit the floor. When something like that happens in a small town, they all stay well out of it, no one is expecting it. I went over and put a final bullet in him, because some of these guys are really tough and you have to make sure of your money. It was all over in seconds. While I had been firing, they had started the car, so I walked to it as calm as could be, and got in. We made sure we didn't drive too fast out of town. We made as if we were going out on the main highway, but then headed off down a side road. We drove for about a quarter of an hour, then left the car by the roadside. We walked for an hour, until we came to a safe house on a farm owned by a friend of the politician who had hired us. We caught a bus back to Medellín about five o'clock the next morning. They sent the gun back to us a few days later. Everything had been well planned and worked like clockwork.

That night we had a huge party. We'd already had the pay-off, so as the saying goes: "the dead to their graves, the living to the dance." It was like Christmas. We bought a pig, crates of beer and liquor, set up a sound system in the street, and gave it all we'd got 'til morning.

STUDY QUESTIONS

1. Why does Antonio believe he gravitated toward gang life? What experiences were influential in shaping his choices in this regard?
2. How does Antonio describe the experience of killing? How does his first experience killing a person compare with some of his statements later in the interview about his work as a contract killer?
3. What role do the police play in supporting the gangs, according to Antonio?

CARMEN NARANJO COTO

13.6 WOMEN'S LIBERATION FROM SERVITUDE AND OVERPROTECTION, 1989

Carmen Naranjo Coto (1928–2012) was an important Costa Rican novelist and poet, whose work was widely read throughout Latin America. During the 1970s, '80s, and '90s, she held a series of high-profile political and cultural roles, serving as the Costa Rican ambassador to Israel, minister of culture, director of the Costa Rican Museum of Art, and director of the Central American University Press. Naranjo played an important role in the Costa Rican women's movement, notably establishing the National Women's Office. In this excerpt from an essay published in 1989, Naranjo thinks through the meaning of feminism in Costa Rica, identifying the home as the key barrier to women's equality.

Critics of feminism say it has concentrated on actions for women who are "with it" or "up to date"—those who all along have been conscious of the problems women face. They claim feminism had to become a kind of escape valve, a way of appeasing the different social strata and muffling their impatience over injustices and discrimination, even though the relief women felt by venting their frustrations offered neither a solution nor an inspiration to seek full incorporation into society.

SERVITUDE: WOMEN'S GRAVEST PROBLEM

To my way of thinking, the core problem of women lies in the human servitude to which they have been subjected throughout history. Servitude does not foster communication, respect for rights, or human consideration. Rather, it cancels creativity and blocks personal and social fulfillment.

Women have always been servants, their image cloaked in domesticity. The architecture of the home clearly fits that image. We see women busy in the bedroom, kitchen, dining room, or some other room dedicated to housework—rarely do they enter the living room, study, or library except to clean these areas and put them in order. Even in recent times, as appliances and new housekeeping techniques have made housework more versatile and creative, duties in the home have remained limited to the exercise of specific skills.

Women's domestic image also carries over to the workplace. In factories, they gather in in large halls, working at product-assembly conveyor belts, where they perform tasks step by step, like mutilated housework.

In the office, women labor to print out the creative works of others. Similarly, in other areas of business, women always serve, translating their experience as buyers into the commercial experience of sellers. Only in exceptional cases and under extraordinary conditions do women move beyond manual labor and enter the world of intellectual contributions.

Of course, manual labor is not humiliating as such, nor does it always represent human servitude.

Source: Carmen Naranjo Coto, "Women's Liberation from Servitude and Overprotection" (1989), in Ilse Abshagen Leitinger (ed.) *The Costa Rican Women's Movement: A Reader* (Pittsburgh: University of Pittsburgh Press, 1997), pp. 29–34.

After all, manual labor itself uses some creative talent; in the highest arts, intellectual and manual labor are combined. Servitude begins when humans are confined to only one type of work, when they are prevented at all costs from going beyond that area which is declared to be their customary tasks. Circumscribed by gender typing, work then brings about human servitude because it sacrifices—through manifold limitations—creative human potential and thus virtually imprisons the worker. Human servitude occurs also when we deny human beings the opportunity of acquiring experience on their own, reasoning that such recourse is simply not permissible for a specific gender.

THE OVERPROTECTION OF WOMEN

The so-called protection of women has placed limits on them in all areas. Ideals proclaiming women's purity and weakness and their inability to suffer and survive have disqualified women at the very moment when they should have begun their apprenticeship for a life full of opportunities and enriching challenges. The extent of the disqualification into which the feminine world has been locked appears in the desolate figure of the widow who must suddenly satisfy all of the spiritual and material demands of her family.

This overprotection of women determines their "appropriate" tasks, modeled after the tasks they fulfill at home. In areas that demand cordiality—a certain touch, the lending of help, the giving of care—women must be involved.

THE TRAGEDY OF HOUSEWORK

Since I am using terms that can be willfully blurred or jumbled, let me clarify myself: I do not underrate housework, which indeed allows creativity and affords enjoyment and personal fulfillment. Working in the kitchen, sewing, weaving, decorating, cleaning, generally improving the home—these activities can be constructive activities, providing a sense of satisfaction and usefully uniting the family. To share obligations, to participate in household duties, to learn to divide housework produces harmony, shared efforts, communication. and broader understanding. It is when household obligations always rest with one person, who then becomes a permanent tireless servant, that they lead to irritated exhaustion. In most cases, the weight of those obligations is misunderstood, and as a result the family is not strengthened but rather weakened or exhausted.

I have frequently pointed to the tragedy that we acknowledge housework only when efficiency is lacking—when bread burns, buttons come off, furniture grows dusty, shirts are poorly ironed, and some tasks are forgotten. We accept the unending routine, performed day after day, with gratitude and silent recognition, simply by failing to notice or honor it, as if it did not merit appreciation. We recognize or, administratively speaking, evaluate that routine only when we criticize, show defects, or complain belligerently about errors or about the partial or total neglect of tasks.

THE GOALS OF WOMEN'S LIBERATION

From various points of view, when we speak about women we must speak about liberation, but not in the sense of breaking with what constitutes a women's intimate being, individual characteristics, possibilities of fulfillment, and free choice. To liberate is not to determine behavior or establish patterns but instead to break with what up to now has been limitation, difficulty, and negotiation. To liberate is to open horizons for a wide array of options.

The term *liberation* has indeed been so poorly understood that many women insist they do not want to liberate themselves. Applauding the traditional role they have played and weighing its privileges and disadvantages, they state themselves to be against all that cuts them off from that role. They fail to appreciate that this role grew out of a history that viewed women as family property, little-wanted beings, precisely because they were deemed to be so limited. Those women do not understand that liberation will not affect their interests and preferences because the goal is not to liberate specific groups of women. The mission is broader: It encourages social change so that all individuals may achieve, on their own, the very best life possible, within their own set of responsibilities toward the meaning of life. To liberate means balancing equality of facilities and opportunities with equality of duties and rights.

Sometimes it seems that in our world we place more value on a perfectly cooked potato than on our chance to offer to women the environment they need to grow and become stronger, to achieve self-realization as human beings. Our current conditions seem to lack respect for interests, callings, or curiosities that differ from traditional conceptions. But all individuals have the right to develop their potential and to orient their creative energy so as to achieve the best results for themselves and society. Limitations, discrimination, and prejudice lead only to frustrations and injustice, which we must eliminate from our communities.

The voices that demand justice have a long history and have expressed their demands clearly in all ages. Women want to go beyond traditional conventions and live in freedom with equality of rights, opportunities, and responsibilities. When we speak about liberating women from ties, bonds, limitations, and prejudices, some critics deliberately misinterpret our words to mean introducing women to licentiousness, social vices, masculine behavior, and some sort of near-barbarism. These critics also contend that female liberation goes against the principles of the family and that it threatens the fundamental bases of society. They harbor strong prejudices against women, considering them basically weak, in need of protection, without spiritual or moral strength, and incapable of judging between good and evil or of acting prudently and with equilibrium. Maybe family and social life was easier for men when they could count on servitude, obedience, and submission of women. But one day, though it may come late, the time of justice will come, and the hand of justice will knock at our door and take over. It is now knocking at the doors of many people, both women and men.

But it is also true that liberating women will mean liberating them from the foolish excuses behind which they have hidden, such as the perception that they are the queens of the home or the power behind the throne. To the contrary, a feminist reading of their situation shows clearly that women are the hidden victims, eternal servants of routine and boredom, riding in the last car of the train, doing laundry or dishes, and preparing delicious foods for others, not for themselves.

Liberating women does not mean putting them on a pedestal, proclaiming them to be divine, exceptional creatures who can be touched only in dreams or mystic visions. Such an image would rob them of soul and body—of everything they have—and would send them into nothingness. To liberate them, in reality, is to strengthen their own development, future, and destiny. It is not to make women into people who merely go along, who are only distant others, but to give them the role of independent interpreter, hand in hand with other interpreters. It is to open a space for their voices, their judgments, their points of view. It is giving them the opportunity of creating and fulfilling themselves.

To liberate women is to free them from traditional roles, double- and triple-shift workdays, exhausting routines, limited geographies, and endless waiting, prohibitions, and fears. It is to fill them with freedoms, hopes, decisions, and joys. It is to show them that their horizons are wide and that they have within them their own spaces in which to grow, to be, to share, and to aspire to carrying out a vocation, a wish, or a mission. Liberating women is to make them look into an illuminated mirror and stop seeing themselves only as a complement to someone else.

STUDY QUESTIONS

1. What evidence does Naranjo use to support her argument that the home is the key factor in women's subordination?
2. How does Naranjo define the concept of liberation? What would true liberation for women look like in her opinion?

SUZANA SAWYER

13.7 SUING CHEVRON TEXACO, 2008

One of the most noteworthy instances of opposition to the dominance of multinational corporations occurred in Ecuador, where Amazonian indigenous people and lowland peasants came together with American lawyers in 1993 to file a major lawsuit against the US oil firm Chevron Texaco, seeking damages for environmental pollution. The lawsuit claimed the company deliberately dumped billions of gallons of toxic wastewater into rivers and streams and abandoned hazardous bio-waste in uncovered pits, making a strategic decision to enhance profits by side-stepping industrial best practices. The contamination had led local indigenous and peasant communities to experience an epidemic of cancers, birth defects, and miscarriages as a result of contaminated water supplies and soil systems. The lawsuit was initially filed in 1993 in New York, but the oil company petitioned to have it heard in Ecuador, a request granted in 2002. The US anthropologist Suzana Sawyer has conducted fieldwork in Amazonian Ecuador since the 1990s and has also played an important role as an activist in the indigenous rights and environmental justice movements. In this excerpt, she provides a firsthand account of the indigenous mobilization around the lawsuit, and details the scene as court proceedings began in the Lagro Agrio courthouse in 2003. After eight years of hearing and investigations, the Ecuadorian court ruled in favor of the Amazonian plaintiffs and upheld damages of $19 billion against Chevron Texaco, a sum later adjusted to just over $9 billion by the Ecuadorian Supreme Court. The oil company immediately appealed, and because Chevron Texaco no longer operates in Ecuador, the judgment had to be pursued through international courts. In 2014, a US District Court held that the Ecuadorian ruling had been based on witness tampering and racketeering; a decision upheld in June 2017 by the Supreme Court of the United States, with the result that the judgment could not be enforced in the United States. However, at the time of this volume going to press, an appeal to enforce the judgment was still pending in Canada and the final outcome remained far from clear. Regardless, the complex and long-running case highlights the frequent negative outcomes of neoliberal economic policies based on deregulation and foreign investment for indigenous and peasant communities, as well as the challenges faced by Amazonian peoples in seeking to use the legal system to pursue environmental justice.

Pablo spoke forcefully as he stood on the flatbed of a large truck seconding as a stage. His words blared through loudspeakers as he rallied a crowd of demonstrators to join his protest chant: "ChevronTexaco, ya viste, la justicia si existe." It was October 2003 and approximately 500 Amazonian peasants and Indians were gathered outside the Superior Court in Lago Agrio, a ramshackle frontier town in the northern Ecuadorian rainforest. Unperturbed by the morning rains, men and women, young and old had traveled to Lago Agrio to mark what they called "the litigation of the century." Inside the courthouse, the opening

Source: Suzana Sawyer, "Suing Chevron Texaco," in Carlos de la Torre and Steve Striffler (eds.) *The Ecuador Reader: History, Culture, Politics* (Durham and London: Duke University Press, 2008), pp. 321–328.

proceedings of a lawsuit against ChevronTexaco had just begun. Filed on behalf of 30,000 indigenous and nonindigenous Amazonian residents, the suit alleged that Texaco recklessly contaminated the local environment and endangered the health of local people during its twenty-odd years of operating in Ecuador.

Carrying homemade placards and swaddled infants, burdened by their stories and ailing bodies, plaintiffs bore witness—often speaking into the microphone—to the despair that Texaco's oil operations had brought them. Yet their presence also gave witness to the power of a social movement capable of both keeping the lawsuit alive and challenging transnational norms of corporate action. Together, marginalized Spanish-speaking peasants and Amazonian Indians demanded that the world's fifth-largest oil corporation be held accountable for its actions in third world places.

Past the guarded metal gates, on the fourth floor of the superior court, 100 people packed a muggy courtroom. The superior court judge sat behind the dais at the head of the room. In front of him sat the legal teams for the opposing sides, each made up of Ecuadorian and U.S. lawyers. Among the spectators, a collection of plaintiffs listened expectantly, periodically relaying news to the demonstrators outside; foreign human rights and environmental activists watched attentively, if skeptically, to what to them appeared to be highly elaborate and arcane trial proceedings; and national and international reporters set up their video cameras and microphones, while security police and bodyguards watched over the crowd. All focused their attention on ChevronTexaco's chief lawyer as he proceeded, over the course of the day, to respond to the lawsuit and negate all charges.

LEGAL WRANGLING IN THE U.S. COURTS

October 2003 was not the first time the plaintiffs had appeared before a superior court. In point of fact, the hearing in Ecuador was the product of a decade-long legal battle over jurisdiction in the United States. In November 1993, a Philadelphia law firm filed the same class-action lawsuit against Texaco Inc. in the New York federal court for having caused environmental degradation and human illness in Ecuador. The lawsuit alleged (as it still does today) that Texaco

made strategic decisions in its New York headquarters to maximize its corporate profits by using substandard technology in its Ecuadorian oil operations. Negligent industrial practices, in turn, the lawyers for the plaintiffs claim, strewed toxic wastes into water and soil systems throughout the region, severely contaminating the environment and jeopardizing the lives of local people.

The lawsuit contended that industrial negligence began in 1964 when Texaco first gained rights to an oil concession in the Ecuadorian Amazon. In 1967, the company—via its subsidiary Texaco Petroleum Company (TexPet)—discovered oil. By 1972, Texaco built the trans-Andean pipeline, connecting Amazonian oil fields with a Pacific port. Over the following twenty-eight years, Texaco produced over a billion barrels of crude, and in the process indelibly transformed the northern rainforest with thousands of miles of seismic grids, over 300 oil wells, more than 600 open waste pits, numerous processing facilities and pumping stations, an oil refinery, and the bare-bones infrastructure essential for petroleum operations. The network of roads linking oil wells facilitated the homesteading of the region by over 200,000 poor Spanish-speaking farmers or *colonos* (colonists). In 1992, Texaco's rights to use the concession ended, the company pulled out of Ecuador, and its operations reverted to the state petroleum company.

Although a number of Texaco's production practices between 1964 and 1992 are questionable, of greatest concern was (and still is) the effect of large, often soccer-field-size, earth-pits. Texaco dug these pits (at least two) alongside each exploratory and production well, and then dumped the sludge, formation waters, and unusable heavy crude that surface during the drilling process—along with the chemical muds and industrial solvents essential for drilling—untreated into these craters. When an oil well was proven to be productive, additional pits were dug at processing facilities where crude is separated out from the waters, sands, and gases also released from the earth. Unlined and open these excavated pits served as holding receptacles for eventual toxic seepage and overflow.

Even during the early years of Texaco's operations, it was standard industrial practice in the United States (and indeed law in Texas, the company's namesake, since 1919) to reinject highly toxic formation waters and subterranean sands at least one mile below the surface of the earth, and to process chemical solvents until they were environmentally safe. According to the plaintiffs' lawyers, Texaco Inc. chose not to implement this technology in order to cut costs. The decision not to reinject toxic formation waters back into the subterranean strata from which they emerged allegedly reduced the company's per-barrel production costs by approximately $3 and saved the parent corporation roughly $5 billion over the course of its operations in Ecuador.

Although Texaco's practices were sufficiently effective to get and keep oil flowing, they were (and continue to be) harmful to the environment and humans. A growing number of studies document the detrimental and deadly effects of oil contamination on Amazonian populations: they report high rates of intestinal disease, miscarriages, birth deformities, and various cancers. Physical disorders, the plaintiffs argue, are a direct result of environmental contamination. According to them, Texaco executives in New York are ultimately accountable for decisions that condemned many Amazonian residents to living in toxic dumps.

At the time of the initial filing of the lawsuit in 1993, Texaco Inc. summarily denied all charges, claiming complete exoneration and motioning (on multiple occasions) that the case be dismissed from U.S. courts. The multinational corporation contended that a subsidiary-of-a-subsidiary-of-a-subsidiary-of-a-subsidiary was liable for operations in Ecuador and not the so-called parent company. This Texaco subsidiary four-times-removed was legally based in Quito, Ecuador's capital, and it was there, the multinational maintained, that Ecuadorian citizens would have to prove wrongdoing and seek restitution.

Three years after its original filing, the case was dismissed from the New York district court in November 1996. Two years later, in October 1998, the Second Circuit Court of Appeals reversed the lower court's decision and reinstated the case. Two years after that, in June 2000, the New York district court dismissed the case once more. In August 2002, the Second Circuit Court of Appeals heard the case once more but this time upheld the lower court's decision and ruled that the case should be heard in Ecuador.

FORGING A "CLASS" OF COMMON INJURY

Although this was not the ruling that the plaintiffs' lawyers had sought, much had changed in Ecuador between 1993 and 2003. When the lawsuit was first filed in New York, "class action" was a foreign concept in Ecuador. Were a collection of people wishing to sue a corporate entity for industrial contamination under Ecuadorian law, they would each have to do so individually; there was no legal mechanism by which they could sue as a group. Consequently, in order for the New York lawsuit truly to have substance, the "class" of the class action had to be constructed in the minds, hearts, and actions of the *colonos* and *indigenas* affected by Texaco's oil operations.

Forging a "class" was not easy, however. Texaco's operations covered a 400,000-hectare area—approximately three times the size of Manhattan. Colonos living in the area constituted a hodgepodge group of individuals who had arrived in the Amazon at various time periods and from diverse regions. They had no preexisting cohesive identity. To complicate matters more, colonos and indigenas were often quite antagonistic toward each other as a consequence of colonos having largely usurped and homesteaded indigenous lands. Despite the odds, in the early 1990s, diverse colono associations, a handful of urban barrio groups, and four Indian federations worked together to form the *Frente de Defensa de la Amazonia*—the organization that represents the plaintiffs.

During the 1990s, the *frente* emerged as a formidable force in the northern Amazon with the guidance and support of Ecuador's regional and pan-national indigenous confederations and a handful of national and international environmental rights organizations (specifically, Acción Ecológica, the progressive church, Oxfam America, and the Center for Economic and Social Rights). Early actions focused on organizing hundreds of workshops in rural communities to educate people about the lawsuit and the U.S. judicial process, the plaintiffs' legal rights in Ecuador and the United States, and the effects of oil contamination on human physiology and ecological systems. In addition, the frente coordinated direct actions in support of the lawsuit. The plaintiffs and their supporters organized marches and mobilizations, protests and occupations, to pressure the Ecuadorian executive branch to support the case, to lobby congress to enact protective legislation, to boycott Texaco gasoline, and to demonstrate to the corporation and the world the moral righteousness of their cause.

As Luz—a community organizer on the road heading north from Lago Agrio toward the Colombian border—recalled, the frente largely emerged among the colonos by strengthening and extending ad hoc groups of women who began lodging complaints with TexPet in the 1970s. "I remember," Luz said, "traveling to the company clinic when my son was an infant and meeting other women there whose babies were also covered in open sores." These women and their children were among the thousands of Amazonian residents who bathed, washed clothes, fished, and cleaned food in rivers whose waters and sediments reek of hydrocarbons. "Our children kept on getting sicker," Luz continued, "as the toxins and contamination got worse. The doctor told my neighbor that her five-year-old son had leukemia. That was when we started to organize ourselves." Wastes from oil operations contain known carcinogens that bioaccumulate. And crude oil's most toxic components have been shown to negatively affect the reproductive and cellular development of all life forms. Children in particular are susceptible to many of petroleum's ill effects. Recent epidemiological studies report an increased incidence of skin and intestinal disease and tumors, miscarriages, reproductive abnormalities, and unusually high incidences of cancer in the region—most notably stomach, larynx, cervical, and, among children, leukemia. The neighbor's son died a few years after being diagnosed. Luz's now thirty-year-old son was one of the demonstrators outside the courthouse standing next to a large banner reading "Amazonia Libre de ChevronTóxico."

DEMANDING ACCOUNTABILITY AND EXERCISING RIGHTS

From his ersatz stage, Pablo bellowed to the demonstrators gathered outside the superior court in Lago Agrio, "The hour of justice has arrived." Behind him a huge black banner read "JUSTICIA" in bold lettering. Both Pablo's words and the banner signaled that many—previously wary of Ecuador's judicial system—increasingly believed that the courts might treat them fairly. Although discrimination and injustice still abounded in Ecuador, much had also changed. Throughout the 1990s and into the next millennium, social upheaval rocked Ecuador; the frente was part of this broad-based social action. Between 1992 and 2003, popular groups—often led by CONAIE—pressed for far-reaching social and political changes, rejecting the neoliberal economic agenda which the government had adopted with unprecedented zeal. In addition to ousting three national presidents (Bucaram 1997, Mahuad 2000, and Gutiérrez 2005), this ever-burgeoning indigenous and nonindigenous movement compelled crucial constitutional reforms and legislative changes.

In the late 1990s, intense social pressure compelled the rewriting of the Ecuadorian Constitution. New articles of the 1998 Constitution state that living in a healthy environment is a collective right (art. 86) and that communities must be consulted and allowed to participate in state decisions that might affect the environment in which they live (art. 88). In 1998, Ecuador also signed the International Labor Organization's Convention 169, which recognizes the collective rights of indigenous peoples and their right to demand recompense should their territory or its resources be undermined. But one law in particular passed in 1999 formed the legal basis for the lawsuit when filed in Ecuador in 2003. The Ley de Gestión Ambiental specifically protects individuals against actions that violate environmental norms. And, it allows individuals to file the Ecuadorian equivalent of a class-action lawsuit—an *acción popular*—*against* entities that have allegedly undermined human health or the environment. Together, these legislative changes made the Ecuadorian court system more sympathetic than ever before to the plaintiffs and their plight.

Circumstances had also changed in the United States. In October 2001 Texaco Inc. merged with the Chevron Corporation. When the new corporation, the Chevron Texaco Corporation, moved its headquarters to San Ramon, California, Amazon Watch—an environmental rights NGO on the West Coast—expanded the U.S. campaign in support of the plaintiffs. The organization flew peasant and indigenous leaders to the United States on multiple occasions. It organized protests in front of corporate headquarters, where the Ecuadorians, carrying a poster-sized faux bill from the "Amazon Rainforest Collection Agency," demanded appointments with ChevronTexaco's CEO. Amazon Watch also organized meetings between visiting plaintiffs and residents of San Ramon. Community and religious leaders from California traveled to the contaminated regions of the Ecuadorian Amazon to see the effects of (now) ChevronTexaco's practices firsthand. With their growing concern, they formed an organization. San Ramon Cares, and have brought local pressure to bear on the corporation that calls their town home. In 2004 and 2005, Amazon Watch coordinated actions with Trillium—a socially responsible investment firm. Having garnered the support of a large state pension fund, they filed shareholder resolutions, and spoke at the annual shareholder meetings to educate stockholders of the lawsuit and actions in Ecuador.

Just as social justice and business concerns in the United States increased public scrutiny of corporate activity overseas, so intriguing developments on the legal front were rewriting the U.S. courts' capacity to extend their power beyond national jurisdiction. When the Second Circuit Court of Appeals decided that the class action should be heard in Ecuador, it made its ruling dependent on certain conditions. According to the plaintiffs' lawyers, because the case they presented was so compelling, the appellate court, in sending the lawsuit overseas, was obliged to circumscribe ChevronTexaco's defense for plausible deniability. The three conditions were (1) that Texaco Inc. submit to Ecuadorian law, (2) that documents obtained during the "discovery" period, which up to then had been confidential, could be used in an Ecuadorian trial, and (3) that the decision of the Ecuadorian court could be enforceable in the United States. In the words of one of the plaintiffs' U.S. lawyers, Cristóbal Bonifaz, "We won a victory when the New York court forced ChevronTexaco to show up [in Ecuador] and comply. Here we have a situation in which an American court forces an American company to appear before a Third World court and comply with whatever comes out of that court."

Many questions remain as to how the ongoing trial in Ecuador will be resolved. As outlined by the corporation's chief lawyer on the first day of the 2003 trial in Lago Agrio, ChevronTexaco (like Texaco Inc. before it) assertively claims that TexPet—not it—is the entity responsible for oil operations in Ecuador. Similarly, the corporation claims that TexPet's operations did not violate any Ecuadorian law and were in accordance with standards used in other tropical countries around the world. And finally, the corporation claims that it or any other entity cannot be sued for alleged activity that occurred between 1964 and 1992 on the basis of a law (Ley de Gestión Ambiental) that was enacted in 1999. Following the Ecuadorian juridical system, laws cannot be applied retroactively. In response to these claims, the plaintiff's chief lawyer, Alberto Wray, replied:

"Regardless of what name used, regardless of what legal disguise deployed, Texaco caused environmental damages to the Ecuadorian Amazon. And the poison is still there today. It is simplistic to claim it is not. The plaintiffs are not against the exploitation of petroleum. Rather they are against the act of pursuing it aggressively, solely for the purpose of economic gain, and toward that end using production technologies that strewed toxic elements into the environment—which in turn caused harm to the people, fauna, and flora there—all the while knowing that there were less toxic ways of working. . . . We are not asking that any law be applied retroactively. To speak of contaminating elements is not to speak of a myth from the past. We are talking about a present danger that is still harming and causing injury to local people, animals, and the environment, and to you Honorable Judge."

Any final outcome of this lawsuit is surely to be long in coming. When the present trial ends, the losing side will appeal the verdict first with the superior court of appeals in Lago Agrio, and then the Ecuadorian supreme court in Quito. As of Spring 2005, however, the *frente*—working with a transnational network of U.S.- and Ecuadorian-based lawyers, social justice groups, and environmental rights organizations—has forged a formidable social movement that is transforming the relations between local communities and multinational capital, and in the process setting legal precedent. As the crowd standing on the street in front of the Lago Agrio courthouse affirmed: "Las pruebas te dimos, con eso te jodimos. Chevron Texaco no puedes, con nosotros nunca juegues."

STUDY QUESTIONS

1. What evidence did the Amazonian plaintiffs provide to support their claim that Chevron Texaco knowingly and deliberately polluted the environment?
2. What obstacles did the Amazonian people represented in the lawsuit face in coming together into a single "class" of common injury for the lawsuit?

GLORIA ANZALDÚA

13.8 TO LIVE IN THE BORDERLANDS MEANS YOU, 1987

As migration from Latin American to the United States expanded and intensified during the last decades of the twentieth century, distinct Latino cultures began to emerge within the United States as immigrants and their children forged new identities. Gloria Anzaldúa was one of the most important writers who gave voice to this identity. One of the founders of Chicana cultural studies, Anzaldúa developed important theoretical reflections on the meaning of cultural hybridity, advancing a concept of the border as a place of innovation and loss in which races, heritages, languages, and spiritualities merge and renew. This poem is drawn from one of her most famous books, *Borderlands/ La Frontera: The New Mestiza*, a semiautobiographical reflection of life on the borders between two different cultures.

To live in the Borderlands means you
are neither *hispana india negra espanola*
ni gabacha, eres mestiza, mulata, half-breed
caught in the crossfire between camps
while carrying all five races on your back
not knowing which side to turn to, run from;

To live in the Borderlands means knowing
that the *india* in you, betrayed for 500 years,
is no longer speaking to you,
that *mexicanas* call you *rajetas,*
that denying the Anglo inside you
is as bad as having denied the Indian or Black;

Cuando vives en la frontera
people walk through you, the wind steals your
   voice,
you're a *burra, buey,* scapegoat,
forerunner of a new race,
half and half—both woman and man, neither—
a new gender;

To live in the Borderlands means to
put *chile* in the borscht,
eat whole wheat *tortillas,*
speak Tex-Mex with a Brooklyn accent;
be stopped by *la migra* at the border checkpoints;

---

gabacha – a Chicano term for a white woman
rajetas – literally, "split," that is, having betrayed your word

burra – donkey
buey – oxen

Source: Gloria Anzaldúa, "To Live in the Borderlands Means You," from *Borderlands—La Frontera: The New Mestiza,* (San Fransisco: Aunt Lute Books) pp.194–195.

Living in the Borderlands means you fight hard to
resist the gold elixir beckoning from the bottle,
the pull of the gun barrel,
the rope crushing the hollow of your throat;

In the Borderlands
you are the battleground
where enemies are kin to each other;
you are at home, a stranger,
the border disputes have been settled
the volley of shots have shattered the truce
you are wounded, lost in action
dead, fighting back;

To live in the Borderlands means
the mill with the razor white teeth wants to shred off
your olive-red skin, crush out the kernel,
    your heart
pound you pinch you roll you out
smelling like white bread but dead;

To survive the Borderlands
you must live *sin fronteras*
be a crossroads.

———————

sin fronteras – without borders

STUDY QUESTIONS

1. How does Anzaldúa present her mixed heritage within the poem?
2. What types of challenges arise from living on the border between cultures, according to Anzaldúa? How are these challenges best overcome?

CHAPTER 14

NEW IDENTITIES, NEW POLITICS, 1980–2016

RIGOBERTA MENCHU

14.1 *I, RIGOBERTA MENCHÚ: AN INDIAN WOMAN IN GUATEMALA*, 1984

Rigoberta Menchú Tum is a K'iche Maya woman who emerged in the 1980s as one of the most internationally renowned indigenous rights activists in Latin America, largely as the result of publication of her testimonial biography with the Venezuelan anthropologist Elisabeth Burgos-Debray. The book, *I Rigoberta Menchú*, excerpted here, was based on multiple in-depth interviews and tells the story of Menchú's life largely in her own words. The book highlights the poverty and discrimination faced by Guatemalan Maya, and details the violence of the Guatemalan state against the Mayan people, which had politicized Menchú's family and which cost her parents and two of her brothers their life. Menchú was awarded the Nobel Peace Prize in 1992 and has subsequently continued to work to bring to justice the Guatemalan leaders responsible for the atrocities of the civil war. Menchú's biography became the subject of intense debate when the US anthropologist David Stoll published a book questioning some of the specific claims of her text, including the passage in which she witnesses the death of one of her brothers. More recently, Stoll's arguments have in turn been questioned by other scholars, and the Nobel Prize committee dismissed calls to revoke her prize. Regardless of this controversy, the book remains one of the iconic pieces of testimonial Latin American literature, and provides important insight into the connection between the indigenous rights movement and state violence. In this excerpt, Menchú reflects on the specific challenges she faced as indigenous women engaged in political activism. Notably, although in this passage Menchú suggests that marriage, motherhood, and activism are not compatible, she did marry many years later and has one son.

Source: Rigoberta Menchu, "Women and Political Commitment," *I, Rigoberta Menchú: An Indian Woman in Guatemala*. Edited by Elisabeth Burgos-Debray and translated by Ann Wright (London: Verso, 1984).

"We have kept our identity hidden because we have resisted"

—*Rigoberta Menchu*

I still haven't approached the subject—and it's perhaps a very long subject—of women in Guatemala. We have to put them into categories, anyway: working-class women, peasant women, poor *ladino* women, and bourgeois women, middle-class women. There is something important about women in Guatemala, especially Indian women, and that something is her relationship with the earth—between the earth and the mother. The earth gives food and the woman gives life. Because of this closeness the woman must keep this respect for the earth as a secret of her own. The relationship between the mother and the earth is like the relationship between husband and wife. There is a constant dialogue between the earth and the woman. This feeling is born in women because of the responsibilities they have, which men do not have.

That is how I've been able to analyse my specific task in the organisation. I realize that many *compañeros*, who are revolutionaries and good *compañeros*, never lose the feeling that their views are better than those of any women in charge of them. Of course, we mustn't dismiss the great value of those *compañeros*, but we can't let them do just whatever they like. I have a responsibility, I am in charge, and they must accept me for what I am. But in this respect I've met serious problems when handing out tasks to those *compañeros*, and I've often found it upsetting having to assume this role. But I really believed that I could contribute, and that they should respect me. All the same, it was difficult for me to say: "Listen, *compañero*, these tasks are for you; and you, *compañero*, these are your defects, what are we going to do about them?" It doesn't mean you dominate a man, and you mustn't get any sense of satisfaction out of it. It's simply a question of principle. I have my job to do just like any other *compañero*. I found all this very difficult and, as I was saying, I came up against revolutionary *compañeros*, *compañeros* who had many ideas about making a revolution, but who had trouble accepting that a woman could participate in the struggle not only in

superficial things but in fundamental things. I've also had to punish many *compañeros* who try to prevent their women taking part in the struggle or carrying out any task. They're sometimes willing to let them participate but only within certain limits. They start saying: "Oh no, not that. No, not here. No." Well, we've had to talk seriously with these *compañeros* to solve that problem.

My mother, of course, didn't know all these ideas, all these theories about the position of women. But she knew all these things in practice. I learned a lot from my mother but I also learned a lot from other people, especially when I had the opportunity of talking to women who aren't from our country. We discussed the organisation of women and we came to the conclusion that many women so often take other people's problems upon themselves and push their own to one side. This doesn't do us any good. It shows us that we must solve our problems ourselves and not ask someone else to come and solve them, otherwise it's dishonest. No-one will solve our problems for us.

The Indian women who have a clear political vision and participate in the leadership of the organisation are realizing this. We're seeing change, revolution, taking power, but this isn't the profound change within society. We women *compañeras* came to the conclusion (because for a time we thought of creating an organisation for women) that it was paternalistic to say there should be an organisation for women when in practice women work and are exploited as well. Women work picking coffee and cotton, and on top of that, many women have taken up arms and even elderly women are fighting day and night; so it isn't possible to say that now we're setting up an organisation so that women can rebel, work or study women's problems. It won't always be like this, of course. That is just the situation we're facing at the moment. Perhaps in the future when there's a need for it, there will be a women's organisation in Guatemala. For the time being, though, we think that it would be feeding *machismo* to set up an organisation for women only, since it would mean separating women's work from men's work. Also we've found that when we discuss women's problems, we need the men to be present, so that they can contribute by giving their opinions of what to do about the problem. And so that they can learn as well. If they don't learn, they don't progress. Our struggle has shown us that many *compañeros* have clear ideas, but if they don't follow in the footsteps of their woman, they'll never have the clarity that she has and they'll be left behind. What is the point of educating women if men aren't there to contribute to the apprenticeship and learn as well? By creating an organisation for women we would be presenting the system which oppresses us with another weapon. We don't want that. We must fight as equals. If a *compañero* is asked a question about *machismo*, he must be able to give a wide balanced view of women, and a woman must be able to do the same for men because the two have been studying the problem together.

That has been my experience anyway. I'm not married but I've taken part in important discussions where we've talked about the problem of men and women, in a mixed group. We think that this is the right path to follow. Naturally, we can't say that this alone will do away with *machismo*, because it wouldn't be true. In all revolutionary countries, socialist countries, wherever you care to name, *machismo* still exists. The whole world is afflicted with this sickness. It's part of society. Part of it we can improve, and part of it we can wipe out. But perhaps it's not possible to solve the problem entirely.

There is something else we are discovering in Guatemala to do with intellectuals and illiterate people. We've learned that we haven't all got the ability of an intellectual: an intellectual is perhaps quicker and able to make finer syntheses. But nevertheless, others of us have perhaps the same ability for other things. Before, everyone used to think that a leader had to be someone who knew how to read, write and prepare documents. And our leaders fell into that trap for a time and said: "I am a leader, it's my job to lead and yours to fight." Well: in every process there are certain exchanges which have to be made. That is not unusual. I think that every movement has gone through the process whereby an opportunist arrives, feels that he is worth more than the others and abuses their confidence. At one time, many of our leaders would come from the capital to see us in the *finca* and say: "You peasants are

stupid, you don't read or study." And the peasants told them: "You can go to Hell with your books. We know you don't make a revolution with books, you make it through struggle."

And that was why we decided to learn many things, and rightly so, because, remember, that now everything was in our hands. We had to make big sacrifices. And so, we peasants have learned to direct our struggle ourselves, and *that* we owe to our understanding of our situation. A leader must be someone who's had practical experience. It's not so much that the hungrier you've been, the purer your ideas must be, but you can only have a real consciousness if you've really lived this life. I can say that in my organisation most of the leaders are Indians. There are also some *ladinos* and some women in the leadership. But we have to erase the barriers which exist between ethnic groups, between Indians and *ladinos*, between men and women, between intellectuals and non-intellectuals, and between all the linguistic areas.

The situation we are in means that our women don't get married because they're expecting something happy, a lovely family, pleasure, or something different from what they already have. No, not at all. They know that a very hard life awaits them. Although for us marriage is something joyful (because the concept our ancestors had was that our race must not die out and we must follow our traditions and customs as they did), at the same time it is something very painful, knowing that when you get married you'll have the responsibility of bringing up your children, and not only of looking after them, but worrying, trying to make do, and hoping they live. In Guatemala, it's unusual for a family not to see some of their young children die.

Well, in my case, I analysed my ideas about not getting married with some of my *compañeros*. I realized that what I said wasn't crazy, that it wasn't some personal mad idea, but that our whole situation makes women think very hard before getting married, because who will look after the children, who will feed them? As I was saying before, we're used to living in a community, among up to ten or eleven brothers or sisters. But there are also cases of women who were left alone because all their brothers and sisters go off and get married, so they're sometimes forced to get married because they know how hard it will be for them by themselves. But knowing that I had to multiply the seed of our ancestors and, at the same time rejecting marriage...that was a crazy idea. I thought I was alone in feeling like this, but when I discussed it with other women, they saw the whole thing of getting married in the same way I did. It is terrible to know that such a hard life awaits you, with so much responsibility to make sure your children live. You can't think any other way in Guatemala: when you get engaged or married, you immediately think of the many children you're going to have. I've been in love many times but it was precisely because of that fear that I didn't jump into marriage. But the time came when I saw clearly—it was actually when I'd begun my life as a revolutionary—that I was fighting for a people and for many children who hadn't anything to eat. I could see how sad it would be for a revolutionary not to leave a seed because the seed which was left behind would enjoy the fruits of this work in the future. But I thought of the risks of having a child. It would be much easier for me to die, at any time or place, if I weren't leaving anyone behind to suffer. That would be sad, because although my community would take care of my child, of my seed, no other person can give a child the love his mother can, however much that person looks after and cares for the child. I was very confused about all this because so many dedicated *compañeros* said they would be there on the day of victory, but I knew that they could give their lives at any time and would no longer be there. All this horrified me and gave me a lot to think about.

I was engaged once but I wasn't sure, because, well, the idea our ancestors had—and it's ours too—is that you don't only look for happiness for yourself but also for your family. I was very confused. Society and so many other things wouldn't leave me alone, I always had a heavy heart.

And then when my parents died, I felt what a daughter feels for a father and mother when they die, and even more so because of the way they died. That's when I decided, although I can't say that it's a final decision because I am open to life. My idea is, though, that there will be time enough after our victory; but at the moment I wouldn't feel happy having a *compañero* and giving myself to him while so many of our people are not thinking of their own personal happiness

and haven't a single moment to rest. This gave me a lot to think about. As I said, I am human and I am a woman so I can't say that I reject marriage altogether, but I think my primary duty is to my people and then to my personal happiness. I know many *compañeros* who have devoted themselves without reservation to the struggle, without thinking of personal happiness. And I know *compañeros* who've gone through bitter moments, who have troubles and worries, but who, nevertheless, are in the struggle and carry on. It could be that I renounced marriage because of the harsh experience of having seen so many friends die. This not only frightens me, it puts me in a panic, because I don't want to be a widow, or a tortured mother. I'm restricted by so many things. It's not just not wanting a child. Many little things have made me think about renouncing all this. I know that our men have suffered too, because many *compañeros* had to give their children away so they could carry on the struggle, or they've had to leave their women in other places, not because they don't want marriage but because they feel it is their duty to fight for their people.

The conclusion I came to was that, while we have so many problems, we shouldn't look for more. There are married women in the struggle, however, who contribute as much as I do, *compañeras* who have five or six children and do magnificent work. Being afraid of all that is a certain trauma I have. I'm even more afraid when I think that if I had a *compañero*, I'd probably love him very much and I wouldn't want it to be for only a week or two because after that he wouldn't be there. While I don't have this problem, I won't look for it. But, as I said, I'm open to life. It doesn't mean that I reject everything because I know that things come in their time and when you do things calmly, they work much better.

As I said, I was engaged once. At one time he wanted a lot of things in life; a nice house for his children and a peaceful life. But I didn't think like that. We'd known each other since we were children, but unfortunately he left our village and had to go to the city. He became a factory worker, and then really turned into a *compañero* with good work prospects who thought differently from the way I and my village thought. So, when I became a revolutionary I had to choose between two things—the struggle or my *compañero*. I came to all sorts of conclusions because I loved this *compañero* and I could see the sacrifices he made for me. It was a more open engagement than was usual for people of my culture. Well, there I was between these two things—choosing him or my people's struggle. And that's what I chose, and I left my *compañero* with much sadness and a heavy heart. But I told myself that I had a lot to do for my people and didn't need a pretty house while they lived in horrific conditions like those I was born and grew up in. Well, that's when we went our separate ways. I told him that it wasn't right for me to stay with him because he had other ideas and we'd never understand each other, since he wanted one thing and I'd always go on wanting another. Then I went on with our struggle and now I'm on my own. But as I said, there'll be a time when things will be different, when we'll all be happy, perhaps not with nice houses, but at least we won't see our lands running with blood and sweat.

STUDY QUESTIONS

1. What challenges has Menchú faced in seeking to assert her leadership as a woman?
2. Why is she ambivalent about marriage and motherhood? In what ways does she fear these roles may limit her ability to be successful as an activist?

JORGE ESTEVES

14.2 OCAMA-DACA TAINO (HEAR ME, I AM A TAINO): PERSPECTIVE OF JORGE ESTEVEZ, A TAINO FROM THE DOMINICAN REPUBLIC, 2006

Indigenous rights movements emerged as powerful factors in regional politics following the quincentenary of Columbus's arrival in 1992. While they were strongest in areas where indigenous peoples formed a large percentage of the population, notably the Andes, Amazon, and Mesoamerican highlands, their reach spread throughout the whole of Latin America. In Caribbean islands like the Dominican Republic, Cuba, and Puerto Rico, where indigenous peoples had suffered catastrophic population collapse in the colonial period, indigenous activists began to assert strong politicized identities as Taino, often using newly available DNA analysis to assert their claims to an indigenous heritage. This activism challenged traditional assumptions that the Taino—the first indigenous group to encounter Columbus—had been completely eliminated by the Spanish. Yet these movements also proved controversial, as some observers and scholars suggested that claims to indigenous heritage in the strongly African-influenced Caribbean islands simply represented a new way to dismiss and deny the importance of blackness. Like other indigenous rights movements, Taino

Source: "Hear Me I Am Taino" in Maximilian C. Forte (ed.) *Indigenous Resurgence in the Contemporary Caribbean: Amerindian Survival and Revival* (New York: Peter Lang Publishing, Inc. 2006)

activism was transnational in focus and reached across national boundaries. In 1998, the United Confederation of Taino peoples was formed, to provide a leadership council for indigenous people across the Caribbean. Jorge Estevez is one of the main leaders of the Taino movement. Originally from the Dominican Republic but now living in the United States, he has worked with the National Museum of the American Indian in New York to collect interviews and artifacts illuminating the Taino culture and legacy in the Dominican Republic and Cuba. In this interview with the Canadian anthropologist Maximilian Forte conducted in the early 2000s, Estevez lays out the biological and cultural factors that underpin his Taino identity, and denounces arguments that the Taino had been exterminated in the aftermath of Columbus as a "paper genocide."

Ocama-Daca Taíno. I am Dominican and I am Taíno. Kiskeya was once the heartland of the Taíno people. Yet the denial of our culture and heritage has been ingrained in all Dominicans with just about every book or magazine article we read on the subject. Historians, teachers, and scholars in all fields, as well as other well-meaning people and institutions, have perpetuated the myth that our indigenous ancestors perished within approximately 30 years of contact with the Spaniards, leaving hardly any trace of our complex culture. We are told that the union between the Spaniards and the African slaves they imported to the islands of the Greater Antilles is what gave rise to the modern-day peoples and culture on these islands. While it does appear true that wars, the encomienda system, slavery, and disease killed off great numbers of my ancestors, the social discrimination practiced by the Spaniards throughout the colonial era, and "paper genocide" practiced by historians ever since, have been just as cruel on my people. With the stroke of their pens, the legacy of my ancestors was wiped out.

I find the notion disturbing that the Taíno are not my ancestors, but rather my "precursors" because they are "extinct." This notion disconnects me, and others like me, from our islands, rendering us, in a sense, immigrants in our own homelands. It also disturbs me when the prehistory of the Caribbean is romanticized so that the Taíno are elevated onto a pedestal so high that no one can reach them—they are placed in the realm of things legendary rather than real, which again, I interpret as an attempt to disconnect indigenous people like me from our ancestors.

So why, despite all these problems, do I and others who are involved in Taíno movements feel such a strong connection to our indigenous ancestors? For me, it is because, since I was a child, my mother and grandmother told me stories of the *campo* (countryside) and our hometown in Jaibón, Kiskeya. They spoke of farming methods, myths and legends, casabe bread, and basket weaving, which are important to life in Jaibón. At the time, I thought these were unique to us in Kiskeya. I later realized that we share these stories and practices with the campo people of Puerto Rico and Cuba. Distinctive words such as *chin-chin, caimito, burén, ciguato, cacata, naiboa,* and *güiro,* among hundreds of others, are unrecognizable to people in other Spanish-speaking countries, yet familiar to us in the Spanish Antilles. Tobacco ceremonies, our aversion to owls, the belief that *cocuyos* (fireflies) are the eyes of the dead, are just a few of the many spiritual beliefs that we share. . . .

Many of us who, today, identify with the indigenous part of our multiethnic heritage, heard stories about a grandmother or other family member who was "a real Indian." Some of us—like me—were told outright that we descend from indios. I became curious and began to look deeper into my history. Much to my dismay, I found notable contradictions between my family's oral histories and the "official" history taught in schools and national museums. Most scholars claim that indios in the Spanish Antilles have long been extinct. I and the others with whom I began to compare notes discovered, however, that there were crucial inconsistencies in the extinction stories, so we began to investigate them. Among the inconsistencies we found in a multitude of books were the claims that the Taíno burned their crops and ran off into the mountains in their desperate effort to escape

Spanish domination. Supposedly the ploy backfired on them, because they were said to have starved to death in those mountains they had called home for thousands of years. Yet the African slaves who escaped into those very same mountains, terrain that was totally unfamiliar to them, survived in the thousands (see, for example, Moya Pons, 1995, p. 41). The above is just one example of the senseless contradictions we have found. The more we research our history and the more we question our elders, the more perceptive we become. We know that the true story of our ancestors has not yet been told, but some scholars are finally beginning to ask the same questions that we have been asking, have finally begun to revise the inconsistencies and errors of the past. Many historians and anthropologists, such as Samuel Wilson and Fernando Luna Calderón, who previously wrote about the plight of the peaceful and gentle Taíno who were wiped out as a result of warfare and disease, are now beginning to realize that they may have perpetuated the myth of Taíno extinction without having weighed all of the facts. They accepted history at face value. Besides, it is much more romantic to write about a vanished race of "noble savages" than it is to contemplate that human interactions in the Greater Antilles were much more complicated than historians described them.

Taíno, who once populated all the islands of the Greater Antilles, died in great numbers, yes, but African and Spanish men were intermarrying with Taíno women in great numbers, too, and producing children who were more disease-resistant than their mothers. It should come as no surprise, then, that so many people of Taíno descent and so many aspects of Taíno culture remain to this day on Hispaniola and the other islands of the Greater Antilles.

Some people, however, including many academics with whom I have communicated, view the current Taíno revival efforts with contempt. They and others accuse us of being "romantics." My associates and I hear this and variants of "fanatics wanting to be Indian" coming frequently from their circles, or the battering ram: they are denying their negritude (i.e., Haslip-Viera, 2002). When we compare the interpretations of those who would deny us our Taíno heritage to our families' oral histories, and when we point out the historical oddities and inaccuracies,

they counter with a series of arguments to blot out the critical facts, using what I can only call circular logic. Recent DNA studies, however, are now providing a line of evidence that cannot be denied.

Recent mitochondrial DNA sequencing studies have revealed that not only are there indigenous genetic markers in the current population of the Greater Antilles, but the quantity is so staggeringly high it directly challenges the "facts" of Taíno extinction (Martinez Cruzado, 2002). Genetic evidence is not brushed off the way the revisionist historians, anthropologists, and their evidence often are, for it is "scientific." Recent DNA studies, however, are now providing a line of evidence that cannot be denied as easily as shared experiences, beliefs, and traditions.

Recently I took a BGA (Bio-Geographical) nuclear test through DNA Print Genomics. This test, according to the company's specialists, provides individuals with the percentages of their genetic background within five generations. My test results showed that I have a significantly high quantity of indigenous genetic markers. In fact, it was explained to me that, just four generations ago, my ancestors were what used to be called "full-blooded" natives. Four generations are roughly 80 to 100 years. That's 400 years after natives supposedly "disappeared" from Kiskeya. While recognizing the importance of genetic studies, I feel that we Taíno, as a people, validate the DNA evidence, not the other way around. This journey of self-discovery that I and so many others are undertaking is about culture, not genes, for genes say little about us as a people. In fact, at the beginning of the Taíno restoration movements (through which we mean to restore the Taíno to their proper place in the histories and societies from which their supposed extinction has erased them), we did not have DNA to back up any claims to native ancestry that were made. All we had were oral traditions and staunch native assertions. The movements took *off* from this, not from a laboratory.

The Taíno restoration movements began in the late 1980s, when individuals of Puerto Rican descent began gathering at cultural events to discuss family oral histories and historical inaccuracies about our ancestors. Among the popular events we attended were the Native American pow-wows (festivals), where some of us found like-minded people who were seeking to learn more about their Taíno heritage. It became evident that an organization needed to be created to pull together all the resources that became available once we started to pool our resources. Some of us began researching and disseminating information, and the numbers grew. This is how the Asociación Indigena de Puerto Rico (Indigenous Association of Puerto Rico), or AIPR, was born.

The AIPR started out well, but almost as soon as it was created it became obvious that its focus varied from individual to individual. Some members were more interested in spiritual aspects, others with academic, and still others with the politics of asserting native identity. The group splintered and became two separate entities: the Maisiti Yucayeque Taíno (MYT) and the Taíno Nation. Within the MYT there were family units or subgroups focusing on culture, such as the Arawak Mountain Singers, a group that performed pow-wow-style music at Native American festivals. The Taíno Nation would, in time, encompass the entire Spanish-speaking Caribbean in scope, evolving more into a "tribal government" in that its leaders make decisions on behalf of all Taíno people and represent Taíno peoples internationally. Soon after the formation of the Taíno Nation and its splinter groups, people of Cuban and Dominican extraction in the US also began joining, bringing with them aspects of Taíno culture

that had almost disappeared from Puerto Rico due to American assimilation. As of this writing, there are at least 25 Taíno organizations with thousands of members from New York to California and from Florida to Puerto Rico, and the numbers are still growing.

For those of us who identify with our Taíno roots, these are exciting times. For more than two decades, Taíno like me, who live in the US, have been working vigorously to reclaim our Taíno culture and identity. New evidence is mounting to prove that we are who we say we are—and not only are our numbers growing; the movement is also spreading back to our home islands.

We celebrate the fact that we are Taíno, for our common Taíno roots are what make us uniquely Dominican, Puerto Rican, and Cuban. We respect and acknowledge our African and Spanish ancestors as well. Understanding that we have tripartite biological, cultural, and linguistic influences does not subtract from, but rather adds to, our human experience. Our Taíno heritage, however, is what makes us a Native Caribbean people.

Taíno heritage stretches across time, since long before the arrival of the European invaders and the African people they enslaved and brought to our ancestors' islands. In such a way, the European and the African became a part of the native Caribbean. We are Caribbean peoples, and our roots will always be indigenous.

STUDY QUESTIONS

1. What conflicts exist between family history and "official" history with regard to the Taino in the Dominican Republic?
2. How important is genetic evidence to Estevez's claim to Taino identity? To what extent does the DNA record complicate traditional understandings of the indigenous past in the Caribbean?
3. How does Estevez respond to the argument that claiming Taino identity means rejecting the African heritage of the Caribbean?

14.3 AFRO-COLOMBIANS AND LAW 70 OF 1993

The struggle for greater rights for racially subordinated groups also encompassed the region's large African descended populations. One of the most powerful and effective Afro-Latin American rights movements developed in Colombia, where black populations along the Pacific coast were able to use the language of indigeneity to make a successful claim to land rights. The passage of Law 70 of 1993 represented one of the greatest achievements of the African-descendant civil rights movement throughout the whole of Latin America. Signed into law by President César Gaviria Trujillo following the promulgation of the 1991 Constitution, which established Colombia as a plurinational state, it recognized Afro-Colombians for the first time as a distinct ethnic group and, based on this shared heritage, supported their claim to an ancestral homeland along the rivers of the Pacific Basin. The law established Community Councils to support collective administration of the common land, placing Afro-Colombian people on a parallel legal footing to indigenous Colombians. It also provided for financial assistance to support education and economic development in the Pacific region. Colombia's ongoing civil conflict disrupted enforcement of the law, and many members of the groups possessing collective title have subsequently been displaced by narcotrafficking and guerrilla warfare, with some analysts arguing that they have been targeted specifically because of the rights held under Law 70. Nevertheless, the legal foundation the law represents remains important, and it has inspired African-descendant rights groups throughout the region.

Senate of the Republic of Colombia

Article I. The object of the present Law is to recognize the right of the Black Communities that have been living on *tierras baldias* [untitled lands] in rural areas along the rivers of the Pacific Basin, in accordance with their traditional production practices, to their collective property as specified and instructed in the articles that follow. Similarly, the purpose of the Law is to establish mechanisms for protecting the cultural identity and rights of the Black Communities of Colombia as an ethnic group and to foster their economic and social development, in order to guarantee that these communities have real equal opportunities compared to the rest of Colombian society. . . .

Rivers of the Pacific Basin. Are the rivers of the Pacific region, which comprise: a) the Pacific flow made up of superficial waters of rivers and creeks that drain directly into the Pacific Ocean and its subsidiaries, the basins of the rivers Mira, Rosario, Chajul, Patia, Curay, Sanquianga, Tola, Tapaje, Iscuandé, Guapi, Timbiquí, Buey, Saija, Micay, Naya, Yurumanguí, Tumba Grande, Tumbita, Cajambre, Mallorquín, Raposo, Anchicayá, Dagua, Bongo, San Juan, Ijua, Docampadó, Capiro, Ordó, Sivirú, Dotendó, Usaraga, Baudó, Piliza, Catripre, Virudo, Coquí, Nuquí, Tribugá, Chori, El Valle, Huaca, Abega, Cupica, Changuera, Borojó, Curiche, Putumia, Juradó, and other smaller tributaries which drain directly into the Pacific Ocean;

b) the basins of the Atrato, Acandi, and Toló Rivers, that flow into the Caribbean.

Rural Riparian Lands. Are the lands bordering the banks of the rivers mentioned in the preceding paragraph that are outside urban perimeters as defined by

Source: Excerpted from Ann Farnsworth-Alvear, et al. (eds.) *The Colombia Reader: History, Culture, Politics* (Durham: Duke University Press, 2017). ProQuest Ebook Central. http://ebookcentral.proquest.comlllbngcu/detall.actlon7docID=4760879. .

the Municipal Councils of the area municipalities in question in accordance with the provisions of Municipal Regulation Code (Decree 1333 of 1986), and any subsequent added laws that develop or amend it and in which the respective community is settled.

Tierras baldias. Are the lands situated within the borders of the national territory belonging to the State and no other owner, and that, having been categorized as such, shall return to the domain of the State in accordance with article 56 of Law 110 of 1913, and any other regulations that augment, develop, or reform it.

Black Community. Is the group of families of Afro-Colombian descent who possesses its own culture, shares a common history and has its own traditions and customs within a rural-urban setting and which reveals and preserves a consciousness of identity that distinguishes it from other ethnic groups.

Collective Settlement. Is the historic and ancestral settling of Black Communities in lands for their collective use, lands that constitute their habitat, and where they currently develop their traditional practices of production.

Traditional Practices of Production. Are the technical, agricultural, mining, forestal extractions, grazing, hunting, fishing, and general harvesting activities of natural resources, customarily used by the Black Communities to guarantee the conservation of their lives and their self-sustaining development. . . .

Article 4. The State will grant collective property to the Black Communities referred to in this Law, in areas that, according to the definitions in Article II, comprise unclaimed lands located along the riverbanks in rural riparian areas of the Pacific Basin as well as those in areas specified in the second clause of Article I of the present Law: lands that they have been occupying in accordance with their traditional practices of production. For all legal purposes the lands, for which collective property rights are established, will be called: The Lands of the Black Communities. . . .

Article 39. In order to offer fair and equitable information about the society and culture of the Black Communities, the State shall be vigilant so that within the National Educational system the Black Communities' own cultural practices and contributions to the history and culture of Colombia are known and promoted.

In the social sciences area at all educational levels, the subject of Afro-Colombian Studies that conforms to the corresponding curricula should be included. . . .

Article 41. The State will support, by providing the necessary resources, the organizational processes of the Black Communities, in order to recover, preserve, and develop their cultural identity.

Article 42. The Ministry of Education will formulate and execute a policy of Ethno-education for the Black Communities, and will create a pedagogical commission to assess said policy with representation of the communities.

Translated by Norma Jackson and Peter Jackson

STUDY QUESTIONS

1. What rationales does the law use to define Black Communities as culturally and legally distinct? Why is this such a significant moment for the legal classification of African-descended peoples in Latin America?
2. What types of education does the law provide for with regard to Afro-Colombian people? What goal does the law seek to advance with these provisions?

EVO MORALES

14.4 TOWARDS A NEW WORLD ORDER FOR LIVING WELL: ADDRESS TO THE SUMMIT OF THE GROUP OF 77, 2014

In 2006 Evo Morales became the first indigenous person to be elected president in Latin America, when he ascended to the presidency of Bolivia. Born into a family of Aymara peasants, Morales rose to prominence in the coca leaf growers' movement. He played an important role in political protests against neoliberal economic policies in the early 2000s, including the Cochabamba protests against the privatization of the water supply and strikes over foreign exploitation of natural gas supplies. Morales was elected as head of the left-wing party Movement for Socialism (MAS), and his presidency was part of a "pink tide" of left-wing governments that emerged throughout Latin America in the mid-2000s, including Rafael Correa in Ecuador, Hugo Chavez in Venezuela, and Lula in Brazil. His campaign focused on the redistribution of gas wealth, and once in office he used increased taxation on gas reserves to fund education and social programs for indigenous and poor communities. Morales's government sought to encourage a model of development based on vivir bien, or "living well," which would emphasize social harmony, environmental health, and the elimination of discrimination as opposed to strictly economic indicators such as GDP. In this 2014 speech to the Group of 77—the UN Coalition of Developing Nations—Morales laid out his vision for a new world order based on a more sustainable and inclusive model of development.

HISTORY OF THE G77:

Fifty years ago, great leaders raised the flags of the anti-colonial struggle and decided to join their peoples in a march along the path of sovereignty and independence.

Those were the times when the world superpowers and multinationals were battling with each other over the control of territories and natural resources in order to feed their growth at the expense of the poverty of the peoples of the south.

In this context, on June 15, 1964, by the end of an UNCTAD meeting, 77 countries (currently 133 plus China) from the south met to enhance their trade bargaining capacities, by acting in a block that advanced their collective interests and respected their individual sovereign decisions.

During the past 50 years, these countries went beyond their statements and promoted resolutions at the UN and embarked on shared actions in favor of development underpinned by South-South cooperation, a new world economic order, a responsibility for climate change and economic relations based on preferential treatment.

In this journey, the struggle for decolonization, as well as for the peoples' self-determination and sovereignty over their natural resources must be underscored.

GROWING WORLD INEQUALITY:

In spite of these efforts and struggles for equality and justice for the peoples around the world, *the hierarchies and inequalities* have grown in the world.

Source: Evo Morales, President of Bolivia, "Towards a New World Order for Living Well," speech. (http://www.worldfuture fund.org/Reports/G77/moralesspeech.html).

Today, 10 countries in the world control 40% of the world's total wealth and 15 multinational corporations control 50% of the global output.

Today, like 100 years ago, acting in the name of the free market and democracy, a handful of imperial powers invades countries, blocks trade, imposes prices on the rest of the world, chokes national economies, plots against progressive governments and applies espionage to the population worldwide.

A tiny elite of countries and multinational corporations control, in an authoritarian fashion, the destinies of the world, its economies and its natural resources.

The economic and social inequality among regions, among countries, among social classes and among individuals has grown abusively.

About 0.1% of the world's population owns 20% of the asset base OF MANKIND. In 1920, a US business manager made 20 fold the wage of a worker; at present, the difference is 331 fold.

THE STRUCTURAL CRISIS OF THE CURRENT WORLD ORDER—AN ORDER THAT IS NOT SUSTAINABLE

This unfair manner of concentrating wealth and this predatory way of destroying nature are also giving rise to a structural crisis that is becoming unsustainable over time.

It is indeed a structural crisis. It impacts every component of capitalist development; in other words, it is a mutually nurtured crisis involving finances, energy, climate, water, food, institutions and values. It is a crisis inherent to the capitalist civilization.

The financial crisis was prompted by the greedy pursuit of financial capital, which led to profound international financial speculation, a practice that favored certain groups, multinational corporations or power centers that amassed wealth.

These financial bubbles that generate speculative gains eventually burst, and in the process, they plunge into poverty the workers who received inexpensive credits, the middle-class saving-account holders who trusted their savings to greedy speculators, who overnight went bankrupt or took their capital to other foreign countries, thus leading entire nations into bankruptcy.

We are also faced with an *energy crisis* that is driven by the excessive consumption in developed countries, the pollution of energy sources and the energy hording practices by multinational corporations.

In parallel, we witness a drop in reserves worldwide and high costs of oil and gas development, while production capacity drops due to the gradual depletion of fossil fuels and global climate change.

The climate crisis is caused by the anarchical capitalist production, the consumption levels and unharnessed industrialization of which, have given rise to excess emissions of polluting gases that in turn have led to global warming and natural disasters with effects on the world all over.

For more than 15,000 years prior to the era of capitalist industrialization, the load of greenhouse gases did not exceed 250 particles per million of molecules in the air.

Since the 19th century, and in particular the 20th and 21st centuries, thanks to the actions of predatory capitalism, this count has risen to 400 particles, and as a result, global warming has become an irreversible process with its aftermath of weather disasters the primary impacts of which are felt in the poorest and most vulnerable countries of the south; specially, the island nations that are being hit by the thawing glaciers.

In turn, global warming is giving rise to a water supply crisis that is compounded by the privatization, source depletion and commercialization of fresh water. As a consequence, the number of people without access to running water is growing fast.

The water shortage in many parts of the planet is causing armed conflicts and wars that further worsen the availability of this non-renewable resource.

The world population is growing, while food production is dropping, and these trends are leading to a food crisis. Add to these issues the reduction of food-growing lands, the imbalances between urban and rural areas, the monopoly exercised by multinational corporations over the distribution of seeds and agricultural inputs, and the food pricing speculation.

The imperial model of concentration and speculation also caused an *institutional crisis* that is described as an unequal and unjust distribution of power in the world; in particular, within the UN system; including, without limitation, the IMF and the WTO.

As a result of all these issues, the peoples' social rights are at stake. The promise of equality and justice for the whole world is increasingly distant, and the survival of nature is being threatened to become extinct.

We have come to a limit, and global actions must be taken urgently to save society, humanity and Mother Earth.

STEPS BOLIVIA HAS TAKEN TO DEAL WITH CRISIS

Bolivia has started to take steps to address these issues. Up to 2005, Bolivia applied a neoliberal policy that gave rise to wealth concentration, social inequality and poverty. As a result, marginalization, discrimination and social exclusion rose. In Bolivia, the historic struggles waged by social movements; in particular, the native, indigenous peasant movement, have helped us launch a Democratic and Cultural Revolution, through ballot win and without the use of violence. This revolution is rooting out exclusion, exploitation, hunger and hatred, and it is rebuilding the path of balance, complementarity, consensus with home-grown identity; i.e., the live-well model.

In 2006, the Bolivian government introduced a new economic and social policy, as enshrined in a new Community-based socioeconomic and productive model, the pillars of which are the nationalization of natural resources, the recovery of the financial profits for application in the benefit of the entire Bolivian people, the redistribution of the wealth, and the active involvement of the State in the economic activity.

In 2006, the Bolivian State and people made their most significant political, economic and social decision; i.e., the nationalization of the country's hydrocarbons, a core decision of our revolution. As a result of this measure, the State participates in and controls the ownership of our hydrocarbons and processes our natural gas.

OLD NEO-LIBERAL ECONOMICS FAIL IN BOLIVIA, NEW MODEL BRINGS PROSPERITY AND GROWTH

Contrary to the neoliberal prescription that economic growth ought to be based on external market demand ("export or die"), our new model has relied on a combination of exports with a domestic market growth that is primarily driven by income-redistribution policies, relaxation and successive raises of the national minimum wage, annual salary increases in excess of the inflation rate, cross subsidies, and transfer vouchers to the neediest.

As a consequence, the Bolivian GDP grew from $9.0 bn. to over $30.0 bn. in the past eight years.

Our nationalized hydrocarbons, economic growth and cost austerity policy have helped the country generate budget surpluses for eight years in a row, in sharp contrast with the recurrent budget deficits experienced by Bolivia for more than 66 years.

When we took over the country's administration, the ratio between the wealthiest and poorest Bolivians was 128 fold. This ratio has been cut down to 46 fold. At present, Bolivia ranks among the top six countries with the best income distribution in our region.

It has been shown that the peoples have options and we can defeat the fate imposed by colonialism and neoliberalism.

These achievements produced in such a short span are attributable to the social and political awareness of the Bolivian people.

NATIONAL AND GLOBAL RECOVERY

We have recovered our nation for all of us. Ours was a nation that had been alienated by the neoliberal model, a nation that lived under the old and evil system of political parties, a nation that was ruled from abroad, as if we were a colony.

We are no longer the unviable country we were described as by the international financial institutions. We are no longer an ungovernable country as the US empire would have us believe.

Today, the Bolivian people have recovered their dignity and pride, and we believe in our strength, our destiny and our own selves.

I want to tell the entire world in the most humble terms that the only wise architects that can change their future are the peoples themselves.

Therefore, we intend to build another world, and several tasks have been designed to establish the live-well society.

STEPS NEEDED TO ESTABLISH A SUSTAINABLE GLOBAL MODEL

FIRST: WE MUST MOVE FROM SUSTAINABLE DEVELOPMENT TO COMPREHENSIVE DEVELOPMENT SO THAT WE CAN LIVE WELL AND IN HARMONY AND BALANCE WITH MOTHER EARTH

We need to conceive a vision that is different from the western capitalist development model. We must move from the sustainable development paradigm to the live-well comprehensive development approach that seeks not only a balance among human beings, but also a balance and harmony with our Mother Earth.

No development model can be sustainable if production destroys Mother Earth as a source of life and our own existence. No economy can be long lasting if it generates inequalities and exclusions.

No progress is just and desirable if the well-being of some is at the expense of the exploitation and impoverishment of others.

What Is "Live-Well Comprehensive Development?"

"Live-Well Comprehensive Development" means the supply of wellbeing for everyone, without exclusions. It means respect for the diverse economies of our societies. It means respect for local knowledge. It means respect for Mother Earth and its biodiversity as a source of nurture for future generations.

Live-Well Comprehensive Development also means production to satisfy actual needs, rather than to expand profits infinitely.

It means to distribute wealth and to heal the wound caused by inequality, rather than widening the injustice.

It means combining modem science with the age-old technological wisdom held by the indigenous, native and peasant peoples that interact with nature respectfully.

It means listening to the people, rather than financial markets.

It means placing Nature at the core of life and regarding the human being as just another creature of Nature.

The Live-Well Comprehensive Development model of respect for Mother Earth is not an environmentalist economy for poor countries, while the rich nations expand inequality and destroy Nature.

Comprehensive development is only viable if applied worldwide, if the States, in conjunction with their respective peoples, exercise control over their energy resources.

We need technologies, investments, production and credits, as well as companies and markets, but we shall not subordinate them to the dictatorship of profit gain and luxury. Instead, we must place them at the service of the peoples in the satisfaction of their needs and for the expansion of the shared goods and assets.

SECONDLY: SOVEREIGNTY EXERCISED OVER NATURAL RESOURCES AND STRATEGIC AREAS

The countries that have raw materials should and can take sovereign control over the production and processing of our raw materials.

The nationalization of strategic companies and areas can help the State take over the management of production, exercise sovereign control over its wealth, embark on a planning process that leads to the processing of raw materials, and distribute the profit among its people.

Exercising sovereignty over natural resources and strategic areas does not mean isolation from global markets; rather, it means connecting to those markets in the benefits of our countries, and not in the benefit of few private owners. Sovereignty over natural resources and strategic areas does not mean preventing foreign capital and technologies from participating. It means subordinating these capital and technologies to the needs of each country.

THIRDLY: WELLBEING FOR EVERYONE AND THE PROVISION OF BASIC SERVICES AS A HUMAN RIGHT

The worst tyranny faced by humankind is the basic services under the control of multinational corporations. This practice subjugates humanity to the specific interests and commercial aims of a minority that becomes rich and powerful at the expense of the life and security of other persons.

This is why we claim that basic services are inherent to the human condition. How can a human being live without running water, power supply or communications? If human rights make us all equal, this equality can only be realized if access to basic services is universal. our need for water, just our need for light and communications, makes us all equal.

The resolution of social inequities requires that both the international law and the national legislation of each country define basic services (such as water, power supply, communications and basic health care) as a fundamental human right of every individual.

This means that the States have a legal obligation to secure the universal provision of basic services, irrespective of their costs or margins.

FOURTHLY: EMANCIPATION FROM THE EXISTING INTERNATIONAL FINANCIAL SYSTEM AND CONSTRUCTION OF A NEW FINANCIAL ARCHITECTURE

We propose that we rid ourselves from the international financial yoke by building a new financial system that prioritizes the requirements of the productive operations in the countries of the South, within the context of comprehensive development.

We must incorporate and enhance banks of the South that support industrial development projects, reinforce regional and domestic markets, and promote trade among our countries, but on the basis of complementarity and solidarity.

We also need to promote sovereign regulation over the global financial transactions that threaten the stability of our national economies.

We must design an international mechanism for the restructure of our debts that help reinforce the dependence of the peoples of the south and strangle our changes of development.

We must replace the international financial institutions, such as the IMF, for other entities that provide for a better and broader participation of the countries of the South in their decision-making structures that are currently managed by imperial powers.

We also need to define limits to the gains from speculation and to the excessive accumulation of wealth.

FIFTHLY: BUILD A MAJOR ECONOMIC, SCIENTIFIC, TECHNOLOGICAL AND CULTURAL PARTNERSHIP AMONG THE MEMBERS OF G-77 PLUS CHINA

After centuries under colonial rule, transfer of wealth to imperial metropolises and impoverishment of our economies, the southern countries are once again gaining critical importance in the performance of the world economy.

Asia, Africa and Latin America are not only home to 77% of the world's population, but also account for nearly 43% share in the world economy. And this importance is on the rise. The peoples of the South are the future of the world.

Immediate actions must be taken to reinforce and plan this inescapable global trend.

What Needs to be Done in the Global South, so that they can have a Greater Share of Economic Prosperity?

We need to expand trade among the southern countries. We also need to gear our productive operations to the requirements of other economies in the South, on the basis of complementarity necessities and capacities.

We need to implement technology transfer programs among the southern countries. Technological sovereignty and leadership that are critical for a new global economy based on justice will not be obtained by any country acting on its own.

Science must be an asset held by the entire humankind. Science must be placed at the service of everyone's wellbeing, without exclusions or hegemony. A decent future for all the peoples around the world will require integration for liberation, rather than cooperation for domination.

For the purpose of discharging these worthy tasks in the benefit of the peoples around the world, we have invited Russia and other foreign countries that are our brothers in needs and commitments to join the G-77.

Our G-77 partnership does not have an institution of its own that gives effect to the remarks, statements and action plans of our countries. For this reason, Bolivia proposes that a Decolonization and South-South Cooperation Institute be established.

This institute will be charged with the provision of technical assistance to the southern countries, as well as the further implementation of the proposals made by the G-77 plus China.

The institute will also supply technical and capacity-building assistance for development and self-determination, and it will help conduct research projects. We propose that this institute be headquartered in Bolivia.

SIXTHLY: ERADICATE HUNGER FROM AROUND THE WORLD

It is imperative that hunger be eradicated and the human right to food be fully exercised and enforced.

Food production must be prioritized with the involvement of small growers and the indigenous peasant communities that hold age-old knowledge in regards to this activity.

To be successful in hunger eradication, the southern countries must lay down the conditions for democratic and equitable access to land ownership, in a manner that monopolies over this resource are not authorized to exist in the form of latifundia. Notwithstanding, acreage fragmentation into small and unproductive plots must not be allowed either.

Food sovereignty and security must be enhanced through access to healthy foods in the benefit of the people.

The monopoly held by multinational corporations over the supply of farm supplies must be eliminated as a way to foster food security and sovereignty.

Each country must make sure that the supply of the basic food staples consumed by its people is secured by enhancing production, cultural and environmental practices, and by promoting people-to-people exchanges on the basis of solidarity. The States have an obligation to ensure the supply of power, the availability of road connections and the access to water and organic fertilizers.

SEVENTH: STRENGTHEN THE SOVEREIGNTY OF THE STATES, FREE FROM FOREIGN INTERFERENCE, INTERVENTION AND/OR ESPIONAGE

Within the framework of the UN, a new institutional structure must be propitiated in support of a new world order to live well.

The institutions that emerged after World War II, including the UN, are in need of a thorough reform today.

International agencies that promote peace, eliminate global hegemonism and advance equality among states are required.

For this reason, the UN Security Council must be removed. Rather than fostering peace among nations, this body has promoted wars and invasions by imperial powers in their quest for the natural resources available in the invaded countries. Instead of a Security Council, today we witness an insecurity council of imperial wars.

No country, no institution and no interest can justify the invasion of a country by another nation. The sovereignty of the States and the internal resolution of the conflicts existing in any country are the foundation of peace and the UN.

I stand here to denounce the unjust economic blockade imposed on Cuba and the aggressive and illegal policies pursued by the US government against Venezuela, including a legislative initiative offered at the US Senate Foreign Relations Committee designed to apply sanctions to this country to the detriment of its sovereignty and political independence; a clear breach of the principles and purposes of the UN Charter.

These forms of persecution and internationally driven overthrows are the traits of modem colonialism, the colonial practices of our era.

These are our times, the times of the South. We must be able to overcome and heal the wounds caused by fratricidal wars stirred by foreign capitalistic interests. We must strengthen our integration schemes in support of our peaceful coexistence, our development and our faith in shared values, such as justice.

Only by standing together will we be able to give our peoples a decent life.

EIGHTH: DEMOCRATIC RENEWAL OF OUR STATES

The era of the empires, colonial hierarchies and financial oligarchies is coming to an end. Everywhere we look, we see the peoples around the world calling for their right to play their leading role in history.

The 21st century must be one of the peoples, the workers, the fanners, the indigenous communities, the youth and the women. In other words, it must be the century of the oppressed.

The realization of the peoples' leading role requires that democracy be renewed and strengthened. We must supplement the electoral democracy with participatory and community-based democracy.

We must move away from the limited parliamentary and party-based governance and into the *social governance* of democracy.

This means that the decision-making process in any State must take into consideration its parliamentary deliberations, as well as the deliberations held by the social movements that carry the life-giving energy of our peoples.

The renovation of democracy in this century also requires that any political action represents a permanent and full service to life. This service constitutes an ethical, humane and moral commitment to our peoples, to the humblest masses.

For this purpose, we must reinstate the codes of our forefathers; i.e., "thou shall not steel or lie and thou shall not be soft or toady."

Democracy also means the distribution of wealth and the expansion of the common goods shared by the society.

Democracy means the subordination of rulers to the decisions of the ruled.

Democracy is not a personal benefit vested in the rulers, let alone abuse of power. Democracy means serving the people with love and self-sacrifice. Democracy means dedication of time, knowledge, effort and even life in the pursuit of the wellbeing of the peoples and humanity.

NINTH: A NEW WORLD RISING FROM THE SOUTH FOR THE WHOLE OF HUMANKIND

The time has come for the nations of the South.

In the past, we were colonized and enslaved. Our stolen labor built empires in the North.

Today, with every step we take for our liberation, the empires grow decadent and begin to crumble.

However, our liberation is not just the emancipation of the peoples of the south. Our liberation is also for the whole of humanity. We are not fighting to dominate anyone. We are fighting to make sure that no one becomes dominated.

Only we can save the source of life and society: Mother Earth. Our planet is under a death threat by the greed of predatory and insane capitalism.

Today, another world is not only possible, but also indispensable.

Today, another world is indispensable because, otherwise, no world will be possible.

And that other world of equality, complementarity and organic coexistence with Mother Earth can only emerge from the thousands of languages, colors and cultures existing in brotherhood among the peoples of the South.

STUDY QUESTIONS

1. What evidence does Morales use to support his argument that the current world order is not sustainable?
2. Why does Morales think it is so important that the nations of the global South play a greater role in international policy? What changes will a shift in global hierarchies lead to in his opinion?

RICHARD GOTT

14.5 *HUGO CHAVEZ AND THE BOLIVARIAN REVOLUTION, 2000*

Perhaps the most influential of the "Pink Tide" governments in Latin America at the beginning of the twenty-first century was that of Hugo Chavez in Venezuela. A hugely polarizing and controversial figure, Chavez served as president of Venezuela from 1999 until his death from cancer in 2013. Chavez drew heavily from the iconography of Simón Bolívar, and presented himself as the head of a Bolivarian Revolution that would bring Bolívar's goals for regional development to fruition. His government nationalized the oil industry, and used the revenues from soaring commodity prices to develop extensive social programming and to support diplomacy by sharing subsidized oil with allied nations elsewhere in Latin America and the Caribbean. Richard Gott is a well-known left-wing British journalist with a long history of covering revolutionary movements in Latin America—notably, Gott was the person who identified Che Guevara's body after he was executed by the Bolivian military in 1967. Gott wrote a series of books covering Chavez and the Bolivarian Revolution that, although written from a very pro-Chavez perspective, provide an important firsthand window into the development of the Chavez regime. In this except from Gott's first book on Chavez, published in London in 2000, Gott recounts the very first interview he conducted with Chavez.

FROM BARINAS TO CARACAS: THE IRRESISTIBLE FLIGHT FROM THE COUNTRYSIDE

When I first interviewed Hugo Chávez in 2000, he was standing in the garden of La Casona, the presidential residence in Caracas, with his back to the house, gazing out towards the small forest of bamboo and palms that fringes the far end of the lawn. Since he is on television most days of the week, making impromptu speeches, greeting protocol visitors at the Miraflores palace, or glad-handing his way through a shanty town, everyone knows what he looks like. They are familiar with his pugilist's face, his generous lips, his beaming grin, and the almost imperceptible asthmatic tick of his mouth as he takes a breath or is caught searching for a word in mid-rhetorical flow. He always appears decisive, and radiates confidence and optimism.

Yet alone on the green lawn he appeared more vulnerable, a monochrome and ambiguous sculpture dressed in a grey suit. He stood absolutely motionless for several minutes, as though gaining strength to face the long day ahead, and seemingly oblivious of the arrival of a stranger. Finally he turned round and walked across the grass to greet me.

He is a master of the surprise gesture and the rhetorical flourish, with a considerable sense of theatre. I was reminded for a moment of *Yo el Supremo* (I the Supreme One), the great Paraguayan writer Augusto Roa Bastos's novel about José Gaspar Rodríguez de Francia, the ascetic Robespierrean president of Paraguay in the early nineteenth century who isolated his country for thirty years from the globalising currents of his time and laid down the solid foundations of its economic development. Chávez has a similar messianic streak.

Source: Richard Gott, *In the Shadow of the Liberator: Hugo Chávez and the Transformation of Venezuela* (London: Verso, and imprint of New Left Books, 2000)

The damp heat of the early morning, the lush colours of a tropical garden, and the verandah columns of a building designed as a replica of a colonial hacienda house of the eighteenth century, all conspired to create the illusion of a time warp. Our lengthy conversation—much of it devoted to his ambitious plan to stimulate development in the countryside—seemed to have a timeless quality to it, as though recalling that this was an issue that presidents and colonial viceroys in Latin America had been wrestling with for centuries.

In an interview, Chávez becomes a cross between an after-dinner raconteur and a university lecturer giving a tutorial, sometimes telling long stories about distant events, sometimes analysing current problems. José Vicente Rangel, his vice-president, had told me that Chávez was "a head of state quite unlike any other." While "most of them have a laconic style and keep a low profile, Chávez is quite the opposite: he accepts a challenge in any area; he really enjoys permanent confrontation; he is an extrovert and an excellent communicator, and he likes polemic and seeks it out." Would I be a sufficiently stimulating interviewer, I wondered. Rangel also said that Chávez was much more of an intellectual than people think, with great creativity. He is a pragmatic romantic, a mixture of passion with calculation."

On that first occasion, we were in tutorial mode, and Chávez delved for my benefit into the history of Venezuela in the twentieth century, explaining how the exploitation of oil in the 1920s had led to the collapse of the rural economy. This in turn had brought an end to Venezuela's old "balanced and harmonious model," whereby the cultivation of coffee, sugar and cocoa in the country had marched in step with the industrial development of the towns. "The government simply gave up on the countryside, and what the history books call the peasant exodus began." Chávez emphasised that "this was not because the peasants wanted to leave, but because the rural areas were abandoned by the government."

He used a personal example close to home. "This is something that I have felt ever since I was a child; I never wanted to move away from my home village, but I had to go; I was drawn into the city by a centripetal force." The aim of his policies, he explained, was "to make this force go in the opposite direction."

Once he had finished sixth grade at school in Sabaneta, he had to leave his home village, to go first to Barinas and then to Caracas. He explained the causes of his move, an explanation that lies at the heart of what he thinks is wrong with the country's development—and what he plans to put right.

"If I wanted to continue studying, which I did, since my father was a teacher, then I would have to go to Barinas, which was a larger town, the state capital. But if there had been a secondary school in Sabaneta, I wouldn't have had to go."

When it came to further education, Barinas had no university. "All my brothers had to travel to the university in Merida, and I had to come to Caracas, to the military academy. Those who didn't leave, stayed behind and stagnated."

The same forces affecting education had also influenced the provision of health care in Sabaneta and Barinas. "People who needed attention had to go to Barquisimeto or Caracas. Even our local sportsmen had to leave. Peasants left when they lost their land to the great haciendas. There was a massive exodus."

The military were subject to the same centripetal force, dragging them to the city. When he was in the army, he said, there was "always a struggle with the *muchachos* who came from the rural areas to do their obligatory military service."

"They were brought to the cities, to the barracks in Caracas, and of course when they saw the city—when they set out on a day off—and saw everything that the city has to offer, they didn't want to return to the country. For there they would have no land and no work, nothing, just a shack to go home to. Military service was another factor that helped to force people into the towns."

Venezuelans have been migrating over many years, Chávez pointed out, to the narrow centre-north coastal strip of the country. "Eighty per cent of the population is now concentrated here," he said. All he wanted to do, he claimed, was to reverse the trend. The principal aim of his revolution was "to occupy the geographic space of the country in a more harmonious and balanced way."

In his first year in office, Chávez proposed a bold scheme to move hundreds of thousands of people from the crowded cities of northern Venezuela to new economic centres in the sparsely populated east and south of the country. He planned to develop "integrated" agro-industrial projects in these empty lands, and he hoped that these would cajole people living in the shanty towns to start a new life in the rural areas. While some early reports suggested that most people wanted to cling to their urban shanties, others suggested that some were thrilled by the prospect of being provided with land and new homes—and the possibility of a fresh start.

Politicians and urban planners have argued for years about what to do with the gigantic urban conglomerations of Latin America, the old capital cities housing millions of people for whom there are few real homes, not much food, and little work. To move urban dwellers back to the country is a tall order, flying in the face of historical experience and of what is now believed to be possible, for few people hanker after the grinding life of the peasant. Yet to populate the rural areas with the country's own population, rather than to bring in fresh settlers from outside, is an ambition that goes back at least as far as the proposals of Simón Rodriguez, Bolívar's tutor, in the early nineteenth century. Chávez's utopian schemes have a venerable lineage.

STUDY QUESTIONS

1. What insights do Gott's reflections on Chavez's personality reveal about the foundation for his popularity with the Venezuelan masses?
2. What role does Simón Bolívar play in the rationalization of Chavez's plan for greater economic development outside the major cities of Venezuela?

MICHELLE BACHELET

14.6 INAUGURAL ADDRESS, 2006

On March 11, 2006, Michele Bachelet became the first woman president of Chile. She was a physician by training who had served as minister of health and minister of defense, and Bachelet's candidacy was profoundly shaped by her family connection to the atrocities of the military dictatorship in Chile. Her father, a general in the Air Force, had served in the Allende government and was kidnapped and tortured by the military. After his death, her mother played an important role as an activist for family members of victims of human rights abuses. Both Bachelet and her mother were also detained and tortured before fleeing into exile in Germany. In her political career, Bachelet was able to emphasize her position both as a victim of human rights abuses and as the daughter of a military leader, and was thus well placed to reconcile Chilean civilians and the military. Bachelet served her first term as president between 2006 and 2010, and was reelected to the presidency in 2014, becoming the first person in almost a century to win two Chilean presidential elections.

Source: Michelle Bachelet, Inaugural Address, 2006 (https://library.brown.edu/create/modernlatinamerica/chapters/chapter-10-chile/primary-documents-w-accompanying-discussion-questions/document-30-inaugural-address-michelle-bachelet-2006/) [*Student translation*]

Palacio de la Moneda

11 March 2006

Thank you men and women of Chile. Thank you for your applause. Thank you for the smiles that you give me. Thank you for the embraces. I feel privileged to receive so much affection. I want to direct my words to all the men and women of Chile, without exclusion.

In times past we were divided amongst one another. We looked at each other with distrust, suspicion, with disdain. In these sixteen years of democracy we have worked together to smooth the rough edges of a divided society, of a society that separated us between us and them.

This is the moment when we all feel as one. Today, the winds have changed. Today, there is nothing more besides the future. A future where everyone belongs, where we can all build a better nation. An inclusive nation, where no kind of diversity will be left out. Where nobody feels that their destiny has been left out in the cold.

We have prepared for a great challenge. The twenty first century has presented new trials, some of which are still unknown. Beyond the technological revolution that is before our eyes and approaching, I think of the ways in which we relate to one another as well. How we interact in community and fight against individualism, indifference, and desperation. The time has come to look at one another, face to face, without resentment or suspicion.

The past is what it is: past. We will never forget it, but our gaze is fixed on tomorrow. A more prosperous tomorrow, more just, more egalitarian, more participative. We know that in four years we will not resolve all problems. That was never in my campaign platform. But we will take a step forward. A great step forward. It will be the government of the citizens. From the neglected to the entrepreneurs, this infinite spectrum of colors, of perspectives and viewpoints, gives our society such richness.

The citizens have in me a president who will always speak the language of truth. Difficulties will emerge, without a doubt, all governments encounter them. Campaigns are made in poetry, but governments are made in prose. Even so, whatever difficulties that may arise, you will not see the relationship between us affected. We will establish a dialogue based on openness and participation. A grand pact between the citizens and their leaders. As you all know, I keep my commitments. I say what I think and I do as I say. On my word as a woman!

Our endeavor will not come without opposition. Parliament is the expression that gives legitimacy to our laws, it does not matter what political overtones the laws have, we will achieve a shared ideal, which is the welfare of all Chileans and justice throughout our land.

Our focus will be put towards children, so that they can learn and develop from a young age and eliminate all traces of inequality. Our endeavors will be put towards those who aspire to have a job, a decent job. Our support will be given to young people filled with talent who want to go to university, who want to learn, who want to forge their own destiny. Our efforts will be with women, because women deserve it. Our efforts will be with our indigenous communities. Our efforts will be with people with any kind of disability. The state should be put to the service to those who suffer the bitterness of defenselessness and on the side of those who wish to rise up. In Chile there will not be one forgotten citizen. That is my promise. We will be active in all the regions. There will not be one town or village that won't receive our concern. If not, men and women of Chile, you can hold me to my word.

You already know: I never had ambitions for power, I have only had the desire to serve. The office that I assume today has been given to me by you. And I feel the weight of that responsibility. Every Chilean is in my mind and my heart at this moment.

I understand very well the reality of my country. I know of dangers and inequalities. I also know of invaluable successes, such as Nobel prizes, artists and creatives who have forged our culture. The tenacity of our athletes. The labor and merit of our professionals and workers, who are the strength of our land. I think of the many who have managed to rise against adversity with great commitment. Everyone, throughout our wide territory, will be the focus of my administration.

Friends, this is a solemn moment for the country. I ask you to turn your heads and look at the illustrious citizens that adorn this plaza. It is the republic, friends, this is the republic.

Over there in front is Diego Portales and the symbol of a nascent republic, small, modest for its time, but vigorous, lover of order, that learned to resolve its differences through the rule of law and not by arms.

Jorge Alessandri, Salvador Allende, and Eduardo Frei Montalva are also in this plaza. An homage to all of them, who symbolize our modern nation, the country of the twentieth century, our call to democracy, and an era of progress and social advancements.

I am the depository of the entirety of a history, that has had its gray and bitter times, but that has managed to recuperate itself. As a Chilean people today, we live better and freer than before. We have had three successful governments. I am proud to continue a path that has brought forth so many fruits. My regards and love to Don Patricio Aylwin and Eduardo Frei Ruiz-Tagle. The Chile that we start building today is based on the foundations that they built yesterday.

My special gratitude also goes to another illustrious citizen, Ricardo Lagos. What great pride we Chileans feel today, upon seeing him leave this palace, cheered by his people. Yes, friends! Cheer louder, because when we applaud a president who has done his duty well we are applauding the entire republic.

Finally, there is one tribute that I cannot stop from giving. On the 12 of March, 32 years ago, my father passed away, Alberto Bachelet Martinez. One day I will be with him again, but I know that he is also here with me right now. In the memory of my father, General Bachelet, I wish to salute the armed forces of Chile, who are an important part of our history and who today are the legacy of all Chileans.

Friends, we are on the verge of making this a developed country, with more justice and better opportunities. The world is watching us. The world observes with careful attention this little country at the South of the planet. A country that knew how to peacefully leave a dictatorship, that knew how to construct a solid democracy, that knew how to rediscover itself, that progresses, and that knows how to bring millions of compatriots out of poverty, in liberty and dignity for all. This little country, the distinguished visitors who accompany us here know, today wishes to take a grand step in its history. A step for prosperity for all of its children, it is certain, but also for a new form of policy making. More inclusive, more participative, more open, more transparent. A policy by and for the citizens.

Men and women of Chile, I know very well that there are many unsatisfied needs. I understand the just aspirations that exist in every family. I wish to bring my experience, my sensitivity, and my effort to the beautiful task of guiding this country towards a better destiny. This is what we want for Chile, and we know that together, we can achieve it.

A new era is born. A time for joy, a time for men, a time for youth and children, a time for women. It is time for everyone in my beloved country, the country of all the citizens.

Thank you friends, thank you very much.

STUDY QUESTIONS

1. How does Bachelet position the historic nature of her victory as the first woman president in her inaugural address? To what extent does she engage gender in her speech?
2. What role does the history of military dictatorship play in her speech? How does this past affect her vision of the future?

CREDITS

3.4: By permission of Oxford University Press, USA

3.5: William Walker, The War in Nicaragua. New York: S. H. Goetzel and Co, 1860.

3.6a: Biblioteca Nacional, Rare Works Division.

3.6c: Biblioteca Nacional, Rare Works Division.

4.1: By permission of Oxford University Press, USA

4.2: Thomas Ewbank, Life in Brazil, Or, A Journal of a Visit to the Land of Cocoa and the Palm (New York: Harper and Brothers, 1856), pp. 436–441.

4.3: Robert Edgar Conrad, Children of God's Fire: A Documentary History of Black Slavery in Brazil, pp. 133–134.

4.4: Miguel Barnet (ed.), Biography of a Runaway Slave (Williamantic, CT: Curbstone Press/Northwestern University Press, [1966] 2016). Translated by W. Nick Hill, pp. 27–37.

4.5: John L. Stephens, Incidents of Travel in Central America, Chiapas and Yucatan, Vol. II. (New York: Harper and Brothers, 1841), pp. 209–217.

4.6: Pérégrinations d'une Paria, by Flora Tristan, was first published in France in 1838; This translation and Introduction: The Folio Society Limited 1986, pp. 251–262.

4.7: Life in Mexico by Frances Calderon de la Barca [aka Frances Erskine Inglis] (1804–1882).

5.1: Juan Bautista Alberdi, translated, "Immigration as Means of Progress," in The Argentina Reader, Gabriela Nouzeilles, Graciela Montaldo, Eds., pp. 95–101. Copyright, 2002, Duke University Press. All rights reserved. Republished by permission of the copyright holder. www.dukeupress.edu

5.2: Denise Helly, The Cuba Commission Report: A Hidden History of the Chinese in Cuba. The Original Language Text of 1876. (John Hopkins University Press, 1993), pp. 66–69.

5.3: Original source: Pehuen Editores, in Elizabeth Quay Hutchison, Thomas Miller Klubock, Nara B. Milanich, and Peter Winn (eds.), The Chile Reader: History, Culture, Politics (Durham, NC: Duke University Press, 2014), pp. 206–209.

5.4: Gertrude M. Yeager (ed.), Confronting Change, Challenging Tradition: Women in Latin American History, Jaguar Books on Latin America, Number 7 (Wilmington, Delaware: Scholarly Resources Inc. Imprint), pp. 30–39.

5.5: Frederick Upham Adams, Conquest of the Tropics: The story of the Creative Enterprises conducted by the United Fruit Company (Garden City, New York: Doubleday, page & Company, 1914), pp. 354–356.

5.6: Archivo Nacional de Costa Rica.

5.7: Channing Arnold and Frederick J. Tabor Frost, The American Egypt: A Record of Travel in Yucatan (1909), pp. 324–333.

5.8a: W. E. Hardenburg, The Putumayo: The Devil's Paradise: Travels in the Peruvian Amazon Region and an Account of the Atrocities Committed Upon the Indians Therein (T. Fisher Unwin, London: Adelphi Terrace, Leipsic: Inselstrasse, 1886), pp. 180–186.

6.1: Theodore Roosevelt, The Platt Amendment, 1902.

6.2: Philippe Bunau-Varilla, Panama: The Creation, Destruction, and Resurrection. Ann Arbor: University of Michigan Library, 1914, pp. 302–303, 334–339.

6.3c: Library of Congress Prints and Photographs Division Washington, D.C. 20540 USA.

6.4: José Martí, "The Truth about the United States," Inside the Monster: Writings on the United States and American Imperialism. Edited and with an introduction by Philip S. Foner. (New York: Monthly Review Press, 1975), pp. 49–54.

6.5: Fanny Chambers Gooch Inglehart, Face to Face with the Mexicans (New York: Fords, Howard, and Hulbert, 1887) pp. 84–96.

6.6: Norma Valle-Ferrer, Luissa Capetillo: Pioneer Puerto Rican Feminist, (New York: Peter Lang, 2006), pp. 76–77.

6.7a: The Henry Ford, Companhia Ford Industrial do Brasil Records.

6.7b: The Henry Ford, Companhia Ford Industrial do Brasil Records.

6.7c: The Henry Ford, Companhia Ford Industrial do Brasil Records.

6.7d: The Henry Ford, Companhia Ford Industrial do Brasil Records.

6.7e: The Henry Ford, Companhia Ford Industrial do Brasil Records.

6.7f: The Henry Ford, Companhia Ford Industrial do Brasil Records.

6.7g: The Henry Ford, Companhia Ford Industrial do Brasil Records.

6.7h: The Henry Ford, Companhia Ford Industrial do Brasil Records.

6.7i: The Henry Ford, Companhia Ford Industrial do Brasil Records.

7.1: John Charles Chasteen, Born in Blood and Fire: Latin American Voices (New York: W. W. Norton & Company, Inc., 2011), pp. 144–150.

9.4: José Carlos Mariátegui, On the Indigenous Problem (1928).

9.5: Gilberto Freyre, The Masters and the Slaves (1933).

9.6: Nicolas Guillén, "Son Number 6" ["Son Número 6", 1947], Yoruba From Cuba: Selected Poems (Leeds, UK: Peepal Tree, 2005) pp. 67–69.

9.8: Erich Lessing / Art Resource, NY.

10.1: Kenneth Karst and Keith S. Rosenn, Law and Development in Latin America: A Case Book. Latin American Studies Series Volume 28, UCLA Latin American Center. 1975. pp. 328–330.

10.2: Excerpt(s) from CHILD OF THE DARK by Carolina Maria de Jesus, translated by David St. Clair, translation copyright © 1962 by E. P. Dutton & Co., Inc. and Souvenir Press, Ltd. Used by permission of Dutton, an imprint of Penguin Publishing Group, a division of Penguin Random House LLC. All rights reserved.

10.3: Abdias do Nascimento, "The Myth of Racial Democracy," in The Brazil Reader, Robert Levine, John Crocitti, Eds., pp. 379–381. Copyright, 1999, Duke University Press. All rights reserved. Republished by permission of the copyright holder. www.dukeupress.edu

10.5: 2005 Aleida March, Che Guevara Studies Center and Ocean Press.

10.6: Excerpt(s) from CHILEAN REVOLUTION by Regis Debray, "Notes" Copyright © 1971 by NLB. "Postscript by Allende" Copyright © 1971 by Random House, Inc. Used by permission of Pantheon Books, an imprint of the Knopf Doubleday Publishing Group, a division of Penguin Random House LLC. All rights reserved.

10.7: From A Theology of Liberation by Gusatvo Gutiérrez Copyright © 1973, 1988 by Orbis Books, Maryknoll, NY 10545. All rights reserved. Reprinted by permission of Orbis Books.

10.8: Excerpt(s) from REVOLUTIONARY PRIEST by John Gerassi, copyright © 1971 by Penguin Random House, LLC. Used by permission of Random House, an imprint and division of Penguin Random House LLC. All rights reserved.

10.9: Presentation of Mujer Integrante Ahora to the International Tribunal of Crimes Against Women, Brussels, March 1976, Documentos del feminsimo del Puerto Rico: fascilimes de la historia (University of Puerto Rico Press, 2001), pp. 296–306.

11.1: National Archives and Records Administration, RG 59, Central File 611. 14/1-1654. Confidential. (https://2001-2009.state.gov/r/pa/ho/frus/ike/iv/20210.htm).

11.2: "Somoza Unveils Somoza's Statue of Somoza at the Somoza Stadium by Ernesto Cardenal," trans. Donald Walsh, taken from The Art Divas (Blog of Rabih Alameddine, http://www.theartdivas.com/2016/somoza-unveils-somozas-statue-of-somoza.html).

11.3: "John F. Kennedy Speeches: Address at a White House Reception for Members of Congress and for the Diplomatic Corps of the Latin American Republics, March 13, 1961," John F. Kennedy Presidential Library & Museum (https://www.jfklibrary.org/Research/Research-Aids/JFK-Speeches/Latin-American-Diplomats-Washington-DC_19610313.aspx).

11.5: Excerpt(s) from MASSACRE IN MEXICO by Elena Poniatowska, translated by Helen R. Lane, copyright © 1971 by Ediciones Era SA de CV, translation copyright © 1975 by The Viking Press, Inc. Used by permission of Viking Books, an imprint of Penguin Publishing Group, a division of Penguin Random House LLC. All rights reserved.

11.6: Latin America and the United States: A Documentary History, eds. Robert H. Holden and Eric Zolov (New York: Oxford University Press), pp. 313–316. By permission of Oxford University Press, USA.

11.7: Margaret Power, Right-Wing Women in Chile: Feminine Power and the Struggle Against Allende, 1964–1973 (University Park, PA: Pennsylvania State University Press), pp. 274.

11.8: The Chile Reader: History, Culture, Politics, eds. Elizabeth Quay Hutchinson, Thomas Miller Klubock, Nara B. Milanich, and Peter Winn (Durham and London: Duke University Press, 2014), pp. 443–449.

11.9: Mellibovsky, Matilde. *Circle of Love Over Death: Testimonies of the Mothers of the Plaza de Mayo*, Translated by Maria and Matthew Proser. Williamantic: Curbstone Press, 1997. pp. 90–102.

12.1: Margaret Randall, Sandino's Daughters: Testimonies of Nicaraguan Women in Struggle, ed. Lynda Yanz (Rutgers University Press, 1995), pp. 59–68, 70–76.

12.2: Reprinted by permission from The Struggle is One: Voices and Visions of Liberation by Mev Puleo, the State University of New York Press © 1994, State University of New York. All rights reserved.